LANGUAGE AND SOCIAL RELATIONS

Language connects people to each other in social relationships and allows them to participate in a variety of activities in everyday life. This original study explores the role of language in various domains of our social life, including identity, gender, class, kinship, deference, status, hierarchy, and others. Drawing on materials from over thirty languages and societies, this book shows that language is not simply a tool of social conduct but the effective means by which human beings formulate models of conduct. Models of conduct serve as points of reference for social behavior, even when actual conduct departs from them. A principled understanding of the processes whereby such models are produced and transformed in large-scale social history, and also invoked, negotiated, and departed from in small-scale social interactions provides a foundation for the cross-cultural study of human conduct.

ASIF AGHA is Associate Professor in the Department of Anthropology at the University of Pennsylvania, and editor of *The Journal of Linguistic Anthropology*.

STUDIES IN THE SOCIAL AND CULTURAL FOUNDATIONS OF LANGUAGE

The aim of this series is to develop theoretical perspectives on the essential social and cultural character of language by methodological and empirical emphasis on the occurrence of language in its communicative and interactional settings, on the socioculturally grounded "meanings" and "functions" of linguistic forms, and on the social scientific study of language use across cultures. It will thus explicate the essentially ethnographic nature of linguistic data, whether spontaneously occurring or experimentally induced, whether normative or variational, whether synchronic or diachronic. Works appearing in the series will make substantive and theoretical contributions to the debate over the sociocultural-function and structural-formal nature of language, and will represent the concerns of scholars in the sociology and anthropology of language, anthropological linguistics, sociolinguistics, and socio-culturally informed psycholinguistics.

Editors	*Editorial Advisers*
Judith T. Irvine	Marjorie Goodwin
Bambi Schieffelin	Joel Kuipers
	Don Kulick
	John Lucy
	Elinor Ochs
	Michael Silverstein

A list of books in the series can be found after the index.

LANGUAGE AND SOCIAL RELATIONS

ASIF AGHA
University of Pennsylvania

CAMBRIDGE UNIVERSITY PRESS
Cambridge, New York, Melbourne, Madrid, Cape Town, Singapore,
São Paulo, Delhi, Dubai, Tokyo, Mexico City

Cambridge University Press
The Edinburgh Building, Cambridge CB2 8RU, UK

Published in the United States of America by Cambridge University Press, New York

www.cambridge.org
Information on this title: www.cambridge.org/9780521576857

First published 2007

A catalogue record for this publication is available from the British Library

ISBN 978-0-521-57176-0 Hardback
ISBN 978-0-521-57685-7 Paperback

CONTENTS

List of figures   *page* viii
List of tables   x
Acknowledgments   xiii
Typographical conventions   xv

   Introduction   1
1 Reflexivity   14
   1.0 Introduction   14
   1.1 Reflexive activity   16
   1.2 Text-level indexicality and interactional tropes   24
   1.3 Reflexive activity in interaction   27
   1.4 Deixis and representation   37
   1.5 Performativity   55
   1.6 Reflexive processes across encounters   64
   1.7 Large scale cultural formations   77

2 From referring to registers   84
   2.0 Introduction   84
   2.1 Referring   85
   2.2 Propositional stance and role alignment   96
   2.3 Denotational categories   103
   2.4 Norms of denotation and interaction   124
   2.5 Dialect, sociolect and denotational footing   132
   2.6 Retrospect and prospect   142

3 Register formations   145
   3.0 Introduction   145
   3.1 Three aspects of registers   147
   3.2 Metapragmatic stereotypes   150
   3.3 Stereotypes and socialization   155
   3.4 Stereotypes and ideology   157
   3.5 Entextualized tropes   159
   3.6 Fragmentary circulation   165

3.7   Reflexive social processes and register models   167
3.8   Sociological fractionation and footing   171
3.9   Semiotic range   179
3.10 The enregisterment of style   185
3.11 Conclusion   188

4   The social life of cultural value   190
4.0   Introduction   190
4.1   Received Pronunciation: basic issues   191
4.2   Metadiscourses of accent   195
4.3   The emergence of a standard   203
4.4   The transformation of habits of speech perception   206
4.5   The transformation of habits of utterance   219
4.6   Asymmetries of competence and perceptions of value   223
4.7   Changes in exemplary speaker   224
4.8   The sedimentation of habits and the inhabitance of agency 228

5   Regrouping identity   233
5.0   Introduction   233
5.1   From 'identity' to emblems   234
5.2   Emblematic figures of identity   237
5.3   Role designators and diacritics   246
5.4   Emblematic readings   254
5.5   Interaction rituals as emblems of group status   260
5.6   Emergent, stereotypic and naturalized groupings   268
5.7   Enregistered identities and stereotypic emblems   272

6   Registers of person deixis   278
6.0   Introduction   278
6.1   Metapragmatic stereotypes and standards   279
6.2   Reflexive processes within pronominal registers   286
6.3   Emblems of social difference   293
6.4   Troping on norms   295
6.5   Social boundaries   298

7   Honorific registers   301
7.0   Introduction   301
7.1   Variation and normalization   302
7.2   Lexeme and text   304
7.3   Pronominal repertoires   308
7.4   Phonolexical registers of speaker demeanor   310
7.5   Registers of referent-focal deference   315
7.6   Deference to referent: text-defaults   317

7.7	Textually composite effects	322
7.8	Social domain	332
7.9	Speech levels	334

8	Norm and trope in kinship behavior		340
	8.0	Introduction	340
	8.1	From kinship systems to kinship behavior	341
	8.2	Lexicalism, codes, and the genealogical reduction	346
	8.3	From kinship terms to text-patterns	350
	8.4	Normalized tropes	356
	8.5	Renormalization and standards	368
	8.6	Society-internal variation	372
	8.7	Sign and metasign in kinship behavior	375
	8.8	From cultural kinship formations to any cultural formation	382

Notes	386
References	408
Index	419

FIGURES

1.1 Metasemiotic motivation of icons   *page* 22
1.2 Metasemiotically motivated co-occurrence effects:
    text-level indexicality   24
1.3 Reflexive descriptions of speech co-text and context   32
1.4 Self-reported strategies for modeling next-turn behavior
    (Swedish)   35
1.5 Communicative transmission through a speech chain   67
1.6 Communicative networks in mass communication   69
1.7 Dyadic conversation   70
1.8 A biographic history of encounters   70
1.9 Soliloquy and inner speech   71
2.1 Referential vs. attributive uses   92
2.2 Text configurations as referring signs   93
2.3 Multi-channel sign-configurations and participant
    alignments   101
2.4 Structural sense classes of English noun   114
2.5 Deictic signs: denotational and interactional schemas   118
2.6 Denotational stereotypes as social regularities   121
2.7 Referential prototypes   122
2.8 Reanalysis of Thai syntactic patterns into 'high' and 'low'
    registers   130
2.9 Role configuration and denotationally-mediated
    footing   138
3.1 Three levels of engagement with register phenomena   149
3.2 Gender tropes in Lakhota   161
3.3 Register-mediated alignments: reanalysis and
    self-differentiation   173
3.4 Javanese Wayang Kulit: ritual comportment as implicit
    typification   184
3.5 *Calvin and Hobbes* on registers, voicing, tropes and
    recirculation   188
4.1 Bateman cartoon, 1920   198
4.2 Diagrammatic motivation of co-occurring variables   211

5.1   Role designators and diacritics   249
5.2   Textually cumulative models of personhood   252
5.3   Title page, *Elements of Elocution* by John Walker,
      1806 edition   274

TABLES

1.1 Propositional content and propositional act   *page* 41

1.2 Non-selective deixis: from definite past queries to 'nomic' truths   43

1.3 Categorial text-defaults for common English deictics   47

1.4 Categorial text-defaults and cross-linguistic comparison   48

1.5 Co-textual specification of denotational schema   49

1.6 Role fractions of speaker   50

1.7 Predicate modalization and the explicit performative locution   57

1.8 Cross-cultural comparisons of performative locutions   62

2.1 Reflexive evaluations presupposed in choice of location-referring term   95

2.2 Denotational text as a performed diagram of interactional text   99

2.3 Distributional structure and sense categories   112

2.4 Structural sense classes of suffix   115

2.5 Thresholds of normativity   126

2.6 Tamil caste sociolects and denotational footings   137

2.7 Register contrasts in Norwegian   139

3.1 Typifications of language use   151

3.2 Phonolexical registers of speaker gender in Koasati   160

3.3 Lexical registers of speaker gender in Lakhota   160

3.4 Some features of 'Sports announcer talk'   164

3.5 American military register   166

3.6 Some dimensions of register organization and change   169

3.7 Mirror-image alignments in Egyptian Arabic: a case of inverse iconism   174

3.8 Reanalysis in stereotypic values of second person polite pronouns (Javanese)   176

3.9 Javanese kasar 'coarse' vocabularies   181

3.10 Javanese kasar 'coarse' prosody   182

3.11 Multi-channel indexical icons in Javanese   183

4.1 Phonolexical changes in RP vowels: selected examples   194

4.2	Popular media mis-spellings of U-RP words	197
4.3	Accent speech levels in Britain	200
4.4	Patterns of accent evaluation and role alignment in West Wirral	201
4.5	Rough estimates of genre circulation	217
5.1	Greeting form as emblem of speaker's status	263
5.2	Emblems of piety and honor	266
5.3	Processes that operate over role diacritics and emblems	272
5.4	Enregistered indices of refinement linked to 'Received Pronunciation'	273
6.1	Common genres of metapragmatic discourse about pronouns	281
6.2	Person-referring pronominal forms in Thai	285
6.3	Pronominal registers in European languages	287
6.4	Text configurations marking politeness in French	287
6.5	Reanalysis of Italian second-person pronominal address	289
6.6	Levels of second person pronominal deference in Maithili	290
6.7	Second person pronominal levels in Urdu	290
6.8	Honorific nouns used as 'pronouns' in Urdu	292
6.9	Norms of appropriateness reported for Yiddish address	296
6.10	Social groups and dispensation rights in Swedish	299
7.1	Metapragmatic data used in the study of honorific repertoires	306
7.2	Malayalam honorific 'pronouns'	309
7.3	Phonolexical registers in Samoan	311
7.4	Enregistered phonolexical styles in Standard Teherani Persian	313
7.5	Referent-focal deference: a cross-linguistic approximation	318
7.6	Cross-linguistic distribution of lexemic honorific forms	321
7.7	Honorific forms whose appropriate use depends on two interactional variables	330
7.8	Conjoined focus in Japanese verbs of giving	331
7.9	Textually 'superposed' effects and interactional tropes	332
7.10	Javanese [−human] common nouns	333
7.11	Addressee honorifics in Javanese: repertoire contrasts	334
7.12	Korean speech levels: the early Standard system	335
7.13	Korean speech levels: contemporary Cihwali	336
7.14	Lexeme cohesion and speech levels (Tibetan): five ways of saying 'Mother went to the house'	337
7.15	Javanese speech levels: early Standard	338
7.16	Acceptability of 'mixed' speech levels by social domain of evaluator: 'conservative' vs. 'modern' speakers	339

8.1	Common patterns of addressee-referring and third person kinterm usage	352
8.2	Role inhabitance and referential gloss (English)	354
8.3	Role inhabitance and referential gloss (Vietnamese)	355
8.4	Address inversion in Japanese: referring to self as addressee would or should	359
8.5	Recentered affinal address (Bengali): addressing others as someone else would	361
8.6	Address recentering in Japanese	362
8.7	Patterns of kinterm usage	365
8.8	Address recentering in Hindi	374

ACKNOWLEDGMENTS

A first draft of this book was completed while I was a Fellow at the Stanford Center for Advanced Study in the Behavioral Sciences during 2003–04. In addition to the opportunity to work full time on the book, the Center and its extraordinary staff helped create conditions for writing and reflection that were no less than ideal. Faculty grants from the University of Pennsylvania and the University of California, Los Angeles made possible sabbatical leaves at earlier stages of writing. I am immensely grateful to these institutions for their support.

Conversations with other Fellows at the Center, especially Thomas Welskopp, Walter Johnson, Jane Hill, and Webb Keane, remained a daily source of intellectual stimulation while the book was being written. Judith Irvine, Stanton Wortham, Douglas Glick, Robert Moore, Irene Applebaum, Sabina Perrino, Michael Lempert, Luke Fleming and Constantine Nakassis read the first draft of the manuscript and responded with comments. At an earlier stage, James Kurichi provided insights into Malayalam and Ed Keenan into Malagasy. Bob Agajeenian and Andrew Schwalm worked as my research assistants. I am grateful to them all.

Thanks also to my two Cambridge editors, Judith Ayling, who first invited me to write a book proposal and then accepted it, and Andrew Winnard, who, with a kindness bordering on friendship, saw it through to the form that now lies in your hands.

Some of the material in this book has been presented at various conferences over the years, and earlier versions of parts of the argument have appeared in print. The basic view of registers underlying Chapter 3 was first presented at a panel organized by Alessandro Duranti at the American Anthropological Association's annual conference in November 1997; a portion of the chapter (perhaps two-thirds of the current version) was published as Agha 2004 in an anthology that eventually emerged from this panel. Different portions of Chapter 4 were presented at the Ethnohistory seminar at the University of Pennsylvania in November 1999, at a panel organized by Greg Urban at the American Anthropological Association in November 2000, and at the Anthropology Department Colloquium of the University of Chicago in March 2002. I'd like to thank

Ben Lee, Richard Bauman and Sue Gal for stimulating comments during these presentations and Michael Silverstein for comments on an earlier version, published as Agha 2003. A portion of Chapter 7 was first presented to the Japanese Association of Sociolinguistic Sciences in March 2002 and published in their proceedings as Agha 2002. I thank Sachiko Ide and Kuniyoshi Kataoka for the invitation to present my work at the conference and for their extraordinary hospitality during my visit. About half the material in Chapter 8 was first presented at the Symposium About Language in Society at the University of Texas, Austin, in April 2005, and is scheduled to appear in their proceedings. I am immensely grateful to the organizers of these symposia and to members of audiences for feedback and discussion.

This book is dedicated to my son Omar Sheheryar Agha, now 11, who helped me find examples of register phenomena in *Calvin and Hobbes* comic strips, and, when they were found, helped me find lots of other things too, so many that even Calvin and Hobbes had some trouble guessing what they were.

TYPOGRAPHICAL CONVENTIONS

I use **boldface**
For technical terms when first introduced and occasionally thereafter to remind the reader of their technical senses

'Single quotes'
1. For glosses of expressions and utterance-acts
2. For quotations from authors (except when numbered and set on a different line)
3. For everyday usages and terminologies on which I wish to comment

Italics
1. For forms of words and expressions in orthographic representation
2. For expository emphases

"Double quotes"
To clarify levels of embedding in reported speech

As for the linguistic data cited in this book, I have used IPA conventions whenever possible, but have left intact the conventions used by the many authors I cite when these depart from them.

INTRODUCTION

Social relations vary across human societies in ways that are limitlessly varied, endlessly susceptible to reanalysis, periodic stabilization and change. Yet they are highly systematic in each locale for persons who recognize themselves as so related. The goal of this book is to show that such possibilities of variation and change, and their actual determinacy for particular social actors, can only be explained given an adequate conception of the role of language in human affairs. Doing so requires that we move beyond a variety of folk-views of language that exist among its users in particular times and places; for instance, that language is primarily a collection of words; that language is abstract, mental, devoid of materiality; that it stands apart from the 'things' that it inertly represents. We will be building towards a rather different conception of language here, a view that focuses on the materiality of language and its relationship to other material things, on classifications of behavior that can be inhabited through behavior, and on processes whereby classifications of behaviors, and of those whose behaviors they are, can be maintained or modified within the order of social interaction in which they are experienced.

It has often been supposed that the variability of social relations observed across societies and history can be tamed by means of various top-down approaches, as in the creation of taxonomies of 'kinds of society' viewed as explanations of what people do; or by enumeration of ever more abstract cognitive universals believed to constitute structures of mind independent of human action; or by resort to principles of functional explanation through which actions tend to certain equilibria and yield particular social formations as homeostatic results. There is no difficulty even today in making up such stories about society. The difficulty is, rather, that in order to appear plausible such accounts must ignore vast realms of human experience attested in the ethnographic and historical record, or harness such variation to evolutionist metaphors, or lay claim to the greater rationality of their own moment in the history of the human experiment even as this moment slips away.

This book builds in a different direction. I argue that the organization of social life is shaped by reflexive models of social life, models that are made

1

through human activities and inhabited through them, though not always by the same persons. If the term 'model' seems a bit abstract there are many other terms – idea, image, discourse, position, response, habit, ideology, practice – that are variously appropriate in its place. All these terms convey the notion of an enacted representation, a thing made somewhere through some activity conveying something about another. One of the curious things about language is that it allows us to formulate models of phenomena that are highly abstract, even timeless; one of the curious things about our folk-views of language is their tendency to neglect what is obvious to our senses, namely that any such representation, however general in import, must be conveyed by a perceivable thing – i.e., be materially embodied – in order to become known to someone, or communicable to another. These moments of being made, grasped, and communicated are the central moments through which reflexive models of language and culture have a social life at all. And persons who live by these models (or change them) do so only by participating in these moments.

These moments are of focal interest throughout this book. This focus does not replace other concerns. It orients them. I discuss a large number of traditional topics in this book, matters of longstanding interest to students of language, culture and society. But I propose that careful attention to such moments of making and unmaking allows us to solve many of the most vexing problems we face in conceptualizing our subject matter. Despite the fact that some reflexive models of human behavior perdure or persist through time, some even for a long while, and despite the fact that some among them persist through arrangements that formulate them as timeless, exceptionless, essential, dominant, and so on, the central and inescapable fact about human societies is the diversity of reflexive models of behavior that co-exist within each society (and thus across societies) at any given time. This diversity is partly a result of the fact that persons have interested stakes in – they seek to own, disown, maintain or re-evaluate – the models by which they live, though it has other sources too. Such diversity is the taxonomist's nightmare. But this is as it should be, because, when it comes to culture, taxonomy is taxidermy.

Our goal here is to consider culture as a living process, as a thing whose arrangements are continually renewed – though not always at the same rate, or all at once – through the form-giving fire of human activities. The notion of activity relevant here is semiotic activity – the use of enacted representations in the sense discussed above – through which reflexive models of behavior are made, inhabited, and re-made by the semiotic labor of persons oriented to historical institutions. In many ways, this book is an attempt to argue that human activities yield material precipi-tates and projections (things made through activity, 'artifacts' of various kinds) that carry semiotic value or significance to those who perceive them. This point is fairly obvious for the case of durable artifacts. Yet human beings make artifacts of different degrees of durability, whose cultural meanings and consequences persist for different scales of time. If human beings are artifact makers, the artifacts they most readily make are enacted representations, including utterances and discourses. As individuals, we do this countless times a day and think nothing of it; but those patterns of individual activity that we call institutions do it in a more complex, sometimes puzzling way, and often with far greater consequence. It is therefore all the more important to see that utterances and discourses are themselves material objects made through human activity – made, in a physical sense, out of vibrating columns of air, ink on paper, pixels in electronic media – which exercise real effects upon our senses, minds, and modes of social organization, and to learn to understand and analyze these effects. It is true that utterances and discourses are artifacts of a more or less evanescent kind (speech more than writing). But these are questions of duration, not materiality, and certainly not of degree or kind of cultural consequence. Things that last for seconds can have effects that last for years. Even physical tokens of discourse that have a fleeting durational existence (such as spoken utterances) can order and shape social relations of a much more perduring kind, ones that persist far longer than the initial speech token itself, whether through uptake in the subsequent activities of others, by incorporation into widely routinized practices that rely on and replay them, or by conversion into artifacts of a more durable kind. Every argument in this book assumes the materiality of language and other signs. But I reject the privileged status typically accorded in contemporary discussions of materiality to the narrow special case of durable objects. Such an emphasis, which fixates on the physical persistence of the durable object, obscures the processes through which its sign-values emerge or change. Last year's hat doesn't make the same fashion statement this year. It's the same hat. Or is it? Everyone agrees that fleeting signs (such as spoken utterances and gestures) acquire contextual significance from their more durable physical setting. It remains to be seen that the semiotic values of durable objects (the kinds of things one can put on the mantelpiece, or trip over in the dark) are illuminated for their users by discourses that appear evanescent even when their effects are not. In this book, I attempt to make clearer attributes of language that shape the significance of perceivable objects across thresholds of durability in various ways, whether by allowing fleeting signs to borrow significance from ones that persist, or vice versa, or by making evanescent sign-values more durable, or by causing enduring cultural phenomena to fade into disrepute and disuse. It will soon become clear that many of these attributes make language so exquisite an instrument for doing work – for acting and interacting, for making and unmaking, for imbuing objects (including discourse itself) with value – that its products, or 'works,' are far more accessible to our everyday awareness than the instrument itself.

Chapter 1 introduces basic concepts of reflexive activity, its varieties, and a way of conceptualizing the scales of sociohistorical process in which its effects (products, models, 'works') are experienced. Chapter 2 develops themes pertaining to the issue of enacted representation, the character of acts of referring (to 'things') as interpersonal achievements, the sociology of denotation, and the normativity and authority of forms of representation. Chapter 3 develops an account of register formations, viewed now as systems of socially significant signs (involving language and non-language) that are formed, maintained, and reanalyzed through reflexive activities. The account presented in these three chapters expands our conception of what a register is (beyond the traditional view that registers are sets of socially valued words and expressions) to a model where the kinds of signs that comprise registers, the processes of valorization that establish their sign-values, and the persons for whom they function as signs are all shown to be features of a register not fixed once and for all but variables whose values are defined and negotiated through reflexive processes within social life. These aspects of the model allow us to conceptualize register formations as *cultural models of action*, as stereotypic ways of performing 'social acts' of enormous range and variety, a variety exhibited not merely in their intelligible social consequences but also in the range of phenomenal behaviors in which they are embodied.

Chapter 4 develops an account of enregisterment, the process whereby one register formation comes to be distinguished from other modes of activity, including other registers, and endowed with specific performable values. Whereas all the other chapters in the book take a comparative look at phenomena in different languages and societies, the comparative focus of Chapter 4 is on different historical periods of a single language/society. The next few chapters examine different types of enregistered signs. Chapter 5 focuses on the social logics that underlie enregistered emblems of 'identity,' and on matters of self- and other-positioning that emerge out of these logics. Chapters 6 and 7 take up honorific register formations, cases where enregistered signs are linked in ideologically explicit ways to matters of respect, status, power and rank. Chapter 8 discusses processes of enregisterment that bear on matters of kinship. The chapter illustrates the enormous range of interpersonal relations that can be established through kinship behaviors (the use of kinterms and associated non-linguistic signs), both behaviors that conform to norms of kinship and those that trope upon them. Behaviors of the latter kind establish forms of propinquity that are 'kinship-like' only in certain respects, but which, through further processes of reflexive reanalysis, can be re-evaluated as new norms of kinship for certain social purposes, thereby resetting the standard to which further analogues of kinship are referred.

This dialectic of norm and trope is central to social processes discussed throughout this book. The sense in which social processes are *limitlessly* varied, as I claimed in my opening sentence, is not that they vary randomly or that 'anything goes.' This is far from the case. To see this we have to recognize two distinct issues. First, although cultural models are often normalized by social practices so as to constitute routine versions of (even normative models for) the social behaviors of which they are models, they can also be manipulated through tropes performed by persons acquainted with such models to yield variant versions, and the range of these tropic variations is potentially limitless. The second point is this. The existence of cultural models and tropic variants also involves sociological asymmetries. Not all norms that exist in a society are recognized or accepted by all members of that society. Similarly, not all behaviors that trope upon norms occur equally routinely or are intelligible equally widely; not all intelligible tropes are ratified by those who can construe them; not all the ones that are ratified come to be presupposed in wider social practices, or get normalized in ways that get widely known. Each of these asymmetries imposes some further structure on the first process I described. I argue in this book that if we understand this dialectic of norm and trope in semiotic terms, and if we know how to study these asymmetries in sociological terms, the fact that cultural models vary in (potentially) limitless ways is no cause for distress. Rather, a recognition of this fact and the ability to explain its consequences helps us to understand better the sense in which culture is an open project, the ways in which forms of social organization are modifiable through human activities, and, through a recognition of the various 'positionalities' generated by these asymmetries, to recognize that the processes whereby cultural variation comes about make untenable any form of radical relativism that presumes the perfect intersubstitutability of social 'positions.'

I use the expression 'a language' in this book to refer to the kinds of phenomena to which we ordinarily refer by means of words like French, Chinese, Arabic, or Tagalog. The term has no further technical specificity. None is needed since more precise claims about reflexive processes are formulated in the terminology of sign-functions introduced in Chapter 1. When I use the generic term 'language,' my intent is to say: Pick any language that you like. But I do not use this term for what is called 'Language' by some linguists ('grammar' will do here; more on this below); if my arguments prove persuasive, the epistemological status of the capital-L construct will need to be re-thought. I specifically refer to matters of grammar and grammatical organization by using those terms. Other more specific terms like 'dialect' and 'sociolect' are introduced in the text.

A different set of considerations apply to the term language 'use.' The term is an imperfect way of talking about events of semiosis in which language occurs. As we examine the orderliness of such events we find that there are several ways in which the unity of this construct, this thing called language 'use,' breaks down. First, the term 'use' is itself ambiguous between an act of performing an utterance and an act of construing it; here 'use' breaks down into 'performance and construal' or 'act and response.' Second, to say that language is being used is generally to point to the fact that an array of signs is being performed and construed by interactants, of which language is but a fragment; when language occurs in 'use,' it occurs typically as a fragment of a multi-channel sign configuration, whose performance and construal, enactment and response, constitutes the minimal, elementary social fact. Third, much of what is traditionally called the data of 'usage' by linguists and others consists, in fact, of the data of reflexive models of usage (e.g., norms and standards of usage) to which the actual practice of using language does not always conform even in the society where such data are gathered. These issues require that we distinguish different varieties of usage – an instance of usage, a habitual usage, a normative usage, a tropic usage – in conceptualizing the kinds of work that is accomplishable through language itself.

This book presents methods and frameworks for analyzing many aspects of language. I offer extended discussion of examples from a variety of linguistic and sociohistorical locales, relying on the work of many others. Many of these data are summarized in tables, with source authors and texts indicated at the bottom of the table. At various points in the exposition I have found it convenient to highlight certain features of the argument by setting them off from the text as summaries of the discussion. These are cross-referenced in the text with a preceding S for summary by chapter and summary number (as S 1.1, S 1.2, etc., in Chapter 1, and so on). I have tended to highlight by way of summary those features of the discussion in a particular chapter to which discussions in other chapters make reference. The intention is to provide pointers and flags foregrounding a few selected themes so that the reader can re-visit issues which animate discussions elsewhere in the book. In all cases the summaries offer synopses of points discussed and exemplified at greater length in the body of the text. But they differ among themselves in other respects. In most cases the summaries occur immediately after the discussion summarized. In a few cases, they highlight themes preemptively, offering synopses of materials that follow in the next two or three pages. In one or two instances the summary highlights issues discussed in a previous chapter in order to formulate a bridge or connection to the material now at hand. Although these summaries always offer a synopsis of issues illustrated by examples, they sometimes state synopses in formulations more general than local examples appear to warrant; this is invariably because the local examples are instances of a more general phenomenon, of which additional examples from many languages and societies, cross-referenced to the summary, occur later. So whereas all of these summaries have a common expository function (that they are synopses of local parts of the text) they are also variously, and additionally, flags, pointers, connectors, bridges to other parts of the text, and sometimes generalizations which unite together different portions of a more extended argument. The reader may be able to use these summaries in various ways. But they are not intended as self-standing claims isolable from the empirical cases which furnish their point, nor as adipose verities of some armchair theory in which we may come to find some everlasting rest (which is when they would become most adipose).

A great deal of ink has been spilled in the last forty years in pursuing the assumption that the study of language is the study of 'rules' or 'constraints' on language. As with any fad, the time for this one has come and gone. There is a simple trick that forms the basis for – and explains the popularity of – the fad. The trick itself has two parts. Here's how to do it. First, redefine what the word language means, preferably fixating upon a fragment or feature of language – let's say the concatenation system of language, its syntactic and phonotactic aspects – and call this fragment 'language' (or even 'Language'). Second, redefine the study of this fragment as the study of some restricted type of data about it, let's say the study of decontextualized intuitions about it. If you've done this carefully enough, you can now amaze and amuse your friends by pulling a vast number of rules and constraints out of the hat of introspectable intuitions. And, now, the statement 'the study of language is the study of constraints' appears to be true. But a more accurate way of stating this truth is 'the study of decontextualized intuitions can isolate plenty of features of a concatenation system that appear as inviolable constraints to those intuitions.' You can also do this for discourse. So, in your first step, you can redefine 'discourse' as some genre of discourse, let's say 'conversation.' And in your second step, you can define your privileged data type as 'transcripts of conversation.' You can now come up with all kinds of formalizable constraints on discourse itself – the examples are right there, after all, in those very transcripts! – and appear to prove that the study of discourse is the study of constraints on conversation structure as long as you don't worry about the question: For whom?

Suppose now that someone else does this, and you are part of the audience. Even if you spot the trick, you will find yourself in an awkward position. You might for instance find yourself inhabiting what Nietzsche calls a 'reactive' position, a position defined by the thing to which you are reacting. You might for instance find yourself saying 'there are no rules or constraints' or 'there's no such thing as syntax' or 'conversation has no structure' or something along these lines. This would be an over-reaction. The real issue is that if the study of language proceeds by fetishizing restricted data about fragments of language the possibility that such a study could reveal something about social relations among persons across diverse languages and cultures simply vanishes. A better response is to locate the narrowed purview within a wider one. To observe, for example, that when syntacticians claim to describe the concatenation rules of a 'language' they are not describing a language at all, but only a socially locatable register of a language (often the register called 'the Standard Language'), and the question of how they come to have any particular intuitions about it is part of what a social theory of language must explain. Or to observe that when the role of discourse in society is approached from the standpoint of some specific genre, such as 'face to face conversation,' the models identified as models of discourse make opaque discursive processes that connect persons at different scales of social grouping and historical time *through* that conversational encounter, but also through encounters whose genre characteristics are entirely different. An even better response is to make explicit the limits within which specific theories of language can explain aspects of it, so that the fruits of attachment to singular ideals can be enjoyed without nearby fields falling fallow. These are issues I take up in more detail later, especially in Chapters 1 and 2.

We shall do better to think of semiotic norms of language not as rules or constraints but as conditions on the construal of messages as signs. Such conditions are only satisfied for persons *for whom* these messages function as signs. You may not know the language your interlocutors are using. Or you may know it quite well, but speak a different register of it, and be inclined to call the register they are using by a specific name ('legalese' or 'baby talk,' for instance) and get only part of their gist. Every such register of a language has a describable grammar, which may differ only fractionally from Standard register, if a Standard exists, and only in some limited structural realm, such as lexicon or phonology; but this *fractional difference* itself conveys social information, is itself diacritic of social contrasts, which may also become commodified in various ways, even named as emblems of distinct social identities. Issues of register difference are discussed in Chapter 3. The social life of such commodity forms is the main focus of Chapter 4. And issues pertaining to social diacritics, emblems and identities is the topic of Chapter 5.

Reflexive operations can fractionally transform a norm, and such operations can recursively be iterated through further semiotic activity. This point is implicit in what I said earlier about the dialectic of norm and trope. Much of the complexity of the ways in which language can clarify social relations for users derives from the capacity of language users to acquire a reflexive grasp of particular aspects of a semiotic norm – *what* the norm is, *for whom* it is a norm, *when* the norm applies, and so on – and to treat such a reflexive grasp as a subsequent basis for communicating messages, even when the message consists of the act of upholding a contrastive norm as a diacritic of self. If we approach these issues by taking a 'view from nowhere' (Nagel 1986), we end up right there. Nowhere. We can only study the intelligibility of social relations for social actors by making reflexive processes a central focus of the study. The two-fold approach I suggested earlier – a linguistically informed approach to the semiotic character of these processes, and an ethnographically informed approach to the sociological positions they generate – helps us see that radical relativism (much like Platonic realism) is just a variant of the view from nowhere.

Aside from issues of reflexivity, three broad themes inform discussions of semiotic processes throughout this book. The first one is that language and non-language are intermingled with each other in communicative acts in ways more varied and intimate than common sense suggests. Much of the goal of the first two chapters is to make clear that these relationships, though diverse, can be characterized in precise ways. A second broad theme is that cultural formations are reproduced over social groups through communicative processes that unfold one participation framework at a time. It is sometimes supposed that culture is reproduced through communication in discrete and invariant 'concept'-sized chunks. Yet if cultural representations are formulated through semiotic acts, they become communicable only through participation frameworks. Hence to acquire them is to take a footing with respect to them. If cultural representations 'move' through space and time through semiotic activities they do so only through the footholds they find in participation frameworks. These footings and footholds reshape and resize them in various ways. I argue at a number of points in this book that, given their orientation to participation frameworks, semiotic acts (of whatever representational character) themselves generate various roles (stakes, stances, positions, identities), and relationships among roles (alignments, asymmetries, power, hierarchy). I discuss several different ways in which such effects, of different degrees of constancy or evanescence, can emerge, the semiotic conditions under which they do so, and the kinds of processes through which they are made to last, or are undone. In Chapter 2, I show that differential uses of a grammatical system itself generates types of asymmetry in society. Other mechanisms of footing and role alignment are discussed in Chapters 3 and 4. In Chapter 5 I discuss this issue in more generalized terms, showing that *any* perceivable behavior, whether linguistic or non-linguistic, can make facts of 'positionality' palpable in social interaction. The goal of these discussions is to make clear that semiotic activity generates roles and relationships in several, rather different ways, and that these require different kinds of analyses; and that we can study these phenomena in as careful a way as we like by attending to the thing to which interactants attend, namely semiotic activity itself.

A third broad theme is that language mediates social relations not only among persons who are co-present but also among persons separated from each other in time and space. Social relations are mediated by signs that connect persons to each other, allowing persons to engage with each other by engaging with signs that connect them in a semiotic encounter. What makes something a semiotic encounter in my sense is not the fact the people meet each other or come together in face to face settings. (Sometimes they do, of course, and when they do, we have the special case of face to face encounters. But this is just one possibility among many.) What makes something a **semiotic encounter** is the fact that a particular sign-phenomenon or communicative process connects persons to each other. (Even in the special case of face to face encounters it is not the fact of co-presence but the fact that one person's semiotic activity is audible and visible to another that creates the possibility of social inter-action; blindfolds and earplugs readily dispose of this possibility even when co-presence is maintained.) Persons encounter each other by encoun-tering signs that connect them to each other. They may encounter each other to different degrees. In our electronic age, persons are connected to each other in semiotic encounters of varying degrees of directness, imme-diacy, mutual awareness, and possible reciprocation. Each of us encounters countless others indirectly in mass media representations. Many encoun-ters are non-immediate in the sense that they involve intermediaries (known or unknown) that relay messages serially across a chain of communicative events. It is now commonplace for millions of persons to simultaneously inhabit a single interactional role without having any awareness of each other's existence (e.g., a mass television 'audience'). And although social interaction is sometimes reciprocal – i.e., all parties have the entitlement or opportunity to respond to those who engage them – this is not always the case in either face to face or electronically mediated interactions. Persons may thus be connected to each other through signs at varying degrees of separation by criteria of co-presence, directness, inter-mediation, mutual awareness, and the capacity to respond to each other. And language mediates social relations of diverse types across all such cases. These issues are introduced in 1.6 and developed further in later chapters.

Taking reflexive processes seriously also helps us get beyond some unproductive conundrums that haunt social theory. One of these is the so-called micro-/macro- divide. Each side has its proponents. Some social theorists believe that the micro-analysis of interaction if pursued relent-lessly enough may one day help explain large scale issues that matter to all of us. Some think that the true calling of social theory is to make macro-sociological generalizations, and that micro-analysts are wasting their time, or worse. Yet although these debates are often fierce they are not always clear about what the micro-/macro- divide is, or how it can be defined.

Part of the reason that the micro-/macro- divide is vexing is that it appears so natural, and yet so difficult to pin down. It seems natural because it appeals to a particular framework of part-whole reasoning that has long seemed plausible in twentieth century social theory, a framework where large scale phenomena are supposed to be composed of small scale phenomena and derive all of their causal structure from them. In yet other ways, the micro-/macro- distinction is an epistemological divide, one that separates different classes of social theory from each other through constraints placed by their underlying assumptions on what they can reveal about social processes. Yet the distinction is difficult to pin down because the prefixes *micro-* and *macro-* are correlative terms which cannot be defined on any absolute scale of largeness or smallness, only contextually and relationally, like *near* and *far*. Ad hoc definitions are always possible, of course. Many believe that face to face encounters are micro-phenomena and the emergence of nation states macro-phenomena. But these are merely differences of sociohistorical and demographic scale. Once we attend to matters of scale it is readily apparent that every macro-phenomenon is a micro-phenomenon with respect to a phenomenon at a larger scale. Differences of scale cannot by themselves constitute a divide.

Taking reflexive processes seriously means that the assumption that smaller scale phenomena causally shape larger scale phenomena, but not vice versa, also becomes implausible. In section 1.6 I argue that small scale reflexive activities have semiotic consequences that perdure beyond an encounter and become known to larger groups of people; in this respect a single encounter is an element of a larger process, and contributes to the shape of that process. You might say that this amounts to a part-whole argument, and in one sense it does. However a single semiotic encounter in my sense is not necessarily an event of micro-interaction. It may be. But, given the definition I just gave, it may also connect millions of people to each other, as in the case of a television broadcast or in other forms of mass communication. So there is a part-whole structure here but it does not correspond to the micro-/macro- relationship proposed in interactionist approaches to social theory. Nor does it involve a scheme of part-whole causal explanation. This is because a 'whole' is often a functional element of a 'part'.

To see this we have to see that semiotic encounters become occasions in which communication can occur only under certain conditions. Just 'being there' doesn't make communication happen. Take a case of oral communication in which polite speech is being used. One kind of condition on politeness being conveyed by the utterance is that expressions that occur in the utterance need to have become valorized in a specific way through a larger social process as polite forms for at least some people (what is polite for one sub-group is often rude for others); another condition is that the particular individuals who happen to be there, who perceive these signs as audible speech, need to have gone through particular trajectories of socialization so as to belong to the relevant groups, that is, to have become individuals for whom these forms count as polite (or rude). These are two entirely different kinds of large scale processes. And both serve as conditions on the communicative possibilities available in the smaller scale encounter. In this sense, the 'macro-' level is part of the 'micro-' level. It is presupposed within the current encounter as a condition on there being communication at all.

At some points in this book I talk of small scale encounters shaping larger scale processes; at other points I describe large scale processes through which particular types of registers emerge and become usable in face to face encounters. Thus relationships across scales that differ as smaller-to-larger and larger-to-smaller both matter. And a social theory of language that recognizes these relationships and explores their consequences gets rid of the epistemological boundaries that separate social theories that do not.

When people invoke the micro-/macro- divide they are sometimes thinking of other things too. For instance, to many anthropologists, an account of how the deictics *I* and *you* work in English is clearly an account of a 'micro-' phenomenon. Why? Well *I* and *you* are just little words. How about an account of all English deictics? Oh, that's still just a few words; and it's only English. How about a framework for reasoning about deixis in all human languages? (Notice that such a framework, if accurate, would help us understand how more than six billion people anchor themselves hundreds of times every day with respect to their referential and interpersonal realities in acts of reference.) Still not 'macro-' enough? My impression is that it isn't. My impression is that for many anthropologists, 'macro-' things are things denoted by certain types of nouns. If I'm writing about 'modernity' or 'hierarchy' or 'globalization' that's clearly 'macro-'. Notice that these nouns are abstract nouns, not deictics; they bathe their referents in a numinous glow of vastness and mystery. (If I point out that modernity hasn't reached all six billion yet, it won't help.) Part of my argument in this book is that phenomena of these kinds, phenomena grouped under vast notional rubrics in this way cannot be studied empirically unless the forms of social-semiotic activity through which they are expressed, and the processes through which such activities become valorized so as to be able to express them are clearly understood. These activities need not depend on the use of abstract nouns, or have abstract nouns as names. As long as they are organized as practices in which many people engage, they are large scale social practices in the relevant sense. Most such practices don't come with ready-made, naturally occurring, everyday names – abstract or otherwise – and for those that do, the everyday names with which we try to pry into them, or pry them open, mislead us. We can understand their social consequences only if we understand their semiotic organization. This argument is developed over the course of this book and culminates in the discussion in Chapter 8.

You might say that what we ordinarily call 'language' also constitutes a vast notional rubric. This is perfectly true. That is why a social analysis of language always encounters ideologies of language that co-exist with the phenomenon itself and which themselves require analysis (in both semiotic and ethnographic terms) in order for the social phenomenon of language to be understood. And that is why a lot of the work that I do in the pages that follow involves looking at ideologies of language.

We know that social relations can be expressed by all kinds of things – gifts, clothing, cars, handshakes, land mines. Why emphasize the role of language? If we regard social relations not merely from the vantage of those scattered moments – whether warm or explosive – in which they rise to focal awareness or to forms of civic summary by individual persons, but regard them instead as positions held or taken within cultural projects in which others also play a part, and if we take seriously the idea that the intelligibility and efficacy of social relations depends on the character of reflexive processes that connect persons to each other – and I claim that we must do this to study social relations of any kind, however expressed – then we can scarcely proceed without an understanding of a type of semiotic activity that gives reflexive processes their greatest complexity and elaboration for humans. This activity, the activity of using language, plays a central role in connecting social persons to each other at every scale of geographic and historical remove, in classifying and valorizing perceivable objects so that social relations can be expressed through them, and, since reflexive operations can be iterated, in formulating models of sociohistorical reality that diverge fractionally within the very order of interpersonal semiotic activity that gives rise to them, thereby linking social semiosis to forms of positional difference, contestation and politics. Understanding the various reflexive relationships expressible through language and the social processes to which these possibilities give rise is our first task, the main business of Chapter 1.

I

REFLEXIVITY

1.0 Introduction

In every human society certain uses of language make palpable highly specific kinds of social effects such as the indication of one's relationship to persons spoken to or spoken about, or the presentation of self as belonging to some identifiable social group, class, occupation or other category of personhood. In such cases particular features of utterance appear to formulate a sketch of the social occasion constituted by the act of speaking. Our sense that the people that we meet are persons of certain kinds, that they differ from us in status or group-affiliation, that they establish recognizable roles and relationships in their encounters with us are all social effects mediated by the utterances they produce. Unavoidably, such effects depend also on accompanying non-linguistic signs (such as gesture, clothing, features of setting) which comprise a context for construing the effects of speech. In general, therefore, the social effects mediated by speech are highly context-bound or **indexical** in character: they are evaluated in relation to the context or situation at hand, including those aspects of the situation created by what has already been said or done. Either an utterance is felt to be appropriate to the situation as already understood, or it alters the context in some recognizable way, transforming it into a situation of an entirely different kind. We may speak, in particular, of **social indexicality** when the contextual features indexed by speech and accompanying signs are understood as attributes of, or relationships between, social persons.

In this book I use the term **social relations** for this domain of enactable roles and relationships. The more encompassing term is useful because 'roles' and 'relationships' are correlative ways of talking about persons. To identify a person's role is potentially to infer relationships to others such as oneself. To identify a relationship is to recognize connections between persons, to view them in roles that vary as the relationship unfolds. Human languages have a variety of properties that delineate social relations in this sense. These clarify diverse aspects of our social being. They allow us to negotiate our dealings with others in particular encounters and hence over many encounters; they allow us to establish identities recognized by others, to maintain these identities over time or to depart from them; they permit the treatment of diverse objects as valued goods or commodities through which describable social identities and relationships are expressed. The goal of this book is to discuss the ways in which language plays a part in these possibilities.

It will be evident that in order to do this we need to become clearer about the processes whereby images of role and relationship come to be associated with language in the first place. Yet our everyday terminology for talking about these issues is quite unsatisfactory. Most language users can recognize the social indexical effects of speech more easily than they can describe *how* they recognize them. If ideas about language are at issue, they are often unarticulated ideas. We might do better, perhaps, by speaking of habits of evaluation. But whether we speak of ideas or habits (or find, as we shall, that we can dispense with neither notion) it is clear that we are dealing with the social value of language for persons connected to each other through its use, as speakers or hearers of spoken utterances, as writers and readers of written ones, and so on.

Utterances are social in several senses. In a very basic sense, utterances are social because they are signs that function as connectors. They form a connection or a bridge between – they semiotically **mediate** relations between – persons who interact with each other through them. The connection is perceivable (audible as sound, legible as script); it has physical and durational characteristics which allow for differences in the propinquity, number and types of persons it connects (viz., oral vs. televised vs. printed speech); it may mediate social relations at a small or large sociohistorical scale; it is accompanied by non-linguistic signs, upon which its intelligibility often depends. But utterances are social in a second, more specific sense too, the sense to which I alluded in my opening paragraph. They formulate a sketch of the social occasion in which they occur; they make social relations construable as effects of their occurrence. Such effects are of more than one type and require different types of analysis.

In one type of case the effect is **stereotypically** associated with the semiotic display; many people are socialized so to recognize it. In such cases widespread schemes of speech valorization associate particular forms of speech with commonplace value distinctions (e.g., good vs. bad speech, upper-class vs. lower-class speech), which are known to a large number of speakers. The ability to recognize such effects depends on a prior history of socialization through which persons become acquainted with such culture-internal values; if you lack the requisite background you cannot recover the distinction. For such cases, the task for a social theory of language is two-fold: on the one hand to explain how the use of speech is interpreted in the light of such value systems; and, on the other, to explain how particular systems of speech valorization come into existence in the first place and, once formed, exist as cultural phenomena over the course of some period for some locatable group of social persons.

But language use has a second kind of social effectiveness as well. In this type of case the social effects in question are mediated by **emergent** features of current semiotic activity. No socially widespread scheme of speech valorization underlies the construal. We shall see in Chapter 2 that even ordinary referential uses of language – cases where speech is used to pick out and characterize entities in the world – pervasively mediate interpersonal effects of this kind. In such cases social relations are mediated by an emergent organization of signs that co-occur in the current interaction; they are not mediated by the stereotypic values of any single sign. For example, when one person succeeds (or fails) in drawing another's attention to a referent, or characterizes a referent in a way that the other accepts (or rejects), or uses a referring expression that the other understands (or doesn't), the relative behavior of the two individuals constitutes a form of emergent alignment between them. A variety of such positions, stances, alliances and boundaries readily emerge around acts of referential communication in our everyday experience of language use, but most of them last only for a moment or two and give way to others, often following each other in rapid succession across phases of interaction. Others last longer, as we shall see, in ways that depend on the macro-social organization of interpersonal encounters. All such effects are highly palpable and consequential while an interaction is under way but the sign-configurations that mark them are less easily discussed out of context, particularly in the more evanescent cases. Nonetheless social effects of this kind do have a principled organization that a social theory of language must describe.

Whether we are dealing with stereotypic or emergent social effects, or with the way in which they are laminated together in some stretch of semiotic activity, our ability to describe such effects depends on **reflexive** uses of language. Such uses of language are reflexive in the sense that language is both a semiotic mechanism involved in the performance of these effects and in their construal. The purpose of this chapter is to characterize some of the more basic issues linked to the apparently simple observation that the social life of language, and of language users, is pervasively organized through and around reflexive activities.

1.1 Reflexive activity

Human beings routinely engage in forms of **reflexive activity**, namely activities in which communicative signs are used to typify other perceivable signs. Reflexive acts differ among themselves in a variety of ways, such as the kinds of signs through which they are expressed, the kinds of phenomena they typify, the explicitness with which they do so, and the degree to which they constitute commonplace practices. In the sections below I show that we cannot understand the variety of social relations enactable in social life without coming to grips with the range of reflexive relationships expressible through speech. Let us take the special case of reflexive linguistic activity, or metalinguistic activity, as our point of departure.

Metalinguistic activity

To speak of **metalinguistic activity** is to speak of a vast range of meaningful behaviors that typify the attributes of language, its users, and the activities accomplished through its use. All attempts to understand the properties of language require the use of metalinguistic devices, of which the technical terminologies employed by linguists are a special case. A variety of metalinguistic activities occur naturally in social life as well, and are readily recognized as such. Metalinguistic routines such as requesting, formulating and interpreting word glosses are a commonplace of everyday experience; in the case of parent-child interaction such activities are necessary for the acquisition of vocabulary items by children. Yet the role of metalinguistic activity in shaping and propagating cultural regularities other than the lexicon is less obvious to our everyday intuitions.

The study of language as a social phenomenon must include the study of metalinguistic activity for a simple reason: language users employ language to categorize or classify aspects of language use, including forms of utterance, the situations in which they are used, and the persons who use them. Such reflexive classifications shape the construal of speech (and accompanying signs) for persons acquainted with them. Institutionalized metalinguistic practices play a distinctive role in expanding this circle of acquaintance, in making reflexive classifications more widely known. But before we turn to the analysis of such large scale social processes it is necessary to attend to the range and variety of reflexive activity itself. Let us begin with metalinguistic acts in the least restrictive sense of the term.

Any act which typifies some aspect of language is, by definition, a metalinguistic act. Notice that this broad and minimal definition commits us only to the object typified by the act, i.e., 'some aspect of language.' It tells us nothing about the form of the act itself. From this standpoint, metalinguistic acts necessarily typify aspects of language, though they need not themselves be linguistic utterances. An eyebrow raised in response to a remark implicitly evaluates the import of that remark and is, to this extent, a metalinguistic act. But it is not an instance of language use. In contrast, a response like 'You sound silly!' is both a metalinguistic evaluation and a

The point holds quite generally, not just for verbs, as in the examples in (2), but for metapragmatic uses of nouns and adjectives too. Thus when we look across cultures we find that terms such as *politeness, refinement* or *respectability* are commonly used to describe specific uses of language; but the same terms are used to describe non-linguistics activities as well, such as bowing, putting palms together, dressing appropriately and so on. For example, in Thai, the term *mâi suphâap* 'impolite' is predicable of utterances and kinesic activity but also of physical objects: 'casual sandals and revealing or immodest women's clothes ... are called *mâi suphâap* 'impolite' and symbolize a lack of concern and respect for authority' (Simpson 1997: 42). Here diverse objects – specific forms of utterance, gesture clothing, footwear, etc. – which can themselves be displayed as signs in behavior are grouped together under a metasemiotic typification. They comprise the **semiotic range** of the typification. The typification is a **metasign**, a sign typifying others, which motivates a likeness among objects within its semiotic range (Figure 1.1). Diverse objects are now signs of a particular type of conduct. They are **object-signs** with respect to the metasign that groups them together as signs of the same type of conduct.

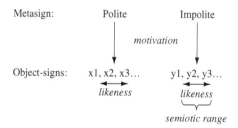

Figure 1.1   *Metasemiotic motivation of icons*

Metasemiotic typifications of this kind motivate a type of **cross-modal iconism** whereby forms of speech (y1) are likened to object-signs of other kinds (y2, y3, etc.), such as paralanguage, gesture, body comportment or artifactual accompaniment. Many kinds of metasemiotic activity can achieve this effect, as we shall see; the Thai case here, involving a regularity of predication, is just the simplest kind of example.[6]

The fact that language may be used as a metasemiotic notation for both linguistic and non-linguistic signs has the consequence that for many social phenomena (such as 'politeness' or 'power' and so on) reflexive activity blurs the boundaries between language and non-language at the level of object-signs, i.e., behavioral displays. Many kinds of behavior become motivated as signs of 'politeness' and the like, each capable of indexing a comparable social fact for those acquainted with the scheme of metasemiotic typification.

In many cases, a range of objects thus grouped into a likeness can co-occur with each other as signs in social interaction. The fact that sign repertoires in different semiotic channels receive a unified (or at least overlapping) metasemiotic treatment often has the consequence that acts of using certain kinds of socially valued speech appear most felicitous and appropriate when the speech variety co-occurs with certain *non-linguistic* displays; in such cases, the occurrence – display, enactment – of certain non-linguistic signs may even be treated, culture-internally, as a prerequisite on the appropriate use of corresponding linguistic signs, and vice-versa. We are observing, in other words, that:

Summary 1.3
Overlaps in the metasemiotic treatment of otherwise disparate signs provide criteria on the appropriate co-occurrence of such signs.

One common type of situation where this occurs is the case where normative traditions of etiquette specify restrictions on the behavioral display of signs in many channels. The following example from Javanese is a sample of metasemiotic discourse that describes canons of semiotic display among the *Priyayi*, the traditional Javanese aristocracy:

(3) A complicated etiquette dictates the way a person sits, stands, directs his eyes, holds his hands, points, greets people, laughs, walks, dresses, and so on. There is a close association between the rigor with which the etiquette of movement is observed and the degree of refinement in speech. The more polite a person's language, the more elaborate are his other behavioral patterns; the more informal his speech, the more relaxed and simplified his gestures.

(Poedjosoedarmo 1968:54)

This example is more elaborate than the previous Thai case in a variety of ways and I shall have more to say about it later (1.6). One thing is similar however. A unifying form of metasemiotic treatment (here, a normative code of etiquette) imbues diverse object-signs (the manner of sitting, standing, gaze, laughter, dress, speech, and so on) with comparable values (the capacity to index refinement in performance). Among the issues that require further discussion are the nature of the processes whereby such icons become semiotically elaborated (i.e., acquire a more diverse semiotic range), become widely known (acquire, as I shall say, a larger social domain), or are treated as authoritative by some among those acquainted with them.[7]

The important point for the moment is that once interactants have criteria on the comparability of signs, the actual sequential deployment or performance of such signs itself carries information. Let us consider this point in more detail.

1.2 Text-level indexicality and interactional tropes

Metasemiotic schemes of the above kind permit various types of manipulation in the order of interaction itself. The very fact that a scheme of typification can motivate likenesses among otherwise disparate signs (i.e., can treat all the x's in Figure 1.1 as 'polite' and all the y's as 'impolite') has the consequence that, relative to the scheme of motivation, *the comparability of co-occurring signs* in the temporal flow of behavior itself carries information. In simple terms: any observer acquainted with the scheme can evaluate an order of co-occurring signs – which may include signs in many channels, and thus comprise **a multi-channel text** – for internal likeness and unlikeness of effect among its partials. The top line in Figure 1.2 illustrates the case where all the signs displayed in behavior are judged to have the same indexical values. Here the order of text is **indexically congruent**. The lower line illustrates the non-congruent case.

Evaluations of textual congruence or non-congruence take as their object of evaluation an order of co-occurring signs made sensible or perceivable through timebound activity. To speak of co-occurring signs as an order of **text** is to observe that they have a unifying **texture** i.e., fit together in some way. This is another way of saying that a larger whole is evaluable for the congruence of its parts. The criteria of likeness or 'fit' may be quite various.[8] But when such criteria are indeed available, a textual order contains, or conveys, indexical information that is not reducible to the indexical values of any of its parts. To speak of **text-level indexicality** in this sense is to speak of a wholly emergent type of information that reflexively shapes the construal of behavior while the behavior is still under way.

Such text-level indexical effects are completely **non-detachable** for purposes of construal: They are not preserved under decontextualization. If you isolate a piece from the total textual process that motivates the effect, the semiotic partial thus 'detached' appears to have no property that could explain the text-level effect, no matter how carefully you inspect it! The effect depends on the comparability of co-occurring signs – by criteria of congruence/non-congruence – and therefore vanishes when the sign is isolated and inspected by itself. In matters of etiquette the non-congruent case in Figure 1.2 is best exemplified by the phenomenon of the 'fatal breach': imperfect mastery of a code of etiquette often allows a person to

Congruent: ...... x1 ...... x2 ...... x3   —————————→

                                                  time

Non-congruent: ...... x1 ...... y2 ...... x3

Figure 1.2 *Metasemiotically motivated co-occurrence effects: text-level indexicality*

observe many of its niceties in performance, to display the self as refined in many ways, until such moment as a single mis-step (y2 in the figure) indexes that imperfect mastery, relegating the person to a less authentic status (a social climber, parvenu) in the judgment of others.

Any approach to interaction that does not attend to text-level indexicality remains incomplete in the sense that it fails to capture a large part of what it seeks to explain. For during social interaction, attention to text-level indexicality allows participants to formulate **emergent reflexive models** of what is happening, who their interactants are, what they're doing, what they intend by their doings, what they actually achieve, and so on, over an interval of semiotically mediated interaction; such a textually diagrammed model of interaction, or **interactional text** (Silverstein 1993), is shaped by inferences from many co-textual cues and therefore differs significantly from the effects of any particular one. Indeed, cases where textually diagrammed models of interaction are inconsistent with the effects of localizable signs are sometimes puzzling or confusing to those at the receiving end of the message, and such puzzlement or uncertainty can be exploited by the sender of the message as a way of controlling or dominating interlocutor.

A particularly dramatic instance of this occurs in the case of interactional tropes of veiled aggression such as irony and sarcasm. The example below is from Paul Friedrich's classic study of pronominal usage in Russian. After giving a systematic account of norms of usage associated with the Russian pronouns *vy* (polite) and *ty* (non-polite) Friedrich observes that such norms are often manipulated in encounters to yield complex interactional tropes, such as the one recalled below by Tolstoy from an encounter between an old countess and a young prince:

(4) This and other cases in my data point to important discriminations not covered by my system: those of sarcasm and irony. Under certain circumstances the opposite of the expected usage could confuse, humiliate, or affront an addressee ... This is illustrated by a passage from the twentieth chapter of Tolstoy's *Childhood*.

> Grandmother had a singular gift of expressing her opinion about people under certain circumstances by using the plural and singular pronouns of the second person together with a certain tone of voice. She used *vy* and *ty* contrary to general custom, and on her lips these shades of meaning acquired an entirely different significance. When a young prince walked up to her she said a few words calling him *vy* and looked at him with an expression of such contempt that if I had been in his place I would have become utterly confused ...

(An ancient countess would normally use *ty* to a young prince.)

(Friedrich 1986: 280)

It is readily seen that the overall effect in question is a laminated interactional trope, the result of two distinct tropes – one performed through a linguistic sign, the other through a kinesic act – that are superimposed upon one another.

The first of these is the trope of hyperpoliteness achieved by 'the opposite of the expected [pronominal] usage': Since the countess and the prince do not differ in class (both are aristocrats), the salient status asymmetry between them is one of age; the prince is younger and would normatively expect his older interlocutor to use the non-polite pronoun *ty* in addressing him. By using *vy* the countess is troping upon this norm (performing a usage that is not congruent with co-textually motivated expectations) in the direction of excessive politeness. The second trope is motivated by kinesic accompaniment: the expression of 'contempt' is utterly non-congruent with the excessive politeness performed through the linguistic trope. These two performed signs – the pronoun *vy* and the facial expression – index models of social relations that are mutually inconsistent. Together they constitute the trope of veiled aggression: the contemptuous glance implements a form of aggression, the pronominal politeness counts as its veiling. Tolstoy remarks that in this scenario he would have become 'utterly confused.' Creating such confusion among interlocutors is a characteristic feature of strategies of veiled aggression cross-culturally (Agha 1997). Any act that successfully implements more than one model of its own significance creates a tension in the interlocutor, curtailing the avenues of unambiguous response available in the next turn.

Such text-level effects differ from item-level effects in that they can only be 'calculated' or reckoned by appeal to a sign-configuration – a semiotic array or text involving two or more co-occurring signs – that emerges or unfolds during the course of interaction. Now, it may seem that to speak of co-occurring signs in this way is potentially to open up a vast can of worms. Many signs of diverse kinds typically co-occur with utterances in interaction. Which of these are relevant?

Even when the values of co-occurring signs are non-congruent – so that one marks rudeness, the other excessive politeness – the text-level construal **converges** when such co-occurring signs have the same **indexical focus**, that is, convey information *about the same interactant*; and, independently of the first issue, converges in a second way when the effects in question are understood as having the same **indexical origo**, that is, are understood as *performed by the same interactant* (see 1.4 for a more inclusive definition of origo and focus, of which these are special cases). Thus in the above example, the two sign-elements – facial expression and pronominal usage – are non-congruent in social import (one is rude, the other polite) but convergent in both indexical origo and focus. The countess is the origo or source of both effects since she is the one who performs the gaze and utterance. And the prince is the focus of these semiotic acts since the countess' act of 'calling him *vy*' establishes the prince as the referent/addressee of the second person pronoun, and the directionality of the countess' gaze (when she 'looked at him with an expression of . . . contempt') establishes him as the focus of her kinesic disapprobation.

In general therefore when we speak of text-level indexicality we are concerned not only with mere facts of co-occurrence (in some physical sense), not only with the congruence of sign-values (relative, say, to a cultural scheme) but also with the convergence of indexical origo and focus of utterance-acts (within the emergent order of interaction). The example discussed above involves a very simple type of case. In later discussion we will see that the overall patternment of origo and focus may be more complex, and in a variety of ways. For example, different semiotic fractions of an utterance-act may be non-congruent in origo/focus, thus yielding more complex figures of action, such as voicing effects, ventriloquation, hybrid personae, and so on. In the case of elaborate honorific registers, a single utterance may concurrently mark the speaker/actor's relations with multiple interactants, who are all established as distinct foci of indexical deference by segmentable pieces of the utterance. Conversely, in a multi-party interaction, a single individual may become the focus of multiple utterance-acts having the same sign-value (e.g., all acts of disapprobation) even though the origos of these acts may be different individuals (e.g., cases where multiple interlocutors 'gang up' against a single individual) yielding various emergent groupings and alignments in interaction.

This section is intended as an initial orientation to the importance of text-level indexicality. The key point here is that *the co-textual organization of signs* can, as a whole, formulate effects which differ from any effects associated with *text-segments* that occur as its parts. In the case of **interactional tropes** one segment is non-congruent with another, and this effect is interpersonally significant. The relevance of criteria such as convergence of origo/focus to the above examples should also be clear. Other issues pertaining to this type of analysis are introduced later.

1.3 Reflexive activity in interaction

The preceding discussion makes clear that we cannot study the way in which social relations are established in interaction without careful attention to who produces a sign, to whom it is directed, what feature of context it clarifies, and so on. I have also suggested that we can make little sense of overall, cumulative effects in interaction without a careful analysis of (1) the semiotic partials that contribute component effects, and (2) the way in which these components are 'resolved' or unified (to the extent that they are) by the emergent orderliness of co-occurring signs, or text, which induces a higher-level patternment, evaluable by criteria such as congruence of indexical sign-value and convergence of the sign's origo or focus.

Part of the complexity of social life derives from the fact that overall cumulative effects may have component effects that exhibit different reflexive relationships. Our goal now is to understand the nature of this variation and its consequences for social life.

In section 1.1, we considered several types of reflexive relationships – or, meta-sign/object-sign relationships – the most important of which may be summarized as follows:

Summary 1.4
We have so far considered a variety of reflexive acts, including

(a) acts that typify some aspect of language use but are not expressed through linguistic signs
(b) acts that are metalinguistic in import and themselves consist of language use (S 1.1)
(c) acts that metasemiotically group together linguistic and non-linguistic signs, thus motivating icons or likenesses among them (Figure 1.1)

It will be clear that all linguistic acts are semiotic acts, and all metalinguistic acts are metasemiotic acts, though the converse is not true in either case.

I want to focus now on case (b), that is, on reflexive acts that themselves consist of language use. For this case we can now make explicit an assumption that has surfaced several times before, namely the character of such acts as pragmatic signs. Linguistic utterances that occur as messages in speech events comprise an order of **pragmatic signs** insofar as they are *perceivable acts that convey information to someone who perceives them*. We have observed also that **metapragmatic signs** are merely a special case of pragmatic signs; what is special about them is a functional relationship to other signs. In other words, pragmatic signs function metapragmatically insofar as they *convey information about other pragmatic phenomena* (their 'objects' of typification) such as signs that have occurred earlier, or elsewhere, or the effects of such signs. In such cases one pragmatic sign typifies another. The case of reported speech is a familiar example; here, one utterance describes another.

To say that a sign functions metapragmatically is merely to say that some particular embodied sign occurs as a perceivable (audible, visible, etc.) message and that its occurrence tells us something about another pragmatic phenomenon, its object, typifying it in some way. Part of the reflexive power of language consists of the fact that the **object typified** may be deictically near or far, specific or generic, manifestly real or imaginary, or made real (actualized) only later, through subsequent semiotic activities. But the **typifying sign** is itself always materially embodied; it is the perceivable product of an act in every case.

In the sections that follow, I characterize some of the ways in which the products of semiotic activity serve as pointers or guides to (we can think of them as 'directions for finding and understanding') a variety of other semiotic phenomena. We make meaning – or intervene meaningfully in behavior – as we go along. Once formulated in particular phases of social interaction the products of semiotic activity may be negotiated, transformed, ratified, even mutually ratified, by interactants during the course of further interaction. Some among these semiotic products and projections may come to be taken so completely for granted in subsequent semiotic activity that they are no longer in dispute. In some cases cultural processes of communicative transmission bring these constructs to the attention of other members of society, making them more widely known and, thus, presupposable in use by larger segments of the population; when such processes are highly institutionalized, the products of semiotic activity may even come to form a routinely accepted background reality for very large groups of people. In such cases we may speak of **socially routinized metapragmatic constructs** (such as beliefs, habits, norms, ideologies) that are still experienced only through *locatable* semiotic activities, including some which – because they are organized as widely established large scale social practices – routinely reanimate them in comparable ways for many people in *diverse* locales. They are 'constructs' in the sense that they are made and unmade through semiotic activity; they are 'social' constructs in that they are invoked in use and construal by many people. I return to these cases in 1.6.

In the remainder of section 1.3, I wish to focus on semiotic activities whose products typify the very same interactions in which they occur. In every such case the typification alters the interaction in which it occurs, whether in an obvious way (e.g., by describing a feature of that interaction), or in a more subtle manner, through a more implicit typification. I begin with a well known class of explicit descriptions, the case that in common parlance is called 'reported speech,' or, among linguists, **reported speech deixis**. (The technical term captures the fact that reported speech constructions are text-patterns involving deictic elements.) In discussing this special case, I introduce the more general phenomenon of **deixis**, or denotational indexicality, in an informal way through a series of examples. In section 1.4, I turn to a more systematic exposition of deixis (in general) and its role in shaping social-interpersonal realities.

Descriptions that shape interactions

The case of reported speech – or 'one utterance describing another' – is a transparent example of metapragmatic activity because the typification consists of an explicit description and the object typified is depicted as a speech event distinct from the act of utterance. For example, a report of speech such as

(5) '"Let him go!" she insisted'

stipulates the occurrence of a pragmatic speech event distinct from itself. It depicts such event as having had certain characteristics, such as a message-form ('"*Let him go!*" ...'), a speaker deictically formulated as distinct from current speech participants ('... *she* ...' vs. *I* or *you*), a specific character as a type of social act ('... *insist*[ence] ...' vs. *saying, pleading*, etc.), and a deictic temporal remove from the current event, here an occurrence in past time marked by verb tense ('... -*ed*'). Any one of these features (reported message, type of social act, speaker and time) may be more or less specifically delineated on some given occasion, as we saw for the reported speech examples in (2). Nonetheless, a reported speech utterance is, in all cases, a single semiotic event that contains within itself an image of another event which is stipulated to have occurred. Only the metapragmatic sign (the reporting utterance) is actually experienced by someone in every case; the object described (the utterance reported) need never have occurred before, or may have occurred but not in the manner depicted. Thus what is commonly called 'reported speech' is in general better termed 'represented speech' (and sometime even 'constructed dialogue'), a point to which I return at the end of this section.

Part of the power of reported speech constructions lies in the fact that the act of reporting speech effectively transforms the current interaction whether or not the report is accurate. This is because 'accuracy' and 'effectiveness' are quite distinct issues, involving two different semiotic relationships: the first of these involves the axis of **denotation**, the second the axis of **interaction**. The first axis links the description to the thing or event described. The second axis links the speaker of the description to the hearer of the description.

Thus one sense in which reported speech constructions comprise a metapragmatic resource in social interaction is that such constructions may be used in any interaction to denote the characteristics of *other* social interactions in ways which contribute to the shape of the *current* interaction. Specific consequences emerge from the way in which the event described (and hence the 'characters' denoted) and the event of describing (and hence the interactants) are linked to each other. Utterances differ, in other words, in the deictic selectivity (see 1.4) with which they refer to those who are interacting through those utterances. In cases where the utterance's referents are current interactants – e.g., someone's saying *you insulted me* to someone else – certain consequences (explanations, apologies) may follow more typically than in cases where they are not. In a case where the characters referred to are not current interactants – e.g., saying *Ann insulted Bill* to the same person – the relevance of the utterance to the current interaction may not be clear from sentence denotation itself;

however, additional co(n)textually established facts of **role alignment** (e.g., Ann is the hearer's daughter, Bill the speaker's son) may suffice to drive home the implication that a complaint is now being made, yielding similar apologies and explanations by way of response.

But even if the two utterances have comparable effects in the scenarios described, there are sharp differences in the way in which these effects are achieved and the conditions under which they become construable. In the first example, certain deictic features of the utterance – prominently, the pronouns *you* and *me* – link its denotational content to its interactional frame more explicitly than do any forms in the second example. The pronouns achieve this effect by collapsing the distinction between the axes of denotation and interaction. They denote occupants of interactional roles: *you* denotes addressee-of-utterance, and *me* the speaker-of-utterance. Since parts of the utterance *you insulted me* denote the interactants linked together through its use, the relevance of the utterance to the pragmatic occasion of its occurrence is relatively transparent to interactants themselves; the link between denoted and interactional realities is construable by anyone who knows English. But the interactional relevance of *Ann insulted Bill* to the scenario of its utterance cannot be established so precisely by forms that occur in the sentence itself. It is not enough to know English. In the case considered above, only those interlocutors who also know relevant facts of role alignment (that Ann is hearer's daughter, Bill is speaker's son) could possibly incline to the view that the utterance is a complaint.

In general, then, whenever an utterance denotes another speech event the act of producing the utterance shapes the interaction in which it occurs in ways mediated by the mode of linkage between the event denoted and the current event. When the link between the two events is locally explicit in sentence denotation, the utterance presents a simple – relatively decontextualizable – model of the character of its relevance to the occasion of its production. The model is relatively salient even to a hearer who pays little attention to further contextual facts. In contrast, utterances whose relevance to the current interaction is not explicit from their denotation may shape the current interaction in equally powerful ways, but only for those who are able to attend to features of presupposed context (such as facts of role alignment in the above example) that connect the states of affairs denoted by the utterance to the activities and roles that current interactants grasp as their circumstances, transforming the latter only for those who see the connection.

This point may be stated more generally as follows:

Summary 1.5
The less explicit a metapragmatic utterance, the more context is needed to establish its import, or even to recognize *that* it is a metapragmatic act of some kind.

Let me now clarify an issue to which I alluded earlier, namely the question of 'represented' versus 'reported' speech. As we saw above, one reason that the term **represented speech** is a better generic label for this class of phenomena concerns the currently constructed nature of reports; such constructions may or may not prove, upon further inspection, to be accurate. An even more general reason is that representations of speech are commonly called 'reports' only when they deictically formulate the speech that they represent as having occurred in past time (see (5)ff.). But this is a very special case. Representations of speech need not deictically formulate their pragmatic objects as having occurred in past time, or even in an interaction distinct from the current one. The utterances typified may be depicted as occurring in contiguous or proximate phases of the current interaction (e.g., as having occurred in an immediately preceding turn), or as utterances that *will* occur, or as utterances that *could, might, should, might not*, occur. All of these effects can be achieved through various alternative forms of deictic anchoring (notice my use of modal verbs to describe these cases).

Let us first consider cases where reflexive relationships hold among contiguous (or relatively proximate) phases of pragmatic activity. These are cases where the metapragmatic sign (the typifying utterance) occurs in the immediate discursive co-text of its object-signs (the utterances typified), whether before or after them, and its deictic features provide the hearer with a set of 'directions' for where to look in its co-text to find the utterances typified. If we represent successive utterances in discourse by means of boxes or cells, as in Figure 1.3, we can diagram such intratextual relations with arrows linking the text-segments shown as cells. The examples in (a) typify prior discursive activity, those in (b) the characteristics of utterances to follow.

The explicit co-textual descriptions in Figure 1.3 depend on a variety of reflexive cues which occur in the current utterance (the grey cell) and allow hearers to locate and construe the target utterance (the dotted cell). These include: nouns and adjectives used to characterize the pragmatics of contiguous stretches of speech (as *gossip, eloquence*, as a *hint* or a *lie*, as

(a)	(b)
How eloquent! Couldn't have put it better myself!	This is only gossip, but guess what...
That's not what I meant. Can't you take a hint?	You'll never believe what I heard...
You're lying. She never did that!	What I am about to say is confidential...
Stop it! Don't be mean!	Let me tell you something as a friend...

Figure 1.3   *Reflexive descriptions of speech co-text and context*

confidential); tense and mood deictics (past or future tense, subjunctives, purpose clauses, etc.) that specify whether the target utterance is prior or subsequent in time to the current utterance; expressions that deictically denote current interactants (*I, you*), their discursively performed personae (*Don't be mean!*) and social relationships among them (e.g., *Let me tell you something as a friend*).

By using such metapragmatic descriptions of speech context and co-text, and independently of whether the utterance described has just occurred or is yet to occur, language users reflexively shape the flow of subsequent discourse (and relations among discourse participants) by means of acts that intervene metadiscursively within that flow. The examples in Figure 1.3 are of a commonplace sort (we do this sort of thing all the time) and are easily identified as having interpersonal significance (because they rely on explicit description). But our previous discussion – and its summary in S 1.5 – suggests that in addition to such locally explicit forms of reflexive activity, social interaction is also permeated by forms of reflexive activity that require a much more careful reading of a larger semiotic surround – the potentially multi-channel semiotic co-text of the utterance – even to be recognized as reflexive acts.

In such cases the ability to perform relatively non-transparent acts often becomes effective as a form of interpersonal power. We saw earlier that when polite language is used as a form of veiled aggression (as in the Russian case in (3) above) relatively implicit co-textual effects enable a form of control over interlocutor not straightforwardly describable as control. Here the act is hegemonic, a form of effective domination barely describable as such.

But implicitly reflexive acts may also constitute a form of resistance to power. Let us consider some examples. In the cases discussed below speakers who lack entitlements to initiate certain modes of conduct employ implicit metapragmatic strategies in order to circumvent normative constraints. Here the non-transparency of implicit typifications is, once again, the central semiotic resource.

Circumventing norms

In Swedish, as in many languages, the act of switching from formal to informal patterns of address is constrained by **dispensation rules** (Ervin-Tripp 1986), norms that entitle certain categories of interlocutor, but not others, to initiate shifts to informal address. How do people get around such norms? The discussion below is based on Paulston 1976 and describes a situation that existed some years ago, despite my expository use of the historical present.

Paulston observes that a variety of expressions are used in formal address (titles, title and last name, the somewhat ambiguously 'polite' pronoun *ni*); these contrast with patterns of usage involving the informal pronoun, *du*. In cases of status asymmetry, lower status persons norma-tively use formal address – such as Title + Last Name (or T + LN) – for higher status interlocutors, who, in turn, respond with *du*. Such a pattern of non-reciprocal exchange indexically maintains a status asymmetry between interlocutors for the stretch of discourse over which it is sustained; conversely, shifting to a reciprocal pattern (e.g., both individuals using informal *du*) resets the parameters of the social interaction bringing the two individuals on par. But who can initiate such a shift? In many societies, including Sweden, the entitlement to initiate such shifts is normatively linked to interlocutors' relative status: higher status interlocutors can readily propose a shift from formal to informal address, but the act cannot be initiated by a lower status individual without risk of seeming impudent. A number of implicit strategies, which lower such risk, are used in the latter case.

Higher status individuals are well aware of their entitlement to initiate shifts to informal usage, as noted in (6a). A metapragmatic utterance like 'Shan't we put the titles away' is a conventional performative formula that explicitly describes the shift desired. Asking your addressees to 'put the titles away' is euphemistically to ask them to refer to you as *du*. Aristocratic speakers are at ease using such formulaic locutions because their position near the top of the hierarchy entitles them to offer such 'dispensation' to most others. In contrast, interlocutors having lower relative status are aware of their lack of entitlement and use the more circuitous methods described in (6b):

(6)

(a) A member of the high nobility writes as follows: 'Now it is much easier
    to become *du* [i.e., initiate reciprocal *du* usage]. I usually propose it as soon as
    it is practical. I usually say something like: '*Skall vi inte lägga bort titlarna*'
    "Shan't we put the titles away," it is much easier so'.

    (Paulston 1976: 368)

(b) Even though the rules for dispensation rights differ between the social classes,
    it is generally recognized that such rights exist. Consequently people develop
    strategies for forcing dispensation, for manipulating the other into suggesting
    du. . . . One informant commented that he would pretend to misspeak and say *du*,
    and then apologize. He said it never failed that the addressee would ask him to
    please continue with *du*. Another strategy is constant and repeated use of T + LN
    (once or twice in each sentence) which marks the address system for attention. . . .
    A common strategy is some teasing remark like 'Well, you are oldest, I wouldn't
    dare suggest *du*.' There are bound to be many more such strategies.

    (Paulston 1976: 370)

The term 'strategy' is used in a variety of ways in the literature, some of which are quite problematic in that they impute intentions to people

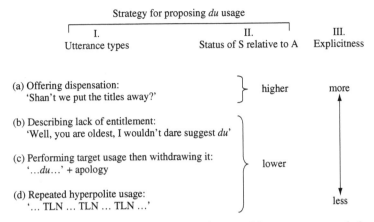

Figure 1.4 *Self-reported strategies for modeling next-turn behavior (Swedish)*

where none exist (Agha 1994). But the cases in (6) are strategies in the simple sense that native speakers describe them as ways of achieving intended ends. They are self-reported as strategies for shaping interlocutor's next-turn behavior. These strategies are listed in columns I and II of Figure 1.4. The strategies cannot be identified with utterance types alone, since they involve text-level indexical effects. They consist of using these utterance types in specific role configurations.[9] The strategies shown differ in the degree of explicitness with which they typify the very act they seek to bring about (column III), differences which, as I now show, depend on the deictic anchoring of denotational content to variables of interaction.

The performative formula in (a) is the most deictically explicit in modeling next-turn behavior: It refers to participants (*we*), describes a speech act (*put the titles away*), and modalizes it as a future-indirect request (*shan't we?*); since the formula is used by the one having higher status (i.e., by a person already entitled to use informal address), the *we* counts as an euphemistic trope for 'you.' Strategy (b) also denotes current interlocutors (*you* and *I*) as well as a speech act (*suggest du*). But from the standpoint of modeling next turn behavior, (b) is less explicit than (a): rather than proposing a shift to reciprocal *du*, the utterance in (b) describes how the current status asymmetry prevents the speaker from proposing it. In the course of such protestations, the speaker's use of the phrase *suggest du* describes the very act which the higher status interlocutor (and only that individual) is entitled to propose. The inference is obvious.

Strategies (c)–(d) are even more implicit in modeling next turn behavior; they provide no descriptions of how subsequent speech might proceed. They perform inappropriate usages: (c) is potentially rude, (d) excessively polite. In contrast to strategy (b), which explicitly describes the norm which it seeks to circumvent, strategy (c) highlights a norm by breaking it, then apologizing for the breach. Strategy (d) neither describes nor breaks the norm associated with *du* usage; but each repeated token of the excessively polite locution Title + Last Name indexes a greater status asymmetry than currently prevails, forcing interlocutor to either accept a potentially embarrassing degree of status-raising or to propose reciprocal *du*; if the interlocutor chooses the latter response the lower-status speaker of (d) will, in effect, have circumvented a norm without describing it.

I observed earlier that language users often seek to shape the future flow of discourse and relations among discourse participants by intervening metadiscursively within that flow. The relatively implicit strategies in Figure 1.4 illustrate an important corollary: very often speakers do this without *describing* anyone's subsequent behavior. The strategies now at issue are implicit to the extent that their denotational content does not formulate a locally unambiguous model of the interactional scenario they seek to bring about. Their strategic character is deniable after the fact. In such cases discerning the metapragmatic qualities of the act is harder for the reason noted in S 1.5. It is not surprising that speakers who self-report reliance on such strategies, as in (6b), view them as relatively effective ways of circumventing norms. Of course, any of these strategies may be unsuccessful (e.g., meet with non-compliance) on particular occasions. But the users of the more implicit strategies value them as modes of resistance to power. For they recognize that when someone has power over them in some *obvious* way (e.g., by virtue of having entitlements they lack) it is always possible to manipulate that exercise of power through implicit typifications – and attempted re-shapings – of the other's subsequent behavior. The cases discussed here illustrate speakers' folk-awareness of a feature of language that has long been known (or, rather, practically grasped, but not theorized as such) in a variety of traditions of rhetorical persuasion, such as the tradition of classical rhetoric since Quintillian (see Agha 1996b), namely that the implicitness of a metapragmatic representation itself yields forms of power over others.

The issue of implicitness has very broad consequences for what we take 'power' to be in lived experience. The forms of interpersonal power now at issue (and we shall consider entirely different varieties later on) depend on the role of deixis in representation. It is worth noting, of course, that power is hardly a unitary concept in the sociological literature. It is a loose notional concept used to describe many different things. In a common definition, power is linked to entitlements, whether the entitlement to choose one's own course of conduct or to shape the conduct of another. But entitlements (such as the 'dispensation' rules discussed above) are merely metagramatic models of how conduct *should* proceed. Social actors' accounts of (their own and others') entitlements are particularly salient to sociologists and anthropologists when they are formulated as explicit metapragmatic statements. Yet we have just seen that it is always possible for social actors to formulate implicit metapragmatic representations of their own and others' conduct, representations that neither describe nor violate norms but are nonetheless effective as means of circumventing them. And the efficacy of these acts depends on the implicitness of deictic representations (as well as text-level indexical effects, as noted earlier). This means that we cannot reduce regularities of conduct to explicit rules of conduct or conceptions of power to rules of entitlement. For strategies of implicit representations themselves yield power over others. They readily shape the behavior of those favored by explicit metapragmatic models. And their effectiveness depends on their non-transparency or implicitness.

In what follows we are not concerned with power in this sense but with the underlying issue, namely the explicitness or implicitness of a representation. At the level of propositional acts, the central issue is one of deixis. We have already seen that deictics link denotational content to ongoing interactional realities. It remains to be seen, however, that all deictics do not link denotation to interaction equally tightly or selectively, and that these differences are of fundamental importance to the way in which discursive representations formulate the outlines of the scenarios in which they occur, and establish the clarity of these outlines for persons caught up in them.

1.4 Deixis and representation

All acts of linguistic representation are scenes in a drama of social relations. Utterances play out parts. They are costumed in symbols. They gesture through deixis. In the middle of this drama, the role played by deixis in acts of representation eludes social actors, more concerned as they are with their parts than with the props through which they are played out.

There is a long tradition of thought about language which supposes that the real work of language is done through its symbolic classifications and that deixis, in contrast, is a somewhat marginal feature of a few odd little words that turn up once in a while. This is hardly the case. No system of symbolic classifications – no matter how semantically complex – can be used to talk about any particular thing in experience without resort to deixis. Deixis is the ground floor of the semiotic architecture whereby language allows language users to talk about specific 'things,' including each other. In general, deictic expressions link talk of things to the ones doing the talking, but they do so in more or less selective ways. The selectivity of the link makes the location, stance and relationship of inter-locutors more or less vivid in different types of deictic representations. We have seen many examples of this already. Our goal now is to understand how deixis works.

The term 'reflexivity' is commonly used in the literature to describe cases where language use facilitates forms of conscious reflection on experiences and activities. We have already seen that this is a very special case. We saw that reflexive acts do not merely reflect upon but also shape activities. And we saw in the last section that clarifying the contributions of language to interpersonal activities requires careful attention to deictic expressions such as pronouns, anaphors, demonstratives, markers of tense, mood and modality (Figures 1.3ff and 1.4ff). These observations raise some general questions: What types of social significance do deictics have? In what sense are deictics reflexive signs?

Many of the more stereotypically 'social' uses of language – such as uses of polite pronouns, terms of address, greetings, the uses of indirection to convey politeness, performative locutions – depend in a fundamental way on widely shared, ideological models of language use that ascribe a specific social significance to patterns of deictic usage. We consider the case of performative locutions in the next section; the other phenomena are dis-cussed later. Yet these phenomena are merely specializations of (typically, normative reanalyses of) far more basic ways in which deictic utterances formulate reflexive models of interpersonal occasions of communication (such as *what* or *who* the referents are; *how* they relate to interlocutors; how interlocutors are linked to *each other*; and so on). It is these more basic functions of deixis that concern us here.

Our focus now is on the role of deixis in **propositional acts**, acts in which we denote things in the world (including each other) during communica-tive interaction. Much of our sense of the concreteness of representations, their universality or particularity, their consequences for us and for our subsequent behaviors depend on the way in which deictics link denoted contents to interactional scenarios.

Deictics as reflexive signs

In discussing personal pronouns earlier I said that deictics collapse the distinction between the axes of denotation and interaction. The geometric metaphor is helpful but need not be taken too literally. The important point here is an issue of functional interdependence: deictic expressions make the construal of utterance denotation dependent on features of the interaction in which the utterance occurs. A deictic utterance reflexively points to variables of utterance context such as where, when and by whom an utterance is produced. For instance, pronouns like *I* and *you* make utterance denotation dependent on variables like speaker and addressee of utterance by denoting these variables; spatial deictics like *here* and *there* denote regions locatable only in relation to the location of utterance; markers of past or future tense, and deictic adverbs like *yesterday* or *tomorrow*, denote temporal intervals that are identifiable only if we know the time of utterance. These and other patterns of deixis often play a critical role in theories of mind, meaning, and politics.[10]

The things on which utterance denotation depends in the above examples (e.g., speaker-of, addressee-of, location-of and time-of utterance) are contextual or **interactional variables** in the simple sense that their values change as speech and interaction unfold. Since the values of these variables change with discursive activity we cannot conceptualize the context of utterance as a static or given thing, i.e., as something established independently of discursive-semiotic activity. Deixis is sometimes characterized as a 'coding' mechanism, though no one has quite clarified what this means. If by 'coding' is meant a necessary relationship between sign and object, then deictics code nothing. Deictics are indexical signs that formulate a sketch of referent that is only interpretable relative to the effects of co-occurring signs. In other words, the issues of text-level indexicality introduced in 1.2 remain critical to the construal of any deictic despite the specificity of its item-level sketch. The indexical sketch formulated by a **deictic form** is organized as a **set of text-defaults** in the sense that the item regularly conveys a set of effects in the absence of interference from co-textual effects. For any deictic, various non-default construals also occur; these are marked *not* by the deictic but by text configurations that contain it, and therefore vanish when the deictic occurs in other text configurations. Let us begin by considering how the default sketch is produced.

A deictic form refers to contextual variables by taking the current utterance-act as a **zero-point** or **origo** of reckoning. Thus *I* refers to whoever produces the current utterance, *here* refers to a region proximal to the current utterance, *yesterday* refers to the calendric day preceding the one in which the utterance occurs, and so on. As the role 'speaker' shifts back and forth in conversation, or as speech participants move through space and time, or establish other points of reference (e.g., other speakers, regions, temporal moments) as origos of reckoning through their own activities, the zero-point in relation to which *I, here* and *yesterday* refer also changes. Deictic expressions provide a **relational centering** of referents (Hanks 1992), a centering relative to an origo, whose default value is 'current utterance' or some dependent variable, such as speaker-of, location-of, time-of current utterance.[11] Since the current utterance is a moving zero-point of reference, we cannot explain the use and construal of deictics without attending to the process through which the zero-point moves, namely the larger framework of activities of which the propositional act is a fragment.

The utterance of a deictic is an act; so also is its construal. We may think of a deictic form as a unit of action (i.e., a form segmentable in the utterance-act) that provides the one construing it with a set of directions for where to look in order to find the referent. Charles Sanders Peirce, the writer who first clarified these issues, formulates this point as a matter of 'collateral observation' on the part of users:

(7) Pronouns are words whose object is to indicate what kind of collateral observation must be made in order to determine the significance of some other part of the sentence. 'Which' directs us to seek the quaesitum in the previous context; the personal pronouns to observe who is the speaker, who the hearer, etc. The demonstrative pronouns usually direct this sort of observation to the circumstances of the utterer (perhaps to the way a finger points) rather than to the words.

(Peirce 1992, v.2: 406)

Recovering the referent of a deictic is generally only a first step in a textually motivated inferential process whereby attention to co-textual cues allows users to 'fill in' further details about referent. Thus, if the hearer of the utterance *I am hungry* later reports to someone else that 'The guy from Portugal was hungry' such a report depends on her locating the referent of *I*, and on collateral observations of further cues that allow her to judge that the referent is a Portuguese male. Any such inference is based on attention to a structure of co-occurring signs, which includes, but is not limited to, the token of *I* which serves as its point of departure.

The distinctive character of deixis, as a type of indexicality, lies in the fact that deictic expressions are **denotational indexicals**, expressions that make variables of utterance denotation dependent on variables of interaction.[12] Two basic types of denotational variables are traditionally distinguished, namely **referents** (entities) and **predicates** (qualities of, and relations among, entities), the two together forming a third, more complex type, namely **propositions** (states-of-affairs predicated of entities). Using these variables as criteria, different utterances can be compared for propositional content even if they differ as propositional acts:

(8) One and the same proposition may be affirmed, denied, judged, doubted, inwardly inquired into, put as a question, wished, asked for, effectively commanded, taught, or merely expressed, and does not thereby become a different proposition.

(Peirce 1992, v.2: 312)

To speak of the 'same proposition' in this sense – more precisely, of the same **propositional content** – is to speak of features of utterance significance that are abstractable from matters of interactional anchoring. What differs

Table 1.1. *Propositional content and propositional act*

utterance	propositional act				
	propositional content	interactional anchoring			
		i	*j*	*tense*	*mood*
(a) You mailed the letter	mail (x_i, y_j)	Adr.	P	past	indicative
(b) She mailed a letter	mail (x_i, y_j)	Ant.	$\sim$P	past	indicative
(c) Mail the letter!	mail (x_i, y_j)	Adr.	P	–	imperative
(d) Did she mail a letter?	mail (x_i, y_j)	Ant.	$\sim$P	past	interrogative
(e) Will she mail the letter?	mail (x_i, y_j)	Ant.	P	future	interrogative
		$\underbrace{\qquad\qquad}_{reference}$		$\underbrace{\qquad\qquad\qquad}_{predicate\ modalization}$	

Ant. = Antecedent, Adr. = Addressee; P/$\sim$P = referent presupposed/not presupposed

in the cases in (8) is the type of interactional anchoring involved and, hence, the overall **propositional act** expressed. The propositional content of an utterance is a fragment or element of its overall significance as a propositional act, namely that fragment which is abstractable from matters of interactional anchoring. Table 1.1 illustrates these differences. All five utterances express a common propositional content: they share the two-place predicate, *(to) mail*, and thus involve talk of two entities, x_i and y_j.[13] But they do not express the same propositional act.

The differences among the propositional acts in (a)–(e) depend on the way in which deictic categories link propositional content to interactional variables. A number of deictic categories occur in each utterance. Each indexes an interactional variable as a text-default in construal. Categories of **mood** index default construals of participant involvement: The indicative mood indexes that the speaker affirms the proposition expressed, the imperative that the addressee must do what the sentence denotes, the interrogative that the addressee produce a verbal response (an 'answer').[14] Categories of **tense** specify temporal relations between the event denoted and the event of utterance, e.g., past, future, etc. Similarly, **noun phrase deictics** anchor the variables x and y to identifiable referents, i and j: the pronoun *you* indexes that the referent i is the addressee; the definite article *the* indexes a presupposition of existence (which the indefinite article, *a*, lacks), thus specifying that a particular letter (e.g., one mentioned earlier) is being talked about; the anaphor, *she*, establishes the referent i as the same entity as referred to by an earlier noun phrase, specifying further that the referent is feminine. Hence the specifications of i and j shown in the middle column are formulated by contrasts between *you/she* in subject position (i = Adr/Ant) and *a/the* in direct object noun phrases (j = ~P/P). Each of these noun phrase deictics provides the hearer with a set of default 'directions for where to look in context,' as it were, in order to find the referent. Yet it does so only in relation to the moment or event of utterance, thus providing a highly relational set of directions. If the utterance is decontextualized from its discursive-interactional frame these directions are more or less useless, i.e., do not help much in settling issues like who is to mail the letter, who has done so, and so on. Particular deictic forms express 'directions for finding the referent' only in the sense that they permit triangulation of referent from a currently perceivable thing (the deictic utterance), allowing hearers to compute the referent from indexical cues contained therein.

Deictic selectivity

Deictic expressions that provide directions of a less specific sort make possible more general kinds of statements. Whereas *the* or *that* are highly specific, the expressions *all* or *every* are not. Peirce refers to this issue as the selectivity of pronouns but, since his definition of 'pronoun' is rather over-broad,[15] the issue is better formulated as the selectivity of deixis:

(9) Along with such indexical directions of what to do to find the object meant, ought to be classified those pronouns which should be entitled *selective* pronouns, because they inform the hearer how he is to pick out one of the objects intended, but which grammarians call by the very indefinite designation of *indefinite* pronouns. Two varieties of these are particularly important in logic, the *universal selectives*, such as ... *any, every, all, no, none, whatever, whoever, everybody, anybody, nobody*. These mean that the hearer is at liberty to select any instance he likes within limits expressed or understood, and the assertion is intended to apply to that one. The other logically important variety consists of the *particular selectives*, ... *some, something, somebody, a, a certain, some or other; a suitable, one*.

(Peirce 1992, v.2: 16)

The contrast between universal and particular selectives illustrates a larger issue, namely that deictics differ in **degree and type of selectivity**. Thus when the universal selective deictics (or universal quantifiers) *any, every, all*, function as noun modifiers (e.g., *All men$_x$*), they provide referential directions to hearer of the form 'pick any x that you like,' where the semantic category of x is specified by the noun (*men*); propositions thus formed contain predicates (e.g., ... *are mortal*) that apply to the entire referential range, i.e., to any x thus found. In contrast, the particular selectives (*some$_x$*, *somebody$_x$*) formulate propositions where the predicate applies to 'at least one x.' Deictic contrasts in utterances therefore yield representations of states of affairs of greater or lesser degree of selectivity.

Since deictics differ in selectivity, acts of deictic usage link the scenario of utterance more or less tightly to a universe of referents, making referents more or less specifically locatable vis-à-vis the here-and-now of utterance. Consider the difference between propositions whose referent, x, is picked out by one of the following expressions: you_x > *that man$_x$* > *the man$_x$* > *some man$_x$*. Each of these choices provide a type of anchoring of referent to utterance/interaction, the anchoring becoming progressively looser as we move rightwards in the series. The first choice (you_x) formulates the individual, x, as co-present, and among those co-present, the one addressed by that very utterance, hence linked tightly to it. The second one (*that man$_x$*) formulates referent as not addressed, but either co-present at some physical remove (e.g., one pointed to by an accompanying finger), or presupposed anaphorically in discourse (i.e., referred to by an earlier utterance); the next one (*the man$_x$*) typically has only the anaphoric function of referring to individuals presupposed in discourse, but when accompanied by other signs (e.g., as part of the definite description, *the man$_x$ she will marry*) may also formulate referents presentatively, introducing a hypothetical person, or one introduced for the first time; *some man$_x$* differs from the others in providing no formulation of address, physical co-presence, uniqueness, or antecedence in discourse, merely the presupposition that a referent x exists and is characterizable as a man.

Like noun phrase deictics, categories of verb deixis also differ in selectivity. When nouns and verbs co-occur in utterances, noun and verb deictics work together to yield composite effects, cumulatively linking referents more or less tightly to the scenario of utterance. These cumulative effects are illustrated in Table 1.2. Notice that all five utterances have a common propositional content, that is, specify referents of the class denoted by *bird*, and actions of the type denoted by *(to) sing*. But they differ in the interactional anchoring formulated through deixis, that is, in the way in which deictic categories selectively link variables of propositional content to a universe of referents and events/activities.

Example (a) unites several types of highly selective deictic anchoring, including anchoring of utterance to addressee through the interrogative

Table 1.2. *Non-selective deixis: from definite past queries to 'nomic' truths*

	Mood +/–interrogative	Determiner +/–definite	Tense +/–past	(Number) +/–specific
(a) Did the bird sing?	+	+	+	+
(b) The bird sang	–	+	+	+
(c) A bird sang	–	–	+	+
(d) A bird sings	–	–	–	+
(e) Birds sing	–	–	–	–

'+' = specified; '–' = unspecified; parentheses mark non-deictic category form, specifying that a response or 'answer' is expected in the next turn; anchoring to a definite referent through choice of determiner, specifying that a given bird is being talked about; and anchoring to a moment in past time, specifying a particular act of singing. This high degree of selectivity is progressively relaxed in the other cases. Examples (b)–(e) are not in the interrogative mood and therefore do not model the addressee's next-turn behavior (viz. that a specific response is expected, as in (a)), thus formulating a lower degree of addressee involvement. The absence of definite determiner in (c)–(e) formulates referent in less concrete terms than the other cases, i.e., as some bird or birds, not a particular contextually presupposed referent. The absence of past tense marking in (d)–(e) formulates the predicated event as less selectively locatable with respect to the moment of utterance and not, as in (a)–(c), as having occurred in past time. This makes temporal construal subject to the usual indeterminacies of the so-called 'present' tense. Example (d) formulates the event as either contemporaneous with time of utterance (the 'immediate present' construal) or as contemporaneous with some other, cotextually established time frame, such as a specific moment in past time (the so-called 'historical present'), or a recurrent time, whether present past or future (the 'habitual' construal). The last example, *Birds sing*, illustrates the pattern of **nomic truths**, or timeless truths, formulated through pervasive non-selectivity of deictic categories in both noun phrase and verb; thus (e) exhibits all of the non-specificity of (d) plus the formulation of propositional content as applying to all birds at all times. The nomic construal is also possible for *A bird sings*, when the subject is understood generically (or as –specific, hence a case different from (d); see last column) as referring not to an individual bird but to the entire class of birds as such, as in talk of biological species or natural kinds, viz., *A bird sings, a lion roars*.

The nomic pattern is the least deictically selective of the ones considered here. It permits talk of referents (things, times, places, etc.) that are not locatable in a determinate way with respect to the current speech scenario and, hence, presented in generic, abstract or collective terms. The pattern is pervasively employed in a more specialized form in a variety of genres concerned with universalizing claims – such as proverbs, apothegms, myths, scientific generalizations – imbuing statements in these genres with the capacity to represent seemingly vast realms of human or physical nature, a capacity often reflexively reanalyzed in culture-specific models of their effects as the power and authority of those who make such statements.

The above examples also bring to the fore two critical issues. First, *deictic non-selectivity is a type of deictic import*, not the absence of deictic import. Universal statements or nomic truths are deictically non-selective ('pick any x that you like').[16] This is precisely their deictic import. Second, *the absence of morphological deictics is not the absence of deictic import*.

Non-selective deixis is often marked by the absence of a localizable morpheme in a position of expectable occurrence. Thus in some universal statements (*Birds sing, Snow is white*), no deictic determiner (like *the* or *that*) occurs in the subject noun phrase; here, the deictic import 'pick any x that you like' is expressed by a grammatical pattern in which the absence of deictic morphemes is significant.[17]

Deictic instructions are far more pervasive in natural language than is consciously grasped by those who follow them. In all utterable sentences of a language many co-occurring constituents provide deictic instructions on how to find referents and assess predicate modalization, though with varying degrees of selectivity and morphological transparency. A discursive representation is a *composite* sketch, or map, in this sense. Language users know how to read it, but they cannot accurately describe how they do so without appeal to an analysis of deictic categories in their language.

We have also seen that the deictic selectivity of propositional acts shapes interpersonal realities by establishing a link between denotational and interactional variables. When the mode of linkage is relatively tight, as when a noun phrase selectively refers to an interactant (e.g., the deictics, *I* and *you*) or when predicate modalization models an interactant's next turn behavior (e.g., the interrogative or imperative mood), the propositional act appears to shape the interaction by referring to it or intervening directly within it. When the mode of linkage is relatively loose, as when talk concerns indefinitely many things, or invokes non-specific time frames, or formulates a universalizing perspective on some state of affairs, propositional content appears to transcend the moment where the propositional act occurs. I have illustrated the latter effect for the special case of timeless truths. A looser connection between denotation and interaction can yield many other types of composite effects too, such as the formulation of an utterance as a generic law, contract, commitment (1.5), or the construal of denotational 'indirection' as a form of stereotypic politeness to interlocutor. I shall have more to say about these cases presently. But before we proceed further we need to become clearer about what we mean by the term *deictic category* itself.

Deictic categories as text-defaults

A deictic category formulates a sketch of referent(s). The sketch is readily complicated by text-level indexicality, that is, by the superimposed effects of accompanying signs. An analogy might help. In optics, we say that superimposed light waves exhibit interference (reinforce or cancel each other), sometimes yielding visible patterns of diffraction. Under text-level indexicality, deictic tokens exhibit interference too, yielding patterns of cumulative reinforcement and cancellation in construal.

A deictic like *now* denotes an interval containing the moment of utterance but does not specify the scale of interval denoted; and similarly for the scale of the region denoted by *here*. But as the deictic (boldface) occurs in different co-textual arrays, the accompanying (italicized) signs differentiate the intervals or regions denoted with greater specificity, thus making plausible the more specific interpretations shown on the right. The construals of denotational scale shown on the right are not construals of the boldface lexemes alone, since these are not specific enough; the specificity of these construals is motivated by the configuration of boldface and italicized expressions in each case.

When the deictic denotes an interactional role, cases of co-textual specification (S 1.6a) delineate the interactional role more finely than the deictic token itself can. Thus deictics like *I* or *me* generically refer to an interactional role variable commonly termed 'speaker of utterance.' Yet the more specific role fractions shown in Table 1.6 – such as animator, principal or author – are readily differentiated by semiotic accompaniments. It is important to see that deictic words like *I* and *me* do not categorically differentiate these role-fractions from each other. The role variable 'speaker' can only be differentiated into more specific variables like 'animator' vs. 'principal' by signs that *accompany* tokens of these pronouns.

Such semiotic accompaniments may themselves may be quite varied. For example, when *me* occurs as a fragment of a larger configuration like *she$_i$ told me$_j$ that S* the textual frame distinguishes the animator, the one who produces the current utterance (here, person j) from the principal, the one to whom responsibility for content is assigned (person i). Similarly, direct reported speech constructions differentiate the animator of the report from the author, the one whose words are being quoted. A number of other semiotic devices – text parallelism, gesture, gaze, posture, corporeal alignment – reflexively differentiate role fractions of speaker and hearer when they occur as semiotic accompaniments of pronominal tokens (see Irvine 1996; Hanks 1996). In all cases, the specification of these role fractions is a co-textually superposed effect, not the effect of a pronoun token alone. This fact is evident from two considerations. First, such effects may be co-textually superposed on the construal of any person

Table 1.6. *Role fractions of speaker*

Animator	the one who physically produces the current utterance
Principal	the one held responsible for utterance propositional content
Author	the one held responsible for utterance wording
Figure	the persona performed through the act of utterance

Source: (Goffman 1981a)

indexing form (e.g., mood, accent), not just pronouns.[20] Second, such superposed effects are non-detachable for purposes of construal. If you isolate the person indexing form from criterial accompaniments, the effect in question (e.g., that 'animator' differs from 'principal') vanishes.

In other cases, co-textual cues substantially modify – even partly 'cancel' (S 1.6b) – the referential sketch performed by the deictic token. Indeed, for each of the deictics listed earlier in Table 1.3, some features among its set of denotational and interactional text-defaults are commonly canceled by the effects of accompanying forms. Thus the deictics a.–f., Table 1.3, tend in their default usage to specify speech participants as 'human'. But cases of represented speech where animals are presented as speaking to each other (as in children's story books) are hardly meaningless; these text-patterns count as tropes of personification. Thus in *Mother Goose*, when Little Robin Redbreast speaks to Pussy-Cat,

(10)   Little Robin Redbreast$_i$ sat upon a tree,
Up went Pussy-Cat$_j$, down went *he$_i$*,
Down came Pussy-Cat$_j$, away Robin$_i$ ran,
Says little Robin Redbreast$_i$: 'Catch me$_i$ if you$_j$ can!'

a variety of cues in the first three lines typify the referents i and j as [+ animate] beings (since they occur as arguments of the animate-subject verbs, *sit, go down, come down, run*), and as [−human] (since they are identified as a robin and a cat). But the italicized cues, largely in the last line, such as the fact that referent i is presented as speaking to j (i.e., as the subject of *say*, a human-subject verb) and as using *me$_i$* and *you$_j$* as referring expressions, formulates i and j as [+human]. The denotational sketch of referents established by the italicized material, is non-congruent with the sketch performed by the rest. Calling the overall usage a **personification** is a way of labeling this non-congruence, namely of pointing out that the referents of this discourse are clearly established as non-human beings, but also, equally clearly, as human-like in certain respects.

The general point at issue here is that referents of discourse are not merely 'things' (as in the folk-view) but things *modeled* through discourse as having certain characteristics. Any such discursively shaped (and hence sequentially unfolding) model of referent consists of local sketches which may or may not be congruent with each other. A denotational text structure that contains non-congruent local sketches as semiotic fractions may prove unintelligible; or, it may be construed as a **denotational trope**, where the non-congruence of local sketches constitutes the trope (a perceived 'deviance,' or text-in-context 'anomaly'), an effect preserved in whatever larger construal is given to the usage.

Reported speech constructions also partly cancel the default interactional construal of deictics that occur in quoted speech. Thus although the default construal of *me* and *you* is that their referents are speaker and addressee of *current* utterance, their occurrence in the reported speech construction in (10) establishes that they are speaker and addressee of the *reported* utterance; the referents of me_i and you_j are therefore understood as 'narrated' participants (a bird and a cat), not 'current' participants (author and reader). The effect is a simple example of the **transposition of origo**, namely a case where co-textual patternment motivates a construal of deictic zero-point distinct from 'current utterance.'[21] Here the criterial co-textual pattern is a reported speech construction, whose presence specifies a non-default interactional frame, the frame of narrated interaction, and thus a distinct set of directions for locating referents of deictics in the framed clause. A variety of other co-textual mechanisms, some far more implicit than reported speech, can implement transpositions of this kind (Hanks 1990). Moreover the event framework *to which* the origo is transposed may be sketched out in more or less specific ways, as 'local space' vs. 'narrated space' vs. 'interactional space' vs. 'narrated interactional space' by signs that accompany deictic usage (Haviland 1993).

The fact that deictic lexemes express a cluster of categories constrains the extent to which non-default construals can be given to text-patterns of usage. I have been observing that cases of defeasibility are in general cases of *partial* cancellation of text-defaults. The reason that this is so, is that a deictic lexeme specifies *a set* of text-defaults, that is, expresses a *cluster of categories*. In cases of intelligible defeasibility, only *some* among the text-defaults are actually canceled in any given communicative event, though different ones may be canceled in different instances.[22] Thus in the immediately preceding example of tropes from *Mother Goose*, the cases where tokens of me_i and you_j exhibit transposition of origo (i.e., 'E^s' is not understood as 'current E^s') are also cases where some features of the denotational sketch (e.g., semantic roles, such as agent/patient of verb) are preserved perfectly, while other features, such as 'human'-ness of referent are, given co-reference with *Robin Redbreast$_i$* and *Pussy-Cat$_j$*, preserved only as fractions of the trope of personification.

Cases of defeasibility are not exceptions to categorial structure. They are not even experienceable at the level of category tokens. They are interaction effects, or superposed effects, at the level of text. If a particular analysis of a category's text-defaults is correct then instances of defeasibility can be explained by considering the semiotic properties of co-occurring signs. If no feature of co-text accounts for such non-default construals then the analysis of categorial effects is wrong and needs to be improved. But an account that does not distinguish categorial from text-level effects gets nowhere at all. This is a characteristic failure of any 'coding' approach, which presumes that deixis consists of necessary relationships between lexical items and referents, and that the contributions of accompanying signs vanish to zero just when the form occurs.

The idiom 'uses of a form' is also highly misleading. The so-called 'use of a form' is never just the use of a single sign; the idiom typically describes a text-pattern in which many other signs make a contribution, and these contributions may partially cancel the categorial effects of the form. Thus, a yes-no question categorially indexes the expectation of a 'yes or no' response by a co-present addressee. In English, such a question is marked by a specific organization of sentence form (e.g., subject-verb inversion, sentence-final intonation rise). What we call a 'rhetorical use' of such a question, is the case where some sign (whether linguistic or non-linguistic) that co-occurs with the question token cancels the effect that a response is expected. For example, no-one may be co-present or ratified as an addressee, as in the case of a dramatic soliloquy; or the predicate which occurs in the question token may characterize a state of affairs manifestly known only to speaker, thus canceling the expectation that a response is expected from anyone co-present. To speak of the 'rhetorical use' of the question is to speak of the effects of a sign-configuration of which the question marker (the syntactic-prosodic marker) is a fragment.

In the case of person deictics, the so-called 'impersonal use of *you*' or the 'use of *we* to refer to addressee' are common examples of cases where text patterns containing tokens of *you* or *we* partially cancel the interactional schema of deixis categorially associated with these tokens. Common cases of the impersonal *you* are cases where forms accompanying the pronoun *you* are deictically non-selective (i.e., denote highly non-specific referents), often employing features of the nomic pattern noted above. Thus in examples such as (11a),

(11)
(a) You$_i$ just <u>can't</u> <u>get</u> <u>children</u> to read <u>these days</u>.
(b) You$_i$ <u>are</u> what you$_i$ <u>eat</u>.
(c) And how <u>are</u> we <u>feeling</u> today?

the nonselectivity of the indefinite plural noun phrase (*children*, as opposed to *your daughter*), of tense deixis (*can't get*, versus *couldn't get*) and of adverbial deixis (*these days*, versus *on her birthday*) motivates the composite effect that the propositional act be understood generically, and that the predicate does not apply (only) to current addressee; hence the referent of *you* is understood in generic terms too (i.e., as 'one'), a cumulative effect partially non-congruent with the default construal of *you* (only *partially* non-congruent since the construal of humanness and semantic roles is still preserved; and the one addressed is not necessarily excluded from the referential range of 'one'). In contrast, when a doctor begins an encounter with a patient by asking *And how <u>are</u> we$_j$ <u>feeling</u> today?*, the underlined predicate motivates the construal that the referent, j, the one whose health is now topical, is the patient addressed (i.e., the one whose health is officially topical in such encounters), not the doctor. The total act is, in a sense, a 'use of *we* to refer to addressee,' though calling it a 'use of *we*' is a highly imperfect description since it leaves out the features of the overall semiotic co-text (the predicate *are … feeling*, plus the presupposed role configuration, doctor speaking to patient) that motivate the non-default construal of *we* in this scenario. But cases (b) and (c) differ from (a) in another respect, a type of difference that illustrates the contrast between the cases described in S 1.6b and S 1.6c above.

In S 1.6c, I noted that deictic patterns may formulate additional construals notionally distinct from the kinds of referential sketches discussed so far. Examples (b) and (c) are idiomatic locutions that specify a further stereotypic image of interactants or of the scenario of interaction. Thus *You are what you eat* is a proverb, whose usage shapes the social interaction in a more specific sense, locating speaker as 'someone performing a type of common lore'; this stereotypic persona or **characterological figure** can be troped upon too, as in cases of irony or humor. Similarly, someone who uses *how are we feeling today?* to talk to a friend with a hangover performs a relationship that tropes upon the doctor-patient relationship stereotypically associated with the idiom, likening one type of interaction to another. Examples of this kind are 'stand alone' utterances, their effects different from the non-detachable effects discussed before; their secondary interactional sketch, or characterological figure, is highly detachable from occasions of use and can be reinserted into different situations in literal or tropic ways to yield characterological figures readily construed by someone acquainted with the stereotype.

In the following examples, highly specific stereotypic images are associated with the referents of third person noun phrases in a manner that constitutes a register of abuse:

(12) [T]he difference between *das* (neuter) and *die* (feminine) *Dorle* 'little Doris' can be indexical of difference in sexual awareness/desirability. Similarly, violation of natural gender is often used to insult or talk down: *Das Mensch* is 'slut' as against *der Mensch* 'human being, man'. Insulting terms for males often take the feminine article and vice versa, examples being *die Memme* 'male coward', *die Tunte* 'homosexual', *der Zahn* 'sexually desirable young girl', *der Fratz, Krott, Teenie* 'very young girls,' etc.

(Mühlhäusler and Harré 1990:73)

All of these tropes are, at one level, shaped by the co-textual non-congruence of determiners and nouns (e.g., in lexical gender), and thus appear familiar from earlier discussion. However, in these cases such co-occurrence has a highly specific kind of stereotypic social meaning, that referents have *sexualized* personae, which is idiomatic to these locutions and stereotypically known to most German speakers.

Cases where deictic text patterns are secondarily reanalyzed into stereotypic indexicals are cross-linguistically common. Thus the view that women use more tag questions than men (Lakoff 1975), or that upper class speakers use polite pronouns differently from lower class speakers (Chapter 6) are both cases where deictic patterns are treated as **stereotypic social indexicals** of the type of person speaking. However, these cases constitute a distinct and larger topic because such stereotypes of social indexicality are not restricted to personifications of speaker type; nor are they limited to patterns involving deixis alone, or even to text-patterns comprised solely of linguistic expressions.

The analysis and study of such cases requires a clarification of sociohistorical processes of **enregisterment**, processes whereby diverse behavioral signs (whether linguistic, non-linguistic, or both) are functionally reanalyzed as cultural models of action, as behaviors capable of indexing stereotypic characteristics of incumbents of particular interactional roles, and of relations among them. These are the more ideologically saturated cases to which I alluded at the beginning of 1.4. One of the main arguments of later chapters is that the phenomena of enregisterment are of much wider consequence in social life than is grasped in traditional definitions of 'registers.' I offer a more empirically adequate definition of register formations in Chapter 3, an account of enregisterment processes in Chapter 4, and, in later chapters, a discussion of enregistered signs of diverse kinds, including signs of 'identity' (Chapter 5) and 'kinship' (Chapter 8).

For the moment, let us approach this larger domain by considering certain patterns of deixis that are enregistered as social indexicals but where the object-signs are not lexical items but text configurations containing deictic and other signs.

1.5 Performativity

I now turn to a class of deictic locutions, so-called **explicit performative locutions**, whose usage transparently creates social facts. When successful, the act of uttering such a locution creates interpersonal realities that endure well beyond the moment of utterance, potentially becoming widely accepted social facts. The effect depends partly on deictic categories, as traditional accounts have emphasized. However, the success of the act also depends on other principles of sign-function – such as matters of text-level indexicality, and cultural enregisterment – that are not adequately theorized in standard accounts. Since each of these principles can mediate social relations independently of the others, an explicit performative locution is a very special type of social indexical sign. It is a hybrid sign, whose effectiveness, or power over users, depends on several concurrent semiotic conditions being met, and vanishes (is defeasible) when one or more of them is not.

These conditions (which jointly give this special case its hybrid character) can be met independently in other sign-phenomena to yield social indexical effects that are more implicit and less transparent to everyday discussion, but which are no less consequential in shaping social relations in behavior.

My goal in this section is to discuss the component principles that give explicit performativity its special character, the better to suggest in later discussion how different combinations of these sign-functions order social indexical phenomena of other kinds. From the standpoint of the expository purposes of this chapter, the material discussed in this section forms a bridge between the kinds of reflexive phenomena discussed earlier, namely cases where utterances formulate a reflexive sketch of the interactions in which they occur (1.4), and the cases discussed in the next two sections (1.6 and 1.7), where large scale semiotic processes make reflexive formations and their effects more widely known.

Explicit performative locutions: the deictic sketch

The philosopher J. L. Austin observed that locutions of the following kind, when uttered by a speaker (person j), transform the social occasion of utterance by creating social facts that persist beyond that occasion:

(13) I_j appoint you$_k$ chairman
     I_j nominate you$_k$ as candidate
     I_j dub thee$_k$ Sir Lancelot
     I_j promise you$_k$ that I_j'll return the book

In the first three cases, the utterance transforms the social role or identity of the one addressed (person k), making that person over into a chairman, a candidate, a knight. In the case of the promise, the relationship is contractual; the utterance creates an obligation on the part of j and, conversely, confers certain entitlements on person k, such as the right to continue pestering j about the book until its return.

Austin was able to identify this phenomenon but unable fully to explain it.[23] He observes, for example, that such utterances appear to have a singular effect: 'There is something which is *at the moment of uttering being done by the person uttering*' (1962: 60). Yet this characterization does not distinguish the utterances in (13) from utterances in general. *All* utterances are ways of 'doing' or accomplishing things. What is distinctive about the cases in (13) is that certain features of their internal organization formulate a sketch of the social occasion of utterance that is highly transparent from the utterance itself. The utterance formulates a socio-pragmatic sketch of the propositional act. The sketch is shaped by three distinct types of deictic elements.

First, these locutions transparently shape social relations among interactants because they contain the participant deictics, *I* and *you*. Thus a locution of the form *She promised him* does not formulate a contractual promise between speaker and addressee but a report of a promise that occurred elsewhere. A second feature is that these locutions are formed through the use of certain deictic verbs – the *verba dicendi* discussed earlier in (2)ff. – which denote speech events and, in denoting them, impute a particular social contour to the event denoted. An act that *nominates* someone to office is sociologically quite distinct from one that *promises* him something. Thus the first two features are that explicit performative locutions contain participant deictics in subject and object position (thus formulating speaker-as-agent and addressee-as-patient), and verbs of speaking that denote the socio-pragmatic contours of the action performed by the one on the other.

The third deictic feature of these locutions is a pattern of verb inflection that identifies the speech event *denoted by* the locution with the event of *uttering* it. All the (matrix clause) verbs in (13) are inflected for denotationally unmarked and deictically non-selective verbal categories, a text-pattern analogous to the nomic inflection discussed earlier.[24] Thus the locutions (a)–(c) in Table 1.7 – which are variously inflected for marked values of tense, voice, aspect and mood – cannot be used to *create* the contractual obligation through the act of utterance. Only (d), which has non-specific verb inflection is used in this manner, in the so-called 'explicit performative' use.

The locution in (d) consists of a particular configuration of verbal categories – indicative mood, non-past tense, active voice – that exhibit no deictic selectivity for how the event denoted (the promise) is located with respect to the event of utterance. It is by no means necessary, therefore, that an utterance of (d) be understood performatively, i.e., as constituting the act denoted. In fact every so-called 'explicit performative' locution is systematically ambiguous between a performative and a

Table 1.7. *Predicate modalization and the explicit performative locution*

	Mood +/–interrogative	Tense +/–past	Voice +/–passive	(Aspect) +/–perfect
(a) You were promised by me ...	–	+	+	–
(b) Have I promised you ...?	+	+	–	+
(c) I have promised you ...	–	–	–	+
(d) I promise you ...	–	–	–	–

' + ' = specified; '–' = unspecified; parentheses mark non-deictic category 'habitual' construal. In the latter construal, which can be specified more explicitly by adverbs (e.g., *I promise you the same thing every time*), the event denoted is understood as recurrent, not as a typification of the act performed in the here and now. Conversely, the habitual construal can be blocked by other adverbs (*I hereby promise you . . .*), thereby motivating the performative construal more specifically. When the habitual construal is effectively blocked (whether by adverbs or other semiotic accompaniments) the utterance of the formula establishes the following default construal: the event denoted by the verbum dicendi is understood as the event of uttering it, and the socio-pragmatics of the verb as specifying attributes of, or relationships among, current interactants.

As with any deictic text-pattern, the reflexive image of the act is highly defeasible. Moreover it is independently defeasible with respect to each of its elements: take away the pronouns and no interactants are denoted; take away the verbum dicendi and no speech-act is explicitly typified in socio-pragmatic terms; take away the non-selective verb deixis (or, even, its non-habitual construal) and the model is understood not as a typification of current utterance but as reported speech. On the other hand, when all of these interactional variables are specified in criterial ways *the event of utterance* may be understood, reflexively, as having the characteristics of *the event denoted*.

I say 'may be understood' here because the *utterance* of a performative locution (with its dense deictic patterning) is only a fragment of the performative act: it is merely 'the leading incident' (to use Austin's phrase) in a larger order of happenings whose shape must be specified by further semiotic accompaniments in order for the utterance to have the effect in question. To see this we have to consider the co-textual accompaniments of the locution.

Text-level indexicality and implicit performativity

Many performative locutions are interactionally effective in creating social facts only when they occur in a larger semiotically shaped scenario of utterance. Thus in the following common examples the performative utterance in quotes is interactionally effective (i.e., yields the right sort of 'uptake' among those co-present) when it occurs in a scenario of the kind described in italics:

(14)
(a) 'I do (sc. take this woman to be my lawful wedded wife)' – *uttered during a marriage ceremony*
(b) 'I name this ship the *Queen Elizabeth*' – *uttered when smashing a bottle against the hull*
(c) 'I give and bequeath my watch to my brother' – *occurring in a will*

In the wrong kind of scenario the utterance will not be effective in the relevant sense, though it may, of course, be a highly effective in some other way (e.g., as a joke). In addition, the effectiveness of the performative act frequently depends on other feature of the scenario of utterance, such as whether speaker and addressee are certain kinds of social persons:

(15)

(a) 'I pronounce you husband and wife' – *that speaker be a priest, etc.*
(b) 'I do (take this woman ...)' – *that speaker not already have a 'living, sane, undivorced' wife (cf. British Common Law)*

Such conditions on effectiveness are not logical or semantic constraints in any sense. They are consequences of the work of particular socio-historical institutions (viz., the Church, Common Law), a type of prior work which constrains the usage of particular performative locutions by setting co-textual conditions on their **appropriate use** (e.g., by normatively codifying role configurations and scenarios of use). As these institutions change or are supplanted by others (e.g., church vs. civil marriages) so do the criterial roles and settings in which these locutions are appropriately used.

Such conditions often include constraints on the sequential structure of discursive co-text. In some cases the successful use of a performative locution presupposes that certain other effects have been enacted through prior utterances, some among which may themselves be achieved through performative locutions. In the case of the multi-party marriage ritual in (16), the performative locution in the last line successfully establishes that the relationship of marriage holds between persons i and j only if it occurs in a particular sequential order in relation to prior turn segments, and the acts performed in these prior segments satisfy the specific conditions on *their* success noted earlier.

(16)

Priest:	Do you$_i$ take this woman$_j$ as your lawfully wedded wife?	Seeking consent
Man:	I$_i$ do	
Priest:	Do you$_j$ take this man$_i$ as your lawfully wedded husband?	Seeking consent
Woman:	I$_j$ do	
Priest:	I$_k$ now pronounce you$_{i,j}$ husband and wife	Establishing marriage

The conditions on the success of such acts include not only relatively local conditions on the appropriate use of particular locutions, e.g., the ones in (15), but more textually global conditions on the orderly arrangement of the entire sequence, e.g., the priest may not attempt to establish the marriage *before* seeking consent. Adherence to the larger text structure is implicitly performative of the fact that certain prerequisites on marriage-ability have sequentially been established (viz., that acts assigning relevant parties to criterial roles of 'consenting adults' have occurred), an effect presupposed in the success of the explicit performative that establishes the marriage at the end. These considerations highlight the special status of explicit performativity versus performativity in general.

We have seen, for one, that there is a distinction between the **implicit performativity of text structure** and the special character of explicit perform-ative locutions. The implicit performativity of text structure is merely another way of talking about text-level indexicality, namely the capacity of a serial arrangement of signs, as a larger whole, to convey information (and constitute acts) not specified by any of its parts. We have seen several examples of this in preceding sections that have nothing to do with explicit performative locutions. But neglect of the issue of text-level indexicality creates a particular difficulty for the doctrine of explicit performativity, namely the problem of so-called 'indirect speech acts' (Searle 1975). The problem is that even utterances that contain no explicit performatives yield performative effects, even though these are not locally denoted in the utter-ance. Thus, to take Searle's example, in an interaction such as the following,

(17)
Student X: Let's$_{X,Y}$ go to the movies tonight
Student Y: I$_Y$ have to study for an exam

Y's utterance appears to count as 'the refusal of an offer'. But unlike a locution like *I refuse your offer* (which is an explicit performative), Y's utterance, *I have to study for an exam*, does not locally denote the perform-ative effect that an offer is being refused. The English sentence *I have to study for an exam* has no properties at the level of isolable grammatical form or propositional content that suffices to explain the effect here achieved; indeed, a moment's reflection will show that the sentence may be used to perform many other acts too, none of which are metapragmati-cally formulated by its localizable form. It is equally readily seen that the effect that an offer is being refused in (17) is an effect formulated by a larger text-structure of which Y's utterance is a fragment: it is only *when* student X has formulated the possibility that 'Y (and X) go to the movies tonight' that Y's utterance (if understood, now, as 'Y has to study for an exam *tonight*') yields the construal that Y is otherwise occupied and therefore cannot go to the movies. But the proposition 'Y cannot go to the movies tonight' is not one that Y has uttered. The construal is, in fact, a textually cumulative inference, recoverable only by taking together the propositio-nal acts performed by X and Y in the sequential order indicated. Most performative effects in discourse are in fact implicitly performative effects based on framing by a text structure (often a multi-party text-structure, i.e., created by many interactants) not on framing by performative locutions explicitly denoting those effects. This issue, which vitiates speech-act theory in its classic form, is discussed in greater detail in later chapters (see especially 2.2 and 5.5).

Cultural enregisterment

Another issue neglected in the standard account concerns the way in which the repertoire of explicit performative locutions comes historically to be differentiated from other expressions in the language and recognized society-internally as having stereotypically performative force. The stereotypic or formulaic character of performative locutions is an issue distinct from their explicitness. What makes these locutions 'explicit' is the fact that a locution-internal metapragmatic frame (participant pronouns + verbum dicendi + non-selective verb deixis) formulates a deictic sketch of the act performed by the utterance. Yet the presence of a locution-internal frame of this kind is neither necessary nor sufficient for an utterance to count as a performative utterance. Thus whereas utterances like *I promise, I swear, I vow*, etc., do function in the manner discussed above, utterances like *I insult you, I humiliate you*, etc., which have the same form, are not stereotypically performative locutions, i.e., are not conventionally used to accomplish the acts they denote. Moreover many conventionally performative locutions have an altogether different form. For example, a notice like *Passengers are warned to cross the tracks by the bridge only* executes a performative act which assigns legally consequential roles to any reader of the notice (that he or she has been warned) and to the issuing authority (that it is free from further legal liability); but the locution has a third-plural passive form. Other performative locutions have a highly truncated form. Thus, when a jury pronounces a man *Guilty!*, or when an umpire cries *Out!* the utterance performs the very act that it denotes, though it lacks the maximally explicit form discussed above; the first example does alternate with a more explicit form (*We find the defendant guilty*), but in the second case the maximal form (*I declare that you're out*), while grammatically possible, is not a performative locution used by umpires. These facts show that the grammatical availability of a deictic pattern is only a kind of minimal, baseline condition for the enregisterment, or recognized existence (cf. 1.7), of conventionally performative locutions within a language community. The routinization of a deictic pattern into an explicit performative locution depends further on the existence of particular institutionalized practices (conducted in some cases by 'institutions' in the narrow sense, such as the Church or the Law) through which deictic possibilities become socially enregistered as stereotypic (or even canonical) ways of doing certain kinds of work.

Table 1.8. *Cross-cultural comparisons of performative locutions*

Performative locutions in English	Aspects of corresponding Ilongot locutions	
(1) Assertives: establish S's beliefs, truth/falsity *predict, conclude, deduce, suggest* I VERB that S	Large class	associated primarily with interactional positioning rather than truth values
(2) Directives: get A to do something *order, command, invite, request*; I VERB you$_i$ [(you$_i$) V$_{ag}$ (NP)...]	Large class	usage of overtly directive locutions not judged harsh or impolite
(3) Commissives: commit S to a course of action *promise, vow, pledge*; I$_i$ VERB you [I$_i$ V$_{ag}$ (NP)...]	Small undeveloped classes of both types	not primarily associated with S's personal (viz., ethical or psychological) commitments but with public acts marking interpersonal relations (often accompanied by gifts, payments, etc.)
(4) Expressives: express S's attitude *thank, congratulate, welcome*; I$_i$ VERB you [nominalization]		
(5) Declaratives: create public roles/ relations *appoint, nominate, declare*; I$_i$ VERB (you) [existential statement]	Small class	used mostly to invoke supernatural forces

Source: (Searle 1976, Rosaldo 1982)

The role of culture-internal enregisterment in shaping performative effects is also evident from the cross-cultural variability of explicit performative locutions. Performative locutions in English belong to several major syntactico-semantic classes, such as the ones shown in the left column of Table 1.8. Using these constructional classes as diagnostic criteria we can identify corresponding performative locutions in other languages. But if we do so, we find that various kinds of ethnotheories of conduct (including views of moral and mental phenomena) are associated with the locutions thus found, and that these often differ from the ones associated with the English locutions. Cross-cultural differences of these kinds suggest that performative locutions (like any other feature of language) are subject to forms of reflexive reanalysis that elaborate (or fail to elaborate) particular locution-types as performative formulae, and interpret their effects in highly culture-specific terms.

The second and third columns of Table 1.8 show some of the ways in which performative locutions used by Ilongot speakers of the Philippines (Rosaldo 1982) differ from corresponding ones in English. Whereas the use of many directive performatives (like *I order you, I command you*) is appropriate in English only in contexts where speaker and hearer differ sharply in social status (typically institution-specific status), the use of corresponding constructions is quite appropriate, even widespread, in everyday family settings among the Ilongot. Similarly, whereas the use of commissives in English (like *I promise you*) is commonly associated with psychological commitments to the act (viz., 'sincerity'), and non-compliance with conceptions of inner moral failure, Rosaldo argues that the notion of a continuous inner self, and the type of interiorized morality it implies, is of little cultural relevance to the use and construal of commissives among the Ilongot. When promises are made it is not the speaker's private psychological intentions but the public act of having made the promise that is critical to the Ilongot conception; and when promises are broken, their breach is linked not to descriptions of inner moral failure but to a language of reparations, to considerations of whether and how the breach can be ameliorated by other public acts such as the giving of gifts or payments. Ideas about personhood and conduct therefore constitute a distinct type of metapragmatic framework for construing the use of performative locutions, a framework relative to which the interactional appropriateness of a particular usage as well as its consequences or entailments (i.e., the kind of social-interpersonal facts effectively created by it) are understood in any given culture.

These considerations show that the kind of social act performed by an explicit performative utterance cannot be understood by attending *only* to its locution-internal metapragmatic frame. The utterance *does* contain an 'internal' metapragmatic framework, an array of grammaticalized deictics (i.e., participant pronouns + verbum dicendi + non-selective verb deixis) which reflexively identifies the act performed with the act denoted. But this is just the most transparent (or locally explicit) framework for construing performed effects. It is neither necessary nor sufficient for construing such effects: not necessary because many conventional performative locutions lack the criterial shape; not sufficient because the appropriateness and success of the act depends also on locution-'external' co-textual conditions, such as features of utterance setting, (14), social categories of speaker and addressee, (15), and the co-textual organization of preceding discourse, (16). Finally, we cannot understand the way in which these features come to be linked to particular locutions, or become conditions on their performative success, without taking into account larger scale sociohistorical practices within that community. In some cases the relevant conditions are set through the work of named institutions such as the Church or Common Law. But in the larger majority of cases the relevant practices are not linked to rigidly codified or named institutions, and thus are not easily described in decontextualized ways by members of the society. Nonetheless, these institutional conditions are readily identified by participants in *explanations of infelicitous usage*, and ethnographic and historical comparison across cultures confirms their contrastive importance.

More generally, and whether or not we can identify the relevant conditions with the work of named institutions, we are considering in all cases the possibility that the prior social history of a language community includes forms of reflexive activity which sets the conditions on subsequent forms of reflexive activity. How is this possible?

1.6 Reflexive processes across encounters

We have been concerned in preceding sections (1.3 and 1.4) with reflexive signs that shape the characteristics of the encounters in which they occur. In 1.5, we considered locutions which appear to create more durable social facts. But how can signs that occur in one encounter shape the way in which *other* encounters proceed? How does reflexive activity have semiotic consequences that *perdure* beyond an encounter?

In much of the rest of the book I discuss a variety of processes through which large scale semiotic formations emerge through the mediation of locale specific activities. These processes have a number of features that differ for different kinds of semiotic formations. These are introduced in subsequent chapters. My concern here is to introduce one elementary feature of such processes, namely the issue of how the social domain of a semiotic regularity may be expanded through semiotic activity itself.

When we say that a sign-form, X, stands for something else, Y, we are talking about a semiotic regularity, namely a 'standing-for' relationship. The semiotic regularity includes a social regularity in the sense that X is taken to stand for Y a population of sign-users. Let us call this population of users, the persons acquainted with the standing-for relationship, the **social domain** of the regularity. The social domain of the standing-for relationship is the population of persons who treat the sign-form X as standing for Y. Can the social domain change as a result of semiotic activity?

The question of the mechanism through which semiotic regularities are transmitted across social populations is relevant even to the simplest cases of lexical innovation. How does a new word, once coined, begin to circulate through social space? How does it begin to recur in disparate events of language use? One area of enormous lexical innovation in contemporary English, for example, is the lexical register of computerese, where terms like *download, zip drive, RAM* and *mouse* now prevail with denotational values quite distinct from those of their ordinary English homonyms. How do the distinctive denotational values of such words and locutions, once established, come to be shared? Now, the existence of a lexical item is, in one sense, an elementary Durkheimian social fact: the existence of the word as something usable in utterances presupposes a collective understanding of its existence. The difficulty with the Durkheimian notion of social fact, however, is the question of how such a collective understanding itself comes about. How, then, does a social regularity of recognition emerge?

Perhaps the most influential contemporary model for thinking about this issue was first worked out by Saul Kripke for the special case of proper names (Kripke 1972), and later extended by Hilary Putnam to a larger class of cases (Putnam 1975). Kripke proposed a particular historical mechanism for explaining how knowledge of a particular denotational regularity – the pairing of name with a referent – comes to be socially shared. Kripke's insight was to see that even this rather elementary discursive fact cannot become a social fact independently of a reflexive historical process through which the social domain of the name-referent pairing is established, or grows, or shrinks. In the discussion below I illustrate these issues for the case of personal proper names. But the discussion makes clear that the underlying principles are easily extended to other types of cases. Let us begin by considering the special case in more detail.

The case of proper names

Proper names are deictic expressions but they are not speech-event deictics or 'shifters.' They are not shifters in the sense that, unlike pronouns and demonstratives (whose reference depends on speech-event variables such as speaker and location of utterance), the reference of a proper name does not shift from occasion to occasion of utterance. Yet proper names are deictic expressions nonetheless. Their deictic properties consist of the fact that proper names indexically denote (their usage appears to point to) a unique individual under certain interactional conditions. It is merely that these conditions (the interactional schema of proper name deixis) cannot be described solely by appeal to variables of the current speech-event. Proper names are **speech-chain deictics** in a sense clarified below.

Before we focus on this issue, however, it is important to see that proper names have additional properties that are not now at issue. For example proper names formulate a denotational sketch of referent by assigning referent to grammatical and cultural classifications. A variety of denotational classifications of referent type – e.g., gender, place or circumstances of birth, religious, tribal or other group affiliation – are lexicalized in personal proper names in languages of the world. These require an entirely different type of analysis, some aspects of which are discussed in the next chapter.

The issue with which we are now concerned is the question of how the uniqueness of pairing of name with referent emerges. This issue constitutes a classic puzzle in the literature on names. It is quite clear, for example, that names are recycled within a language community so that many people have the same name. Why then does a name appear to be associated with a unique individual? The puzzle cannot be solved without recognizing that the cognitive regularity is underlyingly a social regularity: when we say that a name is associated with a unique individual we are saying that some people associate the name with one individual, though others may associate it with someone else. The uniqueness of pairing of name and referent is a regularity that holds for a social domain of persons. And explanations of how this social domain is formed – how, for example, it is differentiated from the larger language community – require appeal to a historical process.

Let us consider the outlines of this historical process for the case of personal proper names. Names are conferred upon persons in a distinct class of performative speech events, called 'baptismal events,' many of which have specific ceremonial prerequisites. In the context of Christian names, for example, the baptismal event takes place in a church, is presided over by a priest, is attended by the child and certain close kin. In such a case the priest is a metadiscursive agent of enormous power in that he is entitled to create a discursive regularity – the pairing of a name with a referent – which has consequences for the way in which the name bearer is correctly referred to in subsequent life.

Yet insofar as a name is conferred upon a person in such a ceremony, it becomes a social fact in a very limited sense. Only the individuals present in the ceremony have a collective understanding that the name is now the name of that child. The general mechanism by which knowledge of a name-referent pairing spreads from this small group of individuals is through further speech events whereby the fact that the name is now the name of a particular person may be learned by others. The overall effect of such a historical chain of speech events is to make a particular kind of linguistic behavior – the act of using a particular name for a particular person – socially replicable through a process of communicative transmission.

The links of the chain are speech events in which social persons occupy roles such as 'sender' and 'receiver' of messages, and the name occurs as part of the linguistic message exchanged by the occupants of these roles. Observe that an individual can relay such a message as its 'sender' only if he or she has been introduced to the name-referent link (i.e., has occupied the role 'receiver' of such a message) in a prior speech event. Figure 1.5

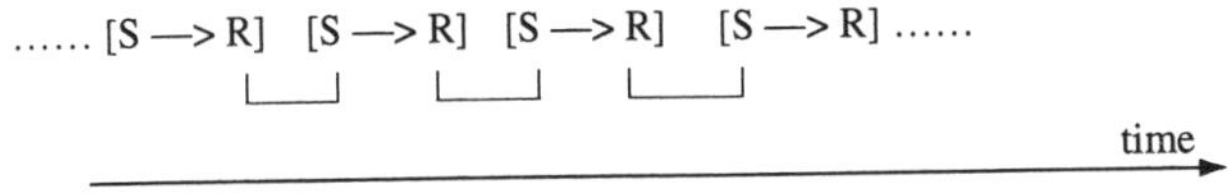

...... [S —> R]   [S —> R]   [S —> R]   [S —> R] ......
           └__┘   └__┘   └__┘

time

Figure 1.5   *Communicative transmission through a speech chain*

illustrates a **participant-linked speech chain** of this type. The chain consists of a historical series of speech events connected together by the permutation of individuals across speech-act roles in the following way: the receiver of the message in the (n)[th] speech event is the sender of the message in the (n + 1)[th] speech event.

The terms 'sender' and 'receiver' (or 'S' and 'R') are variable names for interactional roles: they are names for 'roles' in that different kinds of interactants may occupy positions S and R in different encounters along the chain; they are 'variable names' in that these roles have different specific values in different encounters, values that are indexed by reflexive cues that occur in that encounter.[25] In the case of face to face conversation the sender and receiver are physically co-present as 'speaker' and 'hearer'. In the case of written discourse the roles S and R – more specifically, 'writer' and 'reader' – may be occupied by individuals living centuries apart. Other links may involve public sphere discourses. In the case of a television broadcast that makes the name of a public figure better known, the role of receiver/audience/viewer of the message may be occupied simultaneously by millions of people; and the broadcast may presuppose the cooperation of dozens of people in the role sender of message.

In the case of proper names such a speech chain structure serves to maintain the pairing of a name with a referent over many occasions of language use, thus creating sociohistorical continuities in referential practice. Indeed, the understanding that a name correctly refers to a particular person is socially shared only by members of a given **speech chain network**, i.e., by the class of social persons who have all been receivers of messages belonging to a given speech chain. Co-membership in a speech chain network depends not on knowing one another but on having something common in one's discursive history. All members of a speech chain network need not be acquainted with each other. In the case of proper names, co-members are linked to each other by a continuous history of name transmission, i.e., each member of the network is linked to the baptismal event of name-conferral through a continuous speech chain.[26] An individual need not know *when* that baptismal event occurred, or even *that* it occurred. The social existence of a name-referent link merely *presupposes* an event of name-conferral; it does not in general require its verifiability.[27] In the more general case, co-membership in a speech chain network requires neither conscious knowledge nor verifiability of a shared discursive history by participants themselves, only an awareness of the symbolic values transmitted across the chain.

Other cases

The mechanism of transmission we have been considering is a way of conceptualizing the social expansion of a semiotic regularity. We have been concerned so far with the special case where the semiotic regularity happens to be the pairing of a personal name with a referent through an event of performative nomination. But this is just one type of case among many. Although the details of the account in the preceding section are focused on the special case of proper name deixis, analogous arguments can be formulated for cases that have nothing to do with either proper names or deixis, cases where the sign-object relationships that constitute the semiotic regularity are very different from the ones considered so far. For instance, similar questions pertain to the process whereby the effects of explicit performative locutions come to be recognized as social facts by others. How do the various cases discussed in 1.5 – for example, that someone now bears the title *Sir Lancelot*, or is henceforth the chairman, as in (13); or that two individuals are to be treated as married to each other, as in (16) – come to constitute social facts for persons not present at the ceremonial event that creates them? Analogous questions emerge for the class of social facts established by 'rites of passage' (Van Gennep 1961 [1909]), or rites of performative *re*-nomination, ceremonial events where the roles, statuses, and identities of persons are ritually transformed, e.g., rites of initiation, rites of separation and incorporation into groups, rites of transition through recognized stages of a life cycle, and others. In yet other cases, the social-indexical values of performable signs are formulated or re-formulated through social practices that do not involve performative ceremonies at all (Chapter 4). For any such case, the question naturally arises as to how a semiotic regularity (whether involving the construable status of a single individual, or the values of signs performable by many individuals) once established or transformed through some activity comes to be known to others.

The preceding account of the social transmission of messages across a population can be generalized, in other words, *beyond* the case of proper names to talk about the transmission of any kind of cultural message across social space through semiotic activity itself. Most of the issues relevant to such a generalization are discussed in subsequent chapters. Let me introduce three very basic issues in a preliminary way. One issue concerns the diversity of communicative processes that exhibit chain-like properties. A second issue concerns the extent to which communicative events formulate models of the sociohistorical order in which they occur, including virtual models of their own connection to other events. A third issue concerns the extent to which such models alter the sociohistorical process of which they are a part.

Chains and encounters

In the Introduction to this book, I defined a communicative or semiotic encounter as an emergent social happening constituted in general not by a face to face meeting between participants but by participants' mutual orientation to signs or messages. The reader may find it useful to review that discussion before proceeding. My goal here is to show that communicative encounters – whether they involve two people, or two million – are fragments of communicative chain processes of diverse kinds. It is not useful to conceptualize this diversity through static taxonomies for reasons that will become clearer below. We can nonetheless glimpse the range of issues involved by considering a few simple cases. In the above discussion I noted that particular events in a communicative chain like Figure 1.5 may be quite different from each other. I mentioned events of face to face communication and mass communication, and hinted at the possibility that processes of socialization can also be conceptualized as chain-like in character. Let us consider these differences a little more explicitly.

An event of mass communication is a communicative encounter in which many persons fill a given communicative role. Figure 1.6 illustrates the case where the role R is concurrently inhabited by a number of individuals ($b1$, $c1$, $d1$, etc.).

$$... [S \longrightarrow R] ...$$

$$a \qquad b1...b2...b3...$$
$$c1...c2...c3...$$
$$d1...d2...d3...$$
$$...$$

time

Figure 1.6   *Communicative networks in mass communication*

The term 'mass communication' is often used for events involving electronic and print media, but this is only a special case. Many other kinds of multiparty communicative events, and especially public rituals and ceremonial events, are events of mass communication in the sense intended here. Insofar as a participant in such an event subsequently communicates messages received in the encounter to other individuals in subsequent encounters (e.g., $b1$ communicates with $b2$ who communicates with $b3$; $c1$ with $c2$, and so on), the encounter shown in brackets becomes a branch point in a larger communicative process consisting of many other encounters.

In contrast, a dyadic face to face conversation involves a different kind of communicative chain, one where (1) the communicative events that

.....[S —> R]   [S —> R]   [S —> R]   [S —> R] ......
    a   b   b   a   a   b   b   a

                                            time →

messages exchanged

(1) include oral utterances

(2) occurring in a single encounter

(3) involving only a and b

Figure 1.7   *Dyadic conversation*

define it contain oral utterances; (2) all utterances occur in the same scene/ setting; and (3) the roles S and R are allocated alternatively to just two individuals. Figure 1.7 represents the flow of messages across turns in a single dyadic encounter of this type.

The distinguishing features of this special case make it a highly 'concrete' type of discursive chain, readily abstractable from the rest of social history and apparently amenable to decontextualized forms of transcript-based study.[28] But a dyadic conversation is also a **chain segment** – a segment of larger communicative processes – in the sense that any two individuals who engage in conversation have, of course, participated in various discursive interactions before, and thus bring to the event biographically specific discursive histories. Many features of a person's capacity to produce and understand messages that occur in conversation – to function as competent speakers and addressees of them – are shaped differentially by their prior discursive histories. If a participant lacks the relevant background knowledge, explicit metasemantic or metapragmatic work may be required within the encounter before he or she is able to recover the significance of utterances occurring in it.

When we study processes of socialization we are sometimes interested in the way in which the prior discursive history of a person equips that individual with particular types of semiotic competence. In such cases we are concerned with the sequence of encounters in which that individual has been involved, namely a sequence isolated from a biographic point of view (see Figure 1.8).

...... [S —> R]   [S —> R]   [S —> R]   [S —> R] ......
     b   b   b   b

                                        → time

Figure 1.8   *A biographic history of encounters*

When we consider also the internal structure of such encounters – by considering types of interlocutors (e.g., types of caregivers in the case of childhood socialization), or the genre characteristics of the most routinized form of such interactions (e.g., socialization within the family) – we thereby introduce other variables necessary to an understanding of the communicative process that leads to socialization. But explanations of how particular individuals get socialized cannot proceed without a consideration of their biographic communicative histories.

Many events of a communicative nature, such as soliloquy and inner speech, appear to involve only a single individual. But the capacity of individuals to use language in isolation from other individuals, for example in 'talking to oneself' or as 'inner speech' (without audible utterance), depends on a prior history of language socialization. Thus communicative events of the type illustrated in Figure 1.9 only occur as chain segments of other types of communicative processes, such as those discussed earlier.

$$\ldots\ldots [S \longrightarrow R] \ldots\ldots$$
$$a a$$

--→ time

Figure 1.9   *Soliloquy and inner speech*

It is worth pointing out that many events that are commonly called 'soliloquies' – such as dramatic soliloquies in theatrical performances – are not cases of this type at all. It is true that in the case of theatrical soliloquies only one person may be present onstage and may manifestly be talking to him or herself; but the receivers of the message include (and in the case of the theatre are in fact intended to be) members of the audience offstage, and this fact is indexed by a variety of features of the onstage performance itself. In such a case, one level of metapragmatic framing formulates the event as being of the type shown in Figure 1.9; but other concurrent features of the theatrical performance formulate it as an event (and, the producer hopes, even a chain) of the type illustrated in Figure 1.6.

Notice that we have now explicitly appealed to the question of how an event formulates its own metapragmatics. This issue brings us to the difference between historical chains and virtual models of their chain-like characteristics.

Virtual models in sociohistorical data

We can approach the study of communicative processes in two very different ways. We approach them as **historical chains** when we make independent observations of many actual events and ask how they are related to one another. For example if we are interested in how a rumor or a piece of gossip develops within a group we might look at several events of gossiping (spread out, say, over a cycle of several days) to discover how that rumor grew in the telling. Or if we are interested in language socialization we might consider an individual's communicative history over biographic time in the sense discussed above. Or if we are interested in how a religious text was read in different periods we might compare different commentaries (and thus different events of reading) to discover something about the way in which that text was received in, and shaped, the various cultural milieus in which it played a part. Despite obvious differences, all these efforts are attempts to view the process as a historical chain, i.e., by making independent observations of many events.

A second approach is to consider only a single semiotic event and ask how it formulates its own connection to other events. A chain of events thus identified is a **virtual model** of a chain of events, or a virtual chain. We have seen numerous examples of virtual chains already. Any reported speech utterance formulates a virtual chain, a representation of another utterance which is purported to have occurred. Similarly insofar as the examples in Figure 1.3 typify co-occurring utterances as gossip, eloquence, etc., they formulate virtual models of contiguous utterances. The cases in Figure 1.4 formulate virtual models of next-turn behavior by interlocutor. The performatives in (13) formulate models of the very event in which they occur so that here the event and its model asymptotically converge; but insofar as the social roles and relations formulated are understood as perduring beyond the current event (that a promise is to be kept, that someone is henceforth the chairman), explicit performatives specify virtual models of how subsequent social behavior ought to occur.

To say that an event formulates a virtual model of communicative processes is not to say that the model is inaccurate. In fact questions of accuracy can never be posed by a consideration of the virtual model in isolation from all other facts. We can only assess the accuracy of a virtual model by taking an independent perspective on the events modeled.

Attention to virtual models of events and processes is typically part of any historical research in the ordinary sense of the term 'historical' (i.e., pertaining to the study of events), but it contrasts diametrically with the more restrictive sense in which I have just used the term 'historical' (i.e., based on an *independent* study of many events). To read an archival document is to participate in a semiotic event which contains a virtual model of other events as a representation; but to assess whether the representation is reliable is to evaluate the model by independent appeal to the events represented (e.g., by appeal to other historical records concerning these events). Similarly, in the case of ethnographic research, to ask a person about a particular type of conduct or social practice is to gather a virtual model of the nature of that practice; but the accuracy of the model cannot be assessed without some independent perspective on the conduct or practice of which it is a model.

A virtual model of a discursive event or process can only be evaluated historically (in the narrow sense, i.e., by independent appeal to the events modeled) when features of the current discourse allow a hearer/reader to locate the phenomena modeled (e.g., in terms of time, place, participants, and so on) and thus to acquire some independent perspective on them. This is not possible without deictic directions for finding referents. For example, to ask whether an utterance formulated as reported speech actually did occur, or occurred in the manner reported, is to assess a virtual chain historically; but this is possible only insofar as the current utterance clarifies such details as who allegedly did what to whom when. In the case of archival research, appeals to a variety of deictics (such as person and place names, temporal deictics, calendric expressions) are prerequisites to the simple task of locating documented events in sociohistorical space-time and thus on assessments of the document's accuracy and reliability.

Many social artifacts are so designed as to authenticate facts of the current encounter by formulating **authoritative virtual models** of other events, models that are not easily challenged in everyday life. A simple example is a case where a person is asked to present some form of identification (a driver's license, a passport, etc.) as proof of age. The document records facts of biographic identity which are treated as authentic on the presumption that the holder of the document acquired it through a process that made reference to a baptismal event (e.g., by presenting a birth certificate in order to get a driver's license) and an institution that guarantees its validity. Once presented the document forecloses the possibility of further questions; unless, of course, it exhibits a form of co-textual noncongruence – whether internal (as when it appears to be a forgery) or in relation to other co-occurring indices (such as bearer's visible age) – which leads to questions of an entirely different kind. But such assessments of accuracy are only possible insofar as the 'facts' represented in the current encounter (here documented biographic facts) are specified with sufficient deictic selectivity (name, place and date of birth, etc.) so as to permit independent assessment.

In other cases, virtual models appear authoritative precisely because they forestall any possibility of the discrete locatability of the model in sociohistorical space-time. For example many rituals formulate the activities conducted in them as always having been conducted in that way, as timeless in a certain sense, or as deriving from some ancestral or mythic past that does not belong to the same sociohistorical order as the current event. The ritual models a mode of conduct as having a timeless provenance and validity; and, at the same time, as something experienceable by persons now living only by participation in the ritual itself. The first element, the formulation of a model as somehow apart from the historical order in which it is displayed, is a reflexive relationship which Silverstein 1993 terms the **nomic calibration** of event and model. In the case of rituals such models are not merely *formulated as* timeless or extra-temporal in provenance; they are *formulated by* an extended textual organization of signs unfolding within the ritual, no one segment of which describes the model formulated by the entextualized whole; challenging the model requires some further metasemiotic activity such as its conversion into a descriptive claim which, however, always formulates a message more specific than any that the ritual itself displays. Moreover the implicit entextualized model and explicit descriptive claims about it typically differ in social circulation. For instance, if the ritual is widely experienced (e.g., is ubiquitous and recurrent, or is an event of mass communication in each occurrence) its messages have a social circulation very different from specific descriptions or challenges formulated by particular participants in response to it. In such cases the persistent authority of the model derives both from the difficulty of challenging it and the relatively restricted circulation of individual challenges.

In other cases, processes that explicitly typify social phenomena – such as types of persons, roles, identities, normative behaviors – tend to stabilize these phenomena through explicitly descriptive strategies. For example, descriptive **essentialization** is a common metasemiotic activity or practice that appears to fix the values of complex cultural realities by grouping them into classes and treating some attributes of members (but not others) as necessary or 'essential' to class membership; once interpreted as essences such frameworks of attribution treat other (residual) attributes as 'accidental' or extra-normative. In cognitive terms, an essence is a timeless substrate felt to lie beneath a disorderly play of qualities. In social terms, essentialization is a reflexive activity that normalizes behavior by treating some behaviors as necessary, others as extra-normative to a category or class of social being.

In every society language users employ distinctive metapragmatic vocabularies for talking about the deployment of speech and associated signs in social interaction. Any such vocabulary constitutes an **ethnometapragmatic** terminology used to typify the form and meaning of behaviors, and to classify persons, identities, group membership, and other facts of social being in relation to behavior. These terminologies vary enormously in constructional form, in their **semiotic range** (cf. Figure 1.1), and in the degree to which they are standardized by normative traditions. Yet despite their diversity, such terminologies share some characteristics that are of very general consequence. The very fact that they are terms or vocabularies – lexical items and their phraseological extensions – entails that they are very easily decontextualized from use in one event and recontextualized in other events to form typifications of phenomena occurring elsewhere. They are devices which, by their linguistic design, are pre-eminently capable of circulation through social space and of creating unities among disparate events. They are also devices whose meaning can be codified, linked to criteria of authenticity and essence. Once codified, attributes held essential to the class can be used to evaluate the range of attributes actually displayed by persons in behavior, thus providing normative criteria that convert facts of social difference into measures of rank or hierarchy. Here, for example, is Clifford Geertz's summary of native glosses of two Javanese adjectives, *alus* 'refined, polite' and *kasar* 'coarse,' both of which are critical to norms of deference and demeanor.

(18) *Alus* means pure, refined, polished, polite, exquisite, ethereal, subtle, civilized, smooth. A man who speaks flawless high-Javanese is *alus*, as is the high Javanese [speech] itself. A piece of cloth with intricate, subtle designs painted onto it is *alus*. An exquisitely played piece of music or a beautifully controlled dance step is *alus*. So is a smooth stone, a dog with his hair petted down, a far-fetched joke, or a clever poetic conceit. God is, of course, *alus* (as are all invisible spirits), and so is the mystical experience of Him. One's own soul and character are *alus* insofar as one emotionally comprehends the ultimate structure of existence; and one's behavior and actions are *alus* insofar as they are regulated by the delicate intricacies of the complex court-derived etiquette. *Kasar* is the mere opposite: impolite, rough, uncivilized; a badly played piece of music, a stupid joke, a cheap piece of cloth. Between the two poles the *prijaji* [i.e., a member of the aristocratic class] arranges everyone from peasant to king.

(Geertz 1960: 232)

The wide semiotic range of the terms *alus* and *kasar* generates iconic resemblances and oppositions among a range of otherwise disparate aspects of experience. The metasemiotic treatment also provides a framework for reading persons: if the behavioral signs in the classification are displayed or performed by persons, the classification of things provides a basis for the classification of persons.

Yet these classifications are highly positional. They are formulated by the *priyayi*, the traditional aristocratic class, as Geertz notes. They are further elaborated in traditions of metaphysics, poetry, and religion, where additional terms, such as the abstract noun *rasa* 'feeling; meaning' links the display of 'the truly *alus* character' to an ethos of self-possession, tranquility, control over emotion, viewed now as essential attributes of 'refinement' itself, and thus of those who are identifiable on particular occasions as 'refined':

(19) By taking *rasa* to mean both 'feeling' and 'meaning,' the *prijaji* has been able to develop a phenomenological analysis of subjective experience to which everything else can be tied ... The management of one's emotional economy becomes one's primary concern, in terms of which all else is ultimately rationalized ... Emotional equanimity, a certain flatness of affect, is, then, the prized psychological state, the mark of the truly *alus* character. As the forms which life takes vary from the disordered grossness of animal existence up through the only slightly more refined peasant to the hyper-genteel high-*prijaji*, and, finally, through the divine king to the invisible, intangible, insensible (except mystically), self-sufficient Being of God, so the forms of feeling vary from the vulgar actuality of base passion, through the spiritualized placidity of the true *prijaji* to the ultimate *rasa*, where feeling is but meaning only.

(Geertz 1960: 239)

Between the poles of 'feeling' and 'meaning' lies a great chain of being, a complex diagram of social differences, whereby particular things and persons come to occupy different fixed positions with respect to the 'natural' order. And – unsurprisingly – the *priyayi* themselves have a naturalized position relatively high within this cosmic hierarchy.

From a denotational point of view, metasemiotic discourses of this type treat a variety of sensoria as exhibiting the same characterological qualities (as in (18)), thus formulating them as cross-modal icons in the sense discussed earlier (Figure 1.1). Any of these diverse behavioral signs are **icons** of a single category of personhood (*alus* 'refined') and the display or enactment of these signs in behavior **indexes** something about the actor whose behavior it is, so that disparate things in the world are now formulated as **indexical icons** of a single category of perceivable personhood. Moreover, questions of essence (i.e., what counts as 'truly' *alus* behavior, as in (19)) are formulated by discourses that link perceivable behaviors to transcendent features of mind and cosmic order, thus naturalizing the framework of essences. The behaviors that index the persona are gradient, contingent, varying in thresholds of consistency over interactional time. In contrast, normative cultural readings of these behaviors often view them as naturally motivated icons, as in (3) above.

The sociological effectiveness of such normative schemes often depends on the allocation of authenticity and authority to those who formulate the scheme. In the above case the discourses that link sensoria to essences focus on attributes that are held to be characteristic of the *priyayi* themselves, the very persons who formulate the discourse. The *priyayi* are arbiters of taste because they are exemplars of it. This type of reflexive closure within a system of naturalized essences is, of course, a highly specific case; the special case is not uncommon in aristocratic and hieratic traditions but must be understood as one among many kinds of possible social arrangements that can be realized when discourses of essentialization are naturalized in the attributes of those who produce them.

More generally, any otherwise conventional or arbitrary standing-for relationship within a cultural order of semiosis can be fixed or made durable through a range of metasemiotic processes which bring about the **naturalization** of convention:

(20) ... individuals acting within a [sociocultural] system have a tendency to regard conventions as naturally motivated, that is, as being *objective* rather than socially constituted, *invariant* rather than malleable, *autonomous* rather than dependent, *eternal* rather than historical, *universal* rather than relative, and *necessary* rather than contingent.

(Parmentier 1994:176)

Through discussion of a number of ethnographic and historical cases, Parmentier shows that the tendency to naturalize conventions is a common social practice that tends to stabilize conventions over time. Demonstrating naturalness is itself a kind of metasemiotic work that may take many forms. Common examples include cases where an isolable sign or performed sign structure is recontextualized through a metasemiotic treatment in relation to other sign phenomena of a more abstract or generic order so that the two orders appear, through this treatment, to mutually imply each other in a densely coherent fashion; such a treatment minimizes the appearance of the sign's isolable arbitrariness (or contingent form) and maximizes the appearance of its place (function, purpose) within the more totalizing order (the 'nature' of mind, society, cosmos, etc.). The effectiveness of the strategy is contingent upon the difficulty faced by a hearer of the naturalizing discourse of showing that this second, more totalizing order is itself a model of a historically contingent kind, not something invariant or autonomous of the experience of known individuals in particular times and places. But the strategy is effective only insofar as it is, in fact, ratified; and it is most effective where the ratified construct is presupposed in so many diverse practices that the question of its contingency does not readily arise.

There appear to be no societies in which practices that naturalize conventions do not occur. For such practices are effective in stabilizing not only conventions but social arrangements that depend on their stability, including institutionalized positions of power and authority (and other types of vested interests that can be maintained as long as the naturalized convention lasts).[29]

At the same time no naturalized convention, however densely and rigidly naturalized, persists beyond a particular historical horizon. For demonstrating the naturalness of a convention does not consist only of a process of motivating the attributes of a thing (the conventional sign being talked about) in relation to other experienceable realities. It consists also of the inhabitance of a **footing** or **interpersonal alignment** with respect to other social persons, whether ones described or addressed by the naturalizing discourse. Those addressed respond with a footing too. We shall see in the next two chapters that matters of footing and alignment play an important role in processes through which standing-for relationships are denaturalized, reanalyzed, contested, or otherwise transformed.

1.7 Large scale cultural formations

In the last section we saw that standing-for relationships between perceivable behaviors and cultural realities have a social domain that can be expanded through semiotic activity itself. Insofar as any cultural phenomenon is embodied in perceivable signs, events of its performative expression and construal are semiotic events mediated by human activities. Since

they are semiotic events, particular occasions of expression and construal
may exhibit a variety of reflexive relationships; and since they involve
human activities such events are invariably segments of larger semiotic
chains through which reflexive formulations of value may be maintained
or transformed.

Cultural formations are not static appurtenances of unchanging collections of people. They are dynamically altered by semiotic activities and
practices. Every cultural phenomenon has a social domain at any moment
of its history, susceptible to dialectical variation (and sometimes also
'dialectal' variation) through processes of communicative transmission
that expand or narrow its scale. Talk of variation in 'scale' in this sense is
talk of changes in the social domain of cultural formations through semiotic activity itself. When a cultural construct has a recognizable reality
only for a sub-group within a society, processes of communicative transmission can readily bring the construct to the attention of other members
of society making it more widely known and thus presupposable in use by
larger segments of the population. But the construct can also change
during this process. It may acquire authority, for example, or lose it; or it
may be re-interpreted in one or more ways.

Processes of communicative **transmission** depend on participant linkages between semiotic events. Such processes can alter the social domain
of a cultural regularity through the activities of persons, one participation
framework at a time. In some cases such processes appear to involve
processes of **circulation**. When processes of communicative transmission
expand the social domain of a standing-for relationship, a cultural form
appears to circulate across a group of people through activities that link
them to each other. Yet this is a special case. Taken very literally the term
'circulation' all too easily implies a billiard ball sociology, a conception
inadequate for capturing the effects of transmission in general. Very
frequently the standing-for relationship (i.e., the type of significance
assigned to the cultural form) is altered during the process of communicative transmission itself and, in such cases, no unitary or invariant sign may
be said to 'circulate' globally across the chain. For example the repertoire
of sign-forms that express the cultural construct may grow, shrink, or
otherwise change; or their sign-values may be re-interpreted so that a
scheme of counter-values comes to co-exist society-internally with the
first. Under these conditions it is the **reanalysis** or transfiguration of the
sign phenomenon that dominates the process of communicative transmission even though the observed identity of a fraction of the total phenomenon across locales (such as identity of sign-form) may suggest its
invariant circulation.[30] The term circulation is a useful approximation for
describing the effects of communicative transmission only to the extent
that different phases of a communicative process presuppose that a

cultural form has comparable sign-values; the non-comparability of sign-values is a measure of its reanalysis.

All cultural signs are subject to social transmission – across thresholds of circulation and reanalysis – through semiotic chain processes of the kind discussed above. Once we reconstruct cultural processes in communicative terms and view determinate cultural formations as effects precipitated by reflexive processes, there is nothing surprising or puzzling about the fact that competing models of a cultural phenomenon can come to co-exist within a society as a result of a single continuous historical process. In the next chapter I argue that the society-internal existence of cultural forms need not in general satisfy any condition of invariant sharedness; its semiotic properties need only be fractionally comparable across different social domains in order for the cultural form to mediate patterns of coordinated social interaction.

I noted earlier that acts of value ascription to language can range over generic objects too, formulating them as sets of expressions whose forms and values become socially institutionalized for large social domains of evaluators. Let me illustrate this issue, and the analytic problems it poses, for a particular type of sociocultural formation.

Registers of discourse

All human languages are culturally differentiated into distinct registers of discourse that are associated with particular social practices and categories of persons. Some among them have commonplace names such as 'aristo-cratic speech,' 'bureaucratese,' 'slang,' and so on. Subsequent chapters present a systematic approach to the study of these phenomena. My purpose here is to introduce some basic issues.

Let us begin with the term *register* itself. Before we turn to technical uses of the term, it is useful to consider some ordinary homonyms and variants. In everyday English, the word-form *register* corresponds to several distinct lexemes and derived forms. Some of these are verbs, others nouns:

(21) Some lexemic variants of the term *register* in everyday English
    (a) *to register*$_1$ 'to recognize, become aware of' (verbum sentiendi)
    (b) *to register*$_2$ 'to record, write down' (verbum dicendi)
    (c) *registered, a register, registry, registration, a social register*
       (substantives; various)

The lexemes in (a) and (b) are both metapragmatic verbs (cf. (2) above), though of different kinds. The first one is a verb of cognition that denotes a moment of recognition or awareness by an experiencer typically denoted by a dative noun phrase (viz., 'the point didn't *register on him* at all'). The lexeme in (b) is a verb of speech that denotes an act of writing (or electronic inscription) that yields a perduring record; the act is usually mediated by institutional processes, some among which confer entitlements (viz., 'he *is registered* to vote'). The verbum dicendi denotes cognitive effects too, but of a public rather than a private sort: an act of institutionally recording a fact transforms it into a public fact capable of wider recognition. The verb is attested in intransitive, transitive and ditransitive uses (cf. 'to be registered as Z'; 'For X to register Y'; 'For X to register Y as Z') which imply different thresholds of agentive control over processes that confer durable statuses and entitlements upon individuals. The products of such institutional activities are, in turn, denoted by a variety of substantives, as in (c), that variously capture these cognitive and discursive valences, and dependent forms of entitlement. Thus we have expressions like the modifier *registered* ('she is a *registered* user/pilot/nurse'); the term *registration* for a permit; the term *a register* for a ledger containing many official records as entries. Processes involving individuals become entries in *registers of births, deaths and marriage*; guests sign into *hotel registers* when they arrive; and some people aspire over the course of their lives to become entries in *a social register*, an artifact that names everyone who has, in the relevant sense, 'arrived.'

The technical sense in which I use the term *register* in this book has nothing in particular to do with hotels, births or marriages, of course. But it has everything to do with the way in which behavioral signs (including features of discursive behavior) acquire recognizable pragmatic values that come to be viewed as perduring 'social facts' about signs, and which, by virtue of such recognition, become effective ways of indexing roles and relationships among sign-users in performance.

In the technical usage, however, it is necessary to distinguish registers as products (or precipitates) of human activity from the process through which they are formed. This distinction may be formulated as follows: a **semiotic register** is a repertoire of performable signs linked to stereotypic pragmatic effects by a sociohistorical process of **enregisterment**. To speak of 'a register' (to use the count noun) is to speak of a sociohistorical phase, a moment-interval of a process of enregisterment; the term 'enregisterment' (a deverbal noun of process) makes reasonably transparent the fact that a register's existence is mediated by activities which make known (or 'enregister'), and thus make usable, facts of semiotic value associated with signs. Through much of this book I discuss examples of various **registers of discourse**; however, as we shall see in Chapter 3, discursive registers typically involve non-linguistic signs as well, and are usually fragments of larger semiotic register formations; and, in Chapters 5 and 8, we consider cases where processes of enregisterment yield semiotic formations that do not correspond to discourse registers as classically understood.

A register of discourse is a reflexive model of discursive behavior. The model is performable through utterances in the sense that producing a criterial utterance indexes a stereotypic image of social personhood or interpersonal relationship. The model is formulated by semiotic practices that differentiate a register's forms from the rest of the language, evaluate these repertoires as having specific pragmatic values (e.g., as 'high' vs. 'low' forms of speech) and make these forms and values known to a population of users through processes of communicative transmission. Since such practices are the activities of individuals, any of these features of register organization can be maintained or modified through further reflexive activity, though, typically, institutionally configured forms of such activity tend to be more socially consequential than others. These issues, summarized rather schematically and preemptively below, are discussed in more detail in Chapters 3 and 4.

Summary 1.7
Some technical uses of the word-form 'register':

A *register of discourse*: a cultural model of action

(a) which links speech repertoires to stereotypic indexical values
(b) is performable through utterances (yields enactable personae/relationships)
(c) is recognized by a sociohistorical population

A *semiotic register*: a register where language use is not the only type of sign-behavior modeled, and utterance not the only modality of action. A register of discourse is a special case.

Enregisterment: processes and practices whereby performable signs become recognized (and regrouped) as belonging to distinct, differentially valorized semiotic registers by a population

It will be clear that registers are complex reflexive formations which require different levels of analysis. These issues are introduced at different stages in this book. However, a feature common to all semiotic registers is the assignment of **stereotypic indexical values** to performable signs. In the case of registers of discourse, the relevant performable signs are speech repertoires; their stereotypic indexical values emerge through a reanalysis of speech variation in particular sociohistorical locales; such values may expand in social domain by transmission to other locales through semiotic chain processes; and, in the course of such transmission, may be stabilized by semiotic ideologies and doctrines of essence (e.g., (18) and (19)), or be revalorized or otherwise transformed. Relative to such processes registers grow or shrink in demographic terms, gain hegemonic force or lose it, are replicated uniformly across populations or fractionate into oppositional models of personhood.

Enregistered models of action

To speak of semiotic registers is to speak of cultural models of action. Such models are formulated and disseminated through semiotic activities that evaluate specific behavioral signs as appropriate to particular scenarios of social-interpersonal conduct. We cannot make sense of such reflexive formations without appeal to the meta-sign/object-sign distinction. Much of the cultural point of register models depends on the ways in which they bring together diverse phenomena into unifying rubrics (e.g., unite a number of behaviors into a metasemiotic grouping so that they are treated as expressions of the same, or of analogous, acts), convert one sort of cultural phenomenon into another (e.g., convert speech registers into emblems of political or economic identity), link together public and private domains of experience (e.g., treat overt behaviors as indexical of mental states).

The very special case of **lexical registers** is the case where the object-signs of a register are lexical repertoires. This is the type of case most widely discussed in the literature. However lexical registers are typically fragments of discourse registers involving other types of linguistic signs; and discourse registers are often fragments of more complex semiotic register formations, whose repertoires include non-linguistic signs. One type of complexity emerges from the fact that stereotypes of indexicality are metasemiotic constructs that exhibit a systematic 'leakage' across different types of object-signs, or objects of typification (Agha 1998a). Thus stereotypes about lexical indexicality are extended to, or motivate analogous stereotypes of, phenomenally distinct semiotic phenomena such as speech styles, non-linguistic behaviors, bodily comportment, appurtenances and possessions. In such cases we may speak of different **kinds of enregistered object-signs** to distinguish sign-phenomena which, though phenomenally diverse, are treated as signs of the same semiotic register.

My main focus in most of the chapters that follow will continue to be on the discursive fractions of the semiotic registers I discuss. Both the linguistic and sociological complexity of registers of discourse result from the fact that once a distinct register is culturally recognized as existing within a language, the repertoires of that register can be linked through further reflexive activity by language users to a wider range of enactable effects. For example, the forms of its repertoires may be linked by further metadiscursive activity to stereotypic social personae, or to ethical ideals associated with such personae, both of which can then be indexically invoked in discourse through the utterance of the forms. Or, such forms, once co(n)textualized by other semiotic devices in discourse, may be used to achieve interactional effects which, though dependent on the stereotypic values of the register, are significantly at odds with these values, e.g., the use of honorific language to enact veiled aggression, where utterance denotation formulates an aggressive act but the presence of stereotypically honorific forms counts as its 'veiling.'

Since registers of discourse live – both discursively and metadiscursively – through events of language use, the social significance of discourse registers cannot be understood without some understanding of register-*independent* features of language use. In the next chapter we focus on the social-interpersonal effects of referential acts. There are two main reasons that we turn to a sociology of referring at this stage of the discussion. The first is that when it comes to language use referring takes no holidays. The activity of referring itself has social effects that are invariably laminated upon whatever social effects are mediated by register models of action. Even though registers are sometimes described by language users as if they were self-contained ways of performing roles and relationships, the actual use of any register is unavoidably accompanied by the more implicit index-icalities linked to referring. Hence in any actual semiotic performance the effects of register deployment are superimposed on, and potentially altered by, social indexical effects linked to referring. The second reason concerns the relation between norms of denotational correctness and norms of interactional appropriateness in discursive acts. The latter are, as we shall see, critical to registers of discourse; but to understand how they emerge at all, and how their emergence results in register differentiation, requires a consideration of the former.

FROM REFERRING TO REGISTERS

2.0 Introduction

The purpose of this chapter is to show that everyday acts of referring to things in the world are organized by underlying principles that mediate social relations among speech participants. Referring is an unavoidably 'social' act. Indeed, by the end of the chapter we will see that referring is a social act in several distinct senses of the term 'social.' These require distinct kinds of analysis. In a highly ubiquitous type of case, ordinary acts of referring establish social relations among current speech participants (speakers and hearers of referential utterances) but the forms used to achieve such effects are not widely recognized or discussed out of context as social indexicals at all; here referential usages map out precise distinctions of role and relationship but are not assigned stereotypic social indexical values. In sharp contrast are cases where denotational variants that are usable for referring are widely recognized as belonging to pragmatically distinct registers of a language. In the latter half of the chapter I show that such registers are themselves based on a reanalysis of variation in denotational practices within a community; here the more generalized social functions of referring are re-evaluated to yield the very special case where denotational variants become stereotypically valued as indexicals of speaker's role or relationship to others.

The initial sections of this chapter offer an account of referring as a mode of social semiosis. I argue that the effective use of expressions to refer to things is shaped by interactional principles (2.1), and that acts of referring create emergent interpersonal alignments between speech participants (2.2). In the next few sections I argue that what is normally called 'linguistic structure' is at once a norm of denotation and interaction, not merely a norm of the former type.[1] Grammatical units (units of phonology and morphosyntax) are sociological categories in several ways. First, when we speak of grammatical classifications (whether of sound or sense) we are invariably talking about classifications that are classifications *for* particular social domains of speakers; speakers aware of such classifications can trope upon them in diverse ways. Second, the denotation of many common expressions is fixed by practices in which standards of denotational correctness are backed by sociological principles – such as semiotic divisions of labor, institutionalized asymmetries of power and authority among social actors – which imbue them with types of normativity (2.4). Finally, languages are socio-pragmatically differentiated into registers; thus, accounts of 'linguistic structure' are invariably accounts of a specific register of a language, often the register called the 'Standard Language.' Grammatical analyses that do not recognize the register characteristics of their object of analysis are necessarily incomplete. In 2.5, I show that the differentiation of a language into register partials is itself a social process mediated by various types of interpersonal footings and alignments between language users. In the case of lexical registers, criteria involving the denotational sameness and difference of words and expressions, and norms specifying the use of some word-types and not others, are used to formulate interactional norms, such as norms of appropriate use, and the question of whether or not individuals in fact behave in a norm-consistent manner is used to formulate stereotypes of language users within the processes of register differentiation.

2.1 Referring

In our everyday discourses about meaning we often talk about referring as if it were a relationship between words and things. But words and things are not good candidates for the elementary poles of the referring relation; they are merely the most decontextualizable features of the act of referring. In order to study the social character of referential acts we need a better understanding of the sign-vehicles used in referring and the objects that come to count as their referents.

In the last chapter we saw that the sign-vehicles that mediate acts of referring are typically arrays of signs that co-occur together as text configurations, different elements of which contribute distinct components of a referential sketch, an outline of the identity and characteristics of referents that is often built up cumulatively (e.g., added to, negotiated, edited) over the course of an interaction. 'Words' are merely the most transparent fragments of such text configurations. The referents or things talked about are discursive projections – i.e., they are referents *of* discursive signs – which, once delineated through a semiotic sketch, may turn out to be entities whose existence is verifiable through further semiotic activity, in which case we speak of 'real' things; or their existence may not be verifiable, whether straightforwardly or at all. Such a universe of actual and imaginable entities – whether large or small, near or far, interactionally ratified or contested – is articulated in an immanent fashion through referential acts in any discursive interaction. Calling such entities 'things' is harmless enough, except when it distracts from the semiotic processes whereby entities become referents of a discourse (and thus become present, or relevant, to communicators); or from processes whereby such entities, once identified as now relevant, become manipulable as counters within the game of interaction, permitting various relationships and roles to be exhibited through their manipulation.

The main point regarding referential sign-vehicles – illustrated for the case of deictic usage in Chapter 1, and explored further below – may be summarized as follows:

Summary 2.1
To understand the way in which linguistic expressions contribute to referring requires that we move beyond an expression-centric view of referring (i.e., a view that attends only to the local semanticity of isolable expressions) to a more encompassing, **text-centric** analysis, i.e., a view that treats individual pieces of semiotic text as contributing sketches or images of referents which are filled in or further specified by accompanying signs. The expression-centric view is a useful approximation of the text-centric view only for the special case where the text-segment that suffices to achieve a referential effect is a relatively localizable expression.

The reason that this issue is important is that different levels of co-textual organization within referential acts may accomplish notionally distinct yet concurrent effects. For example, in a scenario such as a police line-up where a victim of a mugging is trying to identify the mugger, the effects of an utterance like *That's the one!* may accurately be described in several distinct ways, viz., as an act (a) of 'picking out a referent,' (b) of 'answering a question' and (c) of 'helping the police identify a suspect.' But these accounts do not appeal to the same level of co-textual organization in the interaction: construal (a) attends only to what the utterance does, (b) also takes into account its relationship to prior utterances, and (c) further attends to the social identities of interactants. All of these construals are mediated by the same utterance but are not construals of the same sign-configuration. They attend to successively more encompassing levels of text-structure, treating more and more of the context of utterance as a semiotic co-text for construing the act performed.

The second point concerns the character of entities sketched out through referential acts. We cannot approach this issue without distinguishing **acts of referring** from the **denotation of expressions** used in such acts. Acts of referring are communicative events anchored to participation frameworks, namely to configurations of persons in roles such as sender and receiver of message. In contrast, the denotation of an expression is its constant capacity to refer to the same type of thing across many acts. Thus the concept of denotation has both a classificatory aspect (involves 'types of things') and a norm aspect (the 'constant capacity' of expressions).

An obvious way of characterizing the classificatory aspect of denotation is to appeal to the logic of classes. This is traditionally done by appeal to the distinction between the semantic intension and extension of a class. The **intension** of a class is a property (or conjunct of properties) that defines membership in the class. Its **extension** is the set of things that are its members. The denotation of an expression may be viewed intensionally as a semantic property that defines class membership; or extensionally, as the set of things to which the expression correctly refers. From this standpoint the denotation of an expression involves a norm of class membership. However the 'norm' aspect of denotation cannot be explained within the logic of classes. The fact that referents are grouped into classes at all, and that such groupings function as social norms, depends on factors of entirely different kinds, such as the capacity of grammatical patterns to organize linguistic form into semantic (denotational) classes (see 2.3), and on facts of social organization that make some among these classifications normative for users (see 2.4).

The critical point for the moment is that, quite aside from the question of the organization of norms, particular acts of referring may or may not be consistent with any given norm. The case where referring conforms to denotational norms is often called 'literal speech' or 'correct reference.' Yet any denotational norm that is recognized by speech participants can also be troped upon to yield significant effects (e.g., to reveal something about the characteristics of referent or of interpersonal relations among interlocutors) even though the act is denotationally anomalous.

The best evidence for the empirical reality of denotational norms is the ability of participants to differentiate acts of literal or correct reference from uses that appear anomalous. In any language community many expressions may be used to pick out a given referent, but some choices are considered more correct than others. Thus if an animal is correctly referred to by the term *dog*, using the term *cat* to refer to it is anomalous. To speak of the 'correct reference' of *dog* is to appeal to the denotation of an expression; but to speak of 'referential uses' is to speak of contextualized acts in which the expression is uttered. Thus referring (or reference) is utterance-dependent in a way that denotation is not:[2]

(1) ... the denotation of an expression is invariant and *utterance-independent*; it is part of the meaning which the expression has in the language system, independently of its use on particular occasions of utterance. Reference, in contrast, is variable and *utterance-dependent*. For example, the word 'dog' always denotes the same class of animals (or, alternatively, the defining property of the class), whereas the phrases 'the dog' or 'my dog' or 'the dog

that bit the postman' will refer to different members of the class on different occasions of utterance.

(Lyons 1995: 79)

Notice that phrases like *my dog, the dog, the dog that bit the postman*, are text configurations that contain the lexeme *dog* (whose denotation is now at issue) as well as deictics that provide users with context-dependent directions on how to find particular referents. Such co-textual cues point to different referents on different occasions of utterance. Lyons observes that such locatable referents are different 'members of the class.' But this is so only in the case of literal usage. The expression *dog* may also be used metaphorically to refer to something which is not a member of the class (i.e., is not normally characterized as a dog). An interactant's ability to spot the difference, *to recognize whether a particular usage is metaphoric or literal*, presupposes acquaintance with the denotation of the expression used and, as we shall see, with wider denotational norms of the language.

Another way of approaching this issue is to consider the difference between successful and correct reference. A referential act is **interactionally successful** if the speaker and hearer have a relatively symmetric grasp of what the referent is.[3] It is **denotationally correct** if the expressions used are employed in a manner conforming to norms of usage. An act of referring may be interactionally successful but denotationally incorrect; or it may be correct by criteria of general usage but unsuccessful in the instance. The case where an act of referring is both successful and correct is, of course, also possible, indeed commonplace; but from a semiotic point of view, this is a special case in the sense that it satisfies both types of criteria.

To view referring in terms of **success** or **failure** is to focus on referring as an interactional achievement. The achievement depends on the recruitment of individuals to participant roles such as speaker and hearer of utterance and consists of the speaker picking out a thing in a manner that the hearer can construe. The achievement can go awry in a variety of ways, resulting in various types of unsuccessful reference. For example the speaker may use a language or a linguistic expression which the hearer does not know, leading to unintelligibility; or the expression may be indexically anchored to context in a manner that picks out more than one candidate referent, resulting in ambiguity or miscommunication. In such cases the utterance creates an interactional asymmetry (e.g., draws a cognitive boundary between speaker and hearer) that shapes the way in which the rest of the interaction proceeds.

In sharp contrast are cases where the act of referring is interpersonally successful (i.e., the hearer is able to recover the referent) even though the expression used is denotationally incorrect (i.e., does not fit the referent). Here is an example made famous by the work of Keith Donnellan:

(2) Suppose one is at a party and, seeing an interesting-looking person holding a martini glass, one asks, 'Who is the man drinking a martini?' If it should turn out that there is only water in the glass, one has nevertheless asked a question about a particular person, a question that it is possible for someone to answer.

(Donnellan 1990 [1966]: 238)

Thus, even when the liquid in the glass is water, person A can use a question like *Who is the man (over there) drinking a martini?* to draw the attention of an interlocutor, person B, to the man holding the glass and thereby elicit a response. The interpersonal accomplishment is quite independent of the intentions or other psychological states of speech participants. Neither A nor B need be aware that the man is drinking water and that the act of referring is, in fact, denotationally incorrect; or A may be so aware, but nonetheless feel that the martini glass is the most salient clue in context for drawing B's attention to the man; or B may be aware that A is mistaken about what the man is drinking but may nonetheless be able to answer A's question.

The example shows that an act of referring may be interactionally successful even though it is denotationally incorrect. The measure of the interactional success of A's act is B's ability to locate the referent, as evidenced in his subsequent behavior (e.g., answering the question). The measure of denotational correctness is the extent to which the referent satisfies the description used by A.

The distinction allows us to see that the social consequences of an act of referring may depend on its degree of interpersonal success, or on its denotational appropriateness, or on both. Referents identified in particular utterances can come to have a social life over the rest of the interaction in the sense that they can be referred to again, whether by the same or by a different participant, whether successfully or not so successfully; or referred to again by a denotationally distinct expression and thus re-characterized, even re-characterized in such a way as to make prior acts of referring to them appear untrue. These cases make palpable various types of interpersonal alignment among co-participants mediated by the denotational patterning of their utterances. Let us consider issues of participant alignment in more detail.

Mutual coordination

An act of referring is successful to the extent that some semiotic device used in the act solves the problem of the **mutual coordination** of participants to referent, e.g., allows speaker and hearer a relatively symmetric grasp of what the referent is. A single speaking turn may or may not suffice, of course, and in cases of failure or partial coordination several additional speaking turns may occur before speech participants feel they have a symmetric enough grasp of referent identity and characteristics that no further referential work is needed. But let us first consider what the problem of mutual coordination implies about the nature of referring in single speaking turns.

One way of approaching this issue is to consider the referential uses of definite descriptions. A definite description, or definite noun phrase, is an expression containing a deictic modifier (e.g., _the_ shirt, _that_ shirt, _John's_ shirt), which specifies that a particular referent is being talked about (vs. an indefinite noun phrase, _a shirt_, which has a generic referent). In addition to the deictic, a definite description contains a nominal expression which characterizes the referent and therefore functions as an embedded predicate. Each of the following descriptions has the general form *The Φ*, where the *Φ* element – the embedded predicate or characterizing component – differs in its degree of formal and semantic complexity.

(3) The man ...
   The man who came to dinner ...
   The man who came to dinner wearing a blue shirt ...
   The man who came to dinner, wore a blue shirt, and sat over there ...

Since the characterizing part of the description may be semantically quite elaborate the philosopher Russell reasoned that definite descriptions pick out referents by adequately typifying the referent, by serving, in effect, as correct semantic labels for them. On this view a definite description *The Φ* picks out a referent, x, by virtue of the referent uniquely satisfying the description, i.e., by virtue of the fact that *Φ* is a correct description of x (and only of x). Descriptions typify things as having certain properties (*Φ*); things get picked out as referents (x) insofar as they have these properties. What could be simpler?

This picture is now understood to be wrong because it seriously underestimates the importance of the mutual coordination problem in the identification of referents. The semantic labeling view assumes that (denotational) correctness is a necessary and sufficient criterion on (interactional) success. But we have already seen a counterexample: in the scenario discussed above, the definite description *The man drinking the martini* successfully picks out a referent of which it is an incorrect description. How can we explain this type of achievement?

Although the problem is intractable within a semantic labeling view, it has a straightforward solution on the view of referring outlined in the previous chapter. The interactional success of an act of referring depends upon the utterance providing the hearer with a set of 'directions' or cues for locating the referent in context, allowing some measure of calibration of the perspective of speaker (person A) with that of hearer (person B). Talk of interactional success is talk of the extent to which A's and B's perspectives on referent are contextually calibrated. In the martini glass example, person A has in fact formulated a sketch of referent for B which is partially confirmed by other signs accessible to B in context, thus allowing B to coordinate his perspective to A's perspective. Notice that A's description, *the man (over there) drinking a martini*, while incorrect, is only partly incorrect: its referent is, after all, a man; and the man is, after all, holding a martini glass; and the liquid contained in the glass is visually indistinguishable from a martini. The interactional success of the act is mediated by A's providing B with a set of directions, formulated through intersubjectively accessible signs (hence, independent of subjective intentions or other psychological states, as noted earlier), which allow B to locate the target referent.

A second difficulty with the semantic labeling view is that the semantic adequacy of the description does not guarantee definite reference no matter how elaborate the description. Definite descriptions often lack definite reference and the question of whether a description has or lacks definite reference cannot be settled, contra Russell, by its semantic content alone; the issue can only be settled by attending, once again, to semiotic cues occurring in the **co-text** of the description used.

Donellan illustrates this point by showing that a single description may be construed with or without definite reference, and that the difference between the two cases – which he calls two 'uses' of the description – cannot be explained by considering any intrinsic feature of the description. Although his demonstration of this point is very clear, Donellan himself lacks a semiotic theory of interaction adequate to explain *how* these 'uses' actually work. I now show that we can make sense of these two uses only by explicit appeal to the capacity of interlocutors to formulate text-in-co(n)text construals of the description, their capacity, in other words, to attend to text-level semiotic cues, cues that occur in the co-text of the description used.

In Donellan's example, both 'uses' are construals of the definite description *The person who murdered Smith* or, more briefly, *Smith's murderer*. In one type of case the description is understood as referring to a unique individual known or alleged to be the murderer. Thus, if Jones has been booked for Smith's murder and is now under trial for the act, person A can use the utterance *Smith's murderer is insane* to get B to realize that Jones is insane. Here the description *Smith's murderer* is construed as picking out a particular individual, Jones. This is the 'referential' use shown in Figure 2.1, (a).

In the second type of case, no one has any idea who murdered Smith. Smith's body has been found, his death appears to be a murder, but no clues are yet available that shed light on the murderer's identity. In this type of context, person A can use the utterance *Smith's murderer is insane* to convey to B that 'whoever murdered Smith' is insane, a construal shown

A's utterance: *Smith's murderer* is insane

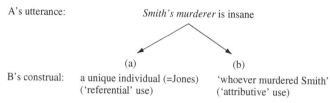

B's construal: a unique individual (=Jones)   'whoever murdered Smith'
                  ('referential' use)   ('attributive' use)

Figure 2.1   *Referential vs. attributive uses*

in (b). Here, the phrase *Smith's murderer* does not pick out a unique individual; it is used attributively, as a way of talking about whoever is responsible.

The example shows that the definite description *Smith's murderer* permits more than one type of construal and that one of these, the attributive use, lacks definite reference. Facts of this kind cannot be captured in a narrowly expression-centric theory of referring – i.e., cannot be explained by appeal to the expression itself – because a single expression permits both uses. How then does person B know whether to construe A's usage as referential or attributive? How can B recover the distinction?

In the above discussion I introduced the distinction by means of context descriptions. I described the 'referential' use by appeal to a context where Smith's murderer has allegedly been identified, and the 'attributive' use by a context where the murderer's identity is unknown. I appealed, in other words, not just to the noun phrase *Smith's murderer* (as an expression with a particular sense) but to an utterance-act in a scenario of use.

Returning to the interaction where A is talking to B, we can now see that B's ability to judge whether A's usage is referential or attributive will similarly depend on his ability to locate the usage in one or the other type of scenario. Donellan suggests that the difference is a function of speaker's intentions (p. 243), but this is wrong. A speaker may intend an act referentially but the hearer may construe it attributively. The difference between the referential and attributive uses is motivated by **text-in-context** relations between an expression and its surround, not by the expression alone, nor – at the level of interpersonal accomplishments – by the intentions of the one uttering it. The two 'uses' are names for the construable effects of text configurations. Figure 2.2 illustrates the special case where criterial co-textual signs are themselves linguistic expressions.

In the two cases shown the same italicized expression co-occurs with two different boldface expressions, each of which provides a distinct set of co-textual 'directions' on how to construe the referent. In (a) the referent, k, is anaphorically formulated as a person the speaker has met by the boldface expression; this motivates the 'referential' use, the construal of k as a specific, known individual. In (b) the boldface expression makes clear

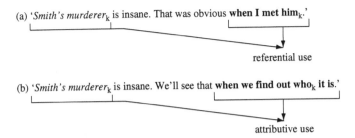

(a) '*Smith's murderer*_k is insane. That was obvious **when I met him**_k.'

referential use

(b) '*Smith's murderer*_k is insane. We'll see that **when we find out who**_k **it is**.'

attributive use

Figure 2.2   *Text configurations as referring signs*

that the identity of k is not known, thus motivating the 'attributive' construal. The distinction is therefore established by text configurations in each case. These examples are purely illustrative, of course. The co-textual cues that discriminate the two construals need not be expressed by signs that are so highly localized (i.e., simple continuous clauses), or by sign-configurations that consist solely of linguistic expressions, or be so very explicit in the way they specify whether referent is a unique individual. In cases where co-textual cues are less transparent, the perspectives of speaker and hearer(s) may fractionally diverge – in one or more types of communicative 'unsuccess' – yielding cognitive asymmetries in their construal of the semiotic act that connects them to each other.

We have seen that a conception of referring centered on the local semanticity of words and expressions (or on speaker's private intentions) is faced with a number of insuperable problems whose resolution requires attention to intersubjective indexical cues formulated by text configurations. But we have so far focused only on the hearer's problem, the problem of construing the reference of an expression that someone else has used. Let us now approach this issue from the point of view of speaker.

Prerequisites on success of referring choices

How do speakers attempt to solve the problem of successful reference? Asking this question brings us to a third difficulty with the semantic labeling view of referring. The difficulty is that appeals to criteria of denotational correctness do not suffice to solve the problem of effective referring choices. Let us approach this issue by looking at the definite descriptions listed in (3) above. Suppose that A wants to tell B about a person who is correctly describable by the most complex description in (3). If you look at the examples again you will see that such a referent is also correctly characterizable by any of the less complex ones, though in a less precise way. Which description should he use? It will be clear that denotational criteria (i.e., correctness of description) can not suffice in solving this problem simply because *all* these descriptions are correct; they differ merely in their degree of specificity and precision. So how complex should the characterization (the Φ element) be in order for A successfully to identify the referent for B?

More generally, the problem concerns not just the complexity of semantic labels but the type of expression to be used. It is true that if the most complex description in (3) correctly describes a referent, so do all the simpler ones; but any such referent may be correctly denotable by other expressions too, such as titles, kinterms, names, and so on. Which among these are to be used on a particular occasion? Which among them is likely to be most effective from the standpoint of successful reference? Interactants do not always solve such problems adequately, of course, and inadequate solutions typically require further interactional work. Nonetheless, the choice of candidate solutions depends upon a particular type of semiotic activity: Speech participants choose referring expressions through practices that involve reading the interactional context of the moment of referring.

We can restate this issue more precisely from a text-centric point of view. At any point in an interaction where the problem of referring to something emerges (e.g., becomes a task for an interactant), a number of semiotically mediated features of the interaction – the locale or setting in which the interaction is recognized as occurring, the way in which particular interactants have displayed or typified themselves or been typified by others, the semiotic activities they have performed, and the results achieved through them – are all available as co-textual presuppositions on further interactional work. It will not do to think of such presuppositions as a static inventory of things (even though the term 'presupposition,' qua noun, tends to reify them). They are, rather, semiotically mediated effects *presupposable by* further co-textual activity; they function effectively as actual *presuppositions of* such activity only insofar as it relies on them. Now the restatement:

Summary 2.2
Candidate solutions to the problem of *which* referring expression to use tend to be more effective (less likely to yield problems in subsequent activity) the more tightly the choice of expression is reflexively calibrated to (formulated through a reading of) co-textual variables presupposed at the moment of referring.

Since the values of such variables are fixed through contiguous activities it is not at all helpful to model presuppositions by means of lists or taxonomies of factors, or to view their effectiveness in referring as the following of a context-independent rule; indeed, to attempt such analyses is to lose sight of how interactants themselves rely on them. Such variables

Table 2.1. *Reflexive evaluations presupposed in choice*
of location-referring term

(a) **Location analysis**: an evaluation of the relative location of speaker, hearer and referent
(b) **Membership analysis**: an evaluation of the social category of hearer; or the relative membership of speaker and hearer in some social category (e.g., whether same or different)
(c) **Topic/activity analysis**: an evaluation of the interlocutor's orientation to the topic or task of the utterance

Source: (Schegloff 1972)

become relevant to the act of referring – or function as conditions on its success – only through a text-in-context construal of their values. Let us consider an example.

Schegloff's work on locational reference – the activity of referring to locations and places in interactions – provides a useful illustration of the more general issue. Schegloff shows that since many denotationally correct ways of referring to places are available to interactants the choice of location-referring term tends to depend on, and thus derives its effectiveness from, the types of co-textual analyses summarized in Table 2.1.

The first of these is a 'location analysis,' an evaluation of the relative location of speaker, hearer and referent. In Schegloff's data, which are based partly on recorded telephone conversations, the receiver of the call (the one who picks up the phone) typically does not know where the caller is. Hence the caller's ability successfully to give place directions to the receiver depends on the two achieving a grasp of their relative location before the receiver of the call can fully parse the caller's chosen place description, or use it to get to the place in question. For example, a caller's description of a street intersection is useless without a clarification of whether the caller is in the same suburb/city/county/etc. as the receiver, or in a different one. The term 'location analysis' describes a type of metapragmatic evaluation of variables of speech context (speaker, hearer and referent), an evaluation of their relative location.

A 'membership analysis' is a distinct type of metapragmatic evaluation, one which focuses on the social category membership of speech participants. In Schegloff's data (where the interactants have not met before) one kind of membership analysis concerns whether or not the hearer is familiar with the broader area/locale in question (e.g., city, neighborhood, etc.), and settling this question is a condition on effectively giving directions to a more specific place such as a house. Thus an interlocutor found to belong to the social category 'a resident of the locale' may be expected to know local landmarks (the local grocery store, drycleaner, elementary school) and these can be used in formulating the place description; but such formulations are less likely to be used, or used effectively, if the hearer belongs to the social category 'a stranger to the locale.' In some cases strangers explicitly evaluate the social category membership of interlocutors before they formulate a place description – by a distinct prior interactional move (e.g., a query such as 'do you live here?') – the results of which allow speaker to attempt a successful place description in a subsequent interactional turn.

Similarly, a 'topic or activity analysis' is an ongoing evaluation of the kind of referent held topical in conversation and the kind of interpersonal work being done through talk of that topic. Particular topics limit (or make relatively narrower) the choice of place descriptions insofar as all possible descriptions are not equally appropriate in relation to the topic. If the mutual orientedness of participants to topic has successfully been achieved in prior interaction, the prior achievement effectively simplifies the subsequent task of choosing descriptions that the hearer can construe; if the co-textual condition has not so far been met, bringing the interlocutor 'back on topic' remains part and parcel of the speaker's task of choosing an effective referring expression.

2.2 Propositional stance and role alignment

Since acts of referring are anchored to – and mutually coordinated with respect to – participation frameworks, a comparable treatment of referents across interactional turns results in the establishment of emergent alignments and stances among participants. In the simplest type of case, when two people agree on a proposition they align with each other; when they disagree they are aligned against each other. A collection of persons in a multi-party encounter often gets sorted into emergent sub-groupings (factions, sides, etc.) by the way in which activities of propositional stance-taking unfold within the encounter. Such groupings may persist beyond the encounter when propositional stances that occur in the current encounter recur in subsequent encounters (among the same or other participants), causing the faction to maintain itself or grow. Such perduring alignments may acquire names or standard descriptions (we might think of political parties here, and what they 'stand for') and even become stereotypic emblems (see Chapter 5) of particular social 'positions,' allowing persons who invoke them to establish their membership in recognized groups through the very act.

Yet the very large majority of interpersonal alignments mediated by propositional stance-taking are extremely evanescent. They neither persist beyond an encounter nor acquire standard names. They are emergent effects of semiotic activity that last for particular moments or phases of interaction and appear to die out in subsequent phases. These are perhaps the most ubiquitous kinds of semiotically mediated social relations we experience in everyday life. An enormous variety of roles and relationships performed in social life are indexical projections of propositional stance-taking activities occurring within particular encounters. Such indexical projections of position, stance, and alignment are entirely effective or consequential within those encounters insofar as they are semiotically construable within them, but they are not durable projections that persist beyond such encounters unless taken up by semiotic-chain processes (see 1.6), which introduce them into other encounters (whether in denotationally explicit terms, e.g., as a named 'position,' or as ritually stabilized habits of comportment), and thus give them a wider circulation and recognition, even recognition as stereotypic emblems of role or relationship in the manner noted above.

The range of encounter-specific alignments – or the variety of social relations indexable through them – can not adequately be described through any decontextualized scheme of conventional labels, such as an inventory of role designators (Chapter 5). The reason is quite simple: co-textual indexicality is a much richer framework for delineating semiotic roles and relationships than semantic labeling. It is richer in the sense that whereas semantic labels are relatively discrete, suggesting all-or-nothing distinctions, co-textually mediated alignments depend on a variety of co-occurring semiotic cues, which are at best **fractionally congruent**, or congruent to fractional degrees, thus permitting gradient thresholds and kinds of alignment.

The following example (from Goodwin and Goodwin 1992) illustrates the fractional congruence of entextualized semiotic cues and of resulting interpersonal alignments.[4] In (4), Dianne is talking about Jeff's cooking. As Dianne begins to characterize the pie as *so good*, Clacia overlaps with an utterance containing two lexically cohesive predicates (*... love it ... love that*).

(4)

1. Dianne: Jeff made en asparagus pie$_R$. It$_R$ was s::**so** $\lceil$: **goo** : d.
2. Clacia: $\lfloor$I love it$_R$. °Yeah I love that$_R$.

Both utterances are indexically anchored to speakers, and exhibit mirror-image stances on referents: The prosodic lengthening and emphases in Dianne's syllables (*s::so: goo:d*) indexes her affectively intensified evaluative stance; and both tokens of *love* in Clacia's utterance have first person subject, expressing Clacia's stance, the repetition marking a comparable affective intensification. This relatively symmetric pattern of interactional moves suggests that the two are expressing comparable stances on referents. They are *aligned with each other* insofar as both typify referents in a positive, affectively intensified manner. But which referents?

Co-textual cues suggest that Dianne and Clacia are not talking about exactly the same thing. Dianne is talking about a specific referent, the asparagus pie that Jeff made on a previous occasion, marked by subscript R; the fact that she is talking about a referent encountered in past time is indexed by predicate deixis, i.e., both finite verbs in her utterance (*made, was*) are in past tense. But Clacia's utterance, which contains non-past predicates, is deictically non-congruent with Dianne's. The thing to which Clacia is referring (R′) is not deictically anchored to past time, to the time of Jeff's activity, and hence is distinct from the particular asparagus pie that Jeff made (R). Clacia is talking about a more generic referent, which is not precisely recoverable (i.e., what Clacia 'loves' may be asparagus pies in general; or pies of any kind; or someone cooking a pie for her; etc.). Yet although R′ is clearly distinct from R, Clacia's affective evaluations continue to maintain alignment with Diane's.

Clacia's generalizing of referent continues in subsequent talk. A few moments later Dianne is describing how Jeff has prepared his asparagus pie; she closes her turn with the same, deictically past predicate as before (*It wz so good*). But Clacia's utterance in line 4 has a subjunctive not a past predicate.

(5)

3. Dianne: En then jus' (cut-up) the broc-'r the asparagus coming out in spokes. = °It$_R$ wz **so** good.

4. Clacia: °°(Oh Go:d that$_R$.'d be fantastic)

Clacia is now speaking hypothetically; her utterance maintains alignment with Dianne's through cohesion at the level of predicate semantics (*so good / fantastic*) but not of predicate deixis (*was* vs. *[woul]d be*). Dianne's use of past tense (*was*) continues to maintain the pie cooked by Jeff as a singular definite referent, but Clacia's use of the subjunctive (*[woul]d be*) generalizes her appreciation to any such referent, e.g., any pie cooked in the manner described.

Such fractional congruence of stances and alignments is only definable over an unfolding text structure containing many semiotic cues, some of which are highly congruent with each other (others less so, or not at all). The pieces that are comparable with each other are not necessarily contiguous. Such comparability of co-occurring – but not immediately contiguous – cues establishes a **metrical structure** (or 'poetic' structure; Jakobson 1960, Silverstein 1985) over textual realtime, to which inter-actants attend and respond in interaction, thus playing out a pattern of mutually calibrated stances and alignments. Such a metrical structure is typically played out at several levels of semiotic organization in any interaction. Let us consider the metrical organization of propositional, prosodic and kinesic cues in the example at hand.

Dianne's utterances in lines 1 and 3 are fractionally congruent in propositional content. Each consists of two propositional units, a description of cooking activities followed by the evaluation *It was so good*. Let us use the symbols a_1 and a_2 for the descriptions of cooking that begin lines 1 and 3, the symbol b_1 for the first token of the evaluation (line 1) and $b_1{}'$ for the second (line 3).

(6)

1. Dianne: Jeff made en asparagus pie$_R$. It$_R$ was s::**so** [:   **goo** : d.
            a_1 b_1

2. Clacia: I love   it$_{R'}$. °Yeah I love that$_{R'}$.
                                  c_1 $c_1{}'$

- - - - -

3. Dianne: En then jus' (cut-up) the broc-'r the asparagus coming out in spokes. = °It$_R$ wz **so** good.
        a_2 $b_1{}'$

4. Clacia: °°(Oh Go:d that$_R$.'d be fantastic)
                                                      b_2

Similarly let us use the symbols c_1 and $c_1{}'$ for the two tokens of Clacia's sentence-proposition *I love X* in line 2; and the symbol b_2 for Clacia's statement in line 4, a choice that highlights the cohesion of predicates, viz., 'X be good' (units b_1 and $b_1{}'$, lines 1 and 3) and 'X be fantastic' (b_2, line 4). We can now represent the exchange in (6) in an approximate way in Table 2.2.

Table 2.2 summarizes the extent to which the mutual coordination of Dianne's and Clacia's interactional moves is expressed through or depends on a reading of the propositional content of their utterances. It highlights three issues. It shows, first, that if we consider the emergent structure of information flow – or **denotational text** – performed in this encounter, we

Table 2.2. *Denotational text as a performed diagram of interactional text*

					INTERACTIONAL TEXT		
I. *Participants:*	II. DENOTATIONAL TEXT			$\Rightarrow$	III. *stances and roles performed by participants*	$\Rightarrow$	IV. *interpersonal alignments*
	Propositions		*Referents*				
1. Dianne:	a_1	b_1	R		D affectively evaluates R	}	C agrees with D
2. Clacia:		$c_1\ c_1{}'$	R'		C affectively evaluates R'		
	...						
3. Dianne:	a_2	$b_1{}'$	R		D affectively evaluates R	}	C agrees with D
4. Clacia:		b_2	R'		C affectively evaluates R'		

Double arrows ($\Rightarrow$) indicate diagrammatic motivation; curly brackets indicate cross turn alignments find that this structure has an internal metrical organization (column II), a type of emergent organization constituted by a fractional congruence of the propositional effects discussed above. Second, even if we consider only this level of detail, column III shows that the participants who make denotational contributions to this unfolding structure inhabit particular propositional stances on referents as they perform these propositional acts. Third, as we look across turn contributions (cf. curly brackets), we see in column IV that the comparability of turn-specific stances maps out interpersonal alignments among participants. Thus by attending to the metrical structure of propositional acts in column II we can identify a second type of semiotic organization, an **interactional text**, an emergent structure of positionalities, stances, and relationships, performatively established through these acts.

As the labeling of columns makes clear, the denotational text is but a fragment of the interactional text; it is the fragment that we identify as the emergent structure of propositional information formulated during interaction. Moreover, the denotational text fragment **diagrams** the larger interactional text in the sense that this very structure of propositional information (column II), when considered relative to its participation framework (column I), motivates a construal of participants' stances and roles (column III) and of relationships between them (column IV). The observations in column IV are based on the metrical comparability of the stances paired in column III; these in turn are construals of the propositional acts shown in column II (the alphabetic symbols are just shorthand for particular propositions and referents as indicated in (6) above) as produced by the participants in column I. Notice that the more specific criteria on metrical congruence discussed in the previous chapter (cohesion, coherence, congruence of origo and focus) all function as criteria on making the observations listed in Table 2.2.[5]

It should also be clear that all the stances, roles and alignments have the character of indirect speech acts in the sense discussed in the last chapter (see example (17)ff., section 1.5). By attending to the implicit performativity of text structure we can now see that an 'indirect speech act' is just a name for the way in which a denotational text diagrams an interactional text without describing it. Moreover, such indirect *speech* acts are often elements of indirect *semiotic* acts of a more diverse kind. That is, an interactional text is diagrammed not only by the metrical organization of sentence-propositional cues (such as the ones considered in Table 2.2) but also by the organization of cues of other kinds. We considered prosodic issues earlier. Let us now consider the kinesic accompaniments of these verbal acts. These are shown in Figure 2.3.

Dianne and Clacia are making eye-contact as the segment begins. Under these co-textual conditions, Dianne's lowering her head, nodding and raising her eyebrow (line 1) indexes a heightened orientation to Clacia

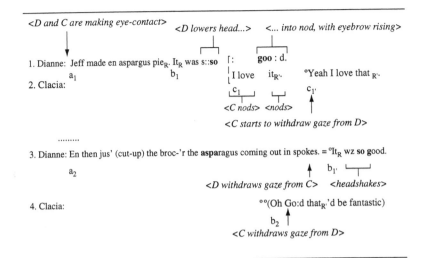

Figure 2.3 *Multi-channel sign-configurations and participant alignments*
Note: Subscripts mark referents; boldface indicates emphases due to change in pitch
or amplitude; colons (:) mark lengthening of preceding segment; brackets across lines
indicate overlap; degree signs (°) indicate lowered volume; italics in angular brackets
< > mark kinesic accompaniments; ellipsis (. . .) indicates intervening material, not
shown; equals sign (=) indicates latching or absence of interval between segments
(Source: Goodwin and Goodwin 1992.)

for the phase of utterance (*s::so: goo:d*) over which these gestures are
contoured. And Clacia's gestures, two nods, contoured over the same
phase, are a kinesically calibrated response. (You can see that Clacia's
response is actually invited or prefigured by Dianne's lowering her head
into a nod, which begins a moment before the response begins.) This
metrical congruence of kinesic signs indexes a heightened mutual orientation. Thus our earlier observations that Clacia aligns with Dianne across
lines 1 and 2 through prosodic cues (as noted in (4)ff.) and propositional
cues (as in Table 2.2) are both part of a larger metrical structure of
alignment. The total act performed constitutes an alignment cued not
only by the prosodic form of audible speech, nor only by its propositional
content; nor, indeed, only by visible gestures; the alignment is an effect of a
multi-channel sign configuration containing all of these elements, an overall performance that is initiated by Dianne and completed by Clacia.

We can now see that inhabiting similar (or different) positions in denotational text is a way of marking social relations at the level of interactional
text. Such 'similarity' of positions is a degree notion, an effect based on text-
metrical comparability of entextualized cues, involving gradient results. Thus
whereas some among the cues performed in this encounter do motivate the

construal of interpersonal alignment shown in Table 2.2 (i.e., that C 'agrees with' D) other semiotic cues are partly non-congruent with this alignment.

For it is obvious that Clacia is doing more than merely agreeing with Dianne: in line 2, Clacia incorporates Dianne's appreciation of a past event into a perspective deictically formulated as timeless; and, whereas Dianne continues to maintain focus on a past event in line 3, Clacia continues to extend her pattern of deictic generalization in line 4, now to all hypothetical scenarios of this denotational type. Similarly, at the kinesic level, although Clacia's double nods align her with Dianne, they are immediately followed in line 2 by Clacia withdrawing her gaze; the pattern of gaze withdrawal is continued by Dianne in line 3, and completed by Clacia in line 4. Thus Clacia doesn't merely 'agree' with Dianne in line 2; she initiates a semiotic pattern which generalizes Dianne's point and draws the topic to a close.

We have already seen that text-level indexicality is a richer framework for delineating interactional text than semantic labeling. Since the orderliness of social interaction depends upon a richer structure of semiosis than is clarified by any scheme of descriptive labels, terms like 'agreement' and 'disagreement' (as well as other labels like 'assessment,' 'repair,' 'ratification' and other terms used by conversational analysts) are little more than provisional ways of highlighting selected aspects of the implicit performativity of text structure. Any interactional move that is fractionally an instance of 'agreement' or 'repair' or 'ratification' (and so on) vis-à-vis another interactional move is, concurrently, an instance of many other acts too because the metrical structure of textual organization – its capacity to diagram types of relationships between acts through a logic of fractional congruence – is itself a structure that classifies acts, though only in a denotationally implicit way. This type of meaningful organization has a reality for interactants independent of whether it is described by them in denotationally explicit terms in the instance. Its intersubjective reality consists of the fact that the behavior of one interactant exhibits a measure of fractional congruence vis-à-vis the behavior of others who perceive it, a feature that is iterated over the course of successive interactional moves. Insofar as this is actually so, the relative behavior of the interactants exhibits the mutual coordination of their actions.

Let me now summarize the main issues illustrated above:

Summary 2.3
In any discursive interaction

(a) the metrical patterning of linguistic and accompanying signs indexes a series of interactional roles and relationships to which interactants respond, *but which they do not describe in that response*; some such effects may well be described by interactants in a subsequent response (or subsequent interaction), but most are not; and yet

(b) by analyzing the metrical structure of the cues to which interactants attend (as evidenced in their responses) we can model the social roles and relationships *implicitly negotiated* by participants during interaction;

(c) such a structure is **emergent** (i.e., consists of the congruence of effects cued by co-occurring signs), but it is also **mutually coordinated** insofar as the behavior of different parties are reflexively calibrated to each other;

(d) our talk of the **fractional congruence** of entextualized effects is a measure of the extent to which local acts *preserve or transform* the structure in play at that moment.

Point (a) is another way of saying that what is often experienced as 'hidden meaning' or 'implicit meaning' in interaction is always mediated by signs that are overt (i.e., perceivable) but are not necessarily either explicit (i.e., denotationally valued) or linguistically expressed. Points (b) and (c) are ways of drawing attention to the contingent orderliness of such semiotic behavior as it is experienced by participants. And point (d) highlights the fact that part of what is orderly – or mutually coordinated – in such behavior is the way in which the behavior transforms over time the social realities experienced through it.

These issues are of central importance not just to the micro-time of interaction but also to the way in which macro-social regularities of culture (such as the transmission of culture from person to person) are precipitated *through* human interaction. For if these patterns are recognizable by participants in particular encounters they are also recognizable across encounters which overlap in participants. We saw in 1.6 that cultural forms are communicable from person to person in interactions, and may be sociohistorically transmitted across a population through participant-linked chains of interactions. We also noted that what is communicated is also frequently transformed through such processes. To recognize that cultural forms remain stable (or relatively invariant) in social life is to recognize the extent to which the form is preserved through a sociohistorical process of transmission (as a 'heritage,' as it were); the transmission of many cultural forms is mediated by institutions that formulate such emphases in a routinized way. For participants to recognize change or transformation is to recognize the semiotic non-congruence of a form encountered over many encounters. I discuss these issues in more detail in 4.3.

2.3 Denotational categories

We saw earlier that acts of referring are traditionally distinguished from the denotation of expressions used in such acts. Whereas referring is a radically contextualized activity, the denotation of an expression is its constant capacity to refer to the same type of thing across many acts. The statement by Lyons quoted in (1) makes this point by saying that referring is utterance- or occasion-dependent but that denotation is 'utterance-independent,' a property associated with an expression 'independently of its use on particular occasions of utterance.' This account of denotation is only partly correct. It is true that denotation is not event-dependent *in the same way* as referring. But it is not true that denotation is altogether event-independent.

It is true, in other words, that the reference of an expression like *dog* (plus suitable deictics) may differ radically from occasion to occasion (Fido on one occasion, Bowser on another) in a way that its denotation does not. But it is hardly the case that the denotation of the expression *dog* is invariant for all speakers at all times and places. For instance, there are plenty of words and expressions in English in which the expression *dog* occurs as an element, and in which its denotation does not involve the class of things to which Fido and Bowser belong. If you are a private eye you may *dog a suspect* all day long, where *dog* means 'to follow and observe'; or, if you are an airforce ace, you may have been in plenty of *dogfights* or 'aerial battles between fighter planes.' In American college slang of the 1980s, the expression *dog* corresponds to a number of lexically distinct nouns and verbs, including *dog out* 'betray, neglect, treat with disrespect,' *dog it* 'for a female to act promiscuously,' *call the dogs* 'to vomit,' *brew dog*, *shroom dog*, and many others (Eble 1996: 69–70). In general, a denotational expression (a meaningful sound shape, like *dog*) may correspond to several distinct lexemes in a language, or may occur in different lexeme collocations. A lexeme is a unit of the denotational identity of words and expressions (see (7)ff. below). Lexemes that belong to different sociopragmatic registers are linked to distinct characterological images of users (the private eye, the airforce ace, the teenager). In such cases, lexemic distinctions also index social-characterological contrasts. Lexemic variants (and the social images associated with them) can be performed and construed in events of language use, but not by all speakers (since many native speakers of English don't know all of these variants), and not felicitously in all events of usage (since some variants, like *dog out*, are treated as normal usages in certain types of interactions but are extra-normative in others). Hence the denotation of an expression is not a Platonic essence that remains invariant for all users and acts of usage. I return to these isssues, and to the norm aspect of denotation more broadly, in section 2.4.

In this section and the next we will be contrasting the ways in which the denotation of an expression is event-independent with the ways in which it is not. The main issues may be stated in summary form as follows:

Summary 2.4

Denotation is event-independent in one sense, but not in another. It is event-independent in that persons acquainted with an expression's denotation can evaluate many referential uses by the same criterion. It is event-dependent in that an expression's denotation is only experienced in events of language use and may thus be debated, disputed, normativized, and even normatively transformed through processes of language use.

Before we can approach these issues, however, it is necessary to get clearer about criteria on the identity of expressions, that is, criteria by which we can decide whether two expressions are of the 'same' type along one or more dimension of categorial content.

Language users commonly view language as involving semantic classifications or 'types' of things. But semantic classifications do not exist as such, i.e., all by themselves. Instead, language is organized by the fact that classifications of sound are linked to classifications of sense. Saussure formulated this point by using the terms *signifier* (classes of sound, form types) and *signified* (classes of sense, semantic types). He characterized the inseparability of the two by a powerful metaphor, the notion that the *signifier* and *signified* are like two sides of a sheet of paper, so that to make a 'cut' in the one (i.e., to alter one) is to make a cut in the other. The point is undeniable. And yet this sheet of paper can be folded over in certain ways and, through a kind of social-semiotic origami, made to represent characterological figures or 'social types' of certain kinds, not usually albatrosses and airplanes as in the case of origami itself, but figures having human and social characteristics, such as the private dick and the airforce ace we just met.

But metaphors will only get us so far. Let us concentrate for now on the fact that denoting expressions are concurrently organized into denotational units of more than one kind. This feature of denotational organization means that questions of the identity and non-identity of expressions (our ability to sort them into 'types') is mediated by more than one criterion. I introduce this issue in an informal way first, then turn to a more precise characterization.

The event-independence of a denoting expression consists of its capacity to set comparable text-defaults across many events of referring. Linguistic expressions are concurrently organized into denotational units of two very different kinds, namely units of phonology and morphosyntax. This feature of language is traditionally called **double articulation**. Both types of units specify text-defaults in events of referring: in the case of phonemic units, these are text-defaults of the sound shape of referring expressions; in the case of morphosyntactic units, phonological shapes are linked to defaults of sense. The fact that linguistic expressions are organized by defaults of more than one kind means that the question of whether two text-tokens are instances of the 'same' expression type is settled by more than one evaluative criterion. A text-token may be canonical with respect to one categorial dimension but defective with respect to another. For instance if two text-tokens are understood as having the default sense of an expression type and one of them also has its default sound shape while the other does not, we say that the first one is a normal token but the latter has been mispronounced. Here the presumed identity of sense is a baseline for evaluating perceived difference in sound shape. When the phonological habits of two social groups differ in this way we sometimes speak of differences of social accent. Similarly, when two text-tokens have the same sound shape, and so appear to be tokens of the same word, but one of them lacks the ordinary sense of that word, we view that token as semantically anomalous; we may regard it as a metaphor or a malapropism. When the variant is used habitually by another social group, we commonly view it as a dialect contrast. Thus differences in usage along categorial dimensions of form and sense diagram differences among their users. In all cases denotational variation in form and sense is interpreted through reflexive models of what this variation means. But whether the variant is treated as idiosyncratic, or seen as emblematic of group differences depends on other factors that shape construal. For instance, particular forms of construal are typically saturated in culture-specific ideologies of *what* is 'normal' (Sapir 1949b) or *who* engages in normal behavior and *when* they do so (Agha 1998a).

In some cases such contrasts are conceptualized not in social group terms but by criteria of interpersonal effectiveness. The fact that phonological and semantic defaults can be troped upon independently in propositional acts is formulated in the tradition of classical rhetoric (Quinn 1982) as the distinction between figures of sound (apocope, syncope, synaloepha, etc.) and figures of sense (metaphor, metonymy, hyperbole, etc.). Here denotational variation is linked to interpersonal ends in oratory on the assumption that the judicious deployment of figures of speech in contexts of public speaking will persuade addressee and audience, or cause them to 'identify' with the stance of the speaker (Agha 1996b).

In the last section we saw that a denotational text diagrams features of the interactional text of which it is a fragment. We are now observing that variation in the form and sense of denotational units can be reinterpreted through metapragmatic models that treat such variation as indexical of characteristics of speaker (qua individual or member of group) or of speaker's relation to interlocutors. In the case of lexical registers, variation in the deployment of word-types in discourse motivates ideological classifications of 'social types' of actions, actors, the relationships between them, and the practices in which they engage. Once institutionally established, such models mediate the actual behaviors of individuals, their self-perceptions – as in-group or out-group, as engaged in proper or improper conduct, as higher or lower status – vis-à-vis others. We are not concerned for the moment with the ideological processes through which the sameness or difference of word choices are reflexively reanalyzed into classifications of persons; we return to these questions in 2.5. Our focus now is on the way in which the denotational organization of language makes possible degrees of likeness or iconism among word-types in the first place.

Language users commonly perceive the denotational organization of language as comprised largely of words, often conceived as elementary building blocks or 'atoms' of meaning. However the denotational properties of words are organized by underlying principles of phonological and morphosyntactic constituency. Words fall into distinct denotational classes by virtue of their grammatical organization. This is the main issue discussed in the next few pages. In exploring this issue we will see, however, that only certain aspects of denotational organization can be identified through a grammatical analysis; other aspects require more overtly sociological methods. Understanding the utility – and limitations – of particular methods of analysis is one of the main goals of the next few pages.

I noted earlier that there are two rather different senses in which denotational units have a social significance. They are social in the first sense simply because they are units *for someone*. They have a social domain. They are recognized as grammatical units of a language by some individuals, not others. A second social aspect of denotation depends on the way in which grammatically structured denotational units play a part in *other* semiotic processes. Thus, phonemes, morphemes and words are denotational units of certain specific kinds. The traditional mistake, typical of any exclusively grammar-centered view of language, is to suppose that this is *all* they are, that denotation is the *only* function they subserve. We have seen in preceding discussion that grammatical types also occur as text-tokens in discourse, a fact on which matters of interpersonal alignment depend (2.2); in the case of register formations, grammatical types are linked to characterological schemes used to interpret roles and relationships among language users (2.5). Yet we cannot understand such forms of reflexive reanalysis without first getting clearer about the way in which grammatical principles shape cross-cutting categories of sound and sense in a language, how such categorizations make fractional variants construable and, finally, how social-semiotic processes treat particular denotational variants as appropriate to certain contexts of action, thus grouping them into distinct registers of the language.

Phonology and morphosyntax

The **phonemes** of a language constitute a basic inventory of sound categories that must occur, in permissible sequences, in order for a denoting expression to count as an utterance of the language. A phoneme is a class of sounds whose members are called **allophones**. The allophones of a phoneme are text-defaults of phonemic sound shape that vary by facts of positional occurrence, whether a particular position in a syllable or in relation to adjacent sounds. Thus the phoneme /t/ in English corresponds to a class of physically distinct sounds, its allophones, which, in American English include the aspirated [tʰ] that occurs in syllable initial position (tin [tʰɪn]), the flap [D] between vowels when the first vowel is stressed (viz., pitted [pʰɪDəd]), the glottal stop [ʔ] before syllabic n or l (kitten [kʰɪʔn]), and others. The phoneme is a class of physically distinct sounds, or a sound category, whose members are text-defaults of sound shape (i.e., are physical sound shapes in which the phoneme is realized under particular co-textual conditions). The class and its members are characterized by giving a **distributional analysis** of facts of allophonic variation, an analysis which pairs members of the class with the positions in which they occur. The above description of the phoneme /t/ and its allophones gives a rough indication of how such statements are formulated, though the details need not concern us here.

A phoneme has a structural function within a language. It distinguishes denotational words and expressions from each other. A phoneme is a **denotationally diacritic sound category** in the sense that contrasts between phonemes (but not allophones) distinguish possible denoting expressions in the language. These contrasts can be highlighted by comparing **minimal pairs**, or pairs of words that exhibit only one phonemic contrast. The units /b/ and /p/ are phonemes of English in that they differentiate a large number of possible words, such as the minimal pair *bit* and *pit*; but the unit /bh/ is not a phoneme of English and *bhit* is not a possible English word. If a word like *bhit* is borrowed from a language where it is phonemically possible (such as Hindi), it is likely to be assimilated to the phonological norms of English.

The phonemic inventory of a language is the repertoire of basic sound categories that differentiate possible denotational expressions from each other. Not all phonologically possible (or phonologically well-formed) expressions actually denote anything in the language. Thus both *binge* and *pinge* are phonologically possible sequences in English, but the latter is not lexicalized as an actual word. The phonological sequence is nonetheless possible and does occur as a part of other words (e.g., *impinge*). And if the sequence were realized as a new word speakers of English would not find it phonologically anomalous (as they would, say, *the bhinge*). Hence the phonemic organization of a language sets defaults on the sound shapes of words, violations of which are contrastively perceived as 'deviations' or 'anomalies.' Such deviations are sometimes personified and imbued with sociological significance. In the case of the phonolexical registers discussed below (2.5), the act of maintaining certain sound shapes is culturally enregistered as defining membership in certain social groups.

In taking the step from possible to actual word, we move beyond the domain of phonology proper (the domain of phonologically well-formed expressions) to the domain of lexicon and morphosyntax. We are now asking whether a possible phonological sequence corresponds to a **denotational sense category** in the language, whether it is a word actually used to denote a thing or a class of things. But our everyday metalinguistic term 'word' is hopelessly imprecise in discussing matters of denotation; it corresponds to many different kinds of denotational units, some of which are given the more technical names indicated below (see also Sapir 1921, ch. 2, and Lyons 1995, ch. 2). Two expressions can be the 'same word' by one criterion, but not by another.

(7) Our everyday term 'word' is used to talk about a variety of distinct types of units, including:

   (a) A unique phonological shape, or expression-type; here 'word' corresponds to **word-form**
   (b) A class of expressions having the same underlying form, or **citation form**
   (c) A phonological shape with a unique morphosyntactic distribution and sense, or **lexeme**
   (d) A complex expression that includes several lexemes, or a **lexeme collocation**
   (e) An expression-type that occurs independently (i.e., is not bound to others), or a **free form**

Types (a) and (b) differ because many word-forms are analytically recognizable as sharing an 'underlying' form, e.g., *is, are, was, will be* are inflected variants of *to be*, the citation-form for this class. Hence in one sense this set of expressions consists of several words (by criteria of phonological shape) and, in another, of a single word (by criteria of citation form). Types (a) and (c) differ because of the problem of **homonymy**, namely the fact that not all phonologically unique expressions have a unique sense. The phonological shape /flaɪ/ corresponds to several lexemes in the language, including an animate noun (*fly₁* 'a type of insect'), an inanimate noun (*fly₂* 'part of a pair of trousers'), an intransitive verb (*fly₃* as in the sentence, *a bird flies*), and a transitive verb (*fly₄* as in the sentence, *he can fly a plane*). All of these have the same word-form. But they are distinct lexemes because they differ in sense. We will see in a moment that their notional senses are differentiated by their morphosyntactic distribution within larger grammatical arrangements.

The term 'word' is also used in morphosyntax to talk about a special type of structural category, namely a **free lexemic form**, or a free form, (e), which is also a lexeme or lexeme collocation in the sense of (c) and (d). A word in this sense corresponds to a unit within a hierarchy of units of morphosyntactic organization – morpheme, 'word,' phrase, clause and sentence – which may be ranked in terms of constituency. The criterion of ranking is that lower ranked units typically (though not necessarily) combine to form higher rank units, so that morphemes form words, words form phrases, phrases yield clauses, and clauses form multi-clause units, or sentences.

The morphosyntactic organization of a language is based on a principle of form-sense combinability which shapes the denotation of complex expressions: when simpler forms are combined to yield more complex forms the denotation of the more complex forms is a function of the denotation of the simpler forms plus the order of their arrangement. This is generally called the principle of **sense compositionality**. The principle can be illustrated through simple examples. Words like *painter, drummer, hitter, sailor, catcher* are expressions that share a sense property: their denotata are 'agents who perform certain actions'. The notional property derives from the fact that nouns of this type are derived from agentive verbs by means of the suffix *-er*, as in (8a). The suffix yields agentive nouns from verbs. Here a principle of form-sense combinability yields the same compositional sense for every expression to which the same concatenation process applies. Although these expressions are equivalent in compositional sense, they are not equivalent in overall denotation; their differences depend on the denotational contrast of the verb stems from which they are derived, viz., *(to) paint*, vs. *(to) drum*, vs. *(to) hit*, etc. The morphosyntactic pattern in (b) similarly imposes a common possessor-possessum sense relationship on expressions otherwise as diverse as *his father, the boy's satchel* and *man's last hope*.

(8)

(a) $[[Verb_{stem}]_{ag} \text{-er}]_N$ agentive noun   painter, drummer,
                                                            hitter, sailor, catcher
(b) $[NP \text{ GEN } NP]_{NP}$ possessor-possessum   his father, the boy's
                                                            satchel, man's last hope
(c) $[[S]\text{'s -ing}]_{NP}$ gerundive nominalization   his being hungry, your
                                                            being late

The third example illustrates the regular contrast between a finite sentence and a gerundive nominal; a finite English sentence (S) yields a gerundive nominal when a complementizer (the discontinuous expression, *'s -ing*) is added to it, the first element (*'s*) to the subject, the second (*-ing*) to the verb (viz., *he is hungry: his being hungry, Sam is late: Sam's being late*). The nominalized sentence can now occur as a constituent of another sentence (viz., [[*his being hungry*]$_{NP}$ *surprised me*]$_S$).

In any language a large number of regularities of form-sense patterning occur that conform to the principle of sense compositionality and, by virtue of such conformity, formulate the sense of a larger expression as a compositional function of the sense and arrangement of its parts. Sense compositionality is not the only principle that shapes the denotation of complex expressions. But a vast number of complex expressions in natural language are sense-compositional, a fact which is the basis of grammatical analysis. It is also the basis of a vast range of semantic classifications that organize the denotational categories of any natural language. The units of form that occur in sense-compositional constructions (such as the suffix *-er* and the configuration *'s -ing*) function as units of **structural sense** in these larger constructions by marking a regular difference of sense between all pairs of constructions that differ only in that unit of form. Thus a series of form contrasts (viz., *paint: painter, drum: drummer*, etc.) exhibits a single sense contrast which we can capture in notional terms ('act': 'actor') or by using grammatical category names ('verb': 'agentive noun').

Every language has many more units of structural sense (or units of form/sense contrast) than it has everyday terms for naming them. This places a constraint on how sense contrasts are best described. Linguists get around these constraints by creating specialized technical terminologies for particular types of form-sense contrast, or by devising descriptive notations other than naming (such as brackets or tree diagrams that show syntactic constituency and constituency-based relations among units), thus innovating in their grammatical metalanguage as required.

The fact that any language has more sense-bearing expressions than it has everyday names for them also places a practical constraint on the capacity of ordinary language users to describe the grammatico-semantic patterning of their own language. Such efforts face other constraints too. For example, many units of structural sense, such as the agentive suffix *-er* in (8a), are only encountered within larger configurations, never in isolation, and thus are not easily glossed.[6] Yet the native speaker can implicitly discriminate the structural sense contributions of the suffix by recognizing, for instance, that *paint* and *painter* differ in the same way as *drum* and *drummer*, and *catch* and *catcher*, and so on. Language users can implicitly discriminate many more units of structural sense than they can explicitly describe in everyday metasemantic discourse.

There are therefore two rather different methods that we can use to discover the denotational properties of an expression in an unfamiliar language. The first is the method of structural sense analysis, which relies on the ability of a native speaker to make implicit discriminations between units. The other relies on explicit metasemantic queries about the meanings of expressions. Both methods allow us to model the denotational norms associated with linguistic expressions, but the methods differ procedurally, and in the limits of their application.

Structural sense

The first method depends on giving a distributional analysis of an item, an analysis of its overall distribution in all complex expression types in the language. The method focuses on norms of structural concatenation in sense-compositional constructions. The basis of this method is that all morphosyntactic expressions in a natural language do not combine with all others to yield complex expressions which are themselves well-formed sense-bearing units. This point is traditionally formulated as follows: structural units differ in their **syntagmatic relations**, or relations of con-catenability, to other structural units; and expressions which have the same syntagmatic properties belong to a **paradigmatic set**, or an equivalence class under concatenation. More simply: asymmetries of concatenation yield grammatico-semantic classes.

The point may be illustrated for the case of classes of noun in English. Viewed in generic terms, a noun is a structural category having certain distributional properties, both properties of external distribution (i.e., with respect to higher rank units like phrase and clause types) and properties of internal structure (i.e., with respect to lower rank units such as suffixes). Thus in the case of simple nouns (i.e., ignoring complex nominalizations) we find that nouns characteristically occur as 'heads' of noun phrases (i.e., either as sole constituents, or as main constituents along with modifiers). But this distributional property defines a **generic** equivalence class, a paradigmatic set which is taxonomically differentiable into more **specific** classes or sub-sets. The structural class 'noun' contains members which differ from each other with respect to the distributional tests indicated in Table 2.3 (i.e., in their capacity to yield well-formed, sense-bearing units in the syntagmatic frames shown). For instance, a [+common] noun char-acteristically takes an article or determiner (*the book, the house*) but other types (such as proper names and pronouns) characteristically do not.

Table 2.3. *Distributional structure and sense categories*

Distributional test	Syntagmatic frame	Paradigmatic class
(a) requires/permits article:	[a/the ___]	+/– common
(b) pluralizability:	[___-s]$_N$ ....is/are ...	+/– count
(c) subject of animate verb	[___ eat/sleep/...]	+/– animate
(d) antecedent of relative pronoun *who*	[___ who (vs. which, etc.)]	+/– human

Similarly, the distinction between 'mass' and 'count' nouns depends on pluralizability. Count nouns are pluralized by localizable word internal treatment – such as the suffix -*s* (viz., *book/books*) or other plural marker (viz., *mouse/mice*) – as well as more configurative types of formal treatment such as concord with modifier (*that book/those books*) and agreement with verb (viz., *the book/books is/are heavy*). In contrast, the denotata of mass nouns are not enumerated by this mechanism (viz., *water/*three waters*); they are enumerated by means of measure phrases (viz., *a cup/three cups of water*), where the head of the noun phrase is a count noun (*cup/cups*), and the verb agrees not with the mass noun in question but with the count noun that heads the measure phrase (*the cup/cups of water is/are on the table*).[7]

Distributional tests of these kinds differentiate the class 'noun' into many sub-classes, which we could name simply as 'class 1,' 'class 2' etc. A more revealing way of naming these classes is to use the structural sense property characteristic of the class as a name for the class, as shown in the last column of Table 2.3. This metasemantic scheme makes clear, in a shorthand form, the way in which asymmetries of concatenation differentiate expressions into semantic classes.

The labeling scheme makes use of a distinctive feature notation, namely symbols of the type $+/-p$, where 'p' is a grammaticosemantic property. The symbols '+' and '−' have a very particular interpretation, called a **markedness convention**: lexemes that are identifiable as members of the class (by criterial distributional tests) specifically and differentially encode the semantic property in question, and this is represented as $+p$; and expressions that are identifiable as non-members of the form-class do not specifically do so, represented as $-p$. However, $-p$ does not mean that non-members specifically encode the opposite property (i.e., in logical notation $-p$ can be glossed as $\sim$ 'p' but not as '$\sim p$'). Thus to say a form (or a class of forms) is [−human] is not to say that the form must refer to 'non-humans', merely to say that the things to which it refers cannot be taken to be 'human' on the basis of the usage itself.

Relative to the markedness convention, our use of grammaticosemantic properties as names for classes (and, indeed, our talk of 'specific and differential coding') is simply a way of talking about the way in which minimal pairs **specify different referential text defaults**: the $+p$ form specifies that the referent has the property 'p' and the $-p$ form fails to do so. This fact about our naming scheme follows from the way in which distributional tests are used to isolate these classes. The constructions used as distributional tests themselves specify referential text-defaults: if you hear a fragmentary utterance like 'the … who …' you are more likely to conclude that speaker is talking about a person than about an animal or place (but a fragment like 'the … which …' leaves the issue open). In using this test as a diagnostic for the class [+human], as in Table 2.3, (d), we assume that expressions that have the criterial distribution (i.e., occur as antecedents of *who*) specify the same referential text-defaults (i.e., +human), and those which lack this distribution do not (hence –human). Thus if we apply the test to a corpus of nouns, we find that expressions like *boy* and *girl* routinely occur as antecedents of *who* (thus, +human), but *bird* and *cow* do not routinely do so (thus, –human).[8]

Yet this in no way implies that such expressions cannot occur in text-patterns that cumulatively yield non-default referential effects. We saw in Chapter 1 (see example (10) and its discussion) that the referents of –human nouns are *personified* when such nouns occur in text configurations where *co-occurring signs* imply that the referent has human, or human-like qualities. Such effects are not exceptions to categorial structure, as we noted before. They are not even identifiable at the level of category tokens. Such effects are based on the interactions of two distinct principles of sign-function, namely textually cumulative reference (based on text-level indexicality) and lexeme-level default reference (based on grammatical categories). Such usages appear to be denotationally incorrect insofar as the cumulative text-level effect is partially non-congruent with the default reference of a lexeme that occurs as a text fragment. The usage may be interactionally unsuccessful (i.e., be unintelligible to interlocutor), or may be successful and understood as an act of tropic reference. As we noted in 1.4, intelligible tropes typically involve a fractional non-congruence between lexemes and co-text. This is because a lexeme is a category cluster of sense dimensions.

A lexeme is a category cluster because sense dimensions cross-classify each other. For instance, by applying the tests in Table 2.3 successively we can sort a corpus of expressions into more and more specific sub-classes in the way shown in Figure 2.4. Each lower node corresponds to a more

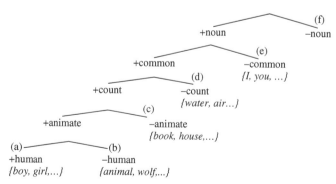

Figure 2.4   *Structural sense classes of English noun*

specific class of expressions. Each sub-class has *all* of the properties specified at nodes superordinate to it, e.g., class (b), {*animal, wolf, . . .*}, is not only [–human], but more particularly, [+noun, +common, +count, +animate, –human]. Since each lexeme is a category cluster of sense dimensions, tropic non-equivalence between lexemes involves fractional congruence. In the case of a tropic utterance such as 'The *man* is a *wolf*,' the two italicized lexemes differ in structural sense – the first is [+human], the second [–human] – but they differ only fractionally since both share the features [+noun, +common, +count, +animate].

Each node in Figure 2.4 corresponds to a class of lexemes. That is, each member of the classes (a)–(f) is a lexeme, not jut a word-form. Given homonymy, lexemes in different classes may have the same phonemic shape, or word-form, but not the same structural sense. Thus as we noted earlier the word-form /flaɪ/ corresponds to two different noun lexemes, *fly₁* (+animate) and *fly₂* (–animate); the former belongs to class (b), the latter to class (c).[9]

The representation in Figure 2.4 is a partial representation of the sense structure of English nouns. It does not show, for example, that certain category clusters are ruled out by **implicational relationships** between form/ sense categories. For example if a lexeme is [+human] it is also [+animate], i.e., the category cluster [–animate, +human] does not occur; the class [+human] is in fact a subclass of [+animate]. It also does not show that the unmarked classes in the figure (the ones having '–' values) are also further differentiable into sub-classes, e.g., the class [–common] includes speech-event deictics and proper names, and each of these is, in turn, further differentiable into [+ /–animate], [+ /–human] and other sub-classes.

This type of model may be used to capture the structural sense contributions of lexemes of any morphosyntactic type, not just the free lexemic forms discussed above. Table 2.4 illustrates its application to suffixes.

Table 2.4. *Structural sense classes of suffix*

Lexeme	Derivational properties	Example	Lexemic sense contribution
-er₁	verbs → agentive noun	paint: painter	[+noun, +agentive]
-er₂	adj → comparative adj	small: smaller	[+comparative]
-ify	noun, adj → verb	electric: electrify	[+verb, +transitive]
-ling	noun → diminutive noun	duck: duckling	[+diminutive]

Limitations of the method

The model of grammaticosemantic meaning that we have been discussing is an extremely powerful way of capturing the structural sense properties of

lexemes. But every model has its limits. We cannot use the model empirically without an appreciation of these limits. Two kinds of empirical
phenomena, the existence of lexemes that are **deictic categories** (or have
indexical denotation) and, for entirely different reasons, the existence of
lexeme collocations that are **idioms**, indicate the limits of structural sense
analysis as a method for capturing the denotation of expressions. To see
what these limits are, let us first summarize some of the issues raised above:

Summary 2.5
We have seen in the above discussion that

(a) part of what we mean by the denotation of a lexeme is its constant
    capacity to specify the denotation of larger expressions;
(b) every lexeme does not combine with every other to yield a well-formed
    sense-bearing unit;
(c) using these two properties together we can partly associate the deno-
    tation of a lexeme with its distribution, and thus learn something about
    the denotation of both elementary lexemes and, by sense composi-
    tionality, of lexeme collocations; and
(d) using markedness conventions we can devise a descriptive scheme which
    interprets lexemic denotation in terms of referential text-defaults.

Each of these statements implies a residue. That (a) and (c) have a
particular purview, or domain of application, is quite clear from the
qualifiers 'part of' and 'partly.' But the limits of applicability of (b) are
more implicit in its formulation. When we say that every lexeme does not
'combine with' every other we are not talking about the possible
co-occurrence (in, say, a physical sense) of form-tokens in utterances.
Observation (b) makes no claims about physical occurrence and
co-occurrence of form-tokens at the level of text. Talk of combinability
in this context is talk of structural concatenation, namely the capacity of
sense-bearing units to yield larger expressions which are themselves
well-formed sense-bearing units, the largest possible sense-bearing unit
being a sentence. The sentence is the largest structural domain of sense-
compositional relationships, and hence forms an upper-limit for grammatical analysis. The actual physical form of an utterance in discourse may
depart from norms of structural sense in a variety of ways. Regularities of
structural concatenation merely entail that when such departures occur the
sense of the complex expression will also depart systematically from the
sense expected by the principle of sense compositionality. Indeed, in some
cases (discussed later) departures from a denotational norm not only occur
but occur commonly because they are interactionally valued. In such cases
regularities of structural concatenation are manipulated in context to yield
special social effects – such as interactional tropes – which may conform to,

or be reanalyzed within register models as conforming to, interpersonal norms of entirely different kinds.

Assumption (c) has another limitation: it does not suffice to explain the denotation of lexeme collocations that have idiomatic content. Idioms are lexeme collocations whose stereotypic denotation does not conform, or does not conform perfectly, to the principle of sense compositionality. Although sense compositionality is pervasive in natural language it is by no means the only principle shaping the sense of complex expressions. Many expressions are **holophrastic lexations**, i.e., have denotational content as a whole which is not reducible by sense compositionality to the sense and arrangements of their parts. For example *kick the bucket* is an idiom meaning 'die' but *kick the ball* is sense compositional. Linguists have come to realize that idiomaticity is a far more pervasive feature of natural language than was previously thought. For example, even the denotation of the familiar expression *dog catcher* is only partly predictable by sense compositionality as 'an X that catches dogs.' Not everyone who catches dogs is a dog catcher. For *dog catcher* is also a municipal title and denotes a type of civil servant (i.e., a 'person employed by the municipality to catch stray dogs'), a fact about its denotation not predictable by sense compositionality. Similarly *lawn mower* is sense compositionally 'an X that mows lawns'; but the additional fact that *lawn mower* denotes an artifact made of metal that has rotors, blades and wheels, is not predictable by sense compositionality. In general, idioms are lexeme collocations whose denotational stereotypes (see next section) differ substantially from denotational properties specified by sense compositionality.

The purview of (d) differs very sharply from that of (a)–(c), and its limitations are of a rather different kind. Whereas a distributional analysis (under assumptions (a)–(c)) allows us to model the denotational properties of sense-bearing units, assumption (d) is a way of linking distributional properties to referential effects. But to say that distributional properties specify referential text-defaults is not to say that nothing else does. We saw in 1.4 that deictic expressions lexically unite two very different principles for specifying referential text-defaults. The denotational schema of deixis is a classification of referent (qua type of 'thing') specified by the denotational category of the deictic. But deictics also formulate an interactional sketch of referent, or locate referent with respect to the interactional scenario of utterance. The latter component of deixis cannot be analyzed under assumptions (a)–(c). This is because the way in which the interactional schema of deixis specifies referential text-defaults depends not on the sense-compositionality of form-types but on the spatio-temporal occasion of token production.

This difference between the denotational and interactional schema of deixis can be highlighted by comparing lexemic deictics with deictics that

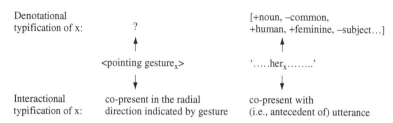

Figure 2.5   *Deictic signs: denotational and interactional schemas*

are not linguistic expressions at all. Thus **ostensive reference** is a type of referential act that can be achieved by a pointing gesture. A pointing gesture is a deictic sign, but not a linguistic expression. It therefore has no structural sense properties (does not semantically classify the referent). Yet it does locate referent in interactional space as shown in Figure 2.5. In contrast a linguistic deictic such as *her* unites two independent kinds of referential text-defaults, a denotational and an interactional formulation of referent. Both the pointing gesture and the word *her* are signs used to refer to things; but the referential effects of the latter differ from those of the former in including a denotational typification of referent as well.

The denotational typification of referent formulated by *her* can be modeled under assumptions S 2.5 (a)–(c), as indicated in Figure 2.5; in this respect, the deictic lexeme is highly comparable to the non-deictic lexemes, *girl, woman*, etc. But the interactional sketch of referent formulated by *her* can only be modeled by appeal to variables of event structure, by appeal to the notion 'utterance' or 'event in which the sign-token occurs'; in this respect the linguistic deictic is more comparable to the pointing gesture. In contrast, the expressions *girl* and *woman* formulate no interactional sketch of referent (in this respect they differ from expressions containing deictics, viz., *this girl, that woman*). Notice also that the denotational typification of referent formulated by *her* is readily preserved under decontextualization but the interactional formulation is not: someone who hears a decontextualized token of *her* may not know who is being talked about, but can still recognize that candidate referents are things of a certain semantic type (female, human, etc.). But someone presented with a close-up photo of a pointing hand is unable to characterize the semantic class of any referents that may successfully have been ostended while the photo was being taken.

Whereas the phenomenon of idiomaticity limits the extent to which we can use assumption (c) to characterize the sense of an expression, the phenomenon of deixis shows that many expressions whose referential text-defaults are interpretable by assumption (d) also set *other* types of referential text-defaults (namely interactional schematizations of referent, as in Table 1.3), which require a different type of analysis. Neither the idiomatic content of expressions nor the interactional schema of deixis can be studied by the methods of grammatical analysis. Thus whereas grammatical analysis is a powerful method for analyzing the structural sense of an expression, the method has definite limits.

Moreover, if by the 'sense' of an expression we mean its denotational class then the sense of an expression is not reducible to its *structural* sense. This is already evident from the case of idioms, the case where the reportable sense (or 'gloss') of an expression differs from its structural sense, that is, from the sense predicted by the principle of sense compositionality. In the next section I discuss two other principles that organize denotational classes, namely their stereotypic denotation and prototypical reference. These considerations foreground the fact that the denotational class of an expression is not merely a semantic but also a sociological construct.

The method of structural sense analysis relies on the implicit metasemantic knowledge of native speakers, that is, on their ability to discriminate form/sense contrasts. But the method does not require that speakers be able to give glosses of all the expressions thus analyzed. Hence distributional methods can be used to analyze the structural sense of lexemes that native speakers cannot gloss directly (such as agentive -*er* and the complementizer *'s -ing*). But denoting expressions that are free forms (see (7e)), and especially those that are continuous free forms, permit a second kind of analysis as well. For such expressions we can formulate metasemantic queries asking speakers to gloss the semantics of the expression.

Stereotypic denotation and prototypical reference

When we encounter an unfamiliar language we often ask questions like 'what does X mean?' or 'what is an X?' where X is a word or other expression. In asking these questions we hope to elicit answers like 'X means Y' or 'an X is a Y' and thus, by recourse to a second expression, Y, to learn something about the denotation of the expression X. There are a number of ways in which the asking of such questions can go awry as an actual field procedure for discovering the sense of an expression. Indeed, for reasons discussed at the beginning of Chapter 1, the responses gathered in such elicitation experiments may not be metasemantic responses at all, or may combine metasemantic with metapragmatic components.[10] In the discussion that follows I am interested in the uses of this procedure where the responses gathered can reliably be construed as metasemantic data.

Under these conditions we can use metasemantic queries to discover something about the **denotational stereotypes** associated with the expression. In the most explicit case the denotational stereotype of an expression (see Putnam 1975) is a set of expressions predicable of it. For example, if we ask a group of English speakers 'what is a wolf?' or 'what does wolf mean?', the metasemantic glosses we gather are likely to include a set of predicates of the following kind:

(9)

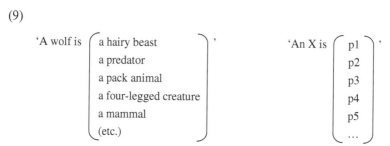

Each predicate defines a class of things (viz., the class 'predator,' the class 'mammal,' etc.). The denotational class *wolf* corresponds to the intersection of these classes; it is a class of entities of which *all* of these properties are predicable (i.e., not merely a 'hairy beast' but also a 'predator,' and also a 'mammal,' and so on). The stereotype corresponds semantically to the Boolean class conjunct of all of the properties found to be predicable of it, or the Venn diagrammatic intersection of all of the classes to which it is said to belong.

(10)

Wolf (x) = hairy-beast (x) & predator (x) & mammal (x) & ...

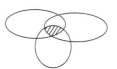

But a model of denotational stereotypy constructed in this way is also a sociological construct. It is constructed by attending to the glossing behavior of a known sample of respondents. Moreover, it is unlikely even in the ideal scenario that all speakers sampled will respond with exactly the same stereotype set. Suppose we were to find that that some subset P′ of the total stereotype set recurs in the responses of many people, but that others (such as the subset P″) are outliers, so that the overall stereotype set has something like a normal distribution. (We can make the example more concrete by supposing that P′ = {p1, p2} and P″ = {p5} from example (9)). This distribution shown in Figure 2.6 illustrates a very simple **social regularity of metasemantic discourse**, a regularity of metasemantic typification observed in a population of speakers. The question of what kinds of regularities we might actually find is, of course, an empirical question. The case of the normal distribution shown here is purely illustrative. The general point here is that a single sample of metasemantic data may show that, for the

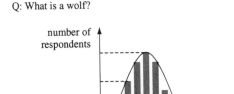

Figure 2.6 *Denotational stereotypes as social regularities*

expression under consideration, some denotational stereotypes are more widely shared than others.

It is worth emphasizing that, from the point of view of the empirical method we are using, denotational stereotypes are publicly observable regularities of metasemantic typification. They are intersubjectively observable facts. They are also 'social facts' (or socially shared facts) in the sense that they have a social domain. To say that a denotational stereotype is socially shared is to say that some of the predicates (or some subsets of predicates, grouped by sense classifications) that occur in the metasemantic activity of one speaker *recur in the activity of many speakers*. The group of such speakers is the **social domain** of the stereotype. The graph shows the case where stereotype P′ has a larger social domain than stereotype P″, i.e., P′ is a typification offered by many more people than is P″. The social sharedness of a denotational stereotype is therefore a degree notion. Moreover the stereotype associated with an expression may grow or shrink over a population of users as we shall presently see.

The notion of denotational stereotype must be distinguished from the partly analogous but fundamentally distinct notion of a **referential proto-type**. The latter notion is analogous because it can also be modeled through metasemantic queries. But the queries are of an entirely different kind. We investigate the denotational stereotypes of an expression by asking what semantic properties are predicable of a class; we investigate the referential prototypes of an expression by asking what objects belong to the class. The difference can be illustrated for the expression *wolf* in the following way. Let us suppose that we have a set of pictures of different animals. Let us give letter names to the different objects (animals) depicted in these pictures (viz., a, b, c, d …). Suppose that we now hold up each of these pictures to a native speaker of the language and ask, in turn, 'Is this one$_a$ a wolf?', 'Is that one$_b$ a wolf?', 'What about this one$_c$?', and so on. By using this procedure we hope to get answers like 'yes' or 'no' for each question, and thus to sort the collection of things into two classes, wolves vs. other animals. Let us now repeat this experiment for a sample of speakers. When

Q: Is that one$_x$ a wolf?

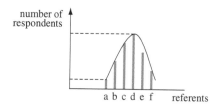

Figure 2.7   *Referential prototypes*

experiments of this sort are carried out (e.g., Rosch 1978) it is generally found that some objects are viewed as members of the class by many more people than are other objects. Such objects are **prototypical referents** of the expression for the population sampled. Thus, like the concept of stereotypic denotation, prototypical reference is at once a semantic and a sociological notion.[11] It is also a degree notion. Figure 2.7 illustrates the case where the largest number of people identify animal d as a wolf, and various (smaller) numbers of respondent identify a, b, c, e, f as wolves. Here d is the most prototypical referent of *wolf*, the others less prototypical in the judgment of speakers. The most prototypical referent is the exemplary member of the class for the population sampled.

Although both are sociological constructs, denotational stereotypes and referential prototypes specify the semantics of a denotational class in two different ways, that is, by specifying attributes predicable of a class in the first case, and by identifying members of the class in the second. This point can also be stated by appeal to the distinction between the semantic intension and extension of a class. We noted earlier that the intension of a class is a defining property (or conjunct of properties), and its extension is the set of things that are its members. An expression's denotational stereotype is a social regularity of intensional classification, identifiable by appeal to properties predicable of it. In contrast, its referential prototype is a feature of its extension, the things regarded as members of the class by a population sampled, the exemplary member of the class being its most prototypical referent.

The denotational category of an expression

The analysis of an expression's structural sense, denotational stereotype and referential prototype are three different ways of modeling the denotational category of an expression. No one among these principles suffices by itself to explain the denotation of all expression types in a natural language.[12] Structural sense is that component of an expression's denotation that is made regular by distributional patterns in the language. Its denotational stereotype is a social regularity of what is predicable of an expression. Its referential prototype is an exemplary referent. The methods used to identify these models are not logically independent, but they are procedurally distinct.[13] And all three models have a sociological dimension in that they are models for someone, or have a social domain.

Linguistic expressions differ in the extent to which principles like structural sense, stereotypy and prototypy shape their referential uses (Silverstein 1987). This point is already implied by our earlier observation that these methods cannot be applied equally easily to all kinds of expressions. Let us consider some specific limitations.

We can use a distributional analysis to specify the structural sense properties of any lexeme (and non-idiomatic lexeme collocation). But the method of metasemantic queries cannot be applied to all lexemes. Lexemes that are not free forms (and, in particular, continuous free forms) are not directly susceptible to analysis by a method of overt queries. Thus a lexeme like agentive -er (which occurs only if a verb stem also occurs), or the verb forming suffix -ify (which combines with adjective and noun stems) have little in the way of reportable stereotypes or prototypes. But they do have a structural sense or grammaticosemantic meaning, specifiable through a distributional analysis, as in Table 2.4.

Some lexemes are amenable to analysis by metasemantic queries, but more readily for stereotypic denotation than for prototypical referents. Consider the case of abstract nouns. For abstract nouns like *truth, justice, beauty, liberty, necessity, intransigence, essence*, etc. we can readily formulate queries like 'what is X?' or 'what does X mean?' and hope to get glosses by way of response. But we can not equally easily hold up extensional instances of these classes (e.g., an instance of beauty or liberty) without also using metasemantic descriptions of the thing we are trying to investigate, and thus, cannot get very far in the use of a method which, by asking questions like 'Is this one an X?', hopes to investigate prototypical reference alone (i.e., in isolation from denotational stereotypes).

For expressions whose denotation is amenable to more than one type of analysis we often find that the results of one type of analysis confirm the results of another. Consider the case of the expression *wolf*. In the preceding discussion we observed that the term *wolf* belongs to a structural sense class defined by the category cluster [+noun, +common, +count, +animate, –human] (see Figure 2.4ff.). We also noted in (9) that its denotational stereotypes include characterizations as some type of X where X is an expression like *beast, predator, animal, creature, mammal*, etc. If we apply the distributional tests noted earlier (Table 2.3ff) to these expression we find that they all belong to the same structural sense class as *wolf*. They are all nouns by the criteria considered earlier, and, in particular, are common, count nouns whose denotata are animate but not specifically human.

In naturally occurring glossing behavior we frequently find that expressions used to gloss particular forms belong to the same structural sense category as the form glossed. This is by no means necessary. The extent to which they do not coincide is a measure of the idiomaticity of the expression. Thus in the case of an idiom like *kick the bucket*, the correct gloss *die* belongs to a different structural sense category (*kick* is transitive, *die* is not).

The ability to give denotational stereotypes can also reshape the structural sense organization of a language. Reanalysis through a **folk-etymology** is a common example of a case where a denotational stereotype imputes sense compositionality to an expression even though it has none, or has one that is no longer transparent. In the case of words like *sand-blind* (< OE *sam-blind* 'semi-blind' or 'half blind') the reanalysis results when an element (OE *sam* 'half') falls out of usage. The expression now appears denotationally analogous to other current expressions such as *snow-blind* and thus to constitute a new equivalence class to which further lexical innovations can in principle be added. In cases of this kind, reflexive processes mediated by the ability to give denotational stereotypes transform the structural sense organization of a language.

Semantic classifications are 'leaky' things (Sapir 1921) because of possibilities of reflexive reanalysis. Yet we cannot understand the social significance of this fact by attending only to the semantic aspect of denotation. For, as we have seen, denotation is at once a semantic and a sociological construct. Let us now focus on the second half of the construct. This brings us directly to the issue of denotational norms.

2.4 Norms of denotation and interaction

I said earlier that the denotation of an expression is the class of entities to which it 'correctly' refers. This statement describes a very special case. When we speak of norms in general we are not always (or only) concerned with evaluations of correctness and incorrectness in the 'normative' sense, i.e., with evaluations linked to codified standards. Normative correctness is sometimes relevant to talk of norms but constitutes a special case. The more general case is better conceptualized as involving different thresholds of normativity, of which at least three gradations may usefully be distinguished, as indicated in Table 2.5.

First, we may speak of social norms in the sense of externally observable correlations. Any observable correlation between two or more variables in the behavior of persons (e.g., people of type X do/say Y) is a norm in this sense. The norm may hold as a statistical pattern in behavior. A pattern of behavior in this sense is the behavior of some category of persons (viz., old vs. young people, Americans vs. Germans, etc.). The pattern can be recognized by anyone who gives concerted attention to a large enough sample of data. However, in practice, most statistical norms that are externally observable are not remarked or noticed by the persons whose behavior displays them. Even a brief glance at any almanac or concordance makes clear that this is so.

A second case concerns patterns of behavior that are reflexively grasped as 'normal' by members of the population whose behavior is at issue. In this case, a reflexive model specifies a **norm for** the social actors whose behavior it is; we might say that the reflexive model **normalizes** some pattern of behavior in the perceptions of these social persons. But when we speak of reflexive models we are often speaking of two social groups, not one. The group of persons whose behavior exhibits the pattern need not coincide exactly with the group that views it as a norm. For example, only a sub-group of the people who behave in a certain way may view that behavior as 'normal.' A reflexive model has associated with it a **social range**, namely persons recognized as displaying the behavior (i.e., a category of actors), and a **social domain**, namely persons who so recognize it (i.e., a category of evaluators). It is not necessary that every member of a population recognize exactly the same norm as holding for a given social range of actors; indeed, competing models may well co-exist society-internally, and recognition of such differences may itself result in further group differentiation.

In the third case, the case of normative standards, the normalization of behavior (the perception that some behaviors are 'normal' or routine, others not) is linked to standards of correctness in the more specific sense noted earlier. Here, a pattern of behavior is not just reflexively normalized (or, recognized as typical) but **standardized**, that is, linked to judgments of appropriateness, to values schemes of 'good' vs. 'bad' behavior, and so on. It should be clear that (c) is just a special case of (b). A normative standard is a particular kind of reflexive model; conversely, any reflexive model can in principle be reanalyzed as a normative standard by some among those who recognize it. For many norms, particular individuals move across these thresholds of recognition as they engage in different tasks or activities (including some that highlight the importance of norms) or, as they move through the life-span (and are exposed to different socializing discourses, as in Figure 1.8), come to different thresholds of awareness, recognition, loyalty, etc., to particular norms at particular moments of lived experience. Hence the distinctions in Table 2.5 do not comprise a taxonomy of norms into which an individual's beliefs and commitments can be sorted in a static way; they are thresholds of norm recognition exhibited by pragmatic-metapragmatic relationships in overt semiotic behaviors. By appeal to such behaviors we can differentiate thresholds of normativity by asking questions like: How is a breach of

Table 2.5. *Thresholds of normativity*

(a) A norm of behavior:	An externally observable pattern of behavior e.g., a statistical norm or frequency distribution in some order of behavior
(b) A normalized model of behavior:	A reflexive model of behavior, recognized as 'normal' or 'typical' by (at least some) actors, i.e., is a *norm for* them
(c) A normative standard:	A normative model, linked to standards whose breach results in sanctions; a norm codified as a standard

norms treated? By whom? How widely is it treated the same way? How, if at all, is it described? What consequences, if any, follow from the breach?

Deviations from a statistical norm in the sense of (a) are wholly unremarkable for those who create the pattern, unless the statistical norm is, in addition, linked to a reflexive model, i.e., is viewed as normal by at least some of the actors involved, and thus is reanalyzed as a case of type (b). Deviations from a normalized pattern in the sense of (b) are felt to be deviations by those who create the pattern because their reflexive grasp of what is typical or routine behavior provides a criterion of what to expect. But departures or deviations from normative standards in the sense of (c) are not merely felt deviations from what is expected; they are felt deviations against which certain sanctions are also to be expected. These may take various forms (e.g., disapprobation, ridicule, social exclusion, penalties). The expectability of the sanction (its frequency, exceptionlessness, etc.) is a measure of the extent to which something really does function as a standard in the sense of (c) versus the case where it is imagined to be one, but no longer is.

It will be evident that differences of thresholds of normativity can be identified in any type of behavior. What about the case of denotational practices? We noted earlier that the denotation of an expression is only experienced in events of language use (S 2.4). The events relevant to understanding denotational norms are metasemantic events; they are therefore observable behaviors of persons that permit a sociological description. A common mistake in studying metasemantic behaviors is to suppose that metasemantic regularities, once identified, have a universal social domain within the entire language community. But the question of whether any such regularity has a provenance that extends beyond the sample population for which it is first identified is an empirical question. The more general issue is that denotational norms have a describable positionality; they are exhibited and articulated in the behaviors of some persons and institutions, not others.

In treating metasemantic evaluations as a function of the category of evaluator, we are considering them as regularities of behavior involving social persons. And once we attend to the reflexive models of behavior that occur in such data we often find that the most common or widely attested glosses are not necessarily regarded culture-internally as correct. Differences between common and correct denotation cannot be explained by resort to any narrowly metasemantic approach, such as a logic of classes, or a distributional analysis. Understanding this difference requires attention to social relations, including relations of power and authority, holding among different categories of metasemantic evaluators. In taking this step, however, we are moving beyond metasemantic questions alone to a consideration of metapragmatic frameworks of sense normalization (and even standardization, in the sense distinguished above). Let us consider this point in more detail.

Common vs. correct denotation

Putnam 1975 argues that the denotation of many common expressions in language is fixed by certain institutional practices that require sociological description. His discussion focuses on the case of natural kind terms and the institution of 'expertise' associated with them in modern societies.

Natural kind terms are expressions denoting things that occur in nature, such as metals (*aluminum, molybdenum, gold*, etc.), animals (*tiger, leopard, tapir*, etc.), and so on. Putnam argues that many common denotational stereotypes about these expressions are in fact incorrect. For example many people may gloss the expression *gold* as 'a yellow metal' even though the metal is nearly white and its yellowness (in commercial varieties) derives from impurities such as copper. The gloss that *gold* is 'a white metal' is also reportable culture-internally but it is more common in the glossing behaviors of experts (chemist, metallurgists, etc.) than in those of ordinary speakers. Similarly, most speakers of English can report that *aluminum* 'is a metal'; but describing the difference between *aluminum* and *molybdenum* is a less straightforward matter for most people. When doubts and disputes arise among ordinary speakers, the common tendency is to appeal to glosses offered by experts. Thus whereas everyone is able to offer some stereotypes of natural kind expressions, all the stereotypes observable in glossing behavior do not have the same degree of authority for language users. The institution of expertise fixes the **authoritative stereotypes** of a denoting expression. For many natural kind terms these differ substantially from the most common stereotypes observable across the language community as a whole.

Similarly many non-specialists who can readily gloss a natural kind term (even gloss it correctly) cannot distinguish exemplary referents from things that superficially resemble them (viz., real gold vs. fool's gold). It is by no means necessary that people who wear gold, or buy and sell gold, be able to recognize whether the object is in fact gold, or just how much gold it contains. All that is necessary is that some persons in society be able to perform the task and be able to provide reliable criteria on settling doubts and disputes when they arise. In such cases the institution of expertise becomes a way of specifying criteria on exemplary referents, and of identifying, even fixing, a **canonical prototype** for a denoting expression; and this may differ, again, from the prototype identified most commonly in the community as a whole.

Considerations of these kind have several implications for a sociology of referring. They show, for instance, that in order for an expression to have correct denotation as a matter of social fact (and independently of whether denotation is regarded intensionally or extensionally, i.e., in terms of stereotypes or prototypes) it is by no means necessary that every user of the expression have identical competence in its use. Folk-theories of denotation (such as the view that denotation involves a 'class concept' that lies 'in the head' of every speaker) tend to essentialize intersubjective, social practices of specifying denotation as facts about individuals abstracted from those practices. But when we examine the actual behavior of individuals we find substantial **asymmetries of competence** which, as we can now see, are neither surprising nor puzzling from the standpoint of the social norm. For, as Putnam shows, the denotation of at least some expressions is fixed by mechanisms of social authority that involve a Durkheimean **division of labor** linked to the institution of expertise: some sub-groups are socially allocated the role of 'experts' and the majority of speakers rely on these individuals for authoritative glosses and identifications of exemplars.

More generally, mechanisms of expertise ensure that events of referring can become mutually coordinated with each other even where asymmetries of denotational competence exist. But they commonly do so by establishing recognizable power relationships among categories of speakers. When doubts and disputes about denotation arise, language users can engage in some further activities through which such doubts or disputes can be settled. In the cases that Putnam considers, such disputes are settled by appeal to a **reference standard** specified by a sub-community of experts. In the case of natural kind terms such metasemiotic experts are often scientists or persons having specialized technical skills. However, systems of normativity (even ones involving reference standards) may differ substantially for other types of semiotic expressions, or be articulated through very different kinds of sociological arrangements.

In Standard Language communities the allocation of expertise tends to be distributed over very different categories of individuals (prescriptivists, lexicographers, language mavens) as well as official institutions (national academies, school boards); and it is typically experienced in a sedimented form through the experience of certain text-artifacts (dictionaries, school-books, manuals of prescriptive grammar). In such artifacts the institution-alized allocation of expertise to individuals can be externalized in certain ways so that the denotational stereotypes they record can acquire a wide circulation; and the ascribed locus of expertise can be transferred or shifted so that it is experienced in an alienated form as the authority of texts. Yet the physical existence of dictionaries and handbooks (viewed purely as physical artifacts) is of little consequence to social life. For such artifacts are themselves precipitates of the workings of institutions through entitled roles of 'author'-ship. And they have social consequences mainly by virtue of being linked to a 'reader' in an event of reading, and through subsequent events, where the erstwhile reader, linked now to other social beings in further communicative activity, produces utterances constrained in some way by that event of reading. Hence the artifacts that disseminate these normative discourses have a social life only through the mediation of speech chains linking persons to each other.

We can now see that whereas the semantic character of denotational norms involves classifications, their sociological character depends on the exchange (circulation and/or reanalysis) of messages. Institutions tend to stabilize denotational stereotypes in a variety of ways; for example, by expanding the circulation of a given stereotype over large populations, by naturalizing the authority of the stereotype through mechanisms such as 'expertise.' However any such mechanism of stabilization unavoidably yields to change and reanalysis over time through mechanisms based at least partly on matters of footing and interpersonal alignment among interactants. I discuss issues of reanalysis at various points in this book, beginning with some elementary features of this process in the next section. But let us first observe that such principles apply to more than just 'words.'

The above discussion focuses on the production of codifications for a highly restricted class of denotational expressions, namely free lexemic forms. What about the codification of denotational units at other levels of grammatical organization? The overall grammatical organization of a language (its phonology and morphosyntax) is so much less transparent to ordinary users than the special case of free lexemic forms that the articu-lation of denotational stereotypes rarely extends to more than a small fraction of the total grammatical organization of a language. As Boas observed, grammatical organization remains, for the most part, recalci-trant to everyday reanalysis (Boas 1996 [1911]). But this simply means that in any given instance of reanalysis only a very tiny fragment of grammat-ical structure can readily become the object of folk-reasoning. Under conditions of institutional codification, where many individuals engage in folk-reasoning about language in patterns of large scale coordinated activity (e.g., in a prescriptivist tradition), this fragment can substantially be expanded.

It is important to see, moreover, that the reanalysis and codification of even a tiny fragment of grammatical organization can have massive social consequences. A useful illustration of this point may be found in Anthony Diller's discussion of diglossic differentiation of Thai syntax into 'high' and 'low' interactional registers (Diller 1993). Diller shows that the high syntactic register of Thai derives from a Sanskritized nineteenth-century courtly speech. This type of speech, under further reanalysis from Latin and English models in the twentieth century, comes to be recirculated in bureaucratic and epistolary discourses that reach a wider audience. More recently, these features have become standardized in prescriptive grammars and traditions of pedagogy, and are now institutionalized in the metadiscursive practices of schooling. A simplified representation of this process is given in Figure 2.8.

The reanalysis results in the diglossic differentiation of patterns of morphosyntactic organization into a 'high' and a 'low' register of speech. The two registers are differentiated by a number of morphosyntactic features (including constituent order, topicalization, null anaphora, reflexivization, cross-clausal control, and others). But the register contrast cannot be defined only by appeal to contrasting grammatical patterns. The register contrast is also a sociohistorical regularity. It is formulated and disseminated by institutions, as the diagram indicates for the case of H register.

The fact that the register distinction is shaped by a sociohistorical process entails that both registers are not fluently known to all Thai

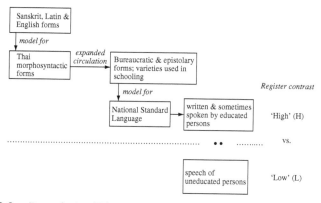

Figure 2.8   *Reanalysis of Thai syntactic patterns into 'high' and 'low' registers* (Source: Diller 1993)

speakers. Contemporary access to register norms depends on differential access to those institutionalized sites where register competence is reproduced. For example, fluency in the H register requires years of specialized schooling. In contrast, the uneducated speakers at the bottom of Figure 2.8 are out of the loop of these circulatory processes and hence lack the **competence to speak** H fluently. Yet they typically have a passive acquaintance with its forms – the **competence to recognize** such forms as H – through primary schooling and, as Diller puts it, the 'omnipresence of mass media.' Facts of social differences in competence (and, more particularly, in competences of two different kinds) are critical to the way in which many register differences become commodity forms, that is, come to be treated as scarce goods (since certain forms are recognized as 'high' forms by many more persons than actively command them), and therefore as objects sought after in their own right.

Under these conditions processes of enregisterment link denotational norms to norms of interactional appropriateness. Thus the 'high' variety is normatively appropriate to certain venues of social life: 'If a Thai is to finish school, pass important examinations, be in line for bureaucratic promotions, understand (or create) official documents, make official presentations, give or even comprehend formal speeches, interviews or lectures, then there must be active mastery of syntactic aspects of the H register complex'; and 'in the higher echelons of administrative and commercial bureaucracies, etc., one needs to be able to "speak in H" fluently as well.'

Yet the 'high' or educated register is by no means appropriate to all settings. Anyone who commands the high register needs to know when not to use it in order to be successful as a member of society: 'For educated speakers, the more L-like register complex would be appropriate for the informal and more personal communicative needs of modern urban life. The ability to shift appropriately is crucial. It would be socially infelicitous (if not disastrous) to use H in situations where an L-like register was the appropriate one – say in the market. Misuse of H is recognized and referred to by the derogatory term *dàtcarìt* 'affectation', 'putting on airs'. Thus it is not the case – as yet, at least – that for urban speakers the H register is on the verge of entirely replacing the L one' (Diller 1993: 415).

Under conditions of diglossic differentiation native speaker intuitions about denotational well-formedness (what linguists call 'grammaticality judgments') are therefore cross-cut by intuitions about interactional appropriateness. Diller points out that approaches to grammar in which syntactic competence is naturalized as something shaped by 'an innate bioprogram' or linked solely to 'neurological maturation processes' can not, even in principle, yield an empirically adequate account of syntactic regularities. For, the metalinguistic data of native speaker intuitions on which such analyses are based are, in part, the data of metapragmatic awareness of register differences, and these features require a sociological analysis of the circulation of normative discourses within society and of the positional access of individuals through trajectories of socialization to such intuitions as they have about 'correctness.'

Leaving aside issues of correctness in the normative sense let us now consider a much more generalized kind of social significance linked to denotational choices in speech.

2.5 Dialect, sociolect and denotational footing

Denotational norms are sociocentric phenomena in that their definition requires appeal to social collectivities. But they only become relevant to acts of referring relative to participation frameworks. The terms dialect and sociolect describe forms of variation in the denotational system of a language community. The question naturally arises as to how such variation becomes relevant to forms of social organization as these are understood by members of a society. It is important to see that the mere existence of dialects is not, by itself, relevant to answering this question. Dialects may exist and be describable by linguists but groups speaking these dialects may be separated in various ways so that cross-dialect contact among persons does not occur and the existence of dialect differences is not even suspected by most (in principle, by *any*) speakers of the language. Dialect differences are relevant to social life only insofar as they are experienced through communicative events. How such relevance is construed society internally is an empirical question that will have different answers in different sociohistorical locales. But attempts at answering these questions require a consideration of two rather distinct issues.

The first issue is the one already noted: dialect differences become relevant to social organization only insofar as they are experienced in discursive interactions, whether directly or in a more indirect fashion (e.g., through mass mediated speech chains and networks); the question remains of how the nature of this experience should be theorized. This is the main issue discussed in the present section. A second issue concerns the way in which interactional differences in dialect forms are evaluated as indexing specific schemas of social identity and groupness; a fuller treatment of this issue is given later (especially 3.1–3.3, 4.4). My concern here is to show that we cannot satisfactorily explore the second issue without taking the first as our point of departure.

Denotational footing and role alignment

We have already seen that individuals who happen to be co-participants in a given encounter may have entirely different trajectories of socialization within the language community and thus may differ substantially in their command of (at least fractions of) the denotational system in play within that encounter (viz., differences of lexis, morphosyntax, pronunciation, etc.). It follows that differences in the denotational norms a speaker knows – or, at least, exhibits in performance – are potentially indexical of social differences and alignments among interactants.

Such differences are sometimes exploited strategically to create social partitions or boundaries within an interaction, but social boundaries can result willy-nilly too. In multi-party encounters where multilinguals and monolinguals come together as co-participants, practices of codeswitching and codemixing mark off monolingual interlocutors as out-group (or non-participants) with respect to certain utterances, whether intentionally or not; the social boundaries enacted in such cases may coincide with differences of propositional uptake and thus involve cognitive boundaries too. But even in encounters among monolinguals, alternations of dialect and sociolect commonly yield social boundaries and alignments of a more subtle type.

In all such cases perceived sameness of speech aligns or groups participants together; perceived differences mark boundaries (of whatever kind). These issues may be summarized as follows:

Summary 2.6
Comparable uses of a denotational system in interaction performatively diagram symmetric **role alignments** among speech participants (e.g., co-membership in an identity or social grouping). Conversely, non-comparable usage diagrams asymmetric alignments (performed differences, social partitions or boundaries) among participants.

Talk of **symmetric** and **asymmetric** alignments in this sense involves considerations of metrical patterns of interactional text mediated by the likeness and unlikeness of denotational behavior across categories of speaker (Agha 2005). Since denotational expressions may be evaluated as like or unlike each other by using any of the categorial dimensions discussed earlier as criteria (their phonemic shape, their structural sense, stereotypic denotation or prototypical reference) *there are as many types of perceivable likeness and unlikeness possible in performance as there are categorial dimensions laminated together in the expressions used.* However, ideologies of language that reanalyze such variation into lexical register distinctions tend selectively to attend to only a few contrasts in any given case, and to imbue them with highly specific characterological values that are known to those who belong to the social domain of the register.

The points summarized in S 2.6 are really just a consequence of pursuing the text-centric perspective on discourse discussed in preceding sections.

But there is a difference. In earlier discussion we were interested in *comparable treatments of referents* across interactional turns (i.e., how one person's typifications of referent correspond to another's). We gave particular attention to questions such as (1) how participants inhabit propositional stances on referents (i.e., identify and characterize them) and (2) how differences of inhabited stance map out relationships among interlocutors (thus diagramming alignments among participant positions).

We are no longer concerned with referents, or things spoken about. Our interest now lies in the *comparability of denotational units themselves*, irrespective of the 'things' that count as their referents. How do differences of denotational choice among speakers diagram facts of interactional positioning and alignment? I refer to cases of this kind as matters of **denotational footing**.

Since denotational choices are invariably anchored to participation frameworks denotational footing is merely a special case of the more general phenomenon of interactional role alignment. In the more general case, role alignments may be achieved by a variety of semiotic mechanisms (such as the referential and kinesic alignments discussed earlier). We are now concerned with the special case where interpersonal alignments are diagrammed through contrasts among denotational units across utterances. Goffman 1981a remarks on a special variety of denotational footing – the case of denotational contrasts at dialect/sociolect boundaries – by citing the work of Blom and Gumperz (1986 [1972]) on code switching. These remarks, once properly theorized within a reflexive view of language, open up a way of conceptualizing the significance of dialect/sociolect contrasts from an interactional point of view, and their enregisterment as indexicals of 'social kinds' within a process of register differentiation.

Dialect and sociolect

Differences of dialect and sociolect depend partly on contrasts among denotational units of various types (phonemic, lexemic, morphosyntactic, etc.)[14] in the speech habits of language users. They depend on other contrast too. But studies of dialect/sociolect variation have traditionally paid special attention to denotational variation (for reasons discussed below), using these facts to differentiate groupings or '-lects' within a language community. What is the social significance of these facts? How do facts of denotational variation come to be imbued with group-differentiating social-indexical values? There are two rather different ways in which these questions may be approached.

The standard approach in variationist sociolinguistics is to attempt a demographic interpretation of linguistic variation. From this point of view, a **sociolect** is a set of linguistic features that mark the social provenance of speaker along any demographic dimension, such as class, profession, gender, or age. A **dialect** is a special type of sociolect, the case where the demographic dimensions marked by speech are matters of geographic provenance alone, such as speaker's birth locale, extended residence and the like. In both cases facts of speech variation are treated as indexical of speaker types. But indexical for whom? Under what conditions?

On the traditional variationist view sociolects and dialects are conceived as attributes of social aggregates that can in principle be distinguished by the analyst without attention to the reflexive activities of their members. Phoneticians can describe formal differences among dialects and sociolects without considering metalinguistic judgments other than their own. Moreover, on this view, the social meaning of dialects and sociolects (i.e., the thing that they mark) is the existence and differentiability of groups.

There is no difficulty in identifying formal distinctions of sociolect or dialect in a pre-selected structural domain of a language by using methods of these kinds. Yet the social interpretation of these results is highly problematic. One difficulty is that the method underlying this approach cannot be used to answer questions of how such observations, if accurate, correspond to perceptions of groupness on the part of language users. These questions cannot be answered by an approach for which the formulation of externally observed correlations – whether statistically modeled or not – is the principal goal from the very outset. There are two reasons for this limitation, one obvious, one less so.

The first reason is that language users are themselves 'correlationsists' *par excellence*. The question of who speaks in what manner is a matter of ubiquitous concern in everyday social life. The asking and answering of such questions is a common form of reflexive practice that formulates models of behavior that co-exist with that behavior, are presupposed and troped upon in that behavior, and thus themselves constitute a distinct order of sociocultural fact which must, from the outset, be part of the object of study. Sociolects and dialects are routinely and readily converted into registers – culture-internal models of personhood linked to speech forms – by reflexive processes that occur naturally in all societies, though the social dimensions of such registers (social domain, institutionalization, etc.), their repertoire characteristics and social values, the degree of naturalization and essentialization of such values, and other dependent features, can themselves differ substantially from case to case. Differences among registers are discussed in more detail in the next two chapters; our concern here is with the first step, the reflexive construal of such '-lects' *as* registers.

A second limitation of correlationalism is that the linguistic features for which it seeks demographic correlates are themselves certain types of extractabilia – mainly denotationally valued units and segments – abstracted from events of communication. There is nothing wrong with paying attention to denotational segments such as phonemes and lexemes in explaining social uses of language; it is in fact impossible to imagine an approach to language study that ignores them. Yet the extractability of denotational pieces of language from contexts of use obscures the processes of reanalysis through which social indexical values are assigned to these pieces. Language is an eminently decontextualizable phenomenon, but this is only one feature of its social life. Pieces of a natural language are readily extractable from acts of language use in such a way that the process of extraction preserves denotationally organized fractions of entextualized form and meaning (e.g., phonemic sound shapes, structural sense) from the totality of semiotic effects mediated by those acts. We can even inspect certain types of text-defaults (e.g., canonical allophones, 'literal' meanings) in relative isolation from features of textuality. But an exclusive focus on these extractabilia obscures the processes whereby denotational units come to be associated with social-indexical values.

In any interaction in which denotational contrasts occur, perceptions of sameness and difference of usage potentially diagram perceptions of sameness or difference of interactant roles and relations. Such contrasts comprise an emergent framework of **role diacritics** (or indices of distinction), which may be given a positively characterizable social meaning through a system of **role designations** (or descriptions) in a variety of ways (see Chapter 5). Yet the diagrammatic effects themselves emerge in the here-and-now of usage and may vanish thereafter; it is by no means necessary that they have broader social consequences. They can, of course, also become more widely enregistered – converted into more widely known classifications of personhood linked to speech – through semiotic chain processes, even become transformed or assimilated into more perduring frameworks of social essence and human nature associated with highly institutionalized registers.

Let us approach this range of possibilities by way of some examples.

Tamil caste sociolects and interpersonal footings

The case of Tamil caste sociolects in Table 2.6 illustrates a cross-linguistically common type of phenomenon. Here the forms regularly employed by one group are treated by a second group as having interactional-pragmatic values absent for those who regularly use them.

The Iyengar (Brahmin) variety of Tamil differs from the Mudaliyar variety in a number of ways. The Brahmin variety tends to calque lexical repertoires from Sanskritic loan words characteristic of Written-Formal registers of Tamil. It also formally overdifferentiates denotational units by

Table 2.6. *Tamil caste sociolects and denotational footings*

I. Gloss	II. Mudaliyar (Non-Brahmin)	III. Iyengar (Brahmin)
(a) drinking water	taṇṇi	tiirtõ
water in general	taṇṇi	jalõ
non-potable water	taṇṇi	taṇṇi
(b) worship	puuse	puuje
food	sooru	saadõ
eat	tinnu	saapḍu
(c) worship	puuse	puuje 'worship' // puuse 'punishment for children'
food	sooru / saadõ	saadõ 'food' // sooru 'food (pejorative)'
eat	tinnu / saapḍu	saapḍu 'eat' // tinnu 'guzzle, etc. (pejorative)'

Notes: '/'= pragmatically but not semantically contrastive variant;
'//'= pragmatically *and* semantically contrastive variant
Source: (Ramanujan 1968)

phonological and lexical processes, sometimes yielding structural sense partitions absent in the Mudaliyar variety; the greater lexemic differentiation of Iyengar words for water in (a) is a simple example. The Mudaliyar variety in contrast tends to make fewer lexical and phonological distinctions, to assimilate loan-words to Tamil phonology and to overgeneralize derivational patterns. The Brahmin variety is structurally fastidious and discriminating; the non-Brahmin variety simplifies form/sense distinctions through assimilation and overgeneralization.

In the situation of the 1960s that Ramanujan describes, some forms from each variety are used by speakers of the other variety too, but with distinct interactional effects:

(11) The Mudaliyārs tried to imitate the speech of the brahmins to elevate themselves in the social hierarchy. Even now it is a common scene in some of the Mudaliyār families for the older people to reprimand the younger generation for speaking like sudras [untouchables] when they don't speak like brahmins ... But if the castes in group IV [fishermen] and V [padayachi] tried to imitate the brahmins, they would be subject to ridicule.
(Pillai 1965: 65; cited in Ramanujan 1968, n. 9)

Thus when Iyengar forms like *saadõ* and *saapḍu* occur in Mudaliyar speech (column II, set (c)) they express a form of self raising actually encouraged in some Mudaliyar homes, but ridiculed if attempted by lower sub-castes. Although these forms are semantically non-contrastive

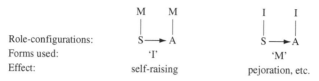

Figure 2.9   *Role configuration and denotationally-mediated footing*

(with *sooru* and *tinnu*, respectively) in Mudaliyar speech, they are sharply contrastive in pragmatic effect.

On the other hand, when Mudaliyar (non-Brahmin) forms occur in Iyengar (Brahmin) speech they comprise a language of pejoration:

(12) In fact, many of the N[on] B[rahmin] forms are constantly used in B[rahmin] homes only with emotional charges: when one is angry with a child or when one is ironic or pejorative.

(Ramanujan 1968: 472)

In this case, perceived differences of interactional persona are partially reanalyzed as contrasts of *stereotypic denotation* as well, as indicated by the contrastive glosses in column III, set (c). Hence for the Iyengars, the lexical contrasts are *both* pragmatically and semantically contrastive.

In both cases, the pragmatic contrasts involve matters of denotational footing. That is, in both cases, variation in choice of denotational units has the interpersonal effects characterized in (11) and (12). Such footings are highly non-detachable from the interactional role configurations in which they are intelligible. As Figure 2.9 shows, Iyengar forms (such as *saadō* and *saapḍu*) imply self-raising only when used by Mudaliyars. And the Mudaliyar forms (cf. *puuse, sooru, tinnu*) have pejorative meanings only when used among Iyengars. Thus the pragmatic effects now in question (self-raising vs. pejoration/irony) are not the effects of lexical items as such. They are forms of footing mediated by text-in-context relationships; they are construable only by reading lexemes in relation to role configurations presupposed at the moment of use.

Such effects depend on the performance of an 'incorrect' identity. Only when the figure of personhood performed through speech is non-congruent with facts of identity readable independently of speech does the effect becomes construable. Such effects are highly robust under text-in-context conditions but are non-detachable from these conditions. If we focus on these forms as extractabilia – as lexemes regarded in isolation from criterial interactional settings – their social construal becomes undecideable.

Under conditions of textuality, however, figures of personhood indexically associated with these forms provide a framework for construing their social meaning. In each of the in-group scenarios discussed above (i.e., speech within Mudaliyar homes, or within Iyengar homes) the use of out-group speech diagrams a departure from a group-internal norm; to this extent, we have asymmetries of denotational usage that performatively diagram social differences. How these difference are construed depends on who performs them, and on inferences about current speakers mediated by the stereotypic values of the forms used. The use of speech that is stereo-typically lower caste often counts as pejoration or irony; the use of higher caste speech counts as self-raising up to a certain threshold of difference (and as ridiculous beyond it). The specific construals discussed above, while attested in ethnographic work and presumably robust during the 1960s, are not the only ones possible; and the question of how this system of denotational footings has fared since the 1960s – how, if at all, it has been maintained or reanalyzed in subsequent social history – requires considerations of an entirely different kind, some features of which are discussed in Chapter 4.

Norwegian dialects and social difference

Our second example is the classic study by Blom and Gumperz (1986 [1972]) of the differential use of two Norwegian dialects in a single language community; the situation described here is also one prevailing during the 1960s. The first of these, Ranamål (R), is a local dialect of Norwegian spoken in Hemnesberget, a small industrial town in northern Norway. The second speech variety, Bokmål (B), is Standard Norwegian, which is not locale-specific. As in the previous example, the contrast between these varieties is traditionally formulated by linguists by appeal to contrasts between deno-tational words, as indicated in Table 2.7. The two varieties have almost the

Table 2.7. *Register contrasts in Norwegian*

Gloss	National Standard (Bokmål, B)	Local variety (Ranamål, R)
I	jœjj	og
you	dœjj	deg
he	hann	hanj
she	hunn	ho
if	viss	vess
to, toward	till	tell
who	vemm	kem
how	vordan	kelesn

Source: (Blom and Gumperz 1986 [1972])

same morphosyntax but differ in lexis. Some lexical contrasts are due to phonological differences (e.g., R makes more consonantal and vocalic distinctions than B), while others are due to morphological differences (e.g., differences in plural suffixes and certain verb inflections) between the two varieties. A few lexical differences in everyday words (pronouns, adverbs and prepositions) are illustrated in Table 2.7.

Consider now the sociological part of the picture. Residents of Hemnesberget acquire the local variety, R, early on in childhood through language socialization in the family; and the national language, B, through formal schooling, the church, and exposure to national media. All residents effectively command both varieties of the language. Blom and Gumperz found, however, that different social categories of speaker exhibit different patterns of context sensitivity in usage; differences in overt metapragmatic commentary also suggest that different sub-populations associate different values with the same pragmatic repertoire.

Differential patterns of speech valorization index contrastive group identities of evaluators. The majority of people who live in Hemnesberget and claim local descent express a strong identification with the town. They view residence in this locale as 'like belonging to a team characterized by commonalty of descent' (p. 418). For such speakers the ethic of the 'local team' is a defining feature of self-identification. Speakers of this reference group appear consistently to employ the local dialect, R, in conversations among themselves. To use the national Standard in in-group interaction is to be judged negatively: 'For a local resident to employ (B) forms with other local residents is in their view to *snakk fint* or to *snakk jalat* 'to put on airs'.' (p. 419). A second group of speakers – generally wealthier, sometimes laying claim to non-local descent – identify with traditional elites; they tend to use the standard language, B, in conversations among themselves, interpolating forms of the regional R variety in telling local anecdotes, gossip, or jokes; for them, R indexes 'lack of education and sophistication' (p. 419). A third group consists of students who have recently attended university in major cities, and who return to Hemnesberget for summer employment or vacation; these individuals identify with local culture and values but also with the pan-Norwegian values associated with the Standard. Speakers of this type tend to switch back and forth between B and R in conversation among themselves, often using R to talk about casual topics (such as their own drinking habits) but switching to B in talk of supra-local topics (such as industrial development, university life) where their identities as intellectuals are more directly at stake. Here various types of 'topic' and 'membership' analyses (Table 2.1) motivate choice of entire speech varieties (and not merely of referring expressions within a speech variety as in the cases discussed before).

In the 'code switching' framework in which they are working, Blom and Gumperz distinguish two types of switching. They use the term 'situational switching' to describe patterns of dialect alternation in the speech of a single individual that correlate with independent contextual differences of what they call the 'social situation' – roughly, the personnel, social setting (locale) and temporal boundary of the event. Thus switches correlating with in-group vs. out-group interlocutors, or home vs. workplace settings are 'situational' shifts. Second, they use the term 'metaphorical switching' for cases where shifts correlate with the 'topics or subject matters' of talk but not to 'social situation' in their sense; thus, in the last example, the difference between talk of drinking vs. talk of industrial development (which occur in the same 'situation') is a metaphoric switch. Situational switching is assumed to be (1) 'a direct relationship' between language and contextual features (such as personnel and setting), and (2) one constrained by 'social norms,' while metaphoric switching is neither.

The decision to restrict the term 'social situation' to the first set of contextual features (and specifically excluding the topic of talk) rests on *the assumption that the 'social' and 'referential' features of talk are somehow orthogonal or independent of each other*; hence the observation that referential topic itself motivates dialect switching becomes an unmotivated residuum of the initial account, an extra something to be explained, to which the name 'metaphoric' switching is given.

Yet as we have seen throughout this chapter, this assumption is false. The referential and the social-interpersonal effects of speech are intimately linked, and in a number of distinct ways. Let me first summarize two issues discussed in the first part of this chapter, before turning to a third type, the form of inter-dependence characteristic of registers.

First, as we saw in our discussion of definite descriptions and location expressions (2.1), denotational choices (viz., the type of expression used to refer to something) are most effective when calibrated to a reading of the semiotic co-text of language use. Here facts of denotational choice mediate thresholds of intersubjective communicative success and failure, as well as forms of interpersonal footing that depend on these in occasion-specific ways. Second, in the case of referential alignments (2.2), acts that semiotically display a stance on a referent are part of an intersubjective series of displays (an 'interaction') in which the metrical congruence or non-congruence of referential stances itself generates contrastive 'positions' on referents, and alignments among interlocutors (Table 2.2); and such sketches of role and relationship can be further filled in by other semiotic accompaniments (Figure 2.3). In both types of cases textual organization links propositional acts to interactional frameworks. But the semiotic devices and patterns that mediate such links may be much harder to discuss out of context than the effects themselves.

In the third type of case (illustrated through the Thai, Tamil and Norwegian examples) denotational variants are linked to *stereotypic* models of personhood. Here denotational footings are mediated by the enregisterment of dialect/sociolect contrasts as indexical of characterolog- ical and social differences. Facts of enregisterment are minimally evident in norms of appropriateness (e.g., norms that require that particular speech forms and personae be performed in 'in-group' settings); and these can be troped upon in ways that make other discursive personae (and dependent 'situations') recognizable through speech. Here the link between denota- tional variants and 'social situations' is itself formulated by a stereotypic model of language use, which has a specific social domain and can be manipulated during usage to yield tropes intelligible to those acquainted with it. The model is not invariant for all members of the language community, of course. The three cases discussed above are described by the authors cited as having different kinds of social domains: the Tamil forms have stereotypic values in relation to a caste boundary (and perhaps a regional boundary as well); the Norwegian contrast is locale-specific, having little reality for persons residing outside Hemnesberget; and the Thai case appears to have a national significance, invested in it by the institutions through which it lives.

In cases of this kind we are dealing with facts of denotational enregister- ment, the social recognition that denotational contrasts entail interactional contrasts, here differences of speaker type; but they are not all registers to the same degree. What is common to the three cases is the connection between denotational units and characterological figures: in the Thai case, morphosyntactic distinctions discriminate 'high' and 'low' personae; in the Tamil case, lexical forms are linked to performable stereotypes of caste; in the Norwegian case, lexical contrasts differentiate the ethic of the 'local team' from the trans-local impersonality of the Standard. But these cases differ in the extent to which the forms having social meanings constitute widespread registers. The Tamil example, which depends on tropes of other- ness, is part of a complex set of caste dialects (there are many other Brahmin and non-Brahmin castes, and caste dialects too) within which the socio- historical snapshot of Iyengar and Mudaliyar practices given above has a local provenance; these tropes can recur at every caste boundary, but cannot involve the same repertoires at different caste boundaries. Only if a locale- specific variety is transformed into a trans-local variety, as in the Thai case, do contrasts involving that variety become widely intelligible.

2.6 Retrospect and prospect

Let me now list four issues that the above discussion brings to the fore- ground, and which later chapters explore in more detail.

First, we have seen that registers are not unitary phenomena; they cannot be conceptualized in an all-or-nothing way. The enregisterment of denotational variation is itself a degree notion. Sets of denotational contrasts in a language can constitute registers of different degrees of complexity. The discussion in the next chapter shows that this notion of 'degree' cannot be conceptualized in a linear way. Register complexity involves different dimensions of register organization, such as the register's social provenance (how many people recognize it), the elaborateness of its repertoires, and the types of sign-values (or stereotypically enactable effects) associated with these repertoires.

A second point concerns the link between the register organization of a language and its grammatical organization. As we begin to explore register phenomena in the next few chapters we'll see that the enregisterment of *denotational* contrasts in language is but a special case. Distinctions of register (and style) are not limited to denotational units. We have merely observed here that they include them. But the fact that they include them has the important consequence that we cannot study the grammatical organization of a language independently of its register organization. Attempts to do so tend to conflate 'grammaticality' with pragmatic infelicity; and, more to the point, tend to obscure the system of social relations embedded in the denotational norms of a language.

A third issue concerns the range of sign-phenomena that can be assimilated to register models. So far most of our detailed discussion has focused on cases where register distinctions are linked to contrasts among lexical forms. (The Thai case involves syntactic patterns too, but we haven't really examined these patterns in any explicit way). In the next chapter we consider in more detail cases where register models are extended to more complex linguistic patterns, and to non-linguistic signs as well.

Finally, from one point of view, register models are ideologically stabilized systems of footing. They are stabilized (or, rather, stabilized-for-a-while) by institutional processes that link figures of personhood and relationship to specific performable signs. And, to the extent that they are stabilized at all, they are stabilized only for a specific social domain of sign-users. The social domain may vary in demographic terms from case to case (a caste group, a town, a nation). The apparent stability of a register formation is experienced by members of its social domain as the fact that comparable stereotypic figures are readable from the performance of its repertoires. And yet register models make intelligible tropic performances of role and relationship too. And unlike the concept of metaphoric switching discussed above, register tropes are not limited to shifts in topics. They permit tropic reformulations of any aspect of the 'social situation' – including tropes of who is talking to whom, what the entailed social setting is, what kind of activity or social practice is now under way – through text-level manipulations of register tokens. These issues are discussed in more detail in the next chapter.

These considerations suggest a comparative framework for studying register formations of many kinds. All register formations are cultural models of action in the sense that they link features of conduct to stereotypically enactable effect. Yet they differ from each other along the dimensions just discussed. Some register contrasts are highly locale specific (functionally effective as contrasts for very few people), while others are widely recognized and widely deployed in performance. Diferent register formations treat *different features of perceivable conduct* as signs of the register; and enregistered signs differ substantially in *the kinds of pragmatic effects* that are enactable through their performance. Several types of register formations that differ in these ways are discussed in the chapters that follow. In Chapters 4 and 5, I discuss systems of enregistered signs that are treated culture-internally as emblems of identity. My focus in Chapter 4 is on the special case of accent as a marker of social identity; in Chapter 5, I generalize this discussion to consider the ways in which any kind of perceivable sign can be linked to evaluations of identity. In Chapters 6, 7 and 8, I consider systems of enregistered signs that are indexical of interpersonal relationships among language users. In cases where the relationship modeled by the register formation is one of deference (Chapters 6 and 7) lexical registers often play a prominent role; yet lexical registers of deference are almost invariably linked to systems of speech style, so-called 'speech level' systems, where larger text-patterns of usage are treated by users as part of the same register formation. In Chapter 8, I consider enregistered models of kinship. Here both lexemes and text-patterns are involved, but the lexemes (kinship terms) need not vary in form or sense across register boundaries. Kinship behaviors are generally linked to enregistered models of action not through lexical register contrasts but through the differential valorization of text-patterns of usage – *who* you use a particular kinterm for, *which* of several possible kinterms you use, *when* a particular usage is appropriate – some among which are treated as norms of kinship behavior. These discursive norms are readily extended to non-linguistic kinship behaviors through the meta-semiotic use of kinterms (i.e., usages that classify non-linguistic behaviors as signs of kinship). And norms of both types can readily be troped upon by persons acquainted with them to yield a wider range of social-interpersonal effects than register stereotypes taken by themselves might imply. The next chapter introduces these basic dimensions of register organization and variation in a systematic way.

3

REGISTER FORMATIONS

3.0 Introduction

The purpose of this chapter is to develop a fuller account of register phenomena and the methods by which they are studied. Some features of register formations were summarized earlier in 1.7 and 2.6. We noted that registers are cultural models of action that link diverse behavioral signs to enactable effects, including images of persona, interpersonal relationship, and type of conduct. The first part of this chapter focuses on registers of discourse. Once we understand the processes through which models of sociability come to be associated with speech the fact that register models readily extend to other types of signs is easily understood. Let us begin, however, with the most obvious way in which facts of register variation are encountered in social life.

Language users often employ labels like 'polite language,' 'informal speech,' 'upper-class speech,' 'women's speech,' 'literary usage,' 'scientific term,' 'religious language,' 'slang,' and others, to describe differences among speech forms. Metalinguistic labels of this kind link speech repertoires to enactable pragmatic effects, including images of the person speaking (woman, upper-class person), the relationship of speaker to interlocutor (formality, politeness), the conduct of social practices (religious, literary, or scientific activity). They hint at the existence of cultural models of speech – a metapragmatic classification of discourse types – linking speech repertoires to typifications of actor, relationship and conduct. This is the space of register variation conceived in intuitive terms.

Writers on language – linguists, anthropologists, literary critics – have long been interested in cultural models of this kind simply because they are of common concern to language users. Speakers of any language can intuitively assign speech differences to a space of classifications of the above kind and, correspondingly, can respond to others' speech in ways sensitive to such distinctions. Competence in such models is an indispensable resource in social interaction. Yet many features of such models – their production and maintenance through social practices, their socially distributed existence, their ideological character, the way in which they motivate tropes of personhood and identity – have tended to puzzle writers on the subject of registers. In this chapter and the next we shall see that a clarification of these issues – indeed the very study of registers – requires attention to **reflexive social processes** whereby such models are formulated and disseminated in social life and become available for use in interaction by individuals. Let me first introduce some of the relevant issues in a preliminary way.

Individuals become acquainted with registers through processes of socialization that continue throughout the life span; hence every member of a language community cannot identify all of its registers with equal ease, let alone use them with equal fluency. Such differences depend on the particular life-course and trajectory of socialization of the individual speaker, e.g., uneducated speakers tend to be unfamiliar with literary registers, older speakers don't know current youth slang, and scientific and technical terminologies often require years of specialized training to master. An individual's **register range** – the variety of registers with which he or she is acquainted – equips a person with portable emblems of identity, sometimes permitting distinctive modes of access to particular zones of social life. In complex societies, where no fluent speaker of the language fully commands more than a few of its registers, the register range of a person may influence the range of social activities in which that person is entitled to participate; in some professions, especially technical professions, a display of register competence is a criterion on employment. Differences of register competence are thus often linked to asymmetries of power, socioeconomic class, position within hierarchies, and the like.

A variety of registers in English and other languages have been studied and documented in recent years. Some of these are known only to specialized communities of speakers; others are more widely known. Some lack official names, others have their own dictionaries. Some are highly valued in society; others, such as varieties of slang, are derogated by prescriptive institutions but positively valued by their users. Some registers are widely recognized as the habits of particular groups. Others, such as Standard English, are promoted by institutions of such widespread hegemony that they are not ordinarily recognized as distinct registers at all. In a common ideological view, Standard English is just 'the language,' the baseline against which all other facts of register differentiation are measured. Yet from the standpoint of usage Standard English is just one register among many, highly appropriate to certain public/official settings, but employed by its speakers in alternation with other varieties – such as registers of business and bureaucracy (Nash 1993), journalism and advertising (Ghadessy 1988), technical and scientific registers (Halliday 1988), varieties of slang (Eble 1996, Gordon 1983), criminal argots (Maurer 1955,

Mehrotra 1977) – which are linked to distinct spheres of social life. As we saw in the last chapter (Figure 2.8ff.), a Standard Language is contextually appropriate only to certain occasions and types of interactions; yet the institutions which maintain its existence link the register to socioeconomic (and other) entitlements, to images of national unity, to ideals of rationality, beauty and other types of social essence, and promote it from early on in the life cycle (e.g., through primary schooling) as a normative criterion for judging all other uses of language. The entitlements and ideals linked to the Standard are often matters of pre-eminent interest to members of society, a feature which tends to naturalize perceptions of the register as a baseline against which other registers appear as deviant, defective varieties of the language.

The above discussion lays out in a rather impressionistic fashion several issues that pertain to the existence and use of registers in social life. Some of the main issues, which are highlighted in the following summary, are discussed in more detail later on in the chapter.

Summary 3.1
Some common characteristics of register phenomena:

(a) No fluent speaker of a language commands more than a few of its registers.
(b) Most speakers can *recognize* more registers than they can *speak*.
(c) An individual's register range permits entry into a range of social practices.
(d) Registers are linked to distinct spheres of activity by judgments of appropriateness.
(e) Some registers are 'more equal' than others. They are institutionally formulated as baseline norms, relative to which other registers appear deviant or defective.

Let me now offer a more precise characterization of registers, beginning with the issues summarized earlier in S 1.7.

3.1 Three aspects of registers

A register formation is a reflexive model of behavior that evaluates a semiotic **repertoire** (or set of repertoires) as appropriate to specific types of conduct (such as the conduct of a given social practice), to classifications of persons whose conduct it is, and, hence, to performable roles (personae, identities) and relationships among them. The repertoires of a register are often linked to systems of speech style, and to non-linguistic accompaniments (such as dress) that constitute larger semiotic styles, including the special case that Weber called a 'style of life.' I return to non-linguistic repertoires and semiotic stylization in 3.9 and 3.10. My main concern now is with the special case of discourse registers.

From the standpoint of language structure, discourse registers differ enormously in the type of repertoire involved, e.g., lexemes, prosody, sentence collocations, and many registers involve repertoires of more than one kind; from the standpoint of function, distinct registers are associated with social practices of every kind, e.g., law, medicine, prayer, science, magic, prophecy, military strategy, commerce, patterns of consumption, the observance of respect and etiquette, the expression of civility, status, ethnicity, gender. Given this range, a repertoire-based view of registers remains incomplete in an essential respect: such a view cannot explain how particular repertoires become differentiable from the rest of the language, or how they come to be associated with social practices at all. These features are identified by appeal to **metapragmatic stereotypes** of speech, i.e., culture-internal models of utterance indexicality associated with speech variants. These models set indexical text-defaults on the construal of utterances for persons acquainted with them.

The **utterance** or use of a register's forms formulates a sketch of the social occasion of language use, indexing stereotypic features such as interlocutors' roles, relationships, and the type of social practice in which they are engaged. If the current scenario of use is already recognizable as an instance of the social practice the utterance appears appropriate to that occasion; conversely, switching to the register may itself reconfigure the sense of occasion, indexically entailing or creating the perception that the social practice is now under way. A register's tokens are never experienced in isolation during discourse; they are encountered under conditions of **textuality** (co-occurrence) with other signs – both linguistic and non-linguistic signs – that form a significant context, or **co-text**, for the construal of the token uttered. The effects of co-occurring signs may be consistent with the text-defaults indexed by the register token, augmenting its force; or, the sign's co-text may yield partially contrary effects, leading to various types of partial cancellation, defeasibility, hybridity or ironic play (see 3.5).

Like other cultural models, registers are **historical formations** caught up in group-relative processes of valorization and countervalorization, exhibiting change in both form and value over time. For instance, when prestige registers used by upper-class/caste speakers are imitated by other groups, the group whose speech is the sought-after variety often innovates in its own speech habits, seeking to renew or transform the emblem of distinction (Honey 1989, Errington 1998). Competing models of register value sometimes exist within societies as well (Hill 1998, Irvine and Gal 2000) and contribute to historical changes in register systems. In any given phase or historical stage of its existence, a register formation involves a **social domain** of persons (e.g., a demographic group) that is acquainted with the model of speech at issue; the boundaries of this social domain may change over time or remain relatively constant, depending on the kinds of institutions that facilitate register competence in society (see 3.3).

Each of the above paragraphs lays out a distinct perspective on register formations that I discuss in more detail below: a **repertoire** perspective, an **utterance** perspective, and a **sociohistorical** perspective. All three are necessary, of course, since registers are repertoires used in utterances by particular sociohistorical populations.

We may think of these 'perspectives' on registers as corresponding to different levels of engagement with registers by users (Figure 3.1). Language users are often able to identify at least some of the repertoires of a register, but this is simply one type of engagement with its forms. In actual events of use, a register's forms are encountered as fragments of utterances and are thus embedded within text-in-context relationships that serve as conditions on event-specific construals. Encounters with utterances are moments within larger sociohistorical processes through which particular forms acquire recognizable values for particular social domains of users and thus become available for effective use in utterances. Forms of participation in such sociohistorical processes (especially matters of socialization, discussed below) themselves constitute a set of conditions on an individual's ability to use and construe a register. In register-mediated encounters with each other, individuals are 'located' with respect to all three levels at once.

The upward arrow in Figure 3.1 indicates that the repertoire fragment of a register is much more easily typified by users than the effects of contextualized utterances, and much more so than the sociohistorical circumstances through which register distinctions emerge and become known to individuals. Even users who can easily identify a register's forms are much less able to characterize the range of effects they can interpret through text-in-context evaluations of utterances. For instance, text-patterns that count as interactional tropes are harder to describe out of context than stereotype-consistent patterns (for reasons discussed in 3.5); common stereotypes associated with any register therefore tend to underspecify the range of effects indexable through its use. Finally, the set of sociohistorical processes through which a register comes to be known to

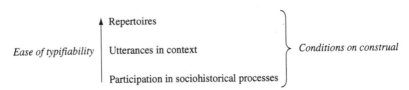

Figure 3.1   *Three levels of engagement with register phenomena*

individuals are the hardest to characterize without systematic study. Anyone can overcome this limitation given sufficient effort; but in practice most users of a register are not able systematically to characterize its socio-historical features.

Thus as we approach the study of registers we find that folk-descriptions of registers tend to distort the social realities lived through them. Indeed, interactants linked to each other through the use of a register may differ among themselves in one or more of these ways – in the repertoires they effectively command, in the extent to which they attend to ongoing text-in-context relationships (their sense of what is being done here-and-now through register use) and in their sociohistorical location with respect to register models (e.g., acceptance of the dominant model, commitment to a scheme of counter-valorization, etc.) – and, thus, may not all be 'co-participants' to the same degree, or experience themselves as participating in the same model of interactional text. These issues become central to the character of registers as ideological formations (3.4).

Let us first consider a more basic question. How are registers identified by linguists?

3.2 Metapragmatic stereotypes

In order to find samples of a register the linguist requires a set of directions for locating instances of language use where tokens of the register occur and a criterion for differentiating these from other types of speech. Here the linguist must turn to the competence of language users. Traditional discussions of registers have long relied on the assumption that language users make 'value judgments' (Halliday 1964) about language form, that they are able to express 'evaluative attitudes towards variant forms' (Ferguson 1994: 18). The linguist's identification of registers depends on the metalinguistic ability of language users to discriminate forms across register boundaries and to assign pragmatic values to variant forms.

The unit data point on which register identification depends is an act of **metapragmatic typification** by a language user, an act that typifies the pragmatics of speech forms. Although such metapragmatic data are necessarily **overt** – in the sense of palpable, perceivable – they may or may not be linguistically expressed; and, if linguistic in character, such behaviors may or may not be denotationally **explicit** with respect to the properties ascribed to the register's forms. In their most explicit form, such evaluations consist of metapragmatic discourses, i.e., accounts which *describe* the pragmatics of speech forms. Several genres of metapragmatic discourse occur naturally in all language communities, e.g., verbal reports and glosses of language use; names for registers and associated speech genres; accounts of typical or exemplary speakers; proscriptions on usage;

standards of appropriate use; positive or negative assessments of the social worth of a register. The explicitness of such data often provides a useful initial picture of register distinctions in a language; but several other types of more implicit data (see below) need to be considered before a fuller picture can emerge. And these implicit data are no less overt in the sense defined above.

The study of such reflexive behaviors allows linguists to distinguish a register's repertoires from the rest of the language and to reconstruct metapragmatic models of speech associated with them by users. We have considered a variety of such reflexive behaviors in Chapter 1 and discussed their characteristics in some detail. Let us now focus on the way in which attention to such behaviors provides data on the identification and study of registers.

Typifications of use

Linguists working in different traditions have tended to rely on a variety of reflexive behaviors in studying register phenomena. A few of the more commonly used varieties are listed in Table 3.1. Since these data are quite diverse in kind, the fact that they comprise an order of reflexive behaviors has not always been properly theorized by those who rely on them. Some

Table 3.1. *Typifications of language use*

1. Everyday reflexive behaviors, such as
   (a) use of register names
   (b) accounts of usage/users
   (c) descriptions of 'appropriate' use
   (d) patterns of 'next turn' response behavior
   (e) patterns of ratified vs. unratified use

2. Judgments elicited through
   (f) interviews
   (g) questionnaires
   (h) 'matched guise' experiments

3. Metadiscursive genres such as
   (i) traditions of lexicography
   (j) grammatology
   (k) canonical texts
   (l) schooling
   (m) popular print genres
   (n) electronic media
   (o) literary representations
   (p) myth
   (q) ritual

traditions are theoretically committed to the use of only one or the other type of data, but, in actual practice, rely on other types as well. It must be understood, however, that *each* of these forms of data offer partial and incomplete understandings of the phenomena they typify; each data point is an instance of reflexive behavior that provides a virtual model of behaviors occurring elsewhere (see 1.6) and thus requires evaluation in relation to other data types before a better understanding of its social significance can emerge. We are only able effectively to rely on one type of data by relying also on other types (a strategy whereby the limitations of each is overcome by resort to others), and by documenting the sociological provenance of each 'data point' as we uncover it (thus socially locating the reflexive behaviors on which we rely). The fact that we rely on multiple types of reflexive behavior as data and attempt to locate each data point sociologically is critical to understanding the ideological character of reflexive behaviors and their organization into widespread social practices.[1]

A common limitation of register names is that they tend to be quantifier-free: if a speech variety is commonly characterized as 'women's speech' the characterization does not reveal whether *all* women use it, or *only* women use it, whether they use it *always*, and so on. Yet because of their deictic non-selectivity register names are readily given a 'nomic' reading by language users (see 1.4 and 1.6), leading to their construal as universal norms (the 'all-only-always' construal), sometimes described as constraints on action, sometimes as facts of exceptionless behavior; these forms of misrecognition are readily reproduced in linguistic studies of register phenomena, particularly if the semiotic characteristics of this data type are not understood. Accounts of other's usage, as in Table 3.1(b), are often permeated by facts of voicing, footing and other alignments between those who give such accounts and those whose behavior they describe; such accounts become usable as data only given an analysis of these features (see Agha 1998a). Accounts of appropriate use, as in (c), are usually statements about standards of behavior, not accounts of the range of behaviors that actually occur; yet an exclusive reliance on such accounts easily confounds the two. In cases (d) and (e), the behaviors that orient us to facts of value implicitly evaluate the indexical effects of co-occurring forms (as 'next turn' responses to them, for example) but do not describe what they evaluate; such data, while invaluable, are therefore unusable without some independent perspective on the pragmatic properties of the forms which occasion the response. Such implicitly reflexive behaviors often include non-linguistic semiotic activity as well, such as gestures, or the extended patterning of kinesic and bodily movements characteristic of ritual responses to the use of many registers. All such behaviors are metalinguistic in nature since they tell us something about the properties of speech forms whether by decontextualizing the forms and describing their properties or by evaluating their effects while the forms are still in play. Such evaluations tell us something, in particular, about the pragmatics of speech, i.e., the capacity of speech forms to index recognizable images of actor, activity, etc., thus belonging to the class of metapragmatic typifications of speech.

The data in (f)–(h) are forms of reflexive data created through direct interventions by the analyst and thus require efforts to minimize the extent to which their character as interventions shapes the results obtained (Briggs 1986). The various types of metadiscursive genres in (i)–(q) are common sources of data on registers, though all of them obviously do not occur in every society; each of them presupposes particular technologies of mass communication in the sense discussed earlier (see Figure 1.6ff) through which typifications of language use (whether explicit or implicit, canonical or playful, prescriptive or extra-normative) are brought to the attention of mass audiences. Data of these kinds become usable in the study of registers only when an analysis of their denotational content is linked to an analysis of their interactional-sociological features (viz., the allocation of authority, circulatory provenance, audience, etc.). These issues are discussed in some detail in the next chapter. It should already be clear however that insofar as such typifications have a mass circulation they play a different kind of role in establishing the register as a social formation, in maintaining or expanding the social domain of its users, and in providing individuals with common intuitions about the significance of usage.

Stereotypes of indexicality

A register is a social regularity: a single individual's metapragmatic activity does not suffice to establish the social existence of a register unless confirmed in some way by the evaluative activities of others. In identifying registers, linguists observe not only that certain kinds of metapragmatic typifications *occur* in the evaluative behavior of language users but that certain patterns of typifications *recur* in the behaviors of many speakers. But in talking of recurrent typifications we have moved beyond individual acts of typification to the order of stereotypes of indexicality. In a manner analogous to the metasemantic stereotypes (or stereotypes of denotation) discussed in 2.3, the metapragmatic stereotypes (or stereotypes of indexicality) discussed here (see also Agha 1998a) constitute reflexive models of interpersonal behavior that set text-defaults on the construal of behavior for persons acquainted with them. But unlike the former, which specify default *characteristics of referent*, stereotypes of indexicality formulate readings of the *social occasion of speaking*. Before we turn to the issue of text-defaults (3.5), two aspects of such stereotypes are worth emphasizing: the *sense* in which they are social regularities, and the fact that they are social regularities *because* they are expressed in publicly perceivable (or 'materially embodied') signs.

To speak of **metapragmatic stereotypes** is to say that social regularities of metapragmatic typification can be observed and documented as data. The simplest kind of social regularity takes the following form: all members of a population sampled typify criterial speech forms in the same way, e.g., assign the same metalinguistic predicates to the forms at issue (viz., 'is slang,' 'is polite,' 'is used by older persons,' etc.); or all treat the use of these forms as appropriate to a given scenario of use. Yet situations where regularities of typification are found to be sociologically symmetric in this way comprise a very special case. In the more general case the scheme of valorization exhibits various forms of **sociological fractionation**, including cases where one group resists the scheme of values upheld by another (counter-valorization), or reanalyzes and thus transforms such values in fashioning norms for itself (see 3.4, 3.8). The assumption that a register's forms and values are modeled symmetrically by all speakers (i.e., are 'uniformly shared') is often a default assumption in many works in the literature. But the extent and degree of sharedness is an empirical issue that requires systematic study in each case. The very possibility of such study lies in the fact that register stereotypes are evidenced in overt (perceivable) metapragmatic activity.

From an empirical standpoint, metapragmatic stereotypes are not ideas in the head. The main evidence for their existence lies in overt (publicly perceivable) behaviors that evaluate the pragmatic properties of linguistic expressions. There is no doubt that such reflexive activity precipitates various kinds of reportable 'beliefs' among individuals; but individuals experience these beliefs with varying degrees of intensity, durational constancy and force over the course of a life span, and have commitments about them that fade in and out of conscious awareness as they move through particular domains of register-mediated activity. Moments of introspectable awareness naturally give rise to the question of sharedness of register models as individuals try to come to grips with their own beliefs vis-à-vis those of others, or with questions of 'what happened' (or, in cases of infelicitous outcomes, 'what the heck happened?') during episodes of register-mediated social interaction. But the orderliness of social life around facts of register use is not in general a 'sharedness' problem. It is a **mutual coordination** problem, a question of how partially overlapping perspectives on a register's forms and values can yield orderly forms of interaction among its users.

The fact that metapragmatic stereotypes are expressible in publicly perceivable signs is not just a matter of convenience to the analyst interested in identifying and studying registers. It is *a necessary condition on the social existence of registers*. Let us consider why this is so.

3.3 Stereotypes and socialization

Since the collection of individuals that we call a society is constantly changing in demographic composition (due to births, deaths and migrations, for example) *the continuous historical existence* of a register depends upon mechanisms for the replication of its forms and values over changing populations (e.g., from generation to generation). The group of 'users' of a register continuously changes and renews itself; hence the differentiable existence of the register, an awareness of its distinctive forms and values, must be communicable to new members of the group in order for the register to persist in some relatively constant way over time.

A minimal condition on such processes is that the typifications of speech through which register values are communicated to others, and hence circulated through society, be embodied in sensorially perceivable signs. Such processes depend upon interaction between people mediated by artifacts made by people – whether directly, as in the case of conversation (here the artifact, or thing made, is an utterance), or more indirectly through the production and use of more perduring artifacts (books, electronic media, other semiotically 'readable' objects) that link persons to each other across large stretches of space and time (Sapir 1949a). In linking persons to each other such semiotic artifacts also link persons to a common set of representations of speech, both explicit and implicit ones, thus making possible the large scale replication of register stereotypes across social populations.

Institutions of replication

To speak of the socialization of individuals to registers and of the replication of registers across populations is to look at the same issue from two different points of view. The latter large scale perspective, focusing as it does on social practices and institutions, helps explain demographic regularities of individual competence. The spread of register competence in society is linked to metalinguistic institutions of diverse types, both formal and informal ones. These differ in the principles of recruitment whereby individuals come to be exposed to the process of socialization and hence, in the regions of social (demographic) space to which individuals competent in the register typically belong.

Prescriptive socialization within the family plays a critical role in the early acquisition of many registers. In the case of honorific registers (see Chapter 7) metapragmatic activity that prescribes appropriate use occurs commonly in most societies (see, e.g., Morford 1997, Smith-Hefner 1988). In the most transparent cases such acts are formulated as denotationally explicit injunctions to child as addressee; but other, more implicitly prescriptive activity – jocular accounts of defective speech (Agha 1998a), the implicit 'modeling' of speech for bystanders (Errington 1998) – occurs as

well. By communicating register distinctions to children such metapragmatic activity expands the social domain of register competence from one
generation to the next within the family unit.

Processes of register socialization continue throughout adult life as well.
One cannot become a doctor or a lawyer, for example, without acquiring
the forms of speech appropriate to the practices of medicine or law, or
without an understanding of the values – both cognitive and interactional
ones – linked to their use. In these cases the process of language socialization typically includes extended affiliation with educational institutions,
such as law school or medical school, through which individuals acquire
the ability to use profession-specific registers of the language. Overt
prescription plays a role in these settings but other types of more implicit
metalinguistic activity occur routinely as well (Mertz 1998). Once acquired,
proficiency in the register functions as a tacit emblem of group membership throughout adult life and, in cases such as law or medicine, is readily
treated as an index of achieved professional identity.

In societies with written scripts and mass literacy a variety of normative
public institutions – such as educational institutions, traditions of lexico-
graphy and grammatology, school boards and national academies – serve
as loci of public sphere legitimation and replication of register stereotypes
over segments of the population. The effect is particularly marked for
prestige registers such as the Standard Language. When effective such
methods may result in the growth or rise of a register formation in society
by extending a more or less uniform competence in a prestige register over
relatively large segments of the population. Yet processes of register
dissemination and replication are inevitably constrained by principles
that limit the participatory access of individuals to criterial institutions
(e.g., mechanisms of gatekeeping in élite schools). Hence, in practice,
register stereotypes and standards are never replicated perfectly over a
population of speakers.

Social asymmetries

All speakers of a language do not acquire competence in all of its registers
during the normal course of language socialization. In the case of registers
of respect and etiquette, only individuals born into privileged circumstances
tend to acquire competence over the most elaborate locutions. In the case
of registers of scientific discourse competence over technical terminologies
typically requires years of specialized schooling. In the case of registers
associated with particular venues of commercial activity (viz., the stock
exchange, the publishing house, the advertising firm) proficiency in specialized terms is usually attained through socialization in the workplace.
In many societies, certain lexical registers function as 'secret languages'

(viz., thieves' argots, the registers of religious ritual, magical incantation, etc.) since their use is restricted to specialized groups by metapragmatic proscriptions against teaching their forms to outsiders.

Thus two members of a language community may both be acquainted with a linguistic register, but not have the same degree of competence in its use. Many speakers can recognize certain registers of their language but cannot fully use or interpret them. The existence of registers therefore results in the creation of social boundaries within society, partitioning off language users into groups distinguished by differential access to particular registers and the social practices they mediate, and by asymmetries of power, privilege, and rank that depend on access to such registers and practices.

3.4 Stereotypes and ideology

I observed earlier that registers often have an ideological – hence 'distorting' – character.[2] How does the 'ideological' aspect of registers relate to the notion of stereotypes of use discussed above?

To say that stereotypes of register form and value exist is merely to say that socially regular patterns of metapragmatic typification can be observed and documented as data. Such models are not false or incorrect in any definitional sense. The question of whether a system of stereotypes is ideological – in the sense of 'distorting' – is empirically undecidable if an order of internally-consistent stereotypes is viewed in isolation from all other observable facts. Yet register systems are typically found to be ideological formations – in several senses – when subjected to further kinds of empirical analysis. Why should this be so?

Let us first approach this issue from the standpoint of the analyst. I observed earlier that the activity of formulating hypotheses about register stereotypes employs diverse kinds of data. *There is no necessity that the results of these data should be wholly consistent with each other for all speakers.* Indeed the logical basis of the claim that some order of stereotypes is ideological is that two (or more) sets of metapragmatic data imply the existence of distinct models.

What about the standpoint of the register's users? I now describe a few social-semiotic processes that commonly give rise to ideological tensions within register formations. I turn to ethnographic examples in sections that follow.

The first type of case involves the ideological character of **competing valorizations**: in so far as register models vary society-internally, particular socially positioned models contrast with each other as alternative systems of normativity. *Each* is ideological from the perspective of *every* other in so far as it gets the (normative) facts incorrect. Why do competing models of normativity co-exist in societies? Two kinds of reasons are very common. The first is merely a result of the asymmetries of replication noted above: individuals differ in their access to institutions through which register competence is reproduced over historical populations (e.g., some are born in élite families, attend élite schools; others lack these opportunities). Another reason is that systems of normative value invariably serve the interests of some speakers, not others; they are therefore subject to manipulation, differential allegiance, and society-internal competition. These factors often play a critical role in the sociohistorical transformation of register systems.

A second ideological aspect of registers derives from the open-ended possibilities of **functional reanalysis**: registers are open cultural systems in the sense that once a distinct register is culturally recognized as existing within a language, its repertoires are susceptible to further reanalysis and change. For example when prestige registers spoken by privileged groups are emulated by others they are often perceived as 'devalued' by speakers of that privileged group; the group frequently innovates in its speech, creating hyperlectal distinctions within prestige forms. In the case of repertoires of youth slang, which change very rapidly, forms that were once 'cool' soon become passé and are replaced by new emblems of in-group identity; in this case, competence over current repertoires is frequently reanalyzed as a system of inter-generational positioning. Every such reanalysis is a distortion of a prior stage of the register that now constitutes a new system of enactable values. Such reanalyses diachronically differentiate distinct group-relative models of a register through time. But any such model can be made to persist in time through a mechanism of institutional stabilization (the family, the peer group, the academy, the mass media, etc.). When the products of such reanalyses come to co-exist synchronically within societies they often contribute to systems of competing valorization – alternative models of normativity – in the sense noted above.

A third reason that stereotypes commonly have an ideological character is that stereotype judgments tend to underdifferentiate the semiotic orders of **lexeme** and **text**. Native judgments about discourse registers are often formulated as models of the pragmatic values of isolable words and expressions (e.g., that some words are inherently polite, some not). Yet since lexemes are never experienced in isolation from other signs in interaction, the effects of co-textual signs may on a given occasion of use either be congruent with or, by degrees, may cancel the stereotypic values of the lexeme, which function, at best, as text-defaults on its construal. Register distinctions can thus be manipulated interactionally to achieve effects which – though dependent on the stereotypic values of particular lexemes – are, at the level of text, significantly at odds with such values. Common examples of this are cases such as the use of female speech by males, the use of honorific language to enact veiled aggression, the use of technical terminologies not to do technical work but to tell jokes about their users. In all of these cases the stereotypic values of a register's lexemes are implemented in discourse – they make certain personae recognizable through speech – but the devices in question are contextualized by other framing devices so that the overall effects of entextualized usage depart significantly from the stereotypic effects of the lexemes troped upon.

I now turn to a range of examples that illustrate the issues discussed above.

3.5 Entextualized tropes

One sense in which registers are ideological constructs is that the range of effects that can be implemented through utterances is always much larger than the range of effects commonly reported in explicit stereotypes of use. The reason is simple. When we speak of the effects of utterances in context we are not speaking only of effects implemented by the register's tokens; we are concerned rather with the effects of an array of co-occurring signs of which the register token is a fragment. This larger – often multi-modal – array of signs itself implements semiotic effects that may or may not be congruent with the stereotypic values of the text fragments that we recognize as the register's forms. Let us consider some examples.

Gender indexicals

In many languages differences of speech are enregistered as indexicals of speaker gender. The actual speech forms that index gender are limitlessly varied across languages; gender diacritics may include prosody, lexical choices, sentence patterns, co-occurrence styles and a variety of other features. Yet the fact that gender repertoires vary enormously from language to language is entirely unsurprising once we see that the unity of a register of speaker gender derives not from aspects of language structure but from a metapragmatic model of language use. And any such model can be troped upon in ways intelligible to those acquainted with it.

Table 3.2 illustrates a phonolexical register of gender indexicals. In the native American language Koasati, a phonolexical alternation between forms of -s and its absence distinguishes stereotypically male and female speech in indicative and imperative forms of the verb. Haas 1964 observes that language users readily formulate metapragmatic accounts linking form contrasts to speaker gender and employ such accounts in socializing children to the register: '... parents were formerly accustomed to correct the speech of children of either sex, since each child was trained to use forms appropriate to his or her sex' (1964: 230). When fully socialized,

Table 3.2. *Phonolexical registers of speaker gender in Koasati*

(a) Repertoire contrasts

Gloss	*A*	*B*	*Phonological alternations*
1. 'I lifted it'	lakawwilí	lakawwilí	–
2. 'you are lifting it'	lakáwč	lakáwč	–
3. 'he will lift it'	lakawwā̱ˑ	lakawwáˑs	-ā̱ˑ ∼ -áˑs
4. 'I am lifting it'	lakawwî̱l	lakawwís	-î̱l ∼ -ís
5. 'don't lift it'	lakawčî̱n	lakawčîˑs	-î̱n ∼ -îˑs
6. 'he is lifting it'	lakáw	lakáws	-áw ∼ -áws

(b) metapragmatic stereotypes:

          ↓   ↓

      'female' 'male'

Source: (Haas 1964)

Table 3.3. *Lexical registers of speaker gender in Lakhota*

(a) Repertoire contrasts

Illocutionary force	*A*	*B*
Formal questions	hu̱we	hu̱wo
Command	ye	yo
Familiar command	nitʰo	yetʰo
Opinion/emphasis	yele, ye	yelo
Emphatic statement	kʃto	kʃt
Entreaty	na	ye
Surprise/opinion	yema̱	yewa̱

(b) metapragmatic stereotypes:

          ↓   ↓

      'female' 'male'

Source: (Trechter 1995)

however, adults are entirely aware that the register comprises a model of performable persona, one that can be manipulated in various ways: 'Members of each sex are quite familiar with both types of speech and can use either as occasion demands.' I return to this point below.

Table 3.3 illustrates a register of gender indexicals in Lakhota whose formal repertoires are rather different. In this case the metapragmatic typifications offered by native speakers are highly comparable to the Koasati case (viz., 'male' vs. 'female' speech); but the **object repertoires** of the register (the forms that are objects of native typification) involve contrasts of sentence-final clitics rather than contrasts of verb stem.

In both cases – indeed, in all cases of the enregisterment of gender – the unity of the phenomenon derives not from features of grammatical structure but from a model of expected or appropriate conduct; and, in all cases, actual behavior may or may not conform to the model. But how is behavior that is contrary-to-stereotype construed by interlocutors?

Whereas folk-models of language use often misrecognize social indexical effects as 'coding' relationships between pieces of utterance and its 'external' (non-semiotic) context, actual uses of a register's tokens are invariably construed by criteria of congruence among co-occurring signs, usually within a multi-channel order of entextualization. Contrary-to-stereotype effects are cases where co-occurring signs partially modify the stereotypic effects of the register token, thus formulating a non-default construal *for the overall text configuration*. Such cases need not be construed as tropes. The most straightforward cases of men uttering women's speech (or vice versa) occur when the register's use is framed co-textually by a reported speech construction. 'Thus if a man is telling a tale he will use women's forms when quoting a female character; similarly, if a woman is telling a tale she will use men's forms when quoting a male character' (Haas 1964: 229–230). In such cases the reported speech construction explicitly differentiates the utterer from the character reported (denotes a principal distinct from animator), thus allowing men to utter women's speech, and vice versa, without taking on the characterological attributes of the other gender.

In other cases, wholly implicit framing by co-textual signs gives contrary-to-stereotype behavior a tropic significance; here *the non-congruence of co-textual frame and register token* implies a metaphoric persona for the one uttering that token. In the Lakhota example in Figure 3.2, a form-token of the female register is uttered by a man who unexpectedly sees his two-year old nephew at his house one evening. The man turns to the boy and says 'Look who's come!'. His use of female speech enacts a trope of affective, maternal concern.

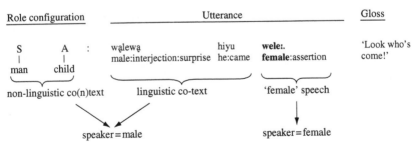

Figure 3.2 *Gender tropes in Lakhota*
(Source: Trechter 1995: 10)

The linguistic utterance is reproduced in the middle column; notice that the man uses male speech in the initial exclamation of surprise but switches to female speech in the segment in which he calls out to the child. The role configuration shown on the left is construable from the co(n)text of utterance, from the visible semiotic surround which clarifies that the person speaking is a man, and the person spoken to, a child. Both the non-linguistic co(n)text and the first part of the utterance form a *multi-channel co-text* for the occurrence of the female form, *wele:*, and the indexical effects of co-text and register token are non-congruent as the arrows show.

The man's use of female speech is tantamount to an interactional trope, the performance of an affective, caring persona often associated with women speaking to young children. But the trope of maternal concern is only recoverable by someone who attends to the multi-channel sign configuration of which the token of female speech is a fragment; the effect vanishes if the register token is decontextualized from the co-textual frame that motivates the construal.

Consider now the following contrast: the enregistered persona associated with the form *wele:* (namely that *speaker is female*) is highly detachable from context, and reportable by any native speaker acquainted with the female register; it is a common, easily reportable stereotype about the form. But the trope of identity (that *speaker is a maternal, affective man*) is contrastively recoverable only by someone who has access to the larger entextualized structure (viz., that the one speaking is a man, that he is speaking to a two-year old, that the child has turned up unexpectedly, that the man has uttered a female form), all of which, as an entire text configuration, motivates the 'maternal, affective' construal. Whereas the stereotypic effect of *wele:* can be discussed by reproducing the lexical form, subsequent discussions of the tropic effect require that the teller reproduce criterial features of the lexeme-plus-text configuration that jointly motivate the trope.

Text-level indexicality is no less important in the case of appropriate or stereotype-congruent usage. The judgment that some usage is **appropriate to context** is never a judgment about an individual form-token; it is a name for a token-to-text relationship. Indeed, in the absence of an evaluation that links a register token to surrounding, entextualized semiotic effects – e.g., without evaluating whether the one using the male forms is everywhere, in every co-textual semiotic respect, a 'man' – we can never evaluate the usage as *appropriate* in any meaningful sense of the term.

Acts of register use superimpose a sketch of context upon a sketch already given. No token use is fully construable without attention to the context semiotically given independently of its occurrence. We call a register's usage 'appropriate to context' when co-textual signs are congruent with, or satisfy, the model of context indexed by the register token; but various types and degrees of non-congruent usage are always possible as well, some of which effectively yield tropes in context. The main issues pertaining to this type of usage may be summarized as follows:

Summary 3.2
Tropes of contrary-to-stereotype usage are effects of text configurations that

(a) are only construable by those acquainted with the stereotypic effects of the form troped upon
(b) depend upon a partial cancellation of the form's stereotypic effects by features of co-text
(c) are harder to discuss out of context than stereotype-congruent effects

Although construals of tropic and appropriate uses both depend on text-in-context evaluations in the instance, subsequent (decontextualized) discussions of tropes tend to require more complex types of explicit metasemiotic work, e.g., reproducing features of co-text that motivate the trope. It is therefore unsurprising that widespread stereotypes of register use tend systematically to simplify the range of effects performable through acts of usage.

Professional registers

Many register contrasts are stereotypically associated with forms of professional conduct, such as the law, medicine, and so on. Although the official rationale for the use of the register may have little to do with the performance of particular roles and relationships, the mere fact of register differentiation in language – that distinct registers are associated with distinct practices – generates paradigms of social identity linked to speech forms. Hence for audiences familiar with the register a competent display of its forms makes palpable a recognizable persona of speaker and a typifiable mode of interpersonal engagement with interlocutors.

A classic early study of such a case is Ferguson's 1983 account of 'Sports announcer talk,' a variety of speech used by sportscasters in radio and television broadcasts. The commercially routinized use of the variety involves a particular kind of electronically mediated setting in which the sportscaster has direct visual access to a sporting event, which unfolds concurrently with the broadcast, and the audience is a large, spatially distributed collectivity that may number in the millions. The dissemination of sports talk through the electronic media is a form of institutional replication that can expand awareness of the register as well. An avid sports fan has more than a passing acquaintance with this variety of talk. Moreover, anyone who is acquainted with the register – not necessarily a

Table 3.4. *Some features of 'Sports announcer talk'*

(a) Omission of sentence-initial deictics (e.g., anaphors, determiners) and present-tense copula: e.g., *[It's a] pitch to uh Winfield. [It's a] strike. [It's] one and one*
(b) Preposed location and motion predicates: e.g., <u>Over</u> *at* <u>third</u> *is Murphy.* <u>Coming</u> <u>left</u> <u>again</u> *is Diamond*
(c) Preponderance of result expressions   e.g., *He throws <u>for</u> the out.*
(d) Epithets and heavy modifiers: e.g., <u>left-handed</u> <u>throwing</u> *Steve Howe . . .; Larry Milburn, <u>3 for 4</u> <u>yesterday</u>, did not face . . .*
(e) Use of the simple present to describe contemporaneous activities   e.g., *Burt ready,* <u>comes</u> *to Winfield and it'<u>s</u> lined to left but Baker'<u>s</u> there and <u>backhands</u> a sinker then <u>throws</u> it to Lopez*

Source: (Ferguson 1983)

sportscaster – can employ it in acts that strategically manipulate roles and identities otherwise indexed as text-defaults through its use.

The following illustrates the use of the register by two young boys who employ sports announcer talk as a way of re-framing their own game playing activities. During the course of games like ping-pong and basketball the boys switch to the register of sports announcer talk in a spontaneous manner. In the excerpt in (1), the two boys, Ben and Josh, indexically depersonalize their current play activity by using last names in describing each other's actions; they also employ many of the devices noted in Table 3.4 to inhabit the persona and mantle of a sports announcer. In this turn-by-turn engagement the players use the register competitively, as part of 'the game.'

(1) Tropes of sports announcer speech (Source: Hoyle 1993)
     Context: The participants are two boys (an 8- and a 9-year old), who use sports announcer register to describe a game of ping-pong as they play it
     Josh: So eleven eight, Hoyle's lead.
               Hoyle serves it!
               Ben Green cannot get it . . . over the net
               and it's twelve eight Hoyle's lead now.
     Ben: Hoyle takes the lead by four.
     Josh: [fast] Green serving.
               [fast] Hoyle returns it.
               THEY'RE HITTING IT BACK AND FORTH!
     Ben: Ach-boo:m!
     Josh: And Ben Green hits it over the table!
               And it i:s thirteen eight.
               Hoyle's lead.

In stretches of talk where the sports announcer register is used there is clearly a second-order game going on – quite distinct from the ping-pong itself – a game which is played entirely through talk, and whose object is to control representations of the first-order game in a persona more authoritative than the boys' own. When problems arise within the ping-pong game itself (e.g., scorekeeping disputes, arguments about the rules, external events that interfere with the game) the boys switch back to everyday speech, thus abandoning the sportscaster persona in favor of the now more pressing concerns of the first-order game (see Hoyle 1993 for further details). Hence the switching back-and-forth between sportscasting and everyday registers corresponds to a switching between imaginary and real identities keyed to specific interpersonal ends within this complex bout of 'play.'

More generally, differential register use is indexically linked during interaction to ongoing activity frames and identities maintained through that use. Since individuals differ in their register range, they differ in their ability to inhabit distinct register-mediated **social personae** in encounters with others, or to perform different **voices** (Bakhtin 1984) or characterological **figures** (see S 3.3 below) as features of self through acts of performance.[3] Interlocutors respond to such personae, voices or figures in ways that depend on their own register range. Taken together, patterns of utterance and response constitute relationships of footing or role alignment at the level of interactional text. In the above example the pattern is agonistic; it comprises a form of interpersonal competition. I discuss other cases and offer a more general discussion in 3.8 below.

3.6 Fragmentary circulation

The young boys who employ the register of sports announcer talk in the above example do not do so consistently or with a full command of its niceties. Indeed the fragmentary nature of their usage – including switching back and forth between everyday and sportscasting registers – constitutes the particular kind of multi-leveled play in which these two individuals are engaged. Yet when registers are used in a fragmentary way in public sphere discourses such usage can have broader sociological consequences too.

When a register that is regularly employed in one social practice is deployed in a partial or fragmentary way in another such a usage may confer some legitimacy – a peppering of prestige – upon its speaker/author, particularly when the target audience is unfamiliar with authentic uses of the source register. The use of statistics by insurance salesmen, or of terms from psychology in popular 'self help' books has something of this character. But such fragmentary use may also have consequences for the competence of the hearer or reader. Thus watching courtroom dramas or war

Table 3.5. *American military register*

Pentagon lexicon ('Militarese')	Standard English
aerodynamic personnel decelerator	parachute
frame-supported tension structure	tent
personal preservation flotation device	life jacket
interlocking slide fastener	zipper
wood interdental stimulator	toothpick
vertically deployed anti-personnel device	bomb
portable handheld communications inscriber	pencil
pre-dawn vertical insertion	a night-time parachute drop
manually powered fastener-driving impact device	hammer

Source: (Lutz 1990)

movies on television does equip the audience with a smattering of legal and military terminology – enough perhaps to recognize some terms and expressions, to engage in language play and jokes – though not usually enough to write a legal brief or, thankfully, to mount a military campaign.

Systematic access to register distinctions requires more careful methods. The data of military terminology in Table 3.5 were gathered through a study of military documents by Lutz 1990. How was the analyst able to find the corpus? By employing native metapragmatic classifications, including terms for speech varieties and their users, as a set of directions for finding published samples of military discourse – Pentagon manuals, defense department contracts, course catalogs at military academies, and others – where elaborate uses of this written register occur. For most English speakers only a fragmentary exposure occurs – mostly through forms of popular media, fiction, and the like – that may acquaint ordinary speakers with the existence of the register, and even a passing familiarity with some of its forms, viz., *surgical strike* and *collateral damage* are now widely known, especially given media coverage of recent wars. Yet most of the forms in Table 3.5 are unfamiliar and perhaps ludicrous to the Standard ear.

Considerations of communicative transmission allow us to link types of exposure to types of competence and to frameworks of value maintenance. Consider the distinction between the competence to speak (or write) and the competence to recognize a register's forms introduced earlier. I noted in S 3.1 that no speaker of a language fully commands more than a few of its registers; thresholds of fluency depend on trajectories of extended socialization mediated by access to criterial institutions as discussed in section 3.3. I also noted that most speakers of a language can passively recognize many more registers than they fluently speak, e.g., are aware of their existence, can identify selected forms and dependent personae, but do not effectively command them in their own speech. The ability to recognize a wider range of registers than one speaks is commonly acquired through these more fragmentary, less extended forms of exposure.

Micro-sociological facts about individual competence of this kind – such as asymmetries between types of competence in a register – can serve to maintain macro-sociological schemes of register valorization under certain conditions. To understand this effect we have to shift our perspective from an individual-centric to a register-centric view on facts of competence. Thus for most register formations, the competence to recognize the register's forms has a wider social distribution (i.e., is an ability possessed by many more persons) than the competence to use its forms. In the case of prestige registers (e.g., forms of upper class speech), forms of the register are widely recognized, and associated with prestige, even by persons who do not fluently speak them. The fact that the register is positively valued by a group larger than its fluent speakers readily creates conditions where the register, now a scarce good, becomes a sought after commodity – even one that can be purchased for a price, through schooling, elocution lessons and the like – and thus create a trend that maintains the value of the register for a time. These effects are easily misrecognized as involving macro-social 'market' principles (Bourdieu 1991); yet they are contingent upon micro-sociological facts of footing and role alignment through which 'market' values are maintained and undergo change. These issues are discussed in more detail in the next chapter.

3.7 Reflexive social processes and register models

In a review of the early literature on registers Douglas Biber observes that 'most register studies have been atheoretical' (1994:36), tending to employ static taxonomic and descriptive schemes rather than principled definitions. Recent work has focused more on reflexive semiotic process and institutions through which register distinctions are effectively maintained and transformed in social life. Let me now comment on the way in which the reflexive approach to registers presented here improves upon and moves beyond the limitations of earlier, more static approaches.

Static vs. dynamic models

The term 'register' was first coined by T. B. W. Reid in the course of a discussion of functionally significant differences in language use. Reid proposed that differences of utterance-form involve differences of 'register' whenever distinct forms are viewed as appropriate to 'different social situations' by users (Reid 1956). Although the intention behind the definition was to illuminate forms of action – e.g., Reid speaks of 'systems of linguistic activity' as his larger space of concern – Reid's formulation remained incomplete in several respects: It lacked a theory of how speech was linked to 'social situations' in the first place, how such links were identified by the analyst, and how register use could meaningfully extend beyond the special case of 'appropriate use.' I have observed above that the link between speech and situation involves a metapragmatic model of action (3.1); that its recovery by analysts is based on the study of socially situated reflexive data (3.2); and that the significance of utterances is inevitably a matter of patterns of entextualization, some among which trope upon the model itself (3.5).

Other difficulties with earlier views – particularly anxieties about 'the discreteness of registers and the validity of register boundaries' (Ferguson 1982:55) – derive from Reid's choice of terminology itself. The term *register* is a pluralizable count noun of English that formulates a suggestion about the social phenomenon that it denotes – a default Whorfian projection, or implication about denotatum (see Silverstein 1979, Lee 1997) – that is fraught with difficulties: the pluralizability of the term implies that *register-s* are collections of objects – like *button-s* and *pebble-s* – that can be identified and enumerated in an unproblematic way. Yet unlike collections of pebbles the registers of a language have a differentiable existence only insofar as – and as long as – they are treated by language users as functionally recognized partitions within the total inventory of its expressive means. The countable-and-pluralizable view of registers has other misleading implications, viz., that each register is a closed set of forms, that each member of the set is endowed with 'inherent' pragmatic values, and so on.

Now every register does involve a repertoire of forms. But the boundaries of the register depend on the social-semiotic processes described earlier (see 3.3 et passim). A register exists as a bounded object only to a degree set by sociohistorical processes of enregisterment, processes whereby its forms and values become differentiable from the rest of the language (i.e., recognizable as distinct, linked to typifiable social personae or practices) for a given population of speakers. From the processual perspective sketched above it should be clear that worries about the discreteness of register boundaries are fruitless and misplaced since there exist in every society social-semiotic processes through which various kinds of boundaries and limits associated with registers can be reset in regular ways. Relative to such processes, every register exhibits various kinds of growth and decline, expansion or narrowing, change or stabilization. Three dimensions of register change are particularly noteworthy, as indicated in Table 3.6.

The repertoire characteristics of a register, dimension A, include features such as the repertoire size, grammatical range, and semiotic range of the register. As registers become centered in formal metadiscursive

Table 3.6. *Some dimensions of register organization and change*

A. **Repertoire characteristics**
   - *Repertoire size*: number of forms
   - *Grammatical range*: number of form-classes in which forms occur
   - *Semiotic range*: variety of linguistic & non-linguistic signs associated with use
B. **Social range** of enactable (pragmatic) values
   - *Indexical focus*: Stereotypes of speaker-actor, relation to interlocutor, occasion of use, etc.
   - *Images* (or icons) stereotypically attached to indexical sign-forms: for speaker-focal indexicals, persona types (male/female, upper/lower class, etc.); for interlocutor-focal indexicals, types of relationship (deference, intimacy, etc.)
   - Positive or negative values associated with the register
C. **Social domain(s)**: Categories of persons acquainted with the register formation
   - *Domain of recognition*: persons who recognize the register's forms
   - *Domain of fluency*: persons fully competent in the register's use

institutions – such as national academies, schooling, traditions of lexico-graphy, the work of corporations – the repertoires of the register may grow over time, such elaboration resulting in part from processes of institutional codification.

Changes in pragmatic value, dimension B, are cases where the stereo-typic effects of usage undergo a degree of functional reanalysis and change. When Standard Languages arises out of regional dialects – such as Parisian French or London English, to take familiar European cases – the derived national Standard no longer effectively marks speaker's locale but comes to index the non-specificity of speaker's place of origin. In most societies, and for the majority of speakers, regional dialects are acquired first through socialization in the family and the national Standard acquired later through formal institutions such as schooling. Hence competence in the Standard language commonly becomes emblematic of additional attributes, such as speaker's class or level of education; such attributes sometimes function as status entitlements – facilitating access, for exam-ple, to select social circles, higher-wage employment, upper echelons of government service, and other privileges (see Honey 1989a) – that are less accessible to those speaking non-Standard varieties of the language.

These changes are often linked to changes in the social domain(s) of the register, namely dimension C in Table 3.6. Facts of collective awareness and competence in a register are mediated by large scale communicative processes (section 1.7) that influence a register's demographic expansion or decline; these vary enormously for different types of registers. A few examples may be cited to illustrate the larger point. Formal institutions often play an official role in expanding fluency in prestige registers of a language – through programs that expand literacy, primary education, or specialized training for particular professions. But other more informal and seemingly disinterested types of institutional mechanisms expand register awareness as well. Specific genres of public media (including entertainment genres) serve as carriers for many kinds of popular registers, serving to expand at least a passing acquaintance with its forms over larger populations. In the case of Anglo-American teenage slang, genres such as pop music, the movies, teen lifestyle magazines and the like have, since the 1950s, made possible the creation of national teenage slangs which have forms that are common to youth populations in many different geographic locales (Hudson 1983).

Thus although dimensions such as A.-C. can in principle be characterized for any register, any such account is merely a sociohistorical snapshot of a phase of enregisterment for particular users. Changes along these dimensions are typically linked to one another. Indeed, as the social domain of a register (C) changes – e.g., as in the social expansion of scientific registers of chemistry or medicine in recent times, or through the disappearance of once firmly institutionalized form of discourse, such as alchemy – both the repertoires and the stereotypic effects of their use are inevitably transformed.

Reanalysis and regrouping

The fact that these dimensions of register organization are inter-linked has a number of consequences for the study of registers in social life. Let me introduce the main issues here before turning to examples in the next section.

The first issue concerns the group-relative existence of a register: registers are only identifiable as having determinate forms and values *for a social domain of evaluators.* Since registers are identified by appeal to reflexive evaluations of speech, the social category of evaluator is always part of the same observation through which forms and values are identified. Claims about a register's social domain are empirical hypotheses that may be formulated more or less precisely depending on the kinds of methods used; and further observations may reveal the limitations of an earlier picture, as in any empirical study. Yet it must be understood that the social domain of a register at a given time is a reflexively shaped, historical object. Indeed, insofar as evaluators themselves perceive schemes of valorization in group-relative terms, such perceptions may transform the characteristics of the social domain over time – at rates varying inversely with the register's institutional entrenchment and inertia – leading to further group-differentiation.

A second issue concerns the way in which the pragmatic values associated with a register's forms (dimension B in Table 3.6) can themselves be transformed through reanalysis across distinct **orders of indexicality** (Silverstein 1996a). We noted earlier that register models pervasively link contrasts among speech forms to differential judgments of appropriate use. A schema of appropriate use (an 'n[th]' order indexical value) can be re-motivated with respect to further contextual variables (such as *who* treats it as appropriate, *when* it is appropriate, etc.) to yield a contrastive schema of value (an 'n + 1th' order value) to which interlocutors attend, or upon which they take a stand; and the latter indexical value – which may be linked to the same sign-form, but, more typically, is linked to a form-configuration that overlaps with the first – is performatively expressible in the same semiotic act in which the former is expressed; see Figure 3.3ff. for an example. The discussion in the next section also shows that these distinct value schemes *may or may not have the same social domain*, i.e., may or may not be evidenced in the evaluative behaviors of the same persons.

A third issue concerns the **fractal recursivity** of registers (Irvine and Gal 2000), a phenomenon that results from the recursive iteration of reflexive processes. Once we regard register formations as precipitates of reflexive semiotic processes, it becomes evident that the production of register models can proceed through iteration – e.g., through successive reflexive 'takes' on an nth model that yield an n + 1th model in each moment of reanalysis – potentially without limit. Registers are open cultural systems in this sense, awareness of whose existence can yield new forms of interpersonal expression and social being.

A dynamic conception of register formations entails a dynamic conception of social groups (5.6). Yet the effectiveness of any such reanalysis is constrained by its intelligibility; and its social consequences depend on its scale. An individual can trope upon a register formation in any way he or she pleases. But its interpersonal effects depend on matters of uptake and response. And its most *widespread* social consequences depend on how such up-'takes' are incorporated into institutions that reproduce the register.

Before we turn to a fuller consideration of these issues it is important to see that matters of stability or change are never questions of form-value relationships at a single level. Let us consider this issue in the light of some examples, and then return to questions of innovation and change.

3.8 Sociological fractionation and footing

The above considerations should make clear that registers are social formations, but not necessarily *sociologically homogenous* formations. To say that they are social formations is to observe that those metapragmatic stereotypes of speech and other signs that are criterial in the identification of registers *have a social domain*, i.e., are evidenced in the behavior of a population of evaluators. Most register stereotypes do not have a maximal distribution (e.g, are not invariant for *all* speakers of a language); yet a population over which an $n + 1^{th}$ order stereotype *diverges* is frequently found to comprise a *unified* social domain with respect to an nth order value. I have already argued that competing models of features of a register commonly co-exist within the same society, each potentially ideological or distorting from the perspective of the other. It remains to be seen that such models are intelligible as variants only insofar as they are fractionally congruent: they are recognizable as competing schemes of valorization by virtue of the fact that they presuppose underlying commonalities.

Becoming someone else: what's different?

A simple case of this type occurs when distinct stereotypes are associated with a form's usage in distinct sub-domains of a language community. For instance, in the case of honorific registers, it is commonly observed that two speakers will identify the same form as honorific but will specify different conditions on its appropriate use. Now, both kind of evaluations – that a form 'is honorific' and that it 'is appropriately used under such-and-such conditions' – are metapragmatic typifications of the form's pragmatic values. The point at issue now is that both may be socially regular – may function as stereotypes – but for *different* social domains of evaluators.

Morford's (1997) study of Parisian French provides an example. In Morford's data, speakers of French readily agree that the pronoun *vous* is polite in pragmatic effect (and that *tu* is not specifically polite); this, then, is a metapragmatic stereotype about the lexeme, *vous*, one having a society-wide social domain. The persons who assent to the lexeme stereotype can be divided into sub-groups with respect to differing standards of appropriate use. Morford shows that a particular pattern of *vous* usage – 'having your children say *vous* to you' – is held to be unacceptable by lower-class speakers; it is described as snobbish, a way of putting on airs. In contrast, traditional upper-class speakers view this pattern as indexical of the family's distinctive class position.

In this case stereotypes of lexeme value are the same for the two groups: both agree that *vous* is a polite lexeme. But stereotypes of appropriate use by children diverge by social class; these differences are reanalyzed as emblems of contrastive family status. Figure 3.3 shows that the object of *differential* evaluation is not the lexeme *vous* but the more complex semiotic array above the bracket – the utterance of *vous* in a particular role configuration – of which the lexeme is a fragment.

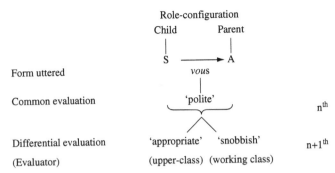

Figure 3.3 *Register-mediated alignments: reanalysis and self-differentiation* (Source: Morford 1997)

Awareness of these facts can lead to strategic tropes of identity management on the part of persons who *otherwise* self-identify with one group or the other. Thus Morford reports the case of an upper-class individual who, when seeking to enter politics, asks his children to switch from *vous* to *tu* in addressing him in public; the goal here is strategic, an effort to perform a more demotic image of his own class origins in the electoral process. Just as the class-emblematic stereotypes shown in Figure 3.3 (namely that a child's use of *vous* for parents is appropriate only for upper-class speakers) presuppose the lower-order stereotype (that *vous* is a polite lexeme), the politician's strategy indexically presupposes awareness of the higher-order class emblem, which it now seeks to manipulate. Notice also that in choosing this as an electoral strategy, the upper-class politician seeks a particular form of role-alignment in his public sphere image, i.e., invites a degree of identification by *working-class* voters.

A parallel case – now involving age and generation, rather than class – is reported in Swedish by Paulston 1976. In the period in which the study was conducted (ca. 1970), the use of the polite pronoun *ni* was already undergoing reanalysis and replacement by the use of informal *du* in most social situations. In address among strangers, the use of *ni* still remained the norm for older, upper-class speakers; the use of *du* for strangers was expanding, but associated largely with younger speakers. Awareness of the stereotype allowed a range of interactional tropes, such as the following: 'Even some 70-year-old-upper-class ladies find it agreeable to be addressed as *du* in the street; they say it makes them feel younger' (1976: 367). The capacity of the usage to make someone 'feel younger' is a direct consequence of the existence of a culture-internal stereotype associating a pattern of usage (*du*-for-strangers) with young people; note that by 'pattern of usage' we here mean, again, a lexeme-in-a-role-configuration.

The stereotype provides a framework for evaluating the unexpected usage and yields the trope of perceived identity as a performed effect.

Both the tropes discussed above involve cases where a stereotypic indexical value is assigned to a lexeme-in-a-role-configuration, viz., that *vous*-for-parents is upper-class, that *du*-for-strangers indexes youth. In both cases, the association of specific characterological figures with patterns of usage also makes possible the inhabitance of tropic identities through acts that manipulate the pattern. But the cases we have so far considered are occasional and event-specific; they involve observations about single individuals. Let us now consider cases where role alignments involve regularities of group behavior. In both cases discussed below attempts to 'borrow' lexemes are attempts to inhabit role-configurations (speaker types) indexically associated with the lexeme.

Owning and belonging to identities

The manner in which social personae become linked to the forms of a register frequently reveals something of the larger social processes that connect groups to each other. Register models that hold for particular users in one locale may become objects of scrutiny and response by users in another locale if the two are linked to each other through a social-communicative process. When different segments of a population have different interests or stakes in the values linked to a speech repertoire, the transformation of its values reflects (and, if effective, promotes) such positional stakes.

The case of pronominal registers in Egyptian Arabic (Alrabaa 1985) is particularly interesting from this point of view (Table 3.7). Alrabaa's study is a questionnaire-based investigation of metapragmatic stereotypes of use associated with pronominal contrasts. At the level of stereotypes of speaker persona, upper-class and lower-class youths offer different models of usage that are, moreover, mirror images of each other. Upper-class youths

Table 3.7. *Mirror-image alignments in Egyptian Arabic: a case of inverse iconism*

	Group₁: Upper-class youths	**Group₂**: Lower-class youths
Stereotype of self-report	claim to use solidary *inta/ inti* forms	claim greater use of the formal *haḍritak/haḍritik* pronouns
Stereotype of others' usage	say that lower class speakers use the *inta/inti* forms	say that upper/middle class speakers use the *haḍritak/haḍritik* forms
Ideological positioning	egalitarian (self-lowering)	stratificational (self-raising)

Source: (Alrabaa 1985)

claim to use the solidary-informal forms *inta/inti* 'you (m./f.),' which they believe lower-class speakers to use; and lower-class speakers lay claim to the more polite-formal lexemes *ḥaḍritak/ḥaḍritik* 'you (m./f.); polite,' which they perceive as upper/middle class usage. Thus a comparison of stereotypes of self and other usage reveals that each social group ideologically formulates a self-positioning modeled on perceptions of the other.

The likening of one's own speech to another's is a commonplace type of reported iconism; it is commonly observed for *some* category of persons in almost every society. What is interesting here however is that these two social groups appear to exhibit **inverse icons** of each other's perceived usage in claiming forms as their own. In interviews, upper-class youth describe themselves as adopting what they perceive to be 'the system of "the people" (*al-sha'b*),' thus professing an egalitarian impulse, while lower-class youth are drawn toward 'what they presume to be the middle-class values' (Alrabaa 1985: 649), thus exhibiting a more stratificational ideology. Each group ideologically professes an alignment to characterological images of the other, the two together exhibiting an ironic form of role reversal.

These aspirations to persona and personhood appear to be responses to a larger sociocultural process consisting of the circulation of metapragmatic representations of persons and identities in genres of public sphere discourse. For example, upper-class youth get their images of lower class speech through the mass media:

(2) In off-the-record comments during our interviews, both older and younger upper-class informants did often express a conviction that lower-class informants would be 'looser,' less formal, etc. This upper-class belief is also reflected in many movies and television comedies, which frequently present a stereotype of the bawdy, raucous lower-class character who addresses all listeners as *inta/inti* = [German] *Du*, [French] *tu*.

(p. 648).

Notice, however, that not everyone aware of the lower-class stereotype claims it as a model; socioeconomic class is not the only factor relevant here. For, among upper-class speakers, both older and younger informants are aware of stereotypes of lower-class speech, but only *younger* upper-class informants align their own self-images with lower-class stereotypes in the mid-1980s milieu on which Alrabaa is reporting. For them, the ideological stance is one of egalitarianism vis-à-vis those perceived as lower-class; yet the stance of these younger speakers is also one of generational differentiation within the ranks of the upper-class itself, i.e., younger vs. older. The two stances are mutually consistent here, i.e., are empirically inhabitable through a single strategy, though the egalitarian impulse is the more widely reported by upper-class youth in their interview responses. Such multiplicity of role alignment reflects the multiplicity of engagements with real or imagined others that is characteristic of social life, a point to which I return below.

Table 3.8. *Reanalysis in stereotypic values of second person polite
pronouns (Javanese)*

	ca. 1920	ca. 1960	ca. 1980
Élite	sampéyan	panjenengan	panjenengan
Villager	ndiká	sampéyan	sampéyan/panjenengan

Source: (Errington 1998, Table 3.2)

Consider by way of contrast the rather distinct pattern of revalorization illustrated for Javanese pronouns in Table 3.8. All the forms listed in the table were 'polite' pronouns for certain groups at certain times. The pattern of their revalorization reflects inter-group alignments of two broad kinds, patterns of other-appropriation by villagers (positive alignment), and self-differentiation by élites (negative alignment); and these patterns are iterated over time. Errington observes that in the early twentieth century the rural pronoun *ndiká* was already beginning to be displaced in village speech by the élite form *sampéyan*. By the logic of self-differentiation, a new term, *panjenengan*, emerged in élite usage at this time and was used increasingly as an alternative to *sampéyan*, effectively replacing it by the 1960s. By the logic of other-appropriation, *sampéyan* had become routine in village usage by the 1960; and by the 1980s *panjenengan* had been assimilated (as a variant) as well. Whereas in the nineteenth century *sampéyan* was an élite form appropriate for equals and superiors, it was by late twentieth century 'stereotypically part of low *básá* usage,' its usage viewed as indexical of membership in lower-status groups lacking competence in high *básá* registers (Errington 1998:48).

If we consider the series of changes in stereotypic value over time it is evident that we are not talking merely of the value of lexemes but of alignments among social groups which engage each other through a series of historical tropes. Three issues are particularly noteworthy in the Javanese case. First, élites and villagers both engage in a pattern of form replacement which is comparable in one respect: each group deviates from an established usage in favor of a form not hitherto used by them. But, second, the target of change reflects the stakes of users: whereas villagers tend towards recognizably élite forms (in a series of 'self-raising' or stratificational moves analogous to the Egyptian case) the élites themselves shift towards apparently new forms in patterns of persistent hyperlectal self-differentiation. The third point is that not all features of this process of role alignment are transparent to users: in the mid-1980s, Surakartan élites perceive the change in value of *panjenengan* as a case of 'devaluation'; yet changes in *sampéyan*, while historically analogous, are not transparent to them as changes of the same type because they occurred much earlier.

Footing, figures and role alignment

The above examples illustrates a number of issues involving register use that require discussion. Let me first highlight them by way of summary as a point of departure.

Summary 3.3

The **social range** of a register (see Table 3.6) includes characterological figures of personhood linked to speech, a feature that has several consequences for register use:

(a) by endogenizing figures of personhood, register models make social personae performable through speech, i.e., perceivable as effects dependent on speech;

(b) characterological figures linked to registers motivate patterns of role alignment in interaction at both micro- and macro-sociological scales of social life;

(c) observable patterns of role alignment are potentially overdetermined in subsequent construal given the complex space of self-and other-contrasts in which they occur;

(d) some patterns of role alignment are avowed or claimed by (some among) those who produce them; and yet

(e) two different members of a group may resort to entirely different conscious strategies of role alignment but nonetheless contribute to the same overall shift

First, the issue of figures and personae. In his discussion of participant roles Goffman uses the term 'figure' for an image of personhood that is clearly differentiated from 'animator' in contexts of character depiction (Goffman, 1974, 1981a); his examples include acts of claiming an identity for self, the differentiation of a past from a present self in story-telling, the portrayal of a character by an actor in the theatre. I use the term **characterological figure** in a related sense to speak of any image of personhood that is performable through a semiotic display or enactment (such as an utterance). Once performed, the figure is potentially detachable from its current animator in subsequent moments of construal and re-circulation. When the social life of such figures is mediated by speech stereotypes, *any* animator can inhabit that figure by uttering the form, as in S 3.3 (a), in a way intelligible to others acquainted with the stereotype.

This feature of registers requires a rethinking – or generalization – of Goffman's concept of 'footing.' Goffman describes footing as (1) an alignment among those co-present, (2) articulated typically through utterances: 'A change of footing implies a change in the alignment we take up to ourselves and the others present as expressed in the way we manage the production or reception of an utterance.' (Goffman 1981a:128). Yet as Goffman is aware relations of footing are not indexed only by utterances; they are effects projectable by a variety of semiotic displays some among which contain 'no speech event at all' (p. 144). This is well and good, for as we shall see in the next section, register-mediated footings are readily expressed through non-linguistic signs too. But what about the co-presence assumption?

The concept of footing draws attention to alignments among persons mediated by their semiotic activities. Since the term 'footing' is derived from a body-part term, it implies that all relations of interpersonal align-ment depend on the co-presence of corporeal bodies; but this assumption is too strong. The number of personae involved in matters of footing is larger than the number of physical persons – or animators – co-present in the here-and-now. We saw in Chapter 1 that acts of finding a footing with an interlocutor are often mediated by representations of the speech of an absent third party; here footings between persons co-present depend on figures *denoted* in speech.

In the case of register-mediated footings, characterological figures are manifest indexically through the mediation of speech stereotypes; they are not denoted at all. The endogenization of characterological figures within registers has the consequence that *footings among animators* emerge during interactional time through *alignments with performed figures*. The presence of biological individuals – bodies and all – is by no means irrelevant; yet relations between two persons having such bodies are mediated by a middle term, a persona stereotypically attached to a semiotic display.

In their most ubiquitous operation enregistered semiotic displays medi-ate persona effects without drawing attention to themselves. But their presence is salient by foregrounding in the case of tropes. Thus in the Lakhota example discussed above a biological male becomes tropically re-figured as female-like in certain respects because he manifestly uses female speech. And in the case of the boys who use sports announcer register, most turn-segments of each boy's talk exhibit a tropic persona to which his interlocutor responds in a subsequent turn with a comparable trope, the two turn-segments thus exhibiting a *symmetric* form of role alignment. Each animator strives to inhabit a figure performed by the other. The two become party to a game of outdoing each other whose competitive qualities depend on the symmetric inhabitance of a single role, a version of which (not necessarily a wholly authentic version) happens to be part of each boy's register range.

The Egyptian and Javanese examples make clear that larger scale foot-ings among groups depend on patterns of role alignment with enregistered figures too. Recognizable positional identities can be incorporated as one's own by adopting speech patterns alleged to be the speech of another; and such alters can be maintained over time as images of self through tropes of *amour propre*, an 'ownership' of signs of self. But these signs and the selves they make present are also alienable through expropriation by others. Such types of group-relative footing can therefore be maintained as constant facts of self vs. other identity only as long as the personae attached to the semiotic display remain apparently constant in value relative to the dialectical give-and-take of stereotypic values in social life. These issues illustrated the point summarized in S 3.3 (b).

It should also be clear that facts of role alignment are not always effects of strategic choices. The French example (the case of the politician) appears to be a clear example of a strategic choice; here a father seeks to animate a figure of himself through the speech of his children in order to become a candidate with which an electorate may identify. But the Swedish case (of the elderly lady who feels younger when addressed by *du*) does not concern strategic choices by speakers, ventriloquated or otherwise. It concerns the way in which a person addressed comes to find herself readable in the light of a usage, whatever strategic intent the speaker might have had in using it. A fuller discussion of these issues may be found in Agha 2005.

We have also seen in the Egyptian case that a single discursive choice may be overdetermined – need not have a unique construal – for role alignments vis-à-vis others. Some among these construals may be grasped more vividly than others by users on particular occasions of register-mediated interaction. Some among these may even be claimed as programmatic facts of identity. And, from the point of view of register change, many kinds of alignments – meaningful to those performing them in diverse ways – can contribute to a single pattern of overall 'drift' (Sapir 1921), cumulatively reinforcing it as a synchronized trend in a single, seemingly concerted or internally uniform pattern of directed change.

3.9 Semiotic range

Let us now focus on the semiotic range of a register, the range of semiotic devices that count as elements of its repertoires. Linguists have long been interested in the *linguistic* signs that belong to a register's repertoires. Yet the identifiability of these repertoires (both for linguists and users) depends on cultural models of speech pragmatics, and such models are readily extended to accompanying non-linguistic signs too. In practice, a register's linguistic repertoires often comprise only a part of its semiotic range; in such cases the register's linguistic repertoires are routinely (even appropriately) deployed in conjunction with criterial non-linguistic signs.

Registers of oral discourse differ from written registers in the kind of semiotic range possible. In written registers of scientific prose, for example, specialized forms of non-linguistic (pictorial, diagrammatic) display co-occur with the use of specialized terminologies, a feature of scientific discourse that influences its lexico-syntactic conventions as well. A variety of non-linguistic devices – photographs, typography, specialized uses of color, serial arrangement, other visual signs – co-occur routinely with distinctive linguistic repertoires in many other written registers, such as those of commercial advertisement (Toolan 1988), 'compressed English' (Sinclair 1988), newspaper headlines (Carter 1988), invoices and service contracts (Bex 1996), and others.

The semiotic range of *spoken* registers is typically linked to the kinds of displays that are possible in face to face interaction. In the case of registers of honorific speech the utterance of honorific expressions in many languages is felt to be most appropriate when accompanied by particular forms of physical and material display, such as prosodic and kinesic activity, bodily comportment, dress, artifactual display, seating arrangement, order of rising and sitting down, and the like (Duranti 1992).

The fact that linguistic and non-linguistic behaviors are grouped together under a scheme of metasemiotic construal and deployment is not itself unusual or peculiar; it appears to be a common feature of register formations of many kinds. We saw in Chapter 1 that normative schemes of etiquette often formulate cross-modal icons of behavior whereby behaviors in diverse semiotic channels are treated as isopragmatic features of a common value scheme. Here for example is an observation about Javanese norms of etiquette discussed earlier.

(3) A complicated etiquette dictates the way a person sits, stands, directs his eyes, holds his hands, points, greets people, laughs, walks, dresses, and so on. There is a close association between the rigor with which the etiquette of movement is observed and the degree of refinement in speech. The more polite a person's language, the more elaborate are his other behavioral patterns; the more informal his speech, the more relaxed and simplified his gestures.

(Poedjosoedarmo 1968:54)

Some of the reasons that models of language use are readily extended to non-linguistic signs have already been discussed in Chapter 1. Thus we noted that metapragmatic terms used to formulate accounts of language are also used to formulate more broadly metasemiotic accounts (S 1.3) and that such overlaps motivate likenesses among otherwise disparate elements of behavior (S 1.4ff.). Such forms of descriptively explicit motivation are hardly the only ones possible, however, or even the most important by themselves. For many (perhaps most) register formations, explicit stereotypes of sign-value have a much narrower circulation and social provenance (e.g., they can be stated by many fewer persons) than the group of persons having some acquaintance with these sign-values. Discourses that *describe* sign-values are neither necessary nor sufficient for furnishing *acquaintance* with sign-values. A variety of schemes of metasemiotic typification typically co-exist within a society and furnish different categories of persons with different thresholds of competence in the use and construal of a given register. These issues are discussed in more detail in the next chapter. Let us focus here on a few aspects of this process for the Javanese case noted above.

Motivation of semiotic range and circulation of sign stereotypes

In the discussion of Javanese in Chapter 1, we considered a number of features of élite (*priyayi*) discourses regarding norms of demeanor. We noted for example that the ethnometapragmatic terms *alus* 'refined, polite' and *kasar* 'coarse' are used to articulate – in particular, *describe* – norms of deference and demeanor. Such descriptions typify behaviors in diverse sign-channels. For example, the term *kasar* 'coarse' is used to describe semiotic behaviors of many kinds, including uses of lexical repertoires as well as prosodic patterns. *Kasar* lexemes (Table 3.9) are associated with highly negative stereotypes of use and user: '*Kasar* words are always considered vulgar. They are not usually used by the upper class. Even lower class people usually use them only in anger' (Poedjosoedarmo 1968). The lexical contrast is therefore conceptualized – particularly by upper-class persons – as differentiating a system of speaker-focal demeanor indexicals, i.e., as forms that make palpable characterological attributes of speaker. The term *kasar* also describes prosodic features (Table 3.10) that index similar speaker attributes. Specific values of a variety of prosodic variables, including speech tempo, volume and dynamic range, are treated as instances of *kasar* 'coarse' behavior, and gradiently opposed to contrastive prosodic values viewed as *alus* 'refined'. Hence from the

Table 3.9. *Javanese kasar 'coarse' vocabularies*

	Gloss	*Ngoko* 'ordinary'	*Kasar* 'coarse'
Nouns:	Eye	mripat	*mata*
	Mouth	tjangkem	*tjatjat*
	Stomach	weteng	*wadhoq*
Adjectives:	Dead	mati	*modar*
	Pregnant	meteng	*mblendheng, busong*
	Stupid	bodho	*gablag*
Verbs:	Eat	mangan	*mbadhag*
	Copulate	saresmi	*laki*

Source: (Poedjosoedarmo 1968: 64)

Table 3.10. *Javanese kasar 'coarse' prosody*

	Alus 'refined'			Kasar 'coarse'
Tempo:	slower	←	→	more rapid
Volume:	softer	←	→	louder
Dynamic range (of intonation):	lesser	←	→	greater

Source: (Poedjosoedarmo 1968: 55)

standpoint of this cultural scheme *kasar* 'crude, coarse' demeanor is exhibited *both* by discrete lexemes (Table 3.9) and by gradable points on a prosodic continuum (Table 3.10). The term *kasar* is now a metasemiotic construct used to typify otherwise disparate phenomenal behaviors. Such behaviors are likened to each other through a metasemiotic classification, which brings diverse object-signs together under unified characterological rubrics; and the contrast of characterological types is further associated with class distinctions.

Some features of aristocratic discourses of *alus* vs. *kasar* behavior (as summarized by Clifford Geertz) were illustrated briefly as examples (18) and (19) in Chapter 1. (The reader may find it useful to review that discussion before proceeding.) We saw that élite discourses formulate a complex diagram of characterological differences linked to a variety of perceivable objects in God's universe. Insofar as these things are perceivable by persons they allow human beings to glimpse essences such as refinement and coarseness, which, although conceived as transcendent facts about the 'natural' order, now become semiotically visible and audible in social interaction. Many of the object-signs discussed in (18), Chapter 1, can be displayed by persons in their own behaviors (e.g., the ones indicated in Table 3.11) and, when displayed, motivate readings of persons as 'refined' or 'coarse'. Recall also that the *alus* variants of these demeanors (the x's in the table) are *prototypically exhibited* in *priyayi* behavior and their *authoritative stereotypes* are also articulated by the *priyayi*; the metasemiotic framework implies a cosmic hierarchy within which the *priyayi* themselves have (unsurprisingly) a rather elevated rank.

Yet the metasemiotic discourses that motivate these correspondences have a very restricted circulation. They are the positional discourses of an élite minority. They are more readily heard in the court and the aristocratic salon, less readily in the street or the marketplace. Most speakers of Javanese are, of course, unable to describe the fine points of *priyayi*

Table 3.11. *Multi-channel indexical icons in Javanese*

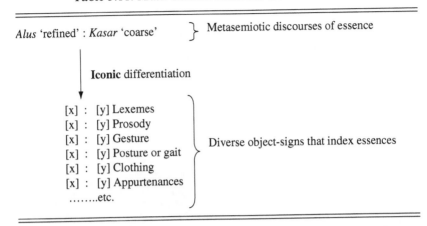

Note: See examples (18) and (19), Chapter 1, for metasemiotic discourses that articulate this model

metaphysics. How then do they associate any sign-values with these behaviors? To what extent are they aware of this cultural scheme at all?

The assumption that the use or construal of a register depends on the 'sharedness' of a uniformly describable cultural scheme is an artifact of a static view of registers (and of culture, more broadly) based on the various types of reification discussed earlier. The orderliness of social life around the existence of register formations does not depend on facts of uniform sharedness but on possibilities of mutual coordination, namely on the extent to which partially overlapping models yield orderly forms of interaction among users. What can we say about other, overlapping, but more widely circulating metasemiotic formulations of this scheme?

One mechanism of circulation more widespread than *priyayi* discourses is the shadow puppet theatre. Poedjosoedarmo offers the following observation in the case of the prosodic styles discussed earlier:

(4) The difference between the two [prosodic styles] is clearly demonstrated in the *wayang* performance, where the well-mannered *satriya*, or knight, uses only *alus* tones, and the impolite giant always speaks in *kasar* tones.

(Poedjosoedarmo 1968: 55)

The *wayang* shadow puppet theatre is an ubiquitous type of ritual performance in which many kinds of iconic likenesses among the values of behavioral signs are implicitly displayed as features of a composite theatrical 'character'. Such implicit patternment in ritual is itself a form of metasemiotic typification, though it involves little or no explicit description of the sign-values typified.

'The puppet characters range between *alus* (extremely refined) and *kasar* (rough and crude). Refined, virtuous characters have small bodies, slitted oval eyes with pupils like rice grains, pointed noses and a modest downward gaze to delicate feet. More vigorous characters look up. Middle size characters may be strong like good kings or princely warriors. For example, this puppet of Karno, one of the hundred Kurewas princes opposing the virtuous Pandawa princes. *Karno* (above) is one of the 'bad' princes, but has many characteristics of the princely *alus* style. More aggressive characters are physically bigger. Their noses and eyes get larger and rounder. Their teeth may show in a snarl. Some large puppets represent physically strong, but virtuous characters. Characters like ogres have only one arm. *Dursosono* (below) displays traits considered *kasar* or crude.'

Karno

Dursosono

Figure 3.4 *Javanese Wayang Kulit: ritual comportment as implicit typification*

(Source: http://www.art-pacific.com/artifacts/indonesi/puppets/kulit.htm)

Some of the semiotically readable features of the 'well-mannered *satriya*, or knight' and 'the impolite giant' are illustrated in Figure 3.4. The character of the knight or prince is formulated through diverse semiotic displays linked to puppet characters (including facial features, delicate bodies, patterns of eye-gaze, dress) through which the essence of *alus* behavior is made pictorially visible and with which ventriloquated features of vocabulary and prosody co-vary in performance. From this standpoint, the Javanese *wayang* ritual is entirely analogous to the Egyptian case discussed earlier, the case where images of pronominal use are circulated through television and the movies. Notice that the quoted material in Figure 3.4 (and the pictures) are from a website (in this case, one designed for Western audiences). Such secondary genres (where one genre is recirculated in another) themselves transform the social domain of the register formation in substantial ways. Moreover, such patterns of recirculation at secondary (or tertiary, or n-ary) remove from the most authentic ritual moment of register use are no less immune from the forms of role alignment, secondary reanalysis, and dependent effects discussed earlier. For most registers, including the Javanese ones, many distinct metasemiotic genres mediate social awareness of enregistered signs. These genres may differ from each other enormously (and along a number of independent dimensions, as we shall see in the next chapter), yet nonetheless prove highly effective in disseminating partially overlapping – or fractionally congruent – images of the register along distinct sociological trajectories of circulation.

Discursive registers are *typically* fragments of broader schemes of semiotic enregisterment to which they are seen as belonging by users and within which they play a role in establishing forms of footing and alignment, and dependent effects, such as power asymmetries, status hierarchies, etc., among those linked to each other through these signs. But given our discussion of normativity in 2.4 – and of the metasemiotic divisions of labor through which power asymmetries can be made to live through signs – the fact that linguistic and non-linguistic signs are linked to one another does not entail that they are seen as so linked (or linked in the same way) by *all* members of a society. In the case of prestige registers, the fact that partially non-congruent models of the register co-exist society-internally can itself maintain power relations among categories of persons. Asymmetries of competence are readily essentialized as differential allocations of 'expertise' or 'authenticity' in matters of register typification and use. Social differences in a register's semiotic range – in characterizations of its range, in performing its range authentically – themselves constitute a powerful social-semiotic mechanism through which register formations mediate social relations within society. For when differences in semiotic behavior are reanalyzed as more or less authentic or more or less correct forms of expression, asymmetries of competence are endogenized into register models as indices of speaker difference, social distinction, or rank. As registers grow in semiotic range such issues can only become more, not less important.

3.10 The enregisterment of style

The term **style** has been used in diverse ways in the sociolinguistics and linguistic anthropology literatures. In some traditions, such as the ethnography of speaking, 'style' is an older term for certain aspects of registers. In variationist sociolinguistics, 'style' – or 'dialect style' – is a name for patterns of variation not correlated with speaker's geographic origins. Since speakers of any dialect exhibit such variation, differences of 'style' are treated as 'superposed' upon dialects (or sociolects) as a type of remainder, and the remainder is not itself susceptible to a correlationist analysis given the problem of 'metaphoric' switching discussed earlier (2.5). These traditions lack a reflexive theory of discursive formations, and the term 'style' – and the single-level discursive phenomenon that it appears to name – cannot be given a clear explanation within their terms.

Despite these difficulties, discussions of style point to a very important domain of discourse organization. If we consider this domain from the standpoint of a reflexive theory of discourse, it becomes apparent that the single term – 'style' – under-differentiates, and thus groups together, three rather distinct phenomena.

First, style is a way of talking about co-occurrence patterns (Ervin-Tripp 1986). Formally, style is identifiable by patterning at many – perhaps *any* – level of semiotic form, whether it be patterning of phonetic, lexical or syntactic elements, or of prosody and kinesis, or of utterance sequences across turns at talk, or of yet more global patterns of interactional-textual components. The fact that stylistic repertoires may be highly varied – by channel of perceptual access, or by level of structure – is no accident. A stylistic pattern is not isolated by repertoire criteria (although, once identified, the analysis of a stylistic pattern requires the study of its repertoires). Styles in this sense are identified by attention to patterns of co-occurrence among semiotic devices. To speak of **co-occurrence styles** in this sense is to speak of the emergent patterning of linguistic and non-linguistic tokens within observable events of semiotic activity and interaction; or, more briefly, to speak of the texture of semiotic patterns in interaction.

From this standpoint *every* utterance has a formal organization that can be described as a co-occurrence style. Moreover such a formal organization, while describable, may not in fact be viewed as significant by language users. The notion of co-occurrence style makes no assumptions about the cultural intelligibility or significance of the pattern described; it involves only a commitment to the describability of formal patterning as such. Hence many more co-occurrence styles are always describable in any corpus of discursive data than language users themselves recognize.

Second, we may speak of **enregistered styles** whenever a co-occurrence pattern is linked to stereotypic indexical values by users. To approach styles from this standpoint requires attention to more than co-occurrence patterns. It requires a study of how such patterns are given distinctive forms of metapragmatic treatment in use; how interlocutors differentially respond to their use; and, in cases where explicit metasemiotic discourses exist, how users *describe* their significance. In short, enregistered styles are co-occurrence styles reflexively endogenized to a register model.

The traditional conception of registers has been sufficiently narrow (i.e., repertoire-centric, not conceived in terms of reflexive processes) that styles in this sense have often been conceived as phenomena to be contrasted with registers. However, the above discussion should make clear that this opposition makes little sense. Every register involves co-occurrence styles, some of which are assimilated into register models as enregistered styles.

Let us take the narrow special case of lexical registers by way of example. Tokens of a lexical register are never encountered in isolation from other signs; they necessarily co-occur with semiotic accompaniments to form co-occurrence styles. Whether or not such patternment is given an additional (i.e., $n + 1^{th}$) construal within the register scheme is an empirical question that may have different answers in different locales and for different sub-populations. Consider for example the fragmentary use of a lexical register in the sense discussed earlier. If a person has only a fragmentary competence in a specialized lexical register, a resulting pattern of co-occurrence – involving, say, admixtures of criterial lexemes with lexemes of another register – is often given a derogatory reading by those fully competent in its use. In the case of honorific lexical registers, for example, the differential use of lexemes (as markers of *respectfulness* to others) is typically re-evaluated as a framework of enregistered sentence styles – typically called **speech levels** in the literature (see Chapter 7) – mastery over which is treated as secondarily indexical of speaker's own status (i.e., is viewed as marking *respectability* of self). Moreover, as the above discussion of Javanese should make clear, such systems of co-occurring signs – and their interpretation for 'level' of stereotypic elegance/refinement/formality, etc. – are not based on covariation of *speech* variables alone. As a register grows in semiotic range a vast number of non-linguistic semiotic accompaniments can become endogenized to the register model, that is, become recognized as co-occurrence patterns that constitute enregistered styles.

Of course, many register contrasts do not depend on lexical contrasts per se (i.e., do not involve a *distinctive* repertoire of free lexemic forms). We have already seen this in the case of 'Sports Announcer' register in English (Table 3.4), a case where the register differs from the Standard Language largely in terms of syntactic patternment as well as other (e.g., prosodic) features not discussed here. A more elaborate and ethnographically better described example is the case of Wolof speech styles discussed by Judith Irvine (Irvine 1990), which involves a wide range of semiotic alternations (including differential use of prosodic patterns, segmental phonology, deixis and modifiers, syntactic patterns) that are stereotypically understood as comprising caste-specific registers of the Wolof language. One of these is linked to a bardic caste (and termed *waxu gewel* 'Griot speech') the other is stereotypically associated with the traditional nobility (termed *waxu géér* 'Noble speech').

Once a co-occurrence style is endogenized to a metapragmatic model – i.e., treated as an enregistered style – a third type of stylistic phenomenon also emerges, namely the phenomenon of **strategic stylization** of one's own speech and demeanor (Rampton 2003, Irvine 2001). This is the phenomenon of register-mediated tropes discussed above, now viewed at the level of co-occurrence patterns. Thus, as we saw in the case of Sports Announcer talk, anyone – not necessarily a sports announcer – who is acquainted with the register can formulate a social persona through the performance of criterial patterns in a way that is non-congruent with independently indexed facts of identity. Much the same is true of Wolof

I watched a Shakespeare play on TV without understanding a word of it. It gave me an idea for a strip, though.

Figure 3.5   Calvin and Hobbes *on registers, voicing, tropes and recirculation*
Note: The remark at the bottom is author's commentary.
(Source: Watterson 1995: 171.)

registers as Irvine shows in some detail. Anyone who performs Griot speech (or, conversely Noble speech) can inhabit the persona of a Griot (or Noble) in ways recognizable within the language community and employ such modes of stylization of persona to achieve strategic ends.

A humorous use of strategic stylization is illustrated in the *Calvin and Hobbes* comic strip in Figure 3.5.

3.11 Conclusion

I have been arguing that register formations inevitably involve models of enactable behavior linked to performable signs of various kinds. Although my main concern has been with registers of discourse I have argued that such models are easily extendable to non-linguistic signs by the same general processes through which they come to be linked to language in the first place. Whether the object-signs are linguistic or non-linguistic, or both, the meta-semiotic processes through which awareness of register classifications are formulated and disseminated invariably involve language use as part of the total process.

I have observed also that registers are historically changing systems that are shaped by processes linking groups to each other in social space. In some cases the social domain of persons acquainted with the register is tightly delimited by institutional processes; other registers have a more amorphous social distribution. Thus to understand the social existence of a register requires some clarity not only about the metapragmatic models that typify its forms and values but an understanding also of the social processes through which such models are institutionally disseminated across social populations.

Finally, the actual use of a register may fully conform to the metapragmatic model associated with its repertoires (e.g., when a legal register is used appropriately in a court of law), or it may not. In the latter case a range of tropes of personhood, enacted conduct, relationship to interlocutor and the like are mediated by the model itself and can be played upon – even manipulated – through contextualization by accompanying signs. This type of flexibility in use is one of the most interesting features of register systems and hence a phenomenon that I have illustrated with numerous examples in the discussion above.

The approach outlined above also makes clear that all talk of 'cultural value' is – from an empirical standpoint – based on observations of reflexive evaluative practices. Language users often formulate essentialistic conceptions of value as 'ideas in the head' and these conceptions often find their way into reports of register phenomena by linguists. Yet we have no empirical evidence for the existence of pragmatic values for any register that is independent of observations of *overt* metapragmatic activity in the sense discussed above. Indeed, our attempts to study the cultural value of speech and other signs rely, from the point of view of method, on socially locatable metasemiotic behaviors – variably institutionalized as recurrent, habitual practices – that differentiate and typify such values for a population of sign-users. Such data are socially locatable precisely because they involve the activities of social persons. Hence, whenever pragmatic values become empirically observable as data, the persons whose activities count as the data are also part of the same empirical observation. Assessments of the social domain of a register are based on this feature of the data of register study.

At the same time, the concept of metasemiotic activity reminds us that the value of speech and other object-signs is not a disembodied abstraction. The cultural values of enregistered signs become empirically observable when they are articulated by sensorially accessible meta-signs (including utterances) that typify these values. Thus, in an empirical sense, the meta-sign/object-sign relation lies at the very heart of the study of systems of register valorization. Once we attend to this empirical criterion, the cultural values of speech and other signs may be seen as phenomena that are neither abstract, nor socially disembodied. Not abstract because they are investigable only through the study of material signs; not socially disembodied, because attending to the social position of the sign-user ensures that our model of culture is, from the very outset, anchored in social space in such a way that the issue of the spatiotemporal distribution of cultural value becomes directly investigable in sociological terms. It is to these considerations that we turn in the next chapter.

4

THE SOCIAL LIFE OF
CULTURAL VALUE

4.0 Introduction

My main concern in this chapter is with processes of linguistic enregisterment, processes through which a linguistic repertoire becomes differentiable
within a language as a socially recognized register of forms. The empirical
case on which I focus is a particular phonolexical register of Standard
British English, nowadays called Received Pronunciation, or RP. I shall be
concerned in what follows with the historical processes through which the
register emerged as a status emblem in British society and became linked
to a distinctive scheme of cultural values. Yet my larger purpose is to draw
attention to a series of reflexive social processes – processes of value
production, maintenance and transformation – through which a scheme
of cultural values has a social life, as it were, a processual and dynamic
existence that depends on the activities of social persons linked to each
other through discursive interactions and institutions. I argue that cultural
value is not a static property of things or people but a precipitate of
sociohistorically locatable practices, including discursive practices, which
imbue cultural forms with recognizable indexical sign-values and bring
these values into circulation along identifiable trajectories in social space.
Though the specific objects of value I consider here are linguistic forms, the
processes of valorization, circulation and reanalysis I describe are quite
general. They apply to – indeed, treat language like – any other cultural form.

   We saw in the last chapter that every register exhibits various kinds of
growth or decline over time, a variety of types of expansion or narrowing,
change or stabilization along one or more dimensions of register organization (e.g., changes in the size and composition of repertoires, in the
range of stereotypic values associated with its forms, in the social domain
of persons acquainted with these forms and values). In this chapter,
I discuss such changes – and the reflexive processes underlying them – for
the historical case of RP. It is worth noting at the outset that no widely
recognized standard of English pronunciation existed in the seventeenth
century; yet by the late nineteenth century the register was well established,
widely seen as a form of semiotic capital in British society. By the end of

this period, competence in RP was widely recognized as a prerequisite for social advancement, as a gateway to employment in the upper echelons of government and military service. How did the register come to be known to its users? How were its values established, maintained or, by degrees, transformed through this process?

In the middle sections of this chapter (4.3–4.6) I focus on the expansionist phase of RP enregisterment, the period roughly between 1760–1900. I return in section 4.7 to more recent changes that suggest that RP is entering a more recessive phase of enregisterment, apparently losing ground to other registers in a changing milieu of class relations. Before we turn to these historical questions, however, let us consider some basic features of contemporary RP.

4.1 Received Pronunciation: basic issues

RP is familiar to anyone living in Britain today as a socially valued accent. The term 'accent' names a folk-concept, however. Although the term is used in everyday discussions of sound patterns, it is neither very precise nor free of ideological distortion. There are at least three ways in which the folk-term distorts the phenomenon it describes.

First, accent contrasts are only perceivable as relational phenomena, but are often described as if they were monadic facts about sound patterns. Not everybody is felt to have an accent. Everyday talk of accents implicitly presupposes a baseline relative to which some sound patterns – but not others – are focally typified as deviant, foregrounded accents. In a common type of case, accent is what other people have; here the phonetic norms of *one's own group* comprise the default baseline of unaccented speech. But the norm can also be externalized as the speech of *some other group*, real or imagined, relative to which one's own speech is felt to be the accented, deviant – even defective – variety by some speakers. This is true for RP, as I presently show.

A second point is that the folk-term 'accent' does not name a sound pattern alone, but a sound pattern linked to a framework of social identities. The social identity is recognized, indexically, as the identity of the speaker who produces the utterance in the instance, and described, metalinguistically, through the use of identifying labels. In the case of geographic accents the most typical labels are derived from names of locales (e.g., 'he speaks with a *Scottish* accent'). But RP is a supra-local accent; it is enregistered in public awareness as indexical of speaker's class and level of education; it is valued precisely for effacing the geographic origins of speaker.[1] The identifying descriptions associated with its forms consist mainly of characterological labels and discourses that identify speakers in terms of the mental, aesthetic and class attributes discussed below.

The third point concerns the conditions under which accents become recognizable to particular individuals. In folk-terms, accents are often described as if they operated in an all-or-nothing way: people either have accents or don't, either have certain social identities or don't. Yet in actual interaction the recognition of speaker type by the hearer of an utterance operates relative to certain contextual prerequisites. Consider the case of geographic accents:

(1) ... a Liverpool working-class accent will strike a Chicagoan primarily as being British, a Glaswegian as being English, an English southerner as being north-ern, an English northerner as being Liverpudlian, and a Liverpudlian as being working-class. The closer we get to home, the more refined are our perceptions.
(Wells 1982, v.1: 33)

Notice that *all* of these characterizations are correct. A person who has a 'Liverpool working class accent' is at once working class, a Liverpudlian, a northerner, English, British and so on. It is the hearer's capacity to ascribe a taxonomically specific identity (e.g., to affix a specific identifying term) to speaker that varies. It varies, moreover, as a function of the hearer's prior history of socialization to speech contrasts. In the case of geographic accents, speech that is 'closer ... to home' is experienced more frequently and, on average, tends to be characterizable in more specific ways. But what about supra-local accents? A prior history of socialization is indeed involved, though it has a different character as I show in some detail below.

Let us begin by considering the issue of exposure to RP: How are the forms of RP experienced by speakers of British English?

Asymmetries of competence

Although RP is routinely heard and widely *recognized* as a valued accent, it is actually *spoken* by a very small proportion of the British population.

(2) RP is, after all, what anyone living in the United Kingdom hears constantly from radio and television announcers and newsreaders and from many other public figures. *Everyone in Britain* has a mental image of RP, even though they may not refer to it by that name and even though the image may not be very accurate. Many English people are also regularly exposed to RP in personal face-to-face contact. For *a small minority*, it is their own speech.
(Wells, 1982, v. 2: 279; emphases added)

Most Britons encounter RP as hearers of RP utterances; only a small minority actually speak it. Indeed, as I show in the next few sections, the *competence to recognize* RP utterances has a wider social domain (i.e., is a competence possessed by many more people) than the *competence to speak* it.

According to some estimates the number of Britons who fully command the RP standard amounts to no more than 3% of the population (Hughes and Trudgill 1987: 3; Milroy and Milroy 1999: 151). Yet RP is widely imitated and approximated in the speech of a larger number of speakers in a series of quasi-equivalent 'paralects' (Honey 1989b). Differences between these '-lects' are socially valued, of course, motivating evaluations of speaker persona along dimensions such as class or educational background. How are boundaries between these types recognized or identified?

The most explicit method involves the use of metadiscursive labels to name discursive varieties. Such labels personify speech by linking sound patterns to attributes of speakers. For example Wells proposes the following labels for internal varieties of RP: *Mainstream RP* for the most common, unmarked variety; *U-RP* for 'U[pper class]' accents (stereotypically spoken by duchesses and elderly Oxbridge dons); *Adoptive RP* for the accent of those who did not speak RP as children; and *Near-RP* for analogous supra-local varieties spoken outside of England (e.g., the educated accents of Scotland, Wales, Australia and South Africa). Wells observes that the boundaries between these types 'may well correspond to our perceptions of social reality rather than to exclusively linguistic and phonetic considerations' (Wells 1982, v. 2: 280). In this case, of course, the metadiscursive labels themselves impose social classifications onto phonetic repertoires. For example, the names for varieties spoken in England link phonetic repertoires to stereotypic categories of speakers, viz., to persons who are in the 'mainstream', or are 'u[pper class]', or have 'adopt[ed]' accents to which they were not born. Observe that phonetic varieties have now become objects – or, object discourses – in relation to a meta-discourse linking speech to social classifications. But what can we say about the phonetic repertoires themselves?

A phonolexical register

The phonetic repertoires of RP are differentiated from those of other accents by phonological rules which take delimited lexical sets as their domain. RP is primarily a *phonolexical* register in this sense.[2] Wells 1982 lists several dozen such rules, including rules for the distinctive treatments of diphthongs, of vowels before /r/, for word-initial /h/ dropping, for the insertion or loss of /r/ in particular positions, as well as rules for a series of vowel mergers and splits that remain confined to particular lexical sets at given moments in the history of phonological change. Phoneticians describe such changes by using lexical items (common members of such lexical sets) as names for the domain of a phonological rule, e.g., the PALM lexical set, the START set, and so on. Two simple examples – one involving a vowel merger, the other a vowel split – are given in Table 4.1.

Thus in the mid-eighteenth century, the word-medial vowel was normatively pronounced [aː] in the PALM set, [aːr] in START, and [æː] (phonemically /æ/) in BATH; but all three sets of words have /ɑː/ in twentieth century RP.

Table 4.1. *Phonolexical changes in RP vowels: selected examples*

(a) Vowel mergers: Medial vowels in three lexical sets

	PALM	START	BATH
mid-18th c.	aː	aːr	aeː
20th c. RP		ɑː	

(b) Vowel splits: In the environment _s#,
<a> ⟶ /ɑː/ in some RP words (*pass, glass, grass, brass*)
<a> ⟶ /æ/ in others (*lass, morass, gas, crass*)

Source: (Wells 1982)

Accent changes involve contingent lexical domains for many reasons. One reason is that such changes do not always extend to the entire stock of words meeting the structural description of a phonological rule. Hence, in the environment _s#, an orthographic <a> is now pronounced /ɑː/ in some RP words, while others retain the older /æ/. The contrast between /æ/ and /ɑː/ now occurs in more than a dozen phonolexical sets in RP, an overall state of affairs referred to as the TRAP-BATH split. Contrasts among internal varieties of RP involve phonolexical sets as well, e.g., the vowel in the TRAP set is pronounced /æ/ in Mainstream RP, but occurs as a diphthong – either [ɛæ] or [eæ] – in U-RP.

The fact that phonological rules operate over specific lexical domains has some practical consequences for performance: Knowing the current prestige forms of RP is partly a matter of knowing the precise lexical boundaries within which particular phonological rules normatively apply. Over- or under-generalization of a rule is socially perilous. The complexity of repertoire variation itself contributes to the differences in competence among speakers noted above.

The examples also show that our ability to describe such phonetic variation requires the use of metadiscursive labels to fix the classes in question. Technical analyses of the register concurrently employ phonetic and sociological modes of reasoning as Wells observes. Yet the two modes can be employed independently as well, and frequently are, by the ordinary language user. One way in which speakers can discern accent contrasts is to attend to phonetic differences audible in utterances. A second method is to use metadiscursive labels – such as Mainstream RP, U-RP, Adoptive RP – which anchor phonetic repertoires to classifications of persons in social space. Of course the technical labels discussed above are not widely known. Let us consider some metadiscursive labels (and more implicit forms of typification) that have a wider social provenance.

4.2 Metadiscourses of accent

The experience of RP in Britain today is mediated by a range of meta-discursive practices that bring register-dependent images of persons into wide circulation in the public sphere. I begin with a set of everyday person-ifying terms, turning then to characterological practices that are partly independent of them.

Everyday personifying terms

A number of personifying terms are very widely known. They are used in everyday descriptions of language use, in prescriptions and proscriptions to others, in public discussions of the 'best' kinds of usage, and so on. These terms are not simply neutral descriptors. They imbue the phenom-ena they describe with specific characterological values. The class includes expressions like *Public School Pronunciation*; terms like *the Queen's English*, the *U / non-U* terminology, *talking proper* and *talking posh*, all of which apply to diction as well as accent; and, of course, *Received Pronunciation* itself. Many of these terms anchor speech repertoires to named positions in social space but differ in the degree of explicitness with which they achieve the effect.

The term *Public School Pronunciation* alludes to a social institution whose products are viewed as exemplary speakers. The term *Queen's English* recalls a Victorian cosmic polity in which differences of rank among the sovereign's subjects were assessed in part by their capacity to uphold a speech standard. Other terms, such as the *U / non-U* terminology (introduced into public debates about language standards by Ross 1954 and Mitford 1956), link speech forms, including accent, to class distinc-tions. In this case, the accent named can be sociologically centered in an explicit way, as in 'U[pper-class] accent'. In contrast, terms such as *talking proper* and *talking posh* do not specify named positions in social space; they describe discursively performable demeanors – 'doing proper' or 'doing posh,' as it were – associated with particular activities, settings and social types.

The term *Received Pronunciation* is rather more implicit in its charac-terological work. It belongs to a small set of idiomatic phrases formed by using the term *received* (in the sense of 'generally adopted, accepted, approved as true,' now rather archaic) as a modifier to nouns that denote cultural forms having a historically normative force (viz., ... *religion / opinion / wisdom / custom / canon*). Though the phrasal idiom is attested as far back as the fifteenth century, the term *pronunciation* was not included in the class of modifiable nouns till the twentieth century. Once accepted in common usage, however, the term *Received Pronunciation* also implies a historical product. It locates a speech variety as something handed down by a tradition about which there is a consensus in the judgment of some contemporary group – its 'receivers,' as it were – who, although unnamed by the term itself, are presumably the best judges of its historical authenticity and value. Hence the term describes a speech variety which is centered elsewhere in social space: it is a discursive variety to which the actual speech of most speakers corresponds only imperfectly (see (2)ff.); it is also a variety whose 'correct' forms and usage (i.e., whose metadiscursive standards) are guaranteed by someone else. The register name thus contributes to a politics of anxiety linked to the register from its earliest inception.

All of these terms link speech to images of persons in various ways. Yet the terms are merely a backdrop to a much wider range of metadiscursive practices linking speech to social personae in everyday life. Some of these practices are not officially 'about' speech at all, but typify discursive personae in the course of 'other' work. Such typifications are inevitably expressed through overt (perceivable) signs, though not always through linguistic expressions; even when such metadiscursive typifications are linguistically expressed, they differ enormously in the denotational explicitness with which they ascribe characterological attributes to the register's forms. Let us consider some examples.

Public sphere metadiscourses

Although RP is indeed an accent which Britons hear 'constantly from radio and television' (as Wells notes above), much of the experience of its forms in the public sphere is accompanied by metadiscursive activity typifying accent forms and values:

(3) In our serious newspapers political columnists and other journalists regularly pass comment on the accents of public figures, while television critics discuss the accents of actors, programme presenters, and other television personalities. The correspondence columns of both national and local newspapers frequently carry letters from readers commenting on various forms of accent – favourably, or, more often, unfavourably – and when the BBC uses people with marked regional accents to present radio programmes or to read the news, waves of protest are expressed in letters of complaint to the BBC and sacks of hate-mail to the presenters themselves . . . Writers of contemporary novels and memoirs use observations about accent as a crucial part of the description of character . . . Most of the characters in Anthony Burgess's recent memoirs are introduced with reference to their accent.

(Honey 1989a: 10)

In all of these cases, phonetic substance is linked to a set of social personae, whether explicitly, as in descriptions of persons and their accents; or implicitly, as in the case of literary treatments, where characters are made palpable to the reader through depictions of accented speech. In some cases implicit typifications are rendered more explicit through 'uptake' and response in subsequent speech events: in the case of the

Table 4.2. *Popular media mis-spellings of U-RP words*

Spelling used for U-RP words	Standard spelling
kebinet office	cabinet office
clawth	cloth
crawss	cross
lawft	loft
hape	hope
arm-air	army
fah	fire
pah of the British empah	power of the British Empire
stains	stones

Source: (Honey 1989a)

BBC announcers who speak with regional accents, particular social personae are only implicitly palpable in the announcer's performance; but in their subsequent letters of complaint and hate-mail, the audiences of these broadcasts describe such enacted personae in highly explicit – sometimes vituperative – terms in the very course of dismissing them. Let us now consider a few other, relatively implicit metadiscourses of accent.

One such case involves the manipulation of spelling conventions in represented dialogue involving U-RP speakers. Words represented as U-RP speech (a.k.a 'Conservative RP') are often mis-spelled in the popular print media, as shown in Table 4.2.

Here the use of mis-spelling constitutes an implicit metapragmatic commentary on norms of speech. For, armed with the folk-view that every word has a correct spelling and a correct pronunciation, the reader can only construe defective spelling as an implicit comment on defects of pronunciation – implicit, because no-one has actually said that the pronunciation is incorrect. The mis-spelling of words also invites inferences about oddity of character (viz., that upper-class speakers are pompous, eccentric, out of touch, etc.) rarely described explicitly in these texts. Such mis-spelling performatively replays folk-stereotypes about the aristocracy in a highly effective way. Yet although these stereotypes are effectively disseminated in the press and easily recognized by readers, they are not actionable. The dissemination of register-based images of persons is here a covert effect of a genre whose official point is just harmless humor.

Consider now an even more implicit case. The cartoon in Figure 4.1 is a metadiscursive representation of improper discursive behavior. Yet it is not itself an instance of language use. The typifying metasigns are entirely pictorial and non-linguistic; but the typified object-signs include speech as well as other behavioral displays. The cartoon depicts the social failure

Figure 4.1 *Bateman cartoon, 1920*
(Source: Bateman 1969)

of the smaller, slim person (let us call him 'Mr. Slim') vis-à-vis the larger, aristocratic gentleman ('Mr. Round'). After the two are introduced in frame 1 on the top left, Mr. Slim (notice the ill-fitting suit, the ill-at-ease expression, the slouching posture) remains anxious and silent for the next six frames; but the gracious Mr. Round (who in contrast is elegantly dressed, socially adept, exudes an amiable grace) has managed to draw Mr. Slim out of his shell with casual repartee by frame 8. Yet as Mr. Slim begins to speak he is all teeth and knuckles, he gesticulates wildly, his speech is obstreperous, over-excited, graceless; we can only imagine his accent! The result is an increasing tension in Mr. Round's demeanor in the last five frames – he frowns, looks askance, scowls at Mr. Slim – resulting, in the final frame, in the brusque dismissal in a puff of smoke.

The cartoon does not isolate accent as an object of metasemiotic scrutiny. It visually depicts the social perils of improper demeanor in many sign modalities (dress, posture, gait, gesture), including speech activity. It reflexively formulates *cross-modal icons or images* of personhood, a contrastive paradigm of two such figures, in particular: one is an image of personhood in which ill-fitting clothing, toothy grins, wild gesture, obstreperous (and, perhaps, crude) speech all go together (Mr. Slim); the other, in which elegant dress, graceful bearing, and well intoned speech are all of a part (Mr. Round). Any British reader of the cartoon knows how accent aligns with these other signs: Mr. Round speaks RP, Mr. Slim very likely does not.

In the foregoing I have discussed a number of public sphere representations that reflexively typify speech and accent in various ways. I have been concerned to show that the everyday experience of accent in Britain routinely contains *reflexive typifications of accent* as part of the experience. Messages containing RP (or alternatives to RP) contain metamessages that typify, comment on, or otherwise characterize speech and accent as pragmatically deployable systems of signs. When the metapragmatic aspect of these messages is relatively implicit or when typifications of speech are linked to typifications of other signs, the fact that the text in question typifies accent may be relatively non-transparent (i.e., less easily reportable in subsequent discourse; see Silverstein 1981) even though the typification is readily recognized in contextualized encounters with the messages themselves.

This culture of reflexive activity does not exist merely at the level of public sphere institutions. It lives through the evaluative activities of ordinary persons. The characterological values of RP are easily elicited from ordinary individuals as well. Let us consider some of these data.

Elicited metapragmatic judgments

RP is not only one of the most storied accents of contemporary times, it is also among the best studied. A number of studies have shown that

Table 4.3. *Accent speech levels in Britain*

Highest ranked

      Mainstream RP ('unmarked' RP)
      Near-RP: educated English accents of Scotland, Wales & Ireland
      Provincial accents (Yorkshire, West Country, Tyneside Geordie)
      Urban accents: London (Cockney), Liverpool (Scouse), Glaswegian

Lowest ranked

Source: (Giles 1970, 1971)

members of the British public typify RP in specific characterological terms and, conversely, employ stereotypes of speech in reasoning about types of persons. These studies are quite heterogeneous in goals and methodology but all make use of elicited metapragmatic data, e.g., questionnaire-based responses to queries about speech and associated demeanor indexicals.

Even the 1972 National Opinion Poll, though not a linguistic survey, provides an initial set of clues. Respondents were provided with a set of eight choices, and asked: 'Which two of these would you say are the most important in being able to tell which class a person is?'. The criterion selected by the largest group of respondents (33%) was 'The way they speak.'[3]

Other studies have focused on accent in particular (Giles 1970, 1971; Giles and Powesland 1975). Several patterns have been reported through the use of 'matched guise' experiments, where speakers are asked to evaluate a sample of discursive data exhibiting differences of accent for selected features, such as persuasiveness of speech, or characteristics of speaker. These experiments indicate that Britons view accents in terms of a stratified model of speaker rank. Unmarked or Mainstream RP is the accent accorded the highest social value; aristocratic or U-RP is generally ranked lower, as are the educated accents of Wales and Ireland ('Near-RP'); provincial accents form a middle region; distinctively urban accents are among the lowest ranked. Table 4.3 offers an approximate picture of some of these results.

Particular accents on this scale are also linked to specific characterological images of persons, including ideas about mental ability and personal habits. Respondents judge RP speakers to be *more* ambitious, intelligent, and confident, cleaner, taller and better looking – even though they are evaluating audiotaped data [!] – but also *less* serious, talkative, good-natured and good-humored than non-RP speakers (Giles 1971).[4]

Similar results occur in studies of accent endorsement and perceptions of speaker's own accent. Newbrook (1999) characterizes the results of his study of West Wirral (Table 4.4) as 'typical' of Northern England. Many more speakers endorse RP than endorse non-RP accents. Moreover, although over half the respondents accurately describe their own speech,

Table 4.4. *Patterns of accent evaluation and role alignment in West Wirral*

Accent endorsement:	Endorse RP 81%	Endorse non-RP 16%	Cannot distinguish 3%	
Accuracy of self-report:	Accurate 59%	Over-reportage 29%	Under-reportage 9%	Dialect error 4%

Source: (Newbrook 1999, Tables 5.2 and 5.4)

the data of inaccurate self-reportage is heavily skewed in favor of RP: 29% of the speakers sampled exhibit over-reportage (i.e., claim to use RP but do not), but only 9% exhibit under-reportage.

We noted earlier that pure RP is actually spoken by a small minority of the population. We can now see that many more people endorse the status emblem and seek to claim it as their own. These data suggest that RP is associated with a characteristic form of role alignment: many more people seek to align their self-image with the characterological figures of RP than with those linked to other accents, including accents that they actually speak.

These studies indicate that RP accent fits within a larger scheme of sociological differentiation linking speech to characterological figures of speaker; they also point to the fact that speech stereotypes motivate patterns of role alignment between speaker and hearer.[5] The data of accent endorsement and self-reportage are sociologically robust but denotationally implicit in specifying the characterological features of accent-linked roles, and alignments with roles, since they reveal them only tacitly. In some cases, however, these alignments show up quite explicitly as focally grasped assessments of self-worth. The following comments by a Glaswegian about his own speech are typical of forms of linguistic insecurity expressed by many who lack fluency in RP.

(4) I mean I'm not a speaker as you can see. I don't ... I'm just a common sort of, you know I'm not ... I've often wished I'd gone to some sort of elocution lessons because I meet so many people in my job and I feel as if I'm lower when it comes to speaking, y' know.

(Macaulay 1977)

Cultural values and metadiscursive processes

I have been observing that the folk-term 'accent' does not name a sound pattern as such but a system of contrastive social personae stereotypically linked to contrasts of sound. In particular the accent called RP is enregistered in cultural awareness as part of a system of stratified speech levels linked to an ideology of speaker rank. These value ascriptions are evident both in public sphere discourses and in responses elicited from individuals. But what is involved in claiming that such cultural values exist at all? For whom do they exist?

In speaking of 'cultural values' I wish to invite no metaphysics of shared belief. To say that pragmatic behaviors – such as uses of a register – have cultural values associated with them is simply to say that certain regularities of evaluative behavior can be observed and documented as data. Indeed, all of the evidence for register values presented above consists of data of observable metapragmatic activity. I have discussed several genres of such activity – the use of register names, journalistic depictions of accent, responses to playback experiments, etc. – in the sections above; they vary enormously from each other, both in form and specific import; some of these are elicited by linguists, others occur naturally as part of the fabric of social life.

Yet all such behaviors are unavoidably positioned, by their very nature, as the activity of socially locatable persons. Insofar as many persons offer comparable typifications of a register formation, these data furnish evidence for the existence of metapragmatic stereotypes – social regularities of metapragmatic typification – identifiable for a particular social domain of evaluators, e.g., a particular sub-population within a society. There is no necessity, of course, that such evaluations always be consistent with each other society-internally; in fact their mutual inconsistency often provides crucial evidence for the co-existence of distinct, socially positioned ideologies of language within a language community.[6]

My concern in the remainder of this chapter is with processes through which register formations change in social domain (e.g., become known to larger groups of people) and the way in which their values change through such processes. In what follows, I pay particular attention to public sphere depictions of RP. But first a word of caution: it is not my purpose to assert that public sphere representations (such as the mass media depictions discussed above) *determine* individual views, or anything of the sort. Contemporary mass media depictions are themselves the products of individuals caught up in larger historical processes; and the 'uptake' of such messages by audiences involve processes of evaluative response that permit many degrees of freedom. I am concerned rather with the ways in which these representations expand the social domain of individuals acquainted with register stereotypes, and allow individuals, once aware of them, to respond to their characterological value in various ways, aligning their own self-images with them in some cases, transforming them in others through their own metasemiotic work.

I argue below that the *dissemination* or spread of a register depends on the circulation of messages typifying speech. Such messages are borne by physical artifacts: in the case of face to face communication, by acoustical artifacts, i.e., utterances; in the mass mediated cases by more perduring text-artifacts – books, magazines, cartoons, musical scores, and the like – that are physical objects conveying information about cultural forms.[7] The circulation of messages depends on interaction between people, whether face to face interactions, or more indirect forms of communication linking persons to each other across larger spans of space and time (Sapir 1949a). Each event in this complex cultural process is a metadiscursive semiotic event with its own forms of recruitment to *roles of communicative participants* (senders and receivers of messages); its own *genre* characteristics; its own *referents*, and in particular, a set of depicted *characterological figures* or stereotypic personae linked to speech.[8] Thus, in the above examples, the individuals who produce the texts discussed (journalists, novelists, cartoonists, etc.) constitute a cadre of *producers or senders* of metadiscursive messages about speech and accent in the public sphere. At the same time, members of the public are recruited willy-nilly to participant roles such as *receiver or hearer* of such messages in the very course of exposure to these media. Some among them subsequently become producers of influential messages in turn, thus reshaping subsequent forms of accent values through their own activities. But the constancy or change of the register over time is mediated by the characterological figures linked to speech in the messages themselves.

The social expansion of the register is mediated, in particular, by processes of *role alignment*. Any social person who is a receiver of such a message can, in principle, seek to align his or her own self-image with the characterological figures depicted in the message; wishing to transform one's own speech in favor of models depicted (e.g., wishing to emulate Mr. Round more than Mr. Slim in Figure 4.1) is a simple type of role alignment in this sense. Each of the characterological depictions of accents in the texts discussed below has a rhetoric that *invites* certain forms of alignment as we shall see; and although there is no necessity to outcomes at the level of individual texts, the density and institutional stabilization of particular metapragmatic genres does appear to produce relatively stable trends for certain periods. One of the most interesting features of the logic of role alignment is that it shows the process of enregisterment to be relatively flexible, yet non-random. During the course of this apparently continuous process, many aspects of RP – its exemplary speakers, its canonical phonetic patterns – change in substantial ways, and do so more than once. Such changes reflect larger scale trends in society, but also amplify them.

Let me now offer a brief sketch of the historical issues as a prelude to a more extended discussion.

4.3 The emergence of a standard

There is a particular, Whiggish history of Received Pronunciation – found in many books on the subject – in which RP is viewed as descending from the prestige variety of English spoken in southeastern England in the sixteenth century, a region including the court in London and the universities at Oxford and Cambridge.[9] Since this speech variety was spoken not by everyone in this region but by a privileged few (such as the London aristocracy, courtiers, those associated with the universities) it functioned at this time as a regional prestige sociolect rather than a dialect common to southeastern England as a whole. But though the sociolect was recommended as a literary standard in the sixteenth and seventeenth centuries, it neither had a large number of speakers, nor recognition as a standard to be imitated by everyone.[10] Even much of the national aristocracy – a landed gentry linked more to their estates than to London – spoke with regional accents without stigma. So the emergence of RP as a *national* standard involved the expansion of the register construct across social categories of users. How was this effect achieved?

The transformation of this regional sociolect into a supra-local variety is the product of a particular cultural history of language standardization, aspects of which I discuss below. We must understand however that the register formation possessed certain features (illustrated for contemporary RP above) at every point in this historical process: The formation has always involved characterological constructs linked to sound (different ones at different times) mediated and disseminated by discourses that circulate through, and are frequently transformed by, the activities of persons linked to each other in particular, institutionalized genres of communicative activity. The events through which these constructs move through society are speech events involving senders and receivers *of* messages, as well as characterological figures – accent personae – typified *in* message content. Though each such event has a limited provenance and reach, the interlinkage of such events over historical time comprises a higher order structure, what I call a speech chain network (1.6), through which the dissemination of RP and associated constructs greatly expands in demographic terms.

It is important to see, moreover, that the formation called RP did not come about all at once. Indeed, the fact that the process of its formation involved several distinct trends – layered upon each other in historical time, motivating each other by degrees – is critical to the way in which the register came into its heyday in the twentieth century. During the eighteenth century, for example, the prestige court sociolect of the sixteenth century came to be championed as the model for a *national* standard of pronunciation. But the prescriptivist arguments advanced in favor of the proposal were written for – and initially read by – a very small portion of the population. In order for these discourses to have any larger consequence they had to be taken up by entirely different types of actors – a rather diverse group of producers of accent metadiscourses, as we shall see – and brought to the attention of a much larger population of persons in roles of receiver (hearer, reader) of such messages.

In the period between 1760 and 1900 a range of genres of accent metadiscourses emerged and flourished; I discuss five such genres below. Though they differ enormously from each other, all of them promote the expansion of RP by formulating social personae linked to sound – a range of characterological figures – to which the 'receivers' of these messages can and do respond with various types of ensuing behaviors, including types of role alignment that bring accent personae to life in the habits of speech production and perception of ordinary individuals.

In Chapter 1 we saw that semiotic regularities that appear as Durkheimean social facts in one locale have a sociohistorical existence mediated by patterns of communicative behavior that connect many locales to each other. Indeed the notion of a speech-chain, and, more broadly, of a **semiotic-chain** – a chain of participant-linked semiotic events, not all of which are speech-events – is a way of talking about the inter-connectedness of locales through behaviors of a communicative sort. In the discussion in section 1.6 we focused on the specific problem of how a particular kind of semiotic regularity (the pairing of a name with a refer-ent) can grow in social domain through semiotic activity itself. I also discussed (1) a number of other semiotic chain processes, such as those involved in mass communication, dyadic conversation, the socialization of individuals, and others; (2) the difference between historical chains and virtual models of chain-like processes; and (3) the way in which certain virtual models formulate authoritative versions of the phenomena they model. The reader may find it useful to review that discussion before proceeding to the sections that follow.

At various points I have found it convenient to talk of such processes as involving the *transmission of messages* across locales. This formulation simply points to a minimal feature of interconnectedness, namely that some sign-phenomenon connects persons to each other. But any process of 'transmission' is at once also a process of social interaction in which the positional stakes of communicators play a role in shaping the future of history of any 'messages' effectively transmitted across a given chain-segment of the larger process.

Such a view of the transmission of messages can be generalized beyond the case of proper names to talk about the transmission of any kind of cultural message across a population. In the following discussion I apply the model to the spatiotemporal movement of discourses about accent. In generalizing from the case of proper names, however, it is important to see that the idea that speech chain processes transmit 'messages' across social space is coherent only to the extent that we have criteria on the identity of messages. In the case of proper names, both criteria of message form and content are necessary.[11] In the case of the discourses of accent discussed below, criteria of message content (i.e., that the discourse typifies accent in some way) are crucial to all cases; in cases where authorities are cited and quoted, the precise form of prior messages is carried over as well. The notion of *identity of messages* must, moreover, be understood by criteria of fractional congruence (see S 2.3 and the discussion following), not in absolute terms; indeed, the fractional non-identity of messages is itself a measure of the transformation of social relations across different periods and locales, as I show in some detail below.

The *demographic profile* of members of a speech chain network is an important variable shaping the social contours of this process. We have already seen that contemporary public sphere discourses of accent link individuals to each other on a mass scale. In the case of electronically mediated discourses the persons recruited to roles of sender and receiver are not single individuals but groups of individuals who may share certain characteristics. For example, in the case of the BBC broadcasts discussed above the role of sender of the message involves the joint activities of many categories of corporate employee; and the receivers of the message may be sorted by broadcast genre – the news vs. the talk show; pop music vs. opera – into specific target audiences that differ from each other in class, age, etc.

The eighteenth- and nineteenth-century metadiscourses discussed below transmit ideas about accent through print artifacts – books, manuals, magazines, newspapers, etc – that can be read at different times by different persons. Yet for any given point in the speech chain, we can estimate several characteristics of social persons occupying roles of sender and receiver (their number, their demographic characteristics, their relative social status, etc.). We can thus estimate the social trajectories through which particular messages moved and the categories of persons they reached. All of the speech-chain linkages discussed below must be understood as involving speech events linking individuals to each other in events of speaking, reading, writing and so on. Yet the account focuses more on the demographic profiles of members of these networks, referring to particular historical individuals only in some cases.

Let us now see how this type of analysis can illuminate the case at hand.

4.4 The transformation of habits of speech perception

There is ample evidence that metadiscourses of accent in eighteenth- and nineteenth-century Britain involved identifiable speech chain trajectories through which accent values moved in space and time. Although the genres I now consider articulate the values of accent for different audiences – and vary in degrees of explicitness, and type of reception by each audience – the structure of speech chain linkages across genres connects the effects in one domain to those in another, creating historical transformations of a more global kind. Let us consider the characteristics of these genres and the connections between them.

Early prescriptivist works

In the second half of the eighteenth century, scholarly writings on English speech and accent – including treatises on elocution, oratory and education, as well as dictionaries – began to proliferate in an unprecedented way. Mugglestone (1995) observes that five times as many works on elocution appeared in the period 1760–1800 than had appeared in all the years before 1760. Whereas several seventeenth-century phoneticians had produced descriptions of English pronunciation (see Dobson, 1968), many of the eighteenth-century writers sought to connect descriptions of pronunciation to prescriptions for national standards. These works eventually had a widespread influence, but only through the intermediation of speech-chain processes involving works from entirely different genres. For, initially at least, these prescriptivist works exerted an influence only within a small discourse community.[12]

The treatment of accent within these works initially faced some difficulties too. Although Samuel Johnson had included pronunciation in his plans for a dictionary, the actual dictionary, published eight years later in 1755, did not cover pronunciation in any systematic way. Johnson's difficulty lay partly in the fact that no accepted orthography was yet available for representing the sounds of English.

The creation of a phonetic notation for use by the general public (as an aid to 'correct' pronunciation) was a central preoccupation of the most influential early prescriptivist, Thomas Sheridan. Sheridan advocated standards of correct pronunciation in a number of works published over the next two decades.[13] In the *Dissertation* of 1761 Sheridan had declared the intent to devise a phonetic notation, for use in a standard dictionary, in order 'to fix ... a standard of pronunciation, by means of visible marks' (p. 29). The dictionary that appeared nineteen years later contained many of the conventions used in lexical entries today, e.g., phonetic re-spelling of every word, marks for syllable boundaries, symbols for consonant and vowel quality.

The development of this phonetic notation and its increasing use in dictionaries of the period led to a rise in public awareness of difference between norms of pronunciation and norms of ordinary spelling. John Walker's *Critical Pronouncing Dictionary* (London, 1791), which employed a more elaborate version of this notation, was to go through over a hundred editions in the course of the next century. Yet such a phonetic notation made 'visible' only half of the social phenomenon of accent, namely sound. The other half, namely the social personae linked to sound, was made visible by other means. These included a series of characterological constructs linking differences of accent to matters of social identity.

One construct that recurs in Sheridan's writings invokes a trans-European framework of *national* identities: Sheridan ascribes social essences such as 'cultivation' and 'barbarism' to specific nations on the basis of the development of institutions regulating forms of oral discourse. The British, he argues, are a barbarous nation since they lack 'proper grammars and dictionaries,' as well as schools and academies where the correct pronunciation might be taught. In these respects, they differ from the 'cultivated' nations of the South (especially Italy, France and Spain), who 'affix the term of barbarism to this country, in the same manner as the Greeks did to the rest of the world; and on the same principle, on account of the neglect of regulating and polishing our speech' (Sheridan 1761: 1).

A second construct is the contrast between 'provincialism' and 'politeness' within Britain itself. The term 'provincial' marks a geosocial trope: 'By Provincials is here meant all British subjects, whether inhabitants of Scotland, Ireland, Wales, the several counties of England, or the city of London, who speak a corrupt dialect of the English tongue' (Sheridan 1761: 2). Only speakers of the prestige London sociolect are 'polite'; all other Britons – whether urban or rural – are 'provincial.' To remedy this problem, Sheridan proposes to write a Grammar and Dictionary of English for

(5) ... use by all schools professing to teach English. The consequence of teaching children by one method, and one uniform system of rules, would be an uniformity of pronunciation in all so instructed. Thus might the rising generation, born and bred in different countries, and counties, no longer have a variety of dialects, but as subjects of one King, like sons of one father, have one common tongue. All natives of these realms, would be restored to their birthright in commonage of language, which has been too long fenced in, and made the property of a few.

(Sheridan 1761: 36)

Sheridan thus proposes that forms of speech that are prestige commodities in his time ('the property of a few') can be redistributed across the nation *through* the use of his Dictionary and Grammar, and so come to serve as emblems, on the one hand, of unity and egalitarianism *within* the nation; and, on the other, of the cultivation of the Briton in the contrast *among* nations. Yet these sentiments imply contradictory views about the social value of accent. The notion that certain nations are 'cultivated' or 'civilized' because they regulate their speech appeals to a framework of hierarchical social differences among nations. And the goal of trying to fuse the social orders within Britain into a harmonious whole through the regulation of speech implies the obliteration of social distinction.

These contradictions were eventually to reconfigure the values of accent, transforming a system of dialect differences into a system of status-differentiating registers. Differences of pronunciation – to say nothing of lexis, and idiom – were hardly obliterated. The total effect of the prescriptivist discourse was to re-configure the values of accent from its earlier role as an index of geographic affiliation to its role as an index of class status, thus transforming a system of regional diacritics into a system of widely enregistered class emblems. For highly educated speakers, a greater likeness of in-group speech did eventually come about; but for every other demographic group, the result was a growing sense of class differentiation across the space of the nation.

But these effects cannot be attributed directly to the work of Sheridan and his associates in the late eighteenth century, for their works were known initially only within a small discourse community, consisting largely of the upper classes, the educated intelligentsia, and specialists on speech and education. The social transformation was mediated rather by other genres of metadiscourse that were linked to early prescriptivist works by a speech chain structure, but themselves had a much larger circulation.

In other words, the mere articulation of ideas is irrelevant to the social transformation with which we are here concerned. In order for such ideas to have social consequences, metadiscursive standards – such as 'cultivated' and 'barbarous' forms of speech – must become available to language users as criteria deployable in everyday events of utterance evaluation. If the accent in a particular utterance differs from the prestige form, a hearer can formulate judgments about the lack of 'cultivation' of current speaker. But the hearer can employ the prestige accent as a criterion only if he or she is acquainted with – has heard, or heard about – the forms and values of the prestige accent itself. Indeed, the social replicability of patterns of accent evaluation presupposes the widespread circulation of comparable metadiscursive standards. Yet the early prescriptive metadiscourses were known initially only within a small discourse community. Hence the effects of this metadiscourse had to reach a much larger audience before the transformation of regional-dialect values into status-register values could effectively occur.

Popular handbooks

By the mid nineteenth century a genre of popular works on speech and accent – including etiquette manuals, handbooks on pronunciation, elocution and 'grammar' – had become well established. The authors of these works read the more scholarly, technical works discussed above, yet wrote in a non-technical style for a much larger audience, seeking to popularize the message which these works had earlier propounded. These works also paved the way for new markets for accent amelioration. As anxieties about accent grew during the nineteenth century growing numbers of orthoëpists and elocution masters appeared as purveyors of semiotic refinement, offering their services for money.

Such accent anxieties are hardly *sui generis* phenomena, of course. They belong to a larger set of anxieties about class emblems of a more varied sort, which grow during this period of increasing social mobility and changing class relations. My goal in this section and the next is partly to show that during this expansionist phase of enregisterment, speech forms were syncretized with a larger range of demeanor indexicals, yielding a semiotic register of comportment of which the discourse register called RP is but a fragment. I return to this aspect of the argument in Chapter 5 (especially 5.7), where I discuss the non-linguistic features of this register in more detail.

In their efforts to make proper speech the business of the common man these works transformed the metadiscursive constructs linking speech to social identity in substantial ways. Rather than relying on a framework of social difference among nations, as Sheridan had done the century before, these works describe the effects of utterance in everyday conversation, focusing on the pragmatic order internal to the speech event itself.

(6) No saying was ever truer than that good breeding and good education are sooner discovered from the style of speaking ... than from any other means.
(*Composition, Literary and Rhetorical, Simplified*, London, 1850; cited in Mugglestone 1995: 1[14])

Many of these works directly address themselves to members of the expanding middle classes. They formulate speech and accent as 'passports,' as means of gaining access to 'good circles':

(7) Accent and pronunciation must be diligently studied by the conversationalist. A person who uses vulgarisms will make but little way in good circles ... A proper accent gives importance to what you say, engages the respectful attention of your hearer, and is your passport to new circles of acquaintance.
(*Talking and Debating*, London, 1856; cited in Mugglestone 1995: 1)

In observing that 'a proper accent' is causally linked to a variety of interpersonal effects, such metapragmatic statements motivate speaker attributes in relation to other pragmatic features within speech-events: a 'proper' *accent* 'gives importance' to *message content* and 'engages the respectful attention' of the *hearer*, thus transforming social relations between *interlocutors*. A single utterance is now a diagram that permits the calculation of many aspects of its pragmatic context. Observe that all of the components thus typified – message form, message content, hearer, speaker – co-occur *within* speech-events (Figure 4.2). The texts typify these components in relation to each other, explicitly relating attributes of one component to

Co-occurring features	Distinctive attributes	Diagrammatic motivation
Accent/message form	[[proper]] vs. [other]	[[ ]] : [ ] : [ ] : [ ] ...
Message content	[[important]] vs. [other]	:: [[ ]] : [ ] : [ ] : [ ] ...
Hearer	[[respectful]] vs. [other]	:: [[ ]] : [ ] : [ ] : [ ] ...
Speaker	[[{successful, well-received, socially mobile, etc.}]] vs. [other]	:: [[ ]] : [ ] : [ ] : [ ] ...

Figure 4.2 *Diagrammatic motivation of co-occurring variables*

attributes of another, viz., the speaker's persona, reflected in forms of proper speech, whose content thereby gains importance, commanding the respect of the hearer. Such accounts motivate indexical icons, or diagrams, for construing the effects of speech.[15] Indexical effects that are in principle distinct are motivated in relation to each other – i.e., are taken to presuppose or imply each other – so that none of the individual effects now appear arbitrary. Each indexical effect is now part of a motivated diagram that grounds the relations between parts. Such metasemiotic diagrams are inherently compelling. They allow the language user to justify or rationalize one type of effect by appeal to another in folk reflection.

A different type of iconic motivation is achieved by popular handbooks that explicitly anchor proper speech to images of class. Etiquette guides were a particularly important source – and resource – for the dissemination of such constructs:

(8) There are certain arbitrary peculiarities of manner, speech, language, taste, &c. which mark the high-born and high-bred. These should be observed and had. They are the signs-manual of good-breeding by which gentlemen recognize each other wherever they meet.

(*Advice to a Young Gentleman on Entering Society*, 1839: 138)

Though it describes familiarity with such habits as an implicit 'signs-manual' – allegedly part of the semiotic competence of the gentleman – the text's own expository work renders the construct accessible to any reader and, especially, to the would-be gentleman addressed by the work. Hence the text transforms both the explicitness and circulation of the construct. Though the signs bearing these values may have seemed 'arbitrary' to the author in 1839, their codification and dissemination through popular genres made them appear 'natural' to many by century's end.

A characteristic feature of etiquette guides is that they link accent to a range of other signs of proper demeanor. The codification of proper demeanor links habits of pronunciation to habits of dress, carriage, gesture, grooming, cosmetics, and numerous other behavioral displays. These texts seek to train the *senses* of gentlemen and ladies, not just their behavior. Learning to read the demeanor of one's interactant is a prerequisite to 'proper' (i.e., interactionally appropriate) behavior. One cannot carry the same 'system of manners' into relations with people of every rank since those of elevated rank have a greater 'delicacy of perception' than the lower ranks.

(9) For example, in a refined circle, the pronunciation of 'beard' according to the analogy of 'feard' would be deemed an evidence of high education: persons of inferior delicacy and knowledge would consider it a mark of low breeding.

   (Advice to a Young Gentleman on Entering Society, 1839: 140)

Thus there are some occasions in life 'in which it is necessary not to be a gentleman' (p. 139). A semiotic reading of the current interactional scenario – and particularly of the interactant's rank – is a prerequisite to performing one's own status and rank in a way readable by the interactant. Notice that this observation is a corollary, for the case of stereotypic social indexicals, of an observation made earlier regarding referring choices (S 2.2): the author of *Advice* is here observing that the interpersonal effectiveness of semiotic choices increases whenever the choice made is more tightly calibrated to (is formulated through a reflexive reading of) variables in play at the moment of utterance.

As signs of demeanor became more explicitly linked to class, the lexicographic definitions of terms like *gentleman* and *lady* shifted from an exclusive focus on inalienable attributes, such as lineage, property and rank, to include behavioral and interactional criteria. As Mugglestone observes (1995: 86), Walker's *Dictionary* of 1791 had defined *gentleman* as 'a man of birth, a man of extraction' and *lady* as 'a woman of rank.' But Ogilvie's *Dictionary* of 1870 defines *gentleman* as '... in the highest sense ... a man of strict integrity and honour, of self-respect, and intellectual refinement, as well as refined manners and good breeding'; and *lady* as 'a term of complaisance; applied to almost any well dressed woman, but appropriately to one of refined manners and education.' Lexical entries such as these clearly anchor names for social positions to features of performed demeanor. They also bespeak an anxiety about degrees of social worth and its misrecognition (cf. a gentleman 'in the highest sense'; lady as 'a term of complaisance'), an anxiety created partly by the fact that the 'signs-manual' of social worth had now become a publicly circulating document, and explicit metasemiotic instruction in the management of such signs was now available to all who could afford it.

What, we might ask, is the relevance of these public texts to our understanding of culture? Neither the notion that dictionaries create new ideas, nor the notion that they transparently reflect common usage stand up to much scrutiny, cherished though they may be as chestnuts of folk-wisdom. We noted in 4.2 and 4.3 that physical text-artifacts such as dictionaries acquire social consequences not by virtue of their physical existence but by virtue of way in which they inform the behaviors of persons connected to each other within semiotic chains, e.g., when a person who reads the text-artifact in an event of reading is, in turn, linked to other social beings in further semiotic activity constrained in some way by that event of reading (e.g., through the use of a pronunciation given in a dictionary entry, the performance of a speech style described in an etiquette guide). Artifacts that disseminate normative discourses have a social life only through the mediation of semiotic chains linking persons to each other. The artifacts disseminate social classifications, which are inhabited by social actors, whose interactions transform those classifications, leading to new artifacts. It is only by considering the movement of such discourses through people and things that we can understand the spread of this culture of language, not by observing some element – such as a mediating artifact, a lexical entry, a precipitated habit or belief – that exists as a fragment or partial of the total process.

Literary works

Novels and other literary works comprise a third genre of metadiscourse about accent. In this case we have direct biographical evidence of speech-chain linkages: many of the most famous novelists were avid readers of works belonging to the first two genres.[16] The general form that metadiscursive activity took within this genre was to foreground selected correlations between speech and social identity through devices such as narrated dialogue and dependent tropes of personification. Narrated dialogue formulates a robust structure of 'voicing' contrasts within the literary work (Bakhtin 1981), a juxtaposition of speech forms from different registers highlighting contrasts of characterological types.

But novelistic depictions of accent do not merely represent the realities of social life, they amplify and transform them into more memorable, figuratively rendered forms. Consider for example the case of /h/-dropping, the most famous index of stigmatized speech. The literary character universally associated with this feature is Dickens' Uriah Heep. Yet, although Uriah Heep is stereotypically linked to /h/-dropping, he does not actually drop most of his /h/'s! In the following exchange from Dickens' *David*

Copperfield the italicized tokens exhibit /h/-dropping, words in boldface preserve /h/:

(10) 'I suppose you are quite a great lawyer?' I said, after looking at him for some time.
'Me, Master Copperfield?' said Uriah. 'Oh, no! I'm a very *umble* person.'
It was no fancy of mine about his hands, I observed; for he frequently ground the palms against each other as if to squeeze them dry and warm, besides often wiping them, in a stealthy way, on his pocket-handkerchief.
'I am well aware that I am the *umblest* person going,' said Uriah Heep, modestly; 'let the other be where **he** may. My mother is likewise a very *umble* person. We live in a *numble* abode, Master Copperfield, but **have** much to be thankful for. My father's former calling was *umble*. **He** was a sexton.'
'What is he now?' I asked.
'**He** is a partaker of glory at present, Master Copperfield,' said Uriah Heep. 'But we **have** much to be thankful for. **How** much **have** I to be thankful for, in living with Mr. Wickfield!'
I asked Uriah if he had been with Mr. Wickfield long?
'I **have** been with **him**, going on four year, Master Copperfield,' said Uriah; shutting up his book, after carefully marking the place where had left off. 'Since a year after my father's death. **How** much **have** I to be thankful for, in that! **How** much **have** I to be thankful for in Mr. Wickfield's kind intention . . .'

Most words in Uriah's speech preserve /h/. Uriah Heep is the literary avatar of /h/-dropping – a folk-icon famously linked to dicta such as 'always be 'umble' – but not consistently a practitioner of it. The actual cases of /h/-dropping represented here occur in tokens of the word '[h]umble'. The word implements a reflexive trope: it semantically denotes the interactional effect indexed by its phonological shape! The trope links an image of social personhood neatly to a single word, one that is repeatable, humorous, memorable, and hence capable of widespread circulation.

A general effect of literary metadiscourses was to create a memorable cast of fictional characters, whose popularity made the link between accent and social character more widely known. These links were foregrounded – even caricatured – through a range of literary tropes. Characters like Dickens' Mr. Micawber and Mr. Pecksniff use the standard language, but with a tendency towards excessive circumlocution and euphemism ('pecuniary difficulties' for 'debt'), which yield what is at times a slightly parodic representation of genteel speech; in the case of Pecksniff we see 'a pseudo-dramatic manner of delivery which, although redolent of the oratorical register, is mainly applied with few exceptions, by Pecksniff throughout his private life, even to those closest to him' (Golding 1985: 118). Similarly, the humility avowed by Uriah Heep and foregrounded through tropic depictions of /h/-dropping stand in sharp contrast to his insolence and desire for respect from others. In such cases, the very inconsistency between different layers of pragmatic function (in Heep's case between his 'umble-ness and the content of what he says to others; in Pecksniff's case, the overextension of public styles to private contexts) constitutes an implicit metapragmatic commentary on the pragmatics of speech style, foregrounding and making visible selected forms of speech, as well as the performed demeanors which count as their effects.

To a reader of the novel there is a message here, of course, a message that links accent to social persona. Yet such works do not describe the value of accent, they dramatize its uses. They depict icons of personhood linked to speech that invite forms of role alignment on the part of the reader. In contrast to the metadiscursive genres discussed earlier, the message has become more implicit in certain ways. Yet it has also become more concrete and palpable to the reader.

Consider now issues of circulation. Though readers of such novels no doubt sought to 'improve themselves,' few would have read them to improve their accent. Novelistic works thus brought the message that speech choices index characterological figures before a much larger segment of society than before, including not only those who read treatises or handbooks on accent, but also those avowing no interest in speech or elocution per se. The recirculation of stock characters in derived genres – such as music, drama, and the like – further expanded social awareness of the cultural form. The 'receivers' of the message also differed in sociological terms. They now included not only the upper classes and the educated intelligentsia but also members of the expanding middle classes.

Penny weeklies

Popular periodicals soon responded to the increasing demand for instruction in matters of speech and lifestyle. Mitchell 1977 argues that the penny weekly journal is perhaps the most significant form of mass literature in nineteenth-century Britain. The first notable journal in this genre is the *Penny Magazine*, launched in 1832; others include the *Penny Satirist* and its successor the *London Pioneer*. By the mid-1850s this popular market was dominated entirely by two penny journals, the *Family Herald* and the *London Journal*, whose combined circulation of three quarters of a million far exceeded that of the most famous novels.[17]

These works transformed the circulation of accent metadiscourse in several new directions. Their lower price brought metadiscourse of accent before an even wider readership, including segments of the lower middle and upper working classes (instrument-makers, merchant's clerks, bookkeepers, navvies, land surveyors, and a host of other professions). This demographic segment grew with the expansion of the railways after the 1840s. Mitchell 1977 argues that many of these magazines were read not by working men but by their housewives; the values gleaned from their pages were very likely passed on to their children in the course of everyday socialization.

The dialogic form (used in novels in depictions of *fictional* characters) is extended in this genre to dialogue involving *real* people, e.g., in letters of advice written by readers to columnists. The readers of these works are aware of the prospect of social mobility. They seek to acquire the manners and forms of etiquette that bespeak a higher status:

(11) The readers of the *London Journal* and the *Family Herald* actively sought information about the values, standards, and mechanical details of living in a milieu that was new to them. Their letters to the correspondence column reveal their conscious mobility. They want to eradicate the traces of their origin that linger in their grammar and pronunciation. They ask the kinds of questions about etiquette and general knowledge that would be impossible for anyone with a polite background and more than a rudimentary education. The advertisers urge them to buy textbooks, life assurance, and fashion magazines, to learn elocution, French, Italian, and music.

(Mitchell 1977: 34)

The capacity of accent to index social distinction is a matter of everyday concern to readers. The recirculation of letters of advice in correspondence columns carries the message that a speech standard exists and is of common concern to others in their position. Moreover, accent is now incorporated into a larger set of prestige commodities that are advertised by sellers and discussed by columnists in overtly characterological terms. Accent thus remains an object of metasemiotic scrutiny and characterization, but not in isolation; it is syncretized with other signs of demeanor to form an array of performable indices sought by those with social aspirations.

The reader's desire to attain these indices of distinction is reinforced by more implicit forms of characterological work; and, in particular, by depictions that invite a form of role alignment between reader and narrated persona. The magazines contain popular short stories that depict characters of somewhat higher social standing than the readers themselves, thus furnishing models for the reader concerned with social mobility:

(12) The 'realistic' short stories usually feature characters of a slightly higher social class than the reader; the tradesman's daughter read about the merchant's daughter to learn how she behaved. Another extremely common heroine is the officer's orphan working as governess. She need not be a bridge into the social elite; her employer is sometimes a grocer instead of a lord. She is an attractive

model, for she demonstrates to the woman of narrow means that ladyhood is not dependent on income, nor destroyed by the necessity of working, but lies in manners and bearing.

(Mitchell 1977: 40)

The primary producers of this genre – editors, journalists, columnists, short story writers – belong to the educated middle class; they employ many of the texts discussed earlier – such as pronouncing dictionaries, etiquette manuals – as instruments of their own professional work; they read the novels and other literary works of the period. They are thus linked to earlier genres by a speech chain structure. Yet they expand the circulation of accent metadiscourses in entirely new directions through their own work. The receivers of its messages include the working classes; the messages themselves contain characterological images that are models of behavior to which readers are drawn by their own group-relative interest, their concern for upward mobility. Accent continues to be typified by these discourses, though it is not treated in splendid isolation from other indices of distinction. It is syncretically coupled with other indexicals by the forms of metasemiotic treatment most common to this genre.

Speech chain linkages among accent metadiscourses, ca. 1750–1870

In transmitting particular messages about the social value of accent, the above genres served to create, within an increasingly larger public, a greater awareness of the importance of accent. Table 4.5 summarizes some features of the circulation of the genres discussed above.

I have argued also that particular texts within these genres were linked together by connections between writers and readers of these texts, thus comprising a speech chain structure over historical time. The larger circulation of the later genres greatly expanded the reach of accent metadiscourses. The prescriptivist works discussed above (treatises, pamphlets, dictionaries) were produced largely in the period 1750–1800; they promulgated accent standards to the aristocracy and intelligentsia. The popular handbooks (etiquette guides, sixpenny manuals) comprised a genre that expanded after

Table 4.5. *Rough estimates of genre circulation*

Genre	Immediate circulation	Demographics: Circulation extends to
(a) Early prescriptivist works	small	(a) aristocracy & intelligentsia
(b) Popular handbooks	larger	+ (b) upper middle classes
(c) Novels & literary works	large	+ (c) middle classes
(d) Penny Weeklies	very large	+ (d) lower middle & upper working classes

the 1830s, and catered to those who aspired to – but did not necessarily belong to – such select social circles. These works were also of interest to novelists who, in turn, brought depictions of accent before the rising middle classes. The penny weeklies combined forms of accent depiction with advice on manners and etiquette, and with advertisements for a variety of products linked to social advancement. Let me now summarize the various kinds of evidence for the speech chain linkages described earlier.

One kind of evidence consists of attestations in the biographical record. In some cases we know that particular historical figures who authored works in one genre employed works in other genres as metasemiotic resources (e.g., that George Bernard Shaw, author of *Pygmalion*, read popular handbooks on elocution and manners, as well as more technical works; see n. 16).

A second type of evidence is attested text-internally in the pattern of citation to other works. There are numerous cases where authors of one genre explicitly cite authors of another, thus explicitly preserving an earlier layer of the metadiscourse in the recirculation of messages across genres. For example, authors of etiquette manuals and novels appeal to the authority of earlier lexicographers such as John Walker. Similarly Henry Alford, the author of *A Plea for The Queen's English*, inveighs against the practice of /h/-dropping by citing the speech of Uriah Heep (the passage to which Alford refers is quoted in (10) above), adding that 'It is difficult to believe that this pronunciation can long survive the satire of Dickens' (Alford 1866: 41). Such patterns of recirculation indicate the prior discursive experiences of the writer. They also ground the epistemic force of the message in a prior authority – in the scholarly or literary acumen of the author cited – thus inviting the reader to align his or her own self-image with a more complex, internally laminated role model, a characterological figure backed through **a chain of authentication** in another authority, understood now both as the 'principal' (Goffman 1981a) and the 'expert' (Putnam 1975) who underwrites the message. In moments like these the pattern of recirculation has begun to appeal explicitly to a semiotic division of labor (see 2.4) whereby the authority of a new cadre of metasemiotic specialists – a system of expertise as yet 'emergent', not yet fully 'dominant' in the sense of Gramsci 1971 – is invoked as a warrant for the author's own prescriptions.

A third kind of link is inferable from the presuppositions of message about accent. For example the authors of the nineteenth-century popular handbooks discussed above *presuppose the existence*, without further argument, of the formal and characterological norms of speech whose reality the eighteenth-century prescriptivists had *hoped to establish*, e.g., that oral speech exhibits phonetic regularities; that accent can mark cultivation; that supra-local standards ought to be imitated no matter where you live. The existence of a pronunciation standard was an ideal-to-be-achieved for the early prescriptivists; for the popularists it is a 'real' baseline against which deviation can be measured in everyday interactions, and linked to a space of minutely differentiated characterological figures, e.g., 'gentlemen' vs. 'the vulgar' vs. 'the vulgar rich.'

4.5 The transformation of habits of utterance

What can we say about the net effect of the genres considered so far? The genres that had wide public circulation – etiquette manuals, literary works and popular periodicals – created a widespread awareness in the reading public of the social value of accent, including an awareness of the social value of the most prestigious accent, RP. These works typically discussed only a few, highly stigmatized features of non-RP speech, such as /h/-dropping. They were neither sufficiently precise in their treatment of accent nor sufficiently comprehensive so as to allow members of the reading public to transform their habits of pronunciation in any systematic way. We might say that these genres replicate the *competence to recognize* accent contrasts and associated values across the space of the nation without replicating the *competence to speak* the most prestigious accent. This latter task required a social institution of an entirely different kind.

The transformation of schooling

There are some obvious ways in which schools are uniquely suited to the replication of speech habits. They are sites of explicitly normative meta-discursive activity to which students are exposed for prolonged periods of time. By the early twentieth century, the British public school had become so centrally linked to the acquisition of RP that the phonetician Daniel Jones proposed the term *Public School Pronunciation* as a name for the accent. But how did schools become institutions fit for the replication of an élite accent?

When the first of these schools were founded – such as Winchester (in 1382), Eton (1440), Westminster (1560), Harrow (1571) – their curricula were focused not on English but on the classical languages, and their students drawn from the 'poor and needy' of the local parish. In contrast, the children of the upper classes studied with private tutors, traditionally at home. Yet by the late nineteenth century, these schools had been trans-formed – both in terms of curricula and student demographics – into an altogether distinct type of institution. These transformations – leading eventually to a 'public school' system designed for the education of élites – have their roots in the metadiscourses and speech-chain structures discussed earlier.

A critical step in the transformation of schooling was the introduction of English into the curriculum; the change was motivated or made plausible by the genres discussed in section 4.4. We have seen that Sheridan, Walker, and their followers had sought programmatically to transform public perceptions of the vernacular tongue. The prescriptivist argument that English had its own rules of 'proper' pronunciation and grammar sought to displace the view that English was – in comparison to Latin and Greek – an inherently vulgar and inconstant tongue. The popular genres discussed above linked the emerging phonetic standard to canons of politeness and etiquette, and to images of class. Hence, by the mid-nineteenth century, Sheridan's proposal (of 1756) that instruction in spoken English be part of a gentleman's education began to seem more natural and self-evident than it had a century before.

The student body and duration of study were also to change. By 1860, the number of boarders (as opposed to day-students) was on the rise. Yet the typical boarder came from local, often poor, families, and stayed only a year or two. After 1870, both trends had been reversed: schools sought to lower the enrollment of local students and, increasingly, to cater to upper and aspiring middle class families; children from these families were sent to boarding schools for longer periods, thus permitting more extended isolation from the discursive milieu from which they came, a more elaborate renovation of speech habits. These changes were partly the result of technological and socioeconomic developments that were independent of perceptions of speech: the expansion of the railways made it possible for more children to attend non-local schools; the expansion of surplus incomes made boarding schools affordable to a larger segment of the population, despite growth in tuition and boarding fees.

Yet metadiscursive representations played a role here as well. For instance, the recirculation of images of schooling in literary works made the public school accent recognizable to a segment of the population larger than those having direct exposure to it:

(13) Because of the amazing popularity of a newly invented literary genre, the school story – read by millions of pupils who themselves had no access to real-life experience of a public school – similar institutions, expectations, and some of the language of public school life, were imported into many other different types of school.

(Honey 1989a: 28)

Here the recirculation of one genre by another changes its effects. The public school story is a literary genre of discursive interaction (between authors and readers) which presupposes the existence of the various genres of discursive interaction that occur within the public school (between teacher and student, among students) but which it now recirculates – albeit in idealized, literary representations – before a much larger segment of the population, thus creating a greater awareness of accent as an emblem of distinction.

The Education Reform Act of 1870 resulted in a sharp increase in the total number of schools, a state of affairs that led to the creation of emblems of self-differentiation on the part of the older, more established, public schools:

(14) Public schools invented distinctive ties for their Old Boys to wear, developed Old Boy Associations and published registers of members' names, but for many purposes these only worked when checking out the products of the better known schools. The most easily manageable, if superficial index of public school status was accent. By the end of the nineteenth century a non-standard accent in a young Englishman signalled non-attendance at a public school, whereas if he spoke RP he was either a genuine member of the new caste of public school men or he had gone to some trouble to adjust his accent else- where, thus advertising the fact that he identified with that caste and its values.

(Honey 1989a: 28)

After 1870, a public school education became an important means for establishing the social credentials of those who aspired to polite society. Men of political power and national eminence who received a privileged education before 1870 had tended to retain traces of their regional accents. But this tendency was to abate in the years to come.

Classroom instruction

With the expansion of schooling itself an increasing number of children were exposed to a common genre of metadiscursive practice, namely class- room instruction. This genre was highly dialogic in one sense: the teacher and students moved across the role of speaker of utterances, the students often reproducing the teacher's utterances within their own speaking turns. But from the point of view of prescriptive metadiscourses of accent, it was the teacher who was, in the relevant sense, the speaker of the metadiscourse, the student its hearer.

The speakers of this metadiscourse were already 'hearers' of the metadis- cursive genres discussed earlier simply by virtue of exposure to newspapers and novels. They were exposed to profession-specific metadiscourses as well, especially those which they encountered in the course of their own training as teachers. The establishment of institutions like teacher's colleges and school boards gave rise to textbooks and pedagogic manuals through which teachers and headmasters were exposed to prescriptive dicta such as the following:

(15) . . . there is no security that the pupils acquire correct pronunciation, unless the teacher be able to give the example. Accordingly the teacher who is anxious to be in this, as in all things, a model, should strive during his preparatory training to acquire a thorough knowledge of English pronunciation. This can only be done by careful observation of good speakers, or, if need be, by a course of lessons with an accomplished and trust-worthy teacher.

(Morrison, *Manual of School Management*, London, 1863: 126)

The pronunciation of the teacher is itself modeled on the accents of exemplary speakers and, once formed, is a model to be replicated among students. Yet in order to accomplish this within the classroom, the teacher has to learn about the organs of replication.

(16) The teacher has to train the vocal organs to produce sounds distinctly and correctly. To do this, he will have to acquaint himself with the functions of the various organs concerned in the production of speech. He will have to be able to detect and correct bad habits and defects of utterance, and show the children how to use tongue, teeth, lips, and palate, in order to articulate distinctly.

(Livesey, *Moffat's How to Teach Reading*, London, 1882; cited in Mugglestone 1995: 299)

An elementary knowledge of articulatory phonetics is now provided to the teacher as a kind of social technology, allowing him not only to monitor his own organs during speech production but to bring the movement of his students' organs into conformity with his own. Thus, the effort to replicate a phonetic standard across the space of the nation literally requires control over the movement of bodily organs. Such control is to be exercised with sufficient regularity within the classroom so as to become internalized in the student as self-control and, eventually, as habit.

But given the variety of regional accents each locale is in a sense uniquely defective when measured against the standard. Hence the teacher receives an elementary training in ethnographic methods of a kind, methods of participant observation that allow him to hunt out the phonetic 'defects' peculiar to each locale and, once identified, to eliminate them within the classroom.

(17) Without waiting to point out all the peculiarities of pronunciation which characterize various districts, we advise the teacher, whenever he finds himself located in a particular parish, to observe carefully the prevalent peculiarities; and, when he has done so, vigorously to set himself to correct them among his pupils.

(Morrison, *Manual of School Management*, London, 1863: 127)

The activities through which this is to be achieved in the classroom are made explicit in pedagogic manuals and schoolbooks of the time. These works are highly explicit in their attempt to isolate features of accent, seeking to train the ear to perceive sounds and the vocal organs to produce them. A textbook of the period (*The First Part of the Progressive Parsing Lesson*, 1833; cited in Mugglestone, 1995: 302) presents the repetitive drilling of vowel sounds as follows:

(18)
TEACHER.   Tell me the vowels sounds in *barn yard*
PUPIL.   *Barn* middle *a*, *Yard* middle *a*

T.	Bee-hive.
P.	*Bee* long *e*, *hive* long *i*.
T.	Blue-Bell.
P.	*Blue* long *u*, *bell* short *e*.

This particular genre of the metadiscourse – then a relatively new genre employing classroom drills in Greek and Latin declension as models for drills in English pronunciation – is highly explicit in its attempt to isolate features of accent, seeking to train the ear to perceive sounds and the vocal organs to produce them. The printed text describes the structure of the discursive interaction which it regiments, detailing both the pattern of turn taking and the messages to be produced in each turn. By replicating such speech events within the classroom, the teacher can, over time, replicate in the student precisely those habits of pronunciation which the metadiscourse defines as the standard.

Observe that whereas genres replicating awareness of the register had already existed for a hundred years (section 4.4), the transformation of schooling after 1870 expanded the social domain of persons having competence to speak it. The demographic domain of replication remained restricted, however, albeit along a different boundary. Fluency in RP was eventually to become an attribute of a group correspondingly larger than the group of persons born into RP speaking families in each generation. Yet mechanisms of gatekeeping continued to restrict access to the 'best' accents only to students of the élite public schools, contributing to latter-day asymmetries in competence over socially distinct 'speech levels' of RP.

4.6 Asymmetries of competence and perceptions of value

I noted in section 4.1 that the competence to recognize the prestige form of RP has a wider social distribution in British society than the competence to speak it. Such asymmetries of competence themselves function as principles of *value maintenance* under certain conditions. Since RP has traditionally been linked to positively valued stereotypic personae (as opposed to slang, for example, which is negatively valorized), its speakers inhabit, through the act of utterance, a social persona recognized as statusful by others. Since the effect is recognized by a group of people larger than those capable of performing it, the forms of RP become objects of value – indeed, scarce goods – that many individuals seek to acquire. Hence the asymmetric distribution of types of linguistic competence itself functions as a principle of value maintenance in society, giving a system of register values a measure of stability in time. A number of factors can influence this pattern of stability-for-a-while, of course, thus resetting the pattern over time. Let me here draw attention to just two considerations, each of which points to a class of processes that influence positional perceptions of value.

First, as the discussion in sections 4.4 and 4.5 shows, such synchronic asymmetries are by no means *sui generis* phenomena. They derive from historical differences in patterns of communicative transmission of the register within the language community, differences mediated by distinctly institutionalized genres of metadiscourse, some shaping recognition, others performance. More people recognize the positive value of the register than speak it because the genres that reproduce the first type of competence have the wider demographic reach. Changes in patterns of communicative transmission can reset the distribution of types of competence and hence its perceived value as a commodity form.

Second, such asymmetries of competence serve as principles of value *maintenance* only if – and *as long as* – the utterable forms of the register continue to be associated with images of personhood judged in 'positive' terms relative to other varieties. The pattern of apparent equilibrium can be reset in various ways: by changes in the space of characterological contrasts, in the specific personae linked to the Standard, in the public sphere metadiscourses that evaluate variation in speech for characterological content, due to changing social relations between 'exemplary' speakers and other social categories of persons. It can be reset, in fact, by any change that alters the conditions under which *responses* to accent stereotypes – and, especially, forms of role alignment with stereotypic figures – occur.

Let us consider some recent changes in RP that appear to be of this type.

4.7 Changes in exemplary speaker

I have been concerned here with the expansionist phase of the enregisterment of RP (ca. 1760–1900), a period in which the register grew in popular recognition and acclaim. I have not discussed the twentieth-century fortunes of RP very much, a period in which it dominated public life in Britain and also exercised influence elsewhere in the English speaking world. More recently RP has begun to give ground to other vernacular accents within England, particularly Cockney, yielding hybrid forms such as Estuary English[18]; this is sometimes depicted as a period of relative decline, what we might call a recessive phase. It is on this phase of enregisterment that I wish to comment briefly here.

For any register, changes of many kinds – of phonetic form, pragmatic values, social domain of users – are almost continuously in progress. Change is cheap, in one sense. I want to suggest, however, that in the case of changes in a prestige standard, changes in exemplary speaker carry a distinctive weight in the public imagination.

There is plenty of evidence that the twentieth-century history of RP has involved several changes in the way the exemplary speaker is characterized or depicted. In the early 1900s Daniel Jones regarded graduates of élite public schools as a reference standard for RP; in the 1930s H. C. Wyld accorded the same status to British Army Officers; in the 1970s A. C. Gimson cited BBC announcers as exemplary speakers. Although these linguists did not have explicitly prescriptivist agendas (the case of Wyld is unclear, however), the presence or absence of prescriptivist intent is hardly relevant. We have seen that prescriptivism in the narrow sense is not the primary engine of enregisterment. Once formulated, characterological figures often acquire a social life of their own, trickling down into popular stereotypes through further patterns of recirculation. Public School Pronunciation continued to be regarded as an exemplary norm, whatever Jones' intent may have been in coining the term.

Consider now the case of the BBC. BBC broadcasts have themselves played a substantial role in replicating images of exemplary speakers, though different ones at different times. The accents performed in BBC radio broadcasts in the 1920s and '30s were closer to conservative accents ('U RP') than later forms. Many BBC announcers of the 1970s and '80s displayed the accent of educated professionals, the variety sometimes called 'Mainstream RP'; its mainstreaming was doubtless a result of this process as well. In this case, larger social changes – such as the rise and expansion of the professional middle classes – played a role in shaping the choices of BBC producers. However, once such choice are made, patterns of exemplification in the mass media themselves amplify the processes of which they are a part, e.g., by furnishing the same model of exemplary speech to very large audiences, thus homogenizing the conditions for subsequent response behaviors and role alignments across a wide social domain. However particular audiences may respond, more of them are responding to the same thing.

Changes in exemplary speaker are the subject of extended commentary in public sphere discourses in Britain today and elsewhere. On 21 December 2000, the British paper *The Independent* published an article whose headline declared that 'Even the Queen no longer speaks the Queen's English.' Here are some excerpts:

(19) *Cor blimey! Even the Queen no longer speaks the Queen's English*
Givin' it large Ma'am! Her Majesty may not be so amused to find that a team of linguists has found her guilty of no longer speaking the Queen's English. A group of Australian researchers analysed every Christmas message made by the Queen since 1952 and discovered that she now speaks with an intonation more Chelmsford than Windsor ... [T]he scientists found that Elizabeth II has dumbed down – albeit unwittingly – to fit in with the classless zeitgeist of New

Labour's Britain ... [They] reported yesterday in the journal Nature
that even the Queen is not immune to the rise of the estuarine English
spoken by southerners. The researchers said: 'The pronunciation of
all languages change subtly over time ... Our analysis reveals that the
Queen's pronunciation of some vowels has been influenced by the
standard southern British accent of the 1980s which is more typically
associated with speakers who are younger and lower in the social
hierarchy.' David Abercrombie, the distinguished phonetician,
remarked in 1963 about the importance of accent as a mark of class.
'One either speaks the received pronunciation or one does not, and if
the opportunity to learn it in youth has not arisen, it is almost
impossible to learn it in later life,' he said. Although the Queen has
resisted the more vulgar aspects of cockney English, such as aitch-
dropping, she has been influenced by it. For example, there is now a
tendency to pronounce the 'l' in 'milk' as a vowel ... A palace
spokesman said: 'We have been made aware of the research and we
leave it for others to assess it.'

The news was recirculated in intense media activity over the next few weeks
both in Britain and overseas. Just three days later, for example, *The Boston
Globe* (24 December 2000) published the following version of the story:

(20) *The Queen no longer speaks the Queen's English. Commonness creeps
into royal accent*
LONDON – Blimey, 'er royal 'ighnes is a right oul' one of us. A team
of Australian researchers has listened to four decades' worth of Queen
Elizabeth's annual Christmas Day addresses and concluded that the
queen is starting to sound more like her subjects. It's not as if she's gone
cockney or mockney ... but neither is she speaking in the clipped,
cut-glass accent that first greeted Britons nearly a half century ago.
Writing in Nature magazine, Jonathan Harrington and two of his
colleagues at Macquarie University in Sydney conclude that the demise
of the Queen's English is part of the process that continues to blur class
distinctions in what was once a class-bound society. The queen, they
say, has not started dropping her H's like a cockney, but she is starting
to pronounce her words like most other English people. They detected
significant differences in 10 out of 11 vowel sounds. When she used
to say 'had' it rhymed with 'bed,' now it rhymes with 'bad.' She, it
seems, is slowly acquiring the flattened vowels and glottal stops of
'Estuary English,' which is peculiar to southeastern England ...

In order to understand the nature of this change it is important to see,
first, that the Queen has never spoken 'the Queen's English' in one
sense: historically, the term itself has functioned not as a label describing the

actual speech of any particular Queen, but a label prescribing a standard of speech to the Queen's subjects, i.e., to commoners.[19] Royals and aristocrats have traditionally distanced themselves from this standard-for-commoners in various ways, e.g., in Victorian times through the phenomenon of aristocratic disfluency, forms of restricted upper-class slang, and a preference for distinctive diction and accent (Philips 1984: 35–51).

What has changed, then, is the pattern of role alignment: the speech of aristocrats now tends *toward* the speech of commoners, not away from it, i.e., 'the Queen's pronunciation ... has been influenced by the ... accent ... more typically associated with speakers who are younger and lower in the social hierarchy.'

Such changes do not occur all at once. They involve a progressive spread of a phonetic pattern, both within a single speaker's habits and across social categories of speakers. Thus David Rosewarne, who coined the term 'Estuary English' (Rosewarne 1984), describes a slightly different picture of attested usage in the early 1990s. At this time, the Queen herself did not exhibit this pattern, apparently, though the Archbishop of Canterbury and Princess Diana definitely 'did it':

(21) John Major is slightly too old to do it. Despite his age, Lord Tebbit still does it, but he says radio and television presenters do it much more than he ever did. Ken Livingstone M. P. and Tony Banks M. P. are proud they both do it. It's so common nowadays that even Dr. Carey, the Archbishop of Canterbury, does it, both in public as well as in private. Mrs. Thatcher certainly has never done it and nor has the Queen, though one of her son's wives flirts with it. As Princess Diana was once heard saying: 'There's a lo(?) of i(?) abou(?)'

(Rosewarne 1994: 3)

Those who take up this pattern evidently do so through the logic of role alignment sketched earlier. Such responses are conceptualized differently in different contexts. They may or may not correspond to conscious strategies on the part of those who perform them; they may or may not be equally 'conscious' or equally 'strategic' in every instance in which they are performed. But they are readily described as adjustments of a self-image by members of these groups and by observers. In some cases they are specifically construed as economic or political strategies:

(22) To paraphrase the words of Stanley Kalms, founder and chairman of the Dixons Group, R. P. speakers in business accommodate towards Estuary English 'to become more consumer friendly'. An example of this was the leadership contest which followed Mrs. Thatcher's resignation. One journalist attributed Mr. Major's success to the 'Prolier than thou' image he created for himself.

(Rosewarne 1994: 4–5)

Reformulating one's persona as more 'more consumer friendly' or 'Prolier' (i.e., more prole[tarian]) are interactional tropes that align the performed image of speaker with that of target audiences and addressees. They belong to the long tradition of characterological tropes that I have discussed in the preceding sections (and for a variety of other registers in 3.8). Such transformations occur one speech-event, one interaction at a time; they respond to local conditions of enregisterment under which highly specific tropes become meaningful responses to interlocutors and audiences, both real or imagined; and, in some cases, such responses are indeed conscious means of accomplishing particular goals. Some among these responses are taken up by institutionalized patterns of recirculation, as in the above examples; and in such cases, the patterns of recirculation may well promote the forms used in these tropes as stable, normalized targets for future generations.

Rosewarne suggests that Estuary English may be tomorrow's RP. This is certainly possible, though in more than one sense. At present, 'Mainstream' RP and Estuary English are centered in very different institutional loci. The demographic profiles of their speakers are also different, despite some overlap. But RP itself is a register that has changed internally in numerous ways over the period discussed above. These changes are, moreover, changes of different *kinds*, involving different *dimensions* of register organization. These include changes in phonetic patterns, exemplary speakers, register names, characterological discourses, as well as changes in the demographic profile of those who recognize the register as a standard to be emulated, versus those able to speak some form of it (whether exemplary or not). RP and Estuary English may well come to approximate one another in one or more of these respects as well; but whether or not they do so, their mode of co-existence at any given point in their history is linked to their modes of dissemination and the logic of socially anchored role alignments between speakers and hearers of utterances, linked to each other through them.

4.8 The sedimentation of habits and the inhabitance of agency

I have been arguing that processes of enregisterment involve a gradual sedimentation of habits of speech perception and production across particular social domains of persons. These processes unfold one communicative event at a time, though certain features of them (such as the possibility of mass circulation of messages) have the consequence that some events within such processes set the initial conditions for very large scale forms of response. In some cases forms of mass circulation are linked to institutional mechanisms of authority as well, mechanisms that align the characterological figures they depict with *transcendent constructs* (such as the 'unity of the nation,' an essence called 'cultivation') that may prove irresistible (even unrecognizable as historically specific constructs); or, mechanisms that anchor the characterological figures they depict in *a chain of authentication* grounded in the authority of others (as in the case of appeals to prior authority; section 4.4). In other cases, the appeal is not to the authority of the 'principal' at all, but to the *desires and interests of the 'receiver' of the message*; thus images of speech are frequently syncretized with images linked to other desirable commodities, and thus propagated without seeming to be of any special interest in themselves.

This account contrasts sharply with any 'top-down' approach to the formation of a standard language. Consider, for example, the version of this approach associated with the writings of Pierre Bourdieu. For Bourdieu 'the legitimate language' is imposed by the institutions of the state upon the socialized habits – or *habitus* – of the individual. The habitus in turn is the experientially sedimented set of dispositions to act, itself formed by factors 'transmitted without passing through language and consciousness' (Bourdieu 1991: 51), and once formed, comprising a set of constraints towards future action continually renewed by the operations of power upon the individual: '. . . a given agent's practical relation to the future . . . is defined in the relationship between, on the one hand, his habitus . . . and, on the other hand, a certain state of the chances objectively offered to him by the social world. The relation to what is possible is a relation to power . . . The habitus is the principle of a selective perception of the indices tending to confirm and reinforce it rather than transform it . . .' (Bourdieu 1990a: 64). The approach has certain well known problems of 'agency' associated with it. These derive partly from the inertial continuity of the habitus (its tendency selectively to attend to indices that reinforce it) and partly because a 'recognition of the legitimate language' is 'inscribed' upon individual dispositions 'by the sanctions of the linguistic market' (Bourdieu 1991: 51). On this view, large scale institutions (the state, the market) are the principal agents of inscription, in which lies their manifest structural 'power,' and the individual, a palimpsest upon which these inscriptions are written and willy-nilly internalized as habitus, thereby appears to lack 'agency.'

I have shown, however, that the habitus simply lacks many of the properties that Bourdieu ascribes to it. First, far from being 'transmitted without passing through language' the social life of the habitus is mediated by discursive interactions. The linguistic habitus is mediated largely by metalinguistic processes, i.e., by discursive events that typify and assign values to speech, though sometimes in ways that are highly implicit. In the case of more implicit typifications, the effects produced may be shaped entirely through discursive activity, and be highly concrete and palpable in the event at hand, but difficult to report out of context. Such cases are therefore non-transparent to the kind of decontextualized reasoning characteristic of Bourdieu's work. The notion that the habitus is 'transmitted without passing through language' is a systematic distortion, not an accidental omission; it reflects an inadequate grasp of the reflexive properties of language itself.

Second, the habitus is not a unitary formation. Indeed the genres that disseminate habits of speech perception and recognition are quite distinct from genres that transmit habits of speech production; they differ both in the metadiscursive operations they employ and in their scales of circulation. Once we understand these differences, some of the principles of 'market'-like value that appear synchronically to maintain the value of specific goods are better understood as effects precipitated by historical differences in patterns of metasemiotic typification and circulation (4.6). The use of registers is linked to a logic of characterological figurements which cannot be reduced to market metaphors. A prestige register may well be a scarce good, but scarcity is only one determinant of perceived value. When Queen and Archbishop, M. P. and Lord, CEO and Prime Minister all shift 'downwards' it is the logic of footing that dominates the logic of scarcity.

Social theories that employ top-down models of causality in explanations of action (e.g., the state inscribes, the market disposes) create the problem of how best to explain the capacity of individuals to determine the course of their own conduct. But the problem is rather artificial, itself an artifact of a top-down view of culture. If we understand human action in semiotic terms, it is readily seen that agency is not a unitary phenomenon. There are several varieties of it. In the case of culturally enregistered models of action we may distinguish at least three distinct types of agency: (1) interpretive ability, or the capacity to interpret others' acts (as evidenced in the intelligibility and 'fit' of one's responses); (2) effective freedom vis-à-vis others; and (3) a reflective grasp of one's own degree of freedom. An individual can 'have agency' in one or more of these senses; and, while having it in one sense, may lack it in another.

Interpreting and responding to another's acts itself involves agency in a sense so primary or basic that it is easily lost sight of. Any act of performing a sign or construing a performance is itself a type of semiotic work; the act is interpersonally effective (felicitous, ratified, etc.) only if certain conditions are met. We saw in the last chapter that appropriate and inappropriate 'uses' of a register both depend on *reading the co-text at the moment of use* (including reading identities of interlocutors, see 3.5); they are, to this extent, irreducibly agentive acts. We saw in this chapter that although RP is stereotypically linked to images of speaker's upper class/refinement, any particular token of RP speech is amenable to entextualized manipulation in ways that allow a multitude of other images of personhood to be performed or construed through a larger text-pattern. Thus, both for the one performing the sign and for the one responding to it, the business of evaluating utterances in relation to co-text is a form of ongoing, moment-by-moment interpretive activity. Agency in this basic sense – the capacity to construe one's semiotic environment and to respond intelligibly to it – is a condition on the very possibility of mutually coordinated social interaction. Yet it is neither symmetrically possessed by all speakers nor uniformly achieved at every moment of interaction. A person who is imperfectly socialized to the stereotypic values of enregistered signs lacks the ability to engage other sign-users in culturally appropriate ways; a person who is perfectly socialized but fails to attend to emergent text-in-context effects undergoes a temporary attenuation of interpersonal possibilities, or degrees of freedom, within the interaction.

Individuals differ also in their agency in the second sense, their degree of effective freedom vis-à-vis others. For example, persons differ in their entitlement to attempt, or to propose that another should attempt, a particular kind of act. If we conflate such normative entitlements with actual behaviors (thus conflating metasemiotic norms with semiotic acts), the possession or lack of entitlements appears to form a set of rigid constraints that limit the behaviors of individuals. In many instances they do. Yet there are a number of ways of getting around these constraints, particularly through implicitly metapragmatic forms of manipulation (see, e.g., Figure 1.4 and discussion). Although effective freedom vis-à-vis others is often constrained by normative entitlements, implicit reflexive strategies are always available for getting around these constraints.

Third, different socially positioned individuals differ in the degrees of freedom they recognize themselves as having. But persons' reportable intuitions about their own place within the social order are not always reliable measures of their effective freedoms. Individuals may regard themselves as powerful yet find themselves highly constrained by specific norms (such as norms of noblesse oblige) or very narrow in their capacity to interpret the acts of others (as in the case of a narrow register range), and thus be powerless in specific zones of register-mediated social life; or find, as when located in recessive phases of enregisterment, that their ability to retain emblems of power requires that they accommodate their behaviors 'downwards' in a rearguard action against another emerging vanguard; or view themselves as powerless, yet belong to that vanguard.

Although individuals differ in these ways (often from themselves, at different moments of self-awareness, in different contexts of register mediated activity) their responses to messages received in the indexical here and now of each encounter are unavoidably agentive acts (in the first sense), acts that require a semiotic reading of the current moment, and result in a 'next' act. As the characterological voices of the past speak to the one engaged in this reading, the next turn (or larger chain segment) is always up for grabs, always potentially a branch point in the social life of the register. Processes of role alignment play a part in each moment of this process. In some among these moments a scheme of prior valorization is simply reproduced without much alteration in future interactions, yielding the special case of inertial continuity (the case where habits are 'confirm[ed] and reinforce[d]') with which Bourdieu is so preoccupied. In other cases, the products of prior events of valorization are transformed to varying degrees, opening up new possibilities of normalized performance and construal. Only some among the trajectories subsequently taken are artifactualized into forms that allow them to be encountered as messages by mass audiences; and only some among the ones encountered frequently are backed by hegemonic voices of authority or desire that invite widespread forms of role alignment. While it is true that institutions like schools, states and markets play a critical role in processes of enregisterment, such institutions are themselves patterns of organization of the semiotic activities of individuals, ones that are reconfigured periodically by external discourses (as in the case of schooling, see 4.5) – and hence by the agentive powers of those who produce such discourses, whether they fully recognize this or not – even though, in local phases of the process, the perception of their own inviolability and autonomy is a form of misrecognition that institutions invite from all those exposed to their institutional work, urging their collective allegiance and surrender, perhaps because it is a form of misrecognition upon which their own – otherwise fragile – continuance so often depends.

5

REGROUPING IDENTITY

5.0 Introduction

In the last chapter we took a close look at accent as an emblem of social identity. We saw that British RP comes to be constituted as an emblem by the connection (established by metasemiotic discourses and practices) between social personae and phonological facts of sound, a connection that treats the latter as diacritics of the former. We saw that over the historical envelope of its existence the emblem changes (both in its sound and persona aspect) through the metasemiotic activities of social actors; and that at any given historical stage, the positional acquaintance of social actors with this emblem makes certain identity readings determinate from facts of utterance. Our goal now is to consider emblems whose diacritics are perceivable signs of *any* kind (not just utterances) and to ask how determinate readings of social identity emerge through their enactment and deployment in conduct.

The main goal of this chapter is to show that a person's social identity, or identities, become determinate only through a class of semiotic processes whereby images of personhood are coupled to or decoupled from publicly perceivable signs. Some among these are images to which persons form attachments, or lay claim, seeking to make them their own; yet the range of images of self construable by others is invariably larger as a matter of principle. In the case of self-images to which persons do form attachments, a person's 'identity' is sometimes linked to a psychobiographical **self-conception**. This internalized self-image is readily essentialized as a fixture – an invariant substrate, even an 'unmoved mover' – lying beneath the vagaries of others' perceptions. But a person's self-conception is not a static thing; it fades in and out of thresholds of awareness and attachment cued by different types of interpersonal activities; it moves through different versions over time, through a great many versions over a life-span; particular versions are frequently displaced, disowned or renewed. Some among them are claimed at particular times as discrete, even fundamental features of self, even fiercely claimed, especially when one's difference from another or one's stakes in a self-image are interactionally at issue. But even when one's self-conception (or, rather, a given timebound version of it) becomes fixed or definite for a while, it is only relevant to social life insofar as it is perceivable by others (Agha 1995).

The term 'identity' in the title of this chapter refers to identity in this public sense, to images of self perceivable by others. It is these perceivable images of self, I argue, upon which social practices of identity ascription depend, and around which variation in internalized self-images also revolves. The term 'regrouping' refers to some of the semiotic processes involved in this type of variation, such as the detachability of identities from those who have them, to the re-grouping of signs that express a particular identity, to changes in the types of 'group' to which individuals perceive themselves, or are perceived by others, as belonging.

The discussion proceeds as follows. I first introduce some basic terminology (5.1). I then show that a person's self-conception differs from a second figure of identity, namely a 'relational self' (the way in which that person is 'read' by others), a figure that is critical to social interaction (5.2). I then consider the connection between social personae and embodied diacritics, and the part played by both in readings of personhood (5.3). I discuss a variety of types of emblematic readings (5.4) and illustrate how these operate in a single ethnographic case (5.5). I consider the implications of this approach for our understanding of social groups (5.6). I conclude with a discussion of the semiotic range of emblems (5.7).

5.1 From 'identity' to emblems

The relevance of identity to social theory lies not in the fact that identity is a unitary phenomenon – a discrete thing – whose characteristics can be described independently of processes of context-bound social action. It is true that our everyday term *identity* is a count noun which, by the usual Whorfian projection, implies a class of enumerable things. It implies the existence of countable and pluralizeable facts of sameness and difference that can become objects of study, and, to some, the existence of a ready-made analytic rubric of some kind. Yet we cannot take the term at face value. Identity is usable as an analytical term only if the rubric can be connected back to the processes through which the things it names get formed. To ignore this problem would be a bit like taking the count noun *climate* at face value. After all, much like identities, climates can be foreign, familiar, desirable, hot, variable, sticky, bothersome, and much talked about, but in order to cope with what happens outdoors we need to understand the processes that give rise to climates. And similarly for identities.

What happens if we don't? Taken by itself, the rubric called identity is inexhaustible. And so we find two impulses in contemporary writing about society, which are really mirror-image twins of each other. First, the impulse to embrace the inexhaustible, an impulse from which the 'currency' of identity as a coin or idiom of social theory derives. And, second, the impulse to turn away from it, to find the act of embracing the inexhaustible *exhausting*. Neither impulse will get us very far. The embrace and its exhaustion are twins.

What is the rubric called 'identity' a name for? What are the things it names? It is a way of talking about the emblematic functions of signs in behavior. An **emblem** is a thing to which a social persona is attached. It involves three elements; (1) a perceivable thing, or diacritic; (2) a social persona; (3) someone for whom it is an emblem (i.e., someone who can read that persona from that thing). When a thing/diacritic is widely recognized as an emblem – when many people view it as marking the same social persona – I will say that it is enregistered as an emblem, or is an **enregistered emblem**. 'Enregistered' just means 'widely recognized,' and there are degrees of it. Emblematic effects can be highly emergent, as in forms of footing, where they are not widely enregistered at all; emblems that are widely enregistered for a population of sign-users can lose this status; and emblems can become naturalized so as to constitute more durable selves.

Things convey identities through acts in which they are emblematic for those connected to each other through those acts. A necktie is a thing. A car. A hat. A sideways glance. An accent. A sob. All things. All perceivable. Too many things. But before the cold front of taxonomy sets in, before one sob leads to another, let us note that things by themselves are not to the point. It's the emblematic functions they have through acts that connect people; that's the point. Although emblems are embodied in diacritics, a single diacritic can yield different emblematic readings under different conditions, a fact from which the complexity of the folk-concept of 'identity' derives. Our focus therefore needs to be not on things alone or personae alone but on acts of performance and construal through which the two are linked, and the conditions under which these links become determinate for actors.

The thing-fraction can also be misunderstood in other ways. Important though they are, objects of sense perception are not the only kinds of perceivable things that have emblematic functions; things *denoted by* objects of sense perception can also have such functions. In Chapter 2 we considered emblematic footings and alignments mediated by *referents* of utterances. Utterances are a very special kind of emblematic sign because, in being perceivable, utterances make the things they denote present or palpable as objects of cognition; such referents can function as diacritics too, that is, are things to which emblematic values can be attached through their treatment as counters within the game of interaction, e.g., through the enactment of referential stances and alignments (2.2). The large majority of such **emergent emblems** are highly evanescent in interaction (they emerge and fade away quickly). But individuals can also formulate **persistent alignments** to such emblems; and such acts can polarize interactants into factional groupings – as when interlocutors take 'positions' on a topic (viz., I prefer Fords, you prefer Chevies; Macintosh vs. IBM computers; apple pies vs. cream puffs; Democrats vs. Republicans), and these groupings, if maintained or made to grow in subsequent encounters through speech-chain processes, can persist beyond an encounter as longer-term totemic partitions and groups.

The case of register-formations discussed in Chapter 3 is very different. From the standpoint of its persona-indexing effects, any register constitutes a class of enregistered emblems. The class consists of those signs in the register's repertoires (Table 3.6) that convey **stereotypic** images of persons (e.g., mark speaker/actor as 'female,' 'lawyer,' 'upper-class,' etc.). We distinguish such formations from each other as distinct 'registers' when we approach them from the standpoint of repertoires; but if we approach them from the standpoint of personae, we are distinguishing enregistered emblems from each other. We saw in 3.9 that register formations typically include both linguistic and non-linguistic diacritics in their semiotic range. Persons can be allocated *enregistered* identities in ways that depend on their register range (the range of enregistered emblems they effectively control), but also in other ways, as when their habitual behaviors are assimilated to a widely known 'reputation' (5.2), or through institutional processes that allocate them certain stereotypic roles within a society on the basis of sign-types routinely (ubiquitously, unavoidably) manifest in their appearance or conduct. A person's enregistered identities often create default perceptions of that person among those acquainted with the relevant stereotypes. But a person's *emergent* identities depend on text-in-context relations between signs that occur in their actual behaviors in particular encounters.

Hence we can make no sense of the emblematic functions of 'things' without first considering whether their emblematic functions are formulated through text-level or stereotypic principles of indexical effectiveness, that is, without an analytic perspective on the conditions under which they function as emblems.

We are observing, in other words, that things that function as emblems differ substantially in the way in which they convey persona attributes, and *for whom* they function as emblems, depending on whether they express stereotypic or text-level effects. In the case of stereotypic indexicals, the persona reading is mediated by semiotic processes of large scale communicative transmission, processes through which particular sign-types become enregistered *as* stereotypic indexicals for particular populations. In the case of emergent or text-level emblematic effects, the reading depends on co-textual relationships among sign-tokens manifest in the current inter-action. In the latter case, a persona is inferred as an attribute of a given actor from **text-level indexical relations** (congruence, coherence, cohesion, etc.) among currently co-occurring **sign-tokens**; here the social domain of the reading is (at most) co-present interactants (i.e., whoever attends to co-textual effects in the current interaction). In the case of stereotypic indexicals, the persona reading is backed by **widespread stereotypes** that formulate the persona as linked to a **sign-type**, and is thus regarded as an attribute of *anyone* who performs the sign on *whatever* occasion; here the social domain of the indexical consists of whoever is acquainted with the stereotype (which may or may not include all of the persons who happen to be co-present).

5.2 Emblematic figures of identity

Given that identity is a variable phenomenon we can only approach it from the standpoint of the semiotic activities through which its variation is exhibited. In 5.0, we briefly considered a particular figure of subjective identity, namely a 'self-conception.' This is a figure of identity that is endlessly recuperable through acts of introspection. While it may appear highly determinate at each moment of introspection, it changes over time. Such a figure can also be reinforced through interpersonal activities of various kinds, including public rituals that reinforce certain self-conceptions among those who participate in them. A self-conception is also a moment or element of an **autobiographical self**. Self-conceptions and autobiographical selves can be of many kinds, of course. I now discuss two examples that point to the range of issues involved in studying these figures.

Self-conceptions

Although self-conceptions are introspectable in subjective ways they are experienced by others only when they are performed through publicly perceivable signs. Such acts of interpersonal expression can reinforce such figures of identity too.

For instance, Haviland 2005 argues that a self-conception is a figure that can be communicated to others through narratives oriented to a history of past encounters and interactions. Haviland discusses narratives gathered from a single Tzotzil speaker, Mol Maryan, gathered over a span of some twenty years, in which Mol Maryan describes his troubled encounters with his son-in-law and eldest son. Acts in which such encounters are told and re-told formulate allegiances, enmities and footings with these kin, and with others. By examining a series of tellings and re-tellings – and attending to the processes of revision and re-editing that go on within them – Haviland shows that certain interpersonal stances can become more repetitive and insistent than others, narrowing the possibilities available to, and constitutive of, a person's developmentally formulated self-conception. In Mol Maryan's case, a historical chain of narrative acts that re-member the past yields a progressively more rigid self-positioning over time, an autobiographical self ever more fixed, less adaptable, congealing eventually into an entrenched interpersonal stance vis-à-vis his immediate kin. More generally, Haviland shows that acts which invoke voices and encounters from the past are strategies of self-positioning in any given present; and that the consistency of such acts over time can itself constitute a stabilized trend over many 'present' moments, and indeed over a lifetime, in ways that shape social relations with persons whose voices they rely upon. In short, an autobiographical self invariably involves footings with others, both in its narratological construction and in its interpersonal manifestation.

Wortham 2005 explores the processes through which an individual's public reputation is formulated, and the implications of this process for a person's internalized self-images. He examines processes through which an individual's public identity is established through a chain of encounters with the very persons who treat the individual as having that identity (now in the sense of 'reputation'). By examining a chain of social interactions that occur within an American high school classroom over the course of a year, Wortham explores the way in which a particular student, Tyisha (who starts the year as a 'good, independent minded student') becomes re-formulated as a 'disruptive' and recalcitrant person, first by the teacher and then increasingly by other students as well. Wortham proposes that the identity trend so constituted emerges over a chain of encounters in which the trend is articulated by participants within those encounters, and increasingly ratified by them, even to the point that the person whose identity (or 'reputation') it is may be forced by degrees to orient herself to it, and willy-nilly even to adopt it in a practical sense as her own (i.e., as a 'self-conception').

An extended meditation on how persons formulate footings with their reputations, and especially, how they manage a 'spoiled identity,' may be found in Goffman 1963.

The relational self

We now consider what is sometimes called **the relational self**, a figure of identity that depends on the ability of persons to assign personae to each other by attending to matters of appearance and conduct. Although self-conceptions and autobiographical selves are not reducible to the relational self, they are mediated by them through narratives produced by the actor in question (whence they become available as data for empirical studies of the self) and also by the orientations others exhibit to a person's relational self, now regarded as a reputation.

The relational self is the living – and ever-moving – center of a person's public identity. All conceptions of social identity are evaluated, sooner or later, in relation to this figure. We shall see presently that the relational self is performed and construed recursively in the give and take of social interaction. But let us first focus on an element of this process, namely the fact that the relational self depends at any moment of performance and construal on the readability of persons.

Reading persons

Like any semiotic activity the activity of reading persons has a text-in-context organization in any given interpersonal encounter; it is shaped by text-level indexical effects. But it is also mediated by stereotypes of indexicality, namely stereotypic social images associated with discrete signs that specify default ways of reading persons who display them.

We have seen in previous chapters that text-level indexical effects are non-detachable from the performed sign-configurations that cue them. In contrast, explicit stereotypes permit a decontextualized form of circulation. They convert contingent and dialectical facts of persona display into seemingly stable categories of personhood. As Erving Goffman puts it: 'Every culture, and certainly ours, seems to have a vast lore of fact and fantasy regarding embodied indicators of status and character, thus appearing to render persons readable' (Goffman 1983: 8). Such 'lore' formulates indices performable in behavior as having stereotypic persona values. But the indices themselves only become relevant to social interaction under conditions of textuality or co-occurrence with other signs, conditions under which text-level indexical effects superimpose a further specificity upon the current construal, partly canceling, deforming, even troping upon stereotypic effects.

For instance, we saw in 3.5 and 3.8 that the dialectic between text-level and stereotypic indexicality is an important dimension of the variability of emergent personae mediated by enregistered signs of role and relationship. If we focus only on stereotypic images, identity (in the sense of the relational self) seems 'fluid'; it appears constantly to exceed them. But we saw through a consideration of a range of cases in 3.5 and 3.8 – cases where men perform images of femininity, boys act like grown-up sportscasters, upper-class politicians strive to appear lower-class in order to get more votes – that if we take into account the text-level cues that mediate such readings this fluidity is non-random; it depends on relations of fractional congruence among co-textual cues. In our everyday encounters with others we readily take such cues into account because they are ready-to-hand. But in moments of decontextualized reflection, the stereotypic values of enregistered signs are the more readily extractable fragments of the semiotic arrays on which our readings of others' identities are based. Hence our most commonplace accounts of identity are, ironically, inadequate as accounts of *how* we achieve determinate readings of persons we encounter.

Demeanor indexicals

In saying that the activity of reading persons involves 'embodied indicators of status and character' Goffman was concerned with the way in which embodied behaviors (including utterances) allow interactants to construe the attributes of the one whose behaviors they are. This way of conceptualizing social personae is rooted in Goffman's concept of demeanor (Goffman 1956).

The concept of demeanor is the notion that an individual's appearance or behavior can be assigned significance by someone who perceives it. Since the thing perceived conveys information about a variable of context, namely the actor whose appearance or behavior it is, the concept of demeanor is an indexical notion. Goffman's concept of demeanor is not limited to any particular type of physical behavior. It is a way of highlighting the connection between attributes displayed through acts and the actor who displays them. Any perceivable feature of conduct or appearance that contextually clarifies the attributes of actor to interactants is, or functions as, a demeanor indicator, or a **demeanor indexical**. Demeanor indexicals are *actor-focal* emblems; they clarify the demeanor of the one who performs the sign. Not all emblems are demeanor indexicals as we shall presently see.

Demeanor indexicals depend on the perceivability of the thing that functions as a sign; they are necessarily embodied in some way. Yet they are limitlessly varied in actual physical form. *Any* kind of perceivable behavioral display (features of gesture, utterance, clothing, appurtenance, etc.) can serve to index characteristics of actor. But the persona readings (or characteristics of personhood) inferable from the display are not established by the fact of embodiment itself. It is not just that demeanor indexicals are physically too varied in kind. It is also that embodiment is simply a condition on the perceivability and manipulability of the display.[1] While the fact that demeanor indexicals function effectively only through perceivable things is important, this fact is of little use in understanding how they convey persona attributes. As we just saw with emblems in general, the thing-fraction of such actor-focal emblems may be imbued with demeanor indexing effectiveness through emergent text-level relationships with co-occurring signs, so that the effect in question is wholly non-detachable from the conditions of its performance; it is not associated with any sign-type abstractable from performance; it is merely the demeanor of that actor, and only of that actor, at that moment of interactional text. Or, it may be based on some type of stereotypic principles of indexical effectiveness, such as stereotypes of speech in the case of discourse registers; or, in the case of possessions displayed in conduct, through principles of commodity valorization that link certain kinds of appurtenances to images of class, income-level, lifestyle, sexual desirability and the like, all of which are not merely readable as features of the current actor's demeanor, but are also (since they are associated with signs-types) readable as attributes of any social person who acquires a commodity of that type, and through acquiring it, inhabits its characterological features as facts of his or her demeanor.

Durable selves and objectifications

Demeanor indexicals differ in durational characteristics as well, both at the level of sign-form and sign-values. Differences in duration of sign-form are obvious enough. Many perceivable features of persons (such as height, weight, skin tone) do not change during an encounter; but other semiotic displays (such as gestural pulses, form and content of utterances) change rapidly over the course of an interaction. The sign-values of these displays – *what* they are treated as indexical of – may also differ in culturally recognized constancy or duration. Every culture has an ontology of personhood which treats some characteristics of persons as more perduring than others. Indeed, from a cross-cultural standpoint, the question of which aspects of people are more stable (temporally constant) than others cannot be settled without appeal to culture-internal theories of personhood. In the case of psychological attributions, common-sense suggests that aspects of current orientation (emotions, attitudes, dispositions) are more transient than aspects of psychic structure (the personality, the self, the soul). Yet the details of these schemes are grounded in cultural frameworks of person-reckoning having a particular history; as social and historical conditions change so do the frameworks that explain and rationalize them (Taylor 1989). In the case of sociological attributions, common sense may suggest that some social characteristics of persons, such as ethnicity, are more permanent attributes than, say, profession; this view is certainly plausible under modern conditions of labor mobility but it is not the view common in cultures having a system of profession-linked castes. Similarly, when we look across cultures we do not find that psychological attributes are always held to be more transient than sociological ones. In some societies, features of caste, ethnicity or gender are **naturalized** in ideas about inherent mental ability, creating situations where folk-theories of psychology serve as the bedrock or foundation for folk-theories of social difference (Irvine 1990). But all personal attributes – whether conceived in mentalistic or group-relative terms, whether naturalized or not – are in the first instance ascribed to specific individuals only by virtue of emblems displayed in appearance or conduct. What we are observing, however, is that such attributes differ substantially in the degree to which they are **objectified** culture-internally as more or less stable (constant, fundamental, essential, etc.) features of personhood. The case where such objectifications are naturalized is the case where they are held to be things in nature, outside the domain of culture and history. But there are other types of objectifications too, such as the treatment of emblematic figures as idealized units of a society.

Role and status

It is now generally recognized that the tendency to objectify attributes signaled by embodied indicators is a chief limitation of earlier forms of social theory as well. One consequence of this recognition is that the terms 'role' and 'status' – once so fashionable in anthropological and sociological studies – are now in a state of disrepute. There are many reasons for this disrepute, but two are especially worth mentioning. It is now evident that role and status cannot be viewed as fixed attributes of individuals because actors semiotically display *a range* of roles and statuses in different kinds of interactional scenarios, and such attributes are, in any case, relevant to the responses of interactants only insofar as they are readable from particular semiotic displays. It is also clear that any theoretical conception that views society, as a whole, as a static ordering of persons with regard to inherent roles and statuses runs into profound difficulties; not only for the reason just noted (that any individual's performances exhibit a range of personae) but also because the internal differentiation of societies into smaller units (families, tribes, corporations, nations) normatively requires that individuals learn to shift among roles and statuses during routine behaviors, so that the static conception makes it difficult to see how the orderliness of social arrangements (a.k.a 'the social order') relates to the type of behavior that comprises it (Nadel 1957, Cicourel 1974).

In the traditional conception, role and status are regarded as stereotypic or idealized attributes of persons. Thus Linton 1936 defines 'status' as a collection of rights and duties, and a 'role' as the proper enactment of a status. A status defines who a person is (child, ophthalmologist) and a role defines what that person is expected to do (go to school, perform eye surgery). The emphasis on rights and duties on the one hand and expectations of proper conduct (and sanctions against improper conduct) on the other makes clear that these definitions focus on idealizations of conduct.

Similarly, Parsons speaks of 'role expectations' as conceptions common to both ego and alter 'of what behavior is proper for each'; and, under conditions of institutionalization, as 'value orientations *common* to members of the collectivity to which both ego and alter belong' (Parsons and Shils 1951: 154). Through its focus on 'role expectations' and 'value orientations' the study of conduct is replaced by the study of models of conduct.

A second difficulty is that the processes through which ascriptions of role and status are attached to persons are not properly theorized. As Linton observes 'it is extremely hard for us to maintain a distinction in our thinking between statuses and the persons who hold them' (Linton 1936: 113). Of course, persons who 'hold' statuses can lose them too. But if the connection between 'what is held' and 'who holds it' is not theorized, roles and statuses are readily misunderstood as categories of person type, often conceptualized as 'units' of a more abstract kind. Parsons says that 'statuses and roles . . . are not in general attributes of the actor, but are *units* of the social system, though having a given status may sometimes be treated as an attribute' (Parsons 1951: 25). His focus is on the structural-function of such 'units' within social systems, not on the processes whereby any one unit comes to be 'treated as an attribute' of any given person. In both Linton's and Parson's formulations, the questions of how roles and statuses are linked to a given individual remains peripheral.[2] And attributes extracted from acts of attribution are readily frozen as facts about 'social systems.'

An underlying difficulty is that statuses and roles are projections from linguistic expressions that function as **role and status designators**. Statuses are best denoted by nouns (child, ophthalmologist) and roles by verb phrases (go to school, perform eye surgery). Because these expressions are denotational categories, statuses and roles appear to form a 'social system' or a 'social structure' by virtue of sense relations among role and status *designators* (synonymy, antonymy, hypernymy, hyponymy, partonomy, etc.). The 'social system/structure' is an ontological projection from facts about sense relationships between certain linguistic expressions, primarily those that function as lexical role and status designators in the language: such lexemes classify 'social' types; they denote facts about normative behaviors, readily reified as a 'system'; and sense relations among them imply various types of 'structure', viz., part-whole, hierarchy, reciprocity, etc.

In the sections below I argue that role and status categories are of little significance to social relations unless linked to emblems, that is, to perceivable behaviors that index social personae (which role/status designators can be used to denote). Emblems are social indexicals in the sense that they convey something about a social person contextually linked to the occurrence of the sign. Such a contextual link may be established in various ways. A person may be linked to the sign because she happens to be wearing it, or has performed it as a gesture, or has produced it as an utterance. In these cases, the emblem functions as a demeanor indexical; it conveys attributes of the actor who performs it. But the link between the emblem and the person whose attributes it reveals can be more indirect. In the case of linguistic utterances, the default focus of the emblem is usually the person who produces the utterance (e.g., if the utterance is refined or vulgar, the attribute is treated as an attribute of current speaker, or animator); but various ways of attaching this effect to others are also possible (e.g., through reported speech frames, patterns of implicit voicing). In the case of more perduring objects, such as clothes and cars, a person may become the focus of indexical attribution in many ways too. A fancy car may mark a particular person's high status because she happens to be driving it, or because she claims to own one, or simply because she is rumored to be the owner. In all cases, the status attribution follows from the emblematic value of the car, plus a mode of contextual linkage to a person. But in some of these cases, the emblematic reading is performatively formulated by someone other than the one made readable by it. The case where a person speaks 'for a group' (e.g., as a leader of the group) is another such case; here the one who performs the emblem is *a member of the set of persons* made readable by the emblem. In such cases, and others, the emblem does not function as a demeanor indexical in the sense defined above.

Some of the main issues discussed above can be summarized as follows:

Summary 5.1

(a) Identity attributes (including roles and statuses) are embodied in things that function as emblems
(b) An emblem can index the attributes of the one who performs it (and is thereby a demeanor indexical) or the attributes of a person or persons linked to it in some other way
(c) An emblematic effect can be based on text-level or stereotypic principles of indexical effectiveness
(d) Emblems mediate various effects that are grasped as **figures of identity**. Some of the ones discussed above include persistent alignments, self-conceptions, autobiographical selves, reputations, durable selves, naturalized selves, institutionalized roles and statuses. There are others too, of course.

Points (a) and (b) are, in effect, ways of distinguishing persona attributes from the persons to whom they are attributed. These attributes are of course ascribed to persons who are connected with these things (e.g., because they have performed them, but also otherwise, as just noted).

Point (c) is a way of distinguishing the social domain of an identity reading, e.g., whether it is knowable only by current interactants (on the basis of text-level effects) or to many people (on the basis of stereotypic effects), where the notion 'to many people' is itself variable in a degree sense. Point (d) is a way of saying that the figures of identity most transparent to everyday reflection are highly dependent and derivative consequences of the social life of emblems, generally articulated through semiotic chain processes. In the sections that follow, I highlight the fact that the process of identity ascription is itself a social-semiotic process of some complexity, and the attributes ascribed are not, by any means, inherent (intrinsic, undisputed, inalienable) facts about persons. Indeed, emblems themselves, and there-fore identity attributions linked to emblems, can change over time at both micro- and macro-scales of social life.

In other words, approaching the problem from the point of view of emblems makes tractable a much wider range of identity phenomena and processes than does the older conception. Let me now summarize, preemptively, some of the issues I take up in the sections that follow.

Summary 5.2
The identity processes discussed in the next few sections include:

(a) *divergent readings*: different evaluators may construe the same sign differently, thus assign different role/status readings to the same person;
(b) *expropriation*: when signs that motivate such readings are alienable from the persons who perform them, so also are the roles/statuses;
(c) *tropes*: performance of role/status emblems can motivate tropes of identity when the co-textual conditions of performance include emblems that partly formulate a different role/status;
(d) *reanalysis*: the diacritics that embody an emblem can be subsumed under new stereotypes of indexicality, resulting in the reanalysis of role/status readings linked to the same diacritics, whether over time, or by social groups that co-exist at the same time.

When none of these processes are operative, individuals appear to have the more durable roles/statuses on which the older conception lingers. But this is a very special case.

On the traditional conception roles and statuses are not merely 'ideal patterns' to which individuals conform, they are also inseparable from each other. A role is merely the 'dynamic aspect' (Linton) or the 'proces-sual aspect' (Parsons) of a status. Since '[t]here are no roles without statuses and statuses without roles' (Linton 1936: 114), to speak of one is necessarily to speak of the other; one is always concerned in such cases with a 'status-role bundle' (Parsons 1952: 25). In the subsequent literature on this subject, the term 'role' is sometimes used for a role/status and sometimes to distinguish the two from each other; and the term 'status' is sometimes used in the above sense (the capacity of rights and duties to define a 'position' in social structure) and sometimes to speak of relative status (e.g., 'A has a higher status than B'), as in discussions of hierarchy. These various usages occur in this book as well. The context makes clear what is meant when the difference matters.

In the remainder of this chapter I use the term role generically to speak of role/status. My concern is to show that role categories are limitlessly defeasible in conduct through facts of contextualization. That is, anything we might call a role can be performed in actual conduct at varying thresholds of conformity to role – including matters of role dissonance, hybridity and ironic play. A second goal is to show that any of these role-fractions or fragments can be further retypified reflexively under new role designations.

If we reify diacritics, emblems, and identities, various forms of part-whole explanation seem plausible, as in older conceptions of 'social system' or 'social structure'. It may appear from the foregoing discussion, for instance, that looking 'downwards' from roles you see emblems, and looking 'upwards' you see figures of identity. It may even seem that there are part-whole relations involved (viz., that diacritics make up emblems, emblems make up roles, roles make up identities). This is simply not so. So a third goal is to show that no part-whole scheme, however conceptualized, can make sense of these phenomena. Briefly, there are two reasons why this is so. All of the elements we are discussing are not objects but sign-functions contracted by objects; in the next section we'll see that even diacritics are not things but sign-functions contracted by things. And, second, these sign-functions can be recursively embedded within each other through semiotic processes of various kinds. Rather than thinking of this issue in terms of 'things' having part-whole relations to each other we must focus instead on reflexive processes that reanalyze semiotic relationships (or sign-functions) into other semiotic relationships. If you re-read the points summarized in S 5.2 from this standpoint, you will see, at least in bare outline, just how I intend to proceed with this argument.

5.3 Role designators and diacritics

The concept of role is not an invention of anthropologists but a concept to which members of all human societies appeal in at least one specific way. All human languages contain a set of naturally occurring linguistic expressions that classify members of the population into categories of persons. In English, the class of **lexical role designators** includes nouns such as *mother, doctor, priest, policeman, tinker, tailor, soldier, spy*. But what is the significance of this fact?

Max Weber observed long ago that we cannot even begin to analyze role designators without first decomposing them into kinds of typical action:

(1) It is necessary to know what a 'king,' an 'official,' an 'entrepreneur,' a 'procurer,' or a 'magician,' does, that is, what kind of typical action, which justifies classifying an individual in one of these categories, is important and relevant for analysis, before it is possible to undertake the analysis itself.

(Weber 1978 [1956]: 18)

To analyze lexical role designators into types of action is to treat them as metapragmatic labels for forms of conduct. There are two very different ways in which we might go about doing this. One method is to attend to native speaker characterizations of the terms that function as role designators in their language. The other is to observe what the persons labeled by a designator commonly do. Neither method is non-linguistic since both take a linguistic expression as a point of departure.[3] Yet whereas the first method seeks to gather further linguistic data (e.g., native glosses of the term) the second tries to anchor linguistic designators to a series of observations of typical modes of conduct. The first gathers **explicit stereotypes about actors**; the second attempts to catalogue forms of **prototypical behavior** associated with a role designator (cf. 2.3 and 3.2). Explicit stereotypes are gathered by attending to what people say about the class or category, prototypical behaviors by attending to the conduct of its members.

In practical terms, neither method is generally adequate when used alone; hence the two methods are often used concurrently. But the distinction between the two methods is very sharp. The first method provides a glimpse of the order of commonplace beliefs; the other yields a profile of typical forms of conduct. There is of course no necessity that the two methods should yield the same result. Indeed the claim, sometimes made by anthropologists, that members of a population adhere to ideologies of personhood often depends on the fact that the models formulated by these two methods diverge from each other (what people are typically said to do is not what they typically do), or from actual conduct (the range of things people actually do is wider than what they are typically said to do *and* what they typically do).

Data of these types can only be gathered by entering into a reflexive process through which persons who make these distinctions are already connected to each other. A recognition of explicit stereotypes and prototypical behaviors associated with role designators is not merely a convenience for the social scientist; it orients the behaviors of social actors too. Yet, as we saw in our discussion of denotational stereotypes and prototypes in Chapter 2, there is an important difference in the way in which these two aspects of an expression's content are experienced. For the case where the expression is a role designator, the main issues may be summarized as follows:

Summary 5.3

Whereas instances of prototypical role conduct are only perceivable while the conduct is under way, explicit stereotypes of conduct permit a decontextualized form of circulation. Explicit stereotypes can be articulated through utterances that are perceivable even on occasions where the forms of conduct they typify do not occur.

For example, an utterance that takes a role designator (e.g., 'a witch') and predicates a property of it ('... is a pagan') recapitulates a familiar stereotype about the role; the further communicability of the stereotype to a hearer depends on the perceivability of utterances ('a witch is a pagan,' etc), not the perceivability of referents (witches).

In general, however, neither role designators nor the stereotypes predicable of them are of much relevance to social encounters unless the role categories they formulate are linked to a set of behavioral signs that allow individuals *to differentiate one kind of role from another*. The perceptual discrimination of a person's role requires access to an order of differentiating marks, or **diacritics**. Lexical role designators are linguistic labels for social kinds that group together a number of different diacritics by assigning class-defining attributes to them. But the behavioral signs that distinguish roles from each other are functional elements of emblems (S 5.1a), namely indices that effectively discriminate roles from each other. Let us use the term **role diacritic** for this type of indexical sign. A role diacritic is simply an indexical that functions in interaction to differentiate one social kind of actor from others, or one role from another.

By distinguishing designators from diacritics we are observing, in effect, that the perceivability and intelligibility of roles in social life depends on the fact that members of society can operate with respect to each other in terms of a two-level structure of semiosis (Figure 5.1). Whereas role designators are linguistic expressions, role diacritics are not necessarily so; they occur in all of the modalities of embodiment characteristic of expressive action generally (represented as $x_1 x_2 x_3 \ldots$ in Figure 5.1). The double arrow is meant to suggest that when individuals operate with respect to each other's personhood, the category of personhood may be recognized by inferences in either direction. By observing that someone is wearing a certain uniform I may infer that he is a policeman; I have inferred a role designation from a diacritic. By knowing that a person is a policeman I may judge his dress to be appropriate (or odd, or flagrant); I have now made sense of a behavioral display in the light of a designation. In general, neither role designators nor diacritics are of much use by

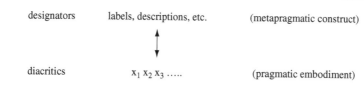

designators   labels, descriptions, etc.   (metapragmatic construct)

diacritics $x_1 x_2 x_3 \ldots$ (pragmatic embodiment)

Figure 5.1   *Role designators and diacritics*

themselves. It is the ability to move across these two levels during inter-action that allows us to infer who we are dealing with.

Although the distinction is purely relational, the fact that role designators are linguistic signs (and diacritics not necessarily so) has important consequences for social life. Role designations are sense-bearing expressions that denote persons or qualities of personhood. The simplest kinds are lexical items, e.g., the lexical role designators to which Weber alludes in (1).[4] But a much larger class of role designating devices consist of extended metapragmatic discourses about persons; these may take the form of narratives belonging to a variety of genres, such as the ones discussed in the last chapter. Many role designating expressions (whether words, descriptions or narratives) emerge as nonce-forms serving occasion specific uses, but some among these come to be treated as standard ways of talking about persons. The fact that role designations and classifications grow and change over time is a critical feature of social life itself. But insofar as they are expressed through language, such classifications are also highly decontextualizable. This is particularly the case for lexical role designators. They are utterable as discrete words with discrete senses; they are organized by semantic relationships with each other (antonymy, hypernymy, taxonomy, partonomy, etc.) and thus formulate classifications that project a reticulated 'logical space' of social differences; they can also become institutionalized and used to articulate normative attributes and distinctions, including matters of rank and hierarchy (e.g., through titles used as designators of rank). Nonetheless, it is a mistake to suppose that we can learn much about social relations by investigating *only* the role designators that function as meta-signs of personhood in a community, just as much, in fact, as to suppose that we can proceed by attending *only* to behavioral displays that count as role diacritics in particular interactions.

By itself a 'diacritic' is a differentiating mark. Role diacritics are semiotic devices that differentiate social personae in figure-ground relationships in interactional text. They are not identifiable out of context, except in certain special cases discussed below. In many cases diacritic contrasts only matter to interactants for fleeting moments of entextualization. Any perceivable phenomenon contextually associable with an individual (e.g., any aspect of appearance, conduct or appurtenance) can foreground a contrastive figure of personhood within an interaction. A common reading of this kind occurs when we are aware that a person's performed demeanor departs in some fleeting way from an interactionally situated role expectation. In this kind of reading, all we have is an indexical phenomenon that differentiates the performance from a condition of role inhabitance that was actually maintained or expected by inference from an earlier phase of interaction. Here the demeanor indexical merely differentiates the performer from a role already in play and, to this extent, plays a diacritic function at that moment.

But this negative, contrastive image can also be positively characterized through a role designation. In this type of case we are no longer dealing with the diacritic alone. A diacritic-under-a-designation is an emblem, a more complex type of sign. A behavior counts as a meaningful emblem of social personhood when the actor is characterizable in some specific way, when a specific designation can be assigned to the diacritic as its meaning. One reason for distinguishing diacritics from emblems is that a single diacritic can come under different designations, be viewed as emblematic of different things by different people. These differences are sometimes matters of contention, but they are not usually random. Let us consider some specific types of cases.

We can best approach these cases by focusing on a single question. It is commonly remarked that everyone has many identities. What does the word 'many' mean in such statements?

How many identities?

A person may have many performable identities. For example a person may have a wide register range in the sense discussed in Chapter 3. In this type of case, the variety of semiotic repertoires that a person effectively commands allows him or her to formulate different stereotypic images of self on different occasions. These images can also be troped upon through further contextualization to yield composite sketches of self that are fractionally non-congruent with such stereotypic signs as contribute to that sketch. We discussed a number of examples of this sort in Chapter 3. Thus, a man who can effectively speak like a woman, like a military person, like a sports announcer, like a lawyer, a doctor, and so on, has a register range of a certain kind. But the actual range of composite sketches performable through contextualization is even larger, since each of these stereotypic figures can be inhabited to different degrees, combined, ironically manipulated, used to tell jokes about enregistered personae, and so on.

An individual's register range equips a person with many identities in the sense of 'many performable identities.' But what about the case where a single behavioral diacritic receives many construals?

To focus on this type of case, let us consider someone who has a narrow register range, someone who (more or less) always speaks the same way. Even a person of this kind has many construable identities depending on who is doing the construing. In this case we are dealing with differences of ascription by others. We discussed issues of identity ascription (for the special case of RP register) in Chapter 4. We also considered cases where a single perceivable diacritic may be read as emblematic of different social attributes by different socially positioned individuals (who, if co-present as participants, will have different 'takes' on the same diacritic). One of the examples discussed earlier is a tendency described by Wells 1982 in people's 'identifications' of accent.

(2) ... a Liverpool working-class accent will strike a Chicagoan primarily as being British, a Glaswegian as being English, an English southerner as being northern, an English northerner as being Liverpudlian, and a Liverpudlian as being working class. The closer we get to home, the more refined are our perceptions.

(Wells 1982, vol. 1, p. 33)

In cases of this kind a single diacritic is characterized through different role designators by differently positioned evaluators. As we noted before, *all* of the labels listed here correctly typify the speaker: a person who has a 'Liverpool working class accent' is at once 'working class,' a 'Liverpudlian,' a 'northerner,' 'English,' 'British' and so on. It is the *hearer's* ability to formulate a taxonomically specific label that varies. In all cases, the accent is a diacritic, perceived by hearer as an index of speaker's otherness; the various designators that Wells lists are simple common-sense defaults of (self vs.) *other*-grouping – for a Chicagoan (American vs.) *British*; for a Glaswegian (Scottish vs.) *English*; for an English southerner (southern vs.) *northern*; for a northerner (generic northerner vs.) a *Liverpudlian* in particular; for a Liverpudlian, a member of the Liverpool *working class*.

Cases of this kind illustrate one feature of the indexical character of acts of other-identification: Such acts depend on socialized habits of reading indexicals that fix the boundary of otherness in an approximate way. A person's prior socialization equips an individual with at least one baseline for construing otherness, that is, with a cultural sense, acquired over a biographic lifetime, of how people at varying degrees of remove from oneself may be distinguished. Differences in socialization (viz., a Chicagoan who has lived in Britain vs. one who has not) are likely to yield differences in the baseline itself, of course.

Let us now consider a very different type of variation.

Identity, when?

Differences of identity ascription do not depend only on matters of *prior* socialization. Such differences often emerge over the time course of an

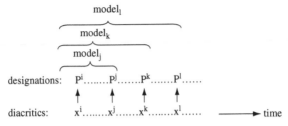

Figure 5.2   *Textually cumulative models of personhood*

encounter through relationships of fractional congruence among signs that co-occur in that very encounter. Within any social interaction the effective specificity of status attribution involves reading many signs that co-occur together, not on reading any one sign. The concreteness of perceived personhood is typically a composite sketch based on an array of co-occurring signs – forming a readable text in performance – such that properties indexed by signs perceived earlier constitute part of the context for construing signs occurring later. For instance, a subsequent utterance may foreground a departure from a role expectation in play from a preceding utterance; in this type of case the sign is diacritic of (or differentiates) a subsequent image (or model) from one just established a moment earlier. Figure 5.2 lays out in schematic form the difference between locally indexed and cumulatively established models of personhood. A more cumulative reading is more specific in import than a more local reading since it takes into account more information.

Taken by itself any local sign (such as x^k/P^k) has an emblematic function insofar as it is an embodied sign (x^k) that indexes a specific persona (P^k); it has a diacritic function insofar as it differentiates one emergent model from another (e.g., $model_k$ from $model_j$). For example, a single indexical can be (1) emblematic of, or specifically convey, a particular attribute (e.g., 'he's angry!') and, at the same time, function (2) as a diacritic that distinguishes that recognition from a prior perception of that person.

Such construals are also interactionally negotiated in the sense that individuals being modeled can intervene to shape the other's act of modeling them. For example, shifts in ascribed persona may result from self-typification (where a designator is offered by the one who performed the diacritic) or through other-typification (where the two are different people). A persona indexed by a sign on some occasion persists beyond that occasion when presupposed in further activity. It persists as a ratified persona when it is presupposed in the activity of those who interact with the one performing it. From the point of view of textuality, the **emblematic function** of an indexical is its capacity to set defaults for subsequent readings of personhood. Its **diacritic function** is its capacity to differentiate further readings from readings already in play.

Reprise

In the discussion above, I have discussed a number of different types of readings of personhood. The main issues may be summarized as follows:

Summary 5.4

A hearer's identification of speaker

(a) can shift because of the speaker's register range;
(b) partly depends on the hearer's own prior socialization;
(c) partly develops and changes during interaction (as further text-in-context construals emerge over the course of the interaction);
(d) is interactionally negotiated by semiotic activities performed by both.

I have presented these as analytically separate cases, but it will be clear that they often interact with each other as fractions of more interesting types of composite effects. Other kinds of principled variation also occur, some of which are described later.

The above considerations present a view of things very unlike our reportable intuitions about how we figure out who we're dealing with. This is because we lack an everyday metalanguage for describing what we do, even though we do it very well every day. Our common ways of describing what we do are mostly limited to the use of role designators (that so-and-so is a person of 'such-and-such-a-kind'). But our ability to perform and construe facts of personhood works differently.

In the discussion following Figure 5.1, I argued that the designator-fraction of a role carries the weight of decontextualized description; the diacritic fraction, of embodied perception; and we move across these levels in making inferences about people. The diacritic-fraction is, moreover, not a thing but *a type of functional relationship expressed by a thing*. As we saw in the discussion of Figure 5.2, a single datum in experience can be emblematic of a specific attribute *while* functioning as a diacritic that distinguishes that recognition from a prior perception. In other cases, certain behaviors are merely diacritics at particular moments; they break an expectation but don't clarify definite or specific attributes at that moment.

The above considerations might suggest that the activity of reading personhood is always shifting, malleable, an impossibly slippery affair. This is not of course the case. There are many ways in which much more definite and clear-cut forms of recognition also occur. Although these cases are more transparent to our everyday intuitions, they are all special cases of one sort or another. In fact, they are transparent *because* a number of distinct principles discussed earlier intersect together to yield special kinds of discrete, readily decontextualizable readings of personhood.

For example, I said earlier that diacritics can not be identified as a discrete, context-independent class of things, except in certain special cases. One type of case occurs when a set of diacritics is configured into an emblem by an explicit metapragmatic discourse. This is most commonly the result of particular kinds of institutionalized work, whereby role diacritics appear to form determinate classes relative to frameworks of role designation. The effect is most common in the case of institutionally codified roles. Let us consider some examples.

5.4 Emblematic readings

If you take a taxicab in the city of Philadelphia you will find a notice posted inside the cab on the partition behind the driver, displayed for the benefit of passengers. Here is an excerpt:

(3) 'Rules for the appearance of drivers':
'A driver will be dressed in clean clothing which will be composed of a shirt with collar, ankle length trousers, slacks/dress, skirts (if gender appropriate), socks or stockings, and clean sneakers. Shorts, bathing suits, tank tops, 'muscle shirts' are strictly prohibited, unless concealed as undergarments.'

The notice is produced by a civil authority, centered in Harrisburg (the state capital) which prescribes normative criteria on appropriate livery for many categories of state-licensed employees. The notice is itself a fragment of a metapragmatic discourse, a stretch of language that legislates boundaries for certain non-linguistic semiotic displays (clothing), specifying appropriate choices and promising sanctions against prohibited ones. There is a phone number that you can call should your driver be wearing a bathing suit. But what is truly remarkable about this case is that the passenger's interaction with the driver is mediated by an explicit metapragmatic discourse physically contiguous to the semiotic display that it regiments; the passenger has but to read the notice to be able to 'read' the role appropriateness of the clothing worn by the driver sitting next to it. In such a case the emblem is highly transparent because the designations and diacritics that comprise it are gathered together so that they can be taken in by a single gaze.

Now, in most social interactions we cannot locate explicit instructions on how to read the interactants within the interaction itself. The writing is not so squarely on the walls. Nonetheless, in any society some perceivable signs are treated as diacritic of certain roles in fairly routine ways. In cases where an encounter does not contain an explicit metapragmatics of this kind, a participant can nonetheless 'read' the others present if he or she is

acquainted with criterial metapragmatic stereotypes through prior socialization, or with an emergent metapragmatics that depends on text-level
indexicality (Figure 5.2). The latter case is highly encounter-dependent in
an obvious way; but the fact that stereotypic readings depend on large
scale cultural processes can easily obscure the fact that they are encounter-
dependent too, at least in one specific, but critical, way.

Cultural prerequisites on readings

In the case of stereotypic readings, prior experiences equip a current
participant with a metapragmatic framework for construing a pragmatic
behavior as a sign of a specific role. But which such framework applies to
the current event? Which portion of one's prior experience is now relevant?
The principle of selection is provided in the current event. It depends on the
experience of the pragmatic sign itself. As the upward arrow in Figure 5.1
shows, the pragmatic sign itself indexes – invokes by presupposition – a
metapragmatic framework *as a condition* on its construal as a sign of a role.
To speak of indexical presupposition in this sense is to say that a role
construal is *conditional upon* acquaintance with a metapragmatic framework. The presupposition may not be satisfied on some occasion, or not
satisfied symmetrically for every interactant: a given interactant may or
may not be acquainted with a framework that construes a behavior as a
sign of a specific role. Or, more interestingly, different co-present interactants
may exhibit asymmetries of acculturation and, starting out with different
frameworks, find it necessary to engage in various forms of negotiation as
to which among these frameworks best provides a characterization of *who*
the person under scrutiny really is, or *what* he or she is up to.

In the taxicab example many people can have a common view of driver
dress code for a peculiar reason. The object-signs typified are co-present
with the metasigns that typify them. Of course a customer may pay no
attention to the notice, or be unable to read English; so co-presence is not
sufficient for the notice to function effectively as a metasign of role
appropriate dress. What we have been observing, rather, is that when the
notice is effective its co-presence with its object-signs plays a part in its
effectiveness. In this unusual type of case, the construal of norm appropriate behavior does not depend on prior socialization to the specifics of
the cab driver dress code (though of course it presupposes prior socialization to countless other cultural conditions, such as the ability to read
English) because the dress code is explicitly described within the encounter
itself.

In the case of stereotypic indexicals more generally many persons have a
common view of an emblem because they are connected to each other
through a processes of communicative transmission through which an

emblem becomes enregistered for a population of sign-users. An **enregistered emblem** is mediated by widespread stereotypes. However, having a 'common view of an emblem' only *sometimes* means having an identical reading. In the more general case, commonalities of reading are relatable to each other only by their fractional congruence. As we saw in Chapter 4, reconstructing the process of enregisterment as a communicative process allows us to see that the replication of enregistered emblems across populations is often linked to their *alteration within* that process. Hence to say that enregistered emblems have a wide social domain is generally to speak of thresholds of fractional congruence between stereotypic models, not to say that they are evaluated identically in all respects by all who are acquainted with them. A number of the most interesting social dynamics mediated by stereotypes (issues of contrastive self-positioning, role alignment, reanalysis, counter-valorization, etc.) all exploit, and in some cases exacerbate, the fractional *non*-congruence of stereotype models too, as numerous examples in previous chapters illustrate.

In the contrastive case of the text-level readings illustrated in Figure 5.2, attributes become linked to diacritics because they are textually diagrammed by an emergent organization of signs within an interaction. Anything which we, from a cognitive point of view, might call an 'emergent emblem' is, from a semiotic point of view, an entextualized emblem. Each of the 'models' in Figure 5.2 is an **entextualized emblem** in this sense, one which motivates an emergent reading of personhood that depends on text-level indexical relations among co-occurring signs. Even if the sign-configuration that motivates the effect is radically contingent or unique, the effect is still recoverable through a process of inference that allows an interactant to treat the many independent signs that constitute that configuration as conveying information about the same actor-origo.

It would be a mistake to suppose that the activity of reading persons can be reduced only to stereotypic or only to text-level processes. If we focus on the ongoing character of such readings it is evident that they rely on both. The difference between the two is that the signs that mediate stereotypic readings are readily discussed out of context. In contrast, when we consider the order of textuality itself, we observe a logic of contrastive figurement of personae of a vastly different kind. We have seen numerous, extended examples of this process in previous chapters. For instance, we saw in Chapter 2 that persona characteristics mediated through referring – such as propositional stances and alignments among interlocutor – are made palpable through *the metrical structure of propositional acts*. In cases of this type, matters of perceivable role and relationship depend on metricized congruence among co-occurring signs (see S 2.3). We saw in Chapter 3 that contrary-to-stereotype construals depend on a textually diagrammed non-congruence between a stereotypic indexical and some other index that co-occurs with the first, conveying information about the same contextual origo, but differing in the information it conveys (3.5). Such composite effects are readily grasped within the order of interaction. However the text configurations that mediate these effects are harder to describe out of context than the effects they yield, precisely because the former are semiotic arrays, frequently complex, and the latter are readily approximated by impressionistic word-long glosses.

Types of emblematic readings

In the terminology of Charles Sanders Peirce, an emblem is an **indexical icon**. It is a performance of a sign that reveals properties or qualities (the iconic part) of the one contextually linked to it (the indexical part). Emblems formulate persons as social actors of specific kinds. They imply groupings and contrasts among persons based on the likeness and unlikeness of behaviors. The term emblem was introduced into the anthropological literature by Singer 1984, who showed that anthropologists since Durkheim have been inclined to view matters of group membership as readable facts about persons and their behaviors. Most of these discussions have tended, however, to focus on special cases. For instance, Durkheim's own account of totemic classifications is a milestone in our thinking about an important special case, the case where widely enregistered (so-called 'conventional') emblems of groupness (e.g., animal totems) become naturalized ways of conceiving group membership and relations between groups, and of reproducing such groupings and relations across time through constraints on marriage. Such examples, as well as other traditionally cited examples of emblems (such as flags, banners, coats of arms), all depend on the fact that certain diacritics of social difference can be given emblematic readings; they are special cases in the sense that these examples are often cited, rightly or wrongly, as instances where the emblem appears to be a socially rigid – apparently invariant – index of social group membership and contrast.

I have been discussing emblems in a wider sense. In this wider sense, emblems are always effective as indices of the social attributes of individuals, but the way in which they index these effects (and for whom they do so) may be quite varied. The examples discussed so far may be grouped into at least the following types:

Summary 5.5
A sign may be emblematic of the social attributes of a person in various ways. For example, the relation between sign and attributes may be

(a) textually diagrammed in an interaction in an **emergent** (potentially, unique) way

(b) widely recognized as **stereotypic** by many persons
(c) **naturalized**, so that questions of its arbitrariness or conventionality no
longer arise

We can now see that the view that emblems are necessarily 'conventional'
signs of identity is a mistake. The doctrine of 'convention' (which is
itself mired in seventeenth-century 'social contract' fictions and other
absurdities[5]) is too blunt an instrument to get us very far. According to
this doctrine two people can recognize a sign as a sign of the same thing
(e.g., the same identity or attribute) only if they share the same 'conventions.'
But this is excessively restrictive.

In cases of type (a), the intersubjective grasp of the attribution is
formulated by an emergent order of entextualized signs; the attribute
is grasped by those who attend to the same emergent text-in-context
relationships. This is the case of entextualized emblems. Here an intersubjective grasp of the attribution depends on mutual orientation to a structure
of information that unfolds while the sign-configuration is in play, not on
conventions known in advance, and not describable later *as a sign-
configuration* as easily as the attributions it mediates. Even if we suppose
that the individual signs that contribute to the sign-configuration are
known to current participants from conventions known in advance, the
sign-configuration and its metrical structure is purely emergent, and its
text-level construal depends on inferences from cues within that emergent
sign-configuration (their convergence, congruence, coherence, etc.; see 1.2),
not on conventions known in advance.

The case in (b) corresponds more closely to the classical notion of
convention, but here we are dealing not with static conventions ('adopted'
once and for all) but with dynamic processes of enregisterment (as discussed in the previous chapter), processes which include mechanisms of
communicative transmission through which a 'standing for' relationship
has a circulation, can become widely known, institutionalized, and so on,
but may also *undergo reanalysis* during this process of transmission, leading to positional, fractionally congruent variants of the sign, so that the
assumption of perfect 'sharedness' (which plays a central role in the
doctrine of convention) becomes irrelevant to the mutual coordination
of behaviors. And in the case in (c), the 'standing for' relationship is treated
not as 'conventional' by sign-users, but as 'natural,' as entirely beyond
contingency or dispute; although processes of naturalization are themselves semiotic processes (see 1.6), they produce effects upon enregistered
signs that are of critical and distinctive importance in shaping the behavior
of sign users, and the doctrine of 'convention' (particularly the notion
of 'arbitrariness' it implies) completely obscures the character of these
effects.

The three possibilities are not mutually exclusive. In any kind of social interaction, features of an actor's performance that function as diacritics can be construed as emergent, stereotypic or naturalized emblems by different socially positioned readings. Different readings do not merely express different 'takes' on who the person is; they also locate the persons doing the readings vis-à-vis each other by highlighting differences in their grasp of the conditions on construing the diacritic as a sign of a role. These differences can also become topics of further interactional work. One person's reading of another may locate her as someone fully an 'insider' with respect to a cultural framework of construal, while other interactants may appear to be 'outsiders' to greater or lesser degrees, able to grasp what is going on only through textually contingent inferences that are relatively partial and incomplete.

We tend to suppose that readings of personhood are cued by isolable signs (single utterances, dress, physical appearance, etc.). Sometimes they are. And yet such isolable signs are often elements of larger patterns of behavior that are configurational wholes that themselves convey information. These larger sign-configurations are often less transparent to subsequent reportability and discussion but are nonetheless critical in establishing determinate identity readings in particular encounters. I turn in the next section to a discussion of these issues in a specific ethnographic case, the case of models of piety and honor in Yemeni society.

My goal in the next section is to examine the ways in which patterns of interaction are metasemiotically linked to models of personhood. In the Yemeni case, these models enregister specific patterns of greeting behavior as indices of specific persona types, and link these greetings to other indices (including non-linguistic ones) through which the same personae can be performed. But beyond the particularities of the greeting ritual (as a specific type of interactional ritual) and beyond the particular characterological constructs associated with greetings and other signs in the Yemeni case lie much more general questions. Let me mention two here: (1) What are the various ways in which a diverse range of indices performable in behavior (including some that are patterns of interactional ritual, and some that are more isolable, less configurational signs) can be linked to readings of personhood in ways that are intelligible to social actors? and (2) What are the various ways in which social actors can inhabit these characterological constructs (whether canonically or through improvised, hybrid variations) in actual lived experience? I do not offer exhaustive answers to either question in the discussion that follows. My hope is, rather, that the answers I do offer for the specific cases I discuss in the remaining sections of this chapter, and elsewhere in this book, will stimulate further research on these questions.

5.5 Interaction rituals as emblems of group status

In every language community there are many ways of greeting a person. These are frequently recognized as differing in pragmatic efficacy. Thus *How do you do?* is a more formal type of greeting than *What's up?* or *How's it hanging?* Now to say that *How do you do?* is more 'formal' than the others is to employ a metapragmatic stereotype as a way of ranking the pragmatics of distinct utterances. The stereotype is readily extended from utterance to utterer so that someone who habitually uses *How do you do?* is evaluated as a more formal *person* than someone who habitually uses the others. The stereotype is also statable through role designators other than 'formal'; for instance, differences among these English examples are commonly described through stereotypes of speaker's class, ethnicity and age.

Such stereotypes often vary society-internally. Any given stereotype not only has a social range describable through role designators (formal vs. informal, upper vs. lower class, older vs. younger) but a contrastive social domain (is formulated by some category of persons). An awareness that different greeting forms exist is often enregistered culture-internally through different positional stereotypes of speaker characteristics. Different forms may well be treated as *diacritic* of role difference by nearly everyone; but their specification as *positive emblems* often differs society-internally. Any language user can recognize many more greeting forms than he or she habitually uses; knowing that an utterance-type counts as a 'greeting' in that society is itself a stereotype of its interpersonal effects that is presupposed in positionally varying models of its more specific, speaker-emblematic effects.

But a greeting is not just an utterance-type. It is an **interactional ritual** in which a particular utterance-type – a greeting initiation – by one person elicits a response from another. In general, greetings are exchanges between interlocutors that comprise an interactional text whose parts, the initiation and response, have a paired structure. A greeting exchange is interactionally complete when a greeting-initiator produces an utterance, the first pair-part, to which a respondent makes a response, the second pair-part, which may be more or less cohesive with the first. In English, the sequence *How are you?[1]/I am fine[2]* has a cohesive pair-part structure when the two pair-parts occur in the order indicated by superscripts, as does *What's up?[1]/Not much[2]*; but other pairings can depart from such smooth, seemingly frictionless unions between initiator and respondent, and formulate various types of role distance instead, e.g., by breaking register (*What's up?[1]/I am fine[2]*), or by a more fundamental break from expected response (*How are you?[1]/Screw you![2]*).

From the point of view of their pair-part structure, greetings are interactional diagrams to which persons in interactional roles of speaker and

respondent contribute turn-fractions; they motivate interactionally negotiated readings of self and other (S 5.4d). These readings are often highly
ordered for members of societal sub-groups; for instance, they are often
linked to emblems of group-relative identity that are more inclusive in their
semiotic range (e.g., link greetings to other kinds of performable signs);
relative to these frameworks, a greeting variant appears to conform to a
larger way of being a person.

Yemeni greetings as diagrams of honor and piety

A particularly clear example of this may be found in Steve Caton's work on
Yemeni greetings (Caton 1986), on which my discussion is based. The
examples below rest on a comparison of two distinct groups, the *sādah*
who are residents of a central Yemeni village, and the tribesmen who reside
in surrounding hamlets. These groups differ in the greeting forms most
typical in in-group usage and in the metapragmatic discourses used to
construe their significance. Let us consider the greeting forms first.

Yemeni greetings are elaborate interactional rituals that take many
turns to unfold, as is the case in many other societies (Irvine 1989 [1974],
Schottman 1995, Perrino 2002). In such cases the pair-part structure of
greetings involves the 'chaining' of utterances (Goffman 1981b: 8) across
many interactional turns.[6] The pattern of chaining is not invariant within
Yemeni society. It is diacritic of social kinds of persons. Caton observes
that greetings among tribesmen typically involve a different pattern of
cross-turn chaining than is common in the *sādah* greeting.

(4) Typical greeting exchange among tribesmen

A		B
1. guwī-t[1]	::	najī-t[2]
'You've been strengthened [by God]'		'You've been saved [by God]')
2. kēf al-ḥāl[1]	::	sallam ḥāl-ak[2]
'How are you?'		'May God bless you'
3. hayy al laḥyah[1]	::	hayy(a) laḥyat-ak[2]
'Long life to you' (literally, '...		'Long life to you' (literally, '...
to the beard')		to your beard')
....[1]	::	....[2]

In the tribal greeting in (4), a greeting-initiator, A, utters a first pair-
part, to which the respondent, B, returns an appropriate second pair-part
(line 1). This pair-part sequence is followed by a second initiation by A, to
which B makes a second response (line 2); this pattern of pair-part chaining
is often repeated for several additional turns. In the tribal pattern, the
respondent B merely completes a pair-part sequence in each line; his
response consists of an appropriate second pair-part but adds no further
elaborations to the pattern initiated by A. The tribal greeting exhibits a
relatively symmetric type of performed structure in this sense.

(5) A *sādah* greeting

A		B		
1. ahlan wa sahlan[1]	::	ahlan-bik[2]	:	hayy allāh man jā[1]
'Hello'		'Hello to you'	:	'May God grant long
				life to one who has come'
2. wa hayyā-k[2]	:	…..[1]	::	…..[2]	:	…..[1]
'And long life					
to you'					
…..[2]	:	…..[1]	::	…..[2]	:	…..[1]

The *sādah* greeting in (5) exhibits a more asymmetric chain structure. Here, after the initiation by A in line 1 (*ahlan wa sahlan[1]*) B produces a second pair-part (*ahlan-bik[2]*), but his turn is not yet complete. Rather than allowing A to initiate the next pair-part sequence (as in (4) above), B himself initiates a second pair-part sequence in his own turn (*ḥayy allāh man jā[1]*) in line 1, which A completes in line 2 with the corresponding second pair-part (*wa hayyā-k[2]*). Thus B's utterance in line 1 exhibits a pattern of next-turn intensification and elaboration of A's prior utterance, which sets the conditions for A's subsequent response.

While A begins his utterance in line 2 with a second pair-part, he typically does not stop there either; he proceeds in line 2, as B has in line 1, by adding a new first pair-part. The pattern of next-turn intensification-and-elaboration, which forms the basic unit of chaining in the *sādah* greeting, has a metrical organization involving simple alternation at the level of speaking turns (A:: B:: A:: B...). After A's first turn, the pattern involves a distinctive pair-part order (...²:¹::²:¹...), and (using a, b, c, as names for propositional acts) a broken chiasmus at the level of denotational cohesion (a:b::b:{c}), where the last element {c} sets the conditions for the beginning of the next such unit, thus forming a composite poetic structure (...B[a²: b¹]:: A[b² :{c}¹]: B[c²: d¹]:: A[d² :{e}¹]...) iterated across several additional turns. This pattern of iteration is shown as 'Pattern II' in Table 5.1.

The first column of Table 5.1 summarizes the two patterns illustrated in (4) and (5) above as patterns I and II, respectively. The lower-case letters indicate propositional acts, with superscripts marking pair-part order as before. The second column summarizes the contrasting effects performed through the two patterns, namely symmetry vs. elaboration/intensification. The final column shows that each pattern is most typical in *in-group* usage. Members of each group are acquainted with the other's greeting pattern and switch to it in inter-group contact, a point to which I return below.

To observe that different patterns of greeting exchange occur is merely to observe a contrast of text-patternment at the level of diacritics. Any observer who attends to the contrast between patterns I and II can recognize that they differentiate those who perform them from one another in

Table 5.1. *Greeting form as emblem of speaker's status*

	Greeting forms			Performed features	Appropriate settings
	A	::	B		
Pattern I	a^1	::	a^2	cross-turn symmetry	in-group usage
[cf. (4)]	b^1	::	b^2		among tribesmen
	c^1	::	c^2		
		etc.			
	A	::	B		
Pattern II	a^1	::	$a^2 : b^1$	next-turn elaboration	in-group usage
[cf. (5)]	$b^2 : c^1$	::	$c^2 : d^1$	and intensification	among *sādah*
	$d^2 : e^1$	::	$e^2 : f^1$		
		etc.			

Source: (Caton 1986)

some way. But whether these patterns convey some further positive content, whether they function as contentful emblems of group status, is not something we can discover by attending to the pristine organization of these form-patterns alone. We require an entry into such metapragmatic frameworks as are employed culture-internally to construe their significance. The appropriateness judgments in the last column of Table 5.1 are already evidence of a metapragmatic framework of a minimal sort: a particular greeting form is judged appropriate by a user when the interlocutor is a certain kind of person. Thus the choice of greeting is emblematic of their relative group membership. Caton shows that a fuller analytic grasp of these emblems requires attention to additional metapragmatic frameworks to which language users appeal in explaining their own behaviors.

The tribesmen and the *sādah* differ in the norms of conduct they consider most distinctive of themselves. Such differences are naturalized *inter alia* in accounts of group origins, and especially in self-avowed genealogies. The *sādah* (pl. of *sayyid*) regard themselves as descendants of the Prophet Mohammed; even the village in which they reside is termed a *hijrah* village, a name that associates them with the Prophet. This genealogy also commits the *sayyid* to an ethos of piety, displayed in a variety of ways in conduct; the ethos of piety is also linked to greeting pattern II, as we shall shortly see. In contrast, a member of the tribes, a *qabīlī*, has a mythical genealogy distinct from the *sayyid's* and, from the point of view of group distinction, a salient commitment to a contrastive inherited ethos: 'As reputed descendants of Qaḥṭan, one of the mythical founders of the Southern Arabs, and of the Ḥimyaritic and Sabaen kings who controlled the ancient incense trade, the tribes consider themselves to be men who have inherited great *šaraf.*'

The ethos of *šaraf* 'honor' requires the doing of 'glorious deeds,' the avoidance of subservience, or of any action by which honor is lost; and by tribal law the maintenance of one's honor may require violence, including revenge killing, an eye for an eye.

The ethos of *šaraf* implies an interactional norm for everyday encounters too: the display of self and the treatment of one's interactant ought to be egalitarian (i.e., ought pointedly to display symmetric relative status) since to raise oneself up or to lower one's interlocutor is potentially to give offence, to lower the other's honor, and thus to put oneself at risk. Notice that the symmetric greeting (pattern I) straightforwardly conforms to this interactional norm. Hence acquaintance with the ethos of *šaraf* makes available a metapragmatic criterion that reads the symmetric greeting as a highly specific sort of 'in-group' emblem, namely an emblem of the membership of both A and B in an emergent grouping, a dyad that uphold the ethos of *šaraf*. The pattern is most appropriate in in-group interactions among tribesmen, among individuals who are intimately acquainted with the broader discourses and norms of *šaraf*, and who, by virtue of their distinctive self-positioning (naturalized in part in a mythical genealogy), attach importance to these ways of performing and reading personae.

The lineage of the *sādah*, who reside in the *hijrah* village, commits them to a contrasting ethos, an ethos of piety. Piety is displayed in a variety of ways, most saliently in the strict observance of conventionally religious practices. Acts that display greater reverence to God, or a more copious scriptural knowledge, or a stricter adherence to religious doctrine are all straightforwardly recognizable as diacritics of a more 'pious' persona by virtue of these displays. But acquaintance with the scriptures also acquaints the *sādah* with specific metapragmatic injunctions about greeting behavior, injunctions that occur in the Qur'ān itself. These require devout muslims to engage in specific forms of greeting behavior in encounters with each other.

Some Qur'ānic injunctions, such as the one in (6), typify the first pairpart of the greeting encounter:

(6) When those come to thee, who believe in Our Signs, say 'Peace be upon you'.
(Surah VI, 53)

The injunction begins by describing a role configuration (one muslim encountering another), followed by a represented speech construction (... say '...') which reproduces the precise form of the utterance to be used as a greeting initiation. Thus the above Qur'ānic verse is an explicit metapragmatic discourse typifying the pragmatics of the greeting *as-salām 'alē-kum* 'Peace be upon you,' formulating it as a normatively appropriate first-pair part in such encounters.

Similarly, the Qur'ānic injunction in (7) is an equally explicit metapragmatic discourse about the second pair-part:

(7) If you are greeted courteously, then greet with a better one, or return it (at least) in kind, God takes account of all things.

(Surah IV, 86)

The statement characterizes a person who responds to a greeting with a 'better one' as a person who finds favor with God. The injunction to respond with a 'better one' suggests a pattern of next-turn intensification and elaboration, which is understood as applying to, but not only to, the lexicogrammatical elaborateness of the second pair-part. For, as Caton shows, the pattern of next turn elaboration and intensification is characteristically observed through many other diacritics of next-turn response in greetings emblematic of a *sādah* persona. These include the use of 'intensifier phrases' which elaborate the greeting's illocutionary force; the use of deictics that nomically universalize the blessing to all muslims, not just current addressee; and of parallelistic 'poetic' features (e.g., consonant and vowel alliteration) that foreground and aesthetically intensify the greeting's phonetic shape. Since the Qur'ānic verse is a metapragmatic discourse in relation to the pragmatic act, any such pattern of next-turn intensification and elaboration counts as a way of replying with a 'better one' and hence as an emblem of the performer's greater piety to an observer acquainted with the metapragmatic discourse.

Unlike the ethos of *šaraf*, the ethos of piety poses no interactional risk: performatively establishing oneself as 'the more pious one' is a way of acquiring higher status in the eyes of God while acquiring higher relative status vis-à-vis interlocutor. Thus whereas the ethos of *šaraf* valorizes symmetric performance of egalitarian relations, the ethos of piety encourages asymmetric performances, amenable to construals of differences in rank (and dependent forms of social stratification) among persons who vie for a higher spiritual status.

Gradient, hybrid and out-group selves

Given all of this, it is very easy to essentialize these parallels and differences into a picture that reads enregistered emblems as 'coding' facts of personhood and group identity. Yet all we really have are relations of contingent alignment among three kinds of contrasts: we have a contrast of greeting patterns (symmetric vs. elaborative), construed as emblematic of specific status content by two different metapragmatic discourses (discourses of *šaraf* vs. piety), which are of special importance to two kinds of nameable persons (the *qabīlī* vs. the *sayyid*). The coding view mistakes facts of contingent alignment among diacritics and designations as necessary relationships; if by 'coding' we mean one-to-one relationships between facts of

Table 5.2. *Emblems of piety and honor*

ascriptions of piety	ascriptions of *šaraf*
↑↓	↑↓
• acts of religious observance • greeting pattern II • use of other patterns of intensification	• acts that preserve and maintain honor • greeting pattern I • allusions to corporeal emblems of honor
• soft tones, even pitch, near-whispers; prosodic indices of 'peace' and 'quiet contemplation'	• loud, creaky voice; high pitch; prosodic indices of 'virility'/'aggressiveness'/'warlike' persona

Source: (Caton 1986)

one kind and another then nothing is coded. These icons are aligned only under certain conditions. This is readily seen by considering three types of non-alignment, the case of role fractionation, hybrid personae, and out-group usage.

Role fractionation is possible because the same group status is iconized by multiple indices, each of which is emblematic of the role. These may be deployed in behavior in a gradiently congruent manner. One can be pious or honorable to different degrees. I noted above that metapragmatic discourses of *šaraf* and of piety treat a variety of performable displays as emblems of each kind. Some of these are summarized in Table 5.2.

Each indexical icon has a semiotic range that includes, but is wider than, the greetings themselves. Thus piety is a quality that can be indexed by acts of religious observance in the narrow sense; and also by greeting pattern II; and also through other patterns of next-turn intensification (e.g., the phrasal intensifiers, universalizing deictics, and alliterations mentioned above). Similarly honor can be displayed and maintained through a range of behaviors discussed above; and also by greeting pattern I, the pattern of symmetric exchange; and also by allusions to corporeal emblems of honor (such as the references to the interlocutor's 'beard' in example (4), line 3). Caton also describes a number of other behaviors, which I have not discussed here, that are emblematic of the two types of performable statuses. For example, a variety of prosodic features are treated as emblematic of distinct speaker personae in the manner indicated at the bottom of Table 5.2.

We have already seen that when a metasemiotically motivated icon of personhood has a range of indices in its semiotic range such overlap of metasemiotic treatment provides criteria on the appropriate co-occurrence of such indices (see, e.g., Figure 1.1ff.) and hence criteria on the internal congruence of role displays. Any given performance may exhibit the role in a highly unified (co-textually congruent) way, or in ways that exhibit varying degrees of role fractionation because only some among the indices criterial for the most unified persona are actually performed. It is not merely that one can be pious or honorable to different degrees; it is also that someone acquainted with the system can display indices that are icons of different social types in behavior and thus perform **hybrid personae**, e.g., pious yet warlike, mindful of *šaraf* yet close to God. Since these effects depend on the co-textual congruence of indexicals (Figure 1.2), and since the criterion of congruence motivates cumulative readings of persona (Figure 5.2) the range of hybrid personae that are *performable and recognizable* through non-congruent indexical displays – and of interactional tropes that depend on them (see example (4), Chapter 1) – is many orders of magnitude greater than the simple scheme of person types that our metapragmatic descriptors (role labels such as *qabīlī* and *sayyid*, discourses that read individuals as 'honorable' or 'pious') might suggest. And differentiable points along this continuum of selves are not pinioned by names.

Let us now consider issues of out-group usage. Notice that we've been talking about 'groups' in two entirely different senses. On the one hand we've been talking about **performed groupings** of individuals in a dyad. Since greeting rituals have a pair-part structure they make palpable the comparability of initiator and respondent as like or unlike each other, as forming an emergent grouping through a performed likeness. On the other hand we have been concerned with **corporate groups** in the sense of recognized collectivities (which may, for instance, be labeled by group names, such as *qabīlī* and *sayyid*). Both senses of 'group' are relevant to issues of in-group vs. out-group usage. Thus if you are a tribesman who can read your interlocutor as also a tribesman then performing and maintaining pattern I is a way of maintaining a performed grouping that, in each phase of interactional text, *preserves* independently readable facts of relative membership in corporate groups, with all the entitlements and expectations that depend on these facts; and similarly for the *sādah* greeting.

But members of the two groups also have frequent contact with each other. The market and mosque of the *hijrah* village are places regularly visited by tribesmen, who recognize that norms of behavior within the *hijrah* village are different from their own. The *hijrah* village is normatively a place with which piety is associated; for the *sādah*, the ethos of piety means that certain forms of violence are normatively forbidden; correspondingly, tribesmen linked together through a blood feud may visit the *hijrah* village and come into passing contact with each other with impunity. It is not uncommon for tribesmen and *sādah* to use each other's greeting forms in out-group contact under these conditions. A more creative type of out-group usage is one where performed groupings are at odds with presupposed facts of corporate group membership. Thus for a *sayyid* not to respond to another *sayyid's* greeting in the manner most appropriate, or to do so with varying degrees of role dissonance, hybridity and so on, is a perfectly intelligible way of marking role distance at the level of performed groupings; how such inappropriate usage is construed (e.g., irony, rudeness, humor, gracelessness) depends on the way in which the act fits into the interactional text currently under way in the encounter.

One reason that the metaphysics of groups has persisted for so long in various forms of social theory is that the very persons under study, the persons who perform and construe emblems of group status, tend readily to describe performed groupings that align with membership in corporate groups as the most natural, motivated, basic types of groupings, particularly in contexts where their contrastive selves or identities are at issue. Thus the valorization of piety vs. *šaraf* is sometimes treated as a system of valorized 'status symbols' that are differentially laid claim to, or owned, in contexts of group differentiation. When asked to comment on whether the tribes had more *šaraf* than the *sādah*, a member of the latter group replies: 'The tribes are famous for their *šaraf* and we can hardly compete with them. For us, it is more important to be a *rajul dīnī*, "a pious (religious) man".' Such ownership can be further motivated by narratives that explicitly rationalize standards of appropriate behavior by appeal to facts of differential genealogy, thus yielding a naturalizing doctrine of group essence; or it may be motivated in a much more implicit way by cases where ritual and ceremonial behaviors, and practices that depend on them, treat the case of appropriate use (where facts of performed and corporate grouping normatively align) as a paradigm or exemplar of the best behavior, and thus a standard to which other performances, occurring elsewhere, ought to conform. But the fact that the users of these status emblems offer naturalizing accounts of this kind does not mean that they do not engage in the denaturalizing, hybridizing practices discussed earlier.

5.6 Emergent, stereotypic and naturalized groupings

The above considerations make clear that we cannot approach the question of how people get sorted into social kinds by taking a static ontology of 'social groups' as our point of departure. It is not that social groups don't exist or that they are not important to social life. It is rather that the existence of social groups is mediated by semiotic processes far richer and more intricate than the repertoire of group names from which the static ontology is derived. In the general case the existence of social groups has a more processual, more event-dependent ontology than the special case implies.

Let us consider the special case first: How do group names imply a static ontology? In every society a small set of role designators – typically nouns and noun phrases – serve as names for social groupings of widely recognized importance. Such groupings are widely recognized because certain institutionalized practices in which many people participate (e.g., marriage, inheritance, property ownership, the allocation of entitlements by the State) make reference to these groupings; such practices therefore invoke classifications to which many people are exposed. The names for social groups to which these practices appeal are widely known and highly transparent to members of society. The ability to invoke such classifications in mutually intelligible ways itself mediates, even maintains, a sense of group unity and cohesion, allowing individuals reflexively to recognize each other, or to recognize persons altogether elsewhere, as belonging to the classes ordered by such acts as invoke them; and their widely known character ensures that such acts occur not only in institutionalized contexts (in practices that cannot proceed without them) but occur also in countless everyday encounters (which could, but thereby do not, proceed without them). But insofar as these widely known group names are merely nouns or noun phrases, the experience of groups mediated by them is an experience of social kinds as 'things,' i.e., the denotata of nouns, which are often formulated by institutional practices as existing independently of the everyday activities that invoke them. In the minimal case, if the same role designators play a part in practices that recur in experience (viz., occur in many locales, at many times in the life cycle, etc.) the denotata of these designators (i.e., groups qua 'things') are self-evidently independent of any instance in which they are referred to and thus apparently independent of the practices that, in each instance, make reference to them. Indeed, some systems of designation are formulated as independent of *all* human activities. Many social practices naturalize the role designations on which they rely in a far more elaborate fashion, thereby gaining power over practitioners to the degree that such naturalizations are accepted. Moreover, although all such systems of role designation change over time, the growth and decline of such systems typically has a dureé (viz., a cycle of emergence, institutionalization, decline) that is much longer than a single encounter. Thus, for these reasons and others, the existence of groups labeled by widely known and institutionally presupposed role designators is easily amenable to reification, to the ascription of a static ontology. The existence of such groups is often a taken-for-granted fact about 'the world as it is' – i.e., a world held to exist independently of human activities – even though it is only made manifest or palpable through semiotic acts of performance and construal.

Let us now consider the general case: What is to say that *any* group exists? It must have members. But if the existence of a group is a function of the existence of its members, the existence of members is a function of recognition. Groups exist insofar as particular individuals are recognizable as their members. The criterion of recognition makes clear that there are many degrees and conditions of group existence. The social consequences of the existence of groups differ by the extent to which their members are in principle recognizable to, or are in fact recognized by, others.[7] In the general case, it must be possible for some person (at least one) to recognize that a particular individual (at least one) belongs to the social kind at issue; the case where many persons can sort many others into a given social kind is more sociologically consequential, of course, but we cannot understand how such cases come about by taking them as our point of departure. Indeed, it is precisely when we approach the question of the existence of groups from the standpoint of locatable events of recognition (i.e., from the point of view of particular events in which individuals sort each other into groups) that we find that the semiotic processes which enable such recognition make appeal to, but are much richer than, systems of role designators used as names for groups.

Most facts of recognizable social grouping are entirely emergent in interaction in the sense that interactants are easily able to sort each other into groupings or classifications on the basis of performed behaviors (i.e., demeanor indexicals displayed in conduct). But the groupings into which co-participants are sorted in this way need not be named by any widely accepted set of simple (e.g., monolexemic) group labels. The paucity of group names is not a problem for social interactants since all kinds of nonce-designations, whether simple or complex, can be formed as needed to augment any repertoire of stock labels. Moreover, the interactional point of recognizing an emergent grouping is usually not to come up with a name for it, but to know how to respond to it in a way that displays one's own placement with respect to it. The fact that most groupings lack widely accepted role designations is a serious problem *only* for social scientists wedded to the static ontology derived from the special case discussed above.

Whereas contingent and emergent facts of relative grouping can be mediated by anything that can function as a role diacritic in behavior, a number of semiotic processes that operate upon such diacritics also occur in social life, serving to make them non-contingent in one or more ways; for example, by linking them to designations that fix the identity of which the diacritic is thereafter emblematic; by institutionalizing the mechanisms through which the social domain of the emblem can be maintained or made to grow; by expanding the class of diacritics that are emblematic of a given role; by normalizing or codifying the emblem for certain social practices; by restricting access to certain diacritics and performable identities; and others. These effects are never achieved all at once, or ever completely for all members of a society. They involve large scale processes of enregisterment of the kind discussed in Chapter 4, processes that are by their very nature internally complicated by counter-processes that co-exist within them. Some among these processes seek programmatically to formulate more **rigidly indexical** emblems of group difference; for example, institutional metasemiotic discourses that seek normatively to fix the official sense of role designators like titles; or seek to codify procedures of 'baptismal' conferral by codifying the kinds of identities and relationships that can be established through performative ceremonies (1.5); or seek to limit the deployment of specific role diacritics only to certain presupposed role designations, as in the case of medieval sumptuary laws that prescribed apparel worn by knights vs. commoners; or make emblems indexically rigid by the degree to which they are presupposed in *other* practices, and viewed even as necessary preconditions on their occurrence.

Many institutionalized metasemiotic practices also appear to stabilize the social order through practices whereby selected diacritics are treated as *inherently* emblematic of the groups they differentiate. As Irvine and Gal (2000) have argued for the case of linguistic emblems, this frequently amounts to a construal or treatment 'as if a linguistic feature somehow depicted or displayed a social group's inherent nature or essence' (2000: 37). Such projects cannot proceed without processes of reinscription over preceding historical projects, including processes of **erasure**, or the elimination of distinctions that make particular erstwhile groupings henceforth marginal or invisible. When effective, or rather, for those for whom they are effective, such institutionalized readings readily formulate **naturalized diagrams** of social differences (either within a society, or in another society, as in the case of colonial encounters; or both, as when the latter serves the interests of the former) so that each classificatory partition appears to correspond, as if naturally, to a unique group essence.

Yet these projects, by their nature, are never complete. They can of course be completely accepted by certain groups for a while, presupposed or institutionalized in at least *their* practices, even acquire authority for others linked to such institutions, but this is not the same thing. They are never complete because they can only exist through semiotic activities in which persons play a part by occupying interactional roles, and in which they are summoned to a sense of their own macro-sociological position within the interpersonal encounter at hand. Each moment-interval in such a process is a semiotic event with a participation framework, subject to processes of role alignment or fractional congruence, whether between participants or between them and the characterological figures conveyed by their acts. A number of these issues have been summarized in earlier sections (especially 3.8, 4.7–4.8). A number of related issues, also involving matters of role alignment and differentiation have been discussed by Bucholz and Hall (2004). In Table 5.3, I summarize the major processes they clarify over the course of an extended and elegant discussion. It will be

Table 5.3. *Processes that operate over role diacritics and emblems*

(a) Adequation	the pursuit of socially recognized sameness
(a′) Distinction	the production of salient differentiation
(b) Authentication	the construction of a credible or genuine identity
(b′) Denaturalization	the production of an identity that appears incredible, non-genuine, hybrid
(c) Authorization	the attempt to formulate an authoritative identity
(c′) Illegitimation	the denial of legitimacy to a recognizable identity

Source: (Bucholz and Hall 2004)

clear that these processes are mediated by signs, that they unfold one semiotic encounter at a time, that they have consequences for trajectories of sameness or difference among persons across encounters, and hence, for the macro-social order that lives as the visible sum of such trajectories (episodically reconfigured – given (a′), (b′) and (c′) – by fits of long division.)

5.7 Enregistered identities and stereotypic emblems

In the above discussion I have focused mainly on senses of the terms 'group' or 'grouping' that are relatively close to the idea of a 'group of persons.' My goal has been to show that the idea of a 'group of persons' cannot be a fundamental (or analytically 'primitive') concept for any social theory. It is a dependent concept, a name for an effect achieved through semiotic activities, maintained or transformed through such activities, and also stabilized, for certain purposes, by naturalized diagrams of the social order.

I want to focus now on a second sense of grouping, one to which I alluded earlier, namely the notion that a set of behavioral diacritics can be grouped into an emblem. Thus, in the Yemeni case, Table 5.2 shows that once discourses about 'pious' or 'honorable' persons group together various behavioral diacritics as emblematic of each of these unified roles, such roles can gradiently be inhabited by anyone capable of performing these diacritics, and recognized by anyone acquainted with the metasemiotic scheme that construes them as characterological emblems.

Similarly in the discussion of Received Pronunciation in the previous chapter I discussed a number of ways in which metadiscourses of accent are not merely discourses about phonetic patterns but are, rather, meta-semiotic discourses that link matters of accent to other diacritics, often formulating multi-channel diagrams of demeanor, social role, and performable identity. Table 5.4 summarizes a few of the features of these

Table 5.4. *Enregistered indices of refinement linked to 'Received Pronunciation'*

- Popular Handbooks diagram likenesses across diverse semiotic variables (Figure 4.2); they also link representations of refinement indexable by speech to refinement in matters of dress, carriage, grooming, cosmetics, and even to abstract essences such as 'taste'
- Literary Works develop these cross-modal diagrams in much more elaborate narrative detail during the course of character depiction; they also give a much fuller articulation of the link between demeanor and social-demographic position within society (class, gender, age, profession, etc.)
- Penny Weeklies are already part of an emerging genre of 'lifestyle' magazines. Here accounts and discussions of accent are linked to various comestibles, appurtenances, skill in foreign languages, music, and a variety of other indices which are prestige commodities that may be purchased for a price (see ch. 4, (11)ff.)

multi-channel diagrams, as articulated in three of the genres we discussed in the last chapter, namely popular handbooks, literary works, and penny weeklies.

These discourses formulate the refinement of speaker-actor through multiple independent diacritics grouped into emblems, just as in the Yemeni case. Thus it is possible to exhibit one's refinement not only through Received Pronunciation but also through the other diacritics listed in Table 5.4 and, therefore, to display it to varying degrees, and in ways susceptible of all the thresholds of congruence and non-congruence (and dependent effects such as role dissonance, hybridity, etc.) discussed earlier.

Discourses of Received Pronunciation have never, in fact, wholly been discourses of accent. The early prescriptivists, Sheridan and Walker, were interested in promoting an overall demeanor through which both voice and gesture would give ultimate expression to the qualities of mind peculiar to 'the gentleman' (a diagramming of bodily hexis that was later extended to 'the lady' too), and in grounding such diacritics in a naturalized ethnopsychology, a 'natural system of the passions,' in which arrays of perceivable outer marks (forms of countenance, tone of voice, gesture, and syllable structure) could be seen as corresponding to specific, interior mental states.

In the early stages of this movement, Sheridan, who was an actor before he became an elocutionist, helped promote a genre of social gatherings in London high society called 'Attic Evenings,' where the well-born gathered together, and with Sheridan's help, trained themselves in elocution and gesture by declaiming the works of Milton and Shakespeare. John Walker attempted to formalize this system into a 'System of the Passions' in his *Elements of Elocution*, as the title page indicates (Figure 5.3).

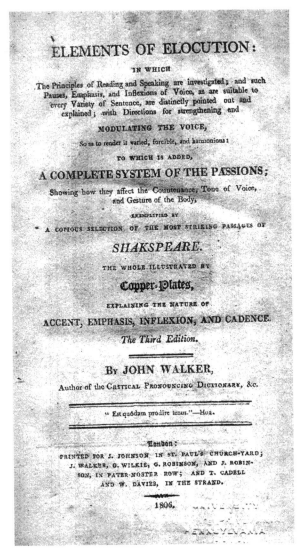

Figure 5.3   *Title page,* Elements of Elocution *by John Walker, 1806 edition*

What Walker calls a 'System of the Passions' is a depiction of 75 different emotions and behavioral stances laid out as a series of encyclopedic entries grounded in a folk-psychology of natural passions and sentiments. Each entry uses as a header a noun linked to a metapragmatic verb – whether to a *verbum sentiendi* (Joy, Delight, Love, Pity, Hope, etc.) or to a *verbum dicendi* (Affirming, Denying, Reproving, Acquitting, Condemning,

Pardoning, etc.) – and employs this noun as a metapragmatic label for a type of behavioral routine. Each entry also contains a fairly detailed description of precisely the forms of gesture, countenance, voice, and intonation that expresses the act in the way most 'naturally' English.

Here is an excerpt from the entry on 'Pity':

(8) Pity is benevolence to the afflicted. It is a mixture of love for an object that suffers, and a grief that we are not able to remove those sufferings. It shows itself in a compassionate tenderness of voice; a feeling of pain in the countenance, and a gentle raising and falling of the hands and eyes, as if mourning over the unhappy object. The mouth is open, the eye-brows are drawn down, and the features contracted or drawn together.

(Walker 1789, vol. 2: p. 308)

Here is 'Hatred':

(9) Hatred or aversion draws back the body as to avoid the hated object; the hands at the same time thrown out spread, as if to keep it off. The face is turned away from the side towards which the hands are thrown out; the eyes looking angrily, and obliquely the same way the hands are directed; the eye-brows are contracted, the upper-lip disdainfully drawn up, and teeth set; the pitch of the voice is low, but loud and harsh, the tone chiding, unequal, furly, and vehement, the sentences are short and abrupt.

(p. 314)

None of the ideas laid out in Walker's text are, of course, of any interest as *ideas*. It is only insofar as these formulations comprise metapragmatic constructs, made tangible through text-artifacts, made public through their transmission, made into elements of everyday ritual practices and thus into signs implicitly communicable to others, and, finally, into models presupposable in behavior by some (but never effectively by all) who are exposed to them, that such formulations, precisely as in the Yemeni case, become living icons realized in the routine behaviors of persons. The models formulated in Walker's text have a complex future history, just as in the case of pronunciation, as they become part of a sociohistorical chain of socially located moments of reception, transmission, and reformulation. While I cannot discuss these issues in the same detail with which I treated accent earlier, let me highlight here, in the briefest way, a few features of this metasemiotic construct and its future history.

As with discourses of accent discussed in the last chapter, there is a recurrent concern in Walker's discourse of bodily hexis with the contrast among nations. As Walker puts it, although the Italians and French are 'confessedly better public speakers than the English,' they 'overcharge their oratory with action' so that 'some of their finest strokes of action would, perhaps, excite our laughter.' These gestures cannot therefore be models for the English. It is rather by appeal to 'feelings of nature' that this diagram of the space of inter-national differences is naturalized in a model of intra-psychic, chthonic forms of 'taste and genius' peculiar to each nation:

(10) The common feelings of nature, with the signs that express them, undergo a kind of modification, which is suitable to the taste and genius of every nation; and it is this national taste which must necessarily be the vehicle of everything that we convey agreeably to the public we belong to.

(Walker 1789, vol. 2: 262)

Finding this national taste in order that 'we' convey ourselves 'agreeably to the public we belong to' is an exquisitely subtle reflexive formulation. Here a transcendent fact of nature (in fact, of 'our own' nature) is summoned to each moment of bodily expression, making possible forms of role alignment in interpersonal encounters (e.g., in messages conveyed 'agreeably') through which 'we' find ourselves becoming a 'public we belong to.' Unlike the Yemeni cases in (6) and (7), where the transcendent backing of the relevant collectivity (the *umma*, the cosmic polity of muslims, those who 'believe in Our Signs') is the voice of God, Walker's text proposes a rather different type of transcendent backing, an appeal to 'feelings of [our own] nature,' which if widely grasped as such – and increasingly deployed through 'the signs that express them' – would make possible the performative coming into existence of a collectivity to which 'we' naturally belong.

The elocutionary movement in Britain was transported to Colonial America and re-interpreted as a register of political oratory, pressed into service, ironically enough, in the rhetorical act of declaring independence from Britain. As Jay Fliegelman has shown, the period of American history in which the *Declaration of Independence* was written is characterized by the quest for 'a natural spoken language that would be a corollary to natural law,' a 'language' or register of political-oratorical self-expression 'composed not of words themselves, but of the tones, gestures, and expressive countenance with which a speaker delivered those words' (Fliegelman 1993: 1–2). In a historical context where the demands of independence had to be grounded in conceptions of political entitlement as well as in a figuration of differences between colonizer and colonized, the naturalizing ethnopsychology of the elocutionary movement was brought to bear on the public act of declaring independence.

As the chairman of the committee that drafted the text, Thomas Jefferson was expected to read the *Declaration* out loud at the Continental Congress on June 28, 1776. In preparing for this momentous occasion, Jefferson, formerly a somewhat anxious orator, relied on the work of the English rhetoricians to supply him with a metasemiotic framework for conceptualizing the task at hand. We know that Jefferson had purchased Thomas Sheridan's *Lectures on Elocution* (1762) during the mid 1760s while preparing for his career in law; and his reading copy of the

Declaration for the June 1776 oration is annotated with precisely the system of 'visible marks' – for rhythmical pauses, emphatic stress and speech melody – recommended by Sheridan in his *Lectures on the Art of Reading* (1775). Fliegelman suggests that many of the metasemiotic constructs distinctive of the English elocutionary movement – its claims to reveal the 'natural' emotions of a people, to provide instruction on how the diacritics that express them can be learned – are employed in post-revolutionary America to formulate a distinctively American style of 'natural sincerity,' of how to 'be oneself.' We cannot explore this history here. Suffice it to note that just as Jefferson's reading copy of the *Declaration* asserts (in propositionally explicit terms) that Americans are to be 'one people' distinct from 'our British Brethren,' the act of reading it, and thus the performative moment of declaring independence from Britain, is saturated in a play of diacritics whereby a discrete, authentic, distinctly American national character is beginning to be formulated as a contrastive externalized self.

6

REGISTERS OF PERSON DEIXIS

6.0 Introduction

The purpose of this chapter is to discuss emblems of social personhood associated with ways of referring to interlocutors. We will be concerned with a number of traditional topics in linguistic anthropology and pragmatics, such as 'polite' pronouns, forms of address and the construal of indirection as a form of politeness. These phenomena all share an underlying property. They are based on a reflexive reanalysis of patterns of deictic usage in human languages. The reanalysis converts **patterns of participant deixis** (i.e., forms that indexically denote speaker or addressee; see 1.4) into **stereotypic social indexicals**, whether indexical of speaker's own attributes or relationship to interlocutor, thus yielding sociocultural **registers of person deixis**. Thus, to take a familiar example, the French pronouns *tu* and *vous* are both deictics that indexically denote addressee as referent; but they differ in stereotypic social indexicality since one is enregistered as 'polite' and the other is not.

The term 'social deixis' is sometimes used to describe these phenomena but the term conflates two distinct indexical layers of the phenomenon (participant deixis vs. stereotypic social indexicality) and therefore makes it difficult to distinguish cases where the two are linked from cases where they are not. One way of distinguishing these two types of indexicality at the outset is to note that contrasts of accent (Chapter 4) involve stereotypes of social indexicality but no deixis. In contrast, the cases discussed in this chapter are all cases where stereotypes of social indexicality take patterns of participant deixis as object-signs and group them under metasemiotic labels (such as 'polite' and 'impolite') thus differentiating the language into distinct registers of deictic usage. Once we make the distinction we can also see that a deictic category and its stereotypic social-indexical values need not have the same social domain. Indeed, the group of people acquainted with the pattern of deixis can very frequently be sub-divided into sub-groups having contrastive stereotypes of the social indexical effects performable through its use.

The study of registers of person deixis has historically been associated with certain essentializing assumptions, such as the view that (1) particular deictics have an inherent, unitary 'social meaning' that is invariant for all speakers, that (2) such register formations constitute closed, internally structured 'systems' of the language (e.g., an 'address system') to which all language users are oriented. These views often have the status of tacit assumptions in the literature, not matters argued for in a programmatic way. It is therefore all the more important to note at the outset that these views are not even remotely plausible in any general account of the phenomena now at issue. My purpose here is to show that reflexive models of social indexicality linked to deixis are, in principle, limitlessly varied and yet highly organized and non-random in social life. They are limitlessly varied in the sense that from any given metapragmatic model further models can be produced iteratively by socially anchored reflexive processes. They are organized in the sense that despite this possibility, and despite the number of variants that actually co-exist society-internally at any given time (this number is not limitless, of course), the possibilities of social interaction that emerge around such variation are themselves mutually coordinated by the fractional congruence of these models.

6.1 Metapragmatic stereotypes and standards

It will be useful to begin by recalling that we are not concerned here with 'stereotypes' in the vernacular usage of this word (cf. 'popular beliefs about persons' etc.). Here is a rough summary of the most pertinent issues discussed in previous chapters:

Summary 6.1
Metapragmatic stereotypes: the term was introduced in Chapter 3 as a technical term for talking about typifications of the pragmatics of language use (3.2) and associated signs (3.9); such typifications constitute stereotypes insofar as they recur in the reflexive evaluations of many language users; the typifications that provide evidence for metapragmatic stereotypes are always overt (perceivable) but not necessarily explicit about (semantically descriptive of) the semiotic behaviors they typify; they do not *in general* correspond to ideas in the head but to habits of evaluative behavior, though they are episodically experienced as 'ideas' too (e.g., when converted into propositional descriptions in inner speech). The social existence of registers depends on the fact that the overtness of stereotypes (even of implicit ones) makes them communicable across large social-demographic scales and timespans. The internal differentiation of register models derives at least partly from the fact that such overt stereotypes are reanalyzed within the process of communicative transmission through which the register lives (3.8).

Our main interest now is in metapragmatic stereotypes associated with ways of referring to interlocutors. This is an area of ubiquitous cross-linguistic and cross-cultural concern on the part of social persons. In any society, even the briefest social interactions commonly begin with acts in which interactants refer to each other. An act of **referring to addressee** is an act of referring of a particular kind, one which assigns the person referred to by an utterance to the interactional role addressee-of-utterance. Since its default origo is the one speaking, and its focus the one referred to as addressee, such an act invariably indexes *some* social relation between speaker and addressee. When the expression used belongs to a distinctive register of deixis, the usage is stereotypically typified, society internally, as indexing a relation to addressee (e.g., deference), and a characterological figure of speaker demeanor (e.g., refined/vulgar, upper/lower class, female/male). In the literature on pronominal politeness and forms of address these effects are sometimes characterized as the 'inherent social meaning' of the form. But such effects are not inherent at all. They are precipitates of native metapragmatic stereotypes whose social domain and range may differ society internally, both at a given time (Table 3.7) and across time (Table 3.8).

Although all studies of registers tend to rely on metapragmatic data (3.2), there are few linguistic categories for which *explicit* metapragmatic reports are more ubiquitous and readily available than for person referring terms.[1] Person deictics are relatively salient to native metapragmatic scrutiny because they exhibit a dense overlap of functional properties: they refer to the very persons picked out as the focus of stereotypic social indexicality. They formulate reference to the very individual to whom deference is paid.

Table 6.1 lists some common types of explicit metapragmatic discourse about second person deictics.[2] Accounts such as these constitute an indispensable resource in the study pronominal deference because they provide some inkling of the stereotypic effects associated with their use.

Metapragmatic discourses of these kinds formulate emblems of social personhood by linking text-patterns of deictic usage to characterological qualities, scenarios of usage and diagrams of social difference among users. They employ adjectives that are predicable of persons (e.g., polite, inferior, intimate), as metalinguistic descriptors designating roles and relationships performed through deictic usage, e.g., 'it [= *tui*] is an *inferior* form of address ...'. They employ [+ human] nouns that name specific social roles and relationships (friend, master, servant, brother, sister) as names for interactional roles of speaker and addressee in events of deictic usage. We saw earlier that explicit metapragmatic discourses comprise only a tiny fragment of the range of public sphere typifications that mediate the social life of registers; thus a fuller understanding of how such stereotypes are formulated, communicated, disseminated and transformed across populations requires a different type of analysis (ch. 4). We

Table 6.1. *Common genres of metapragmatic discourse about pronouns*

Genre	Example
(a) The labeling of pronouns by metapragmatic descriptors (e.g., honorific, polite, formal, crude . . .)	'Bengali has three forms in second person: *apni, tumi* and *tui* all meaning 'you,' the difference being 'honorific', 'ordinary' and 'inferior or intimate' respectively.'
(b) Accounts describing events of usage (e.g., scenarios of 'common' usage, standards of appropriate use, effects of usage)	'This form of address [*tui*] has a wide range of semantic variation beginning from extreme intimacy and affection to utmost crudity and impropriety. It is an endearing form of address inside the family and between friends, but it is an inferior form of address outside the family in most cases.'
(c) Accounts associating different social categories of person with distinct patterns of usage, thus formulating discursive diagrams of sociological difference	'The inferior form *tui* is generally used by superiors to youngers, between intimate friends, in certain families reciprocally by brothers and sisters and by a master to his servant . . . Teachers, for example, use *tui* to their students at school whom they get to know at an early age, but *tui* is never used by teachers at the colleges or at universities.'

Source: (Das 1968: 19–20)

are here concerned with a more limited point, namely that observations of the types listed in Table 6.1 comprise the data of typifications of use, not the data of either the 'inherent meaning' or the 'use' of such lexemes.

In the descriptive practices of linguists and anthropologists data of these kinds are frequently converted into labels for the 'social meaning' of pronouns, such as 'polite', 'male speaking', 'addressee superior,' and so on. When accurate, such labels designate the stereotypic indexical values associated with the lexeme by (some social domain of) speakers. Yet they are often misrecognized as the invariant or inherent meanings of lexemes, and sometimes as constraints on the form of possible physical performances (cf. 'you can't say that!' understood as a constraint on the physical production of utterances). However all such stereotypic values are in fact manipulable, in some cases independently manipulable, in interactional tropes of pronominal usage whenever the indexical effects of a text configuration containing the pronoun is non-congruent with some among the stereotypic values indexed by the pronoun qua text-segment, and the overall non-congruence is interpretable by interlocutors through at least one definite reading.

Such entextualized effects can also be reanalyzed as distinct higher-order indexical norms by distinct sub-populations of users. For example, in discussing Thai pronouns valorized for stereotypic gender indexicality, Cooke observes that these forms 'are comparatively invariable as to sex-meaning value. However *phŏm* 'I (male speaking)' and *dichăn* 'I (female speaking)' are said to be used respectively by female and male homosexuals' (1968: 24). Thus, once masculinity is stereotypically linked to *phŏm* and femininity to *dichăn*, the use of either gender-indexing form by a person of the opposite biological sex itself carries significance for the social domain of persons acquainted with the stereotype; and the practice may well become normalized for a distinct sub-population of users as *also* stereotypic of a hybrid gender identity in in-group usage. Cooke adds: 'Also, *dichăn* is reported to be used by certain male speakers, especially among royalty, without particular effeminate connotations.' Although Cooke does not describe the non-effeminate construal among royalty in any detail (elegance? finesse?), his account does suggest that the form *dichăn* is linked to *more than one* higher-order indexical stereotype, and that these co-exist as normalized behaviors in distinct social strata of the same society.

Through much of their history, studies of pronouns and address have tended to conflate facts of actual usage (performance) with stereotypes and standards of appropriate use (typifications) by employing the term 'language use' or 'usage' for both. Since the 1960s a common field procedure for the study of these phenomena has involved the use of questionnaires and interviews. Data elicited by these methods tell us a good deal about metapragmatic constructs associated with pronouns – such as stereotypes of speaker type, of speaker-addressee relationship, standards of appropriate use – but very little about the *range of acts* that can meaningfully be performed and construed through the deployment of these devices. Although this literature is a valuable source of data on stereotypes of indexicality, the traditional failure to distinguish typifications of behavior from the behaviors typified (e.g., by employing the term 'usage' for both) typically confounds the social relevance of these stereotypes. The difficulty is further compounded by the idiom of 'rules of usage'; the term is often left undefined by those who use it, though a meaning like 'constraints on possible utterances' is often assumed or implied. Such views misunderstand the data of typification on which they are based. For these data reveal something about reflexive models of behavior that are just as relevant to the construal of behaviors that manipulate the model as they are to behaviors that instantiate it. For instance, Das' claim that school teachers use the form *tui* to students whom they know from an early age but that '*tui* is never used by teachers at the colleges or at universities' is best understood as a claim not about the *form of possible utterances* but as a claim about the *inappropriateness of this usage* by teachers to college students in the classroom. It is not that such an utterance cannot be performed, but that *it cannot be performed without intelligible consequence,* i.e., not without a breach in normative expectations regarding addressee-focal deference and speaker-focal demeanor.[3]

From this standpoint, so-called 'standards' of behavior are a variety of stereotypes of use. A great many things are called 'standards,' of course. I argued in 2.5 that the norms of language use cannot be investigated through a taxonomy of norms, or assumed to be static rules uniformly recognized and observed by those whose behavior they involve. We need, at the very least, to distinguish norms for dimensions such as threshold of normativity, social domain and range, and mechanisms of institutional-ization and authority, before we can approach the question of whether such norms function as 'standards' of behavior for those who recognize them as relevant to their behaviors. What we are now observing is that even when these questions are resolved, even when something is arguably a 'standard' of behavior, the standard is not, in general, a constraint on the form of action. It is a principle for construing acts that occur, including acts that are 'appropriate' or standard-congruent, and acts that are not.

Metapragmatic stereotypes and politeness ideologies

Approaches that fail to distinguish typifications of use from the usages typified tend to mistake dominant ideologies of behavior as facts about behavior. Similarly, approaches that treat stereotypes of indexicality as matters of inherent meaning (rather than as reflexive models having spe-cific social domains of evaluators as their provenance) tend to mistake locale-specific models of behavior as facts about entire societies, or worse, as comparative frameworks for studying all societies.

For example Brown and Gilman's (1960) classic account of pronouns is based largely on questionnaires and interviews; hence although the paper investigates stereotypes of indexicality, it reports these facts as facts about 'usage' mediated by the inherent 'semantics' of pronouns (conceptualized as coding relationships between pronoun lexemes and social effects). The authors introduce a metalinguistic convention for describing the social meaning of pronouns in any language: 'As a convenience we propose to use the symbols T and V (from the Latin *tu* and *vos*) as generic designators for a familiar and a polite pronoun in any language' (1960: 254). The convention has two parts: it consists of using the symbols T and V (derived from the Latin forms) as typological labels for lexemic forms in a language, and of using the terms 'familiar' and 'polite' as labels for the social significance of these forms. The convention therefore amounts to a typo-logical claim about form-function correspondences across languages, namely that we can classify all the inflectable second person pronouns in a language into two form-classes (T vs. V), and that the forms labeled T are 'familiar' and the forms labeled V are 'polite.' This formulation quickly leads to intractable difficulties in comparative work.

The most obvious difficulty is that neither the letter names nor the form-function claim have any clear application to languages where the number of pronominal lexemes is larger than two. This point, noted by many writers, is summarized by Braun as follows: 'Many languages, however, have more than two [pronominal] variants. Extending the Brown/Gilman terminology, they might be classified as T and V_1, V_2, V_3 . . . It should further be noted that the 'polite' connotation of a V pronoun is very much dependent on the status of the other variants. V_1 may not be polite when compared to V_2' (Braun 1988: 8). Hence, in such languages, not all the V forms are necessarily polite. We shall see in a moment that this is so for *all* languages, not just for languages having more than two terms.[4]

A second difficulty is that the contrast between the designators 'familiar' and 'polite' is too blunt an instrument for conceptualizing the significance of pronominal contrasts, even in a preliminary way. As we look across languages we find that language users regard pronominal contrasts as involving not just relations among interlocutors (familiarity, politeness, or whatever), but as indexing distinct characterological figures associated with speaker. For example, a range of such figures is associated with Thai pronominal forms in commonplace metapragmatic discourses in Thai society, as illustrated in the third column of Table 6.2. Notice that the Thai examples are like the Bengali ones noted above in that they formulate facts of differential use as indices of types of users. Here we have, again, a diagram of social differences in which differential use is not merely *diacritic* of speaker kind but characterized as positively *emblematic* through role designations of age, urban/rural provenance, gender categories, relative status, and the like.

The sheer diversity of such emblems of personhood makes it evident that we cannot approach the study of pronominal registers by taxonomies based on pre-selected notional rubrics. No single abstract principle explains why these forms (and not some others) have come to be associated with these characterological figures (and not some others) in this language. Table 6.2 is merely a sociohistorical snapshot of a series of reflexive processes through which variation in language use is reanalyzed into a set of emblems of personhood. Hence it is with a consideration of these reflexive processes – particularly, their connection to utterance form and their tendency to reanalyze formal variation into stereotypes of use and users – that we must begin. My goal in what follows is not to describe processes of enregisterment in any single language community (such as Bengali or Thai) in any detail but to discuss a few of the reflexive processes through which such differentiated systems emerge.

Table 6.2. *Person-referring pronominal forms in Thai*

Form & gloss	grammatical category	reported 'social meanings'
(a) *kuu* 'I' *mɨŋ* 'you'	1st singular 2nd singular	Strong nonrestraint terms; used primarily by male and occasionally female intimates and more broadly by rural dialect speakers; otherwise imply anger, coarseness, etc.
(b) *haa* 'I' *khiŋ* 'you'	1st singular 2nd singular	Northern regional dialect nonrestraint terms, equivalent to *kuu* and *mɨŋ*
(c) *chǎn* 'I' *thəə* 'you'	1st singular 2nd singular	Used primarily by women when speaking to equals or inferiors
(d) *raw* 'I' or 'you'	1st or 2nd singular or plural	Used primarily by women as a 1st person term when speaking to intimates; otherwise implies neutrality; used as 2nd person term, usually to inferiors; also plural or generic indefinite
(e) *phǒm* 'I'	1st singular	male speaker; polite, status neutral term used in a wide range of social situations
(f) *naai* 'you' (g) zero form ('I' or 'you')	2nd singular absence of any overt form in NP position	used primarily by males to male equals pragmatically unmarked unless antecedent is ambiguous

Source: (Simpson 1997 and Cooke 1968)

6.2 Reflexive processes within pronominal registers

We have been focusing thus far on *explicit* metapragmatic stereotypes even though, as we have noted several times before, these are not the only kinds of typifications of pronouns that occur in social life. We have given this variety of typification special attention because explicit discourses about pronouns are cross-linguistically ubiquitous for reasons discussed above.

However, when we compare the data of explicit metapragmatic discourse to metapragmatic evaluations of a more implicit kind, we find that explicit stereotypes frequently attribute a social indexical effect to a sign-form *different from* the one that actually marks it. Thus a common tendency across languages is for speakers to describe a polite pronoun as a word even when no single word, and certainly not the pronoun lexeme, suffices to establish the politeness effect. In a common type of case we find a type of metasemiotic reduction whereby *elements of* a larger semiotic pattern are construed as having the same type of efficaciousness as the pattern does *as a whole*. Such a pattern of **metonymic reduction** – i.e., the construal of a part as having the properties of a whole – is a cross-culturally widespread feature of folk-consciousness about pronouns and other signs. The tendency is widespread because language users tend to view referring through the lens of a folk-ideology, the view that referring is a relationship between words and things. We saw in Chapter 2 that this view is ideological in the sense that it distorts the way in which referring to specific things is actually possible during language use. In the general case referring involves a composite sketch of referent based on entextualized arrays of co-occurring semiotic cues, of which words are simply the most readily decontextualized fragments (2.1). Yet the folk-ideology persists due to a common type of metonymic reduction. Such metonymic reduction is also often a critical step in the ideological process through which the stereotype that isolable lexemes are emblematic of social characteristics gains plausibility and force.

Metonymic reduction

Starting with the data of interviews and questionnaires it is easy to document the fact that speakers of French describe the second person pronoun *vous* as a polite word and *tu* as not polite, and that speakers of Russian, German and Italian report the existence of analogous pronominal distinctions as shown in Table 6.3. The stereotypically honorific words are listed in the column labeled 'H'; their polite construal is shown as construal$_1$.

If we compare these decontextualized reports to the data of contextualized construal we get a slightly different result: In actual usage the second person pronoun *vous* appears to vary between a 'polite singular' and a 'plural' construal; the latter is not specifically polite. Each form listed in

Table 6.3. *Pronominal registers in European languages*

	NH	construal	H	construal$_1$ / construal$_2$
French	*tu*	'2nd sg.'	*vous*	'2nd sg. polite' / '2nd pl.'
Russian	*ty*	'2nd sg.'	*vy*	'2nd sg. polite' / '2nd pl.'
German	*du*	'2nd sg.'	*Sie*	'2nd sg. polite' / '3rd pl.'
Italian	*tu*	'2nd sg.'	*Lei*	'2nd sg. polite' / '3rd sg. fem.'

Table 6.4. *Text configurations marking politeness in French*

Text configuration		Metapragmatic construal
number marking	pronoun uttered	
(a) \<singular\>	+ '…vous.…'	'polite'
(b) \<plural\>	+ '…vous.…'	not 'polite'
(c) \<singular\>	+ '…tu.…'	not 'polite'

Examples of the (a) vs. (b) contrast:
participle: (a/b) vous êtes {venu / venus}   'You {sg.POLITE / pl.} have come'
adjective: (a/b) vous êtes {loyal / loyaux}   'You {sg.POLITE / pl.} are loyal'
noun: (a/b) vous êtes {professeur/   'You (sg.POLITE) are a teacher /
  professeurs }   'You (pl.) are teachers'

Note: The examples in the lower part of the table are from Comrie 1975

column H analogously permits more than one contextualized construal. In reality, however, neither construal is ever a construal of the lexeme alone. Let us focus on the French case by way of example.

How does a French speaker know that a token of *vous* is polite or not polite? This difference is never established by the *vous* token alone. The politeness effect of *vous* is indeterminate unless a co-occurring sign, a feature of the co-text of *vous*, establishes the fact that the text configuration *as a whole* marks singular reference to addressee. Only if singular reference is fixed from co-text can a token of *vous* be understood as 'polite.' The text configuration that marks the polite construal is shown as (a) in the top line of Table 6.4; the case where *vous* is not specifically construed as polite is shown as (b). The contrastive case of *tu* usage is indicated in (c).

The examples in the lower half of Table 6.4 show that number marking is *never* fixed by the *vous* lexeme. In the examples shown, numerosity is established by morphological features of predicate that differ for predicate type (whether the predicate contains participles, adjectives or nouns).[5] When addressees encounter such utterances, predicate number marking fixes numerosity of referent and motivates a deference effect. Addressees treat the text configurations establishing singular reference – *vous* plus the predicate in (a), but not in (b) – as specifically polite.

From the standpoint of implicit metapragmatic typifications – 'next turn' evaluative responses in interaction – the construal 'polite (singular)' is thus *the construal of a text configuration*, not the construal of a word-form. The deference effect (politeness) is manifest when a given denotational effect (singular reference) occurs; and the latter effect is marked not by *vous* but by a text configuration containing *vous* (e.g., pronoun plus number marking). Yet from the standpoint of explicit stereotypes the view that '*vous* is a polite word' is an established social fact, readily agreed to by speakers of the language. Folk-consciousness metonymically attributes the significance of the text configuration to a text-segment and essentializes such effects as the stereotypic meaning of the lexeme.[6]

In such cases *textually implemented* contrasts of reference are reanalyzed as facts about *lexemic* contrast in deference. Given the reanalysis, the differences of construal noted in Table 6.3 are perceived as a series of number and person tropes. To the folk-intuitions of the language user each word appears capable of two different meanings. In reality, we have two different text configurations (both of which contain the lexeme) that discriminate the two construals. But the folk theory (one word, two meanings) is much more easily reproduced in decontextualized discussions of the phenomenon. Normative traditions tend to stabilize such tropes, formulating new standards of use linked to the use of particular expressions. When effective such traditions may even result in the replacement of the contrast by one of the patterns that comprise it, thus resulting in an overall simplification in pronominal reference and deference.

However, most accounts of how this happens tend to exaggerate the social domain of the change. A common error in the literature on pronouns is the metalinguistic practice of using names of countries as names for languages, and even as names for pronominal patterns within languages; equally common is the error of equating norms specific to prestige registers of the language (Parisian French, High German, etc.) with the actual practices of the language community as a whole. Thus, it is not uncommon to find typological claims about 'the Italian/French/German systems' of pronominal address in the literature. These accounts are at best descriptions of the Standard language; in reality many actual (so-called) 'systems' co-exist within national boundaries and have differential degrees of normativity for different social domains of language user. For example, in the Italian situation of the 1980s described by Danesi and Lettieri, the lexemic contrasts associated with pronominal usage were in a process of reanalysis from a four-term to a three-term system, as shown in Table 6.5.

Table 6.5. *Reanalysis of Italian second-person pronominal address*

	Singular	Plural			Singular	Plural
Informal	tu	voi		Informal	tu	
			⟶			voi
Formal	lei	loro		Formal	lei	

Source: (Danesi and Lettieri 1983)

Table 6.5 captures only the lexemic fragments of this process of register change. In the situation described by Danesi and Lettieri patterns of pronoun recognition and use differed by variables such as gender, age and social class of the population sampled. For example, upper-class native speakers recognized the form *loro* but 'stated emphatically' that they would use only *voi* in plural address; many lower class speakers did not even know that the form *loro* existed; only non-native speakers (who learned Italian from schoolbooks and manuals) claimed that *loro* is used in plural address. Awareness of the existence of *loro* as a normative form therefore depended at this time mainly on exposure to dictionaries and text-books, which, as the authors show, still maintained the four-term system as the codified norm.

As we look across languages we find a variety of different kinds of situations of fractional congruence and divergence among models of social indexicality linked to pronominal usage. For example Singh describes the following system of speech levels associated with second person pronominal deference in Maithili (Table 6.6). Here each honorific 'pronoun' corresponds to a textual array of cooccurring forms, each a formally discontinuous text configuration of pronoun lexeme and verb agreement. Differences among these text configurations are normatively reanalyzed as distinct levels of deference to referent.

Such stereotypes of social indexicality have the character of positional metapragmatic norms which do not, in general, reflect the actual behaviors of all speakers. Thus although five different speech levels are normatively distinguished in Maithili, the contrast between levels 4 and 5 has a narrower social domain than all the other contrasts; for some speakers, the contrast between 4 and 5 does not exist. Differences in effective competence in speech levels are indexical of speaker kind in all languages having speech level system; however, the specific characterological figures associated with the contrast in Maithili are not discussed by Singh.

In languages where patterns of verb agreement are part of the prono-minal form, deference effects are often expressed by verb elements which

Table 6.6. *Levels of second person pronominal deference*
in Maithili

Text pattern		
Pronoun	verb agreement	Deference level
apnɛ....	-hũ·	Level 1 high honorific
ahãã....	-hũ·	Level 2 honorific
tõ	-ha·	Level 3 neutral
tõ	-hii	Level 4 nonhonorific
tõ	-(h)ɛ̃	Level 5 low nonhonorific

Note: All five text patterns denote addressee (may be glossed as
'you') but differ in deference level, as shown. In utterances
where more than one [+ human] nominal occurs, Maithili
agreement morphology is considerably more complex.
Source: (Singh 1989)

Table 6.7. *Second person pronominal levels in Urdu*

	Verb Agreement			
Pronoun	Imperative	Optative-future	Indicative-present	Denotation and Deference level
(a) āp / ø	-ī e	-ɛ̃	-āĩ	'you (honorific)'
(b) tum / ø	-o	-o	-o	'you (neutral)'
(c) tū / ø	-ø	-e	-ai	'you (nonhonorific)'
(d) ?? āp	-o	–	-o	'you (quasi-polite; substandard)

Note: Only nonpast agreement patterns are shown, and only for second singular
pronouns. For further details see Agha 1998b

also mark other categories such as mood and tense. This is illustrated in
Table 6.7. Let us first focus on rows (a)–(c), which correspond to the
normative system of contemporary Urdu. Notice that the contrast
between pronoun lexemes (āp/tum/tū) corresponds in a one-to-one fashion to the speech level descriptors shown on the right (honorific/neutral/
nonhonorific). Hence when the pronouns actually occur in utterances the
agreement morphology is non-contrastive. This is a case where a historically older system of contrastive text configurations (cf. the French case)
has been reanalyzed into a system where the agreement morphology
appears to be redundant, and the fiction that pronominal contrasts are
established always and only by independent words seems easy to maintain.
However, Urdu is also a language characterized by pervasive null

anaphora. In many contextualized utterances the lexical pronoun simply does not occur, a case represented by the symbol ø in (a)–(c). In such cases it is precisely the agreement morphology that establishes reference and (degree of) deference to addressee.

Moreover non-standard patterns of address exist as well. For example, a fourth level is sometimes created by combining the 'honorific' pronoun āp with the 'neutral' verb endings in -o. This formation is not only sub-standard (in the sense of normatively 'incorrect' or defective) it also does not have a standardized stereotypic construal to which people are social-ized in schooling or in norm-upholding middle class families. As an index of addressee-deference, it appears to lie between levels (a) and (b), of which it is a blend. But as an emblem of speaker characteristics, it has a number of construals which depend on whether the speaker's first language is Urdu (vs. say Gujrati); it is stereotypically associated with non-purists, lower class people, speakers for whom Urdu is a second language, and a variety of additional imagined 'others,' a miscellany of extra-normative beings. Yet in reality the pattern is occasionally produced by monolingual middle class speakers as well (even ones who deny doing so), and its normatively defec-tive character may be construed in a variety of ways, e.g., when used for friends and family members, as a sort of (over-) familiarity among intimates.

Thus to understand the honorific properties of second person honorific forms, we need to move beyond the essentialization of social indexicality as lexical meaning in two distinct ways, i.e., by attending to the text-patterns in which addressee reference can be achieved by such forms,[7] and by attending to cultural processes of enregisterment whereby particular pat-terns of lexeme-in-text become stereotypically valorized. Once we consider both processes together, it becomes clear that even in cases where prono-minal deference appears to be implemented by a single lexeme the defer-ence effect is actually implemented only in a particular text pattern, and only for particular social domains of speakers. Thus in contexts of very high status asymmetry, the 'standard' Urdu pronouns of Table 6.7 do not occur; instead we find a number of common nouns (Table 6.8) used in specific constructions which, as constructional wholes, establish conven-tional reference to a speech participant plus a stereotypic 'social' effect, whether self-humbling (column A forms) or other-raising (column B). The lexical items listed in Table 6.8 are sometimes described as high honorific pronouns of the first and second person. However, lexically, these are simply nouns. They are readily used as nouns in other constructions to refer to non-copresent individuals (e.g., *un kā xādim* 'their servant'). They have no categorial property that necessitates reference to a speech partic-ipant. At the same time, they overlap with pronouns so that when they occur in criterial constructions, these are understood as referring to speaker or addressee and indexing the interpersonal construals shown.

Table 6.8. *Honorific nouns used as 'pronouns' in Urdu*

A.		B.	
Lexeme and sense (referent-humbling)	Tropic use/construal	Lexeme and sense (referent-exalting)	Tropic use/construal
xāqsār 'dustlike' ⎫ nācīz 'nothing' xādim 'servant' ghulām 'slave' bandā 'bondsman' ⎭	reference to speaker + self humbling	sarkār 'master, ruler' ⎫ huzūr 'presence' jenāb 'sir' āqā 'leader, master' ⎭	reference to addressee + other raising

Note: The tropic construals shown are marked not by the lexeme but by text configurations that contain the lexeme. These vary for the different lexemes shown, e.g., any form B + 2nd person agreement marks addressee-raising; for the forms listed in column A self-humbling construals occur with 1st person agreement and also with specialized 3rd person locutions.

The denotational properties of these forms diagram specific interactional construals during use. Since the forms in column A are referent-humbling in stereotypic denotation (i.e., formulate *any* referent as 'low' or humble), their speaker-referring use is construed as speaker-humbling, and, by implication, addressee-deferring as well (i.e., *xādim* 'I = servant = [your] servant'). Similarly, when the forms in column B are used to refer to addressee, they are comparable in reference to the second person pronoun *āp* 'you (H)', though more deferential than it by virtue of their other-exalting denotation. All of these forms are recognizable as literary and aristocratic uses by educated speakers; they are commonly encountered in the literary canon; many though not all are still used in contexts of sharp status asymmetry. Moreover since some of them are recognized as aristocratic, and now somewhat quaint, they are readily susceptible in the practices of urban, middle class speakers, to the forms of lampooning and humor discussed for 'U-RP' register in Chapter 4.

It will be evident that the variety of different construals considered in the above cases can be scaled to one another in one or more ways. In some cases different construals are linked to each other because they overlap in sign-form; in others, construals differ because they involve different stereotypes of indexicality, which, in turn, reflect the relative social positions of sign-user and sign-evaluator. The fact that patterns of person reference exhibit these types of organization is not in general grasped from the positional perspective of the language user. For many speakers, the ideology that words have 'inherent' social meanings – in particular, the usages and values normalized in the speaker's own social domain – is the more comforting, more readily reported, and sometimes fiercely argued-for social fact.

This ideology can be strengthened in various ways. Under conditions of nationalism and language standardization locale-specific speech varieties can be held up as normative models for speakers in other locales so that language users (and linguists) whose intuitions are trained by standard-setting institutions can come to find themselves inclining to the view that normatively defective speech does not in fact occur (or is 'ungrammatical' or whatever); when successful, institutionalized efforts of these kinds may even bring more and more of the discursive practices of a language community into conformity with a single model, thus effectively erasing the divergence between model and reality, at least for a while. These processes are themselves interesting features of social life that deserve systematic study – both in terms of how they unfold and in terms of the consequences they have, when effective.

It is equally important to see, however, that such normalized models rarely, if ever, extend to the speech practices and perceptions of all members of a language community. Even when ideologies of standardization thrive they invariably coexist with facts of society-internal variation, which can themselves be grasped and assimilated to culture-internal models of social difference.

6.3 Emblems of social difference

In any society an awareness of the existence of variation itself results in a type of functional reanalysis, namely the conversion of facts of variation into a framework of role diacritics some of which are given readings as emblems of positive, describable social statuses. In the last chapter we saw that the treatment of differential behaviors as role diacritics involves simply the treatment of differences in semiotic behavior as indices of differences among persons performing the signs. In any community in which multiple patterns of usage co-exist, the treatment of such variation as diacritic of roles requires merely the awareness that someone else's speech differs from one's own. In any interaction in which such differences are experienced, various kinds of *entextualized emblems* can be performed by speaker through intentional strategies that trope upon expectations shaped by co-textual signs; or be treated as speaker attributes by hearers in text-in-context 'solutions' to the problem of how best to construe the unexpected usage performed by speaker. In the case of radically entextual-ized emblems, different co-present hearers, all of whom perceive the utter-ance as diacritic of speaker kind, may well offer different text-in-context solutions to the question of what role designator best describes the person speaking and, thus, may formulate fractionally distinct emblematic readings of the usage encountered. Conversely, in the case of *stereotypic emblems*, all hearers who share a common history of socialization can reproduce the stereotype to which they are socialized and thus find themselves oriented to the same emblematic reading. The two scenarios are not mutually exclusive. For, as we saw before, positive construals of emblems that share a stereotypic fraction may also differ in event-specific ways, thus including radically entextualized construals as fractions too.

It will be evident that in such cases the interesting question is not whether all potential hearers 'share' the same construal; the question is whether the range of construals that actually emerge in an encounter can be calibrated to each other, and reflect some measure of mutual coordination of the activity of construal and response. In practice, in most cases where differences of construing another's identity emerge, much of the subsequent talk between those having different construals consists of the activity of bringing partly divergent perspectives (including, sometimes, aspects of their own trajectories of socialization) into some calibration with each other, and this is typically achieved through some further metasemiotic activity. And in many cases failing to reach agreement is precisely the interactional point, for the act of maintaining the distinctiveness of one's own perspective, as in the display of a more 'discriminating' stance, is itself a mechanism of self-positioning.

In 3.8 we saw that such facts of self- and other-positioning can have large scale sociohistorical consequences too. We saw, for instance, that speakers' perceptions of variation within a language community may themselves contribute to changes in patterns of language use. Under conditions of the enregisterment of behavior – where some social domain of persons recognize that persons of other kinds exhibit different patterns of pronominal usage and normativity – individuals and groups may align their own practices with (or against) those of others. We considered several examples of this phenomenon from French, Swedish, Arabic and Javanese in Chapter 3. Cases of this kind depend on the fact that language users reanalyze individual lexemes as stereotypically appropriate to interactional roles and role configurations. Thus in the Arabic example (Table 3.7), the positional model is mainly a model of *speaker* role: here one social category of person evaluates a pronominal variant as a form *spoken by* another social category of person (and, moreover, lays claim to speaking in the same way). In contrast, in the French example (Figure 3.3), the stereotype associates the lexeme with a more complex role configuration. Here, the stereotype of *vous* usage involves a role configuration of *speaker and addressee types* (a child speaking to parents). Thus, a specific pattern of interactional text – 'a child using *vous* for parents' – becomes a stereotypic emblem of positional identity so that working class speakers describe the pattern as 'snobbish,' while upper-class politicians manipulate the emblem (advise children to switch from *vous* to *tu* in public acts of addressing them) in order to garner working class votes.

6.4 Troping on norms

Metapragmatic representations of language use often typify usage as appropriate to several distinct interactional scenarios. For example, in Table 6.1, Das describes the non-reciprocal use of *tui* as appropriate by master for servant, or by teacher for schoolchildren; and its reciprocal use as normal between intimate friends or between siblings. Similarly Simpson describes the Thai pronouns *kuu* and *miŋ* as used 'by male and occasionally female intimates' or 'by rural dialect speakers'. These norms create a space of analogies. Schoolchildren are not servants; friends are not kin; persons who are intimates are not necessarily rural persons. It is merely that certain norms of usage liken individuals of such categories to each other when they inhabit a criterial participant role. The existence of norms thus creates a space of analogies – whether analogies between persons, between relationships, between social situations – which is almost limitless extendible through tropes that play upon these norms.

During the 1960s and 1970s a number of studies which took metapragmatic representations of speech as their primary objects of study (e.g., interview and questionnaire data, narrated dialogue in literary works) found that norms of usage are often sensitive to multiple, distinct interactional scenarios (Brown and Ford 1964, Slobin 1963, Friedrich 1966, 1986). For example, by examining narrated dialogue in Russian literary works (by Tolstoy, Dostoevsky, Gorki and others) Friedrich found that norms of Russian pronominal usage (as formulated in literary representations) are sensitive to nearly a dozen distinct interactional variables which function together as co-factors mediating pronominal choice (viz., age, generation, sex, kinship status, group membership, relative authority, topic, social locale or setting of interaction, affective relation between speaker and addressee). The other studies mentioned above arrived at similar results. For example, Slobin showed that norms of Yiddish address (as formulated in responses to interviews and questionnaires) are also sensitive to multiple interactional variables which are treated by respondents as co-factors shaping norms of performance and construal.

In a classic synthesis, Ervin-Tripp 1986 showed that configurations of such co-factors cluster in certain patterned ways in these data, describable as paths in a flowchart representation. Each path in such a flowchart represents a configuration of factors to which a given pronominal choice (whether T or V) is sensitive. Ervin-Tripp used the term 'rule' for the set of paths that lead to a particular pronominal choice. However, this formulation is problematic for reasons discussed earlier. The important insight in her paper is not the notion of rule but the observation that metapragmatic typifications associate each utterable form with multiple configurations of contextual factors (the paths in the flowchart). Silverstein 1988 shows that if we disaggregate these paths from each other we can see that each of these configurations can serve as metaphors for each other.

Silverstein's interpretation of the Yiddish case (Slobin 1963) is shown in Table 6.9. Each column corresponds to an appropriateness judgment linking a form (T or V) to a configuration of contextual factors (a 'path' in the flowchart, Ervin-Tripp 1986: 227). The table shows that the use of the form at the top of each column is appropriate when certain contextual readings of factors are independently in play (indicated by '+' in the table; the '−' indicates that a factor does not specifically apply). The reason that there are several columns labeled 'T' is that the form is appropriate for several distinct contextual scenarios, e.g., that the addressee is a child, or a kin of nonascending generation, or a kin with whom speaker is intimate, or a person lower in rank, or a familiar (e.g., an intimate friend), or some possible combination of these. Similarly, the use of V is appropriate when the interaction occurs in a 'status marked setting' (e.g., in a court, in parliament, etc.), or the addressee is non-solidary (i.e., a non-intimate) and either a kin of ascending generation or a non-kin,[8] or is older in age, or some combination of these; V is also the normative interpersonal default, the form used when speaker is unsure of which of these factors apply, as the last column shows. This way of looking at norms has significant consequences for how we think about interaction, and for questions regarding the group-relative character of norms. Let me take these two issues in turn.

First, the issue of interaction. Silverstein's analysis shows that no two tokens of T (or of V) that occur at different points in an interaction are necessarily alike in import. Even if an individual appropriately uses T forms

Table 6.9. *Norms of appropriateness reported for Yiddish address*

	T	V	T	V	T	V	V	T	T	V
addressee child	+	−	−	−	−	−	−	−	−	−
status-marked setting	−	+	−	−	−	−	−	−	−	−
kin			+	+	+	−	−	−	−	−
nonascending gen.			+	−	−					
nonsolidary				+	−	+	−	−	−	−
addressee older							+	−	−	−
addressee lower rank								+	−	−
familiar									+	−

Source: (Silverstein 1988 [cf. Ervin-Tripp 1986, Slobin 1963])

over an entire stretch of discourse, different tokens of T may reflect sensitivity to distinct configurations of emergent situational variables. Hence an individual's turn-contribution cannot be conceptualized as a 'coding' of independent social variables by a linguistic form. Any such form may be used appropriately (i.e., as a response to the fact that the contextual variable occurs independently) or creatively to summon the interpersonal reading in an utterance-dependent way (i.e., making the contextual feature readable as an effect of using the form). The set of creative usages possible includes interactional tropes that liken a known category of respondent to someone else by exploiting the space of analogies created by the multiple values of a given form. A 'T' usage can liken an adult to a child, a stranger to an intimate friend, an older kin to a younger one, and so on. Finally, since pronominal expressions are categorially linked to multiple, alternative configurations of social-contextual factors, which among these effects is interactionally relevant is undecideable until the addressee responds to the current utterance confirming or disconfirming, ratifying or not ratifying, one or more of the social dimensions invoked by the form. At the level of lexemes, the space of tropic analogies appears open-ended and indeterminate; but at the level of interactional text, highly specific social realities do emerge and become interpersonally decideable for interactants as they attend to text-patterns created through acts of usage and response.

The second issue concerns the social domain assumption linked to the very idea of a norm. We have been observing that the social domain of a stereotype of use is, in an empirical sense, the sample of persons who formulate comparable metapragmatic typifications of that use. When we investigate semiotic regularities of usage we have no difficulty *differentiating* stereotypes by social domain, i.e., in identifying two sub-groups who fractionally differ in the values they assign to a form. But we saw in the last chapter that attempts to reify these boundaries fail, and do so for many reasons. One reason that we discussed in some detail is that re-grouping (of self vs. other) is itself a social process in which language users engage. It is not just that social groups have fuzzy boundaries. It is rather that the social domain of the signs that mediate group membership (whether one's own or another's) may be transformed through semiotic activity itself, thus dynamically transforming the possibilities of recognizable group membership and scale of grouping.

In the case at hand, we can see that the very fact that norms of pronominal use create a space of analogies between multiple, independent scenarios of use is itself a principle of potential regrouping. A speaker who is aware of the fact that there are 'n' distinct contextual configurations for which a usage is appropriate can take a contrastive self-differentiating stance by extending the norm to an $n + 1^{th}$ scenario (thus expanding the space of indexical analogies) or restricting it only to n−1 cases (thus narrowing the space of analogies) in practices of other-deference. In such a case the very act of extending or narrowing the norm is a diacritic of self-differentiation. Such diacritics can be converted into stereotypic emblems – even canonical ones – by institutionalized social movements of various kinds. In some cases the conversion of the diacritic into an emblem of community is part of a program or project of bringing into existence new imagined communities, membership in which is made palpable through events of diacritic performance. Thus in Sweden, an expansion in the scenarios of reciprocal T-usage from private to public-institutional contexts had come to be associated by the 1970s with membership in the Social Democratic party (Paulston 1976). In post-colonial Vietnam, a more complex transformation of address practices was programmatically promoted during the 1960s by the incoming Marxist government as a way of replacing the hierarchical forms associated with French Colonial rule, a strategy that sought to formulate a revolutionary 'voice of the people' summoned indexically through practices of other address (Luong 1988).

6.5 Social boundaries

In Chapter 3 we considered a number of examples of interactional tropes that presuppose the existence of multiple society-internal norms of deictic usage, and themselves consist of the selective observance (whether actual or alleged) of *one norm rather than another* in order to reformulate a social identity (e.g., Figure 3.3, Tables 3.7 and 3.8). Let us now consider the converse type of case, a situation where norm multiplicity does indeed exist but is not recognized as such by speech participants, resulting in the creation and maintenance of social boundaries between persons.

The example I consider here comes from the work of Paulston 1976 on Swedish norms of address. Paulston observes that during the early 1970s practices of address in Swedish were undergoing a society-internal reanalysis yielding sociological fractionation (3.8), i.e., the co-existence of *distinct group-relative models* of address. The issue relevant to the current example is the enregisterment of patterns of switching from formal to informal address, or 'dispensation' rights (Figure 1.4ff.), and, in particular, the question of who is entitled to initiate such a switch.

The second column in Table 6.10 shows the class composition of Swedish society ca. 1970, as estimated by the State census. Using this as a baseline, Paulston observed that the upper class had a different ranking of variables for initiating informal address than did the middle and working classes; this is shown in the third column.

For group 1, or upper-class people, the relative *gender* of interlocutors is the most important criterion for who can initiate informal address; thus,

Table 6.10. *Social groups and dispensation rights in Swedish*

Classes	% in 1970	Variables influencing dispensation rights
Social group 1 (upper class)	7.8	gender > age, class
Social group 2 (middle class)	34.7	class > age > gender
Social group 3 (working class)	57.5	class > age > gender

Source: (Paulston 1976)

when a man and a woman meet, it is the woman who is entitled to initiate informal address; relative age and social class, are not themselves ranked for this group. However, for groups 2 and 3 (middle and working classes), social class is itself the most important variable; thus, middle/working class persons will yield to an upper-class person; and a working class person to a middle class person. If the two interlocutors are of the same class, then *age* becomes important (the older person is entitled to initiate informality); and gender is the least important variable for the non-upper classes.

The forms used in formal address (viz., the 'polite' pronoun *ni*, a Title, Title and Last Name) differ from those used in informal address (viz., the pronoun *du*, *du* plus First Name, *du* plus Kinterm). These patterns are known to all concerned. But the fact that acts of switching from formal to informal address involve distinct, class-differentiated norms is not generally recognized society-internally, often leading to miscommunication. In the following example, Mr. Lennart B., an upper-class person, finds himself in an intensely awkward situation with one of his female employees, Mrs. Nilsson.

(1) Herr and Fru (Mr. and Mrs.) Nilsson, members of social group 2 with origin in 3, are caretakers of a farm, owned by Lennart B., a member of the Stockholm upper class. The men are approximately of the same age, and because of his social rank, Mr. B. initiated the use of *du* with Mr. Nilsson and the two now freely exchange *du* and FN. But with Fru Nilsson, Mr. B was stuck. His rules say that a woman initiates *du* no matter what, while Mrs. Nilsson has no such rule. Her rule gives rank precedence and if she does have a rule regarding precedence of sex, it will be that the male initiates. Nor does she use *ni* . . . with the result that she addresses Mr. B as *Direktör B.* in the third person, a practice Mr. B. dislikes intensely.

(Paulston 1976: 369)

With respect to norms of who can initiate informal address, Mr. B. and Mrs. Nilsson belong to distinct social domains of enregisterment. They each have a norm of dispensation that entitles the other to initiate informal address. Hence no-one does, leading to social distance and awkwardness.

A rather distinct type of social boundary can result from the fact that class differentiated norms are frequently reanalyzed, or re-intensionalized, as having distinct types of reportable 'social meanings' in their respective social domains. For older upper-class persons, the pattern of reciprocal *du* usage indexes 'intimacy' or *personal* closeness, and is avoided with strangers; but for the more rank-conscious middle/working classes, the pattern of reciprocal *du* marks in-group 'solidarity,' sometimes reanalyzed more specifically as *class* solidarity. Thus for Mrs. B., the upper-class wife of Herr/Direktör Lennart B., the pattern of sustained non-initiation has a different rationalization than it does for Mrs. Nilsson:

(2) Mrs. B., on the other hand, who knows perfectly well that Mr. and Mrs. Nilsson would prefer to use *du* with her and that it is up to her to initiate as woman and older, refuses to do so. She does not realize that to Mrs. Nilsson *du* means solidarity, not intimacy, and that it is her rank, not her age which keeps Mrs. Nilsson from initiating. To Mrs. B., the semantic of *du* is strongly one of intimacy, and when pressed by her social democratic children for reasons of egalitarianism to become *du* with the Nilssons, she will say 'But I don't know them that well.' Mrs. Nilsson is likely to perceive the distance as one of social class rather than as of personal friendship. And certainly neither of them realize that they don't share the same set of rules.

In this type of case divergent standards of *du* initiation are not merely diacritic of class differences, they are actually given different relational designations (intimacy vs. solidarity) in their respective social domains. Here the issue of social boundaries is no longer a fact solely formed through unrecognized differences of address norms. It has acquired a higher-order rationalization through facts of ownership of norms (3.8), so that even though distinct models of propriety do co-exist, and even though their co-existence is not recognized as such, a perfectly clear pair of mirror-image rationales for why such boundaries exist can be articulated by those divided by them, and thus be made to last as boundaries of an altogether different, more durable kind.

7

HONORIFIC REGISTERS

7.0 Introduction

An honorific register is a reflexive model of pragmatic behavior that selectively associates specific behaviors with stereotypes of honor or respect. In any language, a number of speech forms are regarded by language users as stereotypically honorific indexicals; these comprise the discursive component of the register's semiotic range (3.9). Languages differ in their degree of elaboration of honorific repertoires and the range of stereotypic values associated with their use. In any language community all speakers do not employ honorific speech in the same manner; these differences or diacritics are usually grasped in stereotypes of 'social kind' of speaker, and sometimes ordered within register models as tightly ranked emblems of speaker distinction.

A variety of honorific registers have been discussed in previous chapters. The purpose of this chapter is to consider registers whose linguistic repertoires are more elaborate than the cases so far considered, and to assess some of the ways in which these formations mediate relations of status, rank, and power in social life. Of particular interest are cases where honorific repertoires are structurally elaborated into large lexical sets and grammatical paradigms. This type of semiotic organization makes these systems highly extractable from the interpersonal occasions in which they are used and amenable to elaborate forms of ideological reanalysis.

The fact that honorific registers are reflexive models is evident once we note that their use is neither necessary nor sufficient for paying 'respect' to others. In any society there are many ways of marking respect that do not involve the use of stereotypically honorific indexicals but depend on phenomena of text-level indexicality, such as the referential alignments and denotational footings discussed in Chapter 2. For instance, a vast number (actually, a limitless number) of text-in-context relationships amongst signs which formulate models of propositional stance and alignment among interlocutors (viz., praising the interlocutor's propositional acts for their insight, finesse, perspicacity, beauty, moral worth, etc.) can be construed under various co-textual conditions as expressions of speaker's 'respect' for interlocutor, even when no stereotypically honorific lexemes occur as local segments of the sign configurations that establish these effects. Conversely, even when an honorific form is in fact used on some occasion, co-occurring signs can partially cancel its stereotypic effects leading to laminated tropes of veiled aggression and the like; hence acts in which honorific forms do occur are not, from the point of view of their overall co-textual semiotic effects, necessarily acts of deference. Both kinds of effects – being 'respectful' without using stereotypically honorific forms, using such forms to veil acts of aggression – depend on text-level indexicality to the extent that the construals in question are non-detachable from the emergent (and frequently multi-channel) sign-configurations that motivate them (1.2).

In contrast, stereotypically honorific forms are detachable emblems – frequently word-length emblems – stereotypically treated as 'pertaining to honor or respect' in culture-internal models of behavior.[1] Common encounters with stereotypes are cases where language users typify particular expressions *as* honorific, formulate norms of appropriate use, or treat variation-in-use as emblematic of social characteristics of speaker. Such evaluations formulate metapragmatic models of the effects of speaking. They associate language use with several distinct effects such as the expression of deference, the recognition of another's status, or the display of speaker's own status. Since such effects are linked to one another the folk-models in question are internally motivated to a degree. In such cases different indexical partials that appear to motivate each other may be used to rationalize each other in the culture-internal perspective of the language user (e.g., Figure 4.2). Thus in many societies, the tendency to speak respectfully to others is stereotypically revalorized as an index of the respectability of self; in such cases language users often *justify* their tendency to employ other-respectful speech by appeal to the mantle of their own respectability. Here the speech pattern is more than a counter in the game of other-deference; it is valued as a commodity that must be possessed and, once possessed, displayed as often as possible, such displays themselves constituting significant moves in the second-order game of self-presentation. Some among these models become institutionally dominant in society as standards of respectful – and respectable – behavior.

7.1 Variation and normalization

As we look across languages and societies we find that *any* behavioral diacritic can be treated as indexical of honor or respect in culture-specific models of behavior. Even when the behavioral diacritic is a linguistic expression its valorization as an honorific form often links the expression to a wider range of comparably enregistered semiotic behaviors. The linguistic (and especially the lexical) fraction of the register formation is readily decontextualized from occasions of use. It can be discussed, transcribed, sorted into paradigms, glossed, one lexical item at a time.

Language users tend to view the lexical forms of an honorific register as potent symbols of status and politeness, inherently endowed with social meaning. Much of this ideological sense of the inherent power of words is shaped by metapragmatic constructs to which language users are exposed in the ordinary course of language socialization. Thus prescriptions to children about the best types of speech, about appropriate ways of addressing others, about ways of referring to high status persons are genres of metapragmatic discourse which assign stereotypic indexical values to isolable pieces of language. Such stereotypes are easily reproduced in the speech of adults as nomic-universalizing truths about the nature of deference and demeanor in their society/language/culture as a whole. Such schemes of value assignment are highly bound up with particular metapragmatic projects within a culture, exhibiting a great deal of variability by sociohistorical locale even within a single language community. From the point of large scale diachrony, the myth of the inherent power of words is, nonetheless, itself a stabilizing force that tends to unite together different stages of any historical processes of circulation, (re)valorization and institutionalization.

The social life of these emblems is characteristically mediated by reflexive processes discussed in previous chapters. Although these processes are dialectical and sociohistorical in character the models they yield often appear 'natural' to the language user, whether because they are internally motivated, or institutionally dominant, or presupposed by traditional caste or class hierarchies, or linked to large scale cultural projects (such as modernity, nationalism, colonialism), or through some combination of such factors. However, explicit claims to 'naturalness' are, typically, highly positional. They emanate from distinct sectors of the society in question. They are often voiced by society-internal élites whose privileged social position is served by the appearance of their naturalness, or promoted by Standard-setting institutions that form, through a semiotic division of labor, around such interests. In the early literature on honorifics such naturalized models are frequently reproduced as descriptions of '*the* language' by linguists, or as descriptions of '*the* culture' by anthropologists, especially when such writers rely on positional stereotype models without realizing that they do so. Yet much of the social point of these systems lies in the fact that they are not used symmetrically by all speakers – a fact well documented for the Javanese (Errington 1988), Tibetan (Agha 1998a) and Japanese (Koyama 2003) cases, and for many other systems too (Agha 1994). Such claims to universality and naturalness co-exist with society-internal variation of the types discussed in previous chapters – asymmetries of competence, in standards of appropriate use, etc. – frequently reanalyzing such variation as emblematic of speaker characteristics such as class, gender, age, urban/rural provenance and the like.

Issues of circulation, reanalysis and institutionalization have been discussed in substantial detail in previous chapters. My main interest in the present chapter is to focus on models of an honorific register that are already institutionally dominant in a society. Any given native speaker's judgments about honorific usage inevitably reflects a socially positioned perspective on the register. But if the individual is socialized to its institutionally dominant form, the model evidenced in his or her judgments, while socially positioned, may have a very wide social domain, i.e., may also be evidenced in the metapragmatic judgments of many individuals, and may reflect an institutionally legitimated or official 'position' on the register. Such institutionally dominant models are of special interest because they set the conditions on more types of variation in any society than do other models. Language users may well react to dominant models by differentiating their own discursive practices from them, and thus from each other, in one or more ways; but insofar as such models are dominant, more speakers are often reacting to the same baseline. Let us begin by considering the lexemic repertoires of an honorific register from this point of view.

7.2 Lexeme and text

When linguists and anthropologists identify honorific repertoires in languages the method of discovery requires systematic attention to metapragmatic typifications of speech by native speakers. In the case of lexical registers, the method relies on using native stereotypes of lexeme indexicality as a method for identifying honorific lexemes and as a basis for grouping lexemes into isofunctional pragmatic repertoires (e.g., polite words vs. rude words). Since such activity is the point of entry into the cultural phenomenon under investigation, it is essential that we understand the characteristics of data gathered by these methods and the limits of what they can reveal.

Stereotypes of lexeme indexicality

We saw in 3.2 that the linguist's ability to differentiate a register's discursive repertoires from the rest of the language depends on the reflexive ability of language users to formulate metapragmatic typification of speech. In the case of honorific registers, metapragmatic typifications of all of the types listed in Table 3.1 are potentially of value. However such data are generally unusable without further internal analysis of a variety of features, such as the type of effects associated with a form (e.g., deference to addressee vs. referent), the replicability of a given typification across social categories of consultant (i.e., the social domain of the stereotype), and the normative hegemony of a particular class of stereotype judgments.

In the most explicit cases such typifications *describe* the indexical values associated with a form. Linguists commonly rely on such data in identifying a register's forms. Although some honorific expressions in every language have distinctive grammatical markers (e.g., segmentable affixes) such segmentable markers can themselves be identified as honorific lexemes only on the basis of metapragmatic data. Consequently the only *general* method of identification available to the linguist is one which relies on native speaker typifications that differentiate honorific expressions from the rest of the language. Empirically, the linguist has identified an honorific repertoire when he or she is able to partition the total lexicon of the language into honorific and non-honorific forms in a way consistent with native metapragmatic evaluations. If the linguist is a native speaker of the language such evaluative judgments are available as 'native speaker intuitions,' but these intuitions are useless as data unless they are socially located, just as with any other data type. In the more general case (e.g., fieldwork in an unfamiliar language) the activity of sorting expressions into isofunctional pragmatic repertories relies on field queries employing native metapragmatic terms, on the use of such terms in questionnaires, and on normative traditions of lexicography and grammatology that employ such terms.

A cross-linguistic sample of such terms is given in Table 7.1, (a). Hypotheses about the functions of honorific forms are commonly based (at least in part) on explicit stereotypes of use as well, as in (b). Such accounts frequently take an expression, X, and predicate something of it; the predicate may employ a term from the set in (a), ('is polite,' 'marks respect') or employ social role designators ('elders,' 'parents', 'friends,' 'intimates,' etc.) to typify scenarios of usage. Such accounts occur naturally in most field situations but are easily elicited as well. The use of questionnaires and interviews has been a common method for systematic elicitation of stereotypes of use since the work of Brown and Gilman 1960. Although the data gathered by these methods is often called the data of 'use,' the term is a misnomer. Such data record reportable stereotypes of use, not acts of usage. Questionnaires are particularly valuable as sources of data on stereotypes of use since they gather a corpus of metapragmatic typifications for a sample of consultants; insofar as the demographic profile of each consultant is known such techniques provide a basis for assessing the social distribution of stereotypes of use across a population of speakers (see, for example, Ogino et al. 1985).

Table 7.1. *Metapragmatic data used in the study of honorific repertoires*

(a) Native terms that name discrete repertoires
  Zulu: *hlonipha* 'respect'
  Guugu-Yimidhirr: *Guugu-Dhabul* 'forbidden words'
  Tibetan: *šesa* 'respect; respectful speech, behavior'
  Samoan: *'upu fa'aaloalo* 'respectful words'
  Japanese: *kei-go* 'respect language'; *sonkei-go* 'honoring language'; *kenjoo-go* 'humble language'; *tenei-go* 'polite language'
  Javanese: *ngoko* 'speech; the language'; *madya* 'middle (-polite)'; *krama* 'polite speech, behavior'; *krama inggil* 'high polite'; *krama andhap* 'humble polite'; *basa* 'language, polite language'; *tata-krama* 'politesse, polite conduct, politeness in conduct'
(b) Explicit stereotypes of use, e.g., standards of 'appropriate' use:
  Simple generic types: 'X marks respect to people you're talking to'; 'X is used for talking to superiors/inferiors'; 'X is used for talking to elders/parents'; etc.
  More elaborate narrated scenarios (Bengali, Das 1968: 20): 'The inferior form *tui* is generally used by superiors to youngers, between intimate friends, in certain families reciprocally by brothers and sisters and by a master to his servant. . . .'
  Elicited judgments gathered through questionnaires
  Normative statements in native grammatological and lexicographic traditions

---

Lexemic repertoires

Once a number of languages are investigated in these ways a great many lexemic repertoires can be isolated and treated as data on registers. A cross-linguistic comparison of such repertoires shows that honorific registers differ typologically in a number of characteristics such as **repertoire size** (number of lexemes), **grammatical structure** (type of formation) and **grammatical range** (number of form-classes in which lexemes occur). For instance, honorific titles and terms of address show up in every language; distinct forms of honorific pronoun, proper name and kinterm are fairly common; elaborate honorific repertoires of common nouns, verbs, and adjectives are typologically more restricted. Some of these differences are discussed for a few languages later in this chapter.

Lexemic repertoires, once discovered, are a source of great comfort. They can be laid out into neat lists and paradigms. They can be used to exhibit the existence of a register in some language and even, apparently, to compare registers to each other. But no-one who has actually identified such a repertoire in some language has identified *only* a repertoire of lexemes. Since the identification of repertoires depends on metapragmatic data, such identification is, from the outset, a perspective on not one but three variables, namely a range of stereotypic values associated with repertoires by a social domain of users (variables A, B, and C., Table 3.6).

Once we see this, the initial comfort furnished by tables of lexemes can be supplanted by distress and anxiety. The idea that honorific registers are models of language use which vary by social domain within the societies in which they exist is so distressing that a great deal of the early literature on honorifics has sought to ignore it. Some have even denied this possibility by calling one or more usage 'ungrammatical' even when the usage is a living reality that is merely infelicitous from the standpoint of the normative standard which the author upholds (and sometimes misrecognizes as a fact of 'grammar'). Part of this distress comes from the supposition that in order for a cultural regularity to exist, and to facilitate social interaction, it must uniformly be shared among interactants. Curing ourselves of this idea from the outset is the best way of avoiding the up-down cycle of false comfort and distress.

We saw earlier that perfectly symmetric sharedness is by no means a necessary condition on social interaction; and lack of symmetry in positional models does not imply random divergence. Even when models of honorific register vary society-internally, the variants tend to be fractionally congruent with each other. Thus two users of a language may both recognize a word as a word of their language; may both be able to give the same denotational gloss of it; may both feel that it marks deference to referent; may both feel that using this word rather than another is appropriate in some situation; may both recognize that habitually using this word and words like it is emblematic of a social type of person; may both perceive themselves as persons of that type; may both claim to use it. And so on. However, they may differ from each other in one or more of these respects as well. In general when they do differ, they do not differ in all respects. And if they do, such differences become matters of metapragmatic commentary in the situations in which they encounter each other through its use, and the degree of fractional congruence of their models increases as an effect of that activity.

Text-based perspective

A repertoire perspective on registers provides an initial entry into their study but is inherently incomplete. Honorific lexemes are of little practical utility by themselves since they are neither deployed nor encountered as isolated signs in events of interaction. They are relevant to social interaction only under conditions of textuality or co-occurrence with other signs. The range of effects – and social relations – that are enactable under these conditions is much larger than the range of functions reportable by language users in explicit stereotypes of use. In every language the actual use of honorific lexemes serves many interactional agendas such as control and domination, irony, innuendo, masked aggression, and other types of socially meaningful behaviors that ideologies of honor and respect do not describe. Yet the common-sense stereotype that these forms are 'honorific' in value nonetheless shapes default perceptions of their social relevance.

The utterance of an honorific lexeme is invariably part of a larger semiotic display in which various **textually composite effects** can be recognized in interaction, and all of these are not equally transparent to decontextualized reports of lexeme 'use.' Thus, under conditions of textuality, the effects of co-occurring signs may be consistent with a lexeme's stereotypic indexical force, or may strengthen it (yielding greater politeness than the form alone could achieve), or be at odds with it in some measure, partly canceling its polite force. All three types of effect (consistency, augmentation, and partial defeasibility; see 1.4) are inferred from text-level indexical relationships among co-occurring sign-tokens. Such inferences semiotically presuppose acquaintance with stereotypes of lexeme indexicality as criteria – that is, evaluations of co-textual consistency, augmentation or cancellation of stereotype are only possible for someone acquainted with the stereotype – but they are composite effects, not construals of lexemes. Native speakers have little trouble recognizing all three types of composite effects under conditions of textuality, where the total text configuration – an utterance-in-co(n)text – is the object of metapragmatic evaluation and response. However, in acts of decontextualized reflection about language (where lexemes rather than text configurations are the typical objects of scrutiny) composite effects that are contrary to stereotype are less transparent to native description and report (see S 3.2). Thus for any honorific system the class of enactable and construable effects is, as a matter of principle, larger than the class of explicit stereotypes of use.

7.3 Pronominal repertoires

In the discussion of pronominal registers in the last chapter we saw that *textually implemented* differences in pronominal reference are frequently reanalyzed as facts about *lexemic* contrasts of deference. Thus even in cases where singular pronominal reference is implemented not by a pronoun but by a text configuration containing the pronoun (e.g., pronoun plus number marking), folk-consciousness metonymically attributes the significance of the text configuration to a text-segment and essentializes such effects as the stereotypic meaning of the lexeme. Given the reanalysis, such differences are perceived as a series of number and person tropes. Normative traditions tend to stabilize such tropes, formulating new standards of use linked to the use of particular expressions.

Contemporary European languages exhibit relatively simple repertoires of this kind, though this is evidently a recent phenomenon.[2] In many Asian languages (such as Tibetan, Japanese, Vietnamese, Javanese, Urdu, Thai)

Table 7.2. *Malayalam honorific 'pronouns'*

Form	Range of construals		
	addressee reference	anaphoric reference	other denotation
(a) ńī / tān	'you (sg)'	–	–
ńińńal	'you (pl./sg.HON)'	–	–
tāṅkaḷ	'you (sg.HON)'	–	–
(b) svāmi	'you (HON.)'	–	'master'
ēmānan	'you (HON.)'	–	'master'
yajamānan	'you (HON.)'	–	'master'
(c) tiru-mēni	'you (HON.)'	's/he (HON.)'	'auspicious-body'
tiru-manassǝ	'you (HON.)'	's/he (HON.)'	'auspicious-mind'
tam-purān	'you (HON.)'	's/he (HON.)'	'one's.own-lord'
(d) aviṭuńńǝ	'you (HON.)'	's/he (HON.)'	'from there'
iviṭuńńǝ	'you (HON.)'	's/he (HON.)'	'from here'
ańńuńńa	'you (HON.)'	's/he (HON.)'	'from there'
ańńattǝ	'you (HON.)'	's/he (HON.)'	'from there'

Source: (Chandrasekhar 1970, 1977)

pronominal registers are far more elaborate by criteria of repertoire size (see examples in 6.2). But the size of repertoire is merely a measure of the number of lexicalized tropes co-existing at a particular synchronic stage of the language. For example, Chandrasekhar (1970, 1977) lists over a dozen second person pronouns in Malayalam (Table 7.2). Of these *ńińńal* and *tāṅkaḷ* in (a), formed from the plural suffix (*-kal*), are based on number tropes. The other cases involve person tropes of various kinds. The forms in (b) are all common nouns meaning 'master' which, when used to refer to addressee, merge functionally with pronouns. The forms in (c) are honorific nominals of various kinds which permit deference to both addressee or anaphoric antecedent, unlike those in (b). The deictic adverbs in (d) exhibit a similar range of addressee and anaphor deference in addition to their ordinary use as spatial deictics. Thus all of the expressions in (b)–(d) permit deference to addressee-referent but have other construals as well; they are analogous to second person pronouns only by criteria of partial overlap of function.

Since these kinds of systems are based on the reanalysis of form-classes, it is evident that the term 'pronoun' cannot be used in any precise way to describe them. In languages with elaborate pronominal repertoires we find a range of **person referring honorific forms** which overlap with true pronouns (i.e., categorial participant deictics) by formal (distributional) and functional (referential) criteria. Cross-linguistically, a variety of nominal expressions – nouns, titles, kinterms, body-part terms, spatial deictics – are reanalyzed in this way and come to function as pronoun-like honorific lexemes in particular languages.

Representations like Table 7.2 are useful as summaries of facts of tropic lexicalization within a language, but they can also be highly misleading. They imply that just because a range of uses and construals is attested in a language they are familiar to everyone, used by everyone, used in every genre of discourse, used for every interlocutor type, and so on. This is never the case. For many speakers, one or more of the range of construals of a pronominal form is unfamiliar, or no longer a 'current' usage, or not considered the 'main' meaning; some usages are attested only in literary registers, some occur only in a specialized type of oral discourse (such as myth, folklore), others are associated with specific class, caste or gender identities, and so on.

While an understanding of the lexicogrammatical and textual features of such usages is a necessary first step in understanding their social relevance, it does not get us very far by itself. Very frequently it is the reanalysis of such possibilities into highly concrete emblems of speaker type, and the logic of role alignment linked to events of using and construing them that imbues these forms with the kind of social relevance most transparent to users. We have considered the conversion of pronominal forms into emblems of speaker kind in a number of languages already. In many of these cases, we saw that it is not the lexicogrammatical features of the form but the personification of its usage – and the circulation of this personified emblem in genres of public sphere discourses (see, e.g., Table 3.7ff.) – that explains *why* it is that some persons claim to use one form rather than another, and *what* facts of social self-positioning are implied by such claims.

Once we begin to consider such processes in comparative terms it is evident that many kinds of structural features of language are treated cross-linguistically as stereotypically 'social' indexicals, i.e., as indexing speaker's social identity and relationship to others. Pronominal registers are just one particular structural type. That is to say, processes of stereotype formation, functional reanalysis and stereotype extension apply to many kinds of structural repertoires. We can make little sense of these comparative data by supposing that a particular structural type 'encodes' some particular kind of social relation or identity. Let us now consider these issues for a rather distinct class of register formations.

7.4 Phonolexical registers of speaker demeanor

In Chapter 4, we considered the uses of Received Pronunciation as an emblem of speaker demeanor. Cases where repertoire differentiation depends on phonolexical contrasts among forms emerge whenever phonological rules are restricted to specific lexical sets and the lexical boundary of the

Table 7.3. *Phonolexical registers in Samoan*

	I.	II.		
(a) Repertoires				
'chief, orator'	matai	makai	$t \sim k$	phonological
'village council meeting'	fono	foŋo	$n \sim \eta$	contrasts
'highness (cf. your highness)'	tofa	kofa	$t \sim k$	
(b) Stereotypes of use:	↓	↓		
metapragmatic labels:	tautala lelei 'good speech'	tautala leaga 'bad speech'		
norms of use:	associated with Christianity, literacy, and Western education	appropriate in everyday usage (in homes, at the store, on the road); and in 'traditional' formal settings, such as speechmaking		

Source: (Duranti 1992)

phonological rule is evaluated differently by different social domains of speaker, leading to two possible pronunciations of a word. Such language-structural variation is cross-linguistically very common. But the metaprag-matic constructs through which the diacritic is construed as a speaker emblem can vary enormously across societies, as the examples in the next section show. These systems are 'honorific' in the minimal sense that they involve stereotypes of speaker-decorum and respectability; yet they can also be evaluated as indexical of features of context additional to speaker type, such as speaker's relation to interlocutors, type of setting, etc.

The Samoan case in Table 7.3 involves phonolexical contrasts between lexemes in columns I. and II. based primarily on contrasts between alveolar and velar consonants. This structural fact tells us nothing about the social consequences of using one form of speech or another. Understanding these issues requires attention to the metapragmatic stereotypes of enactable effect indicated in (b).

The role designating metapragmatic terms *tautala lelei* 'good speech' and *tautala leaga* 'bad speech' provide some initial clues to the scheme of valorization linked to usage of the two repertoires. But norms of appro-priate use provide a somewhat fuller picture. So-called 'good speech' is viewed as appropriate to writing, education and Christianity; its use is associated with non-traditional (Western) formal settings such as Church services. In contrast 'bad speech' is appropriate to everyday informal settings (in homes, at the store, on the road) but also to 'traditional' formal settings such as speechmaking. Now the very fact that the term 'bad speech' is used to describe forms used in *traditional* speech-making suggests something of the institutional centering of these metapragmatic constructs. The judgments appear to be positionally centered with respect to the forces of modernity and Westernization that formulate emblems of personhood linked to variation in speech behavior. The repertoires in Table 7.3 are linked to stereotypes of speaker decorum. No robust ideology of other-deference appears to be linked to these forms. Nonetheless, effects pertaining to interpersonal relationships are likely to be projected, if only as emergent role alignments, from facts of relative usage, viz., whether only one person in an encounter uses 'good speech' or both do so.

The Persian example in Table 7.4 involve phonolexical contrasts that are primarily treated as indices of speaker demeanor too, but they are also extended to stereotypes of speaker-interlocutor relations under certain conditions. The styles themselves have no standard names. But text-in-context effects mediated by their use are typified in fully characterological terms as we shall see in a moment.

From a structural standpoint, the shift from style A to style B (the terms are Beeman's) is marked by phonological reductions (deletion, devoicing, and others) that operate in particular syllabic environments (for a discussion of criterial environments see Beeman 1986, ch. 5). One important source of these phonolexical contrasts is the difference between Arabic and Persian patterns of syllable structure. Persian has a large number of borrowed Arabic words. Style A lexemes partially preserve the phonemic and syllabic structure of the source language, but in style B, these contrasts are reduced and Persianized.

At the level of text, the varieties that Beeman calls Style A and Style B are two poles, or extremes of the co-textual patterning of phonolexical shapes in utterances. When none of the lexemes uttered exhibit phonological reduction we have a pure sample of style A; in the converse case, pure style B. Between these two extremes lies a gradable continuum of possibilities. Since the two styles involve phonemic (rather than merely allophonic) variation the contrast between them is relatively transparent to native speakers; it appears moreover that many (if not most) speakers of Standard Teherani Persian can switch between reduced and unreduced forms in discourse, and sometimes do so strategically.

At the level of metapragmatic stereotypes, style A is typified by language users as exhibiting 'proper' demeanor on the part of speaker and, derivatively, as exhibiting deference to those present. One layer of the sense of propriety is motivated by the fact that style A consists of the normatively correct shapes of words (as preserved, for example, in the orthography)

Table 7.4. *Enregistered phonolexical styles in Standard Teherani Persian*

	Style A	Style B		
(a) Repertoires				
1. 'after'	bæ:'d	bæ:d	$/'/\sim\emptyset$	
'pious'	mo:'men	momen		
2. 'fish'	ma:hi:	ma:i	$/h/\sim\emptyset$	
'morning'	sobh	sob		
3. 'patience'	sæbR	sæb	$/r/\sim\emptyset$	phonological contrasts
'how'	četor	četo		
4. 'celebration'	jæ:šN	jæš	nasal $\sim\emptyset$	
'name'	e:sM	es		
5. 'difficult'	sæ:xt	sæx	stop $\sim\emptyset$	
	more lexemes of Arabic etymology	more Persian etyma; Arabic words 'Persianized'		other contrasts
(b) Stereotypically associated with:				
	kæm-ru'i 'restricted expression'	por-ru'i 'free expression'	(actor conduct)	
	zaher 'politesse; self-control'	baten 'inner passions'	(mental disposition)	
	birun 'outside; public'	ændærun 'inside; private'	(social situation)	
(c) frequently used in:				
	national television; religious sermons; political oratory; other ceremonial occasions	interaction with family, intimate friends, casual encounters		

Source: (Beeman 1986)

and style B of sound shapes that appear defective to intuitions trained by graphemic conventions.

The link between sound shapes and the ethic of propriety (and, contrastively, impropriety) is further typified – (re)analyzed, we might say – in more explicitly characterological terms by a range of metapragmatic terms. None of these terms are names for words, syllabic shapes, or sentence-types as such. They function as a commonplace vocabulary for typifying text-in-context effects. For example, style A is associated with the ethic of *kæm-ru'i* 'restricted expression' and style B with *por-ru'i* 'free expression'. These stereotypes treat the enregistered contrast as indexical of speaker persona and relation to interlocutor *but only relative to certain co-textual conditions of use.* For example, the use of style A is judged most appropriate to contexts where (a) status asymmetry between speaker and addressee is independently at issue; (b) self-control is expected; (c) the setting is public and involves non-intimates.

For many speakers such norms of appropriateness clearly function as 'standards' of proper behavior. However style B utterances may be employed in such settings too, a usage that is more highly entailing, less automatized; the utterance may be considered rude, jocular, or otherwise unseemly, depending on the way in which co-textual cues fill in the sense of inappropriateness at hand.

In cases of deviance from expected behavior, the terms *por-ru* 'audacious, brash' and *kæm–ru* 'reticent' are commonly used to typify the stylistic contrast in more explicitly characterological terms. A person is called *por-ru* (literally, 'full face') if he or she deals freely with people to the point of brashness; hence *the unexpected use of style B* in settings (a)–(c) is an example of *por-ru'i* 'brashness, audacity'. A person is called *kæm–ru* (literally, 'little face') or *forutæn* (literally, 'lowering of the body') when he or she exhibits reticence, humility and bashfulness; hence *the unexpected use of style A* in settings that are the converse of (a)–(c) (i.e., symmetric, relaxed, intimate, private settings) is judged unexpectedly decorous, as exhibiting reticence or *kæm-ru'i* in this sense. Such terms comprise a descriptive language for talk of contrary-to-standard behavior, and for formulating judgments about current interlocutors (e.g., calling someone 'brash'); such typifications are often used strategically to typify an interlocutor's prior speech in an effort to reshape subsequent speech style and social relations.

Observe that style A does not in any sense 'code' formal/public situations. Rather the style is simply *appropriate* to such situations insofar as they are independently recognizable as such. That is, insofar as the readable co(n)text of the utterance suggests that asymmetric-proper-nonintimate modes of relationship are already 'in play,' utterances of style A are judged to be indexically congruent with (continue to maintain) such effects. Utterances that tend towards style B entail a gradient movement away from the pole of controlled self-expression, of politesse, or from the presentation of a mannered public persona. The mode of textual implementation of the style makes possible gradient degrees of interactional informality and non-deference. Awareness of stereotypes of appropriate use makes possible the manipulation of such stylistic contrasts to perform effects that are by degrees inappropriate to the model of co(n)text already established and, as a result, capable of reconstituting aspects of the entailed context along dimensions such as (a)–(c) above.

Intuitions of appropriate use are trained by a range of metapragmatic practices, including prescriptive socialization in families and in schooling, and also through highly implicit depictions of speech/speakers in public sphere media. Thus style A is routinely encountered in national television, religious sermons, political oratory and other types of public, ceremonial occasions; and style B in interaction with family, intimate friends, and in casual meetings with acquaintances. Exposure to such routinized forms of implicitly framed speech-in-context – including the special case of explicitly ritualistic and ceremonial routinization – is itself an important social mechanism through which awareness of enregistered values is replicated across populations.

The phonolexical repertoires discussed above are styles of discourse that are enregistered culture-internally as systems of speaker-focal demeanor indexicals. The metapragmatic frameworks that construe them as emblems of speaker kind also treat them as potentially indexical of speaker's relation to, or stance on, persons copresent in the current participation framework, such as addressees and other interactants, as well as on the formality or status-marked character of the setting. The lexicogrammatical repertoires which I discuss in the next two sections allow an additional possibility: they are linked to referent-focal effects in discourse. Thus, using these repertoires, it is possible to index deference to any individual denotable by a linguistic expression – including persons non-copresent, deceased, not yet born, entirely fictitious, etc. – and hence to extend 'honorific' effects beyond immediate participation frameworks.

7.5 Registers of referent-focal deference

When a repertoire of lexemes is culturally differentiated from the rest of the language *as* a referent-focal honorific register, the forms of the register tend cross-culturally to be conceptualized (and practically deployed) as ways of deferring to social persons. Inert, inanimate objects are not *inherently* viewed as worthy of deference in most cases, even though deference to inanimate objects *associated with* honored persons is common everywhere. Thus an underlying stereotypic value associated with honorific registers of this type is that their usage involves deference to persons in some way.

However, honorific expressions are not associated with persons as such. In actual events of language use, honorific lexemes index deference to persons by virtue of the fact that such persons occupy interactional roles with respect to the current utterance. Deference marking is, in this sense, an irreducibly indexical phenomenon. In notional terms any act of deference appears to have the structure 'deference to somebody from somebody'. Such 'somebodys' are identifiable in discourse only as occupants of interactional roles such as speaker, addressee, referent, bystander, and so on. We shall see presently that a variety of semiotic cues serve to make facts of both role occupancy and deference relation manifest or palpable in

discourse, and that such effects can be achieved with extraordinary sub-
tlety in cases of transposition and voiced speech. But these tropic usages
presuppose and manipulate more basic categorial defaults of deference
indexicality.

In previous work (Agha 1993b), I have used the term **focus of deference**
for the interactional role category to which deference is directed, and **origo of
deference** for the interactional role from which deference emanates.
Honorific repertoires differ in whether they mark deference to bystander$_{focus}$,
addressee$_{focus}$, or referent$_{focus}$. Such contrasts involve differences in **categorial text-defaults**, namely differences in the baseline sketch of deference
implemented by a form in the absence of co-textual effects to the contrary.
Any such categorial effect can be troped upon by the effects of semiotic
accompaniments, and even be reanalyzed by reflexive processes so that the
same form can come to have distinct categorial values for a distinct sociohistorical domain of speakers. Such forms of variability are deeply distressing to any 'coding' view of deference (e.g., the view that honorifics are
'direct grammatical encodings of relative social status,' Brown and
Levinson 1987:179) since this view misrecognizes text-defaults as necessary
relationships. So much the worse for the coding view.

Addressee and bystander honorifics are ideologically specialized varieties of honorifics that mark deference to persons co-present. Such devices
are not limited to any particular structural category, *or even to linguistic
expressions.* As we look across languages, we find that a vast variety of
semiotic displays – prosody, phonolexical contrasts, gestures, modes of
bodily comportment, clothing, etc. – are stereotypically associated with
deference to persons co-present. In many cases, such as the Samoan and
Persian examples above, the persons in question need not specifically be
addressees or bystanders. They may be co-present persons of some less
specific kind, such as hearers or perceivers of the semiotic display. In other
cases, deference to addressees or bystanders (in particular) is specified
by culture specific ideologies. In the case of Australian bystander-focal
systems, everyday forms of linguistic and non-linguistic conduct are pro-
scribed in the presence of criterial affinal kin, a scenario where *specialized*
forms of kinesic behavior, bodily comportment, and language use, are
prescribed as alternatives; the restriction to categories of bystander (or
even to kin-as-bystander) is a culture-specific norm (Haviland 1979a).
Similarly, in the case of addressee-focal systems, normative prescriptions
and proscriptions treat behaviors involving a variety of signs and semiotic
channels as deferential to addressee (Errington 1998). These vary enormously across societies. In both types of systems, anything perceivable by
a co-present person can become culturally enregistered as indexical of
deference, and the category of copresent individual can be normatively
specified as something more specific than 'co-present person' (e.g., a kin

copresent as bystander). And if we look across languages at the linguistic fractions of addressee- and bystander-focal registers, we find that the grammatico-semantic class of such expressions can be quite varied.

In contrast, in the case of referent-focal honorifics, the focus of deference need not be copresent (or even alive, or as yet born, etc.). It must be identified *by the utterance used to denote* that person. Hence for such registers, deference and lexemic denotation are more intimately linked; indeed, the grammatico-semantic class of the lexeme shapes its pragmatic text-defaults, as I show in 7.6. Moreover, as we saw in Chapter 2, referring is not a coding relationship between lexical items and things; the way in which a referent is picked out by an utterance depends on the denotation of the lexemes that occur in it, but is also shaped by discourse level processes. Hence lexemic text-defaults of reference (and deference) are also defeasible by discourse-level processes, as I show in 7.7.

All referent-focal honorifics defer to addressee when the addressee is the referent. Thus so-called 'second person honorific pronouns' are referent-focal honorifics which (by virtue of their referring properties) are also addressee-focal in deference effect. Some expressions of this type are not true pronouns at all, but are referent-focal honorifics whose focus of deference varies as the expression is used as a common noun, an anaphor or an addressee-referring form (e.g., Table 7.2, (c)). A number of other kinds of alignment of deferential foci also occur in discourse, including the cases of 'secondary' and 'conjoined' foci discussed in 7.7.

7.6 Deference to referent: text-defaults

Deference to referent is mediated by the denotational class of lexeme. Table 7.5 gives a cross-linguistic summary of the kinds of lexicogrammatical domains in which referent-focal lexemes are most commonly centered (column I) and the kinds of indexical text-defaults associated with their use (column II). Despite the appearance of complexity the principle that organizes these text-defaults is relatively simple. Honorific expressions are stereotypically valued as ways of deferring to people. In the case of referent-focal honorifics, the default focus of deference depends on the way in which the grammatico-semantic properties of the expression associate it with persons. Let us consider the application of this principle to the cases differentiated in (a)–(f) in Table 7.5.

In the case of semantically [+ human] honorific nouns – such as the honorific pronouns, titles and kinterms in (a) – the focus of deference is the person denoted by the noun. Forms of this type have been discussed in the previous chapter and in 7.3, so I will not discuss them any further here.

Verbs specified for [+ animate] subjects (e.g., *come, go, eat, drink, look, throw*), as in Table 7.5 (b), are linked to social persons by virtue of the fact

Table 7.5. Referent-focal deference: a cross-linguistic approximation

I. Grammatico-semantic class		II. Indexical text-defaults	
Major class	Sub-classes	Origo of deference	Focus of deference
(a) [+human] nouns	pronouns, titles, kinterms	speaker	referent of noun
(b) verbs with [+animate]-subject	verbs of cognition and corporeal activity	speaker	referent of subj NP (utterance topic)
(c) verbs with [+animate]-object	verbs of speaking & exchange; other ditransitives and promoted transitives	referent of agentive NP (actor)	referent of dative/accusative NP (receiver)
(d) [−animate] verbs (verbs lacking animate arguments)	non-agentive verbs of physical alteration, displacement, change of state; predicable of natural elements (wind, water. etc);		—*
(e) [−human] nouns	nouns denoting animal and plant species		*
(f) [−human] nouns with 'personal' denotata	nouns denoting body-parts, man made objects, personal possessions, appurtenances		(absorptive)

*not lexicalized; these classes do not productively yield positively valorized honorific variants (see n. 5)

that they are predicable of person.[3] For these verbs, the default focus of deference is the person of whom they are predicated, the referent of the subject NP, or utterance topic. The grammatical formation of honorific lexemes of this type varies considerably from language to language. In the examples in (1), such 'topic-honorific' (TH) verbs and verb-moduli are indicated by boldface. In the Tibetan case the honorific form consists of the verb stem, in Korean of a suffix, and in Japanese of a morpheme configuration. Italics in the English glosses indicate that the focus of deference is the topical referent.

(1)
(a) Lhasa Tibetan
    āma   laà sịmqhāā̱ lʌ **phēè**   sōŋ
    mother H house.H DAT go.**TH** AUX
    '*Mother* went to the house'
(b) Korean
    sensayng-nim kkeyse encey   ttena-**si**-keyss-up-ni-kka
      you–H   NOM.H when   leave-**TH**-will -AH -IND-Q
    'When are *you* going to leave?'
(c) Japanese
    Sakai-san ga Suzuki-san ni chizu-o   **o-kaki-ni nat**-ta
    PN-H NOM PN-H DAT map-ACC Draw-**TH-PST**
    '*Mr. Sakai* drew a map for Mr. Suzuki'

The ditransitive verbs in Table 7.5(c) – typically verbs of speaking and exchange (*give, tell, request*, etc.) – are subcategorized for animate objects (whether direct or indirect objects, i.e., accusative or dative NPs) as well as animate subjects, which are typically [+ human] agentive NPs. The default focus of deference is the referent of the dative/accusative NP (the 'receiver' of the action, the person to whom something is given, of whom a request is made, etc.). For such verbs the default origo of deference (i.e., the one perceived as deferring) is the denoted actor (or referent of agentive NP). Hence verbs of this type project deference as emanating from someone other than the speaker-utterer of the verb token, e.g., for *give*, it is the giver (not the utterer) that is presented as owing deference to the receiver. In the examples in (2), the focus of deference is indicated by the subscript k, and the origo by subscript j.

(2)
(a) Lhasa Tibetan:
    khērāā̱ lʌ   **šụ̈ụ̈**   tụù
    you.H DAT   ask.**RH** AUX
    '[s/he$_j$] has already asked you$_k$[for your permission]'

(b) Korean (Sohn 1988)
    ape-nim, eme-nim   kkeyse   halme-nim kkey
    father-HT mother-HT NOM.H   gr.mo.-HT DAT.H
    yak ul **tuli** -si -ess -up -ni-ta
    pill ACC give.**RH-TH-PST-AH-IND-DEC**
    'Father, mother$_j$ gave pills to grandmother$_k$'
(c) Japanese (Harada 1976)
    Watasi wa Yamada sensei ni   sono koto o **o-tazune si**-masi-ta
    I TOP PN-HON DAT that   thing OBJ ask.**RH-AH-PST**
    'I$_j$ asked Yamada sensei$_k$ about that matter'
(d) Javanese (Errington 1988)
    Kula N -**atur**-i tiyang menika   Bapak
    I   ACT-call.**RH-IO** person.H that.H father
    'I$_j$ call that person$_k$ Bapak'

The use of such verbs projects actor's deference to receiver, but from the speaker's point of view: the actor (or referent of agent NP) need not have spoken or done anything at all; indeed, s/he need not even be alive. In general, it is the speaker who formulates a deference relation as holding between one referent and another. These devices express 'voiced' deference effects in this sense. Since verbs of this type have both animate subjects and objects they yield two honorific forms in many languages, one of type (b) and another of type (c) in Table 7.5. These are sometimes distinguished in native metapragmatic terminologies by distinct register names (e.g., krama inggil vs. krama andhap in Javanese; sonkeigo vs. kenjoogo in Japanese).[4]

Since honorific expressions are used to defer to persons, expressions that do not denote persons exhibit lexical gaps in honorific repertoires. The most common lexical gaps are illustrated in (d) and (e) in Table 7.5. Thus, verbs that lack animate/human arguments and hence are not predicable of persons (verbs like *evaporate, fracture, increase*); or nouns that denote non-human referents (such as terms for animals, minerals, plants) do not productively yield positively valorized honorific forms in referent-focal repertoires.[5]

However the class of [−human] nouns shown in (f) − nouns that denote things associated with persons − form a systematic exception precisely because cultural facts of enregisterment associate honorific expressions with deference to people. And since, unlike the cases in (a)−(c), no person is denoted by these expression their deference focus is highly absorptive: the person understood as deferred to remains indeterminate except by co-textual association. In Tibetan the use of honorific forms of words for appurtenances (e.g., *tea, hat, book, umbrella*) is understood as marking deference to persons co-textually associated with the thing in question, such as the possessor or owner of the object (see Agha 1993b for more details). Since the deference focus of such forms is not transparent at the

Table 7.6. *Cross-linguistic distribution of lexemic honorific forms*

	Referent-focal				Absorptive	Addressee/ Bystander-focal
	[+ human] nouns		[+ animate] verbs		[−human] nouns	(miscellaneous form classes)
	Titles	2nd pro	TH	RH		
I.						
Javanese	+	+	+	+	+	+
Madurese	+	+	+	+	+	+
Sundanese	+	+	+	+	+	+
Japanese	+	+	+	+	+	+
Korean	+	+	+	+	+	+
Persian	+	+	+	+	+	+
II.						
Lhasa Tibetan	+	+	+	+	+	
Ladakhi	+	+	+	+	+	
Mongolian	+	+	+	+	+	
Urdu	+	+	+	+	+	
III.						
Samoan	+	+	+		+	
Nahuatl	+	+	+		+	
IV.						
G-Yimidhirr	+	+				+
Dyirbal	+	?				+
Zulu (hlonipha)	+	?				+
V.						
German	+	+				
Russian	+	+				
French	+	+				
Maithili	+	+				
Uyghur	+	+				
VI.						
English	+					

Note: 'TH' = 'topic honorific' verb (cf. Table 7.5 (b)); 'RH' = 'receiver honorific' verb (cf. Table 7.5 (c)); '+' means that substantial repertoires of the type are attested in the literature.

lexical level such forms are also subject to functional reanalysis to a high degree. Variation in the habitual use of such forms is typically personified – reanalyzed as a system of speaker/actor-focal emblems – and understood as conveying something about the utterer. Thus the frequent use of such expressions is linked, in Tibetan, to stereotypes of speaker refinement

(Agha 1998a); in Javanese to aristocratic or upper-class status (Errington 1988); in Japanese, in at least some urban settings, to stereotypes of high-society elegance and upper/middle class femininity (Shibamoto 1987).

Referent-focal expressions occur in honorific registers in a number of languages. These languages differ in the range of grammatical classes in which such repertoires are well developed. Table 7.6 is an approximate summary of their distribution across a sample of languages. Many of these languages have honorific forms that are not referent-focal, as indicated in the last column. The summary is based on the literature currently available, and is best treated as provisional.

7.7 Textually composite effects

To say that deference indexicals have **categorial** deference effects is to say that honorific expressions regularly specify particular contextual variables as default foci of deference relative to co-text. Categorial effects are gradiently defeasible by co-occurring signs in a variety of ways. The general principle in such cases is that *the emergent semiotic effects of a text configuration containing honorific lexemes* partially diverges from *the categorial effects of the lexemes involved*. The fact that such cases involve partial or fractional non-congruence is important and worth noting at the outset. Since each lexeme is a category cluster of propositional and social-indexical information (see sections 1.4 and 2.3), the significance of accompanying signs is often congruent with *some* categorial dimensions of lexemic content even as it cancels others.

In utterances where the deference effects of co-occurring signs are fully congruent with each other, the overall effect reinforces the effects of its parts. This is the case in the examples in (1) and (2) above, where a number of honorific expressions co-occur with the lexeme highlighted in boldface in each utterance. Thus in the Korean example in (1b), deference to the referent of *you* is marked by a suffix on the pronoun, by an honorific form of the case marker, by the topic-honorific verb-suffix -*si*, and by the addressee honorific suffix -*(s)up*. Similarly in the Tibetan example in (1a), the mother is deferred to by the honorific kinterm, by the honorific form of the word for house (which, by contextual association, is readily understood as the mother's house) and by the topic-deferring honorific verb.

Each honorific utterance is therefore an entextualized map of social relationships, partly mediated by grammatico-semantic values of local utterance-segments and partly by the internal congruence or lack thereof of larger semiotic text configurations. My focus in the discussion that follows is on the latter aspect of these entextualized maps. A number of the textually composite effects I discuss below are not, in fact, consistent with widespread cultural ideologies about the 'function' of these systems.

Many of the effects that are implemented in discourse are not stereotypically 'social' effects at all (e.g., reference maintenance); but even in these
cases, various social-interpersonal effects emerge through text-level indexicality. In some of the other cases discussed below, the effects in question,
while transparently 'social' in character, are not consistent with widespread
stereotypes of *what* the 'social function' of the system is, or, indeed, of *how*
it functions in social life. Such forms of misrecognition are precisely the
kinds of ideological distortions that we would expect from the issues
discussed in 7.2. Let us consider some examples.

Reference maintenance

Any system of referent-focal honorifics serves as a reference maintenance
system under certain conditions. The most elaborate systems permit extensive
null anaphora without loss of propositional information. For example, in
the case of verbs that mark deference to the referent of NP subject, the
occurrence of an overt NP constituent in subject position is merely a default
alignment between grammatico-semantic roles (subject NP), discourse
prominence (topic), and deference indexicality (focus of deference). When
no subject NP occurs, the characteristics of topic/referent can be inferred
from deference indexicality relative to variables of utterance co-text.

In the Lhasa Tibetan example in (3a), where no subject NP occurs, the
predicate 'go' makes clear that the topic is an animate being; its honorific
form makes clear that this referent is, in particular, a person deferred to
by speaker. This semiotic sketch of actant-type motivates the construal of
referent identity relative to discourse presuppositions that are independently in play. For example, if the speaker has been speaking of his father
and daughter in immediately preceding discourse, the use of honorific
expressions in the utterance motivates the construal that it is the father
who went to the house, since he is a category of kin to whom deference is
normatively owed.

(3)
(a) Lhasa Tibetan
    sïmqhāā̀ lʌ   **phēè** sōŋ
    house.H DAT   go.TH AUX
    '[*Someone*] went to the house'
(b) Javanese
    di-**paring**-i
    PASS-give.TH-IND.OBJ
    '[I] was given [it] [by *someone*]'

The Javanese example in (b) illustrates the interaction of recoverable focus
of deference with grammatical voice. Here the presence of the passive voice

marker, *di-*, establishes that the person understood as deferred to is not the verb's (surface) subject but the underlying agent, or giver, which would normally occur as an oblique argument.

A second type of non-default alignment of deference focus and sentence constituents involves cases where the subject refers not to a person but to a thing associated with a human being. In the example in (4a), the head of the subject NP is *salang* 'love,' an abstract noun. The person understood as focus of deference is not denoted by this constitutent, but by its adjunct-modifier *Sensayng-nim uy* 'teacher's'. In other cases, a criterial person may not be denoted by any sentence-internal constituent at all, but be established from prior discourse as a statusful referent now available as a candidate for deference focus. Other utterance indexicals can also foreground certain contextual variables as candidate deference foci without denoting them. In the construal given for utterance (b), the indexical focus of the topic-deferring (TH) form, *-si*, is understood as congruent with the focus of the addressee honorific (AH) form, *-eyo*; that is, the one deferred to by being spoken of (indexed by *-si*) is taken to be the same person deferred to by being spoken to (indexed by *-eyo*), namely addressee.

(4) Differentiation of focus of deference and utterance topic
(a) Sensayng-nim uy salang i   khu-**si-eyo**
    teacher-HT GEN love NOM big-TH-AH
    'The *teacher's* love is big'
(b) Sikan i myech   pwun i   kelli-**si-eyo**
    time NOM how.many minute NOM   take-TH-AH
    'How many minutes will it take [for *you*]'

Each of these alignments of referent and focus of deference can be complicated by non-default readings that are mapped out – or diagrammatically sketched – by the effects of additional co-textual signs in social interaction. In many cases the composite sketch of social relations has more than one plausible solution. Such forms of ambiguity create thresholds of contextual indeterminacy that are often critical to the social goals that speakers seek to accomplish in interaction.

Transpositions of origo

On a coding view of honorific effects, category defaults are viewed as necessary relationships. But in actual discourse, such defaults can be troped upon by text configurations that are non-congruent in overall semiotic effect with the default effects of a text-segment. Thus, for many classes of repertoires, the default origo of deference is the default origo of utterance, namely the one who produces the utterance, i.e., speaker-qua-animator. But in cases of voiced speech, the *origo of utterance* has a non-default value; it is not the animator but some principal or author allegedly distinct from animator, and the difference is established by co-occurring devices (reported speech frames, parallelism, contrasts of voiced speaker, etc.). Hence in such cases, the origo of deference indexicality is still origo of utterance, but a co-textually transposed origo, not the default origo; the transposition is established by co-occurring signs as someone other than the one who produces the utterance, a value to which the origo of all indexicals, not just deference indexicals, is now understood as transposed (see 1.4). The most common scenarios in which this occurs is in cases of 'speech modeling' to children (Errington 1998), cases where a parent uses deferential forms to a child, not in order to mark deference to child but to present a model of speaking which the child should adopt in speech to others, including speech directed to the very parent who formulates the model for the child.

Consider the following examples of Lhasa Tibetan usage which I recorded during the course of fieldwork. The speaker of all three utterances is Nawang Rimpoche, a high-status lama who shares a household with his daughter and grandchildren. On numerous occasions I observed that in speaking to me about his daughter (a young woman by the name of Yankii) he never used honorific forms, as may be seen in one of his utterances, reproduced below as (5a). However he did use honorific forms for her in speaking about her to his granddaughter. A few minutes after he produced the utterance in (5a) in speaking to me, he uttered (5b) and (5c) in talking to Yankii's daughter, his granddaughter, a six-year old girl named Pɛɛma. In both (5b) and (5c), he refers to Yankii as 'mother (hon.)' thus voicing both reference and deference from the standpoint of his granddaughter. The utterance in (5b) was a response to a query from Pɛɛma, just after she had interrupted our conversation, asking about the whereabouts of her mother. Once the act of reference is transposed to addressee-origo by the use of the honorific kinterm, the topic deferring verb phēè is also understood as indexing deference to Yankii from addressee-origo, namely from the standpoint of Pɛɛma.

(5)
(a) yãākii mɔɔmɔ̀ pɛɛ yaqo su̱ qitu̱ù
    PN dumplings very good make AUX
    'Yãākii makes very good dumplings'
(b) āma **laà** qu̱mpaa   **phēè** sōŋ
    mohter H monastery.DAT   go.TH AUX
    '*Mother* has gone to the monastery'
(c) cho̱ **laà**   qiì   āma **laà** lʌ **šüü** tu̱ù
    older.bro H ERG mo.H DAT ask.RH AUX
    '*Older brother* has [already] asked *mother*'

In her immediate response to (5b) the little girl asked her grandfather's permission to go to a neighborhood fair, pointing out that her older brother had already left for the fair and that, by implication, she too should be allowed to go. The grandfather replied with (5c), an utterance which defers to his grandson as well as to his daughter. Yet this too is a case of voiced or transposed deference. In referring to his grandson and daughter, Nawang Rimpoche uses kinterms which his granddaughter would use in referring – and deferring – to them. Within the particular textualized occasion where these shifts occurred, the contextual implication of such voiced deference was quite clear: who was she to insist upon doing as she pleased when her betters must seek permission?

Notice that the act is only *fractionally* non-congruent with default values. All denotational values are completely canonical. The focus of deference is still the referent of the kinterm. It is merely that the origo of deference is not the person speaking but the person addressed. Moreover the construal I have just described is not a construal of the sentence in (5c). It is a construal of an utterance occurring in an interaction in which the interactional role configuration is filled by particular persons in a definite way at the moment of speaking. The construal in question vanishes if the sentence is extracted from this multi-channel sign configuration.

Such voicing effects are fairly commonplace in Lhasa Tibetan usage. One interesting genre-specific usage is attested in religious texts and commentaries as a way of establishing modes of exemplary deference and demeanor. Thus we have examples where an individual uses different honorific forms for the same person in different interactional settings. Example (6) below is linguistically very simple: it involves the alternation between just two words, the honorific pronoun *khoñ* 'he (H)' and the non-honorific pronoun *khyod* 'you (NH)'. Consider the following observation about the uses of these forms:

(6) ... in the work of Gtsañ-smyon he-ru-ka we find the master Mar-pa uses the third person honorific determiner khoñ 'he' when speaking to the young Mi-la ABOUT the lama Rñog-pa and other senior disciples, but switches to the second person unmarked [i.e., not specifically honorific] determiner khyod 'you' when speaking TO them.

(Beyer 1992: 208)

Observe that the contrast here at issue is a contrast not between two lexemes but between two distinct scenarios of language use. In both cases, the master Mar-pa is speaking to his disciples. In the second case, the master uses non-honorific forms in addressing/referring to Rñog-pa and other senior disciples; this is just what we would expect given his higher status. However, in the first case the master uses a referent-focal honorific form in speaking to a junior disciple about senior disciples. The act of deference to referent is here transposed to the standpoint of the addressee, the junior disciple Mi-la. The case at issue here is a type of prescriptive voicing to addressee-origo, i.e., speaking to a junior person in addressee role about persons senior to him in a style that he should normatively employ in speaking of them.

The reason that regularities of deference cannot be reduced to grammatical rules derives from the fact that deference effects are only performed and construed *when* expressions are uttered and heard (or written and read). When we speak of 'utterance' and 'referents' we are moving beyond a grammatical perspective on lexemes to a perspective on co-occurring devices in text. The event structure of interactional roles, viz., who hears the utterance (or reads it), is critical to the construal.

Secondary focus

We noted in Table 7.5 that the grammatico-semantic class of an honorific form gives a partial regimentation to its focus of deference. But grammatical cues, while necessary, are by no means sufficient for recovering many of the most interesting effects mediated by honorific usage. An interesting type of case is the case of secondary focus of deference. An act of deference involves a **secondary focus of deference** when a speaker uses a deferring expression of categorial focus X in order to defer to an individual in some other role, Y. The usage is intelligible only if a co(n)textual relationship between X and Y is independently given (i.e., indexically presupposed) at the moment of utterance. It is therefore completely non-detachable from the utterance event in which it is recognizable.

A common case of this type occurs when a referent-focal honorific form is used to mark deference to a lower status person who is, however, a close kin of current addressee. Thus, in Urdu one may mark deference to a child in speaking to the child's mother in order to mark deference to the mother. Such an effect is completely non-detachable for purposes of construal in the sense that if the sentence type that implements the effect when uttered in a particular scenario (i.e., speaking to child's parent) is extracted from that scenario and presented to a native speaker, the native speaker will not be able to recover the effect and may judge the sentence odd or unutterable. In its most common construal this type of interactional trope marks politeness towards parent. However the overall entextualized effect of such a usage may be more laminated, may contain other interpersonal construals as textually motivated partials so that the overall effect is not, or not straightforwardly, polite. The example in (7) was uttered in the course of a dinner party by an elderly lady (the hostess at whose house the party took place) and addressed to a woman in her late twenties whose two young daughters (both under age ten) were present at the party. The girls were running around with some other children in the parlor, apparently playing a game of tag. The activity was accompanied by loud laughter and raucous shrieks of pleasure. The utterance itself contains a single honorific lexeme, the receiver-deferring honorific verb <u>pesh</u> <u>karna</u> 'to give, serve, present, propitiate (H),' here indexing deference from speaker origo (the elderly lady) categorially to receiver focus (the girls) but also, secondarily, by contextual association, to the person addressed (the girl's mother).

(7) bacciyon ko kuch **pesh kar**-ūn? \<laughing\>
    girls DAT something   give.RH-1°sg;
    'Should I serve something to [your] girls?'

The girls' mother responded to this question with polite laughter, then by an embarrassed apology for the girls' behavior, and finally, by grabbing her daughters by the arm, taking them aside, and scolding them. The subsequent pattern of response makes it clear that the girls' mother construed the elderly hostess' act of deference as hyper-polite, as a type of ironic disapprobation towards her children and secondarily towards herself.

Cases of secondary focus often involve the use of ambiguity to achieve strategic ends. More than one cumulative effect is often at issue, particularly when such usages are performed as elements of highly laminated interactional tropes. For example, in Javanese, referent-focal honorifics (krama inggil) are normatively inappropriate in talking about oneself, one's possessions or kin. However, the use of such forms for one's own kin is judged felicitous – and, in some cases, even appropriate – if speaker transposes *origo of reference* to addressee (i.e., uses a kinterm which denotes addressee's relation to one's kin) and uses the referent-focal honorific form of the kinterm, thus performing deference to a person formulated as *addressee's* kin, and hence, secondarily, to addressee.

(8) ... in some contexts honorific kin term use for one's own relatives can be felicitous: a mother might refer to her newborn in addressing her mother-in-law with the honorific kinterm *wayah* 'grandchild' (ngoko: *putu*) in the phrase *wayah dalem* ... [where *dalem* is also a krama inggil expression] thereby attributing high status to addressee/grandparent through reference to addressee's kin [formulated as 'grandchild'], simultaneously suspending the relevance of her own kin relation to the referent to foreground that between ancestor/addressee and descendant/ referent. For this speaker to refer to her offspring in this context with the phrase *putra kula* 'my child (honorific)', on the other hand, would be a breach of etiquette, because it signifies no kin relation other than that between referent and speaker.
                                                                (Errington 1998: 140)

In this case, the mother defers to her child by formulating the child as addressee's grandchild, and thus, by co-textual association, defers also to addressee. But the usage also foregrounds the relationship between (1) her-affine [=child's-grandmother] and (2) herself-as-child-giver-to-affines, thus highlighting her own importance in an exquisitely layered fashion.

Such layered tropes, while semiotically intricate, are cross-linguistically common. They are discussed in more detail in Chapter 8.

Observe finally that cases of secondary focus appear to be exceptions to the categorial focus of the honorific lexeme, but they are not. They are not even construals of the lexeme. They are construals of a semiotic text configuration, namely an utterance-in-an-interactional-role-configuration. Moreover, the secondary focus of the text configuration presupposes the categorial focus of the lexeme. The former can only be construed by someone who can construe the latter.

Conjoined categorial focus

A superficially similar type of usage may be termed conjoined categorial focus. A lexeme has a **categorially conjoined focus of deference** if its appropriate use depends on the relative status of origo vis-à-vis persons in more than one interactional role.

Utterances involving conjoined focus are like utterances with secondary focus in that both mark speaker's relationship to more than one person through the use of a single form. But the resemblance is only superficial. Whereas secondary focus effects emerge by virtue of emergent role alignments between a categorial focus of deference and persons in other interactional roles (e.g., current referent is current addressee's daughter), cases of conjoined focus (or 'conjoined categorial focus') are cases where a form categorially marks speaker's relation to more than one person. Secondary focus effects may be performed by means of any honorific device under particular co-textual conditions. But only a small subset of the lexemes in a language have a focus of deference that categorially tracks speaker's relations to more than one person.

An example of conjoined focus is the use of honorific kinterms in Japanese, where the choice of appropriate kinterm depends upon the values of both referent and hearer (whether addressee or bystander). Thus each of the kinterm forms in Table 7.7 jointly indexes relations between speaker and referent *and* between speaker and hearer. The kinterms in the middle column are used in referring to one's own kin when speaking to outsiders. The kinterms on the right are used when referring to one's own kin while speaking to other family members, or in direct address (where the kin or family member referred to is the person addressed). Both sets of forms are conjointly sensitive to referent and hearer/addressee.

The sociological boundary of familiars versus non-familiars which this distinction presupposes is actually broader than kinship narrowly defined. It is more generally described as the contrast between *uchi* 'insiders' versus *soto* 'outsiders' of which the contrast between immediate family versus non-family is the prototypical exemplar. Close non-kin of other kinds such

Table 7.7. *Honorific forms whose appropriate use depends on two interactional variables*

Referent	Hearer = Non-family member	Hearer = family member
father	chichi	o-too-san/papa
mother	haha	o-kaa-san/mama
son	musuko	[Name]+chan/san
daughter	musume	[Name]+chan/san
older brother	ani	o-nii-san
older sister	ane	o-nee-san
younger brother	otooto	[Name]+chan/san
younger sister	imooto	[Name]+chan/san

Source: (Inoue 1979: 282)

as friends from childhood may also belong to the domain of one's *uchi* though the boundary to which this domain may be extended beyond family appears to vary by social category of speaker. The tendency to conceptualize such matters in terms of 'groups' is merely another instance of the reification of emergent groupings performable through utterances; from the point of view of performed groupings the actual boundaries of in-group vs. out-group relations can never be fixed or reified in terms of the terminology of 'groups,' even though much naturally occurring metapragmatic discourse about such effects seeks precisely to draw (and re-draw) such boundaries in event-independent ways.

Cases of conjoined focus of this type are systematically related to proscriptions against deference to self as secondary focus. One avoids honorific lexemes in referring to one's kin in the presence of outsiders since forms which defer to one's kin potentially have self as secondary focus of deference. Switching to non-honorific lexemes here marks a conventionalized avoidance of the treatment of self as a secondary focus of deference by contextual association with referent. In other words, cases of conjoined focus of this kind are cases where one kind of metapragmatic construct is re-evaluated as another, i.e., standards of appropriate use applying to text-in-context relationships are re-evaluated as stereotypic properties of lexemes.

In Japanese, proscriptions underlying choice of kinterms are extended to the use of verbs of giving so that contrasts of non-honorific (NH), topic honorific (TH) and relational honorific (RH) verb forms are sensitive to whether or not the receiver of the action belongs to speaker's *uchi* domain as well (see Table 7.8). Note that there is no receiver honorific verb in the middle column (i.e., no honorific verb for actor's deference to receiver)

Table 7.8. *Conjoined focus in Japanese verbs of giving*

		Form appropriate when denoted 'receiver' is	
Deference to referent		S (or S's uchi)	not S (nor S's uchi)
'give'	NH	kureru	ageru
	TH	kudasaru	yaru
	RH	–	shashiageru

when the receiver is speaker or speaker's *uchi*, just as we would expect from the more encompassing proscriptions on deference to self. The verb forms in this paradigm can also be used to form an inflectional pattern in Japanese (i.e., $VERB_1$-te $VERB_2$, where $VERB_2$ is a transactional verb). A number of more complex relations of benefaction, gratitude, reprimand, etc., can be performed through the use of this pattern. Such effects depend partly on facts of lexically conjoined indexical value, and partly on emergent facts of role alignment and secondary focus.

Though the distinction between emergent secondary focus and categorially conjoined focus is quite clear in many cases, the contrast becomes a moot point in cases where the degree of routinization is unclear (whether by criteria of frequency, degree of normativity, or size and characteristics of the norm's social domain). In such cases we might speak of the sensitivity of a usage to persons in secondary interactional roles without commitment to the issue of 'appropriate use' and hence without commitment to the distinction between secondary and conjoined focus. For example, in many cultures the presence of bystanders affects the level of deference to addressee. One speaks higher when others are listening. But such practices tend to be variably centered by social category of speaker. Thus differences among speakers in the extent to which their usage responds to secondary variables may be enregistered as emblematic of speaker type in one social domain (or sub-population), but not in others. Hence the usage may be treated as categorial by one sub-population of users but yield only emergent, textually contingent effects for others.

Many of the types of composite effects discussed above are listed by way of summary in Table 7.9. The effects shown in the table are not the effects of honorific lexemes (qua items of the language). They are effects of text configurations that contain a lexeme plus the criterial co-textual features shown on the right. Such 'superposed' effects are implemented, in other words, by text configurations of which the lexeme-token is a fragment and from which the effect is non-detachable. Everyday metapragmatic discourses about honorific usage tend not to link the use of honorifics to

Table 7.9. *Textually 'superposed' effects and interactional tropes*

Textually superposed effect	Co-textual cues on which construal depends
(a) **Secondary focus** (or indirect deference): deferring to one person in order to defer to another	role alignment between categorial and secondary focus
(b) **Transposed origo** (or 'voiced' deference): deferring to someone from the point of view of another	use of reported speech or other (more implicit) framing devices
(c) **Veiled aggression**: using honorific forms in acts of rudeness, coercion, hostility, etc.	non-congruence between propositional content and honorific indexicality
(d) **Hyperpoliteness**: using higher levels of other-raising or self-lowering than normatively required (as in strategic manipulation; sarcasm, etc.)	norms of appropriate use (for current dyad) known to interlocutors
(e) **Shifts of affective stance**: foregrounding of affective stance or alignment with interlocutors	shifts in honorific usage (e.g., back-and-forth between H and NH forms) in speaking to the same interlocutor
(f) **Reference maintenance**: use of honorific devices as reference-tracking mechanism	null anaphora of NPs plus deference marking in predicate

the effects shown in the table. This is hardly surprising since the effects in question are not the effects of lexemes but of text configurations that are relatively complex and non-transparent to subsequent reportage. However, in more studied forms of culture-internal metapragmatic scrutiny (such as etiquette guides) some of these effects are in fact described in some detail. Hence their non-transparency is a degree notion, easily overcome when events of entextualized use are subjected to systematic scrutiny.

7.8 Social domain

I have noted above that the social domain of register stereotypes is an important variable in the study of register systems. Many kinds of society-internal differences in register competence and use are observed cross-linguistically. I have already discussed some of the factors leading to such differences in Chapters 3 and 4. I now illustrate these points for complex honorific registers with a few examples.

One kind of social difference involves variation in competence over lexemes and associated forms. In the case of honorific terms for parts of the body (cf. Table 7.5(f) and discussion following) Errington shows that all

Table 7.10. *Javanese [−human] common nouns*

Gloss	Ngoko	Krama Inggil (honorific)	% speakers who recognize KI form
tooth	untu	waja	100
eye	mata	paningal	100
mouth	langkem	thuthuk	98
face	rai	(pa)suryan	83
chest	dada	jaja	61
neck	gulu	jangga	61
knee	dengkul	jengku	30
foot	sikut	siku	7

Source: (Errington 1988: 168)

honorific forms are not known to every informant. Using questionnaires/ interview data Errington observed the regularities of metapragmatic judgment listed in Table 7.10. Whereas the *ngoko* (ordinary) forms are widely recognized, the expressions in the *krama inggil* (high honorific) set are not equally well known. Speakers who command the largest repertoires can therefore perform an image of their own distinctive cultivation and higher status simply by exhibiting a mastery of *krama inggil* usage in performance, a display of competence that may itself entitle them to deference from others.

A second kind of variation involves a partial fractionation of stereotype values linked to lexemes: although the lexemes in question are themselves widely recognized the standards of use associated with particular forms exhibit interesting social asymmetries. Thus in the addressee-honorific system listed in Table 7.11 the mid-level *madya* forms (shown in the middle column) are susceptible to competing valorizations among Javanese speakers.

Madya repertoires are evaluated differently from different social positions, both in terms of stereotypes of lexemes (e.g., whether they are 'polite' or not) and in terms of standards of appropriate use. Traditional nobles or *priyayi* view *madya* lexemes as impolite and as appropriate only in speech directed at non-nobles (from whom *krama* honorifics are normatively expected in response). Thus from the positional perspective of traditional nobles *madya* repertoires are stereotypically out-group speech (used for non-nobles); and the pattern of asymmetric exchange (i.e., giving *madya*, receiving *krama*) indexically maintains the nobles' higher status. However non-nobles and younger 'modern' *priyayi* evaluate *madya* speech differently. For such speakers *madya* lexemes exhibit an intermediate level of politeness (rather than impoliteness) whose use is extended from the out-group/asymmetric patterns found among the traditional nobility to patterns of in-group symmetric exchange that index no status differential.

Table 7.11. *Addressee honorifics in Javanese: repertoire contrasts*

Gloss	Ngoko informal/formal	Madya(krama)	Krama informal / formal
'please'	yok / ayo	*ngga*	mangga / sumangga
'again'	(me)nèh/maneh	*melih*	malih
'to'	marang	*teng*	dhateng / dhumateng
'only'	waé / baé	*mawon, men, mon*	mawon / kémawon
passive	di-	*di-*	pun- / dipun-
'what'	pa / apa	*napa*	menapa / punapa
'no'	ra / ora	*mboten*	mboten
'this' (proximal)	ki /iki, kiyi	*niki* ⎫	menika / punika
'that' (medial)	ki / kuwi / iku	*niku* ⎬	
'that' (distal)	ké / kaé / ika	*nika* ⎭	

Source: (Errington 1985, Poedjosoedarmo 1969)

7.9 Speech levels

Speech level systems are systems of enregistered style linked to metapragmatic frameworks that evaluate the **register-cohesiveness** of text as a higher-order index of social role and relationship. In most such systems the cohesiveness of text is evaluated in terms of ideologies of rank and stratification, whether in terms of levels of deference to others, or stratified emblems of speaker rank, or both.

Several kinds of speech level systems have been reported in the literature on honorifics. I discuss three varieties here that are quite common in languages of the world.

Phonolexical and prosodic speech levels

One cross-linguistically common kind of speech level system involves patterns of rankable deference/demeanor based on phonolexical and/or prosodic patterns. We have discussed a number of examples of this kind in previous chapters and sections, such as the case in British English (Table 4.3), Javanese (Table 3.10) and Persian (Table 7.4). Wolof has a system of prosodic speech levels not linked to phonolexical features (Irvine 1990). The Zulu Hlonipha vocabulary is a system of phonolexical repertoires; however the metapragmatic framework and ideology of use is linked to respectful 'avoidance' (Irvine and Gal 2000).

From a typological standpoint languages differ in the kinds of honorific repertoires and speech levels that coexist within them. In Persian and Javanese, phonolexical registers and speech levels co-exist with lexicogrammatical registers of the type discussed in section 7.6. The more complex

Table 7.12. *Korean speech levels: the early Standard system*

Levels	Declarative	Imperative	
Completely raising	-naita	-sose	now archaic
Completely raising	-pnita	–	
Conventionally raising	-eyo	-eyo	
Conventionally lowering	-ney	-key	
Completely lowering	-ta	-ela	
Panmal	-e	-e	ambiguous

Source: (Wang 1990, Table 1; citing Choy 1955)

systems exhibit a greater semiotic range (a greater variety of sign-types) linked to ideologies of honorific value.

Speech levels based on deictic patterning

A second kind of speech level system involves variation in cotextual patterning of deictic elements. Systems of second person pronominal deixis are among the most common varieties. In the last chapter, we discussed some examples of this type from Maithili (Table 6.6) and Urdu (Table 6.7).

These systems are not limited to patterns of pronominal deixis alone. Other deictic categories such as mood and voice are cross-linguistically associated with degrees of politeness as well. In Malagasy, text-patterns involving mood and grammatical voice index deference levels: active voice imperatives are judged harsh and abrupt, and passive and circumstantial imperatives as stereotypically more respectful (Keenan 1996).

In Korean, mood distinctions are grasped through a somewhat more elaborate ideology of speech levels. The system involves textualized co-occurrence relationships between address forms (pronouns, vocatives, etc.) and sentence-final mood endings. Since the language exhibits pervasive null anaphora (the absence of explicit noun phrases in sentences) only the verb plus inflectional endings, including mood endings, are obligatory sentence constituents; hence mood suffixes are treated as citation forms by grammarians. The term 'speech level' was first employed for this system by Martin (1964) but is now widely adopted.

There is of course no single speech level system that can be described for the Korean language as a whole. Most textbook descriptions describe Standard Korean, though even this system is clearly undergoing reanalysis and simplification. The 'early Standard' system in Table 7.12 approximates the Standard prevailing more than half a century ago; although deference distinctions extended to other mood categories as well, only declarative and imperative forms are cited here.

Table 7.13. *Korean speech levels: contemporary Cihwali*

Speech level name	Forms			
	Declarative	Imperative	Interrogative	Propositive
hasio	-pnita	-sio	-(si)pnikka -(si)eyo	-sipsita
	-eyo		-sio	-siciyo
haso	-eyo	-eyo	-eyo	-psita
	-so	-so	-so	
hakey	-ney	-key	-nka	-sey
hayla	-ta	-ela	-na	-ca
panmal	-e	-e	-e	-e

Source: (Wang 1990, Table 7)

Table 7.13 describes more contemporary distinctions prevailing in a village called Cihwali (a pseudonym) lying 300 kilometers southeast of Seoul (see Wang 1990 for other ethnographic details). A comparison of the two tables shows that the 'early Standard' system of speech levels is undergoing a process of reanalysis and change. The changes are quite complex and regionally distinct for various communities of Korean speakers (see also Pei 1992). Many of the variant systems differ not by geographic dialect but by demographic dimensions such as generation and socioeconomic class within dialect regions. Awareness of these differences enregisters these forms as indexical of speaker-type for particular social categories of language users.

We can understand something of the process of reanalysis by considering conflicting metapragmatic judgments associated with these forms. For example, in Cihwali many speakers give conflicting stereotype accounts of the highest level (*hasio*), offering judgments about *lexemes* that conflict with the value assigned to *patterns of exchange*. When speaking of isolated forms, 'gentry' speakers describe the *hasio* level as the only positively honorific level, and *haso* as merging with the other two 'conventionally lowering' levels (*hakey* and *hayla*) below it; *panmal* is ambiguous and neutral in deference for some consultants. However, assessments of patterns of exchange present a different picture. Patterns of *hasio-haso* exchange are treated as marking nearly equal status of interlocutors (this is contrary to the stereotype that *hasio* is much more honorific than *haso*); and patterns of *haso-hakey* and *haso-hayla* exchange are said to mark clear status asymmetries (this is contrary to the judgment that *haso* merges with these two other-lowering levels).

Wang explains the conflicting reports as involving, in essence, a confusion of first-order and second-order indexical values. In actual usage the *hasio* level is now used almost exclusively by the gentry and is stereotypically associated with them; the level is thus treated as a system of second-order indexicals of speaker status. The overvaluing of *hasio* in reports about isolated forms reflects awareness of this speaker-focal indexical effect. But evaluation of patterns of exchange engage more directly with the addressee-focal effects of a given use, evaluating the form used in response as indexical of status asymmetries among interlocutors.

Speech levels based on lexical cohesion

Whereas Korean has a relatively small number of honorific nouns and verbs, languages like Lhasa Tibetan and Javanese have honorific vocabularies consisting of hundreds of lexical items. In these languages honorific forms can occur in many syntactic positions within a sentence thus motivating far more elaborate possibilities of lexeme cohesion (or its absence). In Tibetan for example, the maximally honorific sentence in Table 7.14, (e) is evaluated as a 'pure' honorific utterance; judgments of utterance purity are extended to judgments of speaker refinement; the intermediate or 'mixed' levels in (b)–(d) are evaluated as indexing a variety of categories of sub-standard speaker demeanor (see Agha 1998a). Degrees of cohesion of other-deference are thus converted, by a common form of reanalysis, into indexicals of speaker attribute and social status.

Analogous speech level distinctions occur in Javanese. However the ideological codification of speech levels is more elaborately expressed in native grammatological traditions. Poedjosoedarmo differentiates nine distinct speech levels in Javanese (Table 7.15). Level 1 is 'highest', level 9 'lowest'. Schemes of this kind are normative codifications that treat the sentence-internal cohesion of *lexemes* as diagrams, or indexical icons, of performed role and relative status among *interlocutors*. A hearer of an utterance acquainted with the diagram can read various features of role and relationship by attending to features of the utterance.

Table 7.14. *Lexeme cohesion and speech levels (Tibetan): five ways of saying 'Mother went to the house'*

MOTHER HOUSE-DAT WENT AUX	
(a) āma qhāŋpaa chǐǐ sōŋ	non-honorific sentence
(b) **ā ma laà** qhāŋpaa chǐǐ sōŋ	
(c) āma **si̱ m-qhā̰ā̰** lʌ chǐǐ sōŋ	mixed honorific usage
(d) **ā ma laà** qhāŋpaa **phēè** sōŋ	
(e) **āma laà** **si̱m-qhā̰ā̰** lʌ **phēè** sōŋ	'pure' honorific sentence

Source: (Agha 1998a) Boldface marks honorific lexemes.

Table 7.15. *Javanese speech levels: early Standard*

I. Speech level name	II. Lexical conjugate structure	
	Affixes	Words
1. Mudha-krama 'young krama'	krama	krama+ krama inggil
2. Kramantara 'equal krama'	krama	krama; no krama inggil
3. Wreda-krama 'old krama'	krama+ ngoko	krama
4. Madya-krama 'middle krama'	ngoko	madya+ krama inggil
5. Madyantara 'equal madya'	ngoko	madya; no krama inggil
6. Madya-ngoko	ngoko	madya
7. Basa-antya	ngoko	ngoko; some krama
8. Antya-basa	ngoko	ngoko
9. Ngoko-lugu 'plain ngoko'	ngoko	ngoko

Source: (Poedjosoedarmo 1968) krama 'honorific'; krama inggil 'high honorific'; madya 'middle'; ngoko 'ordinary'

Such readability of role and relationship involves two distinct elements. First, a measure of the intrinsic rank or contrastive level of sentence-type is formulated by criteria of register cohesion among lexemes (affixes and word-stems; column II): the more consistently high honorific lexemes (krama and krama inggil) are used, the higher the sentence level. Second, names for speech levels (column I) employ role designators for kinds of persons ('young,' 'old') and for relative rank among interlocutors ('equal') as names for sentence-types. Speech level names thus reanalyze particular thresholds of lexeme cohesion within sentences as indexing discrete 'levels' of social role and relationship among persons.

Such codifications reflect particular historical stages of (normative) conceptions of usage. The scheme in Table 7.15 (or a similar variant) may well have served as the institutionally dominant model of usage among priyayi in the first half of the twentieth century. But by the 1970s and 1980s the situation had clearly changed (Table 7.16).

The table shows that whereas older priyayi continued to frown on mixed speech levels in the mid-1980s, younger priyayi (who, in the earlier model, allegedly used pure mudha krama, the most deferential level) had come to find mixed usage more acceptable. Such differences of acceptability judgment are not, however, strictly reducible to differences of age. The acceptability of mixed speech had come by now to count as an emblem of egalitarian 'modernity,' a way of devalorizing hierarchical norms of interpersonal engagement. The latter norms, by contrast, had become re-valorized as emblematic of a more 'conservative' voice of tradition.

Table 7.16. *Acceptability of 'mixed' speech levels by social domain of evaluator: 'conservative' vs. 'modern' speakers*

	% age speakers who judge sentence acceptable	
Sentence	older/conservative	younger/modern
(a) **ingkang** saé kados *riyin*	0	77
(b) **piyambakipun** mbèkta *napa?*	25	71
(c) **seratipun sampun** *dugi*, dèrèng?	15	84
(d) ngantos *saniki* dèrèng **wonten**	0	73
(e) **nawi kula kèmawon**, *pripun?*	0	68

Source: (Errington 1985: 147–152) Krama vocabulary in boldface, madya forms in italics.

Once the reanalysis yields a contrastive emblem of personhood – linked to role designations like 'modern' vs. 'conservative' – persons of diverse social categories who align themselves with the project of modernity can now re-formulate their public personae through the use of mixed, erstwhile impure, speech patterns. Thus, as we have seen many times before, judgments of acceptability (and, more narrowly, of 'grammaticality') are by no means extractable from the living process of grouping and re-grouping in which selves and others become recognizable to each other. Although positional intuitions about this process may exhibit a variable grasp of it, or may exhibit a keener, more entrenched grasp of ideals of acceptability than of the processes of enregisterment through which they come to hand, acts of taking social 'positions' can themselves become important social facts in their own right, especially when they function as inhabitable stances or statuses in which persons acquire stakes. Thus social asymmetries and contrasts at the level of cognitive facts (viz. intuitions about speech acceptability) are readily converted into differentiable 'positions' at the level of social facts. The social contrasts may remain latent in implicit habits of action and response, or become explicitly recognized as emblems of named social groups, or remain variably centered between these extremes for distinct sub-populations, not becoming vivid as beliefs and self-images for most persons until (or unless) a more institutionally centered and elaborated framework of metasemiotic stereotypes hails or summons a particular category of persons to the position of a vanguard, the upholder of a new norm, by treating their intuitions and ideals as models for others.

8

NORM AND TROPE IN
KINSHIP BEHAVIOR

8.0 Introduction

In this chapter I outline a reflexive approach to the study of kinship relations. As in previous chapters, the approach sketched here differentiates a reflexive model of semiotic activity from the actual activities that the model organizes and enables for those acquainted with it. Many of the features of semiotic activity discussed in previous chapters – the interanimation of linguistic and non-linguistic signs, the enregisterment of models of action, their 'normalization' for certain practices and contexts of action, the tropic manipulation of norms in behavior – play a critical role in the picture of kinship developed here. A general implication of this approach is that many traditional assumptions regarding kinship – for instance, that every culture has uniformly shared concepts of kinship, or that the comparative study of kinship requires a universal concept of kinship – are shown to be fundamental mistakes that a theory of kinship must move beyond. Debates about 'concepts' of kinship are debates about reflexive models of kinship behavior. We have already seen in previous chapters that models of behavior become relevant to the actual conduct of those acquainted with them only under conditions where text-level indexicality imposes some further structure on acts of their performance and construal. This issue has important consequences for the comparative study of kinship. I argue in this chapter that models of kinship behavior vary by social domain (practices, groups, institutional frameworks) *within* each society; that the actual behavior of individuals who share a given model as a norm does not always conform to the norm that they share; that norms constrain behavior only insofar as they are effective as models of appropriate conduct; that acquaintance with norms also makes possible effective forms of tropic improvisation; and that talk of 'sharedness' generally misrecognizes the fractional congruence of models of behavior for the *identity* of models, or, worse, for the identity of *actual* forms of conduct. The comparative study of kinship cannot take models of kinship as its sole object of study nor presume that any single concept of kinship (and, therefore, any putatively 'universal concept' of kinship, i.e., a model supposed to underlie all culture-specific models) could, in principle, suffice as an explanation of kinship behavior even in any *one* – let alone in *every* – society. For given the possibility of tropic variation, and in a manner analogous to the case of deference behaviors (7.7), any given model of kinship makes intelligible a much larger range of kinship behaviors than what the reflexive model, taken by itself, implies; and some among the tropes made intelligible by the model are themselves normalized as alternative models society-internally. The comparative task, rather, is to understand the processes through which such models are formulated, invoked, improvised upon, and reformulated in social practices within each society; to understand that insofar as acts guided by divergent models are mutually intelligible, variant models are fractionally congruent to one another (e.g., have common presuppositions), thus implying thresholds of unity beneath degrees of variance; and to learn to see that from the fact of their fractional *non*-congruence a large number of sociopolitical consequences follow for social actors who attempt, and sometimes manage, to differentiate themselves (whether as individuals, groups, or institutions) from each other, or find themselves differentiated willy-nilly by processes that re-valorize the behaviors by which they live. A reflexive approach also makes clear that attempts to formulate a 'concept' of kinship by reducing kinship to some specific domain involved in kinship – such as biology or genealogy, to name the usual suspects – cannot possibly succeed; or, rather, cannot succeed without ignoring forms of kinship behavior that are highly principled and cross-culturally common, but whose meaningfulness, ubiquity, and principled character all become inexplicable on any reductionist account.

8.1 From kinship systems to kinship behavior

The study of kinship has long been a major topic – at one time, *the* central topic – in the anthropological study of social relations. From the earliest disciplinary beginnings of anthropology the idiom of kinship has served as a descriptive and analytic framework for characterizing many regularities of meaningful social behavior, including patterns of marriage, co-residence, inheritance, affiliation, and aspects of religious, economic and political activity. The relevance of kinship to such diverse domains of social life is traditionally characterized by invoking an underlying explanatory construct, called a **kinship system**, said to exist in every society. Since the construct is meant to account for many types of behavior, it is rather more abstract than any of the behaviors it explains. On the traditional view, a kinship system is taken to be a genealogical foundation underlying patterns of behavior in diverse spheres of social life, and treated as a discrete, internally structured, unifying framework for studying them.

This conception has faltered in recent years. Today, most anthropologists regard traditional claims about kinship systems to be rather overblown. Some doubt the usefulness of analyzing kinship relations as closed formal systems isolable from the rest of social life, or the plausibility of appeals to shared mental models in explaining how they work, or the view that kinship relations are reducible to genealogical relations. These doubts, which often cluster together, take issue with traditional assumptions regarding the nature of kinship systems – their bounded systematicity, their mentalistic character, their genealogical basis – once held to be unproblematic in kinship studies. The net effect, in any case, is that an earlier consensus regarding the foundational character of kinship systems has died out.

There are good reasons for these doubts. A kinship 'system' is an ontologization of – a model of social reality projected from – highly selected features of language structure and use. The central empirical fact on which all such models depend is the existence of a particular class of lexemes, **kinship terms**, or **kinterms**, found in all human languages. Claims about kinship systems have long relied on the assumption that regularities of kinterm structure and use can be mapped onto, and thus help explain, diverse regularities of human behavior. The reason that the ontological projection is unstable – and its systematicity doubtful – is that traditional views about kinship systems are based on highly *selected* data of kinterm usage and, more poignantly, on a very limited conception of the role of language in human affairs.

The purpose of this chapter is to propose an approach to the study of kinship relations that focuses on the activities through which they are performed and construed. I argue that the range of kinship relations is much larger than the traditional 'kinship systems' approach has recognized, and that neither the genealogical reduction nor a mentalistic approach are particularly useful in understanding it. The difficulty with a 'mental models' approach is that mental models become socially consequential (i.e., have interpersonal effects) only if they are embodied in publicly perceivable semiotic behaviors; a better analysis of how kinship behaviors are performed and construed in context reveals that much of the complexity of kinship relations derives not from disembodied ideas in the head but from models of social relationship inferable from text-in-context relations among perceivable signs.

The difficulty with the genealogical reduction is that kinship terms are frequently used to express relations of fictive or metaphoric kinship that contradict known genealogical facts. I discuss several types of 'tropic' uses of kinterms in this chapter. Simply put, **a tropic use of a kinterm** is an entextualized act in which the semiotic sketch of social relations implemented through the use of a kinterm is non-congruent with a contextual model of social relations independently readable as holding between participants. Such tropes can also become widely recognized or enregistered as acts appropriate to certain contexts and, thus, themselves acquire the status of **normalized models**; and these, in turn, can iteratively be troped upon by those acquainted with them. A fuller analysis of this dialectic – of processes that normalize tropes, and acts that trope upon norms – reveals that kinterms mark social relations in highly principled ways in social life, even though the notion of a 'kinship system' obscures what is principled or systematic about them.

We have seen in previous chapters that this dialectic of norm and trope is central to all social uses of language. Consider the case of pronominal tropes discussed in Chapter 6. Since the work of Brown and Gilman (1960), a large cross-linguistic literature has emerged, which demonstrates that pronominal tropes of various kinds can be normalized in social interaction to yield specialized registers of politeness in languages of the world. We saw in Chapter 6 that many features of register models are mediated by reflexive processes; for instance, that text-patterns that implement denotationally incorrect reference (plural for singular, third person for addressee, etc.) are reflexively reanalyzed as stereotypically polite and interactionally appropriate under certain conditions (when interactant has higher status, when the setting is formal, etc.); that anyone acquainted with the norm of appropriateness can use it to enact interpersonal tropes that indexically reconstitute features of the social occasion of speaking (e.g., treating a stranger as an intimate, a child as an adult, a non-kin as kin) and thereby constitute a space of analogies between contextually presupposed and discursively entailed figures (6.4); that every such register model has a social domain and a historical duration, both of which depend on reflexive processes of transmission, institutionalization, and reanalysis; that when speakers are aware that more than one model of deference to others exists society-internally, contrasts among models are reanalyzed as higher-order indexicals of speaker type, constituting differential emblems of speaker's character, persona or social position (class, gender, rank, refinement, etc.).

The case of kinterm-based tropes is broadly analogous. Yet there are important differences too. Kinterms are common nouns, not deictic expressions; they do not inherently index speech participants and therefore do not mark social relations in the same way (8.3). Yet, at the same time, and precisely because they are common nouns, kinterms can be used metasemiotically to classify (and, more specifically, to articulate normative standards and laws regarding) a range of *other* types of behaviors (including non-linguistic behaviors), thus incorporating them into the domain of kinship. Although this domain is traditionally viewed as the notional domain of 'kinship' (or worse, of 'kinship concepts') it is only empirically investigable through the study of (what I call) kinship behavior.

By **kinship behavior** I mean behaviors *performed* through the use of kinterms or behaviors *construed* through the use of kinterms. Both cases involve 'uses' of kinterms and thus constitute a semiotically unified domain. And, yet, these two varieties of kinship behavior may be phenomenally quite distinct. A typical example of the first kind is a case where a kinterm occurs in an utterance; here the use of a kinterm is a discursive act that formulates a sketch of social relations that depends on the utterance of the kinterm. In behaviors of the second kind kinterms need not occur in acts that performatively establish kinship relations; but they do occur in other practices within the culture that seek metasemiotically to construe such acts. Although kinship behaviors of this kind may be non-linguistic, and phenomenally quite various (e.g., gift giving, divisions of household labor, patterns of inheritance, land ownership, etc.), their status as kinship behaviors derives from the fact that they are construed through discourses of kinship, that is, are metasemiotically typified through the use of kinterms.[1] Thus kinship behavior in my sense includes cases where a kinterm is deployed as a sign-token in interaction, as well as cases in which a kinterm is employed as a metasign grouping together a range of diverse behaviors, including behaviors in which the utterance of a kinterm plays no part. I argue that, despite the fact that kinship behavior is unified by a semiotic criterion (and hence becomes empirically investigable), kinship behavior neither implies a rigid social ontology, nor is necessarily foundational for other types of behavior. In fact the only evidence for isolating it as a distinct realm of social relations is the existence of kinterms and their semiotic and metasemiotic uses.

The demise of an anthropology of 'kinship systems' – sometimes eponymously and confusingly called 'the demise of kinship' (Stone 2004) – is commonly linked to David Schneider's (1984) critique of the assumption that all cultures conceptualize kinship in genealogical terms. The author of a recent survey observes: 'As a result of Schneider's critique, we are left with the following problem: we either have to abandon the assumption that kinship as a system of genealogical relations arising out of procreative activities is a cultural universal, or adopt a wider definition of kinship than a system of relations deriving from the engendering and bearing of children' (Holy 1996: 165). Both proposals present inherent difficulties. The difficulty with the first – with the idea that genealogical kinship is *not* a cultural universal – is that it amounts to a negative proposal; it leaves open the question of how regularities of kinship behavior are to be characterized, and what a comparative study of kinship might then look like. The difficulty with the second is that it seeks a wider *notional* definition of kinship but faces difficulty in specifying the boundaries of this wider concept. Writers who pursue this possibility have proposed, for instance, that the concept of genealogical connection be replaced with the more inclusive concept of 'relatedness' (Carsten 2004, 2000). But the concept of 'relatedness' has no empirical boundaries. All forms of social interaction yield 'relatedness' as a gradient effect; the concept provides no way of distinguishing the particularities of kinship from the generality that meaningful interaction creates various forms of social relatedness among persons.

My purpose here is not to pursue either of these possibilities but to restate the problem. With respect to the first dilemma, I show that a comparative approach to kinship does not require a single universal 'concept' of kinship, only a way of studying reflexive processes through which any given model of kinship can be performed and construed (whether canonically or in improvised variations). And with respect to the second, I propose that the study of kinship is not the study of notional 'relatedness' (whatever that might mean) but the study of kinship behavior in the sense just defined. To make this point explicit I return to Carsten's data towards the end of this chapter, and show that the sorts of cases she describes as examples of 'relatedness' can be understood better in terms of the reflexive approach to kinship behavior I propose here, without getting into problems of how to define the boundaries of 'relatedness' or, indeed, of any other notional construct of this type.

I begin with a critical review of the semiotic assumptions implicit in the genealogical conception of kinship (8.2). I argue that even in cases where kinship behavior consists of the use of language (and, more specifically, of kinterms) the sign-vehicles that express kinship relations are not lexical items (such as kinterms) alone but multi-modal sign-configurations in which kinterms occur as text fragments (8.3). This text-centric approach also clarifies what is meant by 'metaphoric' and 'literal' kinship behaviors, and why the former are cross-linguistically so common. I discuss examples from a number of languages (8.4). I then discuss processes whereby kinship behaviors are linked to norms and standards, and issues of thresholds of normativity involving variants (8.5). Although variant models sometimes take the form of occasion-specific and contingent tropes, tropic variants may themselves be treated as routine or 'normal' by different sub-groups within a society. I discuss a number of cases where the existence of variant kinship norms is itself construed society-internally as a higher-order index of *other* facts about persons (class membership, urban vs. rural affiliation, modern vs. traditional values), that is, is reflexively reanalyzed as emblematic of notionally distinct domains of social organization (8.6). I then turn to a discussion of how a reflexive approach allows us to identify and construe forms of non-linguistic kinship behaviors (8.7). In the final section of this chapter I suggest how the type of reflexive reasoning I employ for the domain of 'kinship' can be generalized and applied to any other notional domain, such as 'modernity,' 'class,' and so on.

Now, to the issues at hand. To say that kinterms mark *any* social relations at all is to make a semiotic claim, one that treats kinterms as signs of something else. There is a simple semiotic theory implicit in the traditional view that kinterms encode genealogical relations. I begin by considering the limitations of this view before proposing alternatives to it.

8.2 Lexicalism, codes, and the genealogical reduction

The view that kinterms encode genealogical relations rests on three assumptions about the semiotic status of kinterms. The first assumption is that the sign-vehicles that mark relations of kinship are lexical items; second, that the 'standing-for' relationship between sign and object is usefully described by the metaphor of 'code'; and third, that the type of relations marked by kinterms are necessarily genealogical relations.

The intuition that kinterms comprise a lexical code for social relations derives from their structural sense properties (2.3). Kinterms are lexico-grammatical units of a language, semantically two-place predicates, which denote a relation between two roles; the set of kinterms in a language formulate a space of inter-relationships by virtue of their sense relations to each other. Thus the kinterm *mother* denotes an individual, y, who bears a kinrelation to another, x, i.e., mother (x, y). The relation has a semantic inverse, which may also be lexicalized as a simple kinterm, i.e., mother (x, y) → child (y, x). If the inverse is not lexicalized in the language, it can be characterized as a semantic type through the use of algebraic and logical notation; if the kinterm is not a simple expression (e.g., *great-great-grand-mother*) it can be decomposed into simpler units through the same notation. By virtue of these properties kinterms and logical kintypes can be used to locate denotata in a grid of logico-semantic relationships. A genealogical grid becomes a syntagmatic environment for specifying arbitrarily complex kinrelations. All of these features of kinterms – that they are lexically relational, that they comprise a semantic space closed under inversion, that their structural sense is compositional – have tended to imply to many writers that repertoires of kinterms comprise a denotational system relatively autonomous of contextual facts of usage.[2]

Yet taken by themselves the lexical semantics of kinterms also suggest a highly misleading view of how kinterms refer to anything at all. The sheer transparency or ease of reportability of facts of lexical sense obscures the critical role played by co-textual indexicals in anchoring kinterm reference to particular social dyads. Indeed, the relationship denoted by a kinterm can be mapped onto a specific social dyad – i.e., be understood as a relation between *particular* individuals – only if the use of the kinterm token is accompanied by indexical forms which provide directions for finding the referent in relation to the event of speaking. For example, in the case of third-person reference, accompanying deictic expressions occur as modifiers to the kinterm (e.g., *my* mother, *her* mother, *John's* mother, *someone's* mother), formulating directions on how to locate the referent of the expression with varying degrees of deictic selectivity (1.4). These considerations draw our attention back to several issues discussed earlier regarding the social-interpersonal character of acts of referring: that acts of referring are typically mediated not by isolable words but by text configurations of which words are fragments (2.1); that they involve co-textual indexical cues which formulate a sketch of referents for interactants, upon which and through which interactants take various stances on referents vis-à-vis each other (2.2); and that a sketch of interpersonal roles and relationships is invariably mediated by referring acts over stretches of interactional text, whether such acts be sense-canonical (or 'literal') or involve a type of text-in-context non-congruence that is effective as an interpersonal trope.

If we ignore co-textual indexical formulations of referent and focus only on matters of lexical sense, it becomes easier to suppose that kinship terms comprise a semantic code – a system of logically structured lexical primes – for characterizing and classifying social relations that are independent of acts of referring, and of the historical process of having, maintaining, and reformulating social relations mediated by any sequence of such acts. The code metaphor suggests that from the semantic space of kinterm denotation we can reconstruct a space of social relations which, once identified from these lexical labels, can be shown to have some independent organization. Thus, lexical structure encodes social structure. Yet the question of whether such social structure is best characterized in terms of biological facts of procreation and parturition, or modes of genealogical reckoning, or land ownership and other economic relations, or through some combination of these and other factors has remained controversial until today. Such controversies are ultimately unresolvable since all code-based views of kinterms – and independently of whether they favor biological or genealogical reductionism – share a common problem.

Any code-based view of kinterms runs into intractable difficulties with indexically creative uses of language, the capacity of certain genres of language use performatively to create kinrelations among persons. Consider for example the classic arguments by W. H. R. Rivers against the reducibility of kinship to biological facts of consanguinity.

(1) Among ourselves such a relationship as that which exists between parent and child, or between brother and sister, can also come into existence by social conventions such as adoption (q.v.), but among many peoples this formation of relationships by social processes may be the habitual practice. A consanguineous relationship may count for little or nothing unless it has been ratified by some kind of social process, or a social process may result in the formation of a

relationship between persons wholly devoid of any consanguineous tie. Thus in the Banks Islands in Melanesia the relationship of parent does not come into existence by the facts of procreation and parturition, but it is such acts as the payment of the midwife, the first feeding of the child, or the planting of a tree on the occasion of a birth that determine who are to be the parents of the child for all social purposes. Similarly, among a polyandrous people like the Todas, it may be *the performance of a ceremony* during pregnancy that determines which of the husbands of the mother is to be regarded for all social purposes as the father of the child. Indeed, the fact of fatherhood is so strictly determined by this ceremony that a male who performs it becomes the 'father' of the child even if he be only a few years of age or have never seen the mother before he is called upon to take part in the ceremony. Kinship cannot be determined and defined by consanguinity even among ourselves, still less among other peoples.

(Rivers 1915: 700; emphasis added)

Rivers is observing here that certain acts of language use involving kinterms have a causal relationship to other acts of kinterm usage. He argues that the conditions on *the appropriate use of a particular kinterm by one person for another* – such as calling someone one's father or mother – may be set by prior semiotic activity through which the kinship tie is performatively established. These observations point to the critical role of semiotic-chain processes (1.6) – the structure of linkage of semiotic events in time – in formulating criteria of appropriateness and correctness on acts of kinterm reference.

Rivers uses this argument to propose that the biological conception of kinship ought to be replaced by a genealogical conception. Yet the alternative he proposes is susceptible to the same difficulty, the problem of indexically creative usage.

Let us first consider what the alternative is. Rivers argues that criteria on the correct use of kinterms within a society are provided by genealogical metadiscourses about kinship terms. One type of kinterm behavior – the use of kinterms in pedigrees – is now treated as a regimenting framework for all other types of kinterm behavior:

(2) Nearly all, if not all, peoples of the world preserve, either in writing or in their memories, a record of those with whom they are related by consanguinity or by those social conventions which, as we have seen, serve the same social purpose. Among many peoples, and especially those of rude culture, the knowledge of relationship thus genealogically determined is far more extensive than among ourselves. Pedigrees preserved in the memories of a rude tribe of cannibals may rival, if not surpass, anything which even the most enthusiastic genealogist is capable of carrying in his mind. Among such peoples it is the facts recorded in the pedigree of a person that largely determine his use of terms of relationship and regulate *all* the social functions which the terms connote.

(Rivers 1915: 700; emphasis added)

The pedigree is a genre of indigenous discourse about kinship which is familiar to Rivers from aristocratic idioms for reckoning social distinction in English society. And the genealogy is a quasi-scientific reconstruction of facts of kinrelation based on analyzing many pedigrees for internal consistency and relative completeness. Pedigrees and genealogies make kinship behaviors extractable from the events and processes in which they are experienced. The pedigree is a genre of ethnometapragmatic discourse that links genealogical facts to proper names, thus anchoring speech-event dependent varieties of deictic kin reference (e.g., 'my/our/his/your father ...') to reference by means of relatively event independent referring expressions ('... is Tom Jones'). A pedigree thus appears to formulate normative denotational criteria on the correctness of many situated acts of kinterm reference. Yet Rivers' assertion that such norms 'regulate *all* the social functions' of kinterms is too strong a claim, one which assumes that all the social functions of kinterm usage depend on acts of genealogically correct reference. Rivers is aware that this assumption is *prima facie* incorrect, since in all human societies kinterms are also used metaphorically, in direct contradiction of known genealogical facts. Hence the reduction of kinship to genealogy famously proposed by Rivers faces the awkward problem of requiring the systematic exclusion of metaphoric usage from the study of kinship so constituted.

(3) The genealogical mode, therefore, is that which furnishes the most exact and convenient method of defining kinship. Kinship may be defined as relationship which can be determined and described by means of genealogies ... The definition of kinship as genealogical relationship will also exclude the metaphorical sense in which terms of relationship are often used by peoples at all stages of culture.

(Rivers 1915: 700–701)

The genealogical model moves away from biological facts of procreation and parturition to a conception of kinship rooted in cultural belief. The model treats culturally reportable facts of kinrelation – such as those described in pedigrees – as the social facts that kinterms encode.

But the problem has been shunted aside, not solved. The difficulties caused by metaphor for a genealogical conception of kinship are entirely parallel to the difficulties posed by adoption for the biological view of kinship: just as events of performative nomination (e.g., adoption) constitute social ties which contravene facts of biology, the metaphoric uses of kinterms performatively formulate interpersonal relations inconsistent with known genealogical facts. In both cases, it is the indexically creative uses of language – matters of performativity and metaphor – that constitute the problem.

In the next section I show that in order to move beyond these problems we need to move beyond lexicalism in two directions: towards a better understanding of the role of textuality in shaping acts of successful kinterm reference, and of the role of metapragmatic standards and ideologies in shaping norms of correct usage.

But first a word on exclusions. We have already seen that the attempt to reduce kinship to genealogy requires the exclusion of metaphoric usage from theoretical consideration. The reason for the exclusion is very simple: acts of metaphoric kinterm reference are by definition inconsistent with genealogical facts and must be excluded if the genealogical reduction is to go through. More surprising, however, is the relative lack of attention given in this tradition to the use of kinterms to refer to speech participants, such as addressee. This is surprising since if kinterms do mark social relations between individuals they do so most concretely when the persons so related are co-present, as in cases of address. Yet models of kinship that seek to reduce kinship to genealogy have historically accorded centrality to acts of third-person kinterm usage in theorizing the phenomena of kinship, treating acts of kinterm address – the so-called 'vocative' use – as peripheral or secondary in formulating the theory itself.

The genealogical model thus conceives of kinterms in a very narrow way. The model treats the lexical sense of kinterms to be the property criterial to the marking of social relations, and genealogical relations to be the only kinds of relations marked. The model is also incomplete since it requires the exclusion of metaphoric usage. Finally, the model gives insufficient attention to the address use of kinterms in formulating its theoretical claims.

I turn now to a discussion of how we may overcome these limitations. I begin with a discussion of the vocative use of kinterms, then turn to matters of so-called metaphoric usage. Throughout, I show that the construal of kinterm usage depends on indexical cues that *accompany* kinterm-tokens in discourse and, hence, that a lexeme-centered focus on acts of kinterm usage cannot account for how social relations are established through these acts.

8.3 From kinship terms to text-patterns

In anthropological discussions of kinship, a distinction is traditionally drawn between the 'referential' or third person use of a kinterm and its 'vocative' use. Although the distinctions between these two types of usage is important, the terminological opposition between the 'referential' and the 'vocative' use – and, especially, the mutual exclusivity it implies – is entirely misleading. The vocative use is simply a special kind of referring use. It is a usage where *the kinterm refers to addressee*. The act aligns effects on the functional planes of semantic denotation (referent is kin) and speech-event indexicality (referent is addressee). But which feature of the act does so?

Unlike second person pronouns, kinterms are neither inherently speech-event indexicals nor specifically addressee-referring forms. The use of the kinterm to refer to addressee requires a distinctive treatment of the kinterm whereby deictic reference to addressee is established by co-occurring indexical cues. Hence it is not the kinterm lexeme alone but a text-pattern containing the lexeme that signals reference to addressee. The types of text-patterns that achieve this effect generally fall into a few well-known types. In some languages a marker of vocative case occurs as an affix to the kinterm stem, e.g., Sanskrit *pita-r* 'father!', a construction where the word stem denoting the genealogical relation (*pitā-*) is formally segmentable from the vocative suffix indexically referring to addresse (*-r*). In other cases a change in lexical shape marks deictic anchoring of reference to addressee, yielding contrasts where one lexical shape may routinely be understood as an address term (e.g., English *ma!*),[3] and other lexical shapes (e.g., *mother*), while usable for address, are not specifically so understood. A third pattern involves the syntactic and prosodic isolation of the kinterm from co-occurring forms, yielding a more configurative pattern of vocative case marking; here, an addressee-referring construal obtains for any lexeme that occurs in this pattern (*Mother/mom/ma, are you ready?*) and contrasts with a third person construal of the lexeme in other patterns. Finally, the kinterm token is often embedded in a sequence of kinesic cues (e.g., eye-gaze, bodily orientation) so that, in the general case, reference to addressee is achieved by a pattern of co-occurring indexical signs, a multi-modal text containing both linguistic and non-linguistic indices.

In considering any such use, the structural sense of the kinterm lexeme must therefore be distinguished analytically from the co-textual cues which identify the referent in the instance. Lexically, kinterms are two-place predicates,[4] which specify a relation between a denoted kin and an origo or zero-point of reckoning, traditionally called 'ego' in kinship studies. Thus the kinterm has the semantic structure KIN (x, y), where the x is the origo of reckoning and y is the referent, viz., KIN (x_{origo}, $y_{referent}$). In the vocative or addressee-referring use, we have a specific alignment of denotational and interactional variables (cued co-textually by the vocative construction) whereby referent is understood as addressee and the origo ordinarily as speaker, viz., KIN ($speaker_{origo}$, $addressee_{referent}$). This case is shown in Table 8.1 (a).

Once we attend to the problem of indexical anchoring of reference it is evident that the so-called 'third person use' – which excludes reference to speech act participants (SAP), i.e., speaker or addressee – also involves an alignment of denotational and interactional variables. The simplest co-textual pattern for unambiguous third person reference is the possessor-possessum construction, Table 8.1(b), a case where both origo and referent are explicitly denoted by noun phrases. In examples like '*John's/your/my . . . mother*,' the origo of reckoning is the possessor denoted by the adjunct-modifier (*John's, your, my*), and the referent (the mother) is formulated as

Table 8.1. *Common patterns of addressee-referring and third person kinterm usage*

Text pattern		Construal
Co-textual cues	Lexeme	
(a) *Vocative*	+ KINTERM (x_O, y_R) ⟶	KIN $(speaker_O, addressee_R)$
(b) *Possessor-possessum*	+ KINTERM (x_O, y_R) ⟶	KIN $(possessor_O, non\text{-}SAP_R)$

R = referent; O = origo of reference; SAP = speech-act participant (speaker or addressee)

neither speaker nor addressee. Calling this type of usage 'third person reference' is simply a way of saying that the value of referent is understood as a non-speech-participant, i.e., KIN $(possessor_{origo}, non\text{-}SAP_{referent})$.

Other types of alignments are also possible. We saw in the last chapter that Japanese kinterms have two lexical forms whose usage depends on whether or not the interlocutor is a kin (more precisely, whether an *uchi* 'insider' vs. *soto* 'outsider'; see Table 7.7ff.). Thus a speaker will use the term *chichi* in third person reference to father when speaking to a close kin, but will use the form *o-too-san* in referring to father before non-kin. Here the act of kinterm reference exhibits a more complex type of polyadic structure (cf. n. 5), formulating relations between speaker and referent in ways sensitive to the category of interlocutor in whose presence the act of referring occurs.

The general point is that the referential effects of kinterm usage always involve a particular alignment of denotational and interactional variables. The 'vocative use' and the 'third person use' of a kinterm are both names for cross-linguistically common entextualized patterns of this kind, the former aligning the kin referred to with addressee, the latter with a non-SAP. The general point may be summarized as follows:

Summary 8.1
In kinterm usage, facts of lexical sense become relevant to the construal of social relations between particular persons *only when* kinterm denotation is referentially anchored to a social dyad identified by co-occurring indexical signs.

That is, kinterm reference involves more than the use of kinterms. The act involves two semiotic components, namely a denotational sketch and an interactional sketch of referent. The lexical sense of a kinterm plays a critical role in the former, but the latter depends on varied co-textual cues. We saw in 2.1 that **denotational correctness** and **interactional success** are two different issues. A particular act of kinterm reference may be indexically anchored in the interaction in a successful and effective way even though the act is denotationally incorrect. That is, an expression like *John's sister* may be interactionally successful in communicating information about a particular, nameable woman, even though (as current interlocutors later discover) the woman in question happens not to be John's sister. Hence the conditions on the interactional success and denotational correctness of the act of kinterm reference are not the same. The usage is interactionally successful if accompanying indexical cues suffice in the instance to identify a particular referent. It is denotationally correct if the referent thus identified happens to be related to origo in a way consistent with the semantics of the kinterm.

The difference is critical to the tropic use of kinterms. In cases of tropic address, for example, the use of kinterm for addressee may be interactionally successful even though the person in addressee role is non-kin to speaker, or is a kin, but of a different genealogical type than the one semantically denoted by the kinterm. Patterns of denotationally incorrect kinterm reference are often culturally valued and even prescribed under particular interactional conditions. One reason that such acts are culturally valued is that denotationally incorrect reference implements interactional tropes of 'voicing' (i.e., are acts formulating reference to individuals from someone else's point of view) and thus yield interpersonal alignments having distinctive sociological effects of their own.

But how are such tropes construed? In the foregoing I have been using the term **cotextual indexical cues** to refer generically to co-occurring signs (whether linguistic or non-linguistic ones) that clarify relevant features of context (such as *who* the origo is, *who* the referent is) and thus formulate an independent sketch of the social encounter in which the kinterm occurs. The act of construing kinterm reference therefore has a text-in-context organization.

Summary 8.2

Acts of kinterm reference always occur under conditions where aspects of the social situation are already understood from accompanying semiotic activity. The semantics of the kinterm simply imposes a further semiotic sketch on the sense of social occasion established by co-textual indexical cues. The co-textual sketch may or may not be congruent with the one performed through the kinterm (see 1.4); correspondingly, the overall construal may suggest that the sketch performed through the kinterm token 'literally' fits its co-text, or effectively transforms it through an interactional trope.

One aspect of the social occasion indexically presupposed from the readable co(n)text is an emergent **model of role inhabitance**, namely a semiotically mediated sketch of who is speaking to whom – including an

Table 8.2. *Role inhabitance and referential gloss (English)*

	Text-pattern		Referential gloss
Role inhabitance	Utterance containing		
S A	kinterm		
(a) aunt child +	'............'	→	(a) '*your mother* told you not to do that'
(b) mother child			(b) '*I* told you not to do that'

'Mommy told you not to do that'

understanding of social relations between persons in roles speaker and addressee – by participants themselves (cf. Figures 3.2 and 3.3). For example, the referential interpretation of an utterance like 'Mommy told you not to do that' can vary by facts of role inhabitance as shown in Table 8.2. In both the cases shown, the word *mommy*, which is stereotypically used by a child, is used by someone who is not a child.

In case (a), where an aunt (or other caregiver) tells a child 'Mommy told you not to do that,' the utterance is construable as '*your mother* told you not to do that.' Here the act of reference to an absent parent is voiced from the perspective of the child addressed, i.e., KIN (addressee$_{\text{origo}}$, non-SAP$_{\text{referent}}$). But if, as in (b), the utterance is produced by a mother speaking to her child – a type of usage common in the register of 'motherese' – the utterance conveys the meaning '*I* (already) told you not to do that.' Here the origo is again the child addressed but the referent is the speaker, viz., KIN (addressee$_{\text{origo}}$, speaker$_{\text{referent}}$).

Observe however that in glossing such utterances as referential tropes we are not talking about the meaning of words, or even of sentences, but of the cumulative effects of text-patterns containing these utterances. For example, in Table 8.2(b), a particular pattern of role inhabitance, namely *that a mother is speaking to her child*, must be established independently of the utterance of the kinterm in order for the kinterm to be construed tropically as referring to self. Languages differ in the range of co-textual conditions (and hence in the settings or social occasions of use) in which such usages are treated as commonplace, readily intelligible forms of behavior.

In a language like Vietnamese, such tropes are not only ubiquitous in everyday usage but are permitted with a much wider range of participation frameworks than in English. For example, the Vietnamese sentence in Table 8.3, *mẹ đã mua cho bố cái mũ hôm qua rồi* 'Mother already bought the hat for father yesterday,' can be interpreted in one of seven different ways depending on co-textually mediated facts of role inhabitance.

Table 8.3. *Role inhabitance and referential gloss (Vietnamese)*

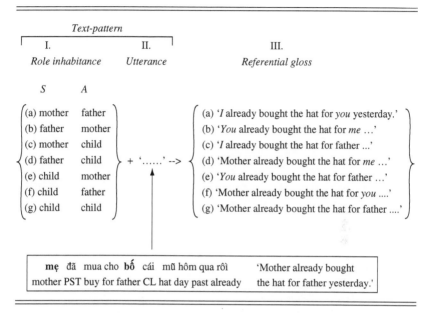

Source: (Luong 1990: 11–12)

The single utterance shown in Table 8.3 appears ambiguous because many pronominal glosses can evidently be given for the kinterms it contains. But what exactly is being glossed? The table shows that the use of pronouns (column III) to gloss the kinterms used (column II) is shaped by co-textual facts of role inhabitance (column I). We can see this by observing that the Vietnamese kinterms cannot be glossed by English pronouns in all cases. If the parents denoted in the utterance are speaking to each other, as in (a) and (b), the kinterms *mẹ* 'mother' and *bố* 'father' are co(n)textually understood as referring to speech participants; hence *both* may be glossed by pronouns in place of kinterms (column III, (a)–(b)). If a parent is speaking to a child, as in (c)–(d), a first person pronoun may be used to gloss a kinterm, but *only* the kinterm denoting the parent in speaker role. Similarly, if a child is speaking to a parent, as in (e)–(f), a second person pronoun may be used to gloss a kinterm, but only the kinterm denoting the parent addressed. Conversely, if two children are speaking about their parents (in their absence) to each other, as in (g), the kin referred to are understood as non-participants, and *neither* kinterm may be glossed with a participant pronoun.

It is very important to note that the referential glosses in Table 8.3 are *not glosses of the Vietnamese sentence alone* (since we have one sentence and seven glosses), but of effects projected by the utterance of a sentence-token in a readable surround. In each case the semantic content of the utterance plus contextually readable – or co-textual – facts of role inhabitance yield a (default) referential gloss as a *cumulative* result. The sign-structure that motivates the gloss is partly linguistic, partly non-linguistic. The glosses therefore represent construals of a textualized multi-modal sign-configuration, a text-pattern which consists not only of the utterance (column II) but also of the set of diverse semiotic cues (including visual cues) that identify the social persons in role speaker and addressee (column I) *independently* of the utterance of any kinterms.

Speech appears tropic or deviant when a larger text configuration motivates a construal for a text fragment that is not congruent with its generic (inherent, decontextualizable) semiotic values. For instance, in case (d) it is the contextually readable fact that the person speaking is the father of the person addressed which motivates the construal of the kinterm *bố* 'father' as 'me.' Notice that 'father' and 'me' are both possible glosses of *bố*. However, 'father' is the only gloss that can generically be given, that is, given independently of further contextual considerations; it is, in fact, the stereotypic denotation of the lexeme. The referential gloss 'me' is only possible in a case like (d), that is, a case where relevant co-textual cues motivate the identity of referent and speaker. It is precisely by relying on such cues that language users find tropes construable.[5]

The above examples illustrate for the case of kinterm usage a fact discussed at length elsewhere in this book: in general, it is not words but text-patterns (or sign-configurations) containing words that signal reference to individuals. Each of the seven text patterns in Table 8.3 has a determinate construal. It is only when our gaze shrinks to a text fragment (a sentence- or word-token) and loses sight of the information that language users themselves employ in construing such cases, that the appearance of ambiguity arises. On the other hand, once we recognize that language users construe acts of reference by relying on a richer structure of information than traditional linguistic and anthropological theory has recognized, we can see that the congruence vs. non-congruence of co-occurring signs provides a measure of the degree to which certain acts appear 'literal' and others usages, perceived as anomalous by one semiotic criterion or another, appear to constitute a space of tropes.[6]

8.4 Normalized tropes

The usages in (a)–(f) in Table 8.3 are denotationally anomalous in that they employ third person nouns in referring to speaker and addressee (for which first and second person pronouns are available, but not used here). At the same time, these tropes are culturally valued in acts of referring where interlocutors have kinrelations to each other. In this sense, the usages in (a)–(f) constitute a set of **normalized tropes**, usages that are denotationally anomalous but interactionally felicitous under certain conditions of role inhabitance (here, encounters between kin).

It is not that Vietnamese lacks pronouns. Rather, in acts of referring to co-present kin, pronouns are normatively avoided in Vietnamese (as in many Asian languages) and kinterms are normatively preferred. The use of pronouns, though possible, is interactionally marked. For example switching to pronouns is frequently a strategy for signaling disapprobation. In the case in (4), a north Vietnamese grandmother has been speaking to her grandchild using the kinterms *bà* 'grandmother' and *con* 'child' for self- and other-reference in preceding discourse. In the text-segment below, she switches to the personal pronouns *mày* 'thou/thee' and *tao* 'I/me'.

(4) (Luong 1990: 128–9)

> **tao** báo **mày** đi tìm cho **tao** cái kéo trong bếp mà **mày** còn ngôì đấy à?
> I tell you go find for me CL scissors in kitchen but you still sit there INT
> 'I have told you to look for a pair of scissors for me in the kitchen. Why
> are you still sitting there?'

The shift in denotational categories – from kinterms in preceding discourse to pronouns in the current segment – marks a temporary suspension of the invocation of kinrelations in acts of reference. This constitutes a recognizable shift in interactional stance, namely the suspension of affective/solidary relations between speaker and addressee maintained by the earlier pattern of kinrelational reference. In the case at hand, the speaker's shift to pronouns is a way of marking exasperation. In contrast, in the usages in Table 8.3, we see a systematic avoidance of pronominal use in favor of kinterm-based reference to speech participants. The general difference between these two types of patterns may be summarized, following Luong 1990, as follows:

Summary 8.3
Whereas reference to speech participants by pronouns denotes social persons by appeal to transient facts of interactional-role inhabitance, reference by means of kinterms anchors interactional positions to more perduring social frameworks by indexically invoking group-relative facts of kinrelationship.

The valorization of perduring social frameworks finds its ideological underpinnings in Confucian ideals of the social order, particularly the doctrine of 'name rectification.' Luong 1990 points out that according to this doctrine '... names or role terms should be appropriately used in

accordance with the order of the universe, and that a person should behave
in accordance with the "name" of his role, for example, as a *bo* (father),
con (son), *vua* (king), *toi* (subject)' (p. 241). What is at stake within this
ideological system is not merely a standard of interpersonal politeness but
an ideological framework that seeks to maintain 'the order of the [social]
universe' through certain discursive practices. The doctrine holds that if
speakers were actually to perform normalized tropes of the kind illustrated
in Table 8.3 the consistency of their usage over time 'would help to
reinforce this order through actors' conformity to the behavioral implications of these role terms' (p. 242). The metapragmatic construct 'reads'
these normalized tropes as ways of maintaining a system of stereotypic role
expectations (a.k.a 'the social order') over historical time.

It is very important to see that Confucian metasemiotic discourses
imbue the text-patterns in Table 8.3 with a range of stereotypic values
they do not themselves possess. They motivate them as object-signs of a
Confucian social order. This issue can be seen even more clearly once we
consider metasemiotic discourses that compete with the Confucian doctrine in seeking to 'read' tropes of kinterm address in entirely different
ways. I discuss some competing discourses in 8.7.

For now, let us return to the text-patterns in Table 8.3 and locate them in
relation to similar tropes in other languages. Since pronouns are available
for reference to speech participants in these cases the use of kinterms
formulates various interactional tropes through the act of referring.
A pervasive trope in the text-patterns in Table 8.3 is the **person trope**, namely
the use of a third person noun (the kinterm) for first and second person
reference. Indeed, in all cases other than (g), one or both kinterms are
construed as involving a person trope. The construal treats the use of a
kinterm as an act of **transposed reference**, a usage that voices reference
from a non-speaker origo, i.e., from the standpoint of someone other than
speaker. In case (c), for instance, the speaker uses the form 'mother' to
refer to herself in speaking to her child, thus voicing the act of reference
from the standpoint of the child. The father's self-reference in (d) is parallel
in voicing effect, i.e., 'for [your] father' = 'for me'. Moreover in both cases
the transposed origo of reference, the child, happens to be a participant in
the interaction.

But in cases (a) and (b) in Table 8.3, the transposed origo is not a speech
participant. Here, the usages recenter address to child-origo simply by
presupposing the existence of a child – someone *for whom* speaker and
addressee are mother and father – although no child is present as a speech
participant (as indicated in column I). Cases of transposed reference therefore differ in whether the indexically formulated zero-point of referential
reckoning is itself a speech participant. Let us consider this contrast in
more detail.

Table 8.4. *Address inversion in Japanese: referring to self as addressee would or should*

Role inhabitance		Utterance	Referential effects	
S	*A*	*kinterm used*	*referent*	*origo of reference*
(a) father	child	Otō-san 'father-HON'	speaker	addressee
(b) uncle	niece	Oji-san 'uncle-HON'	speaker	addressee
(c) grandfather	grandchild	Ojī-san 'grandfather-HON'	speaker	addressee
(d) grandmother	grandchild	Obā-san 'grandmother-HON'	speaker	addressee

Source: (Suzuki 1984)

Address inversion

A common type of transposed reference is the case of **transposition of origo to addressee**. In this case, the speaker employs a referring expression for self which the addressee would normally use in referring to speaker. This type of transposed reference is a very general kind of interactional trope, enactable through many kinds of utterance. The usage has been termed **address inversion** in the kinship literature since the act of reference by speaker is anchored to the standpoint of addressee rather than self, thus appearing to invert the origo of referential reckoning with respect to the interactional frame.

We have already seen examples of address inversion in English (Table 8.2, (b)) and in Vietnamese (Table 8.3, (c)–(d)). Let us now consider the Japanese cases in Table 8.4.

In all four cases the act of referring transposes origo of reference to addressee (last column), and the presence of the honorific suffix *-san* (middle column) makes the voicing structure quite explicit. In case (a), a father speaking to his child uses the kinterm *Otō-san* 'father (H)' to refer to self. Since deference to self is considered inappropriate in Japanese (as in other languages), the choice of *honorific* kinterm to refer to self makes it clear that the speaker is referring to self as the child-addressee would. Thus the referent is speaker and the origo of reference is addressee. Note that the centering of self-reference to addressee-origo is preserved not only at the level of lexeme denotation (i.e., it is the child addressed *for whom* speaker is 'father') but also at the level of deference indexicality (i.e., it is the child who would use the honorific *-san* to index deference to father). The other examples shown are exactly parallel in this regard; they differ in presupposed role configurations, however, thus illustrating something of the range of social dyads for which tropes of this type are normalized patterns of speaking.

An analogous pattern involves the use of titles. In traditional workplace settings, a junior employee will normatively address a senior colleague by using a title, e.g., *Sensei* 'Teacher,' *Oisha-san* 'Doctor', *Kachō* 'Section Chief' (and refer to self by last name); the senior colleague will, in turn, use the same title for self-reference (and pronoun or personal name for his junior colleague) thus employing address inversion as part of larger pattern that maintains the self's higher status. Thus kinship behavior in family contexts is likened to other types of behavior (here, behavior in the workplace) by the fact that the normalized trope of address inversion can be implemented through a range of object-signs (viz., kinterms *and* titles), and functions as a norm of appropriate conduct for a range of social dyads (viz., kin *and* colleagues). This is one reason why systems of social relations exhibited in kinship behavior cannot be hermetically sealed off from other types of social behavior, a point to which I return in S 8.4 below.

Recentered address

A more general type of transposition with kinterms is the trope of **recentering of origo** where the choice of kinterm transposes origo to some culturally appropriate zero-point other than speaker. Unlike cases of inversion, where the zero-point of reckoning is transposed to addressee (and the referent is understood as speaker), cases of recentered address are cases where the origo of reference is not a speech participant (and the referent is the addressee). Recentered address invokes as origo a kinposition specifically distinct from either interlocutor, thus performatively anchoring the current interaction to social positions external to it.

Consider the Bengali examples of recentered affinal address in Table 8.5. In cases (a)–(b), a husband addresses his wife's relatives using the forms that she would use for them. Since the wife is related to these individuals by consanguineal bonds the husband's usage treats consanguineal relations (between his wife and her kin) as a model for affinal relations (between himself and his in-laws).

In (c), the wife employs a similar consanguineal trope in addressing her husband's mother; she addresses her as *ma*, just as her husband would. The case in (d) illustrates a pattern of avoidance. In traditional families the wife has strict avoidance relations with husband's father and elder brother; she does not normatively address them at all. Since consanguineal tropes are not symmetric along the axis of gender (cf. (a)–(b) vs. (c)–(e)), differences in the range of affines to which they apply is itself an index of speaker gender.

The case in (e) is a more laminated trope. In addressing husband's sister or younger brother (particularly if they are senior in age to her) the forms employed by the wife are descriptive appellations that anchor denotation

Table 8.5. *Recentered affinal address (Bengali): addressing others as someone else would*

Role inhabitance		Utterance	Referential effects	
S	*A*	*kinterm used*	*referent*	*origo of reference*
(a) H	WF/WM	baba 'father'/ma 'mother'	addressee	speaker's spouse
(b) H	WB/WZ	dada 'elder brother'/didi 'elder sister'	addressee	speaker's spouse
(c) W	HM	ma 'mother'	addressee	speaker's spouse
(d) W	HF/HeB	–	–	–
(e) W	HyB/HZ	ṭhakur po/jhi 'grandpa's son/daughter'	addressee	speaker's child

Source: (Das 1968) The following standard symbols for kinrelations are used in this table and elsewhere: H = husband, W = wife, F = father, M = mother, B = brother, Z = sister, e = elder, y = younger, S = son, D = daughter. Symbol strings are read compositionally, e.g., FM = father's mother, FyBW = father's younger brother's wife.

Note: All four cases employ consanguineal terms for affinal address, and transpose origo to a kinposition other than speaker. Das' data indicate that the entire range of genealogical tropes in (a)–(e) occur normatively in 'traditional' or 'rural' Bengali usage, and that departures from the norm (e.g., deploying some or none) are indexical of various modern-urban identities.

to the standpoint of her child. Thus, in referring to her husband's younger brother as *ṭhakur po* 'grandpa's son,' or to husband's sister as *ṭhakur jhi* 'grandpa's daughter' a woman voices the act of referring from the standpoint of her child, the individual for whom these persons are indeed the son and daughter of a grandparent. However the woman's stance is also partially preserved as distinct from the child's. The actual kinterms that her child would use for these individuals are *kaka* 'uncle' and *pisi* 'aunt'. Since the use by a woman of these forms for same-generational affines would make her child-like, the woman employs denotationally equivalent descriptive appellations ('grandpa's son,' 'grandpa's daughter'). The usage centers origo to child at the level of denotational content but not at the level of lexical form. The partial centering to child origo highlights the fact that the speaker is a child-giver to the affinal group (and thus has status entitlements within the group) without rendering her childlike in relation to the affines addressed in the instance.

Although the kinterms actually used in cases of recentering denote kin relations different from actual relations between speakers and referents, it should be clear that actual relationships are known to all concerned and *such knowledge is one of the conditions of the construability of the trope.* The utterance formulates a framework of kin reckoning which is tropic in relation to its presupposed context (i.e., presupposed affinal bonds are tropically re-figured as consanguineal ones), whether by the act of

Table 8.6. *Address recentering in Japanese*

Role inhabitance		Utterance	Referential effects	
S	*A*	*kinterm used*	*referent*	*origo of reference*
(a) W	H	Otō-san 'father-HON'	addressee	speaker's son [= addressee's son]
(b) F	FF	Ojī-san 'grandfather-HON'	addressee	speaker's son [= addressee's grandson]
(c) M	S	Onī-chan 'big brother-DIM'	addressee	speaker's youngest son [= addressee's younger brother]

Source: (Suzuki 1984)

inhabiting the standpoint of a spouse (a kin category having consanguineal links to the affine addressed) or by invoking entitlements deriving from having borne a child (a kin category having consanguineal links to both the affine addressed and to speaker).

Recentered address occurs in Japanese as well though it involves a different norm of transposition: here the origo of reference is transposed not to an affine but to the juniormost kinposition within the family. In example (a) in Table 8.6 a wife addresses her husband as 'father,' thus centering reference with respect to their son. In (b) a speaker addresses his father as 'grandfather' by centering address to his son (addressee's grandson). In (c) a mother addresses her son as 'big brother' thus centering address to addressee's younger brother.

The norm of transposing origo to junior kinposition entails that the referent is raised to a kinposition higher than his/her actual relation to speaker along dimensions such as relative age and generation. Insofar as the usage performs both speaker-lowering and referent-raising the trope is understood as a trope of deference. This type of deference marking relies on the existence of status hierarchies within the family in performing tropes of relative status; it is therefore a type of deference quite distinct from the kind implemented by an honorific register of lexemes (Chapter 7). Moreover the two systems of deference marking can be realized in the kinterm in a formally segmentable way. Thus in the case of mother speaking to son in (c), where the addressee is of lower kin status than speaker, the trope of addressee-raising consists of the mother referring to her son as his younger brother would (i.e., as *Onī-* 'big brother') thus marking his higher status relative to a younger sibling; but by adding the diminutive *-chan*, which marks endearment rather than respect (and which contrasts with the honorific -*san*, the form actually appropriate when speaker is a younger sibling), the mother partially preserves a centering of stance to her own standpoint.

Both the pattern of recentering to junior kinposition and the use of diminutive suffixes which partially preserve centering to speaker origo are extended in Japanese to other person-referring forms as well. In modern-urban usage, the pattern extends to the use of the so-called first-person pronoun *boku* 'I'. Thus a parent may address a son as 'I':

(5) ... young couples in Japan these days often call their only son or their youngest son by the first-person pronoun *boku* 'I'. They sometimes even call him *boku-chan*, adding the diminutive suffix -*chan* as though *boku* were a given name. For example, a mother might say to her son, *Boku, hayaku irasshai*, lit., 'Me, come here quickly' or *Boku-chan kore hoshii n deshō*, lit. 'Me+dim. wants this, I suppose?' When she speaks in this way, she is thinking of the boy as he would be called if viewed from the position of the youngest member of the family, in this case the boy himself.

(Suzuki 1984: 146)

In this type of case, the origo of reference is transposed to the juniormost kinposition, which coincides with the referent himself (since he is the youngest or only child). The mother addresses the boy as he would refer to self (i.e., *boku* 'I'). However, the mother's stance is partially superimposed on the boy's since the diminutive -*chan* indexes the mother's affective stance towards her son. Thus cases of recentering may themselves involve subtle composite effects as before, such as the preservation of more than one speech-event origo, here the concurrent expression of addressee-origo reference (*boku*) and speaker-origo intimacy (-*chan*) towards addressee/referent.

Let us now consider cases of kinterm address where current interlocutors are known to have no kinrelations to each other.

Metaphoric and ritual kinship

I use the term **metaphoric kinship** to describe cases where the persons performatively related to each other through the use of kinterms are known to be non-kin. The term **fictive kinship** is also used to describe this type of case, though the latter term is also used more inclusively to cover tropes involving kin (such as cases of inversion and recentering). In my usage, metaphoric kinship is fictive kinship among non-kin, and kinship inversion and recentering are types of fictive kinship among persons who are kin but not of the type denoted by the kinterm.

Acts of establishing metaphoric kinship occur in every known society though there are important cross-cultural differences in their ubiquity, normalization, and institutionalization, as well as in the range of kinterms for which, and in the settings in which, such usages are judged appropriate. Cases of this kind differ from mistakes or confusions about genealogical ties in the following way: in cases of metaphoric kinterm usage, the lack of genealogical relations between origo and referent is contextually known and acknowledged by all concerned at the time of utterance. Such usages reset the social parameters of the interaction by tropically likening relations between non-kin to those between kin. Acts establishing metaphoric kinship, or fictive kinship among non-kin, are quite diverse in kind, varying from the occasional use of terms like *father* to address an elderly stranger encountered on the street, to more institution-specific cases, as in the use of the same term for a priest.

In some cases, particular forms of kinterm address to non-kin are relatively routinized as patterns of **ritual kinship**, which are expressed by both linguistic and non-linguistic kinship behaviors. In these cases particular individuals who are genealogical non-kin are treated as ritual kin; the ritual kin may be specific, known individuals linked to ego through a ceremonial tie, or an open class of persons linked to ego in other ways, such as co-residence in a locale. In the case of the ritual kinship complex called *Compadrazgo* in Latin America, some type of ceremonial 'baptismal' event is generally necessary as a causal pre-requisite on the establishment of the ritual tie; the tie connects specific, known individuals all of whom are generally co-present at the baptismal event. Once effectively established, the ritual tie connects persons in three social positions (the child, the child's parents, a sponsor or sponsors who act as co-parents) to each other, and thus involves three sets of social relations, each normatively linked to distinct types of rights and duties, some reciprocal, some not.

A more generalized pattern occurs in Bengali village society, a case where virtually every co-resident may have ritual kinrelations to every other (e.g., a father's friend addressed as *uncle*, a friend's daughter as *neice*). Frequently a distinctive metapragmatic terminology (e.g., the Bengali term *gram samparke* 'by the relation in the village') is used to introduce ritual but not genealogical kin. In these cases persons are linked together by two kinds of social networks, one consisting of genealogical kinrelations, the other involving generalized but relatively routinized relations of ritual kinship, with membership in the latter networks involving some of the duties, rights and obligations accruing to membership in the former.

Summary of tropes discussed

The patterns of kinterm reference discussed so far are summarized in Table 8.7.

In all four cases the interactional effects listed in column III are intelligible only if the actual kinrelations (or lack thereof) between persons currently in role speaker and addressee (I) are independently known (i.e., are co-textually readable), and the characteristics of utterance (II) can be

Table 8.7. *Patterns of kinterm usage*

I. Co(n)textually readable role configuration	II. Utterance characteristics	III. Textualized interactional effect	IV. Type of address
(a) S & A non-kin	denotes kinrelation	likens non-kin to kin	metaphoric
(b) S & A kin	denotes a kinrelation other than that between S and A	transposes origo of reference to non-speaker	recentered
(c) S & A kin	denotes A's kinrelation to S	transposes KIN (x, y) relation to A-origo, S-referent	'inverted'; refers to self from A's standpoint
(d) S & A kin	denotes S's kinrelation to A	anchors KIN (x, y) relation to S-origo and A-referent	'literal'

evaluated in relation to these indexical presuppositions. The utterance-act indexically formulates a sketch of kinrelations superimposed upon co-textually readable facts and evaluated in relation to them. In case (a), the utterance denotes a kinrelation even though S and A are non-kin; the act metaphorically imposes a social relationship not otherwise holding between them, likening the two to kin. In (b), the act denotes a kinrelation other than speaker's manifest relation to referent/addressee, exhibiting recentered address. In (c), the relation is centered with addressee as zero-point of reckoning. In one obvious sense this is not a case of address at all: the referent is speaker not addressee. But the act of self-reference depends upon an implicit trope of voiced address since it uses precisely the form which interlocutor would use in addressing speaker.

The above considerations make clear that understanding *how* determinate social relations are actually marked by kinterms requires that we move beyond a lexeme-based perspective on language use (and the static conception of social reality it implies) to a consideration of dynamic, multi-modal patterns of semiotic activity involving both linguistic and non-linguistic signs. It will be evident that the choice and construal of a kinterm usage *always* depends on the readability of the co(n)text of utterance by interlocutors. Any particular use employs some semiotically readable and hence indexically presupposable fact of role inhabitance as the basis for an act of referring; the question of whether the act is literal or tropic depends on the congruence, or lack thereof, of the effects indexed by the utterance and the relations given independently of it. In the absence of such a perspective on usage we cannot distinguish the cases shown in Table 8.7 from each other.

The case of 'literal' address in (d) is the special case where the entailments of utterance are congruent with co-textually readable facts. The
traditional approach to this special case mistakes emergent facts of text-
level congruence for facts of lexemic 'coding.' Yet the so-called 'literal' use
is amenable to this simplification only because the entailments of the
utterance are congruent with independently given co-textual presuppositions. Hence the irony of the 'coding' view is that it misrecognizes the
congruence of co-occurring semiotic cues as a relationship of decontextualized denotation between lexemes and social 'reality' – sometimes
ontologized and reified under the name 'social structure' – and treats the
latter as an order of social relations existing independently of events of
semiosis even though it is only revealed through them. In contrast, in all
the other cases shown in Table 8.7 the effects projected by the utterance
are, by degrees, inconsistent with co-textually readable facts of role configuration so that features of the utterance reset the parameters of the
social occasion in systematic ways. Hence the reification readily decon-
structs itself: in any language in which selective attention to patterns of
'literal' kinterm reference persuades the analyst to take a reified view of
social relations (viewed as a 'structure,' or whatever term is used for this),
other patterns of entextualized performance can also be found that formulate social relations external to this reification.

Reflexive reanalysis

It is by no means the case that the various 'uses' I have identified in Table 8.7
exist as a static pickle-jar inventory of 'types' of action. Any of the patterns
in Table 8.7 can be reanalyzed reflexively in a variety of ways, whether
through combination with each other in hybrid forms of semiosis, or by
motivated analogy with other patterns of kinterm usage, or with the use of
other expressions, such as pronouns and titles.

For example, the repertoire of kinterms used for fictive address – cases
(a), (b) and (c) – can become expanded or narrowed in a variety of ways.
Here are some possibilities:

Summary 8.4
Patterns of reanalysis and analogical extension involving kinterm tropes:

- the metaphoric pattern may be superimposed on other fictive uses,
  yielding laminated tropes of 'metaphoric recentering' and 'metaphoric
  inversion'; see example (6) below
- a kinterm-based trope can come to serve as a model for (or be modeled
  on) the use of other expressions, such as pronouns (example (5) above),
  or titles (example (7) below)
- a pattern of fictive use may be analogically extended from acts of address
  to third-person reference (or vice versa)

The domain of kinship behavior exhibits functional leakage through motivated analogies and tropes to other systems of social relations (such as those mediated by the use of pronouns and titles). Kinship is therefore a domain of social relations that is empirically isolable as a distinct domain (by attending to the semiotic and metasemiotic uses of kinterms, as discussed earlier), but not one that is hermetically sealed off vis-à-vis other cultural domains, a point that becomes clear only if we understand the reflexive processes that mediate its existence. This point can be generalized to any cultural formation, a point to which I return in section 8.8.

Attention to reflexive processes also makes clear how behaviors involving kinterm usage may be analogically extended to, or be modeled on, behaviors expressed through other signs, as well as behaviors indexing relations among non-kin. A normalized kinship trope, once enregistered as appropriate to certain interactional conditions, can be reanalyzed in ways that alter its semiotic range (the range of object-signs that express it), its social range (the types of speaker or interlocutor indexed by it), and even its social domain; this point is merely an instance, in the specific case of kinship, of a set of issues pertaining to enregisterment in general, namely the dimensions of register organization and change (see especially Table 3.6ff.). Consider, for example, tropes of affinal avoidance. In the Bengali case discussed earlier (Table 8.5, (d)), a woman has avoidance relationships with certain male in-laws. Such patterns of kinterm-based avoidance may be extended to, or be modeled on, affinal avoidance behaviors expressed through more complex semiotic register formations, including ones whose object-signs include elaborate lexicogrammatical and kinesic repertoires, as in the case of Australian societies (Haviland 1979a, 1979b). Or, acts of avoidance involving specific categories of interlocutors (such as affines) may analogously motivate patterns of avoidance and respect towards other social categories of interlocutors (such as royalty); and may be differently institutionalized (i.e., involve variant models) in different social domains and practices within a single society, as in the case of Zulu *Hlonipha* register (Irvine 1998, Irvine and Gal 2000).

In some cases a series of tropic extensions and reanalyses result in the establishment of an institutionalized form of social relations having many local variants whose interconnectedness only becomes clear if we consider the historical processes that connects them to each other. For instance, the *Compadrazgo* ritual complex in Latin America is historically linked to earlier traditions in Medieval European Catholicism by processes of circulation and reflexive reanalysis on a large sociohistorical scale, elements of which can be reconstructed as a historical series of kinship tropes variously normalized in European institutions of feudalism, property ownership, inheritance, clan affiliation, relations between serfs and kings during the late middle ages (Mintz and Wolf 1967), and later reanalyzed (in fact re-normalized) through the colonial encounter in Latin America in substantially transformed ways.

8.5 Renormalization and standards

Just as with normalized tropes, practices of so-called 'literal' reference (whether to addressee, speaker, or absent third parties) can also be institutionalized in a variety of ways. In the historical literature on kinship, acts of third person literal reference have been given pre-eminent attention (e.g., they pervade the data of pedigrees that are foundational for the genealogical approach). Yet the fact that such data constitute a very special type of kinterm usage – a type of ideologically normalized usage – is not itself theoretically grasped. Like other types of behaviors, acts of kinterm reference can become **standardized**, or linked to social standards, so that actual instances of referring must conform to specific criteria – whether these be criteria of biological, genealogical or classificatory kinship, or some others – and the fit between the act and the standard treated as a normative criterion of correct reference. Recognizing the special character of such cases has several consequences.

For one, we can now see that the entire debate about whether kinterms encode biological or genealogical facts is quite fruitless. It is not a debate about what kinterms 'really' mean. At its best, it is a debate about standards of correct reference. Neither biological nor genealogical criteria suffice to explain all interactionally successful uses of kinterms since acts of successful kinterm reference include acts that trope upon standards. And insofar as it is a debate about correct reference, the criterion of 'correctness' reveals no universal fact about human nature. The criterion is itself formulated by reflexive practices within a society. Different societies (or different sub-groups within a society) may employ different criteria. And it is always possible that biological standards and genealogical standards of 'correct' reference can co-exist with each other in different institutional domains (fertility clinics vs. religious practices vs. laws of inheritance) within a single society, yielding further sociopolitical conflict as a result (Kahn 2004).

The special character of third-person literal usage derives not just from the fact that different standards can co-exist, or that particular standards can be violated. The larger issue is that the third person literal use of kinterms is of no special interest – presents no privileged entry into – the range of social relations mediated by the use of kinterms. The traditional approach not only treats a narrow range of kinship behaviors as its data, it also fails to grasp the social character of practices through which such behaviors are linked to standards.

Standardizing social realities

Appeals to standards are important to social occasions in which persons give pedigrees, state marriage restrictions, or engage in disputes about inheritance, paternity, and the like. On such occasions, patterns of third person kinterm usage are frequently employed to describe norms of social conduct (marriage, inheritance, etc.).

Once we begin to pay attention to the event-structure of acts that seek to standardize social realities it becomes evident that some among these events formulate authoritative reflexive models of *other* social events, even *all* events of a certain type (1.6), such as marrying or inheriting. In some cases discourses of this type employ nomic statements (Table 1.2ff) to formulate universal standards, that is, employ utterance-types in which the absence of deictic selectivity formulates regulative norms as law-like principles applying to all social persons in all times and places. Such discourses formulate 'jural' or legal standards of kinship behavior. The articulation of such reflexive frameworks subserves a highly specific type of social function, the so-called 'official function of kinship' (Bourdieu 1990b). Such acts tend to take an exemplary form in specific scenarios of interaction, such as ceremonial rituals which reproduce normative social arrangements; or family practices that socialize children to what 'our culture' really is; or the habitual practices of those (whether individuals or institutions) who by virtue of their higher standing within the system of extant normative arrangements appear entitled to propose that normative standards of this type are, in fact, features of social reality itself, as it now actually exists, or always has existed, or is pre-destined by cosmological arrangements always so to remain.

In other cases, such discourses seek to describe remote regions of space and time in order to transform the here-and-now. Such acts are more vividly 'rhetorical' in perceived effect. Thus a genealogical reconstruction of the past may serve many present-day purposes for its users; for example, to mobilize certain people to act together as a group, as in contexts of feudal conflict; or to lay a present-day claim to property which is rooted in the past, as in disputes about inheritance. Genealogical metadiscourses involving kinterms are not neutral representations of a social reality that exists independently of them but performative constructions of the past that frequently seek to naturalize present-day relationships. Their jural aspect is unavoidably rhetorical in consequence, even when (perhaps especially when) events of their telling and re-telling become sufficiently alike that the behaviors they model are no longer contested, and the discourses themselves no longer perceived as rhetorical by those grouped by them.

Thresholds of normativity

I have been arguing that tropic uses of kinterms are cases where performed relations are partly non-congruent with presupposed roles and relationships. Such non-congruence resets the parameters of the current interaction by formulating an utterance-mediated sketch of social relations that effectively transforms social relations co-textually manifest as holding among the relevant persons. Of course, particular varieties of tropic usage may themselves become highly routinized for (and even come to count as normative standards for) particular scenarios of role inhabitance, even though the forms that implement them are either denotationally 'incorrect' or interactionally inappropriate in other scenarios. Moreover, one type of tropic usage may employ another type as a model (8.4); or a usage may be recognizably inappropriate to the current interaction, but used nonetheless for occasion-dependent special effects.

In other words, questions of 'thresholds of normativity,' which arise for cases of literal denotation (2.4), also arise for tropes. Explicitly codified standards – whether they are norms of literal or tropic usage – tend to furnish a particularly rigid sense of norms of conduct. But a more socially pervasive type of baseline consists merely of facts of routinization or social habit. And some tropes are not routine at all. It must therefore be understood that claims about whether a usage falls into one or the other of these types is a question that can only be posed for a particular social domain of persons (viz., a group, a community of practice, an institution and those linked to it, etc.). A single type of trope may count as a codified standard in one social domain, as a habitual norm in another, and as a highly non-routine act in another.

In some cases, relatively non-routine tropes count as highly affective acts, charged with emotion and sentiment. For example Suzuki (1984) observes that literal kinterm address in Japanese is appropriate only when addressee is of higher age or generational status.[7] To persons of younger or lower generation, pronouns or personal names are the preferred address forms. However, kinterms may be used for a young stranger with affectively charged force:

(6) Suppose one Sunday a little girl in a park is found lost and crying, unable to find her parents. If an adult happens to pass by, what will he or she say to the girl? It would be quite natural for the passerby to say, 'Don't cry. What's *Onēchan*'s ['Big Sister's'] name? Who was *Onēchan* with?' If the child is a boy, *Onēchan* will be replaced by *Onīchan* 'Big Brother.' This same adult, referring to himself or herself, will use *Obasan* 'Aunt,' *Onīsan* 'Older Brother' etc., depending on his or her own age and sex, as in '*Obasan* will find *Onēchan*'s papa'.

(Suzuki 1984: 136)

The use of *Onēchan* 'Big Sister' for the little girl is an instance of **metaphoric recentered address**; it is metaphoric because she is non-kin to speaker, recentered because its origo is a hypothetical younger brother (and not speaker). The use of *Obasan* 'Aunt' for self is an instance of **metaphoric address inversion**, a usage which employs a kinterm for self-reference which would be used by a niece-addressee; hence the current usage likens the (non-kin) addressed to a niece. Both tropes are affectively charged. The recentering of address to a younger brother formulates the girl found lost and crying as belonging to a family structure; and the act of address inversion affectively formulates the girl as a niece to speaker, as belonging to speaker's family in particular, performing speaker's affective concern in the here-and-now of speaking. The construal of such indexically creative usages depends on familiarity with the normalized values of address recentering and inversion; and the affective meaning depends on the superposition of the sketch of fictive relations on a scenario of role inhabitance in which the addressee's circumstances (viz., that she is a lost child, that she is crying) play a critical part.

A non-routinized usage may be perfectly construable but remain unratified. Consider for example the following metapragmatic judgment regarding address recentering (and potentially inversion) with Thai titles:

(7) A male doctor on a television talk show used the title *mɔ̌ɔ* 'doctor' for first-person reference, which elicited a comment from one of the people watching: 'He calls himself doctor,' indicating that she thought his use of this term to be inappropriate and self-promoting, since it is normally used only as a second-person form.

(Simpson 1997: 47)

As in the cases above, standards of appropriate use continue to serve as criteria on the intelligibility of usage, even if the usage is relatively non-routinized, and even when the total effect performed through the use in the here-and-now of speaking is not ratified by some, or all, hearers.

In addressing kin in Hindi, some relatively non-routinized usages also occur in performing relatively stark affective displays. For example, although tropes that raise children by one or more generation are normatively avoided, they readily occur in acts of scolding:

(8) ... a parent may show displeasure with a child who is behaving too independently or is bossing others about by addressing him or her as *tāū* (FeB), *bābbā* (FF), *dāddī* (FM). Such usages are occasional and situationally determined ... They are unlikely to be used on a regular basis for ordinary address.

(Vatuk 1982: 77)

Observe that Vatuk's description of these cases employs metapragmatic descriptions of the readable surround ('behaving too independently,' 'bossing others') in the very course of characterizing patterns of use. From the point of view of interlocutors, the usage depends on the readability of the co(n)text of use in a similar fashion.

We have been observing that the construal of tropes presupposes acquaintance with norms that apply to the current role configuration.

In some cases the trope may emphasize one feature of presupposed role difference while de-emphasizing another. For example, in traditional (e.g., rural) Hindi address, kin who are junior by criteria of relative age and generation (apart from children) are addressed by given name not kinterm. However in double-bind scenarios where the addressee is known to be junior in generation but older in age, age seniority is recognized by addressing the person by a kinterm that raises the individual in generational terms. In such cases, the speaker uses a form that would denotationally be correct were the addressee of more senior generational status; the trope diagrams a highly specific interactional effect, namely speaker's deference for addressee's age seniority by raising the addressee in generational terms.

It is worth emphasizing finally that we are not talking about the 'meaning' of the kinterm in any of the above cases. We are concerned rather with the felicity or success with which the semantic properties of a kinterm may be superimposed on the semiotically readable features of its co(n)text of occurrence, with some particular performed consequence.

8.6 Society-internal variation

We have seen that norms of many kinds can co-exist with each other even within the same society. Hence to speak of such norms as comprising the 'Bengali system' or the 'Japanese system' is a vast and wholly unnecessary simplification. Norms of appropriate use are cultural models of behavior that typically have an asymmetric social distribution within a society, and such variation is itself culturally significant as a higher-order index of the positionality of the norm, often conceptualized as a fact about the positionality of those *for whom* it is a norm. In saying that such norms exist in a society we are observing merely that such patterns of address are enregistered for – that is, are recognized as patterns by – an identifiable social domain of users; and, insofar as speakers are aware of the existence of society-internal variation, that stereotypic indexical values assigned to them constitute these patterns of action as emblems of group positionality ('distinction,' characterological essence, identity, or rank). Even when such values are conceptualized in normative terms and described as standards of 'correct' behavior, actual behavior may in fact depart from these patterns. Moreover, behavior that counts as a departure-from-norm for one social group may be enregistered as a contrastive norm for another social group.

Variant norms are fractionally congruent. For instance, all cases of recentered address involve transposition of origo to non-speaker; but the *type* of non-speaker origo (i.e., the specific kincategory to which origo of reference is usually transposed) frequently varies society-internally. The capacity of language users to make sense of the latter type of diversity (that is, construe a usage different from one's own, or formulate stereotypes about its users) presupposes a grasp of the former, more generic type of underlying unity.

The cases of Japanese recentering discussed above involve transposition to a junior kinposition, prototypically youngest son. However, social differences in the type of origo performed, and the address terms used to perform it, have been reported in the literature; these appear to be linked to schemas of group differentiation. The tendency to anchor origo to a junior kinposition (Table 8.6) is reportedly widespread in urban middle class address. Fischer observes that transposition to senior origo was also reported to occur in rural settings but was already regarded as 'old fashioned' at the time of writing (Fischer 1964: 122). In the Bengali examples, transposition to speaker's spouse (or, in the relevant case, speaker's child) has long been attested as a routinized norm in rural usage. But the wife's avoidance of father-in-law and brother-in-law (Table 8.5) was already a pattern increasingly under pressure from the growth of female education, movements for social reform, and the influence of city life at the time it was recorded by Das (1968: 23).

We also find that distinct patterns of tropic use are sometimes routinized in different families in ways that index differences in family circumstances, and thus constitute contrastive emblems of 'type' of family. Sylvia Vatuk's study of Hindi kinterm address records a number of patterns of recentering in address to senior kin within extended families (Table 8.8). The major pattern – common to all cases of non-speaker origo illustrated in the table – is that origo of reference is raised one generation above speaker, and the referent thereby downshifted in generational terms. Thus grandparents are addressed with parental terms and actual parents with terms appropriate for more junior kin. However, many of the variants listed are also fractionally non-congruent; that is, the specific patterns of downshifting illustrated in the table are sensitive to additional contextual variables, of which they are contrastively emblematic.

The three cases summarized in Table 8.8 involve three actual families. In all cases the speaker is a child. In cases 1 and 3, the child resides in an agnatic extended family household; in case 2, in an extended family household headed by mother's father. In case 1 the residential locale is a small town, in case 2 a city.

Paternal kinterms are used to address grandparents in all three cases. Yet the genealogical trope is cross-cut by, and thus given further structure by, tropes sensitive to patterns of co-residence. Paternal kinterms are used to address *father's* parents when residence is patrilocal as in (1a–b) and (3a–b), and *mother's* parents when residence is uxorilocal as in (2a–b). In both cases a trope of parental address is laminated upon a trope of deference to the highest ranked members of the extended residential family.

Table 8.8. *Address recentering in Hindi*

Speaker's relation to addressee	Form used for address	Normalized origo
Case 1: agnatic household (small town)		
(1a) grandfather (FF)	pitājī 'father'	speaker's F/FB/FZ
(1b) grandmother (FM)	mā 'mother'	
(1c) father	bhāīsahab 'elder brother'	speaker's FyB/FZ
(1d) mother	bhābī 'brother's wife'	
Case 2: uxorilocal residence (urban)		
(2a) grandfather (MF)	pitājī 'father'	speaker's MB/MZ
(2b) grandmother (MM)	ammājī 'mother'	
(2c) father	pāppājī 'papa' [< Eng.]	speaker (anglicized)
(2d) mother	mammī 'mummy' [< Eng.]	
Case 3: agnatic household includes FeB's family		
(3a) grandfather (FF)	pitājī 'father'	speaker's F/FB/FZ
(3b) grandmother (FM)	mā 'mother'	
(3c) mother	cācī 'aunt (FyBW)'	speaker's FeBS/FeBD
(3d) aunt (FeBW)	mammī 'mummy' [< Eng.]	
(3e) father	bāpūjī 'father'	speaker
(3f) uncle (FeB)	tāūjī 'uncle (FeB)'	

Source: (Vatuk 1982)

The choice of address terms for the parents themselves varies considerably across these cases, involving a number of secondary tropes. In some cases parents are addressed with terms derived from English, (2c–d), a usage characteristic of urban/modern identities (and independent of patterns of co-residence). In some of the other cases the kinterm used for parental address denotes the 'wrong' genealogical category, i.e., not a parent, but a sibling, (1c), a sibling's spouse, (1d), or a junior aunt, (3c).

All of these are tropes of re-centering to non-speaker origo, but the choice of origo is sensitive to further contextual factors. In case 1, the relevant factor is co-residence. Here ego is a young Brahmin girl who has been raised in an extended family headed by paternal grandfather; the residential group includes several of her father's unmarried brothers and sisters. Thus when the girl addresses her parents as 'elder brother' and 'brother's wife', (1c–d), the pattern of recentered address treats her paternal uncles and aunts as origo of reference.

In case 3, co-residence is a factor but so also is kin-reckoning through the male line. Here ego is a young boy living in an extended agnatic household which includes his father's elder brother's family. Paternal grandparents are addressed as in case 1 by parental terms, thus transposing origo of reference to father or father's siblings. But in addressing women in the first ascending generation, the boy centers address to his FeB's children. The two usages are not wholly inconsistent since the fact that FeB is higher in rank than F entails that FeB's children are higher in rank than ego; both cases therefore involve shifting to a higher status zero-point of reckoning. Since the household is agnatic and kin relations are reckoned through the male line, the child emphasizes true genealogical relations with father and paternal uncle (here preserving agnatic reckoning as the basis of literal usage); but in addressing mother and aunt, both of whom have entered the agnatic household through marriage, the child employs kinterms which his older paternal cousins would use for them (here preserving agnatic reckoning as the basis of tropes), addressing his mother as 'aunt' and aunt as 'mother.'

In all these cases, the origo of reference is transposed to a senior kinposition (e.g., ego's uncle, ego's older cousins). As a result, the terms used in address appear to downshift the referent in genealogical terms (e.g., grandfather addressed as 'father,' father as 'brother'). However such tropes are performed only in acts of address, not in cases of third person reference. Thus events of addressing a person imply a different zero-point of reckoning than events of talking about that person. The net effect of this asymmetry is that in face to face address to referent, a person performs a diagram of social order centered not around the self but around an impersonal allocentric position. Although a single allocentric position may be invoked as a zero-point in address to several members of the family there is no necessity that the same allocentric zero-point be invoked in encounters with every member of the family. Indeed, different role alignments may be emphasized in performing address to different individuals.

The cases discussed above appear to be relatively routinized, habitual patterns for the individuals in question. It is readily seen however, that a much larger number of occasion-specific tropes can intelligibly be performed using the same underlying principles. Not all such tropes, while performable, may be ratified by interlocutors; and among those that are ratified in one interaction, not all may become normalized targets in other interactions, whether by the same or by other persons. It should be clear, nonetheless, that quite aside from questions of how and whether event-specific forms of kinterm-mediated footing become widely enregistered as tropes performable in subsequent activity, or even acquire a normativity for a large social domain of speakers, the fact remains that, for any such stabilized genre of interactional footing, further tropic possibilities are always available to interactants acquainted with its enregistered norm.

8.7 Sign and metasign in kinship behavior

In the preceding sections I have considered a number of patterns of kinterm utterance. But, as I argued earlier, kinship behaviors are not limited to utterances containing kinterms. Many kinds of non-linguistic behaviors also count as kinship behaviors. For instance, in many societies care of infants is the mother's responsibility, wage-earning the father's. In such cases a particular division of (non-linguistic) labor is metasemiotically construed through the use of kinterms and treated as emblematic of normative kinship relations.

In some cases specific economic transactions count as kinship behaviors. A classic example is the giving of cattle by the groom's lineage to the bride's lineage among the Nuer (Evans Pritchard 1951):

(9) ... the cattle belong to the lineage, to the sons as a whole, who are links between the ancestors and its as yet unborn members. If the sons are men when their father dies they ought to go on living together round a common kraal... [though] they frequently do not do so. Whether they do so or not, the cattle belong to all of them and should be used when the herd is large enough, to obtain wives for them in order of seniority ...

(1951: 128)

Cattle are the detachable parts of a potential husband just as a child is the detachable part of a wife. In order for the union to occur, the man's lineage must transfer substance to the woman's lineage by giving them cattle in anticipation of her bearing children for the group of cattle givers. Thus before the marriage ritual can itself occur, a set of economic relations have to be transacted, and the transaction is indexically presupposed in the marriage ceremony itself.

Although the act of giving cattle is (at least in part) non-linguistic behavior, its significance as kinship behavior cannot be established without considering discourses that construe it. One cannot discover merely by observing the physical transfer of cattle that it counts as a transaction between lineages (rather than individuals) or that its purpose is the consummation of marriage (rather than a political treaty) or that it is done in anticipation of a child (rather than payment). These facts can only be discovered by attending to metasemiotic discourses about the act, some of which may occur during the transaction; or they may occur only afterwards, or elsewhere. And these discourses are discourses in which kinship terms are employed to make the relevant distinctions.[8]

In such discourses, kinterms function as metasigns typifying some order of perceivable diacritics, their object-signs, imbuing them with kinship values. Proponents of biological and genealogical reductionism argue that a single order of diacritics – whether acts of procreation and parturition on the one hand, or acts of giving pedigrees on the other – constitutes the essence of kinship. But the question of which diacritics actually mark kinship in a given society, or belong to the object-range of signs that are emblematic of kinship, is an empirical question, not something that can be settled in advance. Biology and genealogy are both relevant to diverse kinship behaviors in many societies, though may be relevant to different degrees in different cases; or, may be relevant along with other diacritics of kinship, ones very different from both biological and genealogical ones; and may not be relevant to all cases in all societies. In the Nuer example, the giving of cattle is a diacritic of kinship behavior. Here, something that we normally think of as economic behavior (i.e., involving property ownership and transfer) is assimilated to the domain of kinship.

A more elaborate example involving Yapese kinship is offered by Schneider (1984). Schneider argues that the Yapese kinterms which we would gloss as mother and father are, at bottom, linked to political-economic standards, not genealogical ones. He observes that if the Yapese are asked to provide terms meaning 'the woman from whose womb a child is born' and 'the man who begot him' they will respond to such metasemantic queries by offering the terms *citiningen* and *citamangen*. The anthropologist may now translate them through a second meta-semantic gloss into English as 'mother' and 'father'. But this equivalence is only a matter of extensional overlap. The Yapese terms designate a different intensional class of relata than the English ones do. A man may have only one *citiningen* and only one *citamangen* at a time, and the initial default values of these relatives appear to correspond to 'mother' and 'father.' But when the father dies, the man uses the term *citamangen* for a male successor, the senior-most member of the clan to whom rights to land ownership are now passed on (the term *citiningen* is also alienable and transferable to a different woman, but by a different rule). Thus, the Yapese term *citamangen* marks a politico-economic relationship that only overlaps extensionally, and only in a certain phase of the life-cycle, with our own genealogically conceived kinterm 'father.' Schneider cites cases of this kind to argue effectively against the genealogical reduction. He argues that genealogy is peripheral to the Yapese conception of kinship, that their 'kinship' system is really a system of politico-economic arrangements.

Facts of this kind continue to prove troubling to any theory that supposes that the comparative study of kinship must rest on some foundational 'concept' of kinship, a concept that must be realized in every society in which kinship and its analogues occur.

The above discussion shows this supposition to be without utility. For even in societies where kinship is firmly grounded in genealogical or biological ideologies – or, more realistically, in societies in which genealogical or biological models of kinship prevail in certain institutional loci, dominate certain practices, and compete against each other society-internally – kinship behaviors cannot be reduced to their ideological underpinnings simply because they include behaviors that model social relations through tropes of kinship, through performable and construable analogues of kinship, which are straightforwardly intelligible through text-in-context evaluations to those acquainted with whatever local ideology prevails for the moment in that locale, and are susceptible to a comparative analysis in the manner illustrated above.

Emblematic functions of kinship behavior

In 8.6, I noted that society-internal variation in kinship norms and behaviors is often emblematic of differences in social grouping, that is, is reflexively reanalyzed as revealing something about the urban/rural divide, or about differences in class, modernity, and social 'type' of family. In other cases, variation in kinship behaviors is emblematic not of differences among social groups but of distinctive social practices in which members of many groups may engage.

In all societies, different diacritics of kinship – whether linguistic or non-linguistic ones – matter for different social questions concerning kinship. In her discussion of siblinghood among Malays on the island of Langkawi, Carsten (2004) shows that a range of behaviors – acts of address, the ritual treatment of houses, the activity of breastfeeding – function as diacritics of siblinghood at different points in the life cycle. Since several normalized models of siblinghood co-exist, many different kinds of relationships (whether among non-kin, or among kin who are not siblings) can be modeled on aspects of siblinghood behavior

Patterns of address among siblings serve as models of social relations among spouses:

(10) Older brothers often have affectionate relations with younger sisters, and this has a structural significance in that it provides a model for the relation between husband and wife. Normatively a married couple should use the terms 'older brother' and 'younger sister' to address each other (although they may avoid this in practice); these terms capture the ideal of affection, equality and respect on which marriage should be based. The modeling of marriage on sibling-ship means that affinity has a special status as it is always in the process of being transformed into consanguinity.
(Carsten 2004: 312)

The pattern illustrated here is a trope of recentering. By modeling their address practices on those of siblings, spouses liken affinal relations to consanguineal ones, inhabiting stereotypic relations of affection and respect through the very act. Notice that distinctive patterns of inter-sibling address not only exist in this society but are enregistered as signs of affection and respect that can performatively be summoned in the management of relations among non-siblings.

Questions of siblinghood are linked to other diacritics too. Children are performatively grouped into 'sibling sets' in Langkawi society, whereby they become ratified siblings for future social purposes. This is accomplished through special ceremonial events of a performative nature where the association of children with the house where they are born is fixed by the ritual burial of placentas at birth, a process repeated each time a child is born:

(11) Each child belongs to a set of 'birth siblings' whose existence precedes birth. The child and the placenta, *uri*, are conceptualized as 'two siblings,' *dua beradik*. When a child is born, the *uri* – conceived as the younger sibling – is washed by the midwife and placed in a woven basket together with various ritual objects. It is then buried by the father on the grounds of the house-compound in manner that recalls the burial of human corpses in the graveyard outside the village. The placenta sibling can cause sickness and mood changes in the child. What I would stress here is the way that the sibling set, in this ritual, is anchored to the house.

(Carsten 2004: 312)

Once the ritual is complete, the courtyard and the house of which it is a part are themselves readable as emblems of shared siblinghood. In this case, the emblem is one that perdures in the senses long after the ritual that metasemiotically establishes it as an emblem is over, and remains a point of reference that can be invoked in a variety of ways to assess or assert common siblinghood over the course of a life span.

Siblings cannot marry, of course. But from the standpoint of the incest prohibition, the relevant criterion of siblinghood is entirely different. It concerns the sharing of milk.

(12) Milk feeding also defines the prime category of incestuous relations: kin who have drunk milk from the breast of the same woman may not marry ... The frequency of formal and informal fostering arrangements ... substantially increases the possibility that a child may drink the milk of a woman who is not its birth mother. It is this possibility that gives this definition of incest its particular fascination and horror ... Women often described to me how in the past one might easily have given a child a breast to comfort it, but that now this is not done. If two of the children a woman had breast-fed later married each other, she would bear responsibility for the incest.

(Carsten 2004: 313)

The incest prohibition is not formulated in terms of shared blood but in terms of shared milk. The sharing of milk becomes diacritic of sibling relationships in the context of the incest prohibition. Siblings share other diacritics too. They tend to live in the same house, have their *uri* buried in the courtyard, are raised by common parents, share food, and so on. But foster siblings do not share all of these characteristics. And not all children who share milk share other attributes. This does not imply (contra Carsten 2004) that the 'concept' of siblinghood involves a loose notion of 'relatedness.' It is rather that different diacritics are emblematic of siblinghood in different contexts of action.

We saw earlier that the display of diacritics of kinship are susceptible to determinate readings of kinrelation only insofar as the context of action in which they are displayed is independently readable; that is, a single diacritic of kinship contributes to the construal of a genealogical relation in one type of setting, of metaphoric kinship in another; and is emblematic of class, modernity or urban residence in yet others. We are now observing that normalized standards of appropriate conduct will also emphasize different diacritics for different social purposes. From the standpoint of spousal relations, recentered address with sibling terms is held up as a normative standard. But from the point of view of jural norms that regulate incest, it is the sharing of milk that is treated as the essential diacritic of siblinghood.

Cases of these kinds show that a single category of kinrelation can be given an extensional definition (that is, the questions of which persons belong to the class can be settled) by appeal to a variety of diacritics of role and relationship. The question of what unified 'concept' of kinship (e.g., of siblinghood) exists in this society is a distraction. This is so in at least two ways. On the one hand, the question cannot be answered without first being converted into questions about the linguistic and/or non-linguistic diacritics through which the relationship is expressed in particular contexts, about the metasemiotic processes whereby kinship discourses and practices typify these diacritics, about the ideologies that naturalize such typifications, and about the kinds of higher-order emblems that are formulated through a reanalysis of variation in such practices. On the other hand, the comparative study of particular domains of behavior involving that kinrelation can proceed without worrying about concepts that unify or join these domains to each other; such domains are in any case fractionally congruent with each other as our earlier discussion of kinterm tropes shows. In the Malay case, the question of how couples normatively behave with each other requires considering one set of diacritics; another set of diacritics clarifies membership in 'sibling sets'; and understanding norms of incest requires attention to a third set. These three emblems of siblinghood overlap in their metasemiotic aspect (all are construed through discourses of kinship), but differ at the level of object-signs. And each of them can independently be manipulated in tropes of identity and social relationship without confusion in this society (e.g., spouses who formulate themselves as sibling-like do not worry about placentas or milk; but persons accused of incest might) precisely because of this kind of differentiated reflexive structure.

Regrouping

Paying attention to reflexive processes also helps us see that kinship behaviors can be regrouped into systems of social relations very different from notional kinship by metapragmatic projects that manipulate them for other ends. The case that I wish to discuss now construes patterns of kinship behavior as emblematic of a particular type of nation-state politics.

We saw in earlier discussion (Table 8.3 and S 8.3) that Vietnamese fictive kinship has historically been linked to Confucian ideals of 'name rectification,' and is performatively played out through a distinctive system of normalized tropes. The text-patterns involved are far more extensive than the few examples discussed so far. However, my focus now is not on these text-patterns but on metapragmatic discourses that read them as stereotypic emblems of particular kinds of social order.

We saw in S 8.3 that Confucian doctrines have historically construed address practices in ways that promote an impersonal-hierarchical vision of social relations. Luong (1990) shows that certain features of this system were preserved in the twentieth century by the French colonial government in order to maintain colonial power. The Marxist revolutionary movement which sought to replace the colonial government – and which began its revolutionary struggle in 1930, succeeding finally in 1945 – brought these doctrines partly into question, seeking to transform the polity and the emblems through which it lived.

Both the colonial government and the Marxist underground subscribed to the view that the use of language causally shapes the sociopolitical order. Both imposed penalties (including prison sentences) on writers who engaged in *inappropriate* use of role terms in the public press. However, the Marxist revolutionaries sought to transform public conduct by promoting the use of person-referring forms traditionally considered disrespectful – such as pronouns, epithets, and non-honorific nouns – in referring to members of the colonial establishment. At the same time, the Marxist metadiscourse sought to build a new voice of the people by promoting some among the standards of address that had prevailed during the colonial period, censuring others. In the case of metaphoric address, the use of the more hierarchical kinterms (*chu/co* 'junior uncle/aunt,' *bac* 'senior uncle/aunt,' *ong/ba* 'grand-father/mother,' *cu* 'great grandparent') for non-kin, which had prevailed earlier, was to a great extent supplanted by the use of the more egalitarian sibling terms (*anh/chi* 'elder brother/ sister'), a type of leveling which employed a smaller degree of age and generational distance as a metaphor for greater solidarity within the polity.

Yet these two frameworks for the figurement of politics through uses of kinship, divided though they were by a revolution, remained fractionally congruent. It was not merely that the new dispensation – in which siblinghood became a prominent trope for figuring relations among comrades – was, like the older hierarchical framework that it displaced, merely another system of fictive address and allocentric voicing, one through which a new Marxian 'voice of the people' could be read into variations on an older

Confucian practice. It was also the case that specific forms of fictive address that were once diacritic of the hierarchical colonial order were partially preserved in the new Marxian order, particularly in social scenarios where the revolutionary leader, Ho Chi Minh himself, was at issue, whether as referent or speaker. Ho himself was normatively referred to by means of hierarchical, higher-generation kinterms, such as *bac*, which formulated him as 'senior uncle' to speaker's children; and Ho himself used *chu* and *co* to address his younger comrades as hypothetical 'junior uncle' and 'junior aunt' to his own children (Luong 1988: 248).

In previous chapters we saw that in any such moment of historical transformation, a new framework of social relations becomes salient in all its novelty – even its revolutionary appeal – when the diacritics that formulate the contrast are held up as objects of folk-scrutiny and concern. But even as new differences are staked out through these diacritics, acts of construing diacritics as positive emblems of a new social order invoke metasemiotic frameworks presupposed in both the new and the old regime. Whether it is Thomas Jefferson declaring independence in colonial America (5.7) or Ho Chi Minh in colonial Vietnam, the revolutionary impulse seeks to repossess emblems of the order that it seeks to displace. The diacritics that formulate the initial difference – and which, to the outsider's ahistorical gaze, appear small and arbitrary things (speech prosody and bodily hexis in the one case, kinship tropes in the other) – derive their initial importance from the colonial order of which they are emblematic. But they grow beyond them. The processes through which such emblems expand in their semiotic range (so that more and more forms of perceivable conduct express the new regime, and its lifestyle), or grow in social domain (so that more and more people are socialized to construe them as emblems of the new order) are invariably processes mediated by the semiotic and metasemiotic uses of language, and thus involve participation frameworks, footings and role alignments, new social groupings, and group-relative interests and stakes. By their very nature such processes *differentiate* the new order into its own internal divisions – its positionalities, hierarchies, its own emblems of power – in ways profoundly shaped by the fact that the new social fact does not come about all at once, but unfolds one semiotic act – one participation framework, one regrouping, one alignment – at a time.

8.8 From cultural kinship formations to any cultural formation

Let me begin with a brief retrospect of the argument. In the historical study of kinship, instances of slippage between biological kinrelations (real or presumed) and 'kin-like' relations that clearly do not correspond to biological ones – cases like adoption, descent groups formed through common residence, the levirate and other means of assigning kin to deceased relatives – were known from very early on. But what was to be done with them?

All competing views took the phenomenal existence of kinterms as their point of analytic departure, but many denied that kinterms were important to the analyses they formulated, tending instead to view their formulations as theories of 'kinship' more abstractly defined. Once the abstract noun 'kinship' became the central object of concern, the act of reifying the abstraction as a 'kinship system' was but a short step away. And this abstraction yields explanations fraught with doubt.

The real object of explanation, I have argued, is to give an account of the meaning of kinship behavior as it is grasped by those whose behavior it is. Kinterms are used to perform kinrelations in linguistic utterances, though in ways far more varied than is recognized by traditional theory; they are also used as metasigns that typify other perceivable behaviors, their object-signs, imbuing them with kinship values. Any such moment of typification formulates a model of the behavior that it typifies, isolating it, focalizing it, rendering it intelligible through the use of the metasign. Normalized models are of widespread social consequences. Any such model, enregistered for a social domain of persons, can be modified through further reflexive processes to incorporate behaviors not formerly linked to the model; or to marginalize behaviors once part of it. And during the course of these processes, the kinterms that render such behaviors intelligible are themselves susceptible to intensional reanalysis through changes in stereotypic denotation (e.g., the differentiation of 'mother' into role fractions such as 'ovum donor' vs. 'birth mother' vs. 'legal mother' in recent biomedicine).

If we approach the study of kinship behavior in this manner, we can formulate a comparative method for the study of kinship that allows us to understand how kinship behavior in one society differs from, or is similar to, such behavior in any other; and how it grows and changes through processes of tropism and normalization in any given society over time. The above discussion contains many comparative statements of both types. I have also shown that a comparative approach to kinship does not require a single universal 'concept' of kinship, only a way of studying reflexive processes through which *any given model of kinship* can be performed and construed through semiotic activity, and, therefore, can be maintained and altered over time through that activity.

What holds for kinship also holds for any other notional category – such as 'class,' 'gender' or 'modernity.' We know from the ethnographic record that each such notional construct exhibits elaborate forms of local variation across sociohistorical locales. What counts as an instance of the construct – as an upper-class behavior, as a display of femininity, as a modern outlook – not only differs vastly from locale to locale, these variants often have a profoundly ironic relationship to each other.

There are continuities too, of course. But if we attempt to discover these continuities by focusing only on the object-signs that are diacritic of these behaviors in each locale, we are faced with a profusion of mere differences, an ever proliferating mass (sometimes a morass) of radical discontinuities that can be savored or enjoyed in their uniqueness in each locale (uniqueness is, after all, common), but leave the mind, once satiated, empty. And if we seek to emphasize these continuities by holding fast to our own culture-specific metasemiotic constructs – to pre-conceived, putatively universal 'concepts' of that domain; to cultural evolutionism; or to other features of our own cultural projects that we mistake for nature – we are faced inevitably with the inadequacy of our methods, and, if we pursue them honestly enough, lose confidence in them. Neither pole of this relationship – the object-sign or the metasign – is of very great interest by itself.

In contrast, the approach proposed here takes the meta-sign/object-sign *relationship* to be the basic functional principle through which human conduct becomes meaningful to those whose conduct it is. To speak of the variety of such relationships (and their superposition or lamination in modes of conduct) is to speak of varieties of meaning. To speak of the kinds of 'things' that can contract such sign-relationships for human observers is to speak of the variety of cultural things. All cultural things are historical formations because reflexive operations can be iterated, that is, can follow each other as a sequence of acts, whether they be the acts of one or of many, whether normative or not, whether they maintain or change the cultural form over the interval observed. That is, the very same activities and practices through which such relationships are expressed also yield sociohistorical processes in which the cultural form is transformed for participants, whether dramatically or in subtle ways. Some among these processes maintain the *status quo ante*. Some are processes in which one or more tiers of the cultural formation – a meta-level typification, an object-level enactment, or both – can change over time.

I have tried to show in this book that a number of different notional constructs – such as identity, class, hierarchy, kinship, and others – can be empirically studied in these terms in ways that yield a comparative framework for studying their character in any society. In every case, the notional construct provides, at best, an initial orientation to the phenomena we suppose it to describe (class is not always about class, hierarchy about hierarchy, or kinship about kinship) and that we can understand this feature of culture – that it grows beyond any notional rubric under which, for a time, it may be grouped – by getting clearer about the various relations of 'about'-ness ('standing-for' relations) that are presupposed in, and created by, human semiotic activity itself. Or, what is the same thing, by getting clearer about meta-sign/object-sign relations in human conduct.

I have taken pains in this book to discuss a large number of cultural phenomena in highly explicit terms, both in my theoretical claims and discussions of examples. There are of course numerous phenomena of interest to anthropology and other social sciences that I do not discuss here. Actually, if you take seriously my claim that social relations (in all their concrete, context-bound specificity) do in fact vary (i.e., have, can, and will vary) limitlessly across sociohistorical locales through reflexive processes of the kind described here, then it follows that there is, in fact, an infinite number of very specific 'topics' which this book (and any other) must leave out. And this is no cause for distress. It merely shows that the goal of classifying and cataloguing forms of human conduct in totalizing taxonomies – itself a step-child of the 'view from nowhere' – can get nowhere, at least as long as culture remains a living, growing thing.

A framework that focuses on the reflexive processes through which culture lives and changes for participants urges a different goal. It suggests that we can understand how cultural forms become intelligible to those who create them, and those created by them, by studying their semiotic activities. I have tried to show that by taking signs that mediate the activities of social actors as our point of departure we can travel to all the zones of social life to which the products of their activities go and from which they have come, within the limits of empirical access; that we can traverse sociohistorical regions of belonging and exclusion that are mapped out by trajectories of participation and orientation to fractionally common cultural forms; that we can track the paths of cultural projects that maintain cultural forms, renovate them, or seek to make them grow by displacing and absorbing others. If such an understanding of cultural forms allows us to grasp by bringing near a world that is otherwise remote, the act of grasping them is already an act that intervenes in the world in which these cultural forms (and we) live. To grasp them is to intervene in their lives through our own. Meanwhile, altogether elsewhere, certain semiotic activities and practices are unfolding in someone's backyard or TV screen or nation (yours, perhaps?) and forms of belonging and exclusion are, even now, being re-figured and re-grouped by them. We all have goals. The question remains of whether we grasp the processes that mediate these lives and these goals well enough to arrive where we hope to go.

NOTES

Chapter 1

1 When roles of 'linguist' and 'native speaker' are occupied by the same person, such metalinguistic data become available to the linguist as introspectable 'native speaker intuitions.' The distinctive feature of generative grammar lies not in the use of introspection (or elicitation) as a source of data (see n. 2), but in the privileged status accorded to grammaticality judgments in contrast to other types of data, a decision which, ironically enough, has not been backed by any explicit theory of the boundary between 'grammaticality' in particular and 'acceptability' in general (Lyons 1995: 132–8; Quirk and Svartvik 1966). These commitments have had the unfortunate consequence that much of the work in this tradition has confounded these two types of metalinguistic evaluation, often employing terms such as 'ungrammaticality' to describe cases of pragmatic infelicity.

2 Even though overt argumentation in this tradition typically revolves around this criterion, most actual work in this tradition has been carried out by people working on their native languages, a type of role alignment where native speaker intuitions are unavoidably available as metalinguistic data. Hence here, as in generative grammar (see n. 1), the analyst employs a wider range of metalinguistic criteria than those that are privileged by the theory, including criteria that are programmatically rejected.

3 In general, such naturally occurring metalinguistic activity falls into distinct ethnometalinguistic genres, differing in a number of respects from each other – such as their provenance, degree of explicitness, ubiquity or replicability across social categories of speakers, their authority relative to other genres, and so on – and these characteristics must explicitly be analyzed in order for such accounts to become usable as data. I return to these issues presently.

4 Cross-linguistically, the contrast between metasemantic and other types of statement typically depends on several lexicogrammatical cues which co-occur in the statement. Thus in English the verbs *be* and *mean* transparently function as metasemantic predicates in the 'X verb Y' construction when the verb is specified for timeless-nomic inflections (present tense, indicative mood, active voice, simple aspect, 3rd person), and X and Y are both constituents of the same class (both simple noun phrases, both nominalized infinitival verb phrases, etc.); and, if they are simple noun phrases with determiners, when X and Y both contain indefinite articles. Expression Y frequently contains a specifier (a restrictive relative clause, prepositional phrase or other constituent) which makes it denotationally more specific than X. As each of these conditions is relaxed, the total constructional form moves gradually away from a pure metasemantic equation, merging with statements of other kinds.

5 In saying that large scale formations live through small scale activities I do not wish to propose that large scale social formations lack principles of organization of their own, or that all features of large scale formations are reducible to features of small scale ones. The point, rather, is that large scale formations are *modes of organization* of smaller scale activities, not something apart from them; and although they configure interpersonal activities into widespread social practices (for example, by likening the activities of many individuals to each other through commonalities of socialization, or by uniting them under a common standard), the social realities that are maintained through widespread practices are patterns of the activities of individuals, which, though readily held constant for a while as social patterns (through forms of motivation distinctive to them, e.g., see 1.6, 1.7, 2.4, 2.5, and elsewhere), are never autonomous of (or incapable of change from) the effects of small scale activities.

6 Moreover, a given object-sign may have more than one motivated property. When considering such icons it is essential that we distinguish values attributed to objects by particular forms of metasemiotic treatment, and values independent of such treatment. While it is true that sandals and clothing are associated with politeness in Thai culture, they are assigned other properties as well: they have functionally specific everyday uses, i.e., some are worn around the feet, others around the torso; they have attributes such as color, shape and size, and therefore belong to an aesthetics of 'matching' when worn together; they are manufactured at a cost, and sold in the marketplace for a price. The metasemiotic treatment illustrated in Figure 1.1 superimposes values linked to norms of interpersonal politeness upon values of other kinds – such as those linked to fashion, say, or the display of wealth – whose motivation lies in metasemiotic regimes of a different sort. Which among these multiple values counts as the most relevant in a given interaction is usually settled by the semiotic context of the sign, not by any intrinsic feature.

7 An even more general issue (which I take up in Chapters 4 and 5, and elsewhere) concerns the processes whereby the ubiquitous co-occurrence of sign-tokens in experience can be rationalized by criteria of appropriateness into an explicit metasemiotic scheme of the kind discussed here. Such processes tend to have an ideological aspect simply because any set of facts of *mere co-occurrence* can be judged *appropriate to context* in indefinitely many ways (given the open-endedness of what counts as the context of the sign-configuration and the analogies among signs detectable within it). In some cases criteria of appropriateness are delimited by text-metrical criteria of congruence (1.2), elaborately so in cases of ritual; in such cases, the ways in which co-occurring signs metrically 'fit' together in an emergent way can be reanalyzed as facts of *appropriate* co-occurrence. But when such reanalyses give rise to explicit metasemiotic schemes, they tend, by virtue of the selectivity of explicit descriptions, to functionally transform their object-signs, re-grouping their sign-values in the way discussed here. In some cases, multiple reanalyses co-exist (often serving positional interests), each potentially distorting with respect to the other; in others, one of them may win out as the most widespread model for a while, and even acquire the status of a naturalized norm (1.6).

8 Criteria of congruence are not established only by external classifications (as in Figure 1.1); a number of other types of cases are discussed later in the book. For example, in Chapter 2, we consider cases where criteria of co-textual congruence are established by the semantic values of lexical items used in speech. In these cases specialized types of co-textual congruence – such as 'lexical cohesion' and

'referential coherence' – become important. We have not yet developed these concepts, but the issues will become clear soon enough. Briefly, two lexical items can be evaluated for lexical cohesion if they are like or unlike each other (to gradient degrees) by criteria of grammatico-semantic meaning; here the criterion of likeness is provided by their semantic values within a grammatical system (not by stereotypic grouping under a predicate, as in Figure 1.1). The key issue for now is that criteria of comparability may be of various kinds; but whenever such criteria are available, fragments of a textual order can be compared one to another, such comparability itself comprising a significant type of information about what is being done, by whom, to whom, and so on, through the deployment of these signs.

9 As Figure 1.4 makes clear, the strategic significance of the utterance is non-detachable from its role configuration. The strategy consists in each case not merely of the utterance in column I but of the utterance in a context where the status asymmetry shown in column II is independently given or presupposed. Thus (a) only counts as a 'dispensation' if and when it is used by the higher status interlocutor. And (b)–(d) count as ways of circumventing lack of entitlement if and when they are used by a lower status interlocutor. In other role configurations, the strategic meaning disappears.

10 Beyond these simple examples of person and space-time deixis lie a much wider range of deictic patterns in language, patterns that delineate a variety of ongoing social realities for social actors. These include markings for whether an utterance is the speech or the thoughts of another, what kind of interpersonal stance the other holds, whether such speech/thoughts/stances are those of one person or of many, whether the utterance expresses contingent knowledge or universal truth. It is not surprising, therefore, that reflexive reanalyses of patterns of deixis commonly serve as foundations or axioms for a vast range of cultural projects, including models of mind and subjectivity; of truth, certainty, and objectivity; and for figurations of social collectivities into political formations deictically summoned to a common goal. See Banfield 1982 for a discussion of deictically motivated notions of modernist subjectivity in literature. See Gass 1979 for Freud's uses of the Latin deictics, *ego* and *id*, to formulate role-fractions of the self that speak to each other. A number of additional cases are discussed by Lee 1997: the philosopher Frege's reanalysis of indirect/direct reported speech deixis into the sense-reference dichotomy; Descartes' reanalysis of performative deixis (in the locution *Cogito ergo sum*) into a criterion of self-guaranteeing truth; and uses of the deictic formula *We, the people* by the authors of the American Constitution to performatively summon into existence the political collectivity for which they speak.

11 These dependent variables differentiate deictic sub-classes: spatial deictics (location-of), tense deictics (time-of), person deictics (speaker-of, addressee-of), etc. See Table 1.3 for examples. For non-linguistic deictics, such as gestures, the default origo of reference is the 'current act,' typically understood as the dependent variable 'current actor,' namely 'the one who produces the gesture.' When a gesture accompanies a deictic utterance, the origos of the two sign-tokens may (or may not) converge in a cumulative reading. For example, in the exchange between the Countess and the Prince (example (4)), the expression of contempt and the polite pronoun both have current actor/speaker as origo, i.e., the Countess herself. In cases of mimicry and/or represented discourse such default values can of course be transposed away from the one who produces the physical sign-token, yielding contrasts among role fractions

of 'animator' vs. 'principal' (Table 1.6), as well as more complex footings and voicing effects based on more finely differentiated role fractions.

12 In contrast, many stereotypically 'social' indexicals, such as those involved in register phenomena, do not create this type of interdependence (see Chapters 3 and 4). For example, two utterances that differ only in class-linked registers of 'accent' *denote the same thing*, even though they *index different social images of speaker type* (e.g., images of class). Deictic patterns can become incorporated into register formations too, of course, and, in this type of case, deictic contrasts index *both* denotational-indexical and social-indexical contrasts (see Chapters 6 and 7). But the fact that hybrid forms are possible in no way implies that the principles underlying these two types of indexicality are the same.

13 In the standard semantic notation employed here, the symbols x and y stand for noun phrases, and the subscripts i and j for referents or entities picked out by noun phrases.

14 We are concerned here only with the way in which deictic categories formulate default utterance construals, not with the issue of whether such effects are ratified by interlocutor, nor with effects superimposed by co-textual signs. To make a claim about the one issue is to make no claim about the others, a point which the 'coding' approach to deixis (and to referring more generally; see Chapter 2) misses entirely. This is a point of critical importance and one to which I return towards the end of section 1.4.

15 Peirce uses the term 'pronoun' for any term capable of functioning as a speech-event deictic: 'A pronoun ought to be defined as *a word which may indicate anything to which the first and second persons have suitable real connections, by calling the attention of the second person to it*' (Peirce 1992, v.2: fn., p. 15). In contemporary terminology the term 'deictic' is used for this generic class, the term 'pronoun' (or 'participant deictic') being reserved for the subclass of such terms which specifically refer to speaker and/or hearer.

16 In logical notation, this type of non-selective import is expressed by an overt symbol, the so-called 'universal quantifier', $(\forall x)$.

17 This follows from the fact that linguistic categories are organized into grammatical paradigms so that the absence of an overt form is itself significant relative to the set of contrasts possible in that paradigm. This type of absence is called an 'unmarked' form. Thus in the *Birds sing* example the noun phrase internal contrasts include $[those/these/ some/my/your/ \emptyset/ \ldots birds]_{NP}$, where $\emptyset$ represents the fact that the absence of an overt morpheme is one among the possibilities grammatically available, i.e., $[[\emptyset\ birds]_{NP}\ sing]_S$. This possibility has the least selective construal.

18 My use of the term 'schema' is not related to the psychological usage made fashionable by Kant (viz., 'an a priori rule of the productive imagination'), or to any derived usage of a psychological sort (as in contemporary cognitive theory). The Greek word *schêma* from which all of these theory-specific technical terms are derived has a much broader range of meanings (viz., 'form, figure, appearance; figure of speech; figure of syllogism; geometrical figure'). My own usage here is closer to the way in which the term may be applied to figures, designs, and diagrams (as when an architect might be said to *schematize* features of a building through a line drawing). To speak of schematizations of referent is to speak of performable sketches of referent, enacted or made palpable through utterances. The schematic properties of deictics are not a priori (e.g., the denotational schema is just the cluster of grammatico-semantic properties that are lexicalized in the form), nor psychological features of the form, except

in the derived sense that the sketch performed can be grasped by someone who knows the language.

19 The social domain of a category is the group of persons for whom a form functions as a category of that type. A dialect boundary is a social domain boundary of one kind. The boundary can also be historical, or involve register differences. For example the deictics *hither/thither* in Table 1.3 are now commonly encountered only in literature. In everyday speech their use is superceded by the use of *here/there* plus motion verbs. The general point here at issue (namely, that all linguistic categories are categories *for* a social domain of users) is developed in subsequent sections and chapters. The special case of social domain variation for deictic categories is discussed in Chapter 6, and also in the discussion following Table 7.2.

20 Some examples: in cases of 'voiced' speech, regional accents may be used to mimic the speech of another; and utterances in the interrogative or imperative mood may be formulated as the questions or commands of another. In both cases the author/principal is understood to be different from the current animator. This type of disjuncture is precisely what is called the 'voicing' effect (Bakhtin 1981, 1984; see also Agha 2005).

21 More generally, the origo of action may be understood as a role fraction of speaker other than animator (such as author, or principal), or transposed to addressee, or, as in cases of complex 'voicing' phenomena, to non-present others, whether real or imagined, living or dead, or to institutional and social collectivities of an entirely different kind. In all of these cases, the question of 'who is acting' is settled by co-textual indexical cues that shape models of actor characteristics. These cases are discussed at various points in this book.

22 This fact also informs methods of fieldwork and analysis, which must proceed by considering a range of communicative events, isolate what effects the form has in its most ubiquitous uses, and in cases of defeasibility, isolate, through a series of permutation tests, what fraction of the most ubiquitous *set* of text-defaults is preserved across the range of instances of defeasibility. Any particular claim about text-defaults is, of course, an empirical claim, and, a claim formulated at some stage of analysis may prove later to be wrong. The claim is also meaningful only as a claim about a social domain of language users (e.g., members of a dialect group). Hence the data of communicative events over which it is formulated must be analyzed in sociological terms before they are fully usable as data on the categorial structure of expressions.

23 Austin proposes two explanatory tacks, both of which fail. The first of these, the distinction between two types of *utterances* (performatives vs. constatives) breaks down because constatives turn out to be performatives too. The second, a more abstract distinction between three types of *forces* (locutionary-illocutionary-perlocutionary) suffers from a failure to account for how these 'forces' are expressed in language; to recognize their inter-relationships (e.g., that 'illocution' is just 'sense perlocution,' or a grammatical model of effectiveness, Sadock 1974); or to explain why the causal structure of the model, that 'illocution' causes 'perlocution,' breaks down routinely in both directions, i.e., why 'illocutionary' causes often fail to produce the effects expected, and why 'perlocutionary' effects routinely occur even when no 'illouctionary' forces are present. Austin's view of language remains limited to units of sentence-grammar; it gives little or no consideration to discourse-level phenomena. This difficulty persists in the derived 'speech-act' framework of Searle where explanations of how linguistic codings shape performativity is vitiated by the existence

of 'indirect speech acts,' namely cases where performative effects abound even though none of these codings occur (see ex. (17)ff. in the text). Here a secondary metaphysics of 'intentionality' is invoked, and the concern for linguistic codings abandoned. Both of these accounts are English-only accounts, moreover, lacking any cross-linguistic dimension. For a discussion of why 'speech act theory' has seemed such a plausible ideology of language to its proponents (despite its failure as an account of language) see Silverstein 1979 and Lee 1997.

24 Both text patterns share indicative mood, non-past tense, active voice, and simple aspect. They differ in that the nomic pattern involves third person agreement, but the performative locution has first person subject.

25 Terms such as 'sender' and 'receiver' are not names of people but of interactional role categories inhabitable by social persons in events of communication. Such role categories are indefinitely decomposable into further sub-types; corporeal participants are not. It is now understood that the decomposition of 'sender' and 'receiver' roles into sub-categories such as 'speaker/animator/author/principal ...' or 'hearer/addressee/reader/audience/overhearer ...' cannot be handled by appeal to static inventories of role labels. Their specific construal depends on semiotic cues occurring within messages themselves – the use of pronominal forms, quotation, parallelism, gesture, gaze, posture – which reflexively shape the construal of a participation framework for participants themselves (see Irvine, 1996; Hanks, 1996). I therefore use the terms 'sender' and 'receiver' as names for variables whose specific values are established for participants only by appeal to such cues. It follows that different events in a speech chain will involve different role specifications, shaped in each case by cues that are currently in play.

26 Thus, if I know of two people with the name 'John F. Kennedy' I belong to two distinct speech chain networks – i.e., I have been a 'hearer' of at least two prior speech events, each linked historically to a distinct baptismal event, and thus to two different persons bearing the name – a situation which might lead me to inquire in some subsequent speech event '*Which* John F. Kennedy do you mean?' of my interlocutor.

27 The issue of verifiability of baptismal events does become critical, however, in more specialized areas of cultural life such as historical research, legal proceedings, rights to citizenship, etc. These practices therefore rely on specialized text-artifacts – including public records, such as county registers and birth certificates – that are socially designed to answer questions about the verifiability of baptismal events and of consequent facts of social identity. Yet by their very nature such artifacts are neither accessible to everyone nor called upon in everyday uses of names. In other cases, such as claims to co-membership in a 'fictive lineage' or 'tradition,' aspects of a shared discursive history are not only presupposed but consciously believed and overtly claimed; in such cases, the claims may well be unverifiable, or verifiable and demonstrable as false. And criteria of verifiability may themselves be disputed – and frequently are, as in the case of religious traditions – and even linked to epistemological conflicts that create internal boundaries within the tradition.

28 I say 'apparently' amenable here because no one has, in fact, ever studied conversational transcripts without participating in the larger circulatory processes that make conversational discourse intelligible to its participants. In the case of some traditions of transcript-based study, including some that view transcripts as autonomous and self-enclosed domains of study, this acquaintance is derived by tacit recourse to native speaker intuitions (see n. 2).

29 In some cases the practice of naturalizing conventions is delegated by a division of labor (see 2.4) to a distinct caste or class of 'ethnotheorists' of society who may have no direct stakes in the conventions they analyze but nonetheless have stakes in the forms of explanation offered. Thus in the modern academy theorists who purport to take on such tasks as 'showing the deductive necessity of instituted rules, uncovering concealed practical rationality behind historically transmitted customs, or positing adaptive mechanisms as the real explanation of social practices' (Parmentier 1994: 177) may have little in the way of direct stakes in the rules, customs and practices they rationalize; but they have stakes in the frameworks they use to rationalize them, such as schemata of 'deductive necessity,' 'practical rationality' and 'adaptive mechanisms,' which now appear, through the claims of their universality, as 'natural' ways of reducing conventions to simple logical calculi. Even when comparative evidence (cross-cultural, historical) makes clear that such calculi for explaining customs are specious, and it invariably does, the restricted communities in which they are held plausible have an internal division of labor, and a system of inclusion and exclusion of types of knowledge, whereby attachment to these calculi can be made to persist well beyond the moment of their empirical refutation. In this respect specialized ethnotheories are exactly like the naturalized customs which they seek to explain.

30 A process of communicative transmission may have the appearance of local invariance but nonetheless involve global change. It has the appearance of local invariance whenever messages in adjacent links of a chain are virtually indistinguishable, are asymptotically the 'same message.' Even when this is the case, small differences between adjacent 'messages' may well add up, cumulatively, into massive overall differences. More generally, such questions of change or continuity involve multiple criteria – such as likeness of sign-form or of sign-values, the type of reanalysis involved, the ideological stakes of sign-users in such reanalyses – that enable changes of one type to co-exist with continuities of another, often providing a measure of fractional congruence among divergent models. See 2.2 and 3.8 for further discussion of these issues.

Chapter 2

1 The argument that phonological and morphosyntactic units are denotational units of a language is not a new claim; the sentence-proposition is the traditional domain of grammatical analysis from Saussure to Chomsky (e.g., Saussurean 'signifieds' are denotational classes, Sapir calls grammar a 'referential symbolism,' and Chomsky limits a transformational grammar to 'truth-preserving' transformations). My argument here is that grammatical units (one identified under propositional assumptions) are highly plurifunctional, that is, mark additional types of pragmatic-indexical information, such as deictic and register contrasts, and that the latter cannot be studied by the methods of grammatical analysis.

2 However, it is not accurate to say, as Lyons does in the quote, that denotation is *wholly* utterance-independent; I return to this point in 2.3.

3 My definition of 'successful' reference differs from that proposed by Searle 1969. In Searle's terms, an act of referring is 'successful' if a speaker's referential utterance 'applies' to one and only one object. Searle equivocates on what the term 'applies' means in this definition, settling finally on the criterion of speaker

intentionality (i.e., the speaker's utterance 'applies' to what the speaker 'intends to refer'; p. 83, n. 1); but he provides no empirical criterion for discovering *what* the speaker intends. In contrast with Searle's speaker-centric notion of 'success,' I am concerned here with 'interactional success,' namely the extent to which hearer and speaker exhibit a symmetric grasp of referent in their *relative behavior* during an interaction.

4 Although I rely heavily here on the data and some of the analysis presented in Goodwin and Goodwin (1992), the theoretical framework I develop here is very different from theirs. My goal here is to show that much of what is nowadays called 'conversation analysis' can be subsumed within a richer semiotic theory of interaction, one which pays more careful attention to both the grammatical and text-metrical patterns that constitute the orderliness of linguistically mediated social interaction; and, at the same time, brings together the analysis of linguistic and non-linguistic semiosis within a unified account of multi-channel sign-configurations.

5 Thus in lines 1 and 3 the origo of the utterance-act is Dianne; in lines 2 and 4, Clacia. Lines 1 and 2 are denotationally cohesive in predicate semantics, as are lines 3 and 4. But each pair of lines is not referentially coherent to the same degree (since R ≠ R'); the fractional non-congruence of referent has interactional consequences, as the discussion shows.

6 Hence if you ask a native speaker of English about the semantic properties of the agentive suffix *-er* by formulating a metasemantic query (e.g., by asking 'What does *-er* mean?') you are likely to get various forms of puzzlement by way of response. The native speaker has not encountered the suffix except in larger configurations (words like *painter, drummer*) and is therefore not able to recognize it as an isolable unit of the language, let alone describe its semantic properties.

7 In applying such tests we are not concerned merely with whether the specialized construction occurs or does not occur in speech, i.e., merely with questions of a 'possible form.' We are concerned with regularities of form/sense contrast, i.e., whether a form contrast regularly yields the same sense contrast. Thus the forms *waters, sugars, airs*, do occur in English but not as ordinary plurals of *water, sugar and air*; to speak of *waters* is to speak of bodies of water (viz., *Moses parted the waters. . .*); chemists speak of *sugars* (glucose, fructose, etc.); and *airs* means 'affectations' in phrases like *putting on airs*. Hence the form contrasts *air/airs* implements a different sense contrast than does *book/books*. Similarly pronouns (and proper names) permit determiners under certain special conditions – such as cases of contrastive reference (viz., *the old me, the new me*) – but the use of a determiner with a common noun is far more ubiquitous (and grammatical obligatory for a singular count noun) even when these special conditions do not contextually hold. Hence, once again, the form contrast does not yield the same sense contrast.

8 In this case the denotation of the more complex construction 'the ... who ...' is relatively easily captured by the denotation of a simple expression, the term 'human,' which therefore provides a convenient metasemantic label for both the complex construction and the distributional class of which it is diagnostic. But this is not always so. We noted earlier that every language has many more units of structural sense than it has notional labels for them. In these cases the more convenient descriptive strategy is to use names for morphosyntactic patterns as labels for form/sense distinctions, e.g., in the case of complementizers, we speak, as in (8c), of one type as the 'gerundive' or *'s -ing* construction (*Sam's being*

hungry), another as a *for to* construction (*for Sam to be hungry*), another as a *that*-clause (*that Sam is hungry*). These constructional classes and the lexeme collocations they yield are form/sense categories in precisely the same way as those illustrated in Figure 2.4; but they differ in that they do not correspond to continuous lexical expressions and do not have naturally occurring names. This is sometimes taken as evidence for the autonomy of syntax from semantics, but this is a confusion. All structural sense contrasts are syntactico-semantic contrasts, i.e., are contrasts among syntactic constituents that correspond to semantic contrasts. However, only a few of them can be described by means of naturally occurring metasemantic labels.

9 And if we consider [−noun] categories as well, we find that /flaɪ/ corresponds to two distinct verb lexemes, an intransitive verb, *fly₃* (cf. *the bird flies*) and a transitive verb, *fly₄* (cf. *to fly a plane*). Given sense compositionality, facts of homonymy also have syntactic consequences: when word-forms correspond to more than one lexeme, sentences formed from them correspond to more than one proposition. Thus the sentence *Flying planes can be dangerous* corresponds to two different propositions, or underlying sentences, one in which *flying planes* is understood as 'a plane which is flying' (here the lexeme is the intransitive verb, *fly₃*) and another in which it is understood as 'for someone to fly a plane' (where the lexeme is the transitive verb, *fly₄*).

10 The field procedure relies on using certain constructions (like 'X is Y' and 'X means Y') to formulate metasemantic queries. But as we saw at the beginning of Chapter 1 (see example (1)ff.) constructions that are used metasemantically in a language also have other uses. Thus the use of these constructions to gather metasemantic data presupposes (1) that the relevant constructional forms have been identified in the language, (2) that the distributional conditions under which they function metasemantically are well understood (see n. 4, Chapter 1), (3) that the method of elicitation is sufficiently well structured that metasemantic responses to the query can be distinguished from other responses. For example, if a native speaker responds to the question 'What does X mean?' by saying something like 'Well, X *is a word that only priests use*; they use it to talk about Y' the italicized portion of the response is a metapragmatic gloss on the stereotypic users of the expression (and provides evidence for the existence of a register boundary in the language) whereas the rest of the response appears to formulate a metasemantic gloss on X, typifying its sense as equivalent to (or perhaps overlapping with) the sense of Y.

11 A prototypical referent is a *social* regularity of metasemantic evaluation, i.e., a thing identified by attention to the metasemantic behavior of a sample population. As Rosch observes: 'To speak of a *prototype* at all is simply a convenient grammatical fiction; what is really referred to are judgments of degrees of prototypicality' (Rosch 1978: 40). A single individual's judgments never suffice as data on identification; only by considering the extensional judgments of many individuals is a referential prototype identified – just as the data of *intensional* judgments by many persons provide criteria on the identification of stereotypes. Moreover, as we shall see in 2.4, individuals differ in their judgments about the extension and intension of semantic classes, and these differences are sometimes linked to sociological relationships between these individuals (including asymmetries of power) in establishing authoritative models of correct reference.

12 In cognitive linguistics it has traditionally been assumed that just one out of these three principles – namely, referential prototypes – by itself constitutes a

necessary and sufficient basis for category membership. This is wrong. (The question of whether categories are modeled by Aristotelean or 'fuzzy' logics is not relevant here.) Referential prototypes do not form a *sufficient* basis for category membership since regularities of structural sense and denotational stereotypy (which are largely ignored or remain untheorized in this tradition; see Lucy 1997 on the neglect of distributional criteria in debates about color terms) *also* function as principles of category membership, and frequently run interference with (even cross-classify) facts of category membership. And referential prototypes are not *necessary* principles of class membership since for many linguistic expressions, facts of structural sense and/or denotational stereotypy carry nearly the entire functional load for deciding category membership, and referential prototypes are non-existent, i.e., undecideable by language users (a point discussed a little later in this section).

13 The reasons that they are not logically independent may be summarized as follows: (1) We can never give a distributional analysis (and hence isolate structural sense) without presupposing some metasemantic knowledge on the part of native speakers; and (2) we can never reliably use equational constructions to gather glosses and referent identifications (and hence formulate models of an expression's denotational stereotype or referential prototype) without a grammatical analysis of the conditions under which the constructions employed in our queries function as metasemantic equations (see n. 4, Chapter 1).

14 I have argued in 2.3 that grammatical units – phonemes, as well as lexemes and morphosyntactic patterns – are, from the standpoint of their structural function, denotational units of different kinds. If this point is placed within the context of the argument in previous sections and chapters, it will be clear that this is hardly the *only* function they subserve. We saw that denotational categories are functionally laminated with indexical categories in the case of *deictic expressions* (1.4); that metrical contrasts among *lexemic tokens* mediate emergent role alignments by delineating propositional stances in referential semiosis (2.2); that isosemantic but formally contrastive denotational words (i.e., contrastive *word-form types*, and sometimes also *lexeme types*) mediate register contrasts. This is hardly an exhaustive list, just a summary of some of the non-denotational functions considered so far. In this section I show that the emergence of register contrasts partly depends on a functional reanalysis of denotational footing.

Chapter 3

1 Talk of social 'practices' involves a commitment to the ubiquity and recurrence of certain behaviors. Not all reflexive behaviors are organized equally robustly into widespread practices in this sense. I argued in the Introduction to this book that making the notion of 'language use' empirically tractable requires that we distinguish between thresholds of ubiquity and routinization (viz., an instance of use, a habitual usage, a norm of usage, a tropic usage). Much the same point applies to the notion of reflexive behavior now at issue. An observed reflexive behavior/act may be highly idiosyncratic; or it may be commonplace; or constitute a norm for a population (but see Table 2.5ff.); or it may be intelligible only as a trope upon a norm. To speak of reflexive *practices* is to speak of the social organization of reflexive behaviors; it is therefore a dependent concept, though

one of utmost importance as I argue later in this section. Similar considerations apply to the notion of 'ideology' (3.4).

2 To say that a point of view is 'ideological' is unavoidably to suggest that the point of view is inaccurate or distorting in some way. Yet anthropologists writing on language ideology (Scheiffelin et al. 1998, Kroskrity 2000) often shy away from this position, perhaps because they assume that to allege that a point of view is distorting is to assume a God's-eye, distortion-free position. The alternative commonly adopted is to speak of "the loading of moral and political interests" (Irvine 1989: 255) or to say that ideologies are characterized both by "group relative interests" and by "multiplicity and contention" (Kroskrity 2004, Gal 1998). But these alternatives amount to the same thing: if ideologies make competing claims, variant positions cannot all be equally accurate. So a concept of 'distortion' is assumed, though the term 'distortion' is avoided. My goal here is to show that incorporating ideas of 'distortion' in definitions of ideology in no way presupposes a distortion-free position. Whenever competing models of a cultural phenomenon co-exist in a society, *each* of these models distorts the phenomenon from the point of view of *every* other model. Empirically, to claim that a cultural model is ideological is not to distinguish 'distortion'-laden from 'distortion'-free models (such as, say, scientific models) but to comment on the *mutually distorting character of competing positional models*. Scientific models can be shown to be ideological in precisely this sense too, as when a competing model reveals the interest-bound distortions of another.

3 In the case of linguistic registers, such acts are acts of utterance. However, in the case of semiotic registers more broadly (that is, in cases where the object-signs of the register are not, or are not only, linguistic signs; see 3.9), acts of performance through which characterological figures are exhibited are frequently semiotic behaviors of very diverse sorts. Bakhtinian "voices" (Bakhtin 1984) are special cases of what I call "characterological figures"; the former are linguistically mediated, the latter not necessarily so (see Agha 2005 for further discussion of this point).

Chapter 4

1 Received Pronunciation (RP) may initially be described as the accent associated with the dialect of English generally called Standard British English (SBE). SBE has all of the properties characteristic of prestige varieties in a contemporary 'standard language' community: It contrasts with regional dialects as a 'supra-local' national language; it is widely used in writing and print. For many speakers, SBE is neither the variety acquired first, nor the one used most frequently in casual conversation (Trudgill 1999); yet the variety is preeminent in public life due to its social prestige, its links to education and economic advancement. In all of these ways, SBE is en-register-ed in cultural awareness as a valued commodity. Once acquired, the commodity can be displayed in speech and writing, and such display counts as an index of the status position of speaker/author in many venues of social life. My concern here is not with SBE, however, but with the accent associated with its spoken form.

2 RP is only partially a phonolexical register. As the discussion of repertoire characteristics in the previous chapter makes clear (see Table 3.6ff), elaborate registers typically consist of a variety of repertoire components. In the next chapter (section 5.7) I discuss some non-linguistic signs associated with this

register; the goal of this chapter is to focus on its linguistic aspects. Wells 1982 shows that phonolexical contrasts define a very substantial portion of its linguistic repertoires; however other phonetic features, including suprasegmental prosodic contrasts occur as well. The phonolexical aspects of the linguistic register tend also to acquire a pre-eminence in folk-discussions of RP since language users pay singular attention to the pronunciation of words. The phonolexical component of RP therefore has a distinctive importance at the level of ideological perceptions of the register, both in everyday discussions of accent and in widespread mass-mediated stereotypes; this phenomenon is illustrated at length in this chapter. Analogous phonolexical registers occur in many other languages (see Agha 2002: 39–43), though they are not always ideologically comparable (see Irvine 1998). Our own term 'accent' itself constitutes a highly culture-specific ideological framework for characterizing and discussing register contrasts involving phonolexical and other prosodic features.

3 The remaining criteria, ranked in descending order, are as follows: 'Where they live,' 'The friends they have,' 'Their job,' 'The sort of school they went to,' 'The way they spend their money', 'The way they dress' and 'The car they own' (Reid 1977: 28). Though not specifically mentioned in the questionnaire, perceptions of accent are likely to have played a role in these responses, especially in the ranking of speech habits as number one overall and of schooling (cf. the stereotype of 'Public School Pronunciation') as number five.

4 Observe that for some – though not all – of these evaluative dimensions, RP is ranked *higher* for stereotypes of 'power' (viz., ambition, intelligence, self-confidence, determination) and *lower* for stereotypes of 'solidarity' (good-humor, good-naturedness). Thus stereotypes of RP are broadly comparable to those linked to pronominal registers, as reported by Brown and Gilman (1960) for the European languages on the basis of a similar questionnaire survey. This type of inverse relationship between stereotypes of power and solidarity has now been described for many other status-linked registers, and in a variety of other languages as well (see Agha 1994 for a review of the literature).

5 The stereotype that exemplary speech indexes positive speaker attributes (viz., mental ability, taste, behavioral finesse, social class, caste, etc.) is associated with prestige registers in many other languages too (e.g., Javanese (Errington 1988, 1998; Poedjosoedarmo 1968), Persian (Beeman 1986), Tibetan (Agha 1998a)) though the specific characterological constructs differ from case to case. Also cross-linguistically common are the phenomena of role alignment and the asymmetries of competence noted here for RP.

6 In many cases the scheme of register values exhibits a degree of sociological fractionation (see ch. 3), a process of value competition that reflects the group-relative interests of particular persons (Hill 1998; Agha 1998a). In other cases the sign-values may become rigidly naturalized, whether as attributes of particular groups (e.g., the case where the speech of a privileged group *counts as* the exemplary form), or as impersonal standards, backed by the authority of canonizing institutions (e.g., national academies, school boards, lexicographic traditions); these processes appear to render the cultural formation non-contingent and often expand the social domain of the register.

7 As Lyons (1995: 235) observes, '[t]he term "utterance" can be used to refer either to the process (or activity) of uttering or to the products of that process (or activity).' In the latter, 'product' sense, an utterance is an acoustical artifact, a thing made through human activity in the physical substance of sound. The discursive artifact can carry messages insofar as it is an object of the senses

(Urban 1996) as do other kinds of physical artifact (Appadurai 1986). And although a spoken utterance has a fleeting durational existence (relative to human perceptual rates), it is capable of conversion through the act of recording into more perduring physical artifacts – such as those made of ink and paper – that facilitate the more indirect, spatiotemporally remote forms of communication discussed in this chapter.

8 These notions of characterological figure and role alignment were discussed in more detail earlier (Chapter 3, especially S 3.3 and the discussion following). I am particularly interested in what follows with characterological figures that are stereotypically linked to a speech register, and are thus enactable through a use of that register. The fact that such figures are endogenized to register models makes them detachable from any current animator and thus re-enactable by others in subsequent moments of circulation. And the transformation of register images over time is also linked to the figures with which an individual aligns as an animator, and to the footings established with interlocutors through the act.

9 While there is little doubt that we can identify the *main* source variety in this way, it is equally evident that many other spoken varieties have served as occasional and sometimes dramatic sources of innovation in RP (e.g., the speech of the professional middle classes, London Cockney). All 'single ancestor' accounts of the origins of RP – or, indeed, of any other linguistic register – have an in-principle limitation: they presume a false analogy with biological descent. Biological species can descend from single ancestor species due to constraints on cross-species interbreeding and exchange of genetic materials; but linguistic registers have elements that are easily mixed and recombined across dialect and register boundaries. See Hope (2000) for an elegant discussion of this point. My own argument – that the historical transmission of RP involved metadiscursive processes that *actively reconfigure* particular features of the register and do so, in each instance, in ways that depend on the *local context* of that moment of transmission – avoids this pitfall and provides an alternative.

10 The variety is alluded to by George Puttenham in his *Art of Poesie* (1589) when he recommends the young poet to adopt 'the usual speech of the Court, and that of London and the shires lying about London within 60 miles and not much above.' However even in the seventeenth century the court variety is often perceived as a form of restricted, in-group speech by dramatists and other literary figures who see themselves as out-group. They lampoon it in plays, describe it as 'amusing,' as having 'distended vowels' (Honey 1989b: 585), thus indicating a degree of role distance, or negative alignment with its values.

11 Thus every 'message' which introduces a name-referent pair to someone else must contain a token of the proper name. This is a criterion on the identity of *message form*. In addition, such a message must also contain some semiotic device which introduces the referent (viz., through ostension, definite descriptions, etc.) The latter is a criterion on the identity of *message content* (not message form) since acts of identifying the referent may be accomplished by a variety of sign forms.

12 See Watts 1999 for similar observations about prescriptivist discourses of written Standard English in the first half of the eighteenth century.

13 The titles of these works provide a sense of Sheridan's concerns: *British Education* (1756); *A Dissertation on the Causes of the Difficulties Which Occur in Learning the English Tongue* (1761); *Lectures on Elocution* (1762); *A Plan of Education for the Young Nobility* (1769); *Lectures on the Art of Reading* (1775); *A General Dictionary of the English Language* (1780). In addition to writing

treatises, Sheridan, who was a noted actor, brought these ideas to the theatre as well (Benzie 1972). He also gave lectures on elocution that popularized the view that particular 'tones, looks and gestures constitute a natural language of the passions' (Mohrmann 1969: iv), arguing that education and cultivation are best evidenced in the overall delivery of an utterance. Such a 'culture of performance' was soon transported to the United States and proved influential in early American politics (Fliegelman 1993; Gustafson 1992).

14 I am greatly indebted to Lynda Mugglestone's historical research in the sections that follow. I have consulted many of the sources she cites and have offered a slightly distinct reading of some of them; my conclusions build on her own work, though I extend the argument in rather different directions. In quoting sources cited by her that are unavailable to me I cite the page number from her text.

15 Such semiotic diagrams have been exemplified and discussed in some detail in previous chapters. Let me offer a note on terminology here. In the Peircean terminology (see Peirce 1931–1958), any sign is iconic insofar as the properties of the sign convey something about the properties of the object. Diagrams are complex icons 'which represent the relations ... of the parts of one thing by analogous relations in their own parts' (vol. 2, §277). Peirce argued that geometric figures, algebraic formulae, and even literary fictions are diagrammatic constructs that allow the mind to perceive things in experience as complex wholes, with parts having non-arbitrary relations and affinities to each other: 'The work of the poet or novelist is not so utterly different from that of the scientific man. The artist introduces a fiction; but it is not an arbitrary one; it exhibits affinities to which the mind accords a certain approval in pronouncing them beautiful ... The geometer draws a diagram ... and by means of observation of that diagram he is able to synthesize and show relations between elements which before seemed to have no necessary connection' (vol. 1, §383). The diagrams I discuss here are indexical icons in the sense that they motivate iconic relations (such as likenesess) among variables of the speech event, thus forging non-arbitrary connections between elements indexically co-occurring within the interaction order.

16 As Lynda Mugglestone observes: 'George Gissing read Thomas Kingston-Oliphant's *The Sources of Standard English*, as well as George Craik's *Manual of English Language and Literature*, eagerly absorbing their dictates on the shibboleths and social markers in the spoken English of the late nineteenth century. George Bernard Shaw, "a social downstart", devoted himself to works on elocution in the British Museum, as well as to *The Manners and Tone of Good Society* with its subtitle *Solecisms to be Avoided*, and its advice that "the mispronunciation of certain surnames falls unpleasantly upon the educated ear, and argues unfavourably as to the social position of the offender". Thomas Hardy purchased a copy of Nuttall's *Standard Pronouncing Dictionary*, as well as *Mixing in Society: A Complete Manual of Manners* with its assertion that "the best accent is undoubtedly that taught at Eton and Oxford. One may be as awkward with the mouth as with the arms or legs".' (Mugglestone 1995: 1–2)

17 Sally Mitchell, on whose work I rely here, provides the following estimates: 'If most of the issues were read aloud in the family or passed along to friends, one of the two magazines must have reached nearly one person in three among the literate population. (By way of comparison, the Dickens novel with the greatest immediate sale was *The Old Curiosity Shop* (1840–41) at 100,000 per part).' (Mitchell 1977: 31)

18 Estuary English is an accent that hybridizes Cockney and RP features. Its speakers exhibit a greater tendency towards traditional Cockney patterns – such as /t/ glottalization and affrication, the loss or coalescence of /j/, neutralization of high vowels, and the substitution of /w/ for /l/ in criterial environments – superimposed on General RP patterns. The accent is prevalent in the region of the Thames estuary in Southeastern England. From the standpoint of pure RP loyalists, the accent is viewed as a corruption bespeaking a lowering of general standards and values. However younger speakers from traditionally RP speaking families find themselves increasingly drawn to it.

19 Henry Alford, in his *A Plea for the Queen's English* (1866) is quite explicit on this point. Just as the Queen's Highway is not owned by the Queen, he argues, but 'open to all of common right,' the Queen's English is named after the Sovereign because she is 'the person around whom all *our* common interests gather, the source of *our* civil duties and centre of *our* civil rights.' The various tokens of the pronoun *our* (emphases added) refer to commoners. Hence, he argues, 'the *Queen's English* is not an unmeaning phrase, but one which may serve to teach *us* [i.e., ordinary persons] some profitable lessons with regard to our language, and its use and abuse' (pp. 1–2).

Chapter 5

1 The term 'embodiment' is sometimes restricted in the literature to features of the *human* body. In this peculiar sense 'embodied' means something like 'incorporated into the human body'. This approach seeks to reverse the mentalistic orientation of previous social theories, but finds itself in a narrow, reactive position, entirely caught up in the mind-body dualism which it seeks to transcend. According to this type of essentialism, causes and explanations for why people behave the way they do are 'not in the mind, but in the body'. This corporeal metaphysics is a mirror-image of the intellectualist metaphysics to which it is a reaction: one pole of the dualism simply *replaces* another. In contrast, the view adopted here (following Peirce's critique of dualism and Descartes) is that all signs are *at once* embodied and mentalistic: they are embodied because only physical objects instantiate sign-relationships; they are mentalistic in that the sign-relationship has an import, conveys an idea, to someone. An ethnographic development of these themes may be found in Urban 1996.

2 It is worth noting, however, that talk of 'ascribed' and 'achieved' status in this tradition is an attempt to approach the problem of role/status attribution. This distinction is very useful in thinking about this issue. And yet it is not enough. It is useful because the very act of distinguishing ascribed statuses (those 'assigned to individuals without reference to their innate differences or abilities') and achieved statuses (those 'not assigned to individuals from birth' but on the basis of 'individual effort'; Linton 1936: 115) foregrounds the important issue that the various ways in which individuals are assigned roles/statuses differ in the degree to which the agency of the individual plays a part in the process of assignment. And yet it is not enough because, since roles and statuses are 'ideal patterns,' this account (1) tells us little about how these patterns come into existence or change over time, and (2) neglects the issue of the dialogic engagements of individual actors with their own and others' roles/statuses (at the level of interactional text), through which, as I argue in this chapter, all attributions of

persona, both ones that are fragile and ones that are durable, are linked to those whose personae they are.

3 I am not suggesting that the only way of studying social roles is to take role designators as a point of departure. Rather, I am arguing that *when* we do orient ourselves by taking role designators as points of departure – as Weber proposes, and as is commonplace in ethnographic fieldwork – there are two different ways of proceeding from that point of departure.

4 Our intuition that individuals can be sorted into classifiable social kinds is reinforced by our ability to use role designators as a shorthand for facts of personhood. But even the class of *lexical* role designators is much larger than the set of common nouns to which Weber alludes in the passage in (1). Any semantically [+ human] expression belongs to this class. This includes nominal expressions such as titles, kinterms, proper names and person deictics. Other role designating expressions are not intrinsically nouns, but are expressions predicable of or modifiers of human nouns; names of languages and countries commonly function as role designators when used in this way. In an example like 'He is Welsh' humanness is established by the pronoun, regional group identity by the adjective. Some role designating adjectives are derivationally related to *verba sentiendi* (*happy, sad, angry*) so that their role designating usage ascribes psychological states to persons. Any verb subcategorized for semantically human subjects (e.g., the *verba dicendi, speak, tell, listen*, etc.) are role designating predicates from which nominals can be formed through derivational processes. Many role designators are deictics. Some are speech-event deictics that indexically denote interactional roles (e.g., utterances of 'I' and 'you' are diacritic of the speech-act roles they denote). Proper names are speech-chain deictics that denote unique individuals under certain conditions (see 1.6). Official titles are role designators designed to locate persons in social groupings of an institutional kind, groupings that may officially be inhabitable only one person at a time. Some role designators are not everyday expressions at all but belong to specialized registers of role specifying discourses used by specialists, e.g., terms like *class, caste, clan, gender, moeity*; these terms are given technical, register-specific senses which allow them to function as designators of more abstract social kinds.

5 The notion that common understanding *necessarily* requires shared conventions is associated with the doctrine that conventions and customs are adopted through a 'social contract'; this in turn is linked to a mythic 'state of nature,' a state characterized by the complete absence of shared custom. Thomas Hobbes supposed the state of nature to be a state of continuous chaos and warfare in which there was 'no account of Time; no Arts; no Letters; no Society' and the life of man, correspondingly, 'solitary, poore, nasty, brutish and short,' a state of affairs which he believed to be at once conjectural, and, at the same time, extant among 'the savage people in America' in his time (Bk. XIII, *Leviathan*, 1659). The details of this sometimes mythic, sometimes quasi-historic state are further elaborated by Locke and Rousseau in various ways. Although mainly intended as an account of political formations, the myth appears to motivate the necessity of *convention as such* by counterposing civil society to its savage alternative, to a transcendent and naturalized figurement of social relations in the absence of convention. The state of nature is a transcendent construct in that it belongs to mythic, not human history; and insofar as the 'state of nature' is a model of 'the state of [human] nature [before convention]', the social contract is (was? ought-to-be? must be?) adopted (note the deictic indeterminacy here) in order to escape atavistic human nature. It is the deictic unlocatability of this

perilous state, moreover, that makes the myth of social contract so handy, so omnipresent in such surprisingly different debates. The fact that there's no empirical evidence for it is, of course, irrelevant to those who find it compelling, as with any myth.

6 In this paper Goffman shows that so-called 'adjacency pair' relationships are not 'formal' structures (as Conversation Analysts have supposed) but features of discourse whose emergence and identifiablity is mediated by semiotic cues. Adjacency pairs are local structures of interactional text whereby two contiguous utterances are evaluable by congruence of semiotic cues as 'paired' with each other to some degree, e.g., as a question (a first pair-part) and its answer (a second pair-part). Goffman gives a preliminary typology of types of chaining: for example, 'a two-person interrogative chain,' the case 'where whoever provides a current question provides the next one too' (e.g., person 'a' asks all the questions, viz., $[Q_a] [A_b] [Q_a] [A_b]$...); or 'a two-person sociable chain,' the case 'where whoever provides a second pair part goes on to provide the first pair part of the next pair' (e.g., each respondent adds a question to his answer, viz., $[Q_a] [A_b/Q_b] [A_a/Q_a] [A_b/Q_b]$...). The contrast between these two types of chains differentiates the two Yemeni greeting patterns discussed in the text, though the illocutionary types that occur in turn-segments within Yemeni greetings are far more varied than mere 'questions' and 'answers'.

7 Thus many groups disguise their existence (cf. 'secret societies') by concealing the identities of members and even by restricting knowledge of the criteria on membership to in-group circles. Other groups make public both members' identities and criteria for membership but these are disputed by others (e.g., diplomatic non-recognition of a country). Some groups are widely alleged to have both members and specific criteria for membership, but these are not widely viewed as authoritative (e.g., witches, vampires, aliens), thus calling into question precisely the question of their existence. All such cases depend on the fact that certain signs function as emblems of group status; but the social domain over which such emblems function effectively is more or less problematic.

Chapter 6

1 Such discourses are of course ubiquitous in languages in which the lexical register of honorific forms consists mainly of pronouns, as in the case of the familiar European languages (Table 6.3). But even in languages possessing far more elaborate honorific registers (Chapter 7), pronouns and other participant referring forms are treated as privileged objects of metasemiotic reflection by language users. Thus in the case of Javanese, Errington notes: 'To the most neutral sorts of questions about speech level use – for example, 'How do you speak with X?', where X is the name of an acquaintance, family member, or description of some hypothetical and 'typical' speech partner – speakers typically respond with a specification of pronoun and nothing else.' (Errington 1985: 64) Similarly, in the case of Vietnamese, Luong observes: 'In the metalinguistic awareness of virtually all native speakers, person reference constitutes the most salient domain through which interactional contexts are structured and partly in terms [of] which the native sociocultural universe is reproduced and transformed.' (Luong 1990: 5) Thus, cross-linguistically, person-referring honorific forms are among the most salient to language users as ways of conceptualizing and commenting on the honorific register of their language.

2 Although the examples are selected from a single study they are highly typical of accounts found elsewhere in the literature. Das' study of Bengali is unusually rich and comprehensive, partly because he is a native speaker but also because he has attended to metapragmatic representations of Bengali usage in a wide range of published sources.

3 As we saw in 3.5, the question of whether a particular utterance is 'appropriate' or 'inappropriate' is undecideable if the hearer attends only to the lexeme token itself; it is only by reading the lexeme token in relation to the semiotic co-text of its occurrence that the hearer of the utterance can construe it as one type of act or another. Moreover the specific details of the construal are 'filled in' by the semiotic effects established by cotextual signs. For instance the use of *tui* by a college teacher for a student may be understood as a display of anger or as the loss of self-control if the teacher habitually maintains the normative persona through a pattern of *tui* avoidance in the classroom. But this is not a construal of the current *tui* token alone; it is based on locating the token-occurrence in a prior history or chain of occurrences, relative to which one or more determinate construals become plausible.

4 For many-term systems, the question of whether we extend the typological letter symbols in the way Braun suggests, or as T_1, T_2, T_3 ... vs. V, or in some other way, has no non-arbitrary solution. And in such systems, 'politeness' is a relational (not an intrinsic) property of a form. The latter is also the case with two-term systems. But because the relata are just two terms, the essentializing claim that one form, T, is 'familiar' and the other, V, is 'polite' (For all speakers? In all events of use?) appears initially plausible. However, as we shall see in the next section, this claim is false even for two-term systems.

5 In reality the range of co-textual cues that determine singular reference (and hence the polite construal) is even broader. Comrie 1975 discusses a variety of cues within text-sentences that disambiguate numerosity of referent in several European languages (Polish, Portuguese, Spanish, Dutch, Rumanian). Moreover, additional, more text-configurative cues, including other types of linguistic cues (such as patterns of lexical cohesion from prior discourse) as well as features of the non-linguistic co-text (e.g., fixing of referent by eye-gaze) can play an accompanying role as well.

6 The tension between these two metapragmatic facts – an implicit regularity of contextualized response behavior and an explicit regularity of decontextualized description – is notionally resolved by the claim that there are *two* lexemes that have the shape *vous*, a plural lexeme and a polite-singular. But the homonymy argument is just a way of restating the co(n)textually observed facts since the homonyms can only be distinguished by criterial text configurations. The restatement has no empirical consequences for the study of contextualized interaction; but it is consistent with folk-theories of language structure and use which take referring to be a relationship between words and things (see Chapter 2).

7 The general point here concerns text configurations that refer to addressee, not noun-verb agreement as such. Agreement morphology plays an important role in some languages (such as the Indo-European cases discussed here) but is irrelevant or non-existent in others. In Bantu languages, noun classifier concord plays a role functionally analogous but formally distinct from agreement in the sense illustrated above. In Lhasa Tibetan, where no agreement or concord morphology exists, contrasts involving reflexives, types of pluralization, predicate indexicals, and sentence-final particles indexing participant roles do most of

the work of specifying reference to addressee (Agha 1993a). Similarly distributed cues occur in languages like Chinese, Vietnamese, Thai, and Japanese.

8 The fact that there are three columns in the table where +kin is marked reflects the fact that knowing that your addressee is a kin is not enough information to decide how normatively to address them. You need to consider additional factors. If the kin is of nonascending generation T is used; if a person of ascending generation then, for a non-intimate (i.e., +nonsolidary), the normative choice is V, otherwise T.

Chapter 7

1 As a word of the English language, the term *honorific* is ambiguous. In one sense, the term may be glossed as 'capable of conferring honor or respect' (i.e., positively valued for respect); when used metapragmatically, this usage denotes a commodified, positively valued system of object-signs. In a second, broader sense the term applies to any expression which 'pertains to honor or respect' (whether positively or negatively valued for respect); this broader sense is due to a generic property of the suffix -*ic*, and thus found in many other words of the form *X-ic* (viz., *calor-ic* 'pertaining to calories', *atom-ic* 'pertaining to atoms'). I use the term in the second, more inclusive sense, of which the first is a special case. In the broader sense the term *honorific* applies to any system of signs that pertain to matters of respect, e.g., whether positively or negatively valued for honorific effect (polite/refined or rude/coarse); whether the effect is construed as respect to others (addressee, referent, bystander), or as expressing the speaker's own respectability and, hence, entitlement to respect from others. Much of the older literature has used the term *honorific* (whether exclusively or in large part) for the special case of *positively* valued, *referent*-focal, *lexemic* signs of *deference* to *others*. Each of these italicized expressions marks a typological dimension for which other values are attested in the literature, viz., (a) positively vs. *negatively* valued honorifics, (b) referent- vs. *addressee*-focal indexicals, (c) lexemic vs. *prosodic/kinesic* signs, (d) honorific relations of deference vs. *deprecation*, (e) relations to *others* vs. demeanor of *self*. See note 5 below. In the wider sense used in this book, the term honorific means 'pertaining to honor or respect.' The wider usage is necessary if we wish to locate the special case most commonly discussed in the literature (the case of positively valued referent-focal deference markers) within a comparative framework for studying honorific registers.

2 Although the historical details differ for the different European languages, it is evident that forces of language standardization played a significant role in register simplification during the nineteenth century. Listen (1999) describes several dozen pronominal tropes that existed in different dialects of German between the sixteenth and nineteenth centuries; only a few have survived in modern Standard German. Despite the influence of Standard British English a number of second person pronoun forms (including forms of *thou*) still survive in contemporary 'traditional dialects' in Britain (Trudgill 1999).

3 Such verbs are not specifically [+human]-subject, since they are also predicable of animals. However deference to animals by using such verbs is judged ludicrous in the languages with which I am acquainted. This is not to say that the usage is 'ungrammatical'; it is merely extra-normative from the standpoint of social norms, and therefore highly effective as a joke. The restriction also makes clear

that norms of referent-focal deference are not reducible to structural sense criteria, even though they partly depend on them.

4 For a detailed discussion of how such systems operate in particular languages, see Agha (1993a, 1998a) for a discussion of Tibetan; Errington (1988) for Javanese; Inoue (1979) and Matsumoto (1997) for Japanese. The literature on other languages is summarized with bibliographic citations in Agha (1994). For most such verbs, both arguments are specifically [+ human, +animate], not just [+ animate]; but I have stated the generalization in terms of the weaker condition, since this not always so.

5 However, [–human] nouns are characteristically used in person reference in *negatively* valued honorific registers, including referent-focal registers of *deprecation*, and speaker-focal registers of *taboo* speech (see note 1 for relevant typological dimensions). For example, Leach 1966 notes that animal terms are cross-linguistically common for person reference in acts of abuse and invective; most of the cases he discusses involve referent-focal registers of deprecation (rather than positive deference). In a different vein, Eble 1996 notes several types of [–human] nouns that form compound nouns in registers of American College Slang, viz., *sex machine, study animal*. From the standpoint of word-structure, the second element of the compound noun (*machine, animal*) is a [–human] noun, but the compound noun as a whole denotes persons; here deprecation consists of lexicalized tropes of depersonalization. From the standpoint of metapragmatic norms, such slang registers are treated as negatively valued *taboo* speech from the perspective of Standard-enforcing institutions, though they occur routinely as age-graded emblems in youth practices and sub-culture.

Chapter 8

1 Hence semiotic behaviors in which no kinterms occur – and even behaviors in which no language use occurs – count as kinship behaviors society-internally only insofar as some social domain of actors construe it through discourses of kinship. This constitutes an 'emic' empirical criterion for deciding whether something is in fact kinship behavior for some social domain of persons (i.e., for those whose reflexive typifications provide evidence for the existence of the model). However to say that it counts as kinship behavior in one social domain in no way implies that it does so for all members of society. Recognizing from the outset that reflexive models are *models for* some social domain of persons allows us to understand the positional character of norms and the capacity of society-internal norm differentiation to yield emblems of group distinction (8.6).

2 Facts of lexical sense are sometimes misrecognized as a system of cognitive constraints. On this view, persons using distinct types of kinship terminology – the Crow, Omaha and Hawaiian types, for example – are said to have different kinship systems as mental models. But this is merely a projection from facts of lexicalization to facts of cognition. Thus one might suppose that in a society that has a Hawaiian type of kinterminology (one where siblings and cousins are designated by the same term), users of the language have trouble distinguishing siblings from cousins. This view is no more plausible than the idea that speakers of a language like English, where a single kinterm, *grandfather*, is used for MF and FF, cannot distinguish these logical kintypes from each other; implausible because the term is merely one denoting expression among many, that is, is a

lexation that can easily be replaced by definite descriptions like *my mother's father* and *my father's father* in cases where the difference matters. Nonetheless, the idea that facts of lexicalization imply something about mental models or 'cognitive structure' remains an entrenched folk-theory for the ordinary language user (for reasons discussed in Chapter 2) and is therefore easily elevated to the status of an analytic commitment in certain forms of social theory as well.

3 In this type of case the text-pattern exhibits morphological fusion. The utterance *ma!* consists of a single morpheme. However it is grammatically analyzed as two distinct elements, i.e., *mother* + vocative case.

4 In general, kinterms are n-place predicates which mark polyadic not dyadic relations. However the special case of two-place predicates, which is typologically the most widespread, is the case to which I devote the most attention here. McGregor 1996 describes a number of types of polyadic kinterms in the Australian language Gooniyandi. These include ternary-monadic kinterms, whose usage involves an intermediary or propositus (viz., 'your X who is my Y'), and is generally restricted to contexts where referent is an in-law to whom ego has avoidance relationships; dual-dyadic kinterms denote a pair of individuals by designating their separate relations to ego (through a compound noun) thus making their relations to each other inferrable; ternary-dyadic kinterms relate three individuals. All of these cases involve various types of transposed and recentered origos, some of which are marked by distinct lexical shapes of the kinterm. These cannot, however, be studied by logico-semantic methods of word or sentence analysis since they are, much like the cases discussed in this chapter, further specified (or rendered defeasible) by co-textual accompaniments.

5 To say that tropes are construable by interactants is not, of course, to say that they are *uniquely* construable. In many cases more than one determinate construal is motivated by features of co-text, and the interactional power of the trope lies precisely in the fact that its construal is organized as a structured space of several semiotically motivated possibilities.

6 In a common ideological view of this phenomenon, this space of variation is conceptualized in taxonomic terms, whether by means of a single dichotomy (the 'metaphoric' vs. the 'literal' use of language), or, as in the tradition of classical rhetoric, by an effusive, ever more copious classification of named figures of speech. I have discussed the limitations of static, taxonomic approaches elsewhere (Agha 1996b). The approach developed in this book, and employed in this chapter for the case of kinterm usage, formulates this phenomenon in terms of reflexive processes of normalization and tropism. I argue that various kinds of normalized models can be produced through the reanalysis of 'appropriate' use, and can become, through their institutionalization, effective as 'norms for' particular social domains of language users for a while, and that awareness of a 'normal' form itself motivates tropes of action, some of which may occur only contingently and occasionally in the language community, while others can themselves become normalized targets for widespread social practices. The discussion of normalized tropes in the next section, as well as the material in subsequent sections, exemplify these processes.

7 Suzuki does not specify the social domain of this norm. Is this a norm for urban speakers? Middle class speakers? These are empirical questions that he does not answer. What he does show however is that the tropic usages in (6) are performable and construable within its social domain, that is, by those who do recognize it as a norm.

8 In the preceding discussion I have only been concerned with kinterms of a rather specific type, namely nouns having the semantic structure KIN (x, y). Examples include words like *mother, father, uncle, brother*, etc. These are not, of course, the only kinds of kinterms we find in the languages of the world. For instance, words for groupings, like *family, clan, patriline, moiety*, etc., are also kinship terms. So also are terms that describe kinship practices, such as *wedding, adoption, divorce*, etc.; also, verbs of certain kinds, viz., *marry, disinherit*, etc. There are other kinds too. This point, namely that vocabularies that describe facts and acts of kinship are quite varied in kind, is especially relevant to the question of how metasemiotic discourses of kinship can be isolated as data, and hence relevant to how a varied range of social behaviors, including non-linguistic behaviors, can be identified as belonging to the domain of kinship. It is also worth noting that the metasemiotic behaviors that valorize particular behaviors *as* kinship behaviors extend well beyond the use of lexical items. They include rituals of many kinds, including rites of passage, ceremonies that transform a person's kinship status (like marriage ceremonies), and others. In such cases the metasemiotic behaviors are themselves complex, are frequently extended in duration, and sometimes linked to ritual cycles of other kinds. I discuss a few cases of these types later in the text. Such metasemiotic practices may themselves involve language use in a variety of ways, including uses that only indirectly recall the domain of kinship, or are highly implicit, or consist of patterns of poetic or metrical structure, or belong to specialized registers that are not widely spoken or construed. In other words, such metasemiotic behaviors require many of the kinds of analyses discussed throughout this book before they are usable as data.

REFERENCES

Agha, Asif. 1993a. *Structural Form and Utterance Context in Lhasa Tibetan: Grammar and Indexicality in a Non-configurational Language: Monographs in Linguistics and the Philosophy of Language, vol. 2.* New York: Peter Lang.

1993b. Grammatical and indexical convention in honorific discourse. *Journal of Linguistic Anthropology*, 3(2): 1–33.

1994. Honorification. *Annual Review of Anthropology*, 23: 277–302.

1995. Process and personality. *Semiotica*, 107 (1/2): 125–46.

1996a. Schema and superposition in spatial deixis. *Anthropological Linguistics*, 38 (4): 643–82.

1996b. Rhetoric. In *Encyclopedia of Cultural Anthropology, vol. 3*, ed. by David Levinson and Melvin Ember. New York: Henry Holt.

1997. Tropic aggression in the Clinton-Dole presidential debate. *Pragmatics*, 7(4): 461–98.

1998a. Stereotypes and registers of honorific language. *Language in Society*, 27: 151–93.

1998b. Form and function in Urdu-Hindi verb inflection. *Yearbook of South Asian Languages and Linguistics*, 1: 105–33.

2002. Honorific registers. In *Culture, Interaction and Language*, ed. by S. Ide and K. Kataoka, pp. 21–63. Tokyo: Hituzisyobo.

2003. The social life of cultural value. *Language and Communication*, 23: 231–73.

2004. Registers of Language. In *A Companion To Linguistic Anthropology*, ed. by Alessandro Duranti, pp. 23–45. Cambridge: Cambridge University Press.

2005. Voice, footing, enregisterment. *Journal of Linguistic Anthropology*, 15(1): 38–59.

Alford, H. 1866. *A Plea for The Queen's English.* London and New York: Alexander Strahan Publisher.

Alrabaa, Sami. 1985. The use of address pronouns by Egyptian adults. *Journal of Pragmatics*, 9: 645–57.

Anonymous. 1839. *Advice to a Young Gentleman on Entering Society. By the Author of "The Laws of Etiquette".* Philadelphia: Lea and Blanchard. [Reprinted in London, 1839, with slightly different pagination].

Appadurai, Arjun (ed.) 1986. *The Social Life of Things: Commodities in Cultural Perspectives.* Cambridge: Cambridge University Press.

Austin, J. L. 1962. *How To Do Things With Words.* Cambridge, MA: Harvard University Press.

Bakhtin, M. M. 1981. Discourse in the novel. In *The Dialogic Imagination*, ed. by M Holquist, pp. 259–422. Austin: University of Texas Press.

1984. *Problems of Dostoevsky's Poetics.* Minneapolis: University of Minnesota Press.

Banfield, Ann. 1982. *Unspeakable Sentences*. London: Routledge and Kegan Paul.

Bateman, H. M. 1969. *The Man Who Drew the 20ᵗʰ Century: The Drawings of H. M. Bateman*. Introduced by Michael Bateman. London: Macdonald and Co.

Beeman, William O. 1986. *Language, Status and Power in Iran*. Bloomington: Indiana Univ. Press.

Benzie, W. 1972. *The Dublin Orator: Thomas Sheridan's Influence on Eighteenth Century Rhetoric and Belles Lettres*. Yorkshire: The University of Leeds Press.

Bex, Tony. 1996. Cohesion, coherence and register. In *Variety in Written English*, pp. 90–112. London: Routledge.

Beyer, Stephan V. 1992. *The Classical Tibetan Language*. Albany: State University of New York Press.

Biber, Douglas. 1994. An analytic framework for register studies. In *Sociolinguistic Perspectives on Register*, ed. by Douglas Biber and Edward Finegan, pp. 31–56. New York: Oxford.

Blom, Jan-Petter and Gumperz, John J. 1986 [1972]. Social Meaning in Linguistic Structure: Code-Switching in Norway. In *Directions in Sociolinguistics: The Ethnography of Communication*, ed. by John J. Gumperz and Dell Hymes, pp. 407–34. New York: Blackwell. [Holt, Reinhart and Winston, 1972]

Boas, Franz. 1996 [1911]. *Introduction to Handbook of American Indian Languages*. Lincoln: University of Nebraska Press. [*Handbook of American Indian Languages*. Bulletin 40, Part 1, Bureau of American Ethnology, Washington DC]

Bourdieu, Pierre. 1990a. *The Logic of Practice*. Stanford: Stanford University Press.

1990b. The social uses of kinship. In *The Logic of Practice*. Stanford: Stanford University Press.

1991. *Language and Symbolic Power*. Cambridge, Mass.: Harvard University Press.

Braun, Friederike. 1988. *Terms of Address: Patterns and Usage in Various Languages and Cultures*. Berlin and New York: Mouton de Gruyter.

Briggs, Charles L. 1986. *Learning How to Ask: A Sociolinguistic Appraisal of the Role of the Interview in Social Science Research*. Cambridge: Cambridge University Press.

Brown, Roger and Gilman, Albert. 1960. The pronouns of power and solidarity. In *Style in Language*, ed. by Thomas A. Sebeok, pp. 253–76. Cambridge, MA.: MIT Press.

Brown, Roger and Ford, Marguerite. 1964. Address in American English. In *Language in Culture and Society: A Reader in Linguistics and Anthropology*, ed. by Dell Hymes, pp. 234–44. New York: Harper and Row.

Brown, Penelope and Stephen C. Levinson. 1987. *Politeness: Some Universals in Language Use*. Cambridge: Cambridge University Press.

Bucholz, Mary and Kira Hall. 2004. Language and Identity. In *A Companion to Linguistic Anthropology*, ed. by Alessandro Duranti, pp. 369–394. Cambridge: Cambridge University Press.

Carsten, Janet, ed. 2000. *Cultures of Relatedness: New Approaches to the Study of Kinship*. Cambridge: Cambridge University Press.

Carsten, Linda. 2004 [1995]. The substance of kinship and the heat of the hearth: Feeding, personhood and relatedness among Malayans in Pulau Langkawi. In *Kinship and Family: An Anthropological Reader*, ed. by Robert Parkin and Linda Stone, pp. 309–27. Oxford: Blackwell. [*American Ethnologist* 22(2): 223–242]

Carter, Ronald. 1988. Front pages: lexis, style and newspaper reports. In *Registers of Written English*, ed. by M Ghadessy, pp. 8–16. London: Pinter.

Caton, Steven C. 1986. Salaam tahiiyah: Greetings from the highlands of Yemen. *American Ethnologist*, 13: 290–308.

Chandrasekhar, A. 1970. Personal pronouns and pronominal forms in Malayalam. *Anthropological Linguistics*, 12(7): 246–255.

1977. Degrees of politeness in Malayalam. *International Journal of Dravidian Linguistics*, 6(1): 85–96.

Choy, Hyen-Pay. 1955. *Wuli Malpon* [Our Grammar]. Seoul: Cengumsa.

Cicourel, Aaron V. 1974. Interpretive procedures and normative roles in the negotiation of status and role. In *Cognitive Sociology: Language and Meaning in Social Interaction*, pp. 11–41. New York: Free Press.

Comrie, Bernard. 1975. Polite plurals and predicate agreement. *Language*, 51(2): 406–18.

Cooke, Joseph R. 1968. *Pronominal Reference in Thai, Burmese, and Vietnamese: University of California Publications in Linguistics, 52*. Berkeley: University of California.

Danesi, Marcel and Lettieri, Michael. 1983. The pronouns of address in Italian: Sociolinguistic and pedagogical considerations. *Studi italiani di linguistica teorica ed applicata*, 12: 323–33.

Das, S. K. 1968. Forms of address and terms of reference in Bengali. *Anthropological Linguistics*, 10(4): 19–31.

Diller, Anthony. 1993. Diglossic grammaticality in Thai. In *The Role of Theory in Language Description*, ed. by William A. Foley, pp. 393–420. Berlin: Mouton de Gruyter.

Dobson, E. J. 1968. *English Pronunciation 1500–1700*. Oxford: Clarendon.

Donnellan, Keith. 1990 [1966]. Reference and definite descriptions. In *The Philosophy of Language*, ed. by A. P. Martinich. New York: Oxford. [*Philosophical Review* 75: 281–304]

Duranti, Alessandro. 1992. Language and bodies in social space: Samoan ceremonial greetings. *American Anthropologist*, 94: 657–91.

Eble, Connie. 1996. *Slang and Sociability: In-group Language Among College Students*. Chapel Hill: University Of North Carolina Press.

Errington, J. Joseph. 1985. *Language and Social Change in Java*. Monographs in International Studies, Southeast Asia Series, no. 65. Athens, OH: Ohio University Center for International Studies.

1988. *Structure and Style in Javanese: A Semiotic View of Linguistic Etiquette*. Philadelphia: Univ. of Pennsylvania Press.

1998. *Shifting languages: Interaction and Identity in Javanese Indonesia*. Cambridge: Cambridge University Press.

Ervin-Tripp, Susan M. 1986. On Sociolinguistic rules: Alternation and Co-occurrence. In *Directions in Sociolinguistics: The Ethnography of Communication*, ed. by John J. Gumperz and Dell Hymes, pp. 213–50. New York: Blackwell.

Evans-Pritchard, E. E. 1951. *Kinship and Marriage among the Nuer*. Oxford: Clarendon.

Ferguson, Charles A. 1982. Simplified registers and linguistic theory. In *Exceptional language and Linguistics*, ed. by L. K. Obler and L. Menn, pp. 49–66. New York: Academic Press.

1983. Sports Announcer Talk: Syntactic aspects of register variation. *Language in Society*, 12: 153–72.

1994. Dialect, register and genre: Working assumptions about conventionalization. In *Sociolinguistic Perspectives on Register*, ed. by Douglas Biber and Edward Finegan, pp. 15–30. New York: Oxford.

Fischer, J. L. 1964. Words for self and other in some Japanese families. *American Anthropologist*, 66(6): 115–26.

Fliegelman, J. 1993. *Declaring Independence: Jefferenson, Natural Language and the Culture of Performance*. Stanford: Stanford University Press.

Foucault, Michel. 1971. *The Order of Things: An Archaeology of the Human Sciences*. New York: Pantheon Books.

1972. *The Archaeology of Knowledge*. New York: Harper and Row.

Friedrich, Paul. 1966. Structural implications of Russian pronominal usage. In *Sociolinguistics*, ed. by William Bright, pp. 214–59. The Hague: Mouton.

1986. Social context and semantic feature: The Russian pronominal usage. In *Directions in Sociolinguistics: The Ethnography of Communication*, ed. by John J. Gumperz and Dell Hymes, pp. 270–300. New York: Blackwell.

Gal, Susan. 1992. Multiplicity and contention among ideologies: A commentary. *Pragmatics*, 2(3): 445–49.

1998. Multiplicity and contention among ideologies. *In Language Ideologies: Practice and Theory*, ed. by Bambi Schieffelin, et al., pp. 317–332. New York: Oxford.

Gass, William. 1979. The anatomy of mind. In *The World Within The Word*, pp. 208–52. Boston: Godine.

Geertz, Clifford H. 1960. *The Religion of Java*. Glencoe, IL: Free Press.

Ghadessy, Mohsen (ed.) 1988. *Registers of Written English*. London: Pinter.

Giles, Howard. 1970. Evaluative reactions to accents. *Educational Review*, 23: 211–27.

1971. Patterns of evaluation to R. P., South Welsh and Somerset accented speech. *British Journal of Social and Clinical Psychology*, 10(3): 280–1.

Giles, H. and Powesland, P. F. 1975. *Speech Style and Social Evaluation*. New York: Academic.

Goffman, Erving. 1956. The nature of deference and demeanor. *American Anthropologist*, 58: 473–502.

1963. *Stigma: Notes on the Management of Spoiled Identity*. New York: Simon and Schuster.

1974. *Frame Analysis*. Cambridge, MA: Harvard University Press.

1981a. Footing. In *Forms of Talk*, pp. 124–59. Philadelphia: University of Pennsylvania.

1981b. Replies and responses. In *Forms of Talk*, pp. 5–77. Philadelphia: University of Pennsylvania.

1983. The interaction order. *American Sociological Review*, 48: 1–17.

Golding, R. 1985. *Idiolects in Dickens*. London: Macmillan.

Goodwin, Charles and Goodwin, Marjorie. 1992. Assessments and the construction of context. In *Rethinking Context: Language as Interactive Phenomenon*, ed. by Alessandro Duranti and Charles Goodwin, pp. 147–89. New York: Cambridge University Press.

Gordon, David P. 1983. Hospital slang for patients: Crocks, gomers, gorks and others. *Language in Society*, 13: 173–85.

Gramsci, Antonio. 1971. *Selections from the Prison Notebooks*. New York: International Publishers.

Gustafson, T. 1992. *Representative Words: Politics, Literature and the American Language, 1776–1865*. New York: Cambridge University Press.

Haas, Mary R. 1964. Men's and women's speech in Koasati. In *Language in Culture and Society*, ed. by Dell Hymes, pp. 228–33. New York: Harper and Row.

Halliday, M. A. K. 1964. The users and uses of language. In *The Linguistic Sciences and Language Teaching*, ed. by M. A. K. Halliday, Angus McIntosh and Peter Strevens, pp. 75–110. Bloomington: Indiana University Press.

1988. On the language of physical science. In *Registers of Written English*, ed. by M. Ghadessy, pp. 162–78. London: Pinter.

Hanks, William F. 1990. *Referential Practice: Language and Lived Space among the Maya*. Chicago: University of Chicago Press.

1992. The indexical ground of deictic reference. In *Rethinking Context: Language as an Interactive Phenomenon*, ed. by Alessandro Duranti and Charles Goodwin, pp. 43–76. New York: Cambridge University Press.

1996. Exorcism and the description of participant roles. In *Natural Histories of Discourse*, ed. by Michael Silverstein and Greg Urban, pp. 160–200. Chicago: University of Chicago Press.

Haviland, John B. 1979a. Guugu-Yimidhirr brother-in-law language. *Language in Society*, 8: 365–93.

1979b. How to talk to your brother-in-law in Guugu Yimidhirr. In *Languages and Their Speakers*, ed. by T. Shopen, pp. 161–239. Cambridge, MA: Winthrop.

1993. Anchoring, iconicity, and orientation in Guugu Yimidhirr pointing gestures. *Journal of Linguistic Anthropology*, 3(1): 3–45.

2005. "Whorish old man" and "One (animal) gentleman" The intertextual construction of enemies and selves. *Journal of Linguistic Anthropology*, 15(1): 81–94.

Hill, Jane H. 1998. 'Today there is no respect': Nostalgia, 'respect' and oppositional discourse in Mexicano (Nahuatl) language ideology. In *Language Ideologies: Practice and Theory*, ed. by Bambi K. Schieffelin, Kathryn Woolard and Paul V. Kroskrity, pp. 68–86. New York: Oxford.

Holy, Ladislav. 1996. *Anthropological Perspectives on Kinship*. London and Chicago: Pluto Press.

Honey, John. 1989a. *Does Accent Matter? The Pygmalion Factor*. London: Faber and Faber.

1989b. Acrolect and hyperlect: Education and class as foci of linguistic identity. In *Status and Function of Language and Language Varieties*, ed. by U Ammon, pp. 581–91. Berlin: Walter de Gruyter.

Hope, J. 2000. Rats, bats, sparrows and dogs: biology, linguistics, and the nature of Standard English. In *The Development of Standard English*, ed. by L Wright, pp. 49–56. Cambridge: Cambridge University Press.

Hoyle, Susan M. 1993. Participation frameworks in sportscasting play: imaginary and literal footings. In *Framing in Discourse*, ed. by Deborah Tannen, pp. 114–45. New York: Oxford.

Hudson, Kenneth. 1983. Pop music as cultural carrier. In *The Language of the Teenage Revolution*, pp. 36–52. London: Macmillan.

Hughes, A. and Trudgill, P. 1987. *English Accents and Dialects: An Introduction to the Social and Regional Varieties of English*. London: Edward Arnold.

Inoue, Kyoko. 1979. Japanese: a story of language and people. In *Languages and their Speakers*, ed. by Timothy Shopen, pp. 241–300. Cambridge, MA: Winthrop.

Irvine, Judith. 1989. When talk isn't cheap: Language and political economy. *American Ethnologist*, 16 (2): 248–67.

1989 [1974]. Strategies of status manipulation in the Wolof greeting. In *Explorations in the Ethnography of Communication*, ed. by Richard Bauman and Joel Sherzer, pp. 167–91. Cambridge: Cambridge University Press.

1990. Registering affect: heteroglossia in the linguistic expression of emotion. In *Language and the Politics of Emotion*, ed. by Catherine A. Lutz and Lila Abu-Lughod, pp. 126–61. New York: Cambridge University Press.

1996. Shadow conversations. In *Natural Histories of Discourse*, ed. by Michael Silverstein and Greg Urban, pp. 131–59. Chicago: University of Chicago Press.

1998. Ideologies of honorific language. In *Language Ideologies: Practice and Theory*, ed. by Bambi K. Schieffelin, Kathryn Woolard and Paul V. Kroskrity, pp. 51–67. New York: Oxford.

2001. "Style" as distinctiveness: the culture and ideology of linguistic differentiation. In *Style and Sociolinguistic Variation*, ed. by Penelope Eckert and John R. Rickford, pp. 21–43. Cambridge: Cambridge University Press.

Irvine, Judith T. and Gal, Susan. 2000. Language ideology and linguistic differentiation. In *Regimes of Language*, ed. by Paul V. Kroskrity, pp. 35–84. Santa Fe, NM: School of American Research.

Jakobson, Roman. 1960. Closing statement: Linguistics and poetics. In *Style in Language*, ed. by Thomas Sebeok. Cambridge, MA: MIT Press.

Kahn, Susan M. 2004. Eggs and wombs: The origins of Jewishness. In *Kinship and Family: An Anthropological Reader*, ed. by Robert Parkin and Linda Stone, pp. 362–77. Oxford: Blackwell.

Keenan, Elinor Ochs. 1996. Norm makers, norm breakers: uses of speech by men and women in a Malagasy community. In *The Matrix of Language*, pp. 99–115, Donald Brenneis and Ronald K. S. Macaulay, eds. Boulder, CO: Westview Press.

Kingston-Oliphant, T. 1873. *The Sources of Standard English*. London: Macmillan.

Koyama, Wataru. 2004. The linguistic ideologies of modern Japanese honorifics and the historic reality of modernity. *Language and Communication*, 24(4): pp. 413–435.

Kripke, Saul. 1972. *Naming and Necessity*. Cambridge, MA: Harvard University Press.

Kroskrity, Paul V. 2004. Language ideologies. In *A Companion to Linguistic Anthropology*, ed. by Alessandro Duranti, pp. 497–517. Oxford: Blackwell.

Lakoff, Robin T. 1975. *Language and Woman's Place*. New York: Harper and Row.

Leach, Edmund. 1966. Anthropological aspects of language: animal categories and verbal abuse. In *New Directions in the Study of Language*, E. Lenneberg, ed., pp. 23–63. Cambridge, MA: MIT Press.

Lee, Benjamin. 1997. *Talking Heads: Language, Metalanguage and the Semiotics of Subjectivity*. Durham: Duke University Press.

Linton, Ralph. 1936. *The Study of Man*. New York: Appleton-Century Company.

Listen, Paul. 1999. *The Emergence of German Polite Sie: Cognitive and Sociolinguistic Parameters*. New York: Peter Lang.

Lucy, John A. (ed.) 1993. *Reflexive Language: Reported Speech and Metapragmatics*. Cambridge: Cambridge University Press.

1997. The linguistics of 'color'. In *Color Categories in Thought and Language*, ed. by C. L. Hardin and Luisa Maffi, pp. 320–46. Cambridge: Cambridge University Press.

Luong, Hy Van. 1988. Discursive practices and power structure: Person-referring forms and sociopolitical struggles in colonial Vietnam. *American Ethnologist*, 15(2): 239–53.

——— 1990. *Discursive Practices and Linguistic Meanings: The Vietnamese System of Person Reference*. Amsterdam and Philadelphia: John Benjamins.

Lutz, William. 1990. *Doublespeak*. New York: Harper Collins.

Lyons, John. 1995. *Linguistics Semantics*. Cambridge: Cambridge University Press.

Macaulay, R. K. S. 1977. *Language, Social Class and Education: A Glasgow Study*. Edinburgh: Edinburgh University Press.

Martin, S. E. 1964. Speech levels in Japan and Korea. In *Language in Culture and Society: A Reader in Linguistics and Anthropology*, Dell H. Hymes, ed., pp. 407–415. New York: Harper and Row.

Matoesian, Gregory M. 1999. The grammaticalization of participant roles in the constitution of expert identity. *Language in Society*, 28: 491–521.

Matsumoto, Yoshiko. 1997. The rise and fall of Japanese nonsubject honorifics; the case of "o-Verb-suru." *Journal of Pragmatics*, 28(6): 719–740.

Maurer, David. 1955. *Whiz Mob: A Correlation of the Technical Argot of Pickpockets With Their Behavior Pattern*. Gainsville, FL: American Dialect Society.

McGregor, William. 1996. Dyadic and polyadic kin terms in Gooniyandi. *Anthropological Linguistics*, 38(2): 216–247.

Mehrotra, R. R. 1977. *Sociology of Secret Languages*. Simla: Indian Institute of Advanced Study.

Mertz, Elizabeth. 1998. Linguistic ideology and praxis in U.S. Law School classrooms. In *Language Ideologies: Practice and Theory*, ed. by Bambi K. Schieffelin, Kathryn Woolard and Paul V. Kroskrity, pp. 149–62. New York: Oxford.

Milroy, J. and Milroy, L. 1999. *Authority in Language: Investigating Standard English*. London: Routledge.

Mintz, Sidney and Eric R. Wolf. 1967. An analysis of ritual co-parenthood (Compadrazgo). In *Peasant Society: A Reader*, ed. by Mary N. Diaz Jack M. Potter, George M. Foster, pp. 174–99. Boston: Little, Brown and Company.

Mitchell, S. 1977. The forgotten woman of the period: Penny Weekly family magazines of the 1840's and 1850's. In *A Widening Sphere: Changing Roles of Victorian Women*, ed. by M. Vicinus, pp. 29–51. Bloomington: Indiana University Press.

Mitford, Nancy. 1956. *Noblesse Oblige*. London: Hamish Hamilton.

Mohrmann, G. P. 1969. Introduction. In *A Discourse Being Introductory To His Course of Lectures on Elocution an the English Language, by Thomas Sheridan, 1759*. Los Angeles: University of California.

Morford, Janet. 1997. Social indexicality in French pronominal address. *Journal of Linguistic Anthropology*, 7(1): 3–37.

Morrison, T. 1863. *Manual of School Management*. London.

Mugglestone, Lynda. 1995. *"Talking Proper": The Rise of Accent as Social Symbol*. Oxford: Clarendon.

Mühlhäusler, Peter and Harré, Rom. 1990. *Pronouns and People: The Linguistic Construction of Social and Personal Identity: Language in Society*. Oxford: Blackwell.

Nadel, S. F. 1957. *The Theory of Social Structure*. Glencoe, IL: Free Press.

Nagel, Thomas. 1986. *The View From Nowhere.* Oxford: Oxford University Press.

Nash, Walter. 1993. *Jargon: Its Uses and Abuses.* Oxford: Blackwell.

Newbrook, M. 1999. West Wirral: norms, self-reports and usage. In *Urban Voices: Accent Studies in the British Isles,* ed. by P. Foulkes and G. J. Docherty, pp. 90–106. London: Arnold.

Ogino, T., et al. 1985. Diversity of honorific usage in Tokyo: A sociolinguistic approach based on a field survey. *International Journal of the Sociology of Language,* 55: 23–39.

Parmentier, Richard. 1994. The naturalization of convention. In *Signs in Society,* pp. 175–92. Bloomington: Indiana University Press.

Parsons, Talcott. 1951. *The Social System.* Glencoe, IL: Free Press.

Parsons, Talcott and Edward A. Shils (eds.) 1951. *Towards a General Theory of Action.* Cambridge, MA: Harvard University Press.

Paulston, Christina B. 1976. Pronouns of address in Swedish: social class semantics and a changing system. *Language in Society,* 5: 359–86.

Pei, J. C. Honorific usage in spoken Korean in Yanbian. 1992. *International Journal of the Sociology of Language,* 97: 87–95.

Peirce, Charles Sanders. 1931–1958. *The Collected Papers of Charles Sanders Peirce (8 vols.).* Cambridge, MA: Harvard University Press.

1992. *The Essential Peirce: Selected Philosophical Writings (2 vols.).* Bloomington: Indiana University Press.

Perrino, Sabina M. 2002. Intimate Hierarchies and Quar'anic Saliva (Tëfli): Textuality in a Senegalese ethnomedical encounter. *Journal of Linguistic Anthropology,* 12(2): 225–59.

Phillipps, K. C. 1984. *Language and Class in Victorian England.* Oxford: Blackwell.

Poedjosoedarmo, Soepomo. 1968. Javanese speech levels. *Indonesia,* 6: 54–81.

1969. Wordlist of Javanese non-Ngoko vocabularies. *Indonesia,* 7: 165–190.

Putnam, Hilary. 1975. The meaning of 'meaning'. In *Mind, Language and Reality. Philosophical Papers, vol. 2.,* pp. 215–71. Cambridge, MA: Cambridge University Press.

Puttenham, G. 1589. *The Arte of English Poesie.* London.

Quinn, Arthur. 1982. *Figures of Speech.* Salt Lake City: Peregrine Smith Books.

Quirk, Randolph and Svartvik, Jan. 1966. *Investigating Linguistic Acceptability.* The Hague: Mouton.

Ramanujan, A. K. 1968. The structure of variation: A study in caste dialects. In *Structure and Change in Indian Society,* ed. by Milton Singer and Bernard S. Cohn, pp. 461–74. New York: Wenner-Gren.

Rampton, Ben. 2003. Hegemony, social class and stylization. *Pragmatics,* 13(1): 49–83.

Reid, I. 1977. *Social Class Differences in Britain.* London: Open Books.

Reid, T. B. W. 1956. Linguistics, structuralism and philology. *Archivum Linguisticum,* 8(1): 28–37.

Rivers, W. H. R. 1915. Kin, kinship. In *Encyclopedia of Religion and Ethics,* ed. by J. Hastings, pp. 700–07. Edinburgh and New York: Scribner.

Rosaldo, Michelle Z. 1982. The things we do with words: Ilongot speech acts and speech act theory in philosophy. *Language in Society,* 11: 203–37.

Rosch, Eleanor. 1978. Principles of categorization. In *Cognition and Categorization,* ed. by Eleanor Rosch and Barbara B. Lloyd, pp. 27–48. New York: Lawrence Erlbaum Associates.

Rosewarne, D. 1984. Estuary English. *The Times Literary Supplement, 19 October.*

1994. Estuary English: Tomorrow's RP? *English Today,* 37(10.1): 3–8.

Ross, A. S. C. 1954. Linguistic class indicators in present-day English. *Neuphilologische Mitteilungen*, 55: 20–56.

Sadock, Jerrold M. 1974. *Towards a Linguistic Theory of Speech Acts*. New York: Academic Press.

Sapir, Edward. 1921. *Language*. New York: Harcourt, Brace and World.

1949a. Communication. In *Selected Writings of Edward Sapir*, ed. by David G. Mandelbaum, pp. 104–10. Berkeley: University of California Press.

1949b. Abnormal types of speech in Nootka. In *Selected Writings of Edward Sapir*, ed. by David G. Mandelbaum, pp. 179–96. Berkeley: University of California Press.

Schegloff, Emanuel. 1972. Notes on a conversational practice. In *Language and Social Context*, ed. by Pier Paolo Giglioli, pp. 95–135. Hammondsworth: Penguin.

Schieffelin, Bambi et al. eds. 1998. *Language Ideologies: Practice and Theory*. New York: Oxford.

Schneider, David M. 1984. *A Critique of the Study of Kinship*. Ann Arbor: University of Michigan Press.

Schottman, Wendy. 1995. The daily ritual of greeting among the Baatombu of Benin. *Anthropological Linguistics*, 37(4): 487–523.

Searle, John. 1969. *Speech Acts: An Essay in the Philosophy of Language*. London: Cambridge University Press.

1975. Indirect speech acts. In *Syntax and Semantics, vol. 3*, ed. by Peter Cole and Jerry Morgan, pp. 59–82. New York: Academic Press.

1976. A classification of illocutionary acts. *Language in Society*, 5: 1–23.

Senft, Gunter. 1997. Magical conversation on the Trobriand islands. *Anthropos*, 92: 369–91.

Sheridan, Thomas 1756. *British Education*. Dublin: Printed by George Faulkner.

1761. *A Dissertation on the Causes of the Difficulties Which Occur in Learning the English Tongue. With a Scheme for Publishing an English Grammar and Dictionary Upon a Plan Entirely New. The Object of Which Shall be, to Facilitate the Attainment of the English Tongue, and establish a Perpetual Standard of Pronunciation*. London: Printed for R. and J. Dodsley, in Pall-Mall.

1762. *A Course of Lectures on Elocution*. London: printed by W. Strahan, for A. Millar, R. and J. Dodsley, T. Davies, C. Henderson, J. Wilkie, and E. Dilly.

1769. *A Plan of Education for the Young Nobility and Gentry of Great Britain*. London: Printed for E. and C. Dilly.

1775. *Lectures on the Art of Reading*. London: printed for J. Dodsley, J. Wilkie, E. and C. Dilly, and T. Davies.

1780. *A General Dictionary of the English Language. One main object of which, is, to establish a plain and permanent standard of pronunciation. To which is prefixed a rhetorical grammar*. London: Printed by William Strahan for J. Dodsley; C. Dilly; and J. Wilkie.

Shibamoto, Janet S. 1987. The womanly woman: manipulation of stereotypical and non-stereotypical features of Japanese female speech. In *Language, Gender and Sex in a Comparative Perspective*, ed. by Susan Phillips, Susan Steele and Christine Tanz, pp. 26–49. Cambridge: Cambridge University Press.

Silverstein, Michael. 1976. Shifters, linguistic categories, and cultural description. In *Meaning in Anthropology*, ed. by Keith Basso and Ellen Selby, pp. 11–56. Albuquerque: University of New Mexico Press.

1979. Language structure and linguistic ideology. In *The Elements: A Parasession on Linguistic Units and Levels*, ed. by Paul R. Clyne, William F. Hanks and Carol L. Hofbauer, pp. 193–247. Chicago: Chicago Linguistic Society.

1981. The limits of awareness. In *Sociolinguistic Working Paper, no. 84*. Austin, TX: Southwest Educational Development Laboratory.

1985. On the pragmatic 'poetry' of prose: parallelism, repetition and cohesive structure in the time course of dyadic conversation. In *Meaning, Form and Use in Context: Linguistic Applications*, ed. by Deborah Schiffrin, pp. 181–99. Washington, DC: Georgetown University Press.

1987. Cognitive implications of a referential hierarchy. In *Social and Functional Approaches to Language and Thought*, ed. by Maya Hickman, pp. 125–64. New York: Academic Press.

1988. Demeanor indexicals and honorific register. Unpublished paper, presented at the conference on honorifics, Reed College, 1988.

1993. Metapragmatic discourse and metapragmatic function. In *Reflexive Language: Reported Speech and Metapragmatics*, ed. by John A. Lucy, pp. 33–58. Cambridge: Cambridge University Press.

1996a. Indexical order and the dialectics of sociolinguistic life. *SALSA*, 3: 266–95.

1996b. Monoglot 'Standard' in America: standardization and metaphors of linguistic hegemony. In *The Matrix of Language*, ed. by Donald Brenneis and Ronald Macaulay, pp. 284–306. Boulder, CO: Westview Press.

Simpson, Rita S. 1997. Metapragmatic discourse and the ideology of impolite pronouns in Thai. *JLA*, 7(1): 38–62.

Sinclair, John. 1988. Compressed English. In *Registers of Written English*, ed. by M. Ghadessy, pp. 130–36. London: Pinter.

Singh, U. N. 1989. How to honor someone in Maithili. *Int. J. Soc. Lang.*, 75: 87–107.

Slobin, Dan I. 1963. Some aspects of the use of pronouns of address in Yiddish. *Word*, 19(2): 193–202.

Smith-Hefner, Nancy J. 1988. The linguistic socialization of Javanese children in two communities. *Anthropological Linguistics*, 30(2): 166–98.

Stone, Linda. 2004. Introduction: The demise and revival of kinship. In *Kinship and Family: An Anthropological Reader*, ed. by Robert Parkin and Linda Stone, pp. 241–56. Oxford: Blackwell.

Suzuki, Takao. 1984. Words for Self and Others. In *Words in Context: A Japanese Perspective on Language and Culture*, pp. 111–69. Tokyo: Kodansha International.

Taylor, Charles. 1989. *Sources of the Self: The Making of Modern Identity*. Cambridge, MA: Harvard University Press.

Toolan, Michael. 1988. The language of press advertising. In *Registers of Written English*, ed. by M. Ghadessy, pp. 52–64. London: Pinter.

Trechter, Sara. 1995. Categorial gender myths in Native America: Gender deictics in Lakhota. *Issues in Applied Linguistics*, 6(1): 5–22.

Trudgill, Peter. 1999. Standard English: What it isn't. In *Standard English: The Widening Debate*, ed. by Tony Bex and Richard J. Watts, pp. 117–28. London: Routledge.

Urban, Greg. 1996. *Metaphysical Community: The Interplay of the Senses and the Intellect*. Austin: University of Texas Press.

Van Gennep, Arnold. 1961 [1909]. *The Rites of Passage*. Chicago: University of Chicago Press. [Paris, E Nourry, 1909].

Vatuk, Sylvia. 1982. Forms of address in the North Indian family: An exploration of the cultural meaning of kin terms. In *Concepts of Person: Kinship, Caste and Marriage in India*, ed. by Akos Oster et al., pp. 56–98. Cambridge: Harvard University Press.

Walker, John. 1791. *A Critical Pronouncing Dictionary and Expositor of the English Language*. London: Robinson and Cadell.

1806. *Elements of Elocution*. London: Printed for J. Johnson in St Paul's Churchyard.

Wang, H.-S. 1990. Towards a description of the organization of Korean speech levels. *International Journal of the Sociology of Language*, 82: 25–39.

Watterson, Bill. 1995. *The Calvin and Hobbes Tenth Anniversary Book*. Kansas City: Andrews and McMeel.

Watts, Richard J. 1999. The social construction of Standard English: Grammar writers as a discourse community. In *Standard English: The Widening Debate*, ed. by Tony Bex and Richard J. Watts, pp. 40–68. London: Routledge.

Weber, Max. 1978 [1956]. *Economy and Society, 2 vols.* Berkeley: University of California Press. [*Wirtschaft und Gesellschaft*, 4th edition, Tubingen, 1956]

Wells, J. C. 1982. *Accents of English (3 vols.)*. Cambridge: Cambridge University Press.

Wortham, Stanton E. F. 2005. Socialization beyond the speech event. *Journal of Linguistic Anthropology*, 15(1): 95–112.

INDEX

accent
  and dialect, 106
  as folk-concept, 191–192
  see Received Pronunciation (RP)
address terms, 33, 173–174
agency
  as effective freedom, 230, 231
  as interpretive ability, 230–231
  and normative entitlement, 231
  as reflective grasp of one's own freedom,
    230, 231
allophone, 108
American English, 108, 109
Arabic
  Egyptian Arabic 174–175, 178, 294
  Yemeni Arabic, 259, 261–268, 272, 402n

Bantu languages, 403n
Bengali, 281, 284, 295, 360–361, 364, 367,
  373, 403n
British elocutionary movement, 207, 273
  in America, 274f, 276–277, 398–399n
British English
  Cockney, 200, 224, 226, 398n
  Estuary English, 224, 226,
    227–228, 400n
  geographic accents of, 192, 251
  and national identity, 208, 275–277,
    398–399n
  the Queen's English, 195, 225–227, 400n
  speech levels of, 200, 334
  see Received Pronunciation (RP)

categorial vs. categorical effects, 46
characterological figures, 165, 177,
  181–182, 398n
Chinese, 404n
circulation
  of denotational norms, 129, 132
  fragmentary circulation of register,
    165–167
  of metapragmatic representations, 175
  and reanalysis during transmission, 78

of stereotypes of sign value, 181–185,
  239, 248
  see speech chains
citation form, 109
code-switching, 134, 140–141
Confucianism
  and Vietnamese address terms, 357–358
convention
  doctrine of, 258
  and social contract myth, 401–402n
  reanalysis of, 258
  naturalization of, 76–77
conversation analysis, 18, 386n, 393n, 402n
co-textual cues
  and connected discourse, 32, 32f,
    387–388n
  and deixis, 49
  and descriptions, 91, 141
  and emergent emblems, 237
  and kinship behavior, 346–347, 352, 353
  and linguistic categories, 46
  and performativity, 59
  and register use, 148, 161–162, 403n
  see text-level indexicality
cultural formations, 77–83, 382–385, 387n
  circulation of, 74, 78–79, 97, 155, 183, 183f
  sharedness of, 183, 258, 294, 340
  transmission of, 78–79, 392n
  see registers
cultural value, 201–203

deference indexicals, 315–317
  addressee-focal deference, 316–317
  bystander focal deference, 316
  categorial text-defaults of, 316, 317–322
  coding view of deference, 316, 317, 324
  conjoined categorial focus, 329–331, 332
  denotational class and default deference,
    317–322
  focus of deference, 316
  origo of deference, 316
  referent-focal deference, 315–322,
    404–405n

419

deference indexicals (cont.)
  secondary focus of deference, 327–329, 332
  transposition of deference origo, 324–327, 332
  and text-level indexicality, 301–302, 307–308
  see honorific register, demeanor indexicals
definite descriptions
  attributive vs. referential uses of, 90–92f, 93f
deixis, 29–30, 37–55
  categorial perspective on, 46
  'coding' view of, 39
  deictic form, 39
  deictic selectivity, 42–45
  deictics as reflexive signs, 38–42
  denotational vs. interactional schema, 46–49, 65, 117–118, 118f, 119, 389–390n
  and kinesis, 49
  noun-phrase deictics, 41
  and explicit performatives, 56–58
  reanalysis of, 55, 388n
  referring to addressee, 280
  registers of person deixis, 278
  relational centering of, 39
  deictic role designators, 401n
  'social deixis' as misleading term, 278
  speech-chain deictics, 65
  and stereotypic social indexicals, 278, 389n
  text-defaults of, 39, 45–48, 389n
  textual perspective on, 46, 48–55
  see origo
demeanor indexicals, 240–241
  as actor-focal emblems, 240
  and deference, 181–182
  durability of, 241–242
  honorific registers and speaker demeanor, 310–315
denotation, 86–89, 103–124, 392n
  and asymmetries of competence, 128
  authoritative stereotypes of, 127
  axis of, 29–30
  circulation of denotational norms, 129, 132
  common vs. correct denotation, 127–132, 352
  and division of labor, 128, 392n
  event-(in)dependence of, 87–88, 104–105, 392n
  and expertise, 127–132, 392n
  and institutions of standardization, 129, 392n
  of kinship terms, 346–347
  norms of, 87, 124–132
  and reanalysis, 124, 129, 138
  reference standards, 128

and role alignment, 132–134, 138f, 301, 395n
and sense categories, 109, 112, 115
social significance of, 107
see referring
denotational indexicals, 40
denotational schema, *see* schema
denotational stereotypes, 119–121
  social domain of, 121, 121f
  see intension
denotational text, *see* text
diacritics
  of identity, 235
  and kinship behavior, 376–377, 378, 379–380
  non-detachability of, 249–250, 254
  and role designators, 248–250, 249f
  role diacritics, 136, 248
diagrammatic motivation, 99, 100, 211f, 399n
  see indexical icons
dialect, 106, 132–142
diglossia, 130f, 130–132
dispensation rules, 33, 35f, 298, 299, 388n
distributional analysis, 108, 123
division of labor
  and denotation, 128, 392n
  and honorific standards, 303
double articulation, 105
dyadic conversation, 69, 70, 70f
Dyirbal, 321

emblems, 235, 244–245, 258
  coding views of, 265–266
  in kinship behavior, 378–380
  emergent emblems, 235, 236, 256, 257
  enregistered emblems, 235, 256, 270
  entextualized emblems, 256, 258, 293
  and footing, 235
  and social groupings, 271, 402n
  metapragmatic formulations of, 280–281
  and honorific registers, 302, 310
  as indexical icons, 257
  naturalization of, 241, 258
  persistent alignments to, 236
  and reanalysis, 172, 293, 310, 339, 378, 380
  and role alignment, 236, 375, 382
  and role and status, 243–244
  and stereotypic indexicals, 239–240, 244–245
  and text-level indexicality, 239–240, 244–245
  of social difference, 293–295
  social domain of, 270, 382
  stereotypic emblems, 272–277, 294
  standard language as emblem of class, 169
  see identity

embodiment, 240, 400n
enregisterment, 55, 80, 131, 141–142, 168,
    190, 228, 229, 235, 258, 270, 396n
    and kinship behavior, 367, 375, 383
    of pronominal registers, 278, 286–293,
        294, 298, 299
    of speech levels, 335–337, 338–339
essentialization, 74
    and embodiment, 400n
    and social groups, 271
ethnometapragmatic terminology, 74
etiquette, 23, 24–25, 180
extension, 87, 122
    face-to-face conversation, 69
    see speech chain

figures of identity, 244, 245
    see self, characterological figures,
        personhood
folk-etymology, 124
footing, 77, 177–179
    denotational footing, 132–134, 136–139,
        138f, 141, 301, 395n
    and emblems, 235, 382
    and registers, 143, 152, 165, 167, 185, 230
    and self, 238
    and tropes of kinship address, 375
    see role alignment
free lexemic forms, 109, 110
French, 172–173, 173f, 179, 278, 286,
    287–288, 321

generative grammar, 18
    and grammaticality judgments, 386n
German, 54, 286, 287, 321, 404n
glossing
    and denotational stereotypy, 119–121
    as metalinguistic activity, 17, 19, 111, 120,
        124, 127, 131, 247, 394n, 395n
Gooniyandi, 406n
greetings, 259, 261–268
    pair-part structure of, 260, 402n
    as emblems of personhood, 261–268
    Qu'ran as metapragmatic discourse
        on, 264
groups
    and emergent social groupings, 270
    and emblems of social difference,
        293–295
    corporate, 267
    naturalization of, 268, 270, 271
    ontology of, 268–269
    and role alignment, 271–272
    performed groupings, 267
    and positionality of norms, 372–373, 378
    and regrouping, 170, 380–382
    recognizability of, 269–270, 402n

sense of group unity, 269
    and social domain of stereotypes, 297
    stereotypic groupings, 268–269
Guugu-Yimidhirr, 306, 316, 321, 367

habitus, 229
    and agency, 228–232
    and metadiscourse, 229
Hindi, 371–372, 374
holophrastic lexations, 117
homonymy, 109, 115, 394n, 403n
honorific register, 301, 302, 404n
    and class, 322, 336
    and detachable emblems, 301, 302, 310
    defeasability of categorial effects of, 302,
        308, 322
    grammatical range of, 306
    grammatical structure of, 306
    lexical features of, 302–303, 304–305,
        306–307, 402n
    metapragmatic data, 305, 306
    naturalization of, 303–304
    non-detachable effects of use, 326, 327,
        331–332
    non-linguistic honorific forms, 180, 316
    ordinary speaker awareness of, 280, 402n
    and person referring honorific forms, 309
    phonolexical registers, 310–315
    pronominal repertoires of, 308–310, 402n
    and reanalysis, 289, 301, 308, 309, 310,
        321, 337, 339
    and reference maintenance, 323–324, 332
    repertoire size of, 306
    and self-presentation, 302, 330
    semiotic range of, 180
    social domain of, 304, 307, 331, 332–333
    socialization to appropriate use, 314–315
    and speech levels, 334–339
    speech modeling to children, 321
    stereotypes of use, 304–305, 311, 312
    textually composite effects, 308, 322–332
    and tropes, 324–331, 332
    see deference indexicals, demeanor
        indexicals

iconism
    cross-modal, 22, 22f, 76, 199
    inverse icons, 175
    see metrical structure
identity, 233–234
    diacritics of, 235
    divergent readings of, 244, 245
    and emblems, 234–237
    and emblems of class, 173f, 174–175, 209,
        230, 294–295, 322
    emergent forms of, 236
    enregistered, 236, 272–277

identity (cont.)
  expropriation of, 245
  metapragmatic frameworks for, 254–257,
    280–281
  performance of, 138–139, 147, 174,
    235, 239, 250, 252, 253, 261–268,
    270, 272
  and reanalysis, 172, 245, 281–282
  and self-conception, 233, 237–238
  and speech valorization, 140
  tropes of, 245
  see characterological figures, personhood
ideologies of language, 13, 18, 81, 133, 146,
    286, 292–293
  distorting effects of, 157–159, 396n
  and kinship models, 357–358, 377, 380
  and ideas of normal speech, 106
  and politeness, 283–284, 286
  and register distinctions, 18, 55, 81, 133,
    145, 150, 152, 157–159
  and speech level, 334, 335
idioms, 116, 117, 124
Ilongot, 63
indexical focus, 26, 169, 324
  text-level convergence of, 26
indexical icons, 76, 183, 211, 257, 266, 337,
    399n
  see emblems, personhood, icons of
indirect speech acts, 60, 100, 390–391n
  see performativity
inner speech, 71, 71f
intension, 87, 122
interaction
  axis of, 30
  variables of, 39
interaction ritual, 260
interactional roles, 50, 315, 391n
interactional schema, *see* schema
interpersonal alignment, 77
Italian, 286, 287, 288–289, 303

Japanese, 303, 306, 319–320, 321, 322,
    329–331, 351–353, 359–360, 362–363,
    370, 373, 404n, 405n, 406n
Javanese, 23, 75–76, 176–177, 178, 180, 181,
    182, 183, 184f, 187, 306, 320, 321, 322,
    323–324, 328–329, 332–333, 334, 337,
    338, 339, 397n, 402n, 405n

kinship behavior, 344, 405n
  and affinal avoidance, 360, 367, 373,
    406n
  and class, 373, 378
  Compadrazgo, 364, 367
  diacritics of, 376–377, 378, 379–380
  emblematic functions of, 378–380
  enregisterment of, 367, 375, 383
  and genealogical reduction, 342, 346–350,
    376–377
  and ideology, 357–358, 377, 380
  incest prohibition, 379
  jural standards of, 369
  lexicalist approaches to, 346–350,
    405–406n
  mentalistic approaches to, 342, 405–406n
  metasigns of, 375–382, 383, 407n
  and multi-modal textuality, 351, 356
  non-linguistic kinship behavior, 345,
    375–376
  normalized tropes of, 343, 356–368, 375
  ontologization of, 342, 366
  and pedigrees, 348–349
  performative acts in, 347–349
  and reanalysis, 366–368, 378, 380–382,
    383, 406n
  and reflexive activity, 345
  renormalization and standardization of,
    368–372
  and role inhabitance, 353, 354, 355
  and semiotic chains, 348
  and social domain, 340, 367, 405n, 406n
  society-internal variation, 372–375
  and text-level indexicality, 340, 345,
    349, 350–353
  see tropes of kinship
kinship systems, 341, 344–345, 405–406n
  and cognitive structure, 405–406n
  culturalist critiques of, 344–345, 377
  and social structure, 347, 366
kinship terms (or kinterms) 342, 407n
  argument structure of, 346–347, 406n
  correct vs. successful reference of, 352
  and deictic selectivity, 347
  denotation of, 346–347, 349, 350–353
  honorific kinterms, 329–331
  and address, 296, 350, 353, 370, 371–372
  vocative use of, 349, 350–353, 406n
Koasati, 159, 160
Korean, 319–320, 321, 322, 335–337

Ladakhi, 321
Lakhota, 160, 161, 161f, 178
language, 5, 7–8
language ideologies, *see* ideologies of
    language
language standardization, 128, 146, 293, 404n
language use, 6, 38, 395n
lexeme, 104, 109, 115
  as category cluster, 114
  lexeme collocations, 109
Lhasa Tibetan, 47, 48, 303, 306, 319–320,
    321, 322, 323, 325–327, 337, 339, 397n,
    403n, 405n
linguistic categories, 46, 389n

Madurese, 321, 332
Maithili, 289, 290, 321, 335
Malagasy, 335
Malay, 378
Malayalam, 309
markedness, 113, 389n
  and text-defaults, 113
mass communication, 69, 69f
mass media, 202
  and Received Pronunciation, 202, 225, 397n
  and socialization to register, 170, 175, 314–315
mass vs. count nouns, 113, 114f, 393n
metalinguistic activity, 17, 20, 386n
  explicit vs. implicit, 20, 29, 31, 35, 35f, 36–37, 151, 183, 196–199, 198f, 211–213, 264, 280, 286, 288
  and grammaticality judgments, 18, 131, 339, 386n
  see reflexive activity
metapragmatic signs, 19, 28
  and emblems, 254–257, 280–281
  role designators as, 247
  next-turn behavior, 18, 35f, 151, 152–153, 288
  overt, 150
  typifications of language use, 151–153, 282–283
  and register identification, 150, 304–305
  verba dicendi, 20, 57, 274, 401n
  verba sentiendi, 274
metapragmatic stereotypes, 148, 150–154, 279–284
  conflation with actual usage, 282–283
  and honorific registers, 305, 311, 312
  and mass media, 175
  and politeness ideologies, 283–284
  and role alignment, 174–175, 176–177, 224
  social domain of, 142, 202, 237, 260, 280, 297
  social range of, 260
  sociological fractionation of, 153, 154, 397n
  see registers
metasemantic discourse
  varieties of, 19, 111, 119–121, 123, 127, 386n, 393n, 394n, 395n
  social regularities of, 120, 394n
metasemiotic activity, 21–23, 22f, 387n
  and kinship behavior, 407n
  metasign, 22, 22f, 197–199, 375–382, 383, 384
  object-sign, 22, 22f, 82, 197–199, 384, 387n
  see reflexive activity
metasign, *see* metasemiotic activity
metrical structure, 98, 100, 101, 387n, 407n
  and referential stance, 102–103, 141, 393n
  and participant personae, 256

micro-/macro- scales of analysis, 10–13, 103, 167, 387n
modernity, 12, 303, 312, 338, 345, 383
Mongolian, 321
mood deixis, 41, 43, 290
  and speech-levels, 335–337
mutual coordination, 89–93, 103, 154

Nahuatl, 321
natural kind terms, 127
naturalization, 76–77, 241, 258, 271, 303–304, 392n
Nuer, 376
nomic calibration, 73
nomic truth, 43, 44, 369
norms
  circumventions of, 33
  denotational norms, 87, 124–132
  deviation from, 126
  fractional congruence of, 307, 341, 372–373
  society-internal variation of, 8, 106, 293–295, 345, 372–375, 378
  thresholds of normativity, 125–126, 283, 370–372
Norwegian, 139–142

object-sign, *see* metasemiotic activity
orders of indexicality, 171
origo
  of deference, 316
  of deictic reference, 39, 388–389n
  of social indexicality, 26
  of kinterm, 351
  recentering of, 360, 361, 362, 365, 370, 373–375
  transposition of, 52, 324–327, 332, 358, 359
  see voicing

paradigmatic set (or equivalence class), 112
  generic vs. specific equivalence classes, 112
participant roles, 177, 179
participation framework, 86, 391n
performativity, 55–64, 390–391n
  cross-cultural variation of, 62
  cultural enregisterment of, 61–64
  explicit performative locutions, 55, 56–58
  implicit performativity of text-structure, 60
  and reflexive reanalysis, 62
  'speech-act' theory of, 390–391n
  and text-level indexicality, 58–61
Persian, 312–314, 316, 321, 334, 397n
personhood
  cultural ontologies of, 241–242
  icons of, 76, 199, 215
  textually cumulative models of, 252, 252f
phoneme, 107

poetic structure, *see* metrical structure
power
  as notional rubric, 36–37
  and agency, 229
  and registers, 146, 185
  and resistance, 36
pronouns
  and class distinctions, 172–173, 173f, 298–300
  and kinterms, 357–358
  metapragmatic stereotypes of usage, 174–175, 279–284
  and person referring honorific forms, 309, 402n
  and politeness, 25, 172–174, 176–177, 287–288, 403n
  pronominal tropes 288, 295–298, 308, 343
  and reflexive processes, 286–293
  and social boundaries, 298–300
proper names, 65–68
  and baptismal events, 66, 391n
  as role designators, 401n
  as speech-chain deictics, 65
proposition, 40
  propositional act, 38, 41
  propositional content, 40, 41
  propositional stance and role alignment, 96–103, 301

Received Pronunciation (RP), 190, 272–276, 396n, 397n
  and BBC, 225
  changes in exemplary speaker, 224–228
  changes in habits of perception, 206–219
  changes in habits of utterance, 219–223
  and classroom instruction, 221–223
  asymmetries of competence, 192–193, 219, 223–224
  and cultural values, 201–203
  elicited metapragmatic judgments, 199–201, 397n
  emergence of, 203–206, 398n
  and non-linguistic accompaniments, 273
  everyday personifying terms, 195–196
  metadiscourses of, 195–203
  print representations of, 197
  schooling, 219–223
  accent evaluation and role alignment, 201, 216, 398n
  sources of, 203–204, 398n
reference, *see* referring
referent, 40
  prototypical referent, 122, 122f, 394–395n
  canonical prototype, 128
referring, 85–96
  to addressee, 280, 403–404n
  and descriptions, 90–92f, 93f

denotationally correct reference, 87–88, 352
expression- vs. text-centric views of, 86
interactionally successful reference, 88–89, 352, 392–393n
and kinship behavior, 346–347, 349, 350–353
and location expressions, 95–96
reference maintenance by honorifics, 323–324, 332
semantic labeling-view of, 90–91, 101, 102, 286
and text-configurations, 85, 93f, 403–404n
reflexive activity, 16, 27–37, 32f, 38, 146, 395–396n
  and cultural models, 1–2, 145
  emergent reflexive models, 24–25
  and kinship behavior, 345, 383, 406n
  materiality of, 3
  and norms, 125, 406n
  and pronominal registers, 286–293
  and register models, 167–171
  reflexive processes across encounters, 64–77
  and typification of accent (RP), 199
  see metalinguistic activity, metasemiotic activity
reflexive models, 1–2, 146, 147–148
  and honorific registers, 301
  social domain of, 125
  social range of, 125
  virtual models, 80–81
registers, 79–83, 142–144, 188f, 389n, 396n
  asymmetries of competence and value, 223–224
  change and continuity of, 231–232
  as commodity forms, 131, 216, 223–224, 396n
  competence to speak and recognize, 131, 146, 156–157
  competing valorizations of, 157
  static vs. dynamic models of, 167
  and dialects/sociolects, 135
  and footing, 143, 152, 165, 167, 185, 230
  fragmentary circulation and use of, 165–167
  fractal recursivity of, 171
  as historical formations, 130, 148, 149
  as ideological formations, 55, 143, 145, 150, 152, 157–159, 397n
  institutions of replication, 131, 155–156, 169
  lexical registers, 82, 106, 186
  metapragmatic stereotypes of, 148, 150–154, 279–284
  military register, 166
  'motherese', 354
  of gender, 159, 161

of person deixis, 278
of speaker demeanor, 310–315
professional registers, 163–165
as reflexive models, 146, 147–148, 301
repertoire perspective on, 149, 149f
semiotic range of, 169, 179–185
slang, 79, 104, 145, 146, 158, 170
social asymmetries in access to, 131,
  156–157
social domain of, 148, 169–170, 172
and social personae, 165, 397n
social range of, 169, 177
socialization to, 146, 155–157
sociohistorical perspective on, 149, 149f
sports announcer talk, 163–165
utterance perspective on, 149, 149f
see enregisterment, style
reported speech deixis, 28, 29, 51
represented speech, 32
rhetoric, 36, 106, 406n
rites of passage, 68, 407n
role, *see* role and status
role alignment, 31, 103, 177, 179
  and British English, 201, 216, 227–228,
    230, 398n
  and denotational footing, 132–134, 138f,
    301, 395n
  and emblems, 236, 375, 382
  fractional congruence of, 96–97, 103
  and greetings, 276
  and social grouping, 173, 174–175,
    271–272
  and metapragmatic stereotypes, 174–175,
    176–177, 224
  and propositional stance, 96–103
  and register, 167, 173f, 174–175, 176–177,
    177–179, 185, 201, 231, 397n, 398n
  and social expansion of RP, 203, 215,
    216, 228
  symmetric vs. asymmetric, 133
  and tropes of kinship address, 375
  and tropes of secondary focus, 332
  see footing
role and status, 242–246, 400–401n
  defeasibility of, 246
  durability of, 245
  and emblems, 243–244
  traditional definitions of, 242–243, 245
  role and status designators, 243
role designators and diacritics, 246, 249f,
  401n
Russian, 25, 286, 287, 295, 321

Samoan, 306, 311–312, 316, 321
schema, 46, 389–390n
  denotational vs. interactional schema, 47,
    48, 49, 118f

self
  autobiographical self, 237
  and footing, 238
  and reanalysis of deixis, 388n
  relational self, 238–239
  self-image and public reputation, 238
semiotic activity, 2–3
  emergent effects of, 16
  semiotic chains, 205
  see speech chains
semiotic encounter, 10
  and communicative chains, 69–71
semiotic mediation, 15
semiotic range, 22, 22f, 23, 74
sense categories, 109
  sense compositionality, 110–111
  structural sense, 111, 112–115,
    114f, 123
sharedness
  of cultural formations, 183, 258, 294,
    307, 340
signifier and signified, 105
slang, 145, 146, 158, 170
social contract, 258, 401–402n
social domain
  of a linguistic category, 47
  of any semiotic regularity, 64–65
  of cultural formations, 33–33
  of denotational stereotypes, 121, 121f
  and thresholds of normativity, 125
  and register formations, 148, 169
  transformations of, 170
social indexicality, 14
  stereotypes of, 15
social personae
  and emblematic functions of signs, 235
  gradient performances of, 266
  hybrid personae, 266–267
  objectifications of, 242
  out-group personae, 267–268
  as performable images, 195, 212, 216,
    250, 253
  stereotypic, 236, 237
  see characterological figures, identity
social range, 169, 177
social relations, 10, 14
social structure, 347, 366
socialization, 70, 155–157
sociolect, 132–142
speech act theory, *see* performativity
speech chains, 64–77, 67f, 69f, 70f, 70f, 71f
  biographic history of encounters, 52, 70f,
    70–71, 213, 218
  chain segment, 70
  dyadic conversation, 69, 70, 70f
  historical, 71
  inner speech, 71, 71f

speech chains (cont.)
  participant-linked, 67, 391n
  and metadiscourses of accent, 217–219
  speech chain network, 67, 204, 391n
  transmission of messages through, 67f,
    205, 392n
  virtual model of, 72
speech levels, 187, 334–339
  based on deictic patterns, 335–337
  based on lexical cohesion, 337–339
  based on phonolexical and prosodic
    patterns, 334–335
  in British English, 200
  enregisterment of, 335–337, 338–339
  in Maithili, 289
  in Javanese, 338, 339
  in Korean, 335, 336
  in Lhasa Tibetan, 337
  and register-cohesiveness of text, 334
standard English, 146
standard language, 128, 146, 156, 169, 187
  and honorific registers, 303
  language standardization, 293, 404n
  'top-down' approaches to, 229
status, *see* role and status
stereotypes of indexicality, 153, 236
  and readability of persons, 239–240, 252,
    255–257
  stereotypic social indexicals, 55, 278,
    389n
  linking sign-type to image of personhood,
    237
  see metapragmatic stereotypes
style, 185–188
  co-occurrence styles, 186
  enregistered styles, 186
  strategic stylization, 187
Sundanese, 321
Swedish, 33, 35f, 173–174, 179, 298–300
syntagmatic relations, 112

Tamil, 136–139, 138f, 141–142
tense, 41, 43, 290
text, 24
  denotational text, 99
  interactional text, 25, 99, 100
  multi-channel text, 24, 101, 101f, 102, 159,
    183, 351, 356
  and referring, 85, 93f, 403–404n
  text configuration, 48
  text fragment, 49
  text-in-context, 92, 258
  texture and textuality, 24, 148, 387–388n
  textually composite effects, 308, 322–332,
    356, 403n
text-defaults
  defeasibility of, 49, 51–53, 58

  for deictic categories, 39, 45–48, 390n
  for deference categories, 316, 317–322
  for phonemic categories, 108
  for grammatico-semantic categories, 113
text-level indexicality, 24, 24f, 24–27
  and appropriate use, 162
  and emergent emblems, 237
  and honorific voicing effects, 307–308
  and kinship behavior, 340, 345, 349,
    350–353
  metonymic reduction of, 286
  non-detachability of, 24, 51, 138, 326, 327
  and performativity, 58–61
  and politeness, 287–288, 403n
  and readability of persons, 239–240,
    251–253
Thai, 22–23, 130f, 130–132, 141–142, 282,
    284, 285, 295, 371, 387n, 404n
totemism, 257
tropes, 24–27
  denotational tropes, 51, 106, 115
  gender tropes, 159–162, 161f, 281–282
  honorific tropes, 332
  interactional tropes, 24–27
  kinship tropes,
    see tropes of kinship
  and norms, 5, 8, 25, 295–298
  normalization of, 288, 343, 345, 356–368,
    375, 383
  in novelistic depictions of accent, 214–215
  of pronoun usage, 281, 288
  of register usage, 159–165
  of secondary focus, 327–329
  taxonomic approaches to, 406n
  of transposed origo, 324–327
  of veiled aggression, 25
tropes of kinship, 340, 342–343, 347–349,
    353, 354–356, 383
  address inversion, 359, 365
  fictive kinship, 342, 363, 366, 371, 381
  and 'literal' address, 365, 366
  metaphoric address inversion, 365, 371
  metaphoric kinship, 342, 363–364
  metaphoric recentered address, 365, 370
  and norms, 340, 341, 343, 345, 348,
    368–372, 383
  and nation-state politics, 380–382
  recentered address, 360–363, 365,
    373–375, 378
  ritual kinship, 364
  and thresholds of normativity, 370–372
  transposed reference, 358
Tzotzil, 237

Urdu, 290–292, 321, 327–328, 335
utterance
  and language 'use', 6

as material-sensory artifact, 3, 202, 397–398n
and register-mediated social sketch, 148
Uyghur, 321

Vietnamese, 354, 355, 380–382, 402n, 404n
virtual models of a chain of events, 71–77
   authoritative virtual models, 73
voice, *see* characterological figure
voicing, 27, 109, 152, 188f, 213, 244, 325, 353, 359, 381, 390n
   and kinship behavior, 358

and transposition of origo, 326
in novelistic depictions of accent, 213–214
and 'speech modeling', 325–327

Wolof, 187–188, 303–304
word-form, 109

Yapese, 377
Yiddish, 295, 296
Yucatec Maya, 48

Zulu Hlonipha register, 306, 321, 334, 367

STUDIES IN THE SOCIAL AND CULTURAL FOUNDATIONS
OF LANGUAGE

Editors

Judith T. Irvine
Bambi Schieffelin

1. Charles L. Briggs: *Learning how to ask: a sociolinguistic appraisal of the role of the interview in social science research*
2. Tamar Katriel: *Talking straight: Dugri speech in Israeli Sabra culture*
3. Bambi B Schieffelin and Elinor Ochs (eds.): *Language socialization across cultures*
4. Susan U. Philips, Susan Steele, and Christin Tanz (eds.): *Language, gender, and sex in comparative perspective*
5. Jeff Siegel: *Language contact in a plantation environment: a sociolinguistic history of Fiji*
6. Elinor Ochs: *Culture and language development: language acquisition and language socialization in a Samoan village*
7. Nancy D. Dorian (ed.): *Investigating obsolescence: studies in language contraction and death*
8. Richard Bauman and Joel Sherzer (eds.): *Explorations in the ethnography of speaking*
9. Bambi B Schieffelin: *The give and take of everyday life: Language socialization of Kaluli children*
10. Francesca Merlan and Alan Rumsey: *Ku Waru: language and segmentary politics in the western Nebilyer valley, Papua New Guinea*
11. Alessandro Duranti and Charles Goodwin (eds.): *Rethinking context: language as an interactive phenomenon*
12. John A. Lucy: *Language, diversity and thought: a reformulation of the linguistic relativity hypothesis*
13. John A. Lucy: *Grammatical categories and cognition: a case study of the linguistic relativity hypothesis*
14. Don Kulick: *Language shift and cultural reproduction: socialization, self and syncretism in a Papua New Guinean village*
15. Jane H. Hill and Judith T. Irvine (eds.): *Responsibility and evidence in oral discourse*
16. Niko Besnier: *Literacy, emotion and authority: reading and writing on a Polynesian atoll*

17. John J. Gumperz and Stephen C. Levinson (eds.): *Rethinking linguistic relativity*
18. Joel C. Kuipers: *Language, identity and marginality in Indonesia: the changing nature of ritual speech on the island of Sumba*
19. J. Joseph Errington: *Shifting Languages*
20. Marcyliena Morgan: *Language, discourse and power in African American Culture*
21. Richard Bauman and Charles L. Briggs: *Voices of modernity: language ideologies and the politics of inequality*
22. James Collins and Richard Blot: *Literacy and literacies: texts, power, and identity*
23. Christine Jourdan and Kevin Tuite (eds.): *Language, Culture and Society: key topics in linguistic anthropology*
24. Asif Agha: *Language and Social Relations*

Made in the USA
Lexington, KY
22 March 2012